Essentials of
The Marriage and Family Experience

Essentials of
The Marriage and Family Experience

Bryan Strong
UNIVERSITY OF CALIFORNIA, SANTA CRUZ

Christine DeVault

West Publishing Company

MINNEAPOLIS/ST. PAUL ❑ NEW YORK ❑ LOS ANGELES ❑ SAN FRANCISCO

Copyediting/Indexing: Maggie Jarpey
Composition: Parkwood Composition
Artwork: Miyake Illustration

Cover Quilt: *The Secret Life of Hands*, by Janice Westervelt Campion,
Fiber Artist/Quilt Maker, Newport, KY

WEST'S COMMITMENT TO THE ENVIRONMENT

In 1960, West Publishing Company began recycling materials left over from the production of books. This began a tradition of efficient and responsible use of resources. Today, up to 95 percent of our legal books and 70 percent of our college and school texts are printed on recycled, acid-free stock. West also recycles nearly 22 million pounds of scrap paper annually—the equivalent of 181,717 trees. Since the 1960s, West has devised ways to capture and recycle waste inks, solvents, oils, and vapors created in the printing process. We also recycle plastics of all kinds, wood, glass, corrugated cardboard, and batteries, and have eliminated the use of styrofoam book packaging. We at West are proud of the longevity and the scope of our commitment to the environment.

Production, Prepress, Printing and Binding by West Publishing Company.

Library of Congress Cataloging-in-Publication Data:

Strong, Bryan.
   Essentials of the marriage and family experience/Bryan Strong, Christine DeVault
      p.   cm.
   Includes bibliographical references and index.
   ISBN 0-314-01199-4 (soft)
   1. Marriage.   2. Family.   I. DeVault, Christine.   II. Title
HQ734.S97377   1993
306.8—dc20

92-32555
∞ CIP

Dedication

To Fran Bussard and Terry Crowley

True friends and exemplars, who with grace and good humor
affirm the vitality of marriage and family

CONTENTS IN BRIEF

CONTENTS

Preface

American marriages and families have undergone immense changes over the last generation: the rise of single-parent families; dual-worker families and stepfamilies; the emergence of family violence as an issue; the increasing recognition of ethnic diversity; concern over poverty and families; and heightened awareness of family/workplace conflicts, to name but a few. Since 1979 we have chronicled these changes in various editions of *The Marriage and Family Experience*, hoping that students might better understand their lives and relationships as a result. We continue this chronicle in *Essentials of the Marriage and Family Experience*.

While there is change around us, what does not change is our enduring belief that our families, whatever their form, are the crucibles in which our humanity is born, nurtured and fulfilled. They are what make us human, and they need to be cherished, honored, and supported. This belief provides the underlying theme of this textbook.

We have attempted to present the study of marriage and the family in a manner that enlarges both our personal and intellectual understanding. A functional approach does not exclude an academic approach; nor does an academic approach exclude a functional one. We have tried, in fact, to combine the virtues of both. Ideas allow us to see beyond our own limited experience, and our personal experience breathes life into ideas. We believe that good scholarship encourages individual understanding and that personal exploration encourages intellectual growth. *Essentials of the Marriage and Family Experience* reflects our attempt to unify functionally-oriented and academically-oriented approaches into a single textbook.

We have taken an interdisciplinary approach, since the perspective of a single discipline, such as sociology or psychology, creates only a partial picture of marriage and the family. We have incorporated work from not only sociology and psychology, but also history, economics, communication, folklore, literature, and ethnic studies. To limit ourselves to but one branch of knowledge would leave us much like the blind men who tried to describe the nature of the elephant: each mistook a part for the whole and, while they argued among themselves, the elephant walked away.

We have prepared *Essentials of the Marriage and Family Experience* to meet the various needs of instructors and students. Some instructors are unable to cover all the topics and level of detail found in *The Marriage and Family Experience* because of time constraints. Others supplement (or would like to supplement) their textbook with additional material but are concerned about overburdening their students. Still others wish to use a textbook as but one of several books in their course. By providing instructors with *Essentials*, we hope to offer more choice and flexibility in teaching their courses.

❏ FEATURES OF *ESSENTIALS OF THE MARRIAGE AND FAMILY EXPERIENCE*

We have incorporated current research with the most important issues confronting America's families today. We incorporate America's diverse family systems—both in terms of structure and ethnicity—as an organizing principle throughout the textbook.

Topics include:

❏ African-American, Latino, Asian-American, and Native American families
❏ Dispelling of nuclear family stereotypes
❏ New social science of love and jealousy
❏ Economic and workplace issues, and family/workplace conflicts
❏ Gender roles and ethnicity
❏ Models of family violence
❏ Rediscovering the extended family
❏ Sociological and psychological aspects of health and the family
❏ Family policy
❏ Family strengths
❏ Raising children to be prejudice free

In our research we used computerized library and reference services to supplement our traditional bibliographic research. By utilizing Melvyl, the University of California's on-line catalog (which accesses over 10 million books and periodicals), MEDLINE (the on-line version of Index Medicus), and PsycLit and SocioFile CD-ROM databases, we were able to compile extensive bibliographies of the latest and most important research in marriage and the family. As a result, the fifth edition of *The Marriage and Family Experience* continues to be one of the most comprehensively-researched textbooks in the field.

❏ PEDAGOGY

Over the years we have developed a number of pedagogical features to engage students in exploring the chapters from both an intellectual and a personal perspective. Each chapter includes the following learning tools:

Chapter Outlines

Chapter outlines at the beginning of each chapter facilitate student comprehension.

Focus

Focus boxes feature high-interest topics, such as sexual addiction, family stereotypes, rearing children to be prejudice free, and the relationship between love and sexuality.

Chapter Summary

At the end of each chapter, the main ideas are summarized to assist students in reviewing the chapter material. Key terms are italicized.

Margin Quotes

Quotes in the margins offer unusual, thoughtful, humorous, or provocative insights. A single quotation may spark an intense class discussion or lead a person to reexamine long-held beliefs. Instructors and students alike have remarked that the margin quotes are almost like having a second book.

Glossary

A glossary of key terms is included at the back of the textbook to assist students in their understanding and comprehension. Most of the glossary terms appear in bold face in the text and in italics in chapter summaries.

Resource Center

A resource center at the end of the textbook contains a self-help directory, birth control, sexually transmitted diseases and other topics relating to individual and family well-being. In addition, it contains study guides for marriage and family studies, and African-American, Latino, Asian-American, Native American, and ethnic studies to assist students in their research.

Study Guide

A study guide prepared by Carol Mertens and Mary Willie-Sutton of the University of Iowa with contributions by Linda Green and Suzanne Cobb Platt, both of Normandale Community College, contains chapter goals, review and study questions, key terms, values-clarification exercises, and detailed chapter outlines to expand student learning.

Instructor's Manual

Carol Mertens revised the instructor's manual prepared by Christine DeVault and Bryan Strong. It includes a text bank (with page references), chapter summaries, key terms and ideas, discussion questions and activities, and suggestions for guest lecturers, panels, films, and videos. Appendices include tables of demographic data on aspects of American family life, including African-American and Latino families.

Video Library

Professionally produced videos on various marriage and family subjects are available to qualified adopters.

Transparencies

Transparency masters and acetates, some from the text and some newly-created, enhance the presentation of lectures.

Computerized Test Bank

WESTEST 2.0 computerized test bank is available for IBM PCs, IBM compatibles, and Macintosh computers.

❐ ACKNOWLEDGEMENTS

We would like to acknowledge the assistance of many people in writing this textbook. In doing our research, we were kindly assisted by the reference staff of the Dean McHenry Library at the University of California, Santa Cruz. We would like to thank reference librarians Alan Ritch, Deborah Murphy, Judy Steen, Paul Machlis, and Jaquelyn Maria for their assistance in compiling bibliographies, answering reference questions, verifying citations, obtaining books and journals through interlibrary loan, and assisting us in the use of on-line and CD-ROM bibliographic systems. Jeanie Jordan at Government Documents assisted us in finding census data and researching government publications on Silver Platter's GPO database.

Ruth Gunn Mota, Director of Education, Santa Cruz AIDS Project, provided valuable information about HIV and AIDS. She, the SCAP staff, and a number of people with AIDS in our community, are deeply committed to increasing AIDS awareness among students and the community. We applaud their work.

At West Publishing Company, we would like to thank Carole Grumney, our editor for the last ten years, who has been the soul of patience, as always. We also thank Carole Balach in West's production department, with whom we have been in almost daily contact for months, for her dedication and steadfast optimism.

Our friend and colleague Art Aron, one of the leading researchers in the social psychology of love, assisted us in our love chapter, Terrence Crowley, professor of library science at San Jose State University, continues to assist us in difficult research questions. Fran Bussard, formerly of Chico State University, remains a rich source of insight into personal relationships and communication, not to mention homemade fettucine and peach pie.

We also wish to thank Zoe Sodja, Cheryl VanDeVeer, Judy Burton, Joan Tannheimer, and Valerie Wells for their time and cheerful help inputting the text.

Finally, the authors thank their children—Gabe, Willy, Maria, and Kristin—who over the years have provided hands-on experience in family studies and who continue to challenge and delight as they move us through the stages of the family life cycle. They were toddlers when we first wrote this textbook and are now adolescents! (This took us by surprise.) And once again we would like to thank each other for the support, good humor (the occasional growl notwithstanding), and love given freely in the daily living of life.

❐ REVIEWERS

Both the *Essentials* and *The Marriage and Family Experience* have benefited from the insightful comments and thoughtful suggestions of our many reviewers. They have been exceptionally aware of the dual requirements of a good textbook—academic integrity and student interest—and have helped us maintain our commitment to both. We would like to thank Patty Takeuchi for her insights on Asian-American families, notably Japanese-American families. Professors and consultants who assisted us include, in alphabetical order: Rebecca Adams, Purdue University; Lois Bryant, University of Missouri, Columbia; Sandra Caron, University of Maine; Ann Engin, University of South Dakota; Richard Gelles, University of Rhode Island; Jan Hare, University of Oregon; Ana Matiella, ETR Associates; and Violet Moore, Western Kentucky University. We are greatly indebted to them all. Special thanks to Richard Gelles who painstakingly reviewed our family violence chapter.

❐ Bryan Strong
❐ Christine DeVault

January, 1993

PART 1

Introduction

C H A P T E R 1

The Meaning of Marriage and the Family

There is no more lovely, friendly, and charming relation, communion, or company than a good marriage.

Anonymous

T OWARD THE END OF THE EIGHTEENTH CENTURY, three sportsmen hunting in the woods of Caune, France, were startled by the sight of a young boy gathering roots and acorns. The boy hunched over the ground like a wild animal, naked but for a tattered shirt. As soon as the boy sighted the hunters, he fled and attempted to climb a tree to hide. The hunters quickly captured him and brought him to a neighboring village. He remained in the village a week and then escaped. A few months later he sought refuge in a peasant's dwelling; he was retained and later was taken to Paris.

The boy, who apparently had been abandoned in the woods at an early age, became known as "the Young Savage of Aveyron." He had lived alone from the time he was abandoned, sleeping in the fields and foraging for food. Without human contact, his mental development was little more than that of a one-year-old child. A contemporary (quoted in Itard, 1801 [1972]) described the boy as:

incapable of attention . . . and consequently of all the operations of the mind which depended upon it; destitute of memory, of judgment, even of a disposition to imitation; and so bounded were his ideas, even those which related to his immediate wants, that he could not even open a door, nor get on a chair to obtain the food which was put out of the reach of his hand; in short, destitute of every means of communication . . . his pleasure, and agreeable sensation of the organs of taste, his intelligence, a susceptibility of producing incoherent ideas, connected with his physical wants; in a word, his whole existence was a life purely animal.

When the boy, now named Victor, was brought to Paris, he was put under the tutelage of a young physician named Jean Itard (Malson, 1972). Itard painstakingly undertook to educate the boy in human speech. He taught him to walk and sit, groom himself, open doors, and use instruments and tools. Over the years, he taught the boy how to think conceptually and to express his simplest needs in writing.

The story of Victor and Itard is a reminder of what we tend to take for granted: that the family is the nursery of our humanity. The traits that make us human are not given to us full-blown; rather, they exist potentially in us and are first developed within the family or its surrogate. When Itard took in Victor, he began to undertake the task of socialization, of making him human, one of the basic tasks of the family. If it were not for families that socialize and educate us, we, too, would be like the wild child of Aveyron. We would not know how to speak, how to walk, how to interact with others, how to love.

❒ CONTEMPORARY AMERICAN MARRIAGES AND FAMILIES

Definitions and Incidences

Marriage is a great institution, but I'm not ready for an institution yet.

Mae West

Before we begin examining marriages and families in any detail, it is important to define some of the terms we will be using. Some are so common that they hardly need definition. But as you will see, some terms, such as *family*, are more complex than we usually believe.

COHABITATION. **Cohabitation** technically refers to individuals sharing living arrangements in an intimate relationship, whether these individuals are married or unmarried. Most commonly, however, it refers to "living together" relationships in which unmarried individuals share living quarters and are sexually involved. A cohabiting relationship may be similar to marriage in many of its functions and roles, but it does not have equivalent legal sanctions or rights. In 1990, there were 2.9

million heterosexual couples living together (there were also 1.5 million gay or lesbian couples living together in 1987) (U.S. Bureau of the Census, 1988 and 1991). About a third of the heterosexual couples have children living with them. Over ninety thousand gay and lesbian couples have children living with them.

MARRIAGE. Marriage is a union between a man and a woman: the two individuals perform a public ritual (which means that their union is socially recognized), they are united sexually, and they cooperate in economic matters. The union is assumed to be more or less permanent. If the married couple has children, the children will have certain legal rights. Although gay and lesbian couples may consider themselves married, their marriages are not recognized legally. Recently, San Francisco joined several other critics in recognizing the significance of cohabiting heterosexual relationships and gay and lesbian relationships in its 1991 "domestic partners act."

The incidence of marriage differs according to race and ethnicity (U.S. Bureau of the Census, 1990). In 1988, 111.3 million Americans over eighteen years of age were married. This represents 62.7 percent of the adult population. An additional 13.5 million (7 percent) were widowed. Among whites, 64.6 percent were married and 7.7 percent were widowed. Among African Americans, 46.7 percent were married and 9 percent were widowed. Among Latinos, 61.5 percent were married and 4.3 percent were widowed. In 1980, the latest date for which figures are available, 85.1 percent of Asian Americans, 75.4 percent of Pacific Islanders, and 71.9 percent of native Americans were married (U.S. Bureau of the Census, 1990).

SEPARATION AND DIVORCE. Separation refers to the *physical* separation of two married people. It may or may not lead to divorce. Many more people separate than divorce. Divorce is the legal dissolution of a marriage. Over the last twenty years, divorce has changed the face of marriage and the family in America. The divorce rate is two to three times what it was for our parents and grandparents. About half of all those who currently marry divorce within seven years. Among all Americans, 13.9 million (8.2 percent) are divorced. Among African Americans, 10 percent are divorced; among Latinos, 7.4 percent are divorced.

Divorce has become so widespread that many scholars are beginning to view it as part of the normal life course of American marriages (Raschke, 1987). The high divorce rate does not indicate that Americans devalue marriage, however. Paradoxically, Americans divorce because they value marriage so highly: If a marriage does not meet their standards, they divorce to marry again. They hope that their second marriages will fulfill the expectations that their first marriages failed to meet (Furstenberg and Spanier, 1987).

Contemporary divorce patterns create three common experiences for American marriages and families: single-parent families, remarriage, and stepfamilies. Because of their widespread incidence, these variations are becoming part of our normal marriage and family patterns. They no longer represent deviations or failures as they did for our parents or grandparents; instead they represent part of the normal life course for contemporary Americans. The majority of young Americans will probably have some experience of single-parent families, remarriage, or stepfamilies as either children or adults.

REMARRIAGE. Half of all recent marriages are remarriages for at least one partner (Bumpass, Sweet, and Martin, 1990). Although remarriages are increasing at a faster rate than first marriages, remarriage rates are dramatically affected by race and

If anyone means to deliberate successfully about anything, there is one thing he must do from the outset. He must know what it is he is deliberating about; otherwise he is bound to go utterly astray. Now most people fail to realize that they don't know what this or that really is; consequently when they start discussing something, they dispense with any agreed definition, assuming that they know the thing; then later on they naturally find, to their cost, that they agree neither with each other or with themselves.

Plato, Phaedrus

As to marriage or celibacy, let a man take which course he will, he will be sure to repent it.

Socrates (4th century B.C.)

ethnicity. Remarriage rates for African Americans have been dropping disproportionately during the last twenty years; African Americans remarry at about one-quarter the rate of whites. Latinos remarry at about half the rate of Anglos.

Those who remarry are older, have more experience in both life and work, and have different expectations than those who marry for the first time. About one-third of all children are born to remarried families. Ironically, despite the hopes and experience of those who remarry, their divorce rate is about the same as for those who marry for the first time. Remarriage can also create a stepfamily. When remarriages include children, a person may become not only a husband or wife but also a stepfather or stepmother.

The family is a society limited in numbers, but nevertheless a true society, anterior to every state or nation, with rights and duties of its own, wholly independent of the commonwealth.

Pope Leo XIII (1810–1903)

FAMILY. In Western culture, the **family** traditionally has been defined as a married couple or group of adult kin with children who cooperate and divide labor along gender lines, rear children, and share a common dwelling place. During the twentieth century, Americans have tended to identify the nuclear family as *the* family. But the older (and wider) definition of family also includes other kin, especially in-laws, grandparents, aunts and uncles, and cousins. To distinguish it from the nuclear family, this wider family is known as the extended family.

Until recently, American researchers have focused on the traditional nuclear family, composed of a married couple and their biological children; in this family, the husband is employed outside the home while the wife remains at home performing housework and child-care tasks. The emphasis on the traditional nuclear family as *the* American family has ignored a simple reality: The traditional nuclear family is a minority family form. Today, fewer than 13 percent of contemporary American fami-

The traditional nuclear family, like apple pie, is a powerful cultural symbol. As a reflection of contemporary American families, the traditional family is a minority family.

TABLE 1.1	How Families Have Changed, 1970–1988				
	1970	1980	1988	PERCENT CHANGE 1970–1988	
Population	205,100,000	227,700,000	246,100,000	Up	20
Marriages performed	2,159,000	2,413,000	2,389,000	Up	11
Divorces granted	708,000	1,182,000	1,183,000	Up	67
Married couples	44,728,000	48,643,000	51,809,000	Up	16
Married couples with children	25,541,000	24,501,000	24,600,000	Down	3
Unmarried couples with children present	196,000	424,000	891,000	Up	355
Single-parent families	4,560,000	6,051,000	7,320,000	Up	61
Unmarried couples	523,000	1,600,000	2,200,000	Up	446
Births	3,731,000	3,598,000	3,913,000	Up	5
Births to unmarried women	398,000	600,000	933,000	Up	134

SOURCE: Bureau of the Census, *U.S. Statistical Abstract, 1990*. Washington, DC: Government Printing Office, 1990. U.S. Bureau of Census. Population Reports. P-20. *Marital Status and Living Arrangements, March, 1990*. Washington, D.C., 1991.

lies fit this model! As such, there is no typical American family. Instead, we have single-parent families, stepfamilies, cohabiting families, dual-earner families, families without children, gay and lesbian families, and so on. The majority of Americans are members of one of these other family forms, not the traditional nuclear family.

The most widespread family forms in contemporary America are intact two-parent families, stepfamilies, and single-parent families. By the year 2000 there will be more stepfamilies than any other family form (Pill, 1990). Since 1970, single-parent families have been increasing at four to five times the rate of two-parent families. In 1989, there were 51.8 million two-parent families (including both intact families and stepfamilies) with children under eighteen years. Intact two-parent families represent 47 percent of all families. In 1989, there were 6 million single-parent families. Of our families, 58.1 percent are intact, two-parent families, 15.8 percent are stepfamilies, 21 percent are mother/child families, 2.5 percent are father/child families, and 2.7 percent are other family forms, such as cohabiting or gay or lesbian families (Saluter, 1989). One out of three Americans is currently a member of a stepfamily. By 2000, the number is expected to reach one out of two people.

To include these diverse forms, the definition of family needs to be revised. A more contemporary definition defines the family as one or more adults related by blood, marriage, adoption, or affiliation who cooperate economically, who may share a common dwelling place, and who *may* rear children. Such a definition more accurately reflects the diversity of contemporary American families.

☐ FORMS AND FUNCTIONS OF THE FAMILY

Forms of Marriage and Family

NUCLEAR AND EXTENDED FAMILIES. Society "created" the family to undertake the task of making us human. According to some anthropologists, the **nuclear family,** con-

The traditional nuclear family of the 1940s and 1950s began to be replaced in the 1960s by more diverse family forms, such as single-parent families, stepfamilies and dual-worker families.

sisting of the father/mother/child triad, is universal, either in its basic form or as the building block for other family forms (Murdock, 1967). Other anthropologists disagree that the father is necessary, arguing that the basic family unit is the mother and child dyad (Collier, Rosaldo, and Yanagisako, 1982). The use of arti-

FIGURE 1.1

Model Genogram

This figure represents a sample genogram for a woman named Jenny, a college senior. She and her boyfriend Robert, a musician, are planning to marry, but their relationship is marked by conflict. As soon as one problem gets resolved (or ignored), another seems to crop up. They go back and forth between wanting to marry or break up. The genogram indicates that Jenny's family relationships are marked by closeness and conflict. Her parents and grandparents tended to be noncommunicative; the only way they could open up was through fighting. Their conflicts broke down barriers against intimacy. By contrast, Robert's family was communicative with little conflict. The style in his family was to be open; conflict was not used as a means of achieving intimacy.

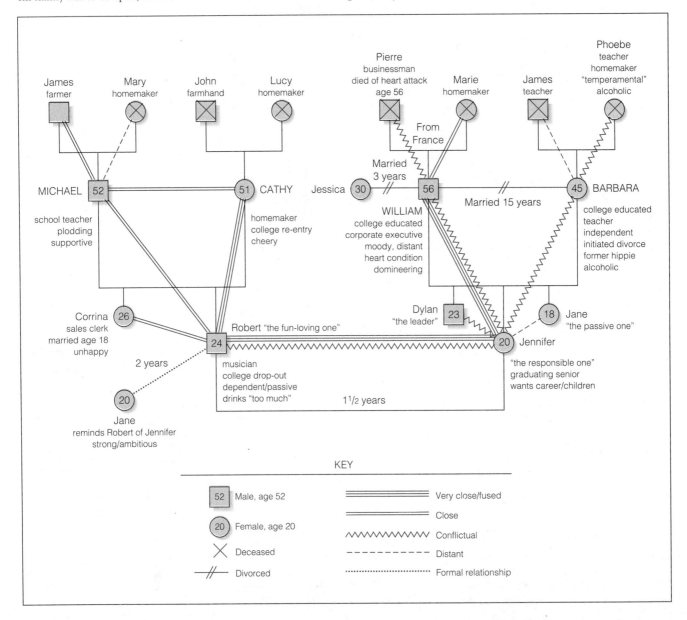

ficial insemination and new reproductive technologies, as well as the rise of single-parent families headed by women, are cited in support of the mother/child dyad.

But whatever its most basic form, the nuclear family is imbedded within a larger family, the **extended family,** which consists not only of the married couple and their children but also of other relatives, especially in-laws, grandparents, aunts and uncles, and cousins. In the majority of non-European countries, the extended family is often regarded as the basic family unit (Murdock, 1967). For many Americans, especially African Americans, Latinos, and Asian Americans, the extended family takes on great importance.

MAPPING FAMILY RELATIONSHIPS: THE GENOGRAM. While we can easily identify family structure in terms of parents, children, grandparents, aunts and uncles, and so on, it is more difficult to discern the emotional structure of families. These emotional structures are especially important, as our families are among the most important influences in our lives. Many of our patterns of interactions, deepest feelings, relationship expectations, and personal standards reflect our family of orientation.

In recent years, family therapists have been using a device called a genogram to look at family relationships. A genogram is a diagram of the emotional relationships of a family through several generations. It is something like a family tree of family interactions. If we can understand the ingrained patterns in our family relationships, we can often understand the nature of our present relationships (Bahr, 1990).

If the marital relationships of our parents and grandparents are marked by conflict, for example, we may unconsciously model our own relationships after theirs. We may experience connection with others through conflict. If their relationships are marked by emotional distance, we may find ourselves distant in our "close" relationships. If their relationships, however, are characterized by warmth and sharing, we may choose similar relationships.

Using the genogram in this figure as a model, draw a genogram of your own family relationships on a large sheet of paper. Use the symbols in the example to indicate relationships. Your genogram should include the following information about you, your parents, and your grandparents:

□ Name and date of birth. If deceased, year and cause of death.
□ Education and occupation.
□ Siblings in each generation.
□ Marital history, including years of marriage, divorces, years of singlehood (including single parenting), and date of remarriage.

MONOGAMY AND POLYGAMY. Within Western cultures, such as that in the United States, the preferred form of marriage is **monogamy,** in which there are only two spouses, the husband and wife. But monogamy is a minority preference among world cultures, practiced by only 24 percent of the known cultures (Murdock, 1967). The preferred marital arrangement is polygamy, the practice of having more than one wife or husband. One study of cultures throughout the world found that 75 percent of these cultures (representing, nevertheless, a minority of the world's population) preferred *polygyny*, the practice of having two or more wives, and 1 percent preferred *polyandry*, the practice of having two or more husbands

(Murdock, 1967). Within polygamous societies, however, plural marriages are in the minority, primarily for simple economic reasons: they are a sign of status that relatively few people can afford. Although problems of jealousy may arise in plural marriages—the Fula in Africa, for example, call the second wife "the jealous one"—there are usually built-in control mechanisms to ease the problem. The wives may be related, especially as sisters; if they are unrelated, they usually have separate dwellings. Women in these societies often prefer that there be several wives: plural wives are a sign of status and, more important, ease the workload of individual wives. This last fact is apparent even in our culture; it is not uncommon to hear overworked American homemakers exclaim, "I want a wife."

Although polygamy sounds strange or exotic, it may not really seem so strange if we look at American marital practices. Considering the high divorce rate in this country, monogamy may no longer be the best way of describing our marriage forms. Our marriage system might be called serial monogamy or modified polygamy, because one person may have several spouses over his or her lifetime. In our nation's past, African slaves tried unsuccessfully to continue their traditional polygamous practices when they first arrived in America; these attempts, however, were rigorously suppressed by their masters (Gutman, 1976). Mormons also practiced polygamy until the late nineteenth century. Even today, an estimated three thousand to ten thousand fundamentalist Mormons continue to practice polygamy despite its prohibition by the church. And one scholar suggests that housekeepers, usually women, perform many of the functions of junior wives for American families (Hochschild, 1989).

Family Functions

Whether it is the father/mother/child nuclear family, a married couple with no children, a single-parent family, a stepfamily, a dual-worker family, or a cohabiting family, the family generally performs four important functions. First, it provides a source of intimate relationships. Second, it acts as a unit of economic cooperation. Third, it may produce and socialize children. Fourth, it assigns status and social roles to individuals. Although these are the basic functions that families are "supposed" to fulfill, families do not necessary have to fulfill them all—as in families without children—nor do they always fulfill them well—as in abusive families.

The word "ordinary" in the dictionary . . . says "familiar; unexceptional; common." Given that set of definitions, it's one of the biggest words in the English language, since life, death, childbirth, love, hate, age, and sex are all familiar, unexceptional and common.

Mary Cantwell

INTIMATE RELATIONSHIPS. Intimacy is a primary human need. As the ancient philosopher Aristotle wrote, "Only an animal or a god can live alone." He appears to have been right. Human companionship strongly influences rates of cancer, tuberculosis, suicide, accidents, and mental illness. Studies consistently show that married couples and adults living with others are generally healthier and have a lower mortality rate than divorced, separated, and never-married individuals (Ross, Mirowsky, and Goldsteen, 1991). This holds true for both whites and African Americans (Broman, 1988).

Marriage and the family furnish emotional security and support. This has probably been true from earliest times. The Book of Ecclesiastes, written thousands of years ago, suggests the importance of companionship:

Two are better than one, because they have a good reward for their toil. For if they fall, one will lift up his fellow; but woe to him who is alone when he falls and has not another to lift him up. Again if two lie together, they are warm; but how can one be warm alone? And though a man might prevail against one, two will withstand him. A three-fold cord is not quickly broken. (Ecclesiastes 4:9–12)

In our families we find our strongest bonds. These bonds can be forged from love, attachment, loyalty, or guilt. The need for intimate relationships, whether they are satisfactory or not, may hold unhappy marriages together indefinitely. Loneliness may be a terrible specter. Among the newly divorced, it may be one of the worst aspects of the marital breakup.

Since the nineteenth century, marriage and the family have become important as the source of companionship and intimacy. They have become a "haven in a heartless world" (Lasch, 1978). As society has become more industrialized and bureaucratic, it is increasingly within the family that we expect to find intimacy and companionship. In the larger world around us, we are generally perceived in terms of our roles. A professor sees us primarily as a student; a used-car salesperson relates to us as a potential buyer; a politician views us as a voter. Only among our intimates are we seen on a personal level as David or Maria. Before marriage, our friends are our intimates. After marriage, our partner is expected to be the one with whom we are most intimate. With our partner we disclose ourselves most completely, share our hopes, rear our children, grow old.

The need for intimacy is so powerful that we may rely upon animals if our intimacy needs are not met by humans. Studies on the role of pets in human relationships suggest that the most prized aspects of pets, especially dogs and cats, is their attentiveness to their owners, their welcoming and greeting behaviors, and their role as confidants—qualities valued in our intimate relationships with humans as well. In fact, one study (Albert and Bulcroft, 1988) found that 87 percent of those who owned pets considered them "family members." One study found that 98 percent of dog owners spent time talking to their pets, 75 percent thought that their dogs were sensitive to their moods and feelings, and 28 percent even confided in their pets (Arehart-Treichel, 1982). Pets give children an opportunity to nurture, and provide a best friend, someone to love. For adults, especially men, they are an outlet for touching; they act as companions and as social catalysts. Dog owners are more likely to interact with strangers when they are with their dogs than when they are without them.

Fidelity is part of every human relationship. It is the strain toward permanence and toward public commitment to permanence that is involved in any relationship beyond the most superficial. Fidelity is a longing for love that does not end.

Andrew Greeley

We form strong bonds within our families. These bonds are reinforced through family and cultural rituals, such as kwanzaa, a winter celebration by many American blacks of their African heritage.

ECONOMIC COOPERATION. The family is also a unit of economic cooperation that traditionally divides its labor along gender lines, that is, between males and females (Ferree, 1991; Thompson and Walker, 1989; Voydanoff, 1987). Although the division of labor by gender is characteristic of virtually all cultures, the work males and females perform (apart from childbearing) varies from culture to culture. Among the Nambikwara in Africa, for example, the fathers take care of the babies and clean them when they soil themselves; the concubines of the chief prefer hunting over domestic activities. In American society, from the last century until recently, men were expected to work away from home while women remained at home caring for the children and house. There is no reason, however, why these roles cannot be reversed. Such tasks are assigned by culture, not biology. Only a woman's ability to give birth is biologically determined. And some cultures practice *couvade*, ritualized childbirth in which a male gives birth to the child's spirit while his partner gives physical birth; in some of these cultures, because the male gives birth to the spirit, his role is considered more important than the female's (Gregor, 1985).

Regardless of what activities men and women do, work traditionally has been divided into "man's work" and "woman's work." This makes the sexes interdependent, cementing their need for each other (Lévi-Strauss, 1956). In tribal societies, where the extended family is the basic producing unit, it is impossible for men and women to survive without each other. In contemporary America, however, interdependence between the sexes has greatly lessened. In earlier times, a man needed a wife to cook his food; today he can make his own dinner or eat out. A woman once needed a husband for economic support; today she can support herself (although most women have difficulty supporting children single-handedly). One result of reduced female dependence on males is that women who work are more likely to divorce than those who remain at home full-time (Spitze, 1991).

We commonly think of the family as a consuming unit, but it also continues to be an important producing unit, although its productive activities are less apparent than formerly. Modern families no longer raise much of their own food, weave their own cloth, or spin their own yarn. We usually do not view the family as a productive unit because of its relative unimportance in the money economy as a whole. The family, for example, pays no wages for its work, nor does it call its members employees. The husband does not get paid for building a shelf or attending to the children; the wife is not paid for fixing a leaky faucet or cooking. Although children contribute to the household economy by helping around the house, they generally are not paid for such things as cooking, cleaning their rooms, or watching their younger brothers or sisters (Coggle and Tasker, 1982; Gecas and Seff, 1991). Yet they are all engaged in productive labor (Zick and Bryant, 1990).

Recently, economists have begun to reexamine the family as a productive unit (Ferree, 1991). If men and women were compensated monetarily for the work done in their households, the total would be equal to the entire amount paid out in wages by every corporation in the United States. Unpaid household work by women in 1990 was worth well over $1 trillion; such work by men was worth $610 billion. Similarly, household assets—homes, cars, appliances, lawnmowers, tools, and so on—produce an annual return equal to the net profits of all U.S. corporations. The household as a productive unit is very much alive. During recessionary periods, for example, family members produce more goods—such as clothes or food—at home than they do during good economic times (Voydanoff, 1991). About 34 percent of the nation's families have a garden, and gardening is the fifth most popular hobby in America. Gardening is rarely seen as one of the family's productive activities because most families don't produce a cash crop, even though families produce over $16 billion worth of vegetables and fruits from their home gardens yearly (Adler et al., 1982).

As a service unit, the family is dominated by women. Because women's work at home is unpaid, the productive contributions of homemakers have been overlooked (Ciancanelli and Berch, 1987; Walker, 1991). Yet women's household work is equal to about 44 percent of the gross national product (GNP), and the value of such work is double the reported earnings of women. Burns (1972) wrote:

The invisible household economy might also be called the matriarchal economy, because it is dominated by women. They perform most of the labor, make most of the household decisions, and are employed as managers for the labor and assets of the household. More than a few observers have noted that the household economy is invisible precisely because it is controlled by women and that present accounting conventions have the effect of demeaning the work and value of women.

If a woman were paid wages for her labor as mother and homemaker according to the wage scale for chauffeurs, nurses, baby-sitters, cooks, therapists, and so on, her services today would be worth more than $50,000 a year. Many women would make more for their work in the home than men do for their jobs outside the home. Because family power is partly a function of who earns the money, paying women for their household work might have a significant impact on husband-wife relations.

REPRODUCTION AND SOCIALIZATION. The family makes society possible by producing and rearing children to replace the older members of society as they die off. Traditionally, reproduction has been a unique function of the family. Yet even this domain has not remained immune to technological change. Developments in artificial insemination and in vitro fertilization have separated reproduction from sexual intercourse. In addition to permitting infertile couples to give birth, such techniques have also made it possible for lesbian couples to become parents.

The family traditionally has been responsible for socialization. Children are helpless and dependent for years following birth. They must learn how to walk and talk, how to take care of themselves, how to act, how to love, how to touch and be touched. Teaching the child how to be human and how to fit into his or her particular culture is one of the family's most important tasks. Without such socialization, we would be like the wild child of Aveyron.

This socialization function, however, is dramatically shifting away from the family. One researcher (Guidubaldi, 1980) believes that the increasing lack of parental commitment to childrearing may be one of the most significant societal changes in our lifetime. With the rise of compulsory education, the state has become responsible for a large part of the socialization of children older than five. The increase in working mothers has placed many infants, toddlers, and small children in day-care, reducing the family's role in socialization. By 1995, scholars estimate that the mothers of two-thirds of all preschool children and three-fourths of all school-age children will be in the work force (Hofferth and Phillips, 1987). Even while children are at home, television rather than family members may be rearing them (Dorr, Kovaric, and Doubleday, 1989).

ASSIGNMENT OF SOCIAL ROLES AND STATUS. We fulfill various *social roles* as family members, and these roles provide us with much of our identity. During our lifetimes, most of us will belong to two families: the family of orientation and the family of marriage. The **family of orientation** (sometimes called the *family of origin*) is the family in which we grow up, the family that orients us to the world. The family of orientation may change over time if the marital status of the child's parents changes. The family of orientation originally may be an intact nuclear family or a

As always, the most automated appliance in the household is the mother.

Beverly Jones

Children . . . have no choice about being born into a system; nor do parents have a choice, once children are born, as to the existence of the reponsibilities of parenthood . . . . In fact, no family relationships except marriage are entered into by choice.

Monica McGoldrick and Elizabeth Carter

The Simpsons are a misunderstood and underrated family.

Homer Simpson

single-parent family; later it may become a stepfamily. The **family of marriage** is the family we form through marriage. (This family had traditionally been referred to as the *family of procreation*, but as many families do not have children or have stepchildren, this older term is no longer an adequate description.) Most Americans will form families of marriage sometime in their lives. Much of our identity is formed in the crucibles of these two families.

In our family of orientation, we are given the roles of child, son or daughter, brother or sister, stepson or stepdaughter. We internalize these roles until they become a part of our being. In each of these roles we are expected to act in certain ways. For example, children obey their parents, sons roughhouse with their fathers, daughters imitate their mothers, siblings help each other. Sometimes our feelings fit the expectations of our roles; other times they do not.

The family roles of offspring and siblings are most important when we are living with our parents, brothers, and sisters in our family of orientation. After we leave home, they gradually diminish in everyday significance, although they continue throughout our lives. In relation to our parents, we never cease being children; in relation to our siblings, we never cease being brothers and sisters. The roles change as we grow older. They begin the moment we are born and end only when we die.

As we leave our family of orientation, we usually are also leaving adolescence and entering adulthood. Being an adult in our society is defined in part by entering new family roles—those of husband or wife, father or mother. These roles are given to us by our family of marriage, and they take priority over the roles we had in our family of orientation. When we marry, we transfer our primary loyalties from our parents and siblings to our husbands or wives. Later, if we have children, we form additional bonds with them. When we assume the role of husband or wife, we assume an entire new social identity linked with responsibility, work, and parenting. In earlier times such roles were considered to be lifelong in duration. Because of divorce, however, these roles may last for considerably less time.

The status or place we are given in society is acquired in large part through our families. Our families place us in a certain socioeconomic class, such as blue collar (working class), middle class, or upper class. We learn the ways of our class through identifying with our families. Different classes see the world through different eyes. In blue-collar families, for example, work may be viewed as a means of earning a living. Work does not necessarily bring fulfillment; rather, it is drudgery undertaken for the sake of the family. Family is an escape from work. In middle-class families, by contrast, work is often seen as something that gives a person a sense of success or failure as an individual; it is a source of pleasure and fulfillment. Work and family may compete for loyalties.

Our families also give us our racial or ethnic identities as white (or Anglo), African American, Latino, Jewish, Irish American, Asian American, and so forth. Families also provide us with a religious tradition as Protestant, Catholic, Jewish, Greek Orthodox, Islamic, agnostic, atheist, and so on. These identities help form our cultural values and expectations.

Why Live in Families?

As we look at the different functions of the family, we can see theoretically that most of them can be fulfilled outside the family. In terms of reproduction, for example, artificial insemination permits a woman to be impregnated by an anonymous donor, while embryonic transplants allow one woman to carry another's embryo. Children can be raised communally, cared for by foster families or child-care workers, or sent to boarding schools. Most of our domestic needs can be satisfied by eating frozen foods or going to restaurants, sending our clothes to the laundry, and hiring help to wash the mountains of dishes accumulating (or growing new life-forms) in the kitchen and to clean the bathroom. Friends can provide us with emotional intimacy, therapists can listen to our problems, and sexual partners can be found outside of marriage. With all the limitations and stresses of family life, why bother living in families?

Sociologist William Goode (1982) suggests that there are several advantages to living in families. First, families offer continuity as a result of emotional attachments, rights, and obligations. Once we choose a partner or have children, we do not have to continually search for new partners or family members who can perform a family task or function better, such as cook, paint the kitchen, provide companionship, or bring home a paycheck. We expect our family members—whether partner, child, parent, or sibling—to participate in family tasks over their lifetimes. If at one time we need to give more emotional support or attention to a partner or child than we receive, we expect the other person to reciprocate at another time. Or if we ourselves are down, we expect our family to help. We further expect that we can enjoy the fruits of our labors together. We count on our family to be there for us in multiple ways. We rarely have the same extensive expectations of friends.

Second, families offer close proximity. We do not need to travel crosstown or cross-country for conversation or help. With families, we do not even need to go out of the house; a husband or wife, parent or child, brother or sister, is often right at hand (or underfoot, in the case of children). This close proximity facilitates cooperation and communication.

Third, families offer us an abiding familiarity with others. Few people know us as well as our family members, for they have seen us in the most intimate circumstances throughout much of our lives. They have seen us at our best and our worst, when we are kind or selfish, understanding or intolerant. This familiarity and close contact require us to make adjustments in living with others. As we do so, we also expand our own knowledge of ourselves and others.

Fourth, families provide us with many economic benefits. They offer us economies of scale. Various activities, such as laundry, cooking, shopping, and cleaning, can be done almost as easily for several people as for one. It is almost as easy to prepare a meal for three people as it is for one, and the average cost per person in both time and money is usually less. As an economic unit, a family can

Home—the place where, when you have to go there, they have to let you in.

Robert Frost (1874–1963)

© Nicole Hollander, *New York Times*

Bob and Carol and Mike and Alice

Two astronauts marooned in space, Bob and Debbie, discover that they both watched "The Brady Bunch" as children. Here, they discuss the show.

Debbie: I often wonder how the Bradys got together. Mike had three boys and Carol had three girls — all with lovely hair of gold, like their mother — so each of them had to have been married previously. What happened to their spouses?

Bob: Well, actually, Mike Brady dumped his wife for Carol the afternoon he met her at the auto show, which, as you can imagine, put his wife's nose out of joint. So one day she just showed up with the three boys and dropped them off in front of the split level. As far as I know, Carol was never married to any of the girls' fathers.

Debbie: And Alice, the housekeeper?

Bob: Defrocked priest? Transsexual psychic healer? The series has never been clear on that. My own theory is that she was robotic. Mike designed her. He was an archi-

tect, you know. He designed the house that the Brady bunch lived in.

Debbie: I loved that house, especially the kitchen. I've always been fond of avocado appliances and bright orange walls. It's amazing how clean that kitchen was with six kids around — and those kids! They'd come home from school, head straight for that avocado refrigerator and take out a piece of fruit. No Ho-Ho's for those cuties.

Bob: Watching too many episodes of "The Brady Bunch" turned me into a soft-centered zombie. I lay on the couch in a state of altered consciousness and let the images of the perfectly thin, perfectly caring Bradys wash away the images of my real family.

Debbie: I wonder what it would take to make the Bradys lose control, to blow the tops of their heads off. I'd like to try. I'd like to stand very close to Mr. and Mrs. Brady and scream, "Get real," to see the veins in Carol's neck stick out (and you know they would). At the same time I always felt a dreamlike state of pleasure staring at their perfect family life.

— N.H.

FOCUS

Stereotyping Families

Each day we are presented with a vast amount of information that we need to organize and make sense of. One of the ways we manage this information is by categorizing it. A **stereotype** is a special kind of category: it is a set of beliefs about the personal characteristics of a group of people. Stereotypes are highly simplified, overgeneralized, and widely-held beliefs about people. Most of us are probably aware of stereotypes about ethnicity and gender. But there are also numerous stereotypes centering around family (Ganong, Coleman, and Mapes, 1990; for family stereotypes on television, see Taylor, 1989a and 1989b, and Fabes, Wilson, and Christopher, 1989).

Probably the most far-ranging family stereotype is that the traditional nuclear family is the only healthy or normal family structure. As a description of American family life, the nuclear family exists more as a cultural symbol or norm than as a reality, yet it has a powerful effect on us. There are numerous consequences.

❏ *The nuclear family stereotype makes other family forms and lifestyles appear deviant or suspect.* Studies indicate that married men and women are generally rated more positively than single individuals. Married persons are perceived as being more mature, more responsible, and better citizens. Similarly, mothers and fathers are viewed more positively than adults who are voluntarily childless. Even the perception of children is affected by whether they are from two-parent or single-parent families: The personalities and behaviors of children from two-parent families were rated higher. Single-parent families are seen as "broken" and stepfamilies as "unhappy." Those who live together are regarded as "immoral," and gay and lesbian relationships are called "perverse." Although family forms and relationships have become increasingly diverse in recent years, cultural stereotypes have remained unchanged (Ganong et al., 1990).

❏ *Nuclear family stereotypes intermingle with stereotypes about ethnicity, affecting our perceptions of African-American, Latino, and other ethnic families.* Such stereotypes are potentially harmful, observed Lois Bryant and her colleagues (Bryant, Coleman, and Ganong, 1988): "When stereotypes are distorted and overgeneralizations are made, the result can be eth- nocentrism or prejudice." Ethnic differences from the nuclear family model are viewed as deviant rather than as expressions of cultural pluralism (Billingsley, 1968; Mirandé, 1985). Common stereotypes depict the African-American family as "unstable, disorganized, and unable to provide its members with the social and psychological support and development needed to assimilate fully into American society" (Dodson, 1988). Stereotypes about Latino families view them as rigid and authoritarian, dominated by macho fathers (Mirandé, 1985). Until recently, these stereotypes have affected much scholarly research (Demos, 1990; Mirandé, 1985). Such stereotypes seriously distort our understanding of families from different ethnic groups.

❏ *The emphasis on family structure tends to distract us from examining what actually goes on within a particular family.* We tend to assume that a family is happy simply because it is intact. But a nuclear family is not necessarily a happy family. Nuclear families may engage in small-scale nuclear warfare. Although they fit the structural norm on the outside, they may be

continued on next page

cooperate to achieve what a single individual could not. It is easier for a working couple to purchase a house than a single individual, for example, because the couple can pool their resources.

Because most domestic tasks do not take great skill (a man can clean the toilet as easily as a woman), most family members can learn to do them. As a result, members do not need to go outside the family to hire experts. In fact, for many family tasks, ranging from embracing a partner to bandaging a child's small cut or playing peek-a-boo with a baby, there are no experts to compete with family members— they tend to be the best.

These are only some of the theoretical advantages families offer to their members. Of course, not all families perform all these tasks or perform them well. But families, based on mutual ties of feeling and obligation, offer us greater potential for fulfilling our needs than organizations based on profit (such as corporations) or compulsion (such as governments).

FOCUS

hiding extensive conflict, alcoholism, incest, abuse, and hatred beneath the surface. We must look beyond a family's structure to see whether it is performing its functions. Is it socializing its children in a healthy way? Is it providing intimacy for its members? A stepfamily or single-parent family may perform the family functions far better than an unhappy but intact nuclear family.

❐ *We may misinterpret the behavior of individuals according to our stereotypes.* We may mistakenly attribute an adolescent's rebelliousness at school to being reared in a "broken home" instead of correctly attributing it to, say, rigid school rules. Or we may ignore behavior that does not fit our stereotypes. If we believe stepmothers are uncaring, we may not notice a stepmother's tenderness or may even interpret it as self-serving.

❐ *Family stereotypes influence how different families perceive and value themselves.* An unhappy traditional family may convince itself that it is a happy family because it fulfills our society's family norms. A happy stepfamily may feel deviant because it is not a biological family. These stereotypes lead single persons, divorced men and women, and

members of stepfamilies to devalue themselves (Cargan, 1986; Coleman and Ganong, 1987; Gerstel, 1987).

❐ *Because we believe that the nuclear family is the family, we ignore the potentially rich family ties offered by our extended family.* We act as if relying on friendship and support from our kin is a sign of dependence and weakness instead of strength and vitality. Scholars also fail to examine the nature of extended family relationships because they focus their research on nuclear families. Those families that do participate in extended family networks, especially African Americans and Latinos, are viewed as somehow deficient for not being self-sufficient (Ellison, 1990; Goetting, 1990; Mirandé, 1985).

❐ *Family stereotypes prevent us from dealing with the changing nature of America's families.* We attribute the problems faced by nontraditional families to their divergence from the traditional nuclear family. Yet many of the problems and stresses experienced by these families are the result of society's failure to give them support and encouragement. A dual-earner marriage, for example, tends to have increased stress because the woman, besides

being wife and mother, has the additional role of worker to fulfill. Society (and often her husband) expects her to continue her primary responsibility for housework and child care. The workplace makes no provision for the special needs of parents, such as child care, paid leave to care for sick children, and so on. Federal policies fail to support child-care initiatives because conservative "pro-family" groups believe such policies would undermine the traditional family by encouraging mothers to work. Single-parent families may be stressful for a mother, not because of the father's absence per se but because of the poverty in which she and her children are trapped.

As long as the traditional nuclear family is upheld as our only ideal family, other family forms will continue to suffer. A first step in eliminating these harmful stereotypes is recognizing that there is no single type of normal American family. We need a new family model that recognizes the diversity of family forms. We need to realize that there are many types of normal American families, embracing different family structures with ethnic variations.

❐ EXTENDED FAMILIES AND KINSHIP

Extended Families

Most people throughout the world live in some form of extended family. Parents and children, the core of the nuclear family, combine with other kin and nuclear families to form extended families. The kinship system is based on the reciprocal rights and obligations of the different family members, such as those between grandparents and grandchildren and mothers-in-law and sons-in-law.

Although American families often exist as some form of extended family, we sometimes don't recognize the fact because we uncritically accept the nuclear family model as our definition. We may even be blind to the reality of our own family structure. When someone asks us to name the members of our family, if we are unmarried we will probably name our parents, brothers, and sisters. If we are married, we will probably name our husband or wife and children. Only if questioned further may we include our grandparents, aunts or uncles, cousins, even friends or neighbors who are "like family." We may not name all our blood relatives, but we will probably name the ones with whom we feel emotionally close. If we live in a stepfamily, we may identify all, some, or none of our steprelations as family, depending on how emotionally close we feel (Pill, 1990).

Kinship System

CONJUGAL AND CONSANGUINEOUS RELATIONSHIPS. Family relationships are generally created in two ways: through marriage and through birth. Extended family relationships created through marriage are known as **conjugal relationships.** [The word "conjugal" is derived from the Latin *conjungere,* meaning "to join together."] In-laws, such as mothers-in law, fathers-in-law, sons-in-law, and daughters-in-law, are created by law—that is, through marriage. **Consanguineous relationships** are created through blood ties—that is, birth. [The word "consanguineous" is derived from the Latin *com-,* "joint," + *sanguineus,* "blood."] Parents, children, grandparents, and grandchildren, for example, have consanguineous relationships. Aunts and uncles may be either consanguineous or conjugal. Our families of orientation and marriage provide us with some of the most important roles we will assume in life. These nuclear family roles, such as parent/child, husband/wife, and sibling, combine with extended family roles, such as grandparent, aunt/uncle, cousin, and in-law, to form the **kinship system.** The kinship system is the social organization of the family.

KIN RIGHTS AND OBLIGATIONS. In some societies, mostly non-Western or non-industrialized cultures, kinship obligations may be very extensive. In cultures that emphasize kin groups, close emotional ties between a husband and wife are viewed as a threat to the extended family. An extreme form of precedence of the kin group over the married couple is the institution of spirit marriage, which continues in China today. In a spirit marriage, according to anthropologist Janice Stockard (1989), a marriage is arranged by families whose son and daughter died unmarried. After the dead couple is "married," the two families adopt an orphaned boy and raise him as the deceased couple's son to provide family continuity. In another Cantonese marriage form, women did not live with their husbands until at least three years after marriage, as their primary obligation remained with their own extended family. Among the Nayar of India, men have a number of clearly defined obligations toward the children of their sisters and female cousins, although they have few obligations toward their own children (Gough, 1968).

In American society the basic kinship system consists of parents and children, but it may include other relatives as well. Each person in this system has certain rights and obligations as a result of his or her position in the family structure. Furthermore, a person may occupy several positions at the same time. For example, an eighteen-year-old female may simultaneously be a daughter, a sister, a cousin, an aunt, and a granddaughter. Each role entails different rights and obligations. As a daughter, the young woman may have to defer to certain decisions of her parents; as a sister, to share her bedroom; as a cousin, to attend a wedding; as a granddaughter, to send a birthday card.

In our own culture, the nuclear family has many norms regulating behavior, such as parental support of children and sexual fidelity between spouses, but the rights and obligations of relatives outside the basic kinship system are less strong and less clearly articulated. Because there are neither culturally binding nor legally enforceable norms regarding the extended family, some researchers suggest that such kinship ties have become more or less voluntary. We are free to define our kinship relations much as we wish. Like friendship, they may be allowed to wane (Goetting, 1990).

While extended families have declined in significance for white middle-class Americans, they continue to be especially important to African-American, Latino, Asian-American, and Native-American families. Among African Americans, for example, extended families provide reciprocal aid and assistance, help with child care, facilitate household cooperation, and give care to aging parents and grandparents (Taylor, 1986 and 1990). They also provide foster care for children whose parents are unable to care for them (Resnick, 1990; Shimkin, Shimkin, and Frate, 1978). Among Latinos **la familia** embraces not only the nuclear but also the extended family. In *la familia*, a**buelos** (grandparents) are especially influential as warm and affectionate figures to their grandchildren (Mirandé, 1985). Among Japanese Americans, despite acculturation and intermarriage, some families attempt to preserve the traditional concept of the **ie** [pronounced *ee-eh*], that is, the family that encompasses not only members of the present extended family but also deceased and yet-to-be born family members (Kikumura and Kitano, 1988). Among Chinese Americans, elders continue to influence younger family members (Huang, 1988).

Despite the increasingly voluntary nature of kin relations, our kin create a rich social network for us. Studies suggest that most people have a large number of kin living in their area (Mancini and Blieszner, 1989). Adult children and parents often live close to each other, make regular visits, and help each other with child care,

Extended families are important sources of strength. Family rituals, such as tamale-making in this Latino family, help maintain kinship bonds.

housework, maintenance, repairs, loans, and gifts. The relations between siblings are often strong throughout the life cycle (Lee, Mancini, and Maxwell, 1990).

We generally assume kinship to be lifelong. In the past, if a marriage was disrupted by death, in-laws generally continued to be thought of as kin. They rallied around the surviving widow or widower, providing assistance and support. The rise of divorce, however, has created a unique phenomenon: ex-kin. When a marriage ends through divorce, what is the role of former in-laws? What kinship ties or responsibilities do former mothers-in-law or fathers-in-law continue to have toward their son's or daughter's former spouse? If there are no children involved, the answer seems to be none. But if the in-law is also a grandparent, the issue becomes more complicated. While relating to their grandchild, how do grandparents relate to their former son- or daughter-in-law—as a relative, friend, acquaintance, stranger, or enemy? Family loyalties may call for them to align themselves against their child's former spouse, but what if a close relationship was formed between the ex-inlaws and the ex-spouse? What if the former spouse needs assistance in child care? In another time, when divorce was considered deviant, shunning the former spouse may have seemed appropriate. But today, divorce is as much a part of the American family system as marriage. Although shunning the ex-spouse may no longer be appropriate (or polite), no new guidelines on how to behave have been developed. The ex-kin role is a **roleless role;** that is, it is a role with no clearly defined rules.

FICTIVE KIN. Blood relationships do not define the type of feelings that a person will have. Instead, they provide a framework to encourage brotherly feelings toward a brother, motherly feelings toward a child, and so on. The strength of kinship ties ultimately depends more on feeling than on biology. A brother or sister can seem like a stranger; a grandmother can be more of a mother than one's biological mother; a parent can be like a brother or sister. The names we call our relatives or friends reflect degrees of feelings (Schneider, 1980).

Feelings of kinship can extend beyond traditional kin (see Chapter 15). We form **fictive kin** (or *pseudo-kin*) by transforming friends and neighbors into kin: "He is like a brother to me," "We are like cousins." In Latino culture, **compadres** and **comadres** (the godparents of one's children) are important figures in the family. Because divorce and geographic mobility are breaking down our ability to interact with in-laws and biological kin, we are beginning to form new kinds of kin (Kempler, 1976; Lindsey, 1982). Single persons may attempt to create families from friends by sharing time, problems, meals, and houses with each other (Lindsey, 1982). They may also create cooperative or communal living arrangements with each other. Single parents may form networks with other single parents for emotional support and exchange of child care (McLanahan et al., 1981). Family networks may be formed in which three or four families from the same neighborhood share problems, exchange services, and enjoy leisure together. An **affiliated family** is a family in which unrelated individuals are treated as family members. In this situation, another person, usually an older widow, widower, or single person, spends time with the family in a role similar to that of an aunt, uncle, or grandparent, joining in family activities, child care, work, meals, housework, or recreation. Often he or she is called by some family name, such as "Auntie," "Gramps," or "Pop" (Kempler, 1976).

⌐ CULTURAL DIVERSITY

Americans come from diverse roots. According to the 1990 census, in identifying their ancestry, Americans cited over 130 ethnic groups. Over 16 million Americans speak non-English languages at home. In 1990, immigration laws were reformed to permit a 45 percent increase in immigration between 1992–1994 and a 35 percent increase in subsequent years. Between 1992 and 1994, 700,000 immigrants will be granted visas yearly; afterward, 675,000 immigrants will be admitted each year. As a result, continued Latino and Asian immigration promises to make ethnicity a major factor in American life well into the next century.

The descendants of nineteenth- and early twentieth-century immigrants, however, are finding their ethnic identities declining in significance as they leave their ethnic neighborhoods for the suburbs, increase their economic status, and marry outside their group. A major study (Lieberson and Waters, 1988) on contemporary ethnic groups in America concluded:

White ethnics, while different from one another on a variety of measures, are still much more similar to each other than they are to blacks, Hispanics, American Indians, and Asians. . . . For whatever cause(s), a European–non-European distinction remains a central division in the society.

During the 1980s, 8.6 million documented immigrants entered the United States, the largest number since 1900–1910, the previous high-water mark (Barringer, 1992). As new immigrants arrive, primarily from Latin America and Asia, they find their ethnic identities major factors in organizing their lives. According to the latest data available, there are at least 16 to 18 million foreign-born Americans. Europeans accounted for 5.3 million, Asians represented 3.8 million (mostly, in numerical order, from the Philippines, Korea, China, Vietnam, and Japan), and Caribbeans totaled 1.8 million (U.S. Bureau of the Census, 1988). Because of the large numbers of undocumented aliens from Latin America, precise numbers of foreign-born Latinos are unknown, although the number may run as high as 7 million. There has been relatively little immigration from black Africa in the twentieth century; most recent-immigrant blacks are from the Caribbean and Latin America.

Families from ethnic groups such as African Americans, Latinos, and Asians often face prejudice and discrimination. Such discrimination has often limited educational and work opportunities for these people. As a result, families from these different ethnic groups often face hardships and challenges that white middle-class families do not.

African-American Families

Unlike the early English, French and Spanish settlers in North America, African Americans arrived in chains. Throughout the New World, the traditional African family forms were severely repressed (Gutman, 1976). At first, some enslaved blacks tried unsuccessfully to continue polygamy, which was strongly rooted in many African cultures. They were more successful in continuing the traditional African emphasis on the extended family, in which aunts, uncles, cousins, and grandparents played important roles. Although the slave system prohibited marriage, enslaved blacks created their own informal forms of marriage. They developed strong emotional bonds and family ties. Slave culture discouraged casual sexual relationships and placed a high value on marital stability. On the large plantations, most slaves lived in two-parent families with their children. To maintain family identity, parents named their children after themselves or other relatives or gave them African names. As time went on, the developing African-American family blended West African and English family traditions (Gutman, 1976). In the harsh slave system, the family provided strong support against the daily indignities of servitude.

We boast of being immigrants . . .when we are no longer subject to the immigrants' ordeal, after we have become certifiable natives and, often, at a time when we and our kind are busily closing the door to others.

Meg Greenfield

We are increasingly becoming a world of migrants, made up of bits and fragments from here, there. We are here. And we have not really left anywhere we have been.

Salman Rushdie

Although there were large numbers of free African Americans—100,000 in the North and Midwest and 150,000 in the South—most of what we know about the African-American family prior to the Civil War is limited to slave families. By the nineteenth century, slave families had lost much of their African heritage. Under slavery, the African-American family lacked two key factors that helped give free African-Americans and white families stability. First, the enslaved African-American family lacked autonomy. Because slave marriages were not legally recognized, final authority in all matters affecting the enslaved families rested with the owner. If the owner decided to break up a family by selling a husband, wife, or children, laws granted him or her that right. As a consequence, the separation of families was a common occurrence. When a woman was pregnant, her owner determined her care during pregnancy and relation to her child after birth (G. Jones, 1985).

Second, the slave family had little economic importance as a unit. Slave families worked for their masters, not themselves. In addition to the field, factory, and household service in which both men and women participated, after these tasks were accomplished women had additional family tasks to perform, such as tending their family garden, preparing meals, and rearing their children.

When freedom came, the formerly enslaved African-American family had strong emotional ties and traditions forged from slavery and from their West African heritage (Gutman, 1976; Lantz, 1980). Because they were not legally able to marry, thousands of former slaves who had "jumped the broomstick" in slave marriage now formally renewed their vows (Litwack, 1979).

African-American families remained poor, tied to the land by the sharecrop system, which kept them in a state of semislavery, and by segregation, which kept them subordinate. Despite poverty and continued exploitation, the Southern African-American family usually consisted of both parents and their children. Extended kin continued to be important: aunts, uncles, grandparents, cousins, and in-laws provided a rich source of affection and kindly assistance through thick and thin.

I am the dream and hope of the slave.

Maya Angelou

The largest ethnic group in the United States is African American. The African-American family, as we have seen, can trace its roots back to the beginnings of the earliest European settlements. Between 1980 and 1990, the African-American population increased by approximately 16 percent. In 1990, there were over 31 million African Americans in the United States. Between 1990 and 2000, the African-American population will increase by 12.8 percent, to 35.2 million (U.S. Bureau of the Census, 1988 and 1990).

The tree of love gives shade to all.

African–American proverb

In the twentieth century, especially after World War II, there was a movement of African Americans from the South to other parts of the country, especially to urban areas (Lemann, 1991). Robert Staples (1991) noted:

Unlike the European immigrants before them, African Americans were disadvantaged by the hard lines of northern segregation along racial lines. Furthermore, families in cities are more vulnerable to disruptions from the traumatizing experience of urbanization, the reduction of family functions, and the loss of extended family support.

In the cities, African Americans were especially vulnerable to economic forces. The postwar technological revolution diminished the need for industrial workers, the backbone of the working-class African-American family. After the mid-1950s, the unemployment rate for African Americans surged to two to three times the rate for whites. As a result, the gradual increase of the African-American middle class has been more than counterbalanced by the demise of the African-American working class, replaced by the underclass (Billingsley, 1988).

The geographical movement out of the South led to a pursuit of individual rather than family goals. The strong tradition of familialism continues, however, as intergenerational ties are emphasized in the African-American family. Kinship bonds are especially important, for they provide economic assistance and emotional support in times of need (Taylor et al., 1991). Women, as well as men, have an important economic role. African-American families, in contrast to white families, have often been dual-earner families as a result of economic need.

As we examine African-American families, much of what they experience, such as high divorce rates or high rates of birth to single women, turn out to be associated with poverty rather than anything inherent in African-American families themselves. Although there seems to be greater marital instability in African-American families than in white families, for example, when divorce rates are adjusted according to socioeconomic status, the differences become minimal. Poor African Americans have divorce rates similar to poor whites, and middle-class African Americans have divorce rates similar to middle-class whites (Raschke, 1987). Thus, understanding socioeconomic status, especially poverty, is critical in examining African-American family life (Bryant and Coleman, 1988; Staples and Mirandé, 1980).

Latino Families

Latinos are the fastest growing and second largest ethnic group in the United States. Between 1980 and 1990, Latino population increased by approximately 35 percent. Most of this increase resulted from immigration from Mexico (Vega, 1991). Between 1990 and 2000, Latinos are expected to increase another 27 percent and number 25.2 million (U.S. Bureau of the Census, 1988). In 1988, there were approximately 19.4 million Latinos in the United States; 12 million were of Mexican descent. Latinos account for 22 percent of the Texas population, 16 percent of the California and Arizona populations, and 14 percent of the New Mexico population. Puerto Ricans are concentrated in the Northeast, especially New York. The greatest concentration of Cubans is found in Florida.

Out of poverty, poetry
Out of suffering, song.

Mexican proverb

For Latinos, la familia *is a central part of their lives. Children are especially valued.*

It is important to remember that there is considerable diversity among Latinos, between those of Mexican, Cuban, Puerto Rican, and other heritages. For example, 40 percent of Cuban Americans earn over $35,000 annually, while only 15 percent of Puerto Ricans and 23 percent of Mexican Americans earn as much. Furthermore, there are 2.5 times as many single-parent families among Puerto Ricans as there are among Mexican Americans. (For an overview of Mexican-American families, see Becerra, 1988; for Cuban American families, see Szapoznik and Hernandez, 1988; for Puerto Rican families, see Sánchez-Ayéndez, 1988.)

> *Frijoles, tortillas, y chile are more American than the hamburger.*
>
> Luis Valdez

Spanish and Mexican settlements date back to the early seventeenth century in the Southwest. Because these areas bordered Mexico and had indigenous Latino cultures, they provided a magnet for Mexican and other Latino immigrants. Latino immigration was very small, however, until the turn of the century (Griswold Del Castillo, 1984). The massive influx of Mexican and other Latino immigrants began after 1945. Attracted by the American demand for workers and uprooted by poverty at home, twice as many Latinos immigrated between 1945 and 1965 as had come to the United States in the previous hundred years. Hope, combined with civil wars, revolutions, repression, poverty, and hunger drove hundreds of thousands from Guatemala, El Salvador, Cuba, Haiti, and other Latin American and Caribbean countries.

As with the European immigrants who preceded them, family networks help sustain the Latino immigrants. Three-fourths of Cuban and half of Mexican immigrants reported assistance from relatives residing in the United States. In fact, Mexican American family networks provide significant community and family links between the United States and Mexico (Vega, 1991). Although *la familia* is centered around the nuclear family, it also includes the extended family of grandparents, aunts, uncles, and cousins who tend to live close by, often in the same block or neighborhood. There is close kin cooperation and mutual assistance, especially in times of need, when the family bands together. Children are especially important; over one-third of Latino families have five or more children. Because Spanish is important in maintaining ethnic identity, many Latinos as well as educators support bilingualism in schools and government. Catholicism is also an important factor in Latino family life. Although there is a tradition of male dominance, day-to-day living patterns suggest that women have considerable power and influence in the family (Griswold Del Castillo, 1984).

Asian-American Families

> *It's not a "melting pot" anymore. . . . (It's) a fusion chamber. We are creating American culture daily.*
>
> Bharati Mukherjee

In 1990 there were approximately 6 million Asian Americans living in the United States; they comprise ten percent of the California population. By 2000, the Asian-American population will increase to 10 million (Lev, 1991). They are an especially diverse group, comprising Chinese, Japanese, Filipino, Vietnamese, Cambodian, Hmong, and other groups. The two largest and oldest groups are the Chinese Americans and Japanese Americans. Other groups, such as Vietnamese, Cambodians, Laotians, and Hmong, are more recent arrivals, first coming to this country in the 1970s as refugees from the upheavals resulting from the Vietnam war. In the 1980s, Koreans and Filipinos began immigrating in larger numbers. Because of their cultural diversity and degree of assimilation, generalizations about Asian Americans are risky. In addition, there has been very little research on Asian-American family relationships. (For an overview of Korean American families, see Min, 1988; for Vietnamese American families, see Tran, 1988; for Hmong families, see Hendricks, Downing, and Deinard, 1986).

Chinese Americans trace their ancestory in the United States to the mid-nineteenth century, when they came as laborers in the gold camps and railroads. (The Chinese word for laborer, *ku-li*, translates as "bitter strength.") Almost all the immigrants were men who had come alone to the "Golden Mountain," sending money home to their wives, who lived with their husbands' parents. Beginning in 1882, anti-Chinese sentiment led to the Exclusion Acts, which restricted Asian immigration. These acts virtually prohibited Chinese women from entering the United States until 1943, resulting in most Chinese men living without intimate marital ties in the United States. By 1930, there were four Chinese men for every Chinese woman in this country; today, the ratio is about equal. More recent immigrants tend to be from Taiwan or Hong Kong rather than mainland China itself.

Contemporary Chinese-American families continue to emphasize familialism, although filial piety and strict obedience to parental authority have become less strong. Chinese Americans tend to be better educated, have higher incomes, and have lower rates of unemployment than the general population. Their sexual values and attitudes toward gender roles tend to be more conservative; they tend to have a strong sense of family.

The second-largest group of Asian Americans is Japanese Americans. First-generation Japanese, called *Issei*, arrived in Hawaii and on the West Coast toward the end of the nineteenth century, where they engaged mostly in agriculture and domestic work. Like the Chinese, they suffered discrimination. In 1924 the Chinese Exclusion Acts were extended to forbid Japanese immigration. *Issei* were prohibited from becoming citizens, and in California, laws were passed to prevent them from owning or leasing farm land. American-born children of *Issei*, called *Nisei*, were granted citizenship, however. When the Japanese attacked the United States in World War II, Japanese Americans were incarcerated in so-called "relocation" camps and their property confiscated. (Only recently—almost fifty years later—did the federal government acknowledge its error and begin making small compensatory payments to the camp survivors.)

Sansei, third-generation Japanese Americans, have experienced more **acculturation** than other Asian-American groups. Almost half of all Japanese Americans, especially women, marry non-Japanese. *Sansei* emphasize *ie* (the Japanese extended family of past, present, and future generations), have high levels of education, and value achievement, diligence, and loyalty. In contrast to their elders, *Sansei* are more independent and individualistic, which sometimes causes cultural tension between the generations. Over a third of their children, *Yonsei*, who are mostly school-age or adolescent, are of mixed marriages, though they often continue to identify themselves as Japanese Americans.

Native American Families

From the beginning of European contact, Native Americans were decimated by invasion, war, famine, and disease. The unique family structures of each surviving tribe were deliberately undermined by the federal government's program of forced enculturation (1870–1930). Missionaries and government agents worked hand in hand to destroy traditional Indian family forms and replace them with the structure and norms of the conventional white nuclear family. As scholar John Price (1981) noted, "Christian missionaries usually tried to eliminate plural marriages and matrilineal customs without understanding the crucial roles these practices had in the normal functioning of native societies." Communal land was turned into private property, regulations were introduced making the man head of the family, and lead-

Question: What is cultural deprivation? Answer: Living in a split level house in suburbia with a color TV.

Native American riddle

Powwows are an important mechanism for the development of Native American cultural identity as well as tribal identity.

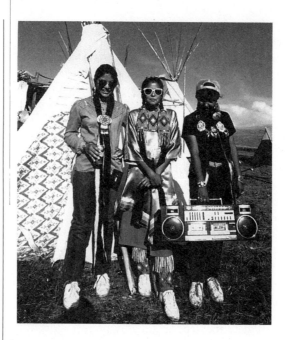

ers no longer came from the clans (extended kin) but were elected. Church activities replaced traditional religious rituals.

Approximately 1.5 million Americans identify themselves as being of native descent. Those who continue to be deeply involved with their own traditional culture give themselves a tribal identity, such as Hopi, Navajo, or Sioux. Those who are more acculturated, such as urban dwellers, tend to give themselves an ethnic identity as American Indians. Most Americans of native descent consider themselves members of a tribal group rather than an ethnic group. And, observed Price (1981), "Specific tribal identities are almost universally stronger and more important than identity as a Native American."

Because of the marked poverty on reservations and pressures toward acculturation, there has been a considerable migration of Native Americans to urban areas since World War II. Today, about half of Americans of native descent live in cities. In the cities, Indians are separated from their traditional tribal cultures and experience great cultural conflict as they attempt to maintain traditional values. Not surprisingly, those in the cities are more acculturated than those remaining on the reservations. Urban Native Americans may attend **powwows,** intertribal social gatherings centering around drumming, singing, and traditional dances. Powwows are important mechanisms in the development of the Native American ethnic identity in contrast to the tribal identity. Urban Native Americans, however, may visit the reservations regularly; in fact, these visits are sometimes described as a specialized form of commuting.

Because of the importance of tribal identities and practices, there is no single type of Native American family. Perhaps the most important factor affecting tribal identities is the degree of acculturation. A study (Miller, 1979) of a group of urban Native American families found that 39 percent were transitional, adopting white values; 22 percent were traditional, maintaining Indian values; 23 percent were bicultural, holding both Indian and white values; and 16 percent were marginal, failing to sustain Indian values or incorporate white ones.

❐ SOURCES OF FAMILY CHANGE

Marriages and families are sensitive to the different forces in society. The most important sources of change are economic, demographic, and gender-role changes (Mintz and Kellogg, 1988).

Economic Changes

The family was once the primary economic unit in society, meeting most of the needs of its members: it provided food, clothing, household goods, and occasionally surplus crops, which it bartered or marketed. Today, the family has moved from being primarily an economic producing unit to a consuming, service-oriented unit. It no longer makes its clothing but buys it; it no longer grows its food but shops for it—or eats out at fast-food restaurants.

Inflation, economic hardship, and an expanding economy have led to married women entering the work force in unprecedented numbers. As a result, the dual-worker marriage and the employed mother have become prominent features of contemporary families. As women have increased their participation in the work force, they have decreased their economic dependency on men. Because working in the labor force provides both income and alternative roles for women, women have been able to increase their marital power.

Demographic Changes

The family has also changed demographically—that is, in terms of the characteristics of its members, such as age, number of children, sex ratio, divorce and death rate (Glick, 1988; Watkins and Menkin, 1987). Four of the most important demographic changes affecting the family have been (1) declining fertility (that is, the number of children a woman bears), (2) increased divorce rate, (3) the gradual aging of the population, and (4) race and ethnicity.

❐ *Declining Fertility.* As women bear fewer children, they have fewer years of child-rearing responsibility. With fewer children, partners are able to devote more time to each other. Parents are able to expend greater energy on each child. And women have greater opportunity for entering the work force.

❐ *Increased Divorce Rate.* The increased divorce rate, beginning in the late nineteenth century (as early as 1900, the United States had the highest divorce rate in the world), has led to the rise of single-parent families and stepfamilies.

❐ *Increased Longevity.* As men and women live longer, they are experiencing aspects of family life that few experienced before. In colonial times, because of a relatively short life expectancy, a husband and wife could expect a marriage to last up to twenty-five years. With today's much longer life expectancy, a couple can remain married for fifty to sixty years. Today's couples can also expect to live many years without children at home; they can expect to become grandparents and as many as one-fourth may become great-grandparents. American women can also expect a prolonged period of widowhood following the death of their husbands. Since men tend to marry women younger than themselves and there are more women than men, most widows will not remarry.

❐ *Race and Ethnicity.* Americans have always had diverse family systems, including the original Native American family systems, the dominant American family sys-

If history repeats itself, and the unexpected always happens, how incapable must man be of learning from experience.

George Bernard Shaw

tem (based on the white English/European heritage), and the African-American family system. To these family systems were added nineteenth- and twentieth-century immigrant family systems. Immigration transformed America from a mainly Protestant country to one of religious pluralism.

Gender-Role Changes

A third basic force altering American marriages and families is changing gender roles, especially women's roles. In colonial times, men were primarily responsible for tilling fields, harvesting crops, and manufacturing work implements. Women were the primary producers of family goods and necessities. If there was a surplus of crops or goods, women marketed or bartered them. But as production of clothing, household goods, tools, and food was transferred to factories and large-scale farms, men and women developed new roles. In the nineteenth century, men and single women increasingly worked in factories and offices. As a result, families were no longer self-sufficient. Instead, they relied on wages brought home by the husband and, in working-class families, by the children. At the same time, women concentrated on mothering and household management. Women were now expected to be responsible for shaping their children's character and tending to the needs of their husbands. These changes led to the "invention" of the male breadwinner and the female housewife.

The emphasis on childrearing and housework as the proper duties of women continued unchallenged until the 1940s. During World War II, however, a massive influx of married women poured into factories and stores to replace men who were fighting. Thus began a trend in which women increasingly entered the labor force. By being less economically dependent on men, women gained greater power in marriage.

The feminist movement of the 1960s and 1970s caused women (whether they identified themselves as feminists or not) to reexamine their traditional assumptions about women's roles. Betty Friedan's *The Feminine Mystique*, published in 1963, became a national sensation. It attacked the traditionalist assumption that women found their greatest fulfillment in being mothers and housewives. The book tapped into fundamental discontent that many white, middle-class women were experiencing in suburbia. These women did everything they were supposed to do—were married, had three children, baked, cleaned, and joined clubs—but many were still dissatisfied. The women's movement challenged the female roles of housewife, helpmate, and mother. Practically, the dual-worker marriage made the traditional division of roles an important question for *all* women. Today, contemporary women have dramatically different expectations of male/female roles in marriage, childrearing, household work, and the workplace than did their grandmothers or even their mothers.

❐ As you begin studying marriage and the family, you can see that such study is both abstract and personal. It is abstract insofar as you learn about the general structure, processes, and meanings associated with marriage and the family. But the study of marriage and the family is also personal: it is *your* present, *your* past, and *your* future that you are studying. It is the family from which you came, the family in which you are now living, and the family that you will create. What R. D. Laing (1972) wrote some years ago may ring true for you today:

The first family to interest me was my own. I still know less about it than I know about many other families. This is typical. Children are the last to be told what was really going on.

As you continue your study of marriage and the family, much of what was unknown in your own family may become known. You may discover new understanding, strength, complexity, and love.

History is the ship carrying living memories to the future.

Stephen Spender

As we near the end of the twentieth century, we see that American families have changed radically during our history as a nation. The most radical change came about in the nineteenth century as we changed from a farming society to an industrial one. Within our own lifetime, families have been undergoing the most significant changes of the twentieth century as the once-dominant traditional white nuclear family has been supplanted by more diverse forms: the single-parent family, the stepfamily, the dual-worker family, and ethnic extended families. Our task as a society is not to decry the "decline" of the traditional family; rather, it is to support and strengthen the contemporary family as it is evolving in today's world.

 SUMMARY

❒ The *nuclear family* consists of the mother/father/child triad. The *extended family* consists of the nuclear family and other relatives. *Monogamy* refers to the marital form in which there are two spouses, husband and wife. *Polygamy* refers to the practice of having more than one husband or wife.

❒ *Marriage* is a socially recognized union between a woman and a man. Its main characteristics are (1) the performance of a public ritual to sanction the union; (2) sexual unification; and (3) economic cooperation. *Divorce* is the legal dissolution of marriage following *separation.* High divorce rates have made single-parent families and stepfamilies important family forms in contemporary America. Divorce, remarriage, single-parent families, and stepfamilies are normal aspects of the contemporary American marriage system. *Cohabitation,* in which an unmarried couple lives together and is sexually involved, has become so common that some regard it as part of the family life cycle.

❒ A *family* may be defined as one or more adults who cooperate and divide labor, share a common dwelling, and may be raising children. Four important family functions are (1) provision of intimacy; (2) formation of a cooperative economic unit; (3) reproduction and socialization; and (4) assignment of status and social roles, which are acquired both in our *family of orientation* (in which we grow up) and our *family of marriage* (which we form by marrying).

❒ Advantages to living in families include: (1) continuity of emotional attachments; (2) close proximity; (3) familiarity with family members; and (4) economic benefits.

❒ *Stereotypes* are highly simplified, overgeneralized beliefs. The strongest family stereotype is that the traditional nuclear family is the norm against which all other families are measured. The consequences of this stereotype include the following: (1) other family forms and life-styles, such as single-parent families and stepfamilies, are misper-ceived as deviant; (2) ethnic family differences are misinterpreted as deviant; (3) behavior may be misconstrued according to stereotypes; (4) those in nontraditional families and life-styles may devalue themselves; (5) the focus on formal structure discourages us from examining whether a family—regardless of its form—fulfills its functions; and (6) society fails to support other family forms.

❒ The extended family consists of grandparents, aunts, uncles, cousins, and in-laws. It may be formed *conjugally,* through marriage, creating in-laws and step-kin, or *consanguineously,* by birth, through blood relationships. Extended families are especially important for African-American, Latino, Asian-American, and Native-American families. The Latino *familia* is an extended family including *abuelos* (grandparents) and *compadres* (godparents).

❒ The *kinship system* is the social organization of the family. In the nuclear family it generally consists of parents and children, but it may also include members of the extended family, especially grandparents, aunts, uncles, and cousins. Kin can be *fictive:* a nonrelated person can be *as* kin, or a relative may fulfill a different kin role, such as a grandmother taking the role of a child's mother. The *affiliated family* consists of related family members and fictive kin. Traditionally, kinship was assumed to be lifelong, but with divorce and remarriage on the rise, kin formed through marriage may change.

❒ Contemporary families are culturally diverse; there are over 130 ethnic groups in America. African Americans and Latinos are the largest ethnic groups, and extended family ties are especially important to these groups.

❒ African-Americans arrived in North America in the early seventeenth century as slaves. They continued the African tradition that emphasized kin relations. Most slaves lived in two-parent families that valued marital stability. The stability of the African-American slave family suffered because it lacked autonomy and had little economic importance. Slave families were broken up by slaveholders, and marriage between slaves was not legally recognized. African-American families formed solid bonds nevertheless.

❏ Since the 1950s, technological changes have decimated the African-American working class, giving rise to the underclass. Many of the problems African-American families experience are the result of low socioeconomic status rather than family structure.

❏ Latinos, who are the fastest-growing ethnic group, emphasize extended kin relationships, cooperation, and mutual assistance. *La familia* includes not only the nuclear family but also the extended family. Catholicism exerts a strong influence on Latino families. Bilingualism helps maintain ethnicity.

❏ Among Asian Americans, Chinese Americans and Japanese Americans have been in the United States the longest. Both groups have experienced great discrimination. Chinese Americans continue to emphasize familial-ism. Japanese Americans, the most *acculturated* of Asian Americans, continue to emphasize the *ie,* the extended family that includes past, present, and future members. Native Americans endured forced enculturation for 60 years as the government and Christian missionaries attempted to assimilate them into mainstream white culture. Tribal identity is their key identity. Poverty forced many off reservations to cities. *Powwows* are social gatherings centering around drumming, singing, and dancing.

❏ Throughout American history, economic, demographic, and gender role changes have significantly affected the family. Economically, the family has moved from being primarily a producing unit to a consuming unit. Demographic effects include declining fertility, increased divorce, increased longevity, and changing ethnic composition. Changing gender roles are reshaping the family as women become more equal in the workplace and at home.

PART 2

Getting Together

CHAPTER 2

Contemporary Gender Roles

OUTLINE

One half the world cannot understand the pleasures of the other.

Jane Austen

L ET US BEGIN WITH A STORY AND A QUESTION. Jason and his father were driving on the highway when suddenly another car veered into their path. The oncoming car struck with such force that Jason's father was killed instantly, and Jason suffered severe head injuries. An ambulance rushed the bleeding boy to the hospital where, fortunately, one of the country's leading neurosurgeons was in residence. Because it was late at night and there was nothing to do, the surgeon was engaged in a friendly poker game with several other physicians. Upon being paged to the operating room, the surgeon cursed and sprinted down the corridor. Entering the operating room, the surgeon exclaimed, "My God! I can't operate on this boy. He's my son." The question is, who was the surgeon?

If you can't figure out the answer, you are probably not alone. The surgeon is Jason's mother. The trick of the story is based on the use of gender-role stereotypes in describing the surgeon. According to traditional female stereotypes, women aren't neurosurgeons, don't play poker, don't curse or sprint down halls. Fortunately, more people each year are able to answer the question correctly as we become increasingly aware of gender-role stereotypes. But you might try the story on friends or classmates to see how well they do.

Our gender roles have a tremendous impact on our lives. They influence our self-image, our dating and marital relationships, our achievement in school and careers, and many other aspects of our lives. In this chapter we look at gender roles, how they are formed, and how they affect us.

❑ STUDYING GENDER ROLES

Until the rise of the women's movement in the 1960s, little interest was expressed in gender roles, and that small interest reinforced traditional notions that woman's place was in the home and man's place was everywhere else (Spence et al., 1985). As a result of the women's movement, however, both the public and researchers began reexamining traditional gender ideas. "In the span of a few years," writes Janet Spence and her colleagues (1985), "inquiries into these matters have grown from a trickle to a torrent."

Initially, this torrent of research focused on women's roles; more recently, this examination has expanded to include male roles, especially male family roles (Losh-Hesselbart, 1987). Previously, researchers showed little interest in male family roles because gender-role stereotypes about men blinded researchers to the actual roles that men play in the day-to-day activities of home life. Researchers assumed that the male role in the family was limited to that of provider.

Most gender-role studies have focused on the white middle class. Very little is known about gender roles among African Americans, Latinos, Asian Americans, and other ethnic groups (Binion, 1990; Reid and Comas-Diaz, 1990; True, 1990; see *Sex Roles* 22: 7–8 [April 1990] for a special issue on gender roles and ethnicity). Students and researchers must be careful not to project gender-role concepts or aspirations based on white middle-class values onto other groups. Too often such projections can lead to distortions or moral judgments. There is evidence, for example, that the traditional woman's role of dependent homemaker has not been an important one for African-American women; instead, African Americans emphasized the "strong" woman who both raised a family and worked outside the home (Gump, 1980; E. Smith, 1982). Similarly, *machismo* has a positive meaning among Latinos, but Anglos often use the term in a derogatory sense.

Before we continue further, we need to define several key terms, because lack of agreement sometimes causes confusion when studying gender roles. These key terms

The great question . . . which I have not been able to answer, despite my thirty years of research into the feminine soul, is "What does a woman want?"

Sigmund Freud (1856–1939)

include *gender, role, gender role, gender-role stereotype, gender-role attitudes,* and *gender-role behavior.* **Gender** refers to male or female. **Role** refers to the culturally defined expectations that an individual is expected to fulfill in a given situation in a particular culture. **Gender roles,** are the roles that a person is expected to perform as a result of being male or female in a particular culture. (The term *gender role* is gradually replacing the traditional term *sex role*). A **gender-role stereotype** is a rigidly held and oversimplified belief that all males and females, as a result of their sex, possess distinct psychological and behavioral traits. Stereotypes tend to be false not only for the group as a whole (all men are aggressive) but for any individual member of the group (Michael may not be aggressive). Even if the generalization is statistically valid in describing a group average (males are taller than females), such generalizations do not necessarily predict whether Jason will be taller than Tanya. **Gender-role attitudes** refer to the beliefs we have about ourselves and others regarding appropriate male and female personality traits and activities. **Gender-role behaviors** refer to the actual activities or behaviors we engage in as males and females. When we discuss gender roles, it is important not to confuse stereotypes with reality and attitudes with behavior.

❒ SOCIALIZATION THEORIES

Gender and Gender Roles

At birth, we are identified as either male or female. This identity, based on genitalia, is called **gender identity,** and we learn it at a very young age. It is perhaps the deepest concept we hold of ourselves. The psychology of insults suggests this depth, for few things offend a person so much as to be tauntingly characterized as a member of the "opposite" sex. Gender identity determines many of the directions our lives will take—for example, whether we will fulfill the role of husband or wife, father or mother. When the scripts are handed out in life, the one you receive depends largely on your gender identity.

Each culture determines the content of gender roles in its own way. Among the Arapesh of New Guinea, both sexes possessed what we consider feminine traits. Men and women alike tended to be passive, cooperative, peaceful, and nurturing. The father was said to "bear a child" as well as the mother; only the father's continual care could make a child grow healthily, both in the womb and in childhood. Eighty miles away, the Mundugumor lived in remarkable contrast to the peaceful Arapesh. "Both men and women," Margaret Mead (1975) observed, "are expected to be violent, competitive, aggressively sexed, jealous, and ready to see and avenge insult, delighting in display, in action, in fighting." She concluded, "Many, if not all of the personality traits which we have called masculine or feminine are as lightly linked to sex as are the clothing, the manners, and the form of head-dress that a society at a given period assigned to either sex. . . . The evidence is overwhelmingly in favor of social conditioning." Biology creates males and females, but culture creates masculinity and femininity.

Although there are a number of ways of examining how we acquire our gender roles, two of the most prominent are social learning theory and cognitive development theory.

Cognitive Social Learning Theory

Cognitive social learning theory is derived from behaviorist psychology. In explaining our actions, behaviorists emphasize observable events and their consequences

Throughout history the more complex activities have been defined and redefined, now as male, now as female—sometimes as drawing equally on the gifts of both sexes. When an activity to which each sex could have contributed is limited to one sex, a rich, differentiated quality is lost from the activity itself.

Margaret Mead (1901–1978)

If you want anything said, ask a man. If you want anything done, ask a woman.

Margaret Thatcher

Women are made, not born.

Simone de Beauvoir

rather than internal feelings and drives. According to behaviorists, we learn attitudes and behaviors as a result of social interactions with others (hence the term *social* learning).

This behaviorist approach has been modified recently to include **cognition**—that is, mental processes that intervene between stimulus and response, such as evaluation and reflection. The cognitive processes involved in social learning include our ability to (1) use language, (2) anticipate consequences, and (3) make observations. By using language, we can tell our daughter that we like it when she does well in school and that we don't like it when she hits someone. A person's ability to anticipate consequences affects behavior. A boy doesn't need to wear lace stockings in public to know that such dressing will lead to negative consequences. Finally, children observe what others do. A girl may learn that she "shouldn't" play video games by seeing that the players in video arcades are mostly boys.

We also learn gender roles by imitation. Learning through imitation is called **modeling.** Most of us are not even aware of the many subtle behaviors that make up gender roles—the ways in which men and women use different mannerisms and gestures, speak differently, use different body language, and so on. We don't "teach" these behaviors by reinforcement. Children tend to model friendly, warm, and nurturing adults; they also tend to imitate adults who are powerful in their eyes—that is, adults who control access to food, toys, or privileges. Initially, the most powerful models that children have are their parents. As children grow older and their social world expands, so do the number of people who may act as their role models: siblings, friends, teachers, media figures. Children sift through the various demands and expectations associated with the different models to create their own unique selves.

Cognitive Development Theory

Unwittingly, the feuding experts and conflicting experiments testify to the truth: we will never have a Sears catalogue of sex differences because human beings are too diverse for labels and measurements. For every trait studied, the differences within each sex are greater than the average differences between the two sexes.

Letty Cottin Pogrebin, Growing Up Free

In contrast to social learning theory, cognitive development theory focuses on the child's active interpretation of the messages he or she receives from the environment. Whereas social learning assumes that children and adults learn in fundamentally the same way, cognitive development theory stresses that we learn differently depending on our age. Swiss psychologist Jean Piaget showed that children's ability to reason and understand changes as they grow older (Santrock, 1983). Lawrence Kohlberg (1969) took Piaget's findings and applied them to how children assimilate gender-role information at different ages. At age two, children can correctly identify themselves and others as boys or girls, but they tend to base this identification on superficial features such as hair and clothing. Girls have long hair and wear dresses; boys have short hair and never wear dresses. Some children even believe they can change their gender by changing their clothes or hair length. They don't identify gender in terms of gentalia, as older children and adults do. No amount of reinforcement will alter their view because their ideas are limited by their developmental stage.

When children are six or seven, they begin to understand that gender is permanent; it is not something you can change as you can your clothes. They acquire this understanding because they are capable of grasping the idea that basic characteristics do not change. A woman can be a woman even if she has short hair and wears pants. Oddly enough, although children can understand the permanence of gender, they tend to insist on rigid adherence to gender-role stereotypes. Even though boys can play with dolls, children believe they shouldn't because dolls are for girls. Researchers speculate that children exaggerate gender roles to make the roles "cognitively clear."

According to cognitive social learning theory, boys and girls learn appropriate gender-role behavior through reinforcement and modeling. But according to cognitive development theory, once children learn that gender is permanent, they independently strive to act like "proper" girls or boys. They do this on their own because of an internal need for *congruence*, the agreement between what they know and how they act. Also, children find performing the appropriate gender-role activities rewarding in itself. Models and reinforcement help show them how well they are doing, but the primary motivation is internal.

❑ LEARNING GENDER ROLES

Gender-Role Learning in Childhood and Adolescence

It is difficult to analyze the relationship between biology and personality, for learning begins at birth. Evidence shows, for example, that infant females are more sensitive than infant males to pain and to sudden changes of environment. Such responses may be encouraged by learning that begins immediately after birth.

In our culture, infant girls are usually held more gently and treated more tenderly than boys, who are ordinarily subjected to rougher forms of play. The first day after birth, parents rate their daughters as soft, fine featured, and small, and their sons as hard, large featured, big, and attentive. Fathers tend to stereotype their sons more extremely than mothers do (Fagot and Leinbach, 1987; Rubin et al., 1974). Although it is impossible for strangers to know the sex of a diapered baby, once they learn the baby's sex, they respond accordingly. In one well-known experiment, three groups played with Baby X (Condry and Condry, 1976). The first group was told that the baby was a girl, the second group was told that the baby was a boy, and the third group was not told what sex the baby was. The group that did not know what sex Baby X was felt extremely uncomfortable, but the group participants then made a decision based on whether the baby was "strong" or "soft." When the baby was labeled a boy, its fussing behavior was called "angry"; if the baby was labeled a girl, the same behavior was called "frustrated." The study was replicated numerous times with the same general results.

PARENTS AS SOCIALIZING AGENTS. During infancy and early childhood, a child's most important source of learning is the primary caretaker, whether the mother, father, grandmother, or someone else. Most parents are not aware that their words and actions contribute to their children's gender-role socialization (Culp et al., 1983). Nor are they aware that they treat their sons and daughters differently because of their gender. Although parents may recognize that they respond differently to sons than to daughters, they usually have a ready explanation—the "natural" differences in the temperament and behavior of girls and boys. Parents may also believe they adjust their responses to each particular child's personality. In an everyday living situation that involves changing diapers, feeding babies, stopping fights, and providing entertainment, it is difficult for harassed parents to recognize that their own actions may be largely responsible for the differences they attribute to nature.

Children are socialized in gender roles through four very subtle processes: manipulation, channeling, verbal appellation, and activity exposure (Oakley, 1985).

❑ *Manipulation:* Parents manipulate their children from infancy onward. They treat a daughter gently, tell her she is pretty, and advise her that nice girls do not fight. They treat a son roughly, tell him he is strong, and advise him that big boys

What are little girls made of?
Sugar and spice
And everything nice.
That's what little girls are made of.

What are little boys made of?
Snips and snails and puppy dogs' tails.
That's what little boys are made of.

Nursery rhyme

If I had knowledge only of the anatomy and cultural capacities of men and women, I would predict that women rather than men would be more likely to gain control over the technology of defense and aggression, and that if one sex were going to subordinate the other, it would be female over male. While I would be impressed with the physical dimorphism—the greater height, weight, and strength of the males—I would be even more impressed by something which the females have and which the males cannot get—namely, control over the birth, care and feeding of babies. Women, in other words, control the nursery, and because they control the nursery, they can potentially modify any lifestyle that threatens them.

Marvin Harris, Cows, Pigs, Wars, and Witches

do not cry. Eventually, children incorporate their parents' views in such matters as integral parts of their personalities.

☐ *Channeling:* Children are channeled by directing their attention to specific objects. Toys, for example, are differentiated by sex. Dolls are considered appropriate for girls, cars for boys.

☐ *Verbal Appellation:* Parents use different words with boys and girls to describe the same behavior. A boy who pushes others may be described as "active," whereas a girl who does the same is usually called "aggressive."

☐ *Activity Exposure:* The activity exposure of boys and girls differs markedly. Although both are usually exposed to feminine activities early in life, boys are discouraged from imitating their mothers, whereas girls are encouraged to be "mother's little helper." Even the chores children do are categorized by gender. Girls may wash dishes, make beds, and set the table; boys are assigned to carry out trash, rake the yard, and sweep the walk. The boy's domestic chores take him outside the house, whereas the girl's keep her in it—another rehearsal for traditional adult life.

It is generally accepted that parents socialize their children differently according to gender (Block, 1983; Fagot and Leinbach, 1987). Fathers more than others pressure their children to behave in gender-appropriate ways. Fathers set higher standards of achievement for their sons than for their daughters; for their daughters, fathers emphasize the interpersonal aspect of their relationship. But mothers also reinforce the interpersonal aspect of their parent/daughter relationship (Block, 1983).

By adolescence, both parents and their teenage children believe that parents treat boys and girls differently. It is not clear, however, whether parents are reacting to differences or creating them (Fagot and Leinbach, 1987). It is probably both, although by that age, gender differences are fairly well-established in the minds of adolescents. Although awareness of differences may be related to parents and adolescents both recognizing the visible changes accompanying puberty—the development of breasts among girls and change in musculature among boys—for parents most of the change is probably cumulative. That is, interactions with their children reflect long-held traditional beliefs about the differences between males and females. One researcher concluded that parental gender-role attitudes for their four-year-old children predicted their attitudes toward their children when they were fifteen years old (Block, 1983).

Various studies have indicated that ethnicity and class are important in influencing gender roles (Zinn, 1990; see Wilkinson, Chow, and Zinn, 1992, for new scholarship on the intersection of ethnicity, class, and gender). More than middle-class families, working-class families tend to differentiate more sharply between boys and girls in terms of appropriate behavior; they tend to place more restrictions on girls. There is evidence that African-American families, more than white families, socialize their daughters to be more independent (Gump, 1980; E. Smith, 1982). Indeed, among African Americans, the "traditional" female role model may never have existed. The African-American female role model in which the woman is both wage earner and homemaker is more typical and more accurately reflects African-American experience (Basow, 1986).

As children grow older, their social world expands and so do their sources of learning. Around the time children enter day-care or kindergarten, teachers and peers become important influences.

Treat people as if they were what they ought to be and you help them become what they are capable of being.

Johann Goethe (1749–1832)

TEACHERS AS SOCIALIZING AGENTS. Day-care centers, nursery schools, and kindergartens are often the child's first experience in the wider world outside the family.

Teachers become important role models for their students. Because most day-care, kindergarten, and elementary school teachers are women, children tend to think of child/adult interactions as primarily the province of women. In this sense, schools reinforce the idea that women are concerned with children whereas men are not (Koblinsky and Sugawara, 1984).

Teachers tend to be conventional in the gender-role messages they convey to children (Wynn and Fletcher, 1987). They encourage different activities and abilities in boys and girls. They give children messages about appropriate activities, such as contact sports for boys and gymnastics for girls. Academically, teachers tend to encourage boys more than girls in math and science and girls more than boys in language skills.

Although schools tend to reinforce traditional gender roles, they can also change them. Among schools that have developed nonsexist curricula, there is significantly less gender-role stereotyping (Koblinsky and Sugawara, 1984; Wynn and Fletcher, 1987). As Tavris and Wade (1984) point out:

Nothing about children's classroom behavior is impervious to change. Using praise and attention as rewards, preschool teachers can get girls to be more independent and both sexes to play more with each other and select both boys' and girls' toys. The effects are surprisingly rapid; simply by moving in a particular area and giving attention to a particular type of play, a teacher, within minutes, can eliminate sex differences in play patterns that were "obvious" all semester. When the teacher withdraws attention or praise, children tend to revert rapidly to their previous sex-typed behavior. Still, the fact that such behavior can be eliminated quickly shows the enormous impact of the environment—including the teacher—on children's day-to-day conformity to sex roles.

PEERS AS SOCIALIZING AGENTS. Peers—the child's age-mates—become especially important when children enter school. By granting or withholding approval, friends and playmates influence what games children play, what they wear, what music they listen to, what television programs they watch, and even what cereal they eat. Peer influence is so pervasive that it is hardly an exaggeration to say that in some cases children's peers tell them what to think, feel, and do. Peers provide standards for gender-role behavior in several ways (Carter, 1987b):

1. *Peers provide information about gender-role norms through play activities and toys.* Girls play with dolls that cry and wet or glamorous dolls with well-developed figures and expensive tastes. Boys play with dolls known as "action figures," such as GI-Joe and Ninja Turtles, with guns, numchuks, and bigger-than-life biceps.
2. *Peers react with approval or disapproval to other's behavior.* Smiles encourage a girl to play with makeup or a boy to play with a football.
3. *Peers influence the adoption of gender-role norms through verbal approval or disapproval.* "That's for boys!" or "Only girls do that!" is severe negative reinforcement when a girl plays with a football or a boy wears an earring.
4. *Children's perceptions of their friends' gender-role attitudes, behaviors, and beliefs encourage them to adopt similar ones in order to be accepted.* If a girl's friends play soccer, she is more likely to play soccer. If a boy's same-sex friends display feelings, he is more likely to display feelings.

During adolescence, peers continue to have a strong influence, but current research indicates that parents are more influential than peers (Gecas and Seff, 1991). Older research viewed peer groups as the family's "enemy" in socializing children for their transition to adulthood. But today, youth culture appears to be adult culture writ small. Youth culture generally reflects the values of adult culture, such as its individualism, consumerism, gender-role attitudes, and so on.

TABLE 2.1	Stereotypic Sex Role Differences Compared to Research Findings
STEREOTYPE	FINDINGS

Aggression

Males are more aggressive. Females are less aggressive.	Strong consistent differences in physical aggression. Inconsistent finding with indirect aggression.

Dependency

Females are more submissive and dependent. Males are more assertive and independent.	Weak differences that are more consistent for adults than for children.

Emotionality

Females are more emotional and excitable. Males are more controlled and less expressive.	Moderate differences on some measures. Overall, findings inconclusive.

Verbal Skills

Females excel in all verbal areas including reading. Males are less verbal and have more problems learning to read.	Moderate differences, especially for children. Moderate differences, especially for children.

Math Skills

Males are better in mathematical skills. Females are less interested and do less well in mathematics.	Moderate differences on problem-solving tests, especially after adolescence.

SOURCE: Frank Cox, *Human Intimacy* (St. Paul, Minn.: West 1984).

Parental influence is especially strong on their adolescent's educational goals and plans for the future. Peer influence is stronger on peripheral issues, such as clothing and hair styles, taste in music, television and films, and recreational activities, such as hanging out, partying, and camping. Parents influence their adolescent's behavior primarily by establishing norms, whereas peers influence them through modeling behavior.

Even though parents tend to fear the worst from peers, peers provide important positive influences. It is within their peer groups, for example, that adolescents learn to develop intimate relationships (Gecas and Seff, 1991). And adolescents in peer groups tend to be more egalitarian in gender roles than parents, especially fathers (Thornton, 1989).

Gender-Role Learning in Adulthood

We forfeit three-fourths of ourselves to be like other people.

Arthur Schopenhauer (1788–1860)

Researchers have generally neglected gender-role learning in adulthood (Losh-Hesselbart, 1987; Sinnott, 1986). Several scholars, however, have formulated a life-span perspective to gender-role development known as *role transcendence* (Hefner, Rebecca, and Oleshansky, 1975).

The role transcendence approach argues that there are three stages an individual goes through in developing his or her gender-role identity: (1) undifferentiated, (2) polarized, and (3) transcendent stages. Young children have not clearly differentiated their activities into those considered appropriate for males or females. As the children enter school, however, they begin to identify behaviors as masculine and feminine. They tend to polarize masculinity and femininity as they test the appropriate roles for themselves. As they enter young adulthood, they begin slowly to

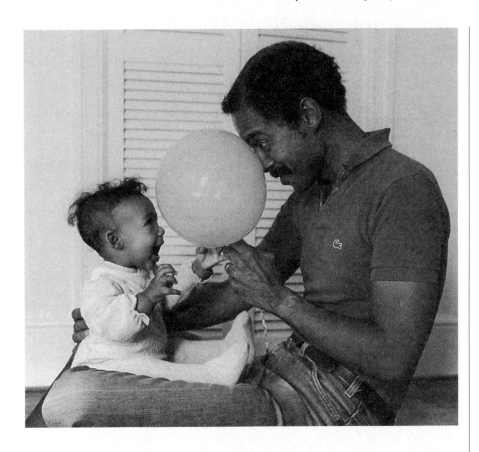

Contemporary fatherhood entails more than merely the provider role. It includes care and nurturing as well.

shed the rigid male/female polarization as they are confronted with the realities of relationships. As they mature and grow older, men and women transcend traditional masculinity and femininity. They combine masculinity/femininity into a more complex transcendent role, a role similar to androgyny (see pages 111–113).

For adults, gender-role development takes place in contexts outside of the family of orientation. In adulthood, college, marriage, parenthood, and the workplace provide new or different sources of gender-role learning.

COLLEGE. The college and university environment, emphasizing critical thought and independent behavior, contrasts markedly with the high school setting, which emphasizes social conformity through dress codes and chaperoned dances and intellectual conformity through noncontroversial, watered-down subject matter. In the college setting, many young adults learn to think critically, to exchange ideas, to discover the basis for their actions. In particular, in the college environment, many young adults first encounter alternatives to traditional gender roles, either in their personal relationships or in their courses. This is especially true for students enrolled in women's studies classes (Losh-Hesselbart, 1987).

MARRIAGE. Marriage is an important source of gender-role learning, for it creates the roles of husband and wife. For many individuals, no one is more important than their partner for shaping gender-role behaviors through interaction. Our partner has expectations of how we should act as a male or female, and these expectations are important in shaping behavior.

Husbands tend to believe in innate gender roles more than wives. This should not be especially surprising, because men tend to be more traditional and less egalitarian about gender roles (Thornton et al., 1983). Husbands stand to gain more in marriage by believing that women are "naturally" better at cooking, cleaning, shopping, and caring for children. But husband and wife influence each other. One study (Mirowsky and Ross, 1987) found that when husband and wife disagree about innate gender roles, both tend to modify their position in the direction of the other. The more one partner believes in the innateness of gender roles, however, the more the other one also does. The mutual influence of husband and wife on each other, the researchers estimate, reduces the disagreement by almost a third in contrast to an unmarried pair.

PARENTHOOD. For most men and women, motherhood alters women's lives more significantly than fatherhood alters men's lives. For men, much of fatherhood means providing for their children. As a consequence, fatherhood does not create the same work/family conflict as motherhood does for women. Men's work role allows them to fulfill much of their perceived parental obligation.

Yet contemporary fatherhood has become more complex. Traditional fatherhood has been tied to marriage. With almost a quarter of all current births occurring to unmarried women and half of all current marriages ending in divorce, what is the father's role for men not married to their children's mother? What are their role obligations as single fathers as distinguished from those of married fathers? For many men, it is painfully unclear, as evidenced by the low rates of contact between unmarried or divorced fathers and their children.

Although women today have greater latitude as wives (it is acceptable to work outside the home), they are still under considerable pressure to become mothers. Once a woman becomes a mother, especially if she is white, she is likely to leave the work force for at least a few months. Even young girls recognize this pressure and accept the notion of working until the arrival of the first child, then combining work and motherhood as the children get older (Archer, 1985). When children are born, roles tend to become more traditional, even in nontraditional marriages. The wife remains at home, at least for a time, and the husband continues full-time work outside the home. The woman must then balance her roles as wife and mother against her own needs and those of her family. Her husband may want her role as wife to take precedence over that of mother, while the children, insistently tugging at her for attention, demand that they be given first priority.

Everybody wants to be somebody; nobody wants to grow.

Johann Goethe

WORKPLACE. Workplaces have their own cultures that influence the way workers and managers feel about themselves as men and women.

It is fairly well established that men and women are psychologically affected by their occupations (Menaghan and Parcel, 1991; Schooler, 1987; Tavris and Wade, 1984). Work that encourages self-direction, for example, makes people more active, flexible, open, and democratic; restrictive jobs tend to lower self-esteem and make people more rigid and less tolerant. If we realize that female occupations are usually low-status with little room for self-direction, we can understand why women are not as achievement-oriented as men. Because men and women have different opportunities for promotion, they have different attitudes toward achievement. Women typically downplay any desire for promotion, suggesting that promotions would interfere with their family responsibilities. But this may be related to a need to protect themselves from frustration, since most women are in dead-end jobs in which promotion to management positions is unlikely.

Household work affects women psychologically in many of the same ways that paid work does in female-dominated occupations such as clerical and service jobs (Schooler, 1987). Women in both situations feel greater levels of frustration owing to the repetitive nature of the work, time pressures, and being held responsible for things outside their control. Such circumstances do not encourage self-esteem, creativity, or a desire to achieve.

□ CHANGING GENDER ROLES

Within the past generation, there has been a significant shift from traditional toward more egalitarian gender roles. While women have changed more than men, men also are changing. These changes seem to affect all classes. Those from conservative religious groups, such as Mormons, Catholics, and fundamentalist and evangelical Protestants, adhere most strongly to traditional gender roles (Spence et al., 1985).

The greatest change in gender-role attitudes appears to have occurred in the 1970s. These roles are continuing to change and become more egalitarian, but at a lesser pace. Between the late 1970s and mid-1980s, support for traditional gender roles for wives has decreased, especially among women. There is still considerable disagreement about the ideal roles for wives and mothers, however. This is especially true for men, who believe maternal employment is harmful to children or to the mother/child relationship (Mason and Lu, 1988).

Despite the continuing disagreement, it is likely that the egalitarian trend will continue (Mason and Lu, 1988; Thornton, 1989). Using an exchange model, researchers Carolyn Morgan and Alexis Walker (1983) suggest that as women increase their participation in the work force, the divorce rate continues to be high, and couples have fewer children, the costs will outweigh the benefits for women maintaining traditional gender roles. Because men benefit from women's increased income, they are more likely to support gender equality.

According to the exchange model, women are more likely than men to support egalitarian gender roles, because women have more to gain and men have more to lose. Men's support for gender equality has increased, but not as much as women's. The cost/benefit ratio of maintaining traditional gender roles continues to favor men in many ways. Employed women desire greater male participation in housework, for example, but as most women know, men display little enthusiasm for such work. Men continue to benefit from their partners' scrubbing the floors, doing the dishes, cleaning the bathrooms, cooking the meals, doing the shopping, changing the diapers, and washing the clothes while they themselves watch television, read the newspaper, or occasionally take out the trash. As long as their partners are willing to do the housework *and* work outside the home, men appear to have little to gain by adopting egalitarian gender roles. Therefore, they are less supportive than women in changing traditional housework responsibilities. Only when the cost becomes too great—involving frustration, fights, guilt—are men likely to accept a more egalitarian or equitable division of household labor.

Traditional Gender Roles

According to traditional gender-role stereotypes, many of the traits ascribed to one sex are not ascribed to the other. Men show instrumental traits—that is, goal-oriented, self-directing traits such as logic and aggression. Women display expressive traits—that is, interpersonal, emotive traits such as compassion and nurturing (Hort, Fagot, and Leinbach, 1990). These personality traits theoretically complemented their traditional roles in the family. Because of this basic difference, men

The things we admire in men, kindness and generosity, openness, honesty, understanding and feeling are the concomitants of failure in our system. And those traits we detest, sharpness, greed, acquisitiveness, meanness, egotism and self-interest are the traits of success.

John Steinbeck, Cannery Row

One's only real life is the life one never leads.

Oscar Wilde (1854–1900)

Femininity expresses the idea that there are things worth living for. Masculinity expresses the idea that there are things worth dying for.

John Wheeler, Touched with Fire

were expected to participate in the world of work and politics. Their central male role was worker; in the family, this role translated to breadwinner. Because women were thought to be primarily expressive, they were expected to remain in the home as wives and mothers.

TRADITIONAL MALE GENDER ROLE. What is it to be a "real" man in America? Bruce Feirstein parodied him in *Real Men Don't Eat Quiche* (1982):

QUESTION: How many Real Men does it take to change a light bulb?
ANSWER: None. Real Men aren't afraid of the dark.

QUESTION: Why did the Real Man cross the road?
ANSWER: It's none of your damn business.

This humor contains something both familiar and chilling. Being a male in America carries a certain uneasiness. Men often feel they need advice about how to act out their male roles; they are unsure of what it means to be masculine.

Central features of the traditional male role, whether white, African-American, Latino, or Asian-American, include dominance and work. Both have consequences for family relationships. Males are generally regarded as being more power-oriented than females. Men demonstrate higher degrees of aggression, especially violent aggression (such as assault, homicide, and rape), seek to dominate and lead, and show greater competitiveness. While aggressive traits may be useful in the corporate world, politics, and the military (or in hunting sabre-toothed tigers), such characteristics, are rarely helpful to a man in fulfilling marital and family roles requiring understanding, cooperation, communication, and nurturing.

The centrality of men's work identity affects their family roles as husbands and fathers. Traditional men see their primary family function as that of provider, which takes precedence over all other family functions, such as nurturing and caring for children, doing housework, preparing meals, and being intimate. Because of this focus, traditional men are often confused by their spouses' expectations of intimacy; they believe that they are good husbands simply because they are good providers (Rubin, 1983).

Rabbi Zusya said that on the Day of Judgment, God would ask him, not why he had not been Moses, but why he had not been Zusya.

Walter Kaufmann

TRADITIONAL FEMALE GENDER ROLE. Although the main features of traditional male gender roles do not appear to have significant ethnic variation, there are striking ethnic differences in female roles.

WHITES. Traditional white female gender roles center around women's roles as wives and mothers. When a woman leaves adolescence, she is expected to get married and have children. Although a traditional woman may work prior to marriage, she is not expected to defer marriage for work goals. And soon after marriage, she is expected to be "expecting." Once married, she is expected to devote her energies to her husband and family and to find her meaning as a woman by fulfilling her roles as wife and mother. Within the household, she is expected to subordinate herself to her husband. Often this subordination is sanctioned by religious teachings. In the New Testament, for example, Paul of Tarsus declared, "Wives, submit yourselves to your husbands as unto the Lord. For the husband is the head of the wife, even as Christ is the head of the Church" (Ephesians 5: 22–23).

The tendency to identify manhood with a capacity for physical violence has a long history in America.

Marshall Fishwick

AFRICAN AMERICANS. The traditional female gender role did not extend to African-American women. This may be attributed to a combination of the African heritage, slavery (which subjugated women to the same labor and hardships as men), and economic discrimination that forced women into the labor force. Karen Drugger (1988) notes:

A primary cleavage in the life experiences of Black and White women is their past and present relationship to the labor process. In consequence, Black women's conceptions of womanhood emphasize self-reliance, strength, resourcefulness, autonomy, and the responsibility of providing for the material as well as emotional needs of family members. Black women do not see labor-force participation and being a wife and mother as mutually exclusive; rather, in Black culture, employment is an integral, normative, and traditional component of the roles of wife and mother.

African-American men are generally more supportive than white or Latino men of more egalitarian gender roles.

LATINAS. In traditional Latina gender roles, women subordinate themselves to males (Vasquez-Nuthall, Romero-Garcia, and De Leon, 1987). But this subordination is based more on respect for the male's role as provider than on dominance (Becerra, 1988). Unlike Anglo culture, gender roles are strongly affected by age roles in which the young subordinate themselves to the old. In this dual arrangement, notes Becerra (1988), "females are viewed as submissive, naive, and somewhat childlike. Elders are viewed as wise, knowledgeable, and deserving of respect." As a result of this intersection of gender and age roles, older women are treated with greater deference than younger women.

GENDER ROLES IN TRANSITION: IMMIGRANT EXPERIENCES. The enormous rise in immigration beginning in the 1980s brought great numbers of Latinos and Asians to the United States. By 1991, over 20 million Americans were foreign born; today, more than 750,000 immigrants are arriving in the United States annually. The process of adaptation to a new environment, culture, and language places individuals under considerable stress. In adjusting to life in the United States, women tend to experi-

If you would marry suitably, marry your equal.

Ovid (43 B.C.–18 A.D.)

ence greater stress than men. Mental health workers attribute women's greater stress to conflicting gender-role expectations and family roles (Aneshensel and Pearlin, 1987).

As Latinas become more acculturated, they adopt more egalitarian gender roles (Vasquez-Nuthall, Romero-Garcia, and De Leon, 1987). First-generation Latinas have held significantly more traditional gender-role attitudes than second- and third-generation Latinas. This traditionalism is reflected in part by the reluctance of first-generation Latinas to work outside the home (Ortiz and Cooney, 1984). Researchers found that for immigrant Latinas, the shift from a culture emphasizing definite male/female gender roles to one with greater freedom has affected their self-identity (Salgado de Snyder, Cervantes, and Padilla, 1990). This shift has been a potential source of both personal and family conflict. As a Latina has demanded greater input in making decisions or has asked her partner's assistance in child care—behavior more typical among Anglos—she has been likely to both encounter resistance from her husband and to feel guilty for violating traditional Latino norms. Asian women, noted Reiko True (1990), struggling to establish themselves in American society, "often find themselves trapped within restrictive roles and identities as defined by Asian cultures or by general American stereotypes."

Although immigrant males also experience stress resulting from changed male/female relationships, their greatest stress tends to be occupational. This difference results from the priority of work roles over family roles for males. Latino males have experienced occupational stress, for example, reflecting their difficulty in finding good jobs or job advancement as a result of language differences, education, or discrimination (Salgado de Snyder, Cervantes, and Padilla, 1990). Although many Asian male immigrants tend to be from white-collar backgrounds, they also experience occupational stress resulting from discrimination and language difficulties.

Gender-role stress increases for both men and women as their children adopt more typically American gender roles. Parents and children may come into conflict about appropriate gender-related behavior because parents tend to be more culturally traditional and their children tend to be more Americanized.

Contemporary Gender Roles

Until recently, most Americans tended to look at men and women as if they were almost distinct species who shared few traits, behaviors, and attitudes. Males traditionally suppressed "feminine" traits in themselves and females suppressed "masculine" traits. What is apparently happening today, especially among women, is that gender roles are becoming more *androgynous*—that is, incorporating both masculine and feminine traits. There is a considerable body of evidence suggesting that androgynous gender roles help us have more flexible and fulfilling relationships and lives.

Contemporary gender roles are evolving from traditional hierarchical gender roles (in which one sex is subordinate to the other) to more egalitarian roles (in which both sexes are treated equally) and androgynous roles (in which both sexes display the instrumental and expressive traits previously associated with one sex). Thus, contemporary gender roles often display traditional elements as well as egalitarian and androgynous ones.

Within the family, attitudes toward gender roles have become more liberal; in practice, however, gender roles continue to favor men, especially in terms of housekeeping and child-care activities (Atkinson, 1987). Some of the most important changes affecting contemporary gender roles in the family are briefly described in the following sections.

WOMEN AS WORKERS AND PROFESSIONALS. Even though the traditional roles for women have typically been those of wife and mother, in recent years (except for black women who have traditionally worked) an additional role has been added: employed worker or professional. It is now generally expected that most women will be gainfully employed at various times in their lives. For most women, entrance into work or a career does not exclude their more traditional roles as wives and mothers. Such work, however, may radically conflict with their family roles. Their work role, for example, requires them to be at the office or factory. Their traditional family roles require them to be at home caring for the husband, house, and children. At some point, unlike most men, women have to make choices. Do their work roles take precedence over their family roles? Women generally attempt to reduce the conflict between work and family roles by giving family roles precedence. As a result, they tend to work outside the home before and after marriage and until the arrival of the first child. Even if a woman is working full time, however, she continues to remain responsible for housework and child care. When a woman's first child arrives, the role of mother is expected to take priority over the role of worker. This expectation continues until the youngest child reaches school age, although half of today's working mothers return to the work force within a year of the birth of their youngest child (Hofferth and Phillips, 1987).

QUESTIONING MOTHERHOOD. Record numbers of women are rejecting motherhood because of the conflicts it creates. It is estimated that between 20 to 25 percent of female "baby boomers" are choosing to remain childless to maximize work opportunities and time with their husbands (Nock, 1987). (This is in contrast to about a 10 percent childlessness rate of the previous generation.) Similarly, women are having fewer children than ever before. Stephen Nock (1987) suggests that women are limiting their fertility or remaining childless because childbearing symbolizes the acceptance and limitations of traditional gender roles.

Women from ethnic and minority status groups, however, are less likely to view motherhood as an impediment. African-American women and Latinas tend to

Cathy © 1989 Cathy Guisewhite. Reprinted with permission of Universal Press Syndicate.

place greater value on motherhood than the white or Anglo majority. For African Americans, the tradition has generally combined work and motherhood; the two are not viewed as necessarily antithetical (Basow, 1986). For Latinas, the cultural and religious emphasis on family, the higher status conferred on motherhood, and their own familial attitudes have contributed to high fertility rates (Jorgensen and Adams, 1988).

GREATER EQUALITY IN MARITAL POWER. Although husbands were once the final authority, wives have greatly increased their power in decision making. They are no longer expected to be submissive but to have significant, if not equal, input in marital decision making. This trend toward equality is limited in practice by an unspoken rule of marital equality: "Husbands and wives are equal, but husbands are more equal." In actual practice, husbands continue to have greater power than wives. Husbands have become what sociologist John Scanzoni (1982) describes as the "senior partner" of that marriage.

BREAKDOWN OF INSTRUMENTAL/EXPRESSIVE DICHOTOMY. The identification of masculinity with instrumentality and femininity with expressiveness appears to be breaking down. In part, this is because the instrumental/expressive dichotomy was a false dichotomy to begin with. This division of traits, developed by sociologist Talcott Parsons (1955), was more theoretical than real. Parsons believed that the more an individual was instrumental, the less he or she was expressive, and vice versa. In reality, instrumentality and expressiveness exist independently of each other (Spence et al., 1985).

While men and women may identify themselves as masculine or feminine, they generally view themselves as possessing both instrumental and expressive traits. As a group, however, men perceive themselves to be more instrumental than do women, and women perceive themselves as being more expressive than do men. A substantial minority of both sexes is relatively high in both instrumentality *and* expressiveness or low in both. Interestingly, the instrumental/expressiveness ratings men and women give each other have very little to do with how they rate themselves as masculine or feminine (Pedhazur and Tetenbaum, 1979; Spence and Sawin, 1985).

EXPANSION OF MEN'S FAMILY ROLES. The key assumption about male gender roles has been the centrality of work and success to a man's sense of self. This assumption has led many researchers to believe that men's primary family role has been that of provider. As a result, until recently there has been little research into men's participation in family life. Unlike research into female role conflicts, the idea that men's work may conflict with family roles has rarely been explored. Although both the public and researchers have expressed concern about the impact of working mothers on the family, few have expressed similar concern about working fathers. In fact, the term *working father* seems redundant, since work is what is expected of fathers (Cohen, 1987).

New research indicates that men consider their family role to be much greater than that of the family breadwinner. As researchers have long pointed out, economic responsibilities are only one small part of men's family lives (Bohannan, 1971; Goetting, 1982). Other dimensions include emotional, psychological, community, and legal dimensions; they also include housework and child-care activities. One study (Cohen, 1987) confirmed the emerging picture of men in families: being a husband and father goes far beyond simple breadwinning. Men indicated that the expressive friendship roles in marriage and nurturant roles in fatherhood were the

Whatever you can do or dream you can, begin it. Boldness has genius, power, and magic in it. Begin it now.

Johann Goethe (1749–1832)

The perpetual obstacle to human advancement is custom.

John Stuart Mill (1806–1873)

The wimp is the man who has a social conscience, who can understand the oppression of women, who is warm and caring, who fixes the family's meals after a rough day at the office. Women don't view such men as wimps; only other men see them that way.

Lucia Gilbert

central elements of their family roles. In fact, only about half of the respondents indicated that "breadwinning" was a husband's major responsibility.

Fathers are increasing their child-care and nurturing activities. More men feel competent in infant care, such as giving bottles, changing diapers, and soothing a crying baby. They spend greater time interacting with their children. But the man's role continues to be "secondary caretaker," and he is more likely to obtain relief from his duties than the mother.

Housework remains a central area of dispute (Atkinson, 1987; Cohen, 1987). While some studies suggest that men are spending more time on housework, rarely is housework divided fifty-fifty. More often than not, women continue to be primarily responsible for cooking, cleaning, shopping, and the like. Men's household work tends to center around automobile maintenance, repairs, and outdoor responsibilities, such as gardening and mowing the lawn (Spence et al., 1985). (But, as one woman asked, how often do you have to repair the toaster or paint the house?)

❑ CONSTRAINTS OF CONTEMPORARY GENDER ROLES

Even though there is substantially more flexibility offered men and women today, contemporary gender roles and expectations continue to limit our potential. Indeed, there is considerable evidence that stereotypes about gender traits have not changed very much over the last twenty years. In the 1960s a classic study of gender-related stereotypes found that college students rated "typical" adult men and women differently. Men were considered to be more instrumental and women were rated as being more expressive (Rosenkrantz et al., 1968). Studies over the years have confirmed that these stereotypes remain strong. Males are perceived as having more undesirable self-oriented traits (such as being arrogant, self-centered, and domineering) than females. Females are viewed as having more traits reflecting a lack of a healthy sense of self (such as being servile and spineless) than males. Only "intellectual" seems to be applied to women more than in the past (Spence et al., 1985).

These limitations are particularly important, as studies suggest that couples who are most traditional in their gender-role attitudes also express the least marital satisfaction (Spence et al., 1985).

Limitations on Men

Men are required to work and to support their families. The male as provider is one of men's central roles in marriage; the provider role is *not* central for women. As a result, men do not have the same role freedom to *choose* to work as women have. Therefore, when the man's roles of worker and father come into conflict, usually it is the father role that suffers (Cohen, 1987; Weiss, 1985). A factory worker may want to spend time with his children to lighten his wife's burdens, but his job does not allow flexibility. Because he must provide income for his family, he will not be able to be more involved in parenting. In a familiar scene, a little boy comes into the father's study to play and the father says, "Not now. I'm busy working. I'll play with you later." When the boy returns, the "not-now-I'm-busy" phrase is repeated. The scene recurs as the boy grows up until one day, as his son leaves home, the father realizes that he never got to know him.

Men continue to have greater difficulty expressing their feelings than women. Men cry less and show love, happiness, and sadness less (Balswick, 1980; Lombardo et al., 1983). When men do express their feelings, they are more forceful, domineering, and boastful; women, in contrast, tend to express their feelings more gently and

Life shrinks or expands in proportion to one's courage.

Anaïs Nin

One half of the world cannot understand the pleasures of the other.

Jane Austen (1775–1817)

In every real man a child is hidden that wants to play.

Friedrich Nietzsche (1844–1900)

quietly. When a woman asks a man what he feels, a common response is, "I don't know," or "Nothing." Such men have lost touch with their inner lives because they have repressed feelings that they have learned are inappropriate.

Male inexpressiveness often makes men strangers to both themselves and their partners. A major complaint of married women is that their husbands do not show them enough affection or attention (Rubin, 1983). Married couples who rate themselves as poorly adjusted tend to be ones in which the husband has poor communication skills (Noller, 1984).

Men continue to expect to be the dominant member in a relationship. Unfortunately, the male sense of power and command does not facilitate personal relationships. Men who are unable to achieve power in their work relationships may seek power and status at home, putting their displaced frustration and anger into their marital relationships. But under such circumstances—without mutual respect and equality—genuine intimacy is difficult to achieve. One cannot control another person and at the same time be intimate with that person. Middle-class men often talk about egalitarian marriages but allow their partners relatively less power in the relationship. A tension exists between ideology and reality.

Limitations on Women

There is considerable evidence that the traditional female gender role does not facilitate self-confidence or mental health. Both men and women tend to see women as being less competent than men. One study found that women generally predicted they would not do as well on a test as the men taking the same test (Erkut, 1983). Another study of 1,850 men and women found that women had significantly lower self-esteem (Hoelter, 1983). A recent study by Carole Gilligan, discussed at greater length in Chapter 8, revealed that the self-esteem of adolescent girls plummetted between the age of nine and the time they started high school (Daley, 1991). Traditional women married to traditional men experience the most symptoms of stress (feeling tired, depressed, or worthless) and express the most dissatisfaction about life as a whole (Spence et al., 1985). The combination of gender-role stereotypes and racial/ethnic discrimination tends to encourage feelings of both inadequacy and lack of physical attractiveness among African-American women, Latinas, and Asian-American women (Basow, 1986).

Because of difference in gender roles, Bernard (1972) has suggested that each sex experiences marriage differently. There is, she argued, a "his" and "her" marriage. Men appear to be more satisfied in marriage than women (Rettig and Bubolz, 1983). More wives than husbands report frustration, dissatisfaction, marital problems, and desire for divorce. More wives than husbands experience anxiety or feel they are on the edge of a nervous breakdown; more wives blame themselves for their poor adjustment than do husbands (Mugford and Lally, 1981; Rubenstein, 1982). Unmarried women, Bernard suggested, tend to be happier and better adjusted than married women. (For a critique of "his" or "her" marriages, see Schumm, 1985.)

Finally, femininity is intimately tied to youth and beauty. As women get older, they tend to be regarded as more masculine. A young woman, for example, is "beautiful" but an older woman is "handsome." Also, culture treats aging in men and women differently: as men age, they become distinguished; as women age, they simply get older. (See Focus, "The Double Standard of Aging.")

Resistance to Change

We may think that we want change, but both men and women reinforce traditional gender-role stereotypes among themselves *and* the other sex (Hort, Fagot, and

It is amazing how complete is the delusion that beauty is goodness.

Leo Tolstoy (1828–1910)

Women have served all these centuries, as looking glasses possessing the magic and delicious power of reflecting the figure of man at twice its natural size.

Virginia Woolf, A Room of One's Own

Leinback, 1990). Interestingly, both sexes react more negatively to men displaying so-called female traits—such as crying easily or needing security—than to women displaying male traits—such as assertiveness or worldliness. And both define male gender-role stereotypes more rigidly than they do female stereotypes. Men do not define women as rigidly as women do men: both men and women describe their ideal female in very androgynous terms (Hort, Fagot, and Leinback, 1990).

Despite the limitations that traditional gender roles place on us, changing these roles is not easy. Gender roles are closely linked to self-evaluation. Our sense of adequacy depends on gender-role performance as defined by parents and peers in childhood ("You're a good boy/girl"). Because gender roles often seem to be an intrinsic part of our personality and temperament, we may defend these roles as being natural even if they are destructive to a relationship or to ourselves. To threaten an individual's gender role is to threaten his or her gender identity as male or female, because people do not generally make the distinction between gender role and gender identity. Such threats are an important psychological mechanism that keeps people in traditional but dysfunctional gender roles.

Lillian Rubin (1983), a prominent psychologist, described her own difficulty in changing roles when her husband changed careers to become a writer and she assumed the primary provider role in the family. At first her husband was relieved to be freed from the financial responsibilities he had assumed for so many years. Then he fell into a six-month depression. Although Rubin was already a successful therapist, writer, and researcher, something in her life "had been altered profoundly." She grew angry. Her work was no longer voluntary. It was necessary to support the family, and she began to hate it. Rubin was stunned by her reaction. She and her husband had planned and agreed on the change; both thought he should be free to pursue his own interests. She wrote:

But speaking the words and living the results are two different things. Suddenly we found ourselves face to face with our inner sense of the way things *ought* to be. Suddenly, we had to confront the realization that we were still dominated by the stereotypic images of male and female roles—images we would have sworn we had, by then, routed from our consciousness.

He struggled with his sense of failure, with the fear that somehow his very manhood had been damaged. I—the liberated, professional woman—was outraged and enraged that he wasn't taking care of me any longer. I felt as if he had violated some basic contract with which we had lived, as if he had failed in his most fundamental task in life—to keep me safe and cared for, to protect and support me.

People can accept minor changes, Rubin found, but deep ones are more difficult.

Smaller changes may be tolerated quite easily. But one that puts a woman in a position of economic superiority and a man in the dependent female role is quite another matter. Most men still can't cope with not being able to support the family, and most women still have difficulty in accepting the need to support themselves.

Finally, the social structure itself works to reinforce traditional gender norms and behaviors. Some religious groups, for example, strongly support traditional gender roles. The Catholic church, conservative Protestantism, orthodox Judaism, and the Mormons, for example, view traditional roles as being divinely ordained. Accordingly, to violate these norms is to violate God's will. The marketplace also helps enforce traditional gender roles. The wage disparity between men and women (women earn about 70 percent of what men earn) is a case in point. Such a significant difference in income makes it "rational" that the man's work role take precedence over the woman's work role. If a man or woman needs to remain at home to care for the children or an elderly relative, for example, it makes economic sense for the woman to quit her job, because her male partner probably earns more money.

All males, without exception, whatever their age, suffer from penis rivalry. . . . This trait has now become a threat to the future existence of the human race. . . . Today our phallic toys have become too dangerous to be tolerated. I see little hope for a peaceful world until men are excluded from the realm of foreign policy altogether and all decisions concerning international relations are reserved for women, preferably married ones.

W. H. Auden (1907–1973)

Man's love is of man's life a part; it is woman's whole existence.

Lord Byron (1788–1824)

Wives, submit yourselves unto your own husbands, as unto the Lord.

Paul of Tarsus (Ephesians 5:22)

Why is it men are permitted to be obsessed about their work, but women are only permitted to be obsessed about men?

Barbra Streisand

FOCUS

The Double Standard of Aging

The double standard of aging (like the double standard of sex) shortchanges women. Society is more tolerant of men who deviate from its standards than of women who do so. Masculinity is associated with independence, assertiveness, self-control and physical ability; with the exception of physical ability, none of these traits necessarily decreases with age. For the most part they intensify as one gains more experience in the world. But femininity is closely associated with attractiveness. Susan Brownmiller (1983) pointed out in her book, *Femininity:*

Feminity is not something that improves with age, for girlishness, with its innocent modesty, its unthreatening impudence, and its promise of ripe sexuality in the rosy future, typifies the feminine principle at its best. Women who rely on a feminine strategy as their chief means of survival can do little to stop the roaring tide of maturity as they watch their advantage slip by.

When Americans marry, a man is likely to marry a woman his same age or younger (in 85 percent of marriages, this is the case; in 75 percent of marriages, the wife is less than five years younger than the husband). The explanation for women marrying older men is related to gender roles. Traditionally, a woman's social status has depended on her husband's; he works and achieves status that reflects on her. Many women have therefore preferred to marry older men, who have probably worked longer and acquired greater status than younger men. Men have traditionally favored younger women because physical attractiveness is an important aspect of the male mate selection process and because our society links the attractiveness of women to their youth.

This arrangement places women at a disadvantage. If a woman marries a man older than herself, she is more likely to become a widow with many years left in her own life. In itself, the loneliness of widowhood can be a burden; but beyond that, it is more difficult for a widow than a widower to find a new partner. As women get older, they become less eligible for marriage because they are considered to have lost their attractiveness and because they have fewer potential partners. An older woman's pool of eligible partners is limited to those of her own age or older. If she were a man, however, she could choose not only from those of her own age group but also from those who are younger.

Instead of seeking to blame one sex for the victimization of the other, we should try to understand the constraints placed on both sexes by rigid gender-role stereotyping.

□ CHANGING CONCEPTS OF GENDER ROLES

Bipolar Gender Roles

The war between the sexes is the only one in which both sides regularly sleep with the enemy.

Quentin Crisp

The traditional view of masculinity and femininity is bipolar: masculinity and femininity are opposite, or mirror images, of each other. Our popular terminology reflects this. When people speak of the "opposite" sex, they suggest that each sex has little in common with the other. Our gender-role stereotypes fit this bipolar pattern, as we have seen: men, aggressive; women, passive; men, instrumental; women, expressive; and so on. According to this view of gender roles, a *real* man possesses exclusively masculine traits and behaviors and a *real* woman possesses exclusively feminine traits and behaviors. Because the sexes have little in common, a "war of the sexes" is the norm.

This older conception does not account for many people having traits ascribed to both sexes and still feeling profoundly masculine or feminine (Heilbrun, 1982). When people believe that individuals should not have attributes of the other sex, males suppress their expressive traits and females suppress their instrumental traits.

As a result, the range of human behaviors is limited by a person's gender role. Sandra Bem (1975) has argued that "our current system of sex role differentiation has long since outlived its usefulness, and . . . now serves only to prevent both men and women from developing as full and complete human beings."

Are men and women as different as traditional gender-role stereotypes portray us? Certainly, we are different biologically and anatomically. Men impregnate and women gestate; men have penises and women have vulvas. But if we reflect on our own lives, whether we are male or female, we will see that men and women have much in common. Men seek intimacy as well as achievement, and women seek achievement as well as intimacy. Each of us contains both instrumental and expressive traits.

Today our ideas of what it means to be male and female are changing. For many, the older gender roles seem archaic, limiting, inappropriate, even dehumanizing. Confusion abounds. What is the new vision of being male and female in America?

Androgynous Gender Roles

Some scholars have challenged the traditional masculine/feminine gender-role dichotomy, arguing that such models are unhealthy and fail to reflect the real world. Instead of looking at gender roles in terms of the bipolar model, they suggest examining them in terms of **androgyny** (Roopnarine and Mounts, 1987). Androgyny is derived from the Greek *andros*, meaning "man," and *gyne*, meaning "woman." It refers to flexibility in gender roles and the unique combination of instrumental and expressive traits as influenced by individual differences, situations, and stages in the life cycle (Bem, 1976; Kaplan, 1979: Kaplan and Bean, 1976). An *androgynous* person combines both the instrumental traits previously associated with masculinity and the expressive traits associated with traditional femininity. An androgynous life-style allows men and women to choose from the full range of emotions and behaviors, according to their temperament, situation, and common humanity, rather than their sex. Males may be expressive. They are permitted to cry and display tenderness; they can touch, feel, and nurture without being called "effeminate." Women can express the instrumental aspects of their personalities without fear of disapproval. They can be aggressive or career-oriented; they can seek leadership, be mechanical or physical.

Flexibility and integration are important aspects of androgyny. Individuals who are rigidly both instrumental and expressive, despite the situation, are not considered androgynous. A woman who is always aggressive at work and passive at home, for example, would not be considered androgynous, as work may call for compassion and home life for assertion.

There is considerable evidence that androgynous individuals and couples have greater ability to form and sustain intimate relationships and adopt a wider range of behaviors and values. Androgynous college students and older individuals tend to have greater confidence in social situations than sex-typed individuals (Puglisi and Jackson, 1981; Spence et al., 1975). Androgynous individuals have shown greater resilience to stress (Roos and Cohen, 1987). They are more aware of love feelings and more expressive of them (Ganong and Coleman, 1987). Also, androgynous couples may have greater satisfaction in their relationships than sex-typed couples. One study found that androgynous couples felt more commitment and satisfaction in their relationships than sex-typical couples (Stephen and Harrison, 1985). Another study found that androgynous couples expressed greater sexual satisfaction than couples with stereotypic sex roles (Rozenweig and Dailey, 1989). Even those couples who generally believed themselves to be stereotypical experienced more sat-

When man lives he is soft and tender; when he is dead he is hard and tough. All living plants and animals are tender and fragile; when dead they become withered and dry. Thus it is said: The hard and tough are parts of death; the soft and tender are parts of life. This is the reason why soldiers when they are too tough cannot carry the day; when the tree is too tough it will break. The position of the strong and great is low, but the position of the weak and tender is high.

Lao-Tse (7th century B.C.)

Because we see characteristics in God that our society identifies as "feminine" as well as those deemed "masculine," it is important to acknowledge the "androgyny" of God. We speak of God's loving-kindness, of tender and nurturing qualities. We hear Isaiah describe God as being like a woman in childbirth, who suffers through the creativity of birth while anticipating the promise that she knows to be present in her child . . . .

Task Force on Human Sexuality and Family Life."Sexuality: A Divine Gift," Episcopal Church Center isfaction if they considered their behavior "feminine" in sexual situations, such as being sexually responsive, expressive, and tender. Transcending traditional male and female behaviors and values, the androgynous couples were more flexible in their responses to each other and to their environment.

It is not clear what proportion of individuals may be identified as androgynous or traditional. Although it has been suggested that androgyny is a white middle-class concept, one study (Binion, 1990) of African-American women indicated that 37 percent identified themselves as androgynous, 18 percent as feminine, and 24 percent as masculine. The remaining were undifferentiated. That such a large percentage were androgynous or masculine, the study argues, is not surprising, given the demanding family responsibilities and cultural expectations that require instrumental and active traits. Another study of college students from India indicated a high degree of androgyny, suggesting cross-cultural validity (Ravinder, 1987).

As Sandra Bem (1974) observed in her pioneering study on androgyny, "In a society where rigid sex role differentiation has already outlived its utility, perhaps the androgynous person will come to define a more human standard of psychological health."

Not all researchers are convinced, however, that androgyny necessarily leads to greater psychological health and happiness. Some have hypothesized that instrumental traits in general, rather than androgyny, may lead to higher self-esteem for both men and women (Orlofsky and O'Heron, 1987). It is not always clear-cut whether androgyny or instrumentality is the most important factor accounting for higher rates of self-esteem, adjustment, and flexibility (Basow, 1985). It will probably be some time before these factors can be tested to everyone's satisfaction.

Androgyny, like other personality theories, assumes that masculinity and femininity are basic aspects of an individual's personality. It assumes that when we are active, we are expressing our masculine side and when we are sensitive, we are expressing the feminine side of our personality. Living up to an androgynous gender role may be just as stultifying to an individual as trying to be traditionally masculine or feminine. In advocating the expression of both masculine and feminine traits, perhaps we are imposing a new form of gender-role rigidity on ourselves. Bem, who was one of the leading proponents of androgyny, has become increasingly critical of the idea. She believes now that androgyny replaces "a prescription to be masculine or feminine with the doubly incarcerating prescription to be masculine and feminine. The individual now has not one but two potential sources of inadequacy to contend with" (Bem, 1983).

❑ Contemporary gender roles are still in flux. Few of us are entirely egalitarian or traditional. Those who are androgynous or who have egalitarian attitudes, especially males, may be more traditional in their behaviors than they imagine. Few with egalitarian or androgynous attitudes, for example, divide *all* labor along lines of ability, interest, or necessity rather than gender. And those who are traditional in their outlook rarely find that wives submit to their husbands in *all* things. Among contemporary men and women, women find that their increasing access to employment puts them at odds with their traditional (and personally valued) role as mother. Women continue to feel conflict between their emerging equality in the workplace and their continued responsibilities at home. Within marriages and families, the greatest areas of gender inequality continue to be the division of housework and child care. But change continues to occur in the direction of greater gender equality. And this equality promises greater intimacy and satisfaction for both men and women in their relationships.

If we do not redefine manhood, war is inevitable.

Paul Fussell

*All are but parts of one stupendous whole
Whose body nature is, and God the soul.*

Alexander Pope (1688–1744)

We unwittingly set the stage for feelings of inadequacy and inferiority. The more rigidly we define ourselves the less likely we are able to cope with the infinite variety of life.

Ernest Rossi

He who knows the masculine but keeps to the feminine will be in the whole world's channel.

Taoist aphorism

SUMMARY

❑ *Gender identity* refers to being male or female. *Gender role* refers to the role a person is expected to perform as a result of being male or female in a particular culture. Gender roles are culturally relative, whereas gender identity is not. *Gender-role stereotypes* refer to rigidly held and oversimplified beliefs that males and females, as a result of their sex, possess distinct psychological and behavioral traits. *Gender-role attitudes* are beliefs that we have about ourselves and others regarding appropriate male and female personality traits and activities. *Gender-role behaviors* are the actual activities or behaviors that we or others engage in as males and females.

❑ The two most important socialization theories are *cognitive social learning theory* and *cognitive development theory*. Cognitive social learning theory emphasizes learning behaviors from others. Cognitive development theory asserts that once children learn that gender is permanent, they independently strive to act like "proper" boys or girls because of an internal need for congruence.

❑ Children learn their gender roles through *manipulation, channeling, verbal appellation,* and *activity exposure*. Parents, teachers, and peers, are important agents of socialization during childhood and adolescence. Ethnicity and social class influence gender roles. Among African Americans, strong women are important female role models.

❑ During adolescence, parents are more important influences than peers. Peers, however, have more egalitarian gender-role attitudes than adults. For students, colleges and universities are important sources for gender-role learning, especially for nontraditional roles. Marriage, parenthood, and the workplace also influence the development of adult gender roles.

❑ Traditional male roles, whether white, African American, Latino, or Asian American, emphasize dominance and work. A man's central family role has been viewed as being the provider. For women there is greater role diversity according to ethnicity. Traditional female roles among middle-class whites emphasize passivity, compliance, physical attractiveness, and being a wife and mother. Work outside the home is acceptable as long as it does not interfere with other traditional role components.

Among African Americans, women are expected to be instrumental; there is no conflict between work and motherhood. Among Latinos, women are deferential to men generally from respect rather than subservience; elders, regardless of gender, are afforded respect. Immigrants face gender-role stress, especially women, as they adapt to American standards.

❑ Contemporary gender roles are more egalitarian. Important changes affecting contemporary gender roles include (1) acceptance of women as workers and professionals, (2) increasing questioning, especially among white women, of motherhood as a core female identity, (3) greater equality in marital power, (4) breakdown of the instrumental/expressive dichotomy, and (5) expansion of male family roles.

❑ Research indicates that gender-role stereotypes have changed little over the last few decades. Limitations of contemporary gender roles on men include the primacy of the provider role, which limits men's father and husband roles; difficulty in expressing feelings; and a sense of dominance that precludes intimacy. Limitations for women include diminished self-confidence and mental health and the association of femininity with youth and beauty, which creates a disadvantage as women age. Ethnic women may suffer both racial discrimination and gender-role stereotyping, which compound each other.

❑ Changing gender-role behavior is often difficult because (1) each sex reinforces the traditional roles of its own and the other sex, (2) we evaluate ourselves in terms of fulfilling gender-role concepts, (3) we have internalized our roles, and (4) the social structure reinforces traditional roles.

❑ *Androgyny* combines traditional male and female characteristics into a more flexible pattern of behavior, rather than seeing the sexes as bipolar opposites. Evidence suggests that androgyny contributes to psychological and emotional health. Some researchers, however, believe that androgyny may impose a double burden of expectation on people. An alternative is to discard the idea that instrumental traits are masculine and expressive traits feminine and think of them as human traits.

CHAPTER 3

Love, Commitment, and Intimacy

*Only love with its science
makes us so innocent.*

Violetta Parra

LOVE IS ESSENTIAL TO OUR LIVES. Love binds us together as men and women, parents and children, friends and neighbors. Its importance can hardly be overrated, for we make major life decisions, such as marrying, based on love (Simpson et al., 1986). Love creates bonds that endure the greatest hardships, suffer the severest cruelty, overcome any distance. Because of its significance, we may torment ourselves with the question, "Is it *really* love?" Many of us have gone through frustrating scenes such as the following (Greenberg and Jacobs, 1966):

YOU: "Do you love me?"
MATE: "Yes, of course I love you."
YOU: "Do you *really* love me?"
MATE: "Yes, I really love you."
YOU: "You are *sure* you love me—you are absolutely sure?"
MATE: "Yes, I'm absolutely sure."
YOU: "Do you know the meaning of love?"
MATE: "I don't know."
YOU: "Then how can you be sure you love me?"
MATE: "I don't know. Perhaps I can't."
YOU: "You can't, eh? I see. Well, since you can't even be sure you love me, I can't really see much point in our remaining together. Can you?"
MATE: "I don't know. Perhaps not."
YOU: "You've been leading up to this for a pretty long time, haven't you?"

Love is both a feeling and an activity. A person feels love for someone and acts in a loving manner. But we can also be angry with the person we love, frustrated, bored, or indifferent. This is the paradox of love: it encompasses opposites. Love includes affection and anger, excitement and boredom, stability and change, bonds and freedom. Its paradoxical quality makes some ask whether they are *really* in love when they are not feeling "perfectly" in love or when their relationship is not going smoothly. Love does not give us perfection, however; it gives us meaning. In fact, as sociologist Ira Reiss (1980) suggested, a more important question to ask is not if one is feeling love but, "Is the love I feel the kind of love on which I can build a lasting relationship or marriage?"

We can look at love in many ways besides through the eyes of lovers, although other ways may not be as entertaining. Whereas love was once the province of lovers, madmen, poets, and philosophers, social scientists have begun to appear on the scene. They have bravely disregarded William Blake's warning:

He who binds to himself a Joy
Doth the winged life destroy;
But he who kisses the Joy as it flies
Lives in eternity's sunrise.

Studying love is no guarantee of finding it. As John A. Lee (1988), a major researcher, explained, "I have studied love because it is my life's most difficult problem. Although I have made much progress, the 'impossible dream' of a truly fulfilling mutual love remains one I have yet to achieve." The study of romantic love is still in its infancy. In the thirty-four years between 1949 and 1983, only twenty-seven articles on love appeared in sociology and psychology journals (Baron, 1983). But now, because the interest in love research is growing at such a pace, one researcher suggests that if Elizabeth Barrett Browning wrote her poem today, she would respond to "How do I love thee?" with "Let me count the articles" (Rubin, 1988). Until recently, researchers failed to investigate love for several reasons (Berscheid and Walster, 1978). First, they did not believe that the phenomenon of

We are shaped and fashioned by what we love.

Johann Goethe

The head is always the dupe of the heart.

François de La Rochefoucauld

Was it not by loving that I learned to love? Was it not by living that I learned to live?

Jorge Amado

love could be subject to scientific examination and prediction. Second, the study of romantic love was taboo; putting love under scientific scrutiny would destroy its mystery. Third, the researchers weren't exactly sure how to study love; they could not envision an appropriate methodology for examining such phenomena as "love at first sight," sexual attraction, and so on.

Love research is also complicated by the kinds of love that different researchers prefer. As John Lee (1988) noted, "The kind of love the researchers like best is the only 'true' love." Because the study of love is still relatively new, there is still no common vocabulary: what one researcher calls romantic love is infatuation to another (Rubin, 1988).

❒ THIS THING CALLED LOVE: THE PHENOMENA OF LOVE AND COMMITMENT

Love and commitment are closely linked in our intimate relationships; they help to create and sustain each other. Love reflects the positive factors—such as caring—that draw people together and sustain them in a relationship. Commitment reflects the stable factors—including love but also obligations and social pressure—that help maintain the relationship "for better or for worse." Although the two are related, they are not necessarily connected. One can exist without the other. It is possible to love someone without being committed. It is also possible to be committed to someone without loving him or her. Yet, when all is said and done, most of us long for a love that includes commitment and a commitment that encompasses love.

Prototypes of Love and Commitment

Despite centuries of discussion, debate, and complaint by philosophers and lovers, no one has succeeded in finding definitions of love and commitment on which all can agree. Ironically, such discussions seem to engender conflict and disagreement rather than love and harmony.

Because of the unending confusion surrounding definitions of love, some researchers wonder whether such definitions are even possible (Fehr, 1988; Kelley, 1983). In the everyday world, however, we do seem to have something in mind when we tell someone we love him or her. We may not have formal definitions of love, but we do have prototypes (that is, models) of what we mean by love stored in the backs of our minds. Researchers suggest that instead of looking for formal definitions of love and commitment, we examine people's prototypes; in some ways these prototypes may be more important than formal definitions. For example, when we say "I love you," we are referring to our prototype of love rather than its definition. By thinking in terms of prototypes, we can study how people actually use the words *love* and *commitment* in real life and how their meanings of love and commitment help define the progress of their intimate relationships.

To discover people's prototypes, researcher Beverly Fehr (1988) asked 172 respondents to rate the central features of love and commitment. The twelve central attributes of love they listed are given in order:

❒ Trust
❒ Caring
❒ Honesty
❒ Friendship
❒ Respect
❒ Concern for the other's well-being

❒ Loyalty
❒ Commitment
❒ Acceptance of the other as he/she is
❒ Supportiveness
❒ Wanting to be with the other
❒ Interest in the other

Love looks not with the eyes, But with the mind.

William Shakespeare, A Midsummer Night's Dream

Only love with its science makes us so innocent.

Violeta Parra

The twelve central attributes of commitment, listed in order, were as follows:

- Loyalty
- Responsibility
- Living up to your word
- Faithfulness
- Trust
- Being there for the other in good and bad times
- Devotion
- Reliability
- Giving your best effort
- Supportiveness
- Perseverance
- Concern about the other's well being

There are many other characteristics identified as features of love (euphoria, thinking about the other all the time, butterflies in the stomach) or commitment (putting the other first, contentment). These, however, tend to be peripheral. As relationships progress, the central aspects of love and commitment become more characteristic of the relationship than the peripheral ones. The central features, observed Fehr (1988), "act as true barometers of a move toward increased love or commitment in a relationship." Similarly, violations of central features of love and commitment were considered to be more serious than violations of peripheral ones. A loss of caring, trust, honesty, or respect threatens love, while the disappearance of butterflies in the stomach does not. Similarly, lack of responsibility or faithfulness endangers commitment, whereas discontent is not perceived as threatening. Researchers have found that love *and* commitment were correlated to satisfaction in romantic relationships (Hendrick and Hendrick, 1988b).

Attitudes and Behaviors Associated with Love

A review of the research finds a number of attitudes, feelings, and behaviors associated with love (Kelley, 1983).

In terms of attitudes and feelings, positive attitudes and feelings toward the other bring people together. Zick Rubin (1970, 1973) found that there were four feelings

The physical expression of love through touching, hugging, kissing, and sexuality is an important aspect of love.

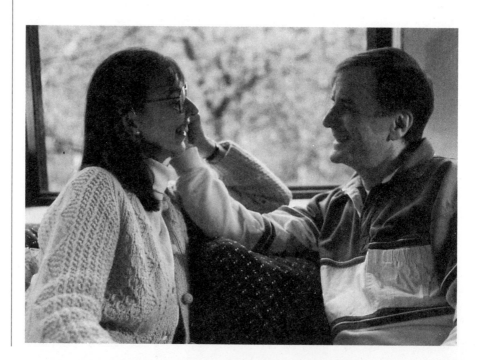

identifying love. These ideas, which correspond fairly well to the prototypical characteristics identified with love, were:

❏ *Caring* for the other, wanting to help him or her;
❏ *Needing* the other, having a strong desire to be in the other's presence and to have the other care for you;
❏ *Trusting* the other, mutually exchanging confidences;
❏ *Tolerating* the other, including his or her faults.

Of these, caring appears to be the most important, followed by needing, trusting, and tolerating (Steck, Levitan, McLane, and Kelley, 1982). Davitz (1969) identified similar feelings associated with love but noted in addition that respondents reported feeling an inner glow, optimism, and cheerfulness. They felt harmony and unity with the person they loved. They were intensely aware of the other person, feeling that they were fully concentrated on him or her.

Love is also expressed in certain behaviors. One study (Swensen, 1972) found that romantic love was expressed in several ways. Notice that the expression of love often overlaps thoughts of love.

❏ *Verbally expressing affection*, such as saying "I love you";
❏ *Self–disclosing*, such as revealing intimate facts about yourself;
❏ *Giving nonmaterial evidence*, such as emotional and moral support in times of need, and respecting the other's opinion;
❏ *Expressing nonverbal feelings*, such as feeling happier, more content, more secure when the other is present;
❏ *Giving material evidence*, such as gifts, flowers, or small favors, or doing more than your share of something;
❏ *Physically expressing love*, such as hugging, kissing, making love;
❏ *Tolerating the other*, such as accepting his or her idiosyncracies, peculiar routines, or forgetfulness about putting the cap on the toothpaste.

These behavioral expressions of love are consistent with the prototypical characteristics of love. In addition, recent research supports the belief that people "walk on air" when they are in love. Researchers have found that those in love view the world more positively than those who are not in love (Hendrick and Hendrick, 1988a).

Factors Affecting Commitment

Although we generally make commitments because we love someone, love alone is not sufficient to make a commitment last. Our commitments seem to be affected by several factors that can strengthen or weaken the relationship. Ira Reiss (1980) believes that there are three important factors: (1) the balance of costs to benefits, (2) normative inputs, and (3) structural constraints.

1. *The Balance of Costs to Benefits.* Whether we like it or not, human beings have a tendency to look at romantic and marital relationships from a cost-benefit perspective. Most of the time, when we are satisfied, we are unaware that we may judge our relationships in this manner. But when there is stress or conflict, we often ask ourselves, "What am I getting out of this relationship?" Then we add up the pluses and minuses. If the result is on the plus side, we are encouraged to continue the relationship; if the result is negative, we are more likely to discontinue it.

2. *Normative Inputs.* Normative inputs for relationships are the values that you and your partner hold about love, relationships, marriage, and family. These values can either sustain or detract from a commitment. How do you feel about a love commit-

Love cannot save life from death, but it can fulfill life's purpose.

Arnold Toynbee (1889–1975)

*Upon my bed by night
I sought him whom my soul loves;
I sought him, but found him not;
I called him, but he gave no answer.
"I will rise now and go about the city,
    in the streets and in the squares,
I will seek him whom my soul loves.
    I sought him, but found him not.
The watchmen found me as they went
    about in the city.
"Have you seen him whom my soul
    loves?"
Scarcely had I passed them,
When I found him whom my soul loves.
I held him, and would not let him go
    until I had brought him into my
        mother's house,
    and into the chamber of her that
        conceived me.
I adjure you, O daughters of Jerusalem,
    by the gazelles or the hinds of the
        field,
That you stir not up nor awaken love
    until it please.*

Song of Solomon 3:1–5

ment? A marital commitment? Do you believe that marriage is for life? Does the presence of children affect your beliefs about commitment? What are the values that your friends, family, and religion hold regarding your type of relationship?

3. *Structural Constraints.* The structure of a relationship will add to or detract from commitment. Depending on the type of relationship—whether it is dating, living together, or marriage—different roles and expectations are structured in. In marital relationships, there are partner roles (husband/wife) and economic roles (employed worker/homemaker). There may also be parental roles (mother/father).

These different factors interact to increase or decrease individuals' commitment to each other. Commitments are more likely to endure in marriage than in cohabiting or dating relationships, which tend to be relatively short-lived. They are more likely to last in heterosexual relationships than in gay or lesbian relationships (Testa et al., 1987). The reason commitments tend to endure in marriage may or may not have anything to do with a couple being happy. Marital commitments tend to last because of norms, and structural constraints may compensate for the lack of personal satisfaction.

For most people, love seems to include commitment and commitment includes love. The two seem to overlap considerably. As we saw, Fehr (1988) found that if a person violated a central attribute of love, such as caring, that person was also seen as violating his or her commitment. And if a person violated a central attribute of commitment, such as loyalty, it called love into question.

Because of the overlap between love and commitment, we can mistakenly assume that if someone loves us, he or she is also committed to us. As one researcher (Kelley, 1983) pointed out, "Expressions of love can easily be confused with expressions of commitment. . . . Misunderstandings about a person's love versus commitment can be based on honest errors of communication, on failures of self-understanding." Or a person can intentionally mislead his or her partner to believe that there is a greater commitment than there actually is. Even if a person is committed, it is not always clear what the commitment means: Is it a commitment to the person or to the relationship, for a short time or for a long time? Is it for better and for worse?

> *The meeting of two personalities is like the contact of two chemical substances; if there is any reaction, both are transformed*
>
> Carl Jung (1875–1971)

❑ HOW DO I LOVE THEE? APPROACHES TO THE STUDY OF LOVE

Researchers have developed a number of ways to study love (Hendrick and Hendrick, 1987). Some of these ways are discussed in this section.

Styles of Love

"How do I love thee?" asked Elizabeth Barrett Browning in one of her poems. She went on to answer her own question:

> I love thee to the depth and breadth and height
> My soul can reach, when feeling out of sight
> For the ends of Being and ideal Grace.
> I love thee to the level of every day's
> Most quiet need, by sun and candle-light.
> I love thee freely, as men strive for right.
> I love thee purely, as they turn from praise.
> I love thee with the passion put to use
> In my old griefs, and with my childhood's faith.

> *Lovers and madmen have such seething brains,*
> *Such shaping fantasies, that apprehend*
> *More than cool reason ever comprehends.*
> *The lunatic, the lover and the poet*
> *Are of imagination all compact. . . .*
>
> William Shakespeare, A Midsummer Night's Dream

Sociologist John Lee has counted the ways differently. "I love thee erotically, madly, playfully, companionately, altruistically, pragmatically," he might say. Lee (1973, 1988) described six basic styles of loving:

❑ **Eros:** love of beauty
❑ **Mania:** obsessive love
❑ **Ludis:** playful love
❑ **Storge:** companionate love
❑ **Agape:** altruistic love
❑ **Pragma:** practical love

In addition to these pure forms there are mixtures of the basic types: Storgic-Eros, Ludic-Eros, and Storgic-Ludis. The six basic types can be described as follows:

Eros. Erotic lovers delight in the tactile, the sensual, the immediate; they are attracted to beauty (though beauty may be in the eye of the beholder). They love the lines of the body, its feel and touch. They are fascinated by every detail of their beloved. Their love burns brightly but soon flickers and dies.

Mania. The word *mania* comes from the Greek word for madness. The Russian poet Lermontov aptly described a manic lover:

He in his madness prays for storms,
And dreams that storms will bring him peace.

For manic lovers, nights are marked by sleeplessness and days by pain and anxiety. The slightest sign of affection brings ecstasy for a short while, only to disappear. Satisfactions last but a moment before they must be renewed. Manic love is roller-coaster love. The French ballad "Plaisir d'Amour" is the manic lover's anthem:

The pleasures of love are but a moment long
But the pain of love endures the whole life through.

Ludis. For ludic lovers, love is a game, something to play at rather than to become deeply involved in. Love is ultimately ludicrous. Love is for fun; encounters are casual, carefree, and often careless. "Nothing serious" is the motto of ludic lovers.

The patron saint of ludic lovers is the poet Sir John Suckling (1609–1642), a favorite of the English court (and the inventor of cribbage), who, when banished, committed suicide. His poem "The Constant Lover" sums up the philosophy of the ludic lover.

Out upon it, I have loved
Three whole days together!
And am like to love three more,
If it prove fair weather.

Storge. Storge (pronounced *stor*-gay) is the love between companions. It is, wrote Lee, "love without fever, tumult, or folly, a peaceful and enchanting affection." It begins usually as friendship and then gradually deepens into love. If the love ends, it also occurs gradually, and the couple often become friends once again. Of such love Theophile Gautier wrote, "To love is to admire with the heart; to admire is to love with the mind."

Agape. Agape (pronounced *ah*-ga-pay) is the traditional Christian love that is chaste, patient, and undemanding; it does not expect to be reciprocated. It is the love of saints and martyrs. Agape is more abstract and ideal than concrete and real. It is easier to love all of humankind in such a way than an individual.

*It lies not in our power to love or hate,
For will in us is over-ruled by fate.*

Christopher Marlowe, Hero and Leander

If you start with the belief that love is the pleasure of a moment, is it really surprising that it yields only a momentary pleasure?

Walter Lippmann, A Preface to Morals

Love gives itself; it is not bought.

Henry Longfellow (1807–1882)

Pragma. Pragmatic lovers are, first and foremost, logical in their approach toward looking for someone who meets their needs. They look for a partner who has the background, education, personality, religion, and interests that are compatible with their own. If they meet a person who meets their criteria, erotic or manic feelings may develop. But, as Samuel Butler warned, "Logic is like the sword—those who appeal to it shall perish by it."

Lee believes that to have a mutually satisfying love affair, a person has to find a partner who shares the same style and definition of love. The more different two people are in their styles of loving, the less likely it is that they will understand each other's love. Research confirms that love styles are also linked to gender and ethnicity (Hendrick and Hendrick, 1986).

Two researchers (Hendrick and Hendrick, 1988a) found that college students in love were more erotic and agapic and less ludic than those not in love. In another study, researchers found that heterosexual and gay men have similar attitudes toward eros, ludis, storge, and mania. The research also confirmed that gay male relationships have multiple emotional dimensions and are not based solely on sex (Adler, Hendrick, and Hendrick, 1989).

Romantic Love and Adrenaline: The Two-Component Theory

Love brings great pleasure. Christina Rossetti wrote:

> My heart is like a singing bird
>   Whose nest is in a watered shoot;
> My heart is like an apple-tree
>   Whose boughs are bent with thick-set fruit;
> My heart is like a rainbow shell
>   That paddles in a halcyon sea;
> My heart is gladder than all these
>   Because my love is come to me.

But love can also be torture, as the Roman poet Catullus complained in the first century B.C.:

> I hate and I love.
> You ask how that can be.
> Yet I do not know.
> But I feel it and I am tormented.

The contradictory nature of romantic love has confused lovers (and those who theorize about love) for centuries. Is passionate love pleasure or pain—or is it both?

The scientific explanation of romantic love was given a boost by Stanley Schachter's *two-component theory* of human emotions. According to his theory, for a person to experience an emotion, two factors must be present: (1) physiological arousal, and (2) an appropriate emotional explanation for the arousal. By recognizing that love is accompanied by physiological arousal, psychologists are able to explain why both intensely positive and intensely negative experiences can lead to love. Stimuli that generate attraction, sexual arousal, jealousy, loneliness, rejection, relief, confusion, and gratitude, for example, can all produce intense physiological arousal. "Thus, these positive *and* negative experiences may all have the potential for deepening an individual's passion for another" (Berscheid and Walster, 1974).

According to the two-component theory of emotions, for a person to experience an emotion there must be (1) physiological arousal and (2) an appropriate emotional explanation for the arousal. What emotions might the couple here be experiencing? Why?

The way people label their physiological responses is important in determining the way they feel. In a situation in which those feelings may reasonably be labeled "love," the person may indeed experience love. We learn to label our physiological responses as we grow up. The adolescent girl may ask, "When I see Willy come into English class, my heart leaps. Does that mean I am in love?" The response is crucial. If the answer is yes, she is going to identify the feeling with love. If a boy gets nervous every time he talks to a particular girl, he may label the nervousness "love" and fall in love; if he labels the nervousness "fear" he will not fall in love with the girl and may even avoid her.

A number of unpleasant situations may generate physiological arousal, including fear, rejection, frustration, and challenge. Similarly, pleasant experiences—attraction, sexual arousal, satisfaction of needs, excitement—may facilitate passion. There are few of us who have not fallen in love or had infatuations as a result of these strange, mysterious, and wonderful physiological arousal mechanisms.

We can turn to Shakespeare (as a social psychologist) for an illustration of the two-component theory. In *A Midsummer Night's Dream*, Titania, Queen of the Fairies, is given a potion that will make her fall in love with the first being she sees when she awakens from her sleep. The love potion is a stimulant that, like certain drugs, induces intense physiological responses. This stimulation is the basis for all love potions and spells, real or imagined. In this aroused state, Titania awakens and her eyes fall on Bottom, who has just been transformed into a donkey:

TITANIA: What angel wakes me from my flowery bed? . . .
Thy fair virtue's force perforce doth move
On the first view to say, to swear, I love thee.
BOTTOM: Methinks, mistress, you should have little reason for that: and yet to say the truth, reason and love keep little company together now-a-days

Of course, Bottom is neither wise nor beautiful; he is a donkey. But love aroused keeps no company with reason—although in a comedy about love, it is reasonable that Titania believes she is in love with a donkey. (We all may make that mistake sometimes!) When the spell induced by the potion is broken (that is, when the physiological stimuli stop), Titania comes to see Bottom as the donkey he truly is. So it is with all romantic love, according to Schacter's theory. It does not endure; indeed, it cannot endure. People cannot sustain the high degree of physiological stimulation. J. K. Folsom (quoted in Hatfield and Walster, 1981) wrote:

Love grows less exciting with time for the same biological reasons that the second run on a fast toboggan slide is less exciting than the first. The diminished excitement, however, may increase the real pleasure. Extreme excitement is practically the same as fear, and is unpleasant. After the excitement has diminished below a certain point, however, pleasure will again diminish, unless new kinds of pleasure have meanwhile arisen.

Because of the physiological arousal that accompanies sexual arousal, we can mistake sexual attraction for love, especially since we are expected to be sexually attracted to those we love. As Erich Fromm (1974) pointed out:

Because sexual desire is in the minds of most people coupled with the idea of love, they are easily misled to conclude that they love each other when they want each other physically. . . . Sexual attraction creates, for the moment, the illusion of union.

Without love, however, the illusion of oneness soon disappears and people are left as far apart as before. In some ways, remarked Fromm (1974), they become even more distant, "because when the illusion has gone they feel their estrangement even more markedly than before."

Why so pale and wan, fond lover?
    Prithee, why so pale?
Will, when looking well can't move her,
    Looking ill prevail?
    Prithee, why so pale?
Why so dull and mute, young sinner?
    Prithee, why so mute?
Will when speaking well can't win her,
    Saying nothing do't?
    Prithee, why so mute?
Quit, quit for shame! This will not move;
    This cannot take her.
If of herself she will not love,
    Nothing can make her.
    The devil take her!

John Suckling (1609–1642)

*Beauty stands
In the admiration of weak minds
Led captive*

John Milton (1608–1674)

The physical responses and sensations accompanying sexual arousal are often labeled as feelings of love.

I am not one of those who do not believe in love at first sight, but I do believe in taking a second look.

Henry Vincent (1813–1878)

Love as Attachment

Attachment theory, the most prominent new approach to the study of love, examines love as a form of attachment that finds its roots in infancy (Hazan and Shaver, 1987; Shaver et al., 1984, 1988). Research suggests that romantic love and infant/caregiver attachment have similar emotional dynamics. Phillip Shaver and his associates (1988) suggest that "all important love relationships—especially the first ones with parents and later ones with lovers and spouses—are attachments. . . ." Based on infant/caregiver work by John Bowlby (1969, 1973, 1980), some love researchers suggest numerous similarities between attachment and romantic love (Shaver et al., 1988). These include the following:

ATTACHMENT	ROMANTIC LOVE
Attachment bond's formation and quality depends on attachment object's (AO) responsiveness and sensitivity.	Feelings of love are related to lover's interest and reciprocation.
When AO is present, infant is happier.	When lover is present, person feels happier.
Infant shares toys, discoveries, objects with AO.	Lovers share experience and goods, give gifts.
Infant coos, talks baby talk, "sings."	Lovers coo, sing, and talk baby talk.
Feelings of oneness with AO.	Feelings of oneness with lover.

Studies conducted by Mary Ainsworth and colleagues (1978, cited in Shaver et al., 1988) indicate that there are three styles of infant attachment: secure, anxious/ambivalent, and avoidant. In *secure* attachment, the infant feels secure when the mother is out of sight. He or she is confident that the mother will offer protection and care. In *anxious/ambivalent* attachment, the infant shows separation anxiety when the mother leaves. He or she feels insecure when the mother is not present. In *avoidant* attachment, the infant senses the mother's detachment and rejection when he or she desires close bodily contact. The infant shows avoidance behaviors with the mother as a means of defense. Sixty-six percent of the infants in the study were secure, 19 percent were anxious/ambivalent, and 21 percent were avoidant.

Shaver and his associates (1988) hypothesized that the styles of attachment developed during infancy continue through adulthood. They conducted several surveys with adults, which revealed similar styles of attachment.

❏ *Secure Adults.* Secure adults found it relatively easy to get close to others. They felt comfortable depending on others and having others depend on them. They didn't frequently worry about being abandoned or having someone get too close to them. More than avoidant and anxious/ambivalent adults, they felt that others generally liked them; they believed that people were generally well-intentioned and good-hearted. In contrast to the other styles, secure adults were less likely to believe in media images of love and believe that romantic love can last. Their love experiences tended to be happy, friendly, and trusting. They accepted and supported their partners. On the average, their relationships lasted ten years. About 56 percent of the adults in the study were secure.

❏ *Anxious/Ambivalent Adults.* Anxious/ambivalent adults felt that others did not get as close as they themselves wanted. They worried that their partners didn't real-

Never seek to tell thy love
  Love that never told can be;
For the gentle wind does move
  Silently, invisibly.
I told my love, I told my love,
  I told her all my heart;
Trembling, cold, in ghastly fears,
  Ah! She did depart!
Soon as she was gone from me,
  A traveler came by,
Silently, invisibly,
  He took her with a sigh.

William Blake (1757–1827)

Love reckons hours for months, and days for years; and every little absence is an age.

John Dryden (1631–1700)

ly love them or would leave them. They also wanted to merge completely with another, which sometimes scared others away. More than others, they felt that it is easy to fall in love. Their experiences in love were often obsessive and marked by desire for union, high degrees of sexual attraction and jealousy, and emotional highs and lows. Their love relationships lasted an average of five years. Between 19 and 20 percent of the adults were identified as anxious/ambivalent.

❑ *Avoidant Adults.* Avoidant adults felt discomfort in being close to others; they were distrustful and fearful of becoming dependent. More than others, they believed that romance seldom lasted but that at times it could be as intense as it was at the beginning. Their partners wanted more closeness than they did. Avoidant lovers feared intimacy and experienced emotional highs and lows and jealousy. Their relationships lasted six years on the average. Between 23 and 25 percent of the adults in the study were avoidant.

In adulthood, the attachment styles developed in infancy combined with sexual desire and caring behaviors to give rise to romantic love.

❑ ASPECTS OF LOVE: FALLING IN LOVE AND UNREQUITED LOVE

Even though love has become an increasingly prominent research topic during the last decade, little research has been devoted to two common aspects of love: falling in love and unrequited love. About 90 percent of college students report having fallen in love and 75 percent have experienced unrequited love (Aron et al., 1989; Aron, Aron, and Allen, 1989).

Falling in Love

In the United States, everyone seems equally likely to fall in love: males and females, young children and the elderly, heterosexuals, gay men and lesbians, whites, African Americans, Latinos, and Asian Americans (Aron, Aron, Paris et al., 1989). Only recent immigrants from areas without the romantic love ethic appear exempt; and even among these immigrants, such as the Hmong, the younger generation is rapidly assimilating romantic love ideals (Meredith and Rowe, 1986). In fact, throughout the world, romantic love is increasingly displacing other forms of love, such as companionate love, as the most valued form of love (Goode, 1963). As such, falling in love—the transition from not being in love to being in love—is critical in the development of intimate relationships.

WHO FALLS IN LOVE? According to the latest research findings, there is little gender difference in overall romanticism. Those who are more expressive—whether they are male or female—tend to be more romantic (Hatfield and Rapson, 1987). More males than females, however, reported never having been in love. And more females than males—64 percent versus 46 percent—reported currently being in love (Hendrick and Hendrick, 1986).

Age seems to have little effect on falling in love. A study of romantic relationships with respondents from the ages of four through eighteen years found little difference in intensity of love between very young children and late adolescents. Males and females experienced the same high emotional levels except at ages ten through twelve years, when the intensity fell dramatically for boys (Hatfield and Rapson, 1987). Among middle-aged men and women, passionate love appears to be as

It is easier to stay out than get out.

Mark Twain

Love is such a tissue of paradoxes, and exists in such an endless variety of forms and shades that you may say almost anything about it that you please, and it is likely to be correct.

Henry Fink, Romantic Love and Personal Beauty

frequent as for younger adults. It is reasonable to suppose that the elderly also may fall in love, although there are no studies of love among the elderly.

Personality traits appear to have a strong influence on falling in love. Attachment styles seem to affect whether one falls in love. In one study (Hazan and Shaver, 1987), the researchers found that almost no avoidants and only 9 to 15 percent of securely attached men and women reported that it was easy for them to fall in love. Twenty to thirty percent of anxious/ambivalents, however, indicated that falling in love was easy. Other researchers used Lee's six styles of love to determine the relationship between falling in love and style of loving. They found that those who had been in love or were currently in love scored higher on ludic (playful) love and lower on eros (romantic/passionate love) and agape (selfless love) compared to those who had not been or were not currently in love (Hendrick and Hendrick, 1986).

Individuals also appear to have a "readiness" to fall in love. Men and women are more likely to fall in love when they have temporarily lowered self-esteem, such as following a breakup, when they are looking for adventure, or when they are desiring to have a close relationship.

WHERE DO PEOPLE FALL IN LOVE? The setting *where* people fall in love appears to be important. Fifty-eight percent of the respondents in one study (Aron, Dutton, Aron, and Iverson, 1989) indicated that the circumstances in which they met were "unusual," and 34 percent said that they felt isolated or special in relation to the people around them. Romantic settings—such as a party, a candlelit dinner, or a deserted beach—give cues that romantic feelings are appropriate. In keeping with the two-component theory of love, one aspect of unusual circumstances is the generation of strong emotion or physiological arousal, which increases the likelihood of attraction.

SELF-DISCLOSURE AND RECIPROCITY. Revealing oneself is important in falling in love, but the mere disclosure of feelings is not the key element. Self-disclosure is most meaningful if you reveal to the other person that you like him or her. Being liked by the other person, whether it is revealed through words, eye contact, or physical contact, is a powerful force to induce you to like someone. In fact, it may be *the most* important factor.

Paradoxically, not being liked can also encourage falling in love. Some men and women respond to the challenge of overcoming another's resistance. In fact, some studies suggest that we like those better who initially disliked or refused us than those who liked us all along.

Unrequited Love

As most of us know from painful experience, love is not always returned. We may reassure ourselves that, as Tennyson wrote 150 years ago, "'Tis better to have loved and lost/Than never to have loved at all." Too often, however, such words sound like rationalizations. Who among us does not sometimes think, "'Tis better never to have loved at all?" Unrequited love is a common experience; a recent study found that about 75 percent of its respondents had experienced it and about 20 percent were currently experiencing it (Aron, Aron, and Allen, 1989). Many people find their lives—and sleep—disrupted by unrequited love.

Unrequited love presents a paradox: If the goal of loving someone is an intimate relationship, why should we continue to love a person with whom we could not

I will reveal to you a love potion, without medicine, without herbs, without any witch's magic. If you want to be loved, then you must love.

Hecaton of Rhodes

The heart is wild. It spins through nebulae that burn like mercury. And it is not vanquished by the darkness it traverses. Love—or even its possibility— requires that we live fantastically.

Earl Jackson, Jr.

No disguise can long conceal love where it exists, nor long feign it where it is lacking.

François de La Rochefoucauld

have such a relationship? Arthur Aron and his colleagues addressed this question in a study of almost 500 college students (Aron et al., 1989). The researchers found three different motivations underlying the experience of unrequited love.

❒ *The Cyrano style*—the desire to have a romantic relationship, with a specific person regardless of how hopeless the love is. In this style, the benefits of loving someone are so great that it does not matter how likely the love is to be returned. Being in the same room with the beloved—because he or she is so wonderful—may be sufficient reason for loving someone who does not reciprocate. This style is named after Cyrano de Bergerac, whose love for Roxanne was so great it was irrelevant that she loved someone else.

❒ *The Giselle style*—the misperception that a relationship is more likely to develop than it actually is. This might occur if one misreads the other's cues, such as mistakenly believing that friendliness is a sign of love. This style is named after Giselle, the tragic ballet heroine who was misled by Count Albrecht to believe that her love was reciprocated.

❒ *The Don Quixote style*—the general desire to be in love, regardless of whom one loves. In this style, the benefits of being in love—such as being viewed as a romantic or the excitement of extreme emotions—are more important than actually being in a relationship. This style is named after Don Quixote, whose love for the common Dulcinea was motivated by his need to dedicate knightly deeds to a lady love. "It is as right and proper for a knight errant to be in love as for the sky to have stars," Don Quixote explained.

Using styles-of-attachment theory, the researchers found that some people were predisposed to be Cyranos, other Giselles, and still others Don Quixotes. Anxious/ambivalents tended to be Cyranos, avoidants were Don Quixotes, and secures were Giselles. Those with anxious/ambivalent attachment styles were most likely to experience unrequited love; those with secure attachment styles were least likely to experience such love. Avoidants experienced the greatest desire to be in love in general, yet they had the least probability of being in a specific relationship. Anxious/ambivalents showed the greatest desire for a specific relationship; they also had the least desire to be in love in general.

❒ JEALOUSY

Does jealousy prove love? Many of us think it does. We may try to test someone's interest of affection by attempting to make him or her jealous by flirting with another person. If our date or partner becomes jealous, the jealousy is taken as a sign of love (Salovey and Rodin, 1991; White, 1980a). But provoking jealousy proves nothing except that the other person can be made jealous. And making jealousy a litmus test of love is dangerous, for jealousy and love are not necessary companions. Jealousy may be a more accurate yardstick for measuring insecurity or possessiveness than love. In William Shakespeare's *Othello*, for example, the jealous Othello murdered his devoted wife because he was misled into believing she was unfaithful. When he discovers that she was innocent, he cries out that "he loved not wisely but too well." But did Othello love too well? Or was he (and she) a victim of his pride and possessiveness?

It is important to understand jealousy for several reasons. First jealousy is a painful emotion filled with anger and hurt. Its churning emotions can turn us inside out, make us feel out of control. If we can understand jealousy, especially when it is irrational, then we can eliminate some of its pain. Second, jealousy can help either

'Tis better to have loved and lost Than never to have loved at all.

Alfred, Lord Tennyson (1809–1892)

My love is like to ice, and I to fire: How comes it then that this her cold so great Is not dissolved through my so hot desire, But harder grows the more I her entreat? Or how come it that my exceeding heat Is not allayed by her heart-frozen cold, But that I burn much more in boiling sweat, And feel my flames augmented manifold? What more miraculous thing may be told That fire, which all things melts, should harden ice, And ice, which is congeal'd with senselesss cold, Should kindle fire by wonderful device? Such is the power of love in gentle mind, That it can alter all the course of kind.

Edmund Spenser (16th Century)

Absence makes the heart grow fonder; then you forget.

Floyd Zimmerman

to cement or destroy a relationship. Jealousy helps maintain a relationship by guarding it exclusiveness. But in its irrational or extreme forms, it can destroy a relationship by its insistent demands and attempts at control. We need to understand when and how jealousy is functional and when it is not. Third, jealousy is often linked to violence (Follingstad, et al, 1990; Laner, 1990). It is a factor in precipitating violence in dating relationships among both high school and college students (Burcky, 1988; Stets and Pirog-Good, 1987). Marital violence and rape are often provoked by jealousy (Russell, 1990). It is frequently used by abusive spouses to justify their violence (Adams, 1990).

Jealousy in Cross-Cultural Perspective

Jealousy appears to be present in all cultures. It differs from culture to culture, however, in its level of intensity and what evokes it. Researcher Ralph Hupka (1981) divides cultures into low-jealousy and high-jealousy ones. Low-jealousy cultures are characterized by sharing attitudes, positive attitudes toward sexual pleasure, and the prizing of children regardless of paternity. High-jealousy cultures, by contrast, are possessive of goods and people, have restrictive attitudes toward sexuality, and require the legitimizing of children through marriage. They place high value on romantic love and marriage as a source of intimacy.

The United States is a relatively high-jealousy society. In a study of 103 men and women (Pines and Aronson, 1983), half described themselves as a "jealous person." In high-jealousy cultures, the husband is permitted to physically assault his wife if she is found having sexual intercourse with another man. In the United States, some states at one time sanctioned murder as justifiable homicide, "a crime of passion," if it was committed by a husband in a fit of jealous rage. Such laws, however, did not ordinarily extend to women. For women, the "crime of passion" was nevertheless murder.

What evokes jealousy differs among cultures. A study of seven nations, including the United States and Mexico, found that flirting, kissing, and sexual relationships evoked jealous responses among all respondents (Buunk and Hupka, 1987). The most intense response was provoked by a partner having sexual intercourse with someone else. Dancing, hugging, and having sexual fantasies about another person evoked more neutral responses. There were not many differences between men and women, except that women were generally more jealous if their partners kissed someone else, whereas men were more upset if their partners had sexual fantasies about someone else.

As discussed in Chapter 1, not all cultures practice **monogamy;** in fact, the overwhelming majority of cultures prefer polygamy. But polygamy is not immune from jealousy. In fact, the words for polygamy and jealousy are often identical in various cultures. In Africa, the Bantu word for jealousy is also used for polygamy because co-wives rarely live together peacefully. And among the Fula in Nigeria, the word for second wife means "the jealous one."

How do polygynous cultures deal with jealousy? To minimize jealous reactions, these cultures generally establish a senior wife, usually the first wife. The other wives are expected to defer to her. Wives are often related by birth, most often as sisters. If they are unrelated, they usually live in separate dwellings. The husband is expected to visit his wives sequentially so that one wife will not be singled out as his sexual favorite. To spend two nights in a row with one wife would be a serious breach of marital decorum.

Some monogamous cultures permit sexual relationships outside marriage under certain conditions. But even these cultures provide mechanisms for curtailing jealousy. Some traditional Inuit (Eskimo) societies sexually share husbands/wives with

There is more self-love than love in jealousy

François de la Rochefoucauld

friends or guests as a means of forming kin-like bonds. Such sharing creates mutual obligations and cements friendship. But sexual sharing is sanctioned by society and is done only with the mutual consent of all involved. In such circumstances, neither husband nor wife experiences jealousy. But both are constantly suspicious of their spouses engaging in *secret* sexual relationships, and these illicit affairs are the source of great jealousy and discord.

What Is Jealousy?

Jealousy is an aversive response that occurs because of a partner's real, imagined, or likely involvement with a third person (Bringle and Buunk, 1985). It functions as a boundary-making mechanism. It sets the boundaries for what a group feels are important relationships that should not be violated (Reiss, 1986).

Jealousy is not a barometer by which the depth of love can be read. It merely records the depth of the lover's insecurity.

Margaret Mead

JEALOUSY: THE PSYCHOLOGICAL DIMENSION. Jealous responses are most intense in committed or marital relationships because both assume "specialness," meaning that one's intimate partner is different from everyone else: It is with him or her that you are most confiding, revealing, vulnerable, caring, and trusting. To have sex outside the relationship violates a sense of exclusiveness, because sex symbolizes "specialness." Words such as "unfaithful," "cheating," and "infidelity" reflect the idea that an unspoken pledge has been broken. This unspoken pledge is the normative expectation that serious relationships, whether dating or marital, will be sexually exclusive (Lieberman, 1987).

As most people know, jealousy is a painful experience. It is an agonizing compound of hurt, anger, depression, fear, and doubt. As one person said (Clanton and Smith, 1977):

I didn't know that anybody could hurt so much and live. I suppose it's jealousy. I didn't know it was like this. I thought jealousy was an idea. It isn't. It's a pain. But I don't feel as they do in Broadway melodrama. I don't want to kill anybody. I just want to die.

Despite its intensity, jealousy is not a primary emotion. Rather, it appears to be a secondary form of anger or fear. When people are asked what they feel when they are jealous, most say they feel angry or afraid. We are taught to label those feelings as jealousy when a relationship is threatened (Hupka, 1984).

Beware, my lord, of jealousy. It is the green-eyed monster that mocks the meat it feeds on.

William Shakespeare. Othello

As our lives become more and more intertwined, we become less and less independent. For some, this loss of independence increases the fear of losing the partner. But it takes more than simple dependency to make a person jealous. To be jealous we also need to lack self-esteem and have a feeling of insecurity, either about ourselves or about our relationships (Berscheid and Frei, 1977; McIntosh, 1989). Insecure individuals tend to feel jealous in their relationships (McIntosh and Tate, 1990). This is true for both whites and African Americans (McIntosh, 1989).

Jealous responses are most intense when they involve sexuality, as Americans tend to be particularly insecure and competitive in this realm (Bringle and Buunk, 1991). Consider, for example, the different responses you might feel if you believe your partner is (1) talking to, (2) holding hands with, (3) kissing, or (4) having sexual intercourse with a potential or real rival. Which activities do you find most threatening? Least? If you are like most people, the more sexual the interaction, the higher the level of jealousy it arouses.

TYPES OF JEALOUSY: SUSPICIOUS AND REACTIVE. Social psychologists suggest that there are two types of jealousy: suspicious and reactive (Bringle and Buunk, 1991).

A man was jealous of his wife, who, despite his jealousies, was always faithful. She gave him no reason to be jealous, but it did not matter; he tormented her with his constant tirades. Finally, one evening she left and was never seen again. But outside the camp, her sons discovered a great rock which resembled their mother. Their father's jealousy, they said, had turned her to stone.

Plains Indian Tale

*Triffles light as air
Are to the jealous confirmations strong
As proofs of holy writ.*

William Shakespeare. Othello

*Here lies the body of Mannie
They put him here to stay;
He lived the life of Riley
While Riley was away.*

Boot Hill epitaph

Suspicious jealousy occurs when there is (1) no reason to be suspicious or (2) only ambiguous evidence to suspect that a partner is involved with a third person. *Reactive jealousy* occurs when a partner reveals a current, past, or anticipated relationship with another person.

SUSPICIOUS JEALOUSY. Suspicious jealousy tends to occur most often when a relationship is in its early stages. At this time the relationship is not firmly established, and the couple is unsure about its future. The smallest distraction, imagined slight, or inattention can be taken as evidence of interest in another person. Even without *any* evidence, a jealous partner may worry ("Is he or she seeing someone else but not telling me?"). The partner may engage in vigilance, watching his or her partner's every move ("I'd like to audit your marriage and family class"). He or she may snoop, unexpectedly appearing in the middle of the night to see if someone else is there ("I was just passing by and thought I'd say hello"). The partner may try to control the other's behavior ("If you go to your friend's party without me, we're through").

Such suspicions often exist without provocation but nevertheless influence our perceptions. Because of suspiciousness, unexceptional events are transformed into evidence of affairs. Telephone hang-ups and wrong numbers are misinterpreted as calls from lovers. Animated conversations with a third party are thought to be lover's talk. Old friends are seen as threats or paramours.

Sometimes, of course, suspicions are valid. That is the terrible thing about suspicions: they can be legitimate. Suspicious jealousy, in fact, may be a reasonable response to circumstantial evidence. (If both partners are non-smokers, for example, the cigarette next to the bed may be actual evidence. "The maid must have left the cigarette. How clumsy of her!" is not a convincing response in such situations.) Bringle and Buunk, in fact, believe that a certain amount of suspicious jealousy may be functional. They observe (Bringle and Buunk, 1991): "Emotional reactions to these [circumstantial] events may forewarn the partner of what will happen if there are serious transgressions and thereby serve the role of *preventing* extradyadic involvements."

On the other hand, the suspicious jealousy may be wholly unfounded. The jealous man or woman may feel out of control and, as a result, his or her self-esteem suffers. "I can't help it. I know it is irrational and I hate myself for it. I am a terrible person. But every time you are out of my sight I think you are seeing someone else." Such jealousy may undermine the relationship. Jealous men and women often try to control their partner's feelings, activities, and movements until their partner feels suffocated, imprisoned in the relationship. Such irrational jealousy can destroy the very relationship it is trying to preserve.

REACTIVE JEALOUSY. Reactive jealousy occurs when someone learns of a partner's present, past, or anticipated sexual involvement with another person. This is usually the most intense jealousy. If the affair occurred in the past, side by side with the present relationship, the unknowing partner may feel that the primary relationship has been based on a lie. Trust is shaken. Every word and event must be reevaluated in light of this new knowledge: "If you slept with him/her when you said you were going to the library, did you also sleep with him/her when you said you were going to the laundromat?" Or, "How could you say you loved me when you were seeing him/her?" The damage can be irreparable.

If the affair is currently ongoing, similar questions arise, but with an important difference. Since the affair is not over, the involved partner may be confronted with a choice: with whom will he or she remain? Sometimes there is no choice: because of the affair, the offended partner breaks off the relationship or marriage.

BOUNDARY MARKERS. As we noted earlier, jealousy represents a boundary marker. It determines how, to what extent, and in what manner others can interact with members of a relationship. It also shows the limits with which the members of the relationship can interact with those outside the relationship. Culture sets the general boundaries of what evokes jealousy, but individuals adjust them to the dynamics of their own relationship. Traditional Moslem culture, such as those in Pakistan and Bangladesh, tends to be the most restrictive. Women are not permitted to leave their homes except with their husband's permission. When they venture into public their bodies must be fully covered, which includes wearing a *chadoor* (veil), and they must be accompanied by relatives. By contrast, American women have great freedom of movement and the ability to dress in any fashion they wish.

Boundaries vary depending on the type of relationship, gender, sexual orientation, and ethnicity. While the majority of people believe sexual exclusiveness to be important in serious dating relationships and cohabitation, it is virtually mandatory in marriage (Buunk and van Driel, 1989; Blumstein and Schwartz, 1983; Lieberman, 1988). Men are generally more restrictive than women; heterosexuals are more restrictive than gay men and lesbians. Although we know very little about the link between jealousy and ethnicity, traditional Latinos and new Latino and Asian immigrants appear to be more restrictive than Anglos or African Americans (Mindel et al, 1988). Despite variations on where the boundary lines are drawn, jealousy functions to guard those lines.

While our culture sets down the general marital boundaries, each couple evolves its own boundaries. For some, it is permissible to carve out an area of individual privacy: a person may have few or many friends of his or her own (of the same or other sex), activities, and interests apart from his or her partner. Other couples do not permit each other to have separate spheres, or do not desire them. But wherever a married couple draws its boundaries, each member understands where the line is drawn and implicitly or explicitly knows what behavior will evoke a jealous response (Bringle and Buunk, 1991). For some, it is having lunch with a member of the other sex (or same sex, if they are gay or lesbian); for others, it is having dinner; for still others, it is having dinner and seeing a movie. For one married partner to pretend to the other that he or she didn't "know" that a particular action (a flirtatious suggestion, lingering kiss, or dinner alone) would provoke a jealous response is often disingenuous.

Gender and Orientation Differences

While men and women both experience jealousy, they differ along both gender and orientation lines.

GENDER DIFFERENCES. Both men and women may fear their partner's attraction to someone else because of dissatisfaction and the desire for sexual variety; women, however, feel especially vulnerable to losing their partner to an attractive rival (White, 1981). Men tend to experience jealousy only when they feel their partners are sexually involved or attracted to other men, while women tend to experience jealousy over intimacy issues as well. Thus, women feel the most jealousy when they believe their partners are both emotionally and physically involved with another woman (White, 1981).

Men tend to react to jealousy by expressing anger. Women more often react with depression. Ira Reiss (1986) suggests that this difference is consistent with cultural restraints prohibiting women from expressing anger. At the same time, it reflects their greater powerlessness vis-a-vis men. As a result, women turn their anger inward, transforming it into depression. In this manner they are able to avoid direct confrontation.

There may be some truth to the belief that women are more jealous than men. But such jealousy is not inherent in being female. It is more likely related to the greater sexual freedom that men are permitted. (Even in marriage, it is more acceptable for men to "roam" because they are believed to be "naturally" more sexual than women.) If women appear to be more jealous than men, it may be because men, granted greater autonomy than women, have more opportunities to evoke jealous responses from women (Reiss, 1986).

GAY, LESBIAN, AND BISEXUAL DIFFERENCES. Gay men and lesbians appear to be less prone to jealousy than heterosexuals. There are two factors accounting for this: First, heterosexual norms place higher value on sexual exclusiveness than do gay and lesbian norms (Hawkins, 1990). (The higher normative value placed on heterosexual monogamy, however, does not prevent heterosexual men and women from having affairs.) In gay and lesbian culture, the model for relationships is not marriage but a "best-friends" model (Peplau, 1988). In the marital model, sexual fidelity is normative, while in the gay/lesbian best-friends model it is negotiable (Kurdek, 1991). As a consequence, many gay men and lesbians are more able to have sexual relationships outside the primary relationship without provoking the same high degree of jealousy.

Second, sex does not necessarily symbolize love. In exclusive heterosexual relationships, sex and love are equated. Sex and love are intertwined for lesbians as well, perhaps reflecting their socialization as women (Nichols, 1987). For lesbians, there appears to be a greater emphasis on the intimacy rather than sexual aspects of relationships. Among lesbian feminists, there is a strong commitment to *not* be jealous. Jealousy is perceived as a patriarchal emotion used to repress female freedom. Thus, the jealous lesbian feminist bears a double burden: jealousy and guilt for feeling jealousy (Wolf, 1981).

For gay men, as for heterosexual men, sex and love can be more easily separated than for women. For them, sex can be more closely related to pleasure than expressions of intimacy. Unlike heterosexual couples, gay male couples in general are presented more or less with the ability to consciously chose to make their relationship exclusive (closed) or nonexclusive (open). While extramarital relationships are often symptomatic of problems among married couples, they are not necessarily symptomatic among gay couples. Rather, nonexclusiveness among gay couples may simply reflect different norms (Kurdeck, 1991; Kurdeck and Schmitt, 1988). Yet, the potential for jealousy exists in open as well as closed gay relationships. To minimize jealousy in open relationships, extrarelational sex is generally compartmentalized so as not to threaten the primary relationship.

Managing Jealousy

Jealousy can be unreasonable or realistic, reacting to genuine threats or events. Unreasonable jealousy can become a problem when it interferes with an individual's well-being or that of the relationship. Dealing with irrational suspicions can be very difficult, for such feelings touch deep recesses in ourselves. As we noted earlier, jealousy is often related to personal feelings of insecurity and inadequacy. The source of such jealousy lies within the individual, not within the relationship. Excessively jealous persons may be helped to some extent by a partner's reassurance, but at some point they must confront their own irrationality and insecurity. If they do not, they may well destroy the relationship they are desperately trying to preserve.

When there are real reasons for jealousy, such as the relationship's boundaries being violated, the cause lies not within the individual, but within the relationship. Clanton and Smith (1977) write:

Jealousy cannot be treated in isolation. *Your* jealousy is not *your* problem alone. It is also a problem for your partner and for the person whose interest in your partner sparks your jealousy. Similarly, when your partner feels jealous, you ought not to dismiss the matter by pointing a finger and saying, "That's your problem." Typically, three or more persons are involved in the production of jealous feelings and behaviors. Ideally, all three should take a part of the responsibility for minimizing the negative consequences.

If the jealousy is well founded, the partner who is its object may need to modify or end the relationship with the third party who caused the jealousy to flare up if the relationship is to be preserved. Modifying the third-party relationship reduces the jealous response and, more importantly, reaffirms the partner's commitment to the primary relationship. If the partner is unwilling to do this, because of lack of commitment or unsatisfied personal needs or problems in the primary relationship, the relationship is likely to reach a crisis. In such cases, jealousy may be the agent for profound change.

There are no hard and set rules for dealing with jealousy. Each person must deal with it using his or her own understanding and insights. As with most of life's puzzling problems, jealousy has no simple answers.

☐ THE TRANSFORMATION OF LOVE: FROM PASSION TO INTIMACY

The Instability of Passionate Love

Ultimately, romantic love may be transformed or replaced by a quieter, more lasting love. Otherwise, the relationship will likely break up and each person will search for another who will once again ignite his or her passion.

THE PASSAGE OF TIME: CHANGES IN INTIMACY, PASSION, AND COMMITMENT. According to researcher Robert Sternberg (1988), time affects our levels of intimacy, passion and commitment.

INTIMACY OVER TIME. When we first meet someone, intimacy increases rapidly as we make critical discoveries about each other, ranging from our innermost thoughts about life and death to our preference for strawberry or chocolate ice cream. As the relationship continues, the rate of growth decreases and then levels off. After the growth levels off, the couple no longer "consciously" feels as close to each other. This may be because they actually are beginning to drift apart, or it may be because they are continuing to grow intimate at a different, less conscious, but deeper level. It is the kind of intimacy that is not easily observed. Instead, it is a latent intimacy that nevertheless is forging stronger, more enduring bonds between them.

But jealous souls will not be answer'd so;
They are not ever jealous for the cause;
But jealous for they are jealous; 'tis a monster
Begot upon itself, born on itself.

William Shakespeare. Othello

Love is a flickering flame between two darknesses. . . . Whence does it come? . . . From sparks incredibly small. . . . How does it end? . . . In nothingness equally incredible . . . The more raging the flame, the sooner it is burnt out.

Heinrich Heine (1797–1856)

Love is patient and kind; love is not jealous or boastful; it is not arrogant or rude. Love does not insist on its own way; it is not irritable or resentful; it does not rejoice at wrong, but rejoices in the right. Love bears all things, believes all things, hopes all things, endures all things.

I Corinthians 13: 4–7

FOCUS

Love and Sexuality

Love and sexuality are intimately connected in our culture (Aron and Aron, 1991). We can see this if we look at some of the words we use to describe sexual intercourse. When we say that we "make love" or are "intimate" with someone, we generally mean that we are sexually involved. But this sexual involvement carries overtones of relationship, caring, or love; it possesses potential richness of meaning. Such meanings are absent in the more technical terms *sexual intercourse* and *coitus* or the obscene *fuck* or *screw*.

Although love and sexuality are connected, researchers have been unable to agree on the nature of that connection (see Aron and Aron, 1991, for a literature review). In the sociobiological perspective, males, who are constantly fertile from early adolescence on, seek to impregnate as many females as possible to insure the continuation of their genes. For males, sex is important. Females ovulate only once a month, however; a single act of intercourse can result in pregnancy, childbirth, and years of childrearing. For women, it is important to be selective about choosing a partner with whom to pass on their genes. Women want partners on whom they can rely for childrearing and support. As a result, love is important for females. Love is their guarantee that males will remain with them to share childrearing tasks. Females trade sex for love, and males trade love for sex.

By contrast, sociologist Ira Reiss (1986) argues that reproduction is secondary to sex. Instead, the essential aspects of sex are pleasure and self-disclosure. The altered consciousness

involved in sexual arousal permits a unique "psychic release." In this, the "elemental physical and emotional disclosures of sexuality can further and deepen psychic disclosures." These deep disclosures help promote and sustain love.

Exchange theorists give sex and love about equal weight in close relationships. Both are interpersonal resources that are exchanged by partners and influence the relationship (Safilios-Rothschild, 1976). Researchers (Rettig and Bulbolz, 1983) found that among married men and women, there was a high correlation between the degree of love and the quality of sex. The greater the love, the better the sex.

Other researchers emphasize love, making sexuality less important in relationships. Hatfield and Walster (1978) view sexuality as somewhat important in romantic love and of little significance in companionate love. And, using Lee's styles of loving, Hendrick and Hendrick (1987) found sex to be related to the love style: erotic lovers were "intense" about their sexuality, whereas pragmatic lovers were "practical." They concluded that "love and sexuality were strongly linked to each other and to both the physical and spiritual aspects of the human condition."

Sex is most highly valued in our culture when it is linked with love. In fact, sex with affection rivals marriage as the accepted moral standard of sexual intercourse. With the "sex with affection" standard of premarital intercourse, we use individualistic rather than social norms to legitimize sexual relations. Our sexual standards are now personal rather than institutional. Re-

searchers report that those in love tend to be less permissive in their sexual attitudes than those not in love. Lovers are also less instrumental in their views about sexuality than those not in love. For lovers, sex is more an expression of intimacy than an exchange of pleasures (Hendrick and Hendrick, 1988).

Relationships change, sometimes dramatically, after an individual first engages in sexual intercourse with a new partner. A person with whom someone has intercourse, even if he or she is a stranger, is no longer like any other person. "After coitus," wrote Gagnon (1977), "the couple will change, with reference to themselves, to each other, and to their surrounding social world." Sexual intercourse represents a new or different degree of intimacy. Each person consciously or unconsciously evaluates what the sexual act means. Does it mean that intimacy has been increased or that boundaries have been violated? Is it a call for greater commitment or for distancing? Is it a sign of love or indifference?

MEN, SEX, AND LOVE

Men and women who are not in an established relationship have different expectations. Men are more likely than women to separate sex from affection. Studies consistently demonstrate that for the majority of men, sex and love are not intimately connected (Blumstein and Schwartz, 1983; Carroll et al., 1985).

Although men are more likely than women to separate sex and love,

continued on next page

PASSION OVER TIME. Passion is subject to habituation: what was once thrilling, whether it be love, sex, or roller coasters, becomes less so the more we get used to it. Once we become habituated, more time with a person (or more sex or more roller coaster rides) does not increase our arousal or satisfaction.

FOCUS

Levine and Barbach (1985) found in their interviews that men indicated that their most erotic sexual experiences took place in a relational context. The researchers quoted one man:

Emotions are everything when it comes to sex. There's no greater feeling than having an emotional attachment with the person you're making love to. If those emotions are there, it's going to be fabulous. . . . They don't call it "making love" for nothing.

Most men in the study responded that it was primarily the emotional quality of the relationship that made their sexual experiences special.

WOMEN, SEX, AND LOVE

Women generally view sex from a relational perspective. In the decision to have sexual intercourse, the quality and degree of intimacy of a relationship were more important for women than men (Christopher and Cate, 1984). Women were more likely to report feelings of love if they were sexually involved with their partners than if they were not sexually involved (Peplau et al., 1977).

While women generally seek emotional relationships, some men initially seek physical relationships. This difference in intentions can place women in a bind. Carole Cassell (1984) suggests that today's women face a "damned if you do, damned if you don't" dilemma in their sexual relationships. If a woman has sexual intercourse with a man, he says goodbye; if she doesn't, he says he respects her *and* still says goodbye. A young woman Cassell interviewed related the following:

I really hate the idea that, because I'm having sex with a man whom I haven't known for a long, long time, he'll think I don't value myself. But it's hard to know what to do. If you meet a man and date him two or three times and don't have sex, he begins to feel you are either rejecting him or you have serious sex problems. . . . But I really dread feeling that I could turn into, in his eyes, an easy lay, a good-time girl. I want men to see me as a grown-up woman who has the same right as they do to make sexual choices.

Traditionally, women were labeled "good" or "bad" based on their sexual experience and values. "Good" women were virgins, sexually naive, or passive, whereas "bad" women were sexually experienced, independent, and passionate.

SEX WITHOUT LOVE

Is love necessary for sex? We assume that it is, but that assumption is one of motives and values. It cannot be answered by reference to empirical or statistical data (Crosby, 1985). The question becomes a more fundamental one: Is sexual activity legitimate in itself, or does it require justification? John Crosby (1985) observed:

Our society and culture . . . have held, at least implicitly, that sexual expression must be justified before it is acceptable. This justification has assumed several forms, including procreation, the expression of marital privilege, and the expression of love and affection. . . . [S]exual pleasure is a value in itself and hence capable of being inherently meaningful and rewarding. The search for extrinsic justification and rationalization simply belies our reluctance to believe that sex is a pleasurable activity in and of itself.

To believe that sex does not require love as a justification, argues Crosby, does not deny the significance of love and affection in sexual relations. In fact, love and affection are important and desirable for enduring relationships. They are simply not necessary, Crosby believes, for affairs in which erotic pleasure is the central feature.

Albert Ellis (1958) similarly argued that, although love and affection are desirable, they are not necessary. People can have satisfying erotic involvement with friends, acquaintances, or strangers, he believed. He made several points in his argument. First, many individuals find great satisfaction in sexual relations without love. Second, the majority of people who find greater satisfaction in sex with love probably do not do so their entire lives. Especially in their youth, such people probably found sex without love satisfying. Third, many people who condemn sex without love have not thought out their views carefully; there are times when they probably would find sex without love very satisfying.

Over a person's lifetime, affectional sex is probably most rewarding, argued Ellis, because it connects people with each other's emotional and intellectual dimensions. "I can easily see, however, even the most intelligent and highly cultured individuals spending a *little* time with members of the other sex with whom they have common sex and cultural but no real love interests" (Ellis, 1958).

If the person leaves, however, we experience withdrawal symptoms (fatigue, depression, anxiety), just as if we were addicted. In becoming habituated, we have also become dependent. We fall beneath the emotional baseline we were at when we met our partner. Over time, however, we begin to return to that original level.

Love and you shall be loved. All love is mathematically just, as much as two sides of an algebraic equation.

Ralph Waldo Emerson (1803–1882)

Love is unjust; justice loveless.

Delmore Schwartz

It is only with the heart that one can see rightly; what is essential is invisible to the eye.

Antoine de Saint-Exupery, The Little Prince

COMMITMENT OVER TIME. Unlike intimacy and passion, time does not necessarily diminish, erode, or alter commitments. Our commitments are most affected by how successful our relationship is. Initially, commitment grows more slowly than intimacy or passion. As the relationship becomes long-term, commitment growth levels off. Our commitment will remain high as long as we judge the relationship to be successful. If the relationship begins to deteriorate, after a time the commitment will probably decrease. Eventually it may disappear and an alternative relationship may be sought.

DISAPPEARANCE OF ROMANCE AS CRISIS. The disappearance (or transformation) of passionate love is often experienced as a crisis in a relationship. A study of college students (Berscheid, 1983) found that half would seek divorce if passion disappeared from their marriage. But intensity of feeling does not necessarily measure depth of love. Intensity, like the excitement of toboggan runs, diminishes over time. It is then that we begin to discover if the love we experience for each other is one that will endure.

Our search for enduring love is complicated by our contradictory needs. Elaine Hatfield and William Walster (1981) wrote:

What we really want is the impossible—a perfect mixture of security and danger. We want someone who understands and cares for us, someone who will be around through thick and thin, until we are old. At the same time, we long for sexual excitement, novelty, and danger. The individual who offers just the right combination of both ultimately wins our love. The problem, of course, is that, in time, we get more and more security—and less and less excitement—than we bargained for.

The disappearance of passionate love, however, enables individuals to refocus their relationship. They are given the opportunity to move from an intense one-on-one togetherness that excludes others to one that includes family, friends, and external goals and projects. They can look outward on the world together.

THE REEMERGENCE OF ROMANTIC LOVE. Contrary to what pessimists believe, many people find that they can have both love and romance and that the rewards of intimacy include romance. One researcher (Knox, 1970), in a study of dating high school seniors, couples married for less than five years, and couples married for more than twenty years, found that romantic love did not die. Instead, its conceptualization changed to include more realistic elements. Intimacy was added to feelings of love. In fact, romantic love was strongest among dating couples and those married more than twenty years.

Romantic love may be highest during the early part of marriage and decline as stresses from childrearing and work intrude on the relationship. Most studies suggest that marital satisfaction proceeds along a U-shaped curve, with highest satisfactions in the early and late periods (see Chapter 7). Romantic love may be affected by the same stresses as general marital satisfaction. In fact, romantic love begins to increase as children leave home (Knox, 1970). In later life, romantic love may play an important role in alleviating the stresses of retirement and illness. Aging adults find that emotional security and loyalty are often more important than sexual intimacy or communication (Reedy et al., 1981).

Intimate Love: Commitment, Caring, and Self-Disclosure

Although love is one of the most important elements of our humanity, it may come and go. Perhaps one of the most profound questions about love is, as novelist Tom Robbins (1980) wrote, how to make it last:

Albert Camus wrote that the only serious question is whether to kill yourself or not. Tom Robbins wrote that the only serious question is whether time has a beginning or end. Camus clearly got up on the wrong side of the bed, and Robbins must have forgotten to set his alarm. There is only one serious question. And that is, Who knows how to make love stay?

The kind of love that seems to stay is what we might call intimate love. In this love, each person knows he or she can count on the other. The excitement comes from the achievement of other goals—from creativity, from work, from childrearing, from friendships—as well as from the relationship. Hatfield and Walster (1981) wrote:

A husband and wife often enjoy being able to count on the fact that, while their friends must contend with one emotional upheaval after another, their lives drift on in a serene, unruffled flow. They enjoy the fact that they can share day-to-day pleasures and that, in old age, they'll be together to reminisce and savor their lives. This portrait is very alluring.

The key to making love stay does not seem to be in love's passionate intensity but in transforming it into intimate love. Intimate love is based on commitment, caring, and self-disclosure.

COMMITMENT.   Commitment is an important component of intimate love, for it is a "determination to continue" a relationship or marriage in the face of bad times as well as good (Reiss, 1980). It is based on conscious choice rather than on feelings, which, by their very nature, are transitory. Commitment is a promise of a shared future, a promise to be together come what may.

Commitment has become an important concept in recent years. We seem to be as much in search of commitment as we are in search of love or marriage. We speak of "making a commitment" to someone or to a relationship. (Among singles, commitment is sometimes referred to as "the C-word.") A "committed" relationship has

Beware, my Lord, of jealousy. It is the green-eyed monster that mocks the meat it feeds on.

William Shakespeare, Othello

There is no love apart from the deeds of love; no potentiality of love than that which is manifested in loving. . . .

Jean-Paul Sartre, Existentialism as Humanism

Having physical limitations does not necessarily inhibit love and sexuality anymore than being able-bodied guarantees them.

She knew a great deal about pulleys and hoists but nothing about love. She went to the library to look up love as she had looked up the mechanical advantages of pulleys. Surely great writers and great lovers of the past had written things worth reading. Here were some of the things great writers had written:

Love begets love
Love conquers all things
Love ends with hope
Love is a flame to burn out human ills
Love is all truth
Love is truth and truth is beauty
Love is blind
Love is the best
Love is heaven and heaven is love
Love is love's reward

"Oh my God," she said aloud in the library and smacked her head. "What does all that mean? These people are crazier than I am!"

Walker Percy, *The Second Coming*

become almost a stage of courtship, somewhere between dating and being engaged or living together.

CARING. Caring is the commitment to place another's needs before your own. As such, caring requires that you treat your partner as an end in himself or herself. It requires what the philosopher Martin Buber called an *I-Thou relationship*. Buber described two fundamental ways of relating to people: I-Thou and I-It. In an I-Thou relationship, each person is treated as a Thou—that is, as a person whose life is valued as an end in itself. In an I-It relationship, each person is treated as an It; the person has worth only as someone who can be used. When a person is treated as a Thou, his or her humanity and uniqueness are paramount.

SELF-DISCLOSURE. When we self-disclose, we reveal ourselves—our hopes, our fears, our everyday thoughts—to others. Self-disclosure deepens others' understanding of us. It also deepens our own understanding, for we discover unknown aspects as we open ourselves to others.

Without self-disclosure, we remain opaque and hidden. If others love us, such love leaves us with anxiety: are we loved for ourselves or for the image we present to the world?

Together, these elements help transform love. But in the final analysis, perhaps the most important means of sustaining love is our words and actions; caring words and deeds provide the setting for maintaining and expanding love (Byrne and Murnen, 1988).

❒ The study of love is only beginning, but it is already helping us to understand the various components that make up love. Although there is something to be said for the mystery of love, understanding how it works in the day-to-day world may help us keep our love vital and alive.

 SUMMARY

❒ *Prototypes* of love and commitment are models of how people define these two ideas in everyday life. The central aspects of the love prototype include trust, caring, honesty, friendship, respect, and concern for the other; central aspects of the commitment prototype include loyalty, responsibility, living up to one's word, faithfulness, and trust.

❒ Attitudes and feelings associated with love include caring, needing, trusting, and tolerating. Behaviors associated with love include verbal, nonverbal, and physical expression of affection, self-disclosure, giving of nonmaterial and material evidence, and tolerance. *Commitment* is affected by the balance of costs to benefits, normative inputs, and structural constraints.

❒ According to John Lee, there are six basic styles of love: eros, *mania, ludis, storge, agape,* and *pragma.*

❒ The *two-component theory* of human emotions suggests that physiological arousal and an appropriate emotional explanation for the arousal must be present for love to occur.

❒ The *attachment theory* of love views love as being similar in nature to the attachments we form as infants. The attachment styles of infants and the love styles of adults are *secure, anxious/ambivalent,* and *avoidant.*

❒ *Falling in love* is the transition from not being in love to being in love. There is little difference in levels of romanticism between men and women, young and old. Attachment style tends to influence falling in love: anxious/ambivalents fall in love most easily. People tend to fall in love in unusual situations or when they have felt isolated or special in relation to others. Disclosure of liking the other person is important in having love reciprocated.

❑ *Unrequited love* is a common experience. There are three styles of unrequited love: (1) the *Cyrano style,* the desire to have a relationship with another, regardless of how hopeless, (2) the *Giselle style,* the misperception that a relationship is more likely to develop than it is, and (3) the *Don Quixote style,* the general desire to be in love. Anxious/ambivalents are most likely to be Cyranos, avoidants to be Don Quixotes, and secures to be Giselles.

❑ Love and sexuality are intimately connected in our culture. According to sociobiology, sex is important for males, love for females; men exchange sex with women for love. Love guarantees females that males will participate in childrearing. Other researchers emphasize the importance of love to both men and women, making sex less important to both. These observers believe attitudes toward sex are related to love styles. Sex is most highly valued in our culture when it is linked to love. Indeed, sex with affection rivals marriage as an acceptable moral standard for intercourse. Men are more likely than women to separate sex from love; women tend to view sex within a relational context.

❑ Jealousy is present in all cultures, which can be divided into low-jealousy and high-jealousy cultures. Extramarital sexual relations evoke the most intense jealous responses in most cultures. Cultures that practice *polygyny* attempt to reduce jealousy among wives by having senior wives, wives closely related by birth, and by customs designed to prevent the husband from practicing; overt favoritism.

❑ Jealous responses are most likely in committed or marital relationships because of the presumed "specialness" of the relationship. Specialness is symbolized by sexual exclusiveness. Jealousy is an aversive response because of a partner's real, imagined, or likely involvement with a third person. It is a secondary emotion, a form of anger or fear. These emotions are labeled jealousy when the relationship is threatened by a third person. As individuals become more interdependent, there is a greater fear of loss. Fear of loss, coupled with insecurity in oneself or in the relationship increase the likelihood of jealousy.

❑ There are two types of jealousy: suspicious and reactive. Suspicious jealousy occurs when there is (1) no reason to be suspicious, or (2) only ambiguous evidence. Reactive jealousy occurs when a partner reveals a current, past, or anticipated relationship with another.

❑ Jealousy acts as a boundary marker for relationships. It provides limits for the partners' interaction with others. Boundaries vary depending on the type of relationship and the gender, sexual orientation, and ethnicity of the partners. Each couple, however, decides on its own boundaries.

❑ Gender differences exist in what evokes jealousy. Women feel more vulnerable to losing their partner to attractive rivals. Men are most jealous over sexual involvement; women, over intimacy issues. Men express jealousy through anger, women through depression. Women may be more jealous than men because men have greater autonomy and more opportunities than women.

❑ There are some differences between gay men, lesbians, and heterosexuals in terms of jealousy. First, heterosexuals place a higher value of sexual exclusiveness as a norm than do the others. Second, sex is less likely to symbolize love for gay men. Third, for many lesbians, especially feminist lesbians, jealousy is perceived as a patriarchal emotion to be avoided.

❑ To manage jealousy, men and women must determine whether their jealousy is irrational or realistic. If it is irrational, they must attempt to treat its source, which is usually personal insecurity. If the jealousy is reasonable, the state of the primary relationship must be evaluated. In this case, a crisis usually ensues in the relationship. The relationship with a third person may need to be modified or ended, or the primary relationship may need to be revised or terminated.

❑ Time affects romantic relationships. The rapid growth of intimacy tends to level off, and we become habituated to passion. Commitment tends to increase, provided that the relationship is judged to be rewarding.

❑ Romantic love tends to diminish. It may either end or be replaced by intimate love. Many individuals experience the disappearance of romantic love as a crisis. Romantic love seems to be most prominent in adolescence and in early and later stages of marriage. Intimate love is based on commitment, caring, and self-disclosure.

CHAPTER 4

Pairing and Singlehood

*Marriage is a great institution,
but I'm not ready for an
institution yet.*

Mae West

ALTHOUGH THEORETICALLY WE HAVE FREE CHOICE in selecting our partners, in reality our choices are somewhat limited by "rules" of mate selection. If we know what the rules are, we can make deductions about whom we will be likely to choose as dates or partners.

There is a game you can play if you understand some of the principles of male/female mate selection in our culture. Without ever having met a friend's new boyfriend or girlfriend, you can deduce many things about him or her, using basically the same method of deductive reasoning that Sherlock Holmes used to astound Dr. Watson. For example, if a female friend at college has a new boyfriend, it is safe to guess that he is about the same age or a little older, taller, and a college student; he is probably about as physically attractive as your friend (if not, they will probably break up within six months); his parents probably are of the same ethnicity and social class as hers; and most likely he is about as intelligent as your friend. If a male friend has a new girlfriend, many of the same things apply, except that she is probably the same age or younger and shorter than he is. After you have described your friend's new romantic interest, don't be surprised if he or she exclaims, "Good grief, Holmes, how did you know that?" Of course, not every characteristic may apply, but you will probably be correct in most instances. These are not so much guesses as deductions based on the principle of homogamy discussed in this chapter.

In this chapter we not only look at the general rules by which we choose partners but we also examine romantic relationships, the singles world, and living together. Over the last decade or two, many aspects of pairing, such as the legitimacy of premarital intercourse and cohabitation, have changed considerably, radically affecting marriage. Today large portions of American society accept and approve of both premarital sex and cohabitation. Marriage has lost its exclusiveness as the only legitimate institution in which people can have sex and share their everyday lives. As a result, it has lost some of its power as an institution.

Each year, more and more adult Americans are single. In 1990, 40.3 million adult Americans—29.9 percent of all men and 22.8 percent of all women—had never married (U.S. Bureau of Census, 1991). Rates of singlehood vary by ethnicity. Among whites, 20.2 percent of the men and 16.8 percent of the women had never married. Among African Americans, 34.3 of the men and 32.1 of the women were single. And among Latinos, 26.9 percent of the men and 21.8 of the women had not married (U.S. Bureau of Census, 1990).

❒ CHOOSING A PARTNER

How do we choose the people we date, live with, or marry? At first glance, it seems that we choose them on the basis of love, but other factors also influence us. These factors have to do with bargaining and exchange. We select our partners in what might be called a marriage marketplace.

The Marriage Marketplace

In the marriage marketplace, as in the commercial marketplace, people trade or exchange goods. Unlike a real marketplace, however, the marriage marketplace is not a place but a process. In the marriage marketplace, the goods that are exchanged are not tomatoes, waffle irons, or bales of cotton; we are the goods. Each of us has certain resources, such as social class, status, looks, and personality, that make up our marketability. We bargain with these resources. We size ourselves up and rank our-

A proposal of marriage in our society tends to be a way in which a man sums up his social attributes and suggests to a woman that hers are not so much better as to preclude a merger or partnership in these matters.

Erving Goffman

selves as a good deal, an average package, or something to be remaindered; we do the same with potential dates or mates.

The idea of exchange as a basis for choosing marital partners may not be romantic, but it is deeply rooted in marriage customs. In some cultures, for example, arranged marriages take place after extended bargaining between families. The woman is expected to bring a dowry in the form of property (such as pigs, goats, clothing, utensils, land) or money; or a woman's family may demand a brideprice if the culture places a premium on women's productivity. Traces of the exchange basis of marriage still exist in our culture in the traditional marriage ceremony when the bride's father pays the wedding costs and "gives away" his daughter.

The traditional marital exchange is related to gender roles. Traditionally, men have used their status, economic power, and role as protector in a trade-off for women's physical attractiveness and nurturing, childbearing, and housekeeping abilities; women, in return, have gained status and economic security in the exchange.

As women enter careers and become economically independent, the terms of bargaining change. When women achieve their own occupational status and economic independence, what do they ask from men in the marriage exchange? Constantine Safilios-Rothschild (1976) suggests that many women expect men to bring more expressive, affective, and companionable resources into marriage. Independent women do not have to settle for a man who brings little more to the relationship than a paycheck; they want a man who is a companion, not simply a provider.

But even today a woman's bargaining position is not as strong as a man's. In 1992 women earned only 72 percent of what men made (and this was a record high!). Women are still significantly underrepresented in the professions. Furthermore, many of the things that women traditionally used to bargain with in the marital exchange—child care, housekeeping services, sexuality—are today devalued or available elsewhere. Children are not the economic assets they once were. A man does not have to rely on a woman to cook for him, sex is often accessible in the singles world, and someone can be paid to do the laundry and clean the apartment.

Women are at a further disadvantage because of the double standard of aging. Physical attractiveness is a key bargaining element in the marital marketplace, but the older a woman gets, the less attractive she is considered. For women, youth and beauty are linked in most cultures. As women get older, their field of eligible partners declines because men tend to choose younger women as mates.

We tend to overlook the bargaining aspect of relationships because, as we said before, it doesn't seem very romantic. We bargain, nevertheless, but usually not openly or consciously. We exchange our social and personality characteristics. To get a sense of the complexity of bargaining in our culture, let's examine the role of physical attractiveness.

Physical Attractiveness

THE HALO EFFECT. Imagine yourself unattached at a party. You notice someone is standing next to you as you reach for some chips. He or she says hello. In that moment, you have to decide whether to engage him or her in conversation. On what basis do you make that decision? Is it looks, personality, style, sensitivity, intelligence, or something else?

If you're like most of us, you consciously or unconsciously base this decision on appearance. If you decide to talk to the person, you probably formed a positive opinion about his or her appearance. In other words, he or she looked "cute," like a "fun person," gave a "good first impression," or seemed "interesting." As Elaine Hatfield and Susan Sprecher (1986) point out:

The beautiful bird gets caged.

Chinese proverb

Physical attractiveness is most important at first meeting. Afterwards it diminishes in importance as people get to know each other better.

I'm tired of all this nonsense about beauty being only skin-deep. That's deep enough. What do you want—an adorable pancreas?

Jean Kerr

Appearance is the sole characteristic apparent in every social interaction. Other information may be more meaningful but far harder to ferret out. People do not have their IQs tattooed on their foreheads, nor do they display their diplomas prominently about their persons. Their financial status is a private matter between themselves, their bankers, and the Internal Revenue Service.

Physical attractiveness is particularly important during the initial meeting and early stages of a relationship. If you don't know anything else about a person, you tend to judge him or her on appearance. (See Berscheid, 1985, for a review of the literature on interpersonal attraction.)

Most people would deny that they are attracted to others just because of their looks. We do so unconsciously, however, by *inferring* qualities based on looks. This inference is based on a **halo effect:** good-looking people are assumed to possess more desirable social characteristics than unattractive people. In one well-known experiment (Dion et al., 1972), students were shown pictures of attractive people and asked to describe what they thought these people were like. Attractive men and women were assumed to be more sensitive, kind, warm, sexually responsive, strong, poised, and outgoing than others; they were assumed to be more exciting and to have better characters than "ordinary" people. Research indicates that overall, the differences in perceptions between very attractive and average people are minimal. It is when attractive and average people are compared to those considered to be unattractive that there are pronounced differences, with those perceived as unattractive being rated more negatively (Hatfield and Sprecher, 1986).

A study (Tanke, 1982) of men from two universities found that among the various traits attributed to attractive women, the trait most affected by their appearance was their sexual behavior. Attractive women were viewed as more sexually warm, exciting, and permissive than unattractive ones. An unpublished study (cited in Hatfield and Sprecher, 1986) found that attractive men and women were believed to have a stronger sex drive, to be sexually permissive, to enjoy multiple sexual relationships, and to play a more dominant role in sexual activities.

THE RATING AND DATING GAME. In casual relationships, the physical attractiveness of a romantic partner is especially important. Hatfield and Sprecher (1986) suggest three reasons why people prefer attractive people over unattractive ones. First, there is an "aesthetic appeal," a simple preference for beauty. Second, there is the "glow of beauty," in which we assume that good-looking people are more sensitive, kind, warm, modest, self-confident, sexual, and so on. Third, we achieve status by dating attractive people. Sociologist Willard Waller (1937) described the process as the "rating and dating" complex. According to Waller, men and women rated potential dates on a scale of one to ten and tried to date the best. The men and women evaluated themselves and others in terms of how their dates ranked.

Several studies (cited in Hatfield and Sprecher, 1986) have demonstrated that good-looking companions increase our status. In one study, men were asked their first impressions of a man seen alone, arm-in-arm with a beautiful woman, and arm-in-arm with an unattractive woman. The man made the best impression with the beautiful woman. He ranked higher alone than with an unattractive woman. In contrast to men, women do not necessarily rank as high when seen with a handsome man. A study in which married couples were evaluated found that it made no difference to a woman's ranking if she was unattractive but had a strikingly handsome husband. If an unattractive man had a strikingly beautiful wife, it was assumed that he had something to offer other than looks, such as fame or fortune.

Taught from infancy that beauty is woman's sceptre, the mind shapes itself to the body, and roaming around its gilt cage, only seeks to adorn its prison.

Mary Wollstonecraft (1759–1797), A Vindication of the Rights of Women

TRADE-OFFS. People don't necessarily gravitate to the most attractive person in the room; they tend to gravitate to those who are about as attractive as themselves. Sizing up someone at a party or dance, a man may say, "I'd never have a chance with her; she's too good looking for me." Even if people are allowed to specify the qualities they want in a date, they are hesitant to select anyone notably different from themselves in social desirability. We tend to choose people who are our equals in terms of looks, intelligence, education, and so on (Hatfield and Walster, 1981). However, if two people are different in looks or intelligence, usually the individuals make a trade-off in which a lower-ranked trait is exchanged for a higher-ranked trait. A woman who values status, for example, may accept a lower level of physical attractiveness in a man if he is wealthy or powerful.

We may daydream of movie-star lovers, but in real life we are more practical. Hatfield and Walster (1981) wrote:

Although we prefer partners who are more desirable than ourselves, our actual choices are influenced by matching considerations. We all tend to end up with partners of approximately our own social value. Thus, our selection of a mate appears to be a delicate compromise between our desire to capture an ideal partner and our realization that we must eventually settle for what we deserve.

Who ever heard of an ugly or pretty man? The beauty of a man is not in his face, but in his character, in his social standing, in his money. Who ever heard of a rich man that was ugly?

Jorge Amado

ARE LOOKS IMPORTANT TO EVERYONE? For all of us ordinary-looking people, it's a relief to know that looks aren't everything. Looks are most important to certain types or groups of people and in certain situations or locations, such as classes, parties, and bars, where people do not interact with each other extensively on a day-to-day basis. Looks are less important to those in ongoing relationships and to those who are older in age. Looks are also less important if there are regular interactions between individuals who, for example, work together or commute in the same automobile (Hatfield and Sprecher, 1986). Looks tend to be especially important in adolescence and youth because of our need to conform. It is at this time that we are most vulnerable to pressure from our peers to go out with handsome men and beautiful women.

Men tend to care more about how their partners look than do women. This may be attributed to the disparity of economic and social power. Because men tend to have more assets (such as income and status) than women, they do not have to be concerned with their potential partner's assets. Therefore, they can choose partners in terms of their attractiveness. Because women lack the earning power and assets of men, they have to be more practical. They have to choose a partner who can offer security and status.

Most research on attractiveness has been done on first impressions or early dating. Researchers are finding, however, that attractiveness may be important in established relationships as well as in beginning or casual ones. Most people expect looks to become less important as the relationship matures, but Philip Blumstein and Pepper Schwartz (1983) found that the happiest people in cohabiting and married relationships thought of their partners as attractive. People who found their partners attractive had the best sex life.

One study (Margolin and White, 1987), however, found that as husbands and wives aged, changes in the wife's physical appearance seemed to have greater impact on the quality of marital sexuality than changes in the husband's appearance. These changes led to greater sexual disinterest, a decline in sexual satisfaction, and, to a lesser extent, unfaithfulness, especially on the part of the husband.

The Field of Eligibles

ENDOGAMY AND EXOGAMY. The men and women we date, live with, or marry usually come from the *field of eligibles*—that is, the people of whom our cultures approves as potential partners. The field of eligibles is defined by two principles: **endogamy,** marriage within a particular group, and **exogamy,** marriage outside the group.

ENDOGAMY. People usually marry others from a large group such as the nationality, ethnic group, or social class with which they identify, because they share common assumptions, experiences, and understandings. Endogamy strengthens group structure. If people already have ties as friends, neighbors, work associates, or church members, a marriage between such acquaintances solidifies group ties. To take an extreme example, it is easier for two Americans to understand each other than it is for an American and a Fula tribesperson from Africa. Americans are monogamous and urban, whereas Fulanis are polygamous wandering herders. But another, darker force may lie beneath endogamy: this is the fear and distrust of outsiders, those who are different from ourselves. Both the need for commonality and the distrust of outsiders urge people to marry individuals like themselves.

EXOGAMY. The principle of exogamy requires us to marry outside certain groups—specifically, outside our own family (however defined) and outside our same sex. Exogamy is enforced by taboos that are deeply embedded within our psychological makeup. The violation of these taboos may cause a deep sense of guilt. A marriage between a man and his mother, sister, daughter, aunt, niece, grandmother, or granddaughter is considered incestuous; women are forbidden to marry their corresponding male relative. Beyond these blood relations, however, the definition of incestuous relations changes. One society defines marriages between cousins as incestuous, whereas another may encourage such marriages. Some states prohibit marriages between stepbrothers and stepsisters as well as cousins; others do not.

Style is the physiognomy of the mind, and a safer index to character than the face.

Arthur Schopenhauer (1788–1860)

HETEROGAMY AND HOMOGAMY. Endogamy and exogamy interact to limit the field of eligibles. It is further limited by society's encouragement of homogamy. **Homogamy** refers to the tendency to choose a mate whose personal or group characteristics are similar to ours. **Heterogamy** refers to the tendency to choose a mate whose personal or group characteristics differ from our own. The strongest pressures are toward homogamy. As a result, those we choose for partners tend to follow certain patterns. As George Bernard Shaw wrote, "Fashionable ladies fall in love with acrobats and have to marry colonels. Shop assistants fall in love with countesses and are obliged to marry shop girls." These homogamous considerations generally apply to heterosexuals, gay men, and lesbians alike in their choice of partners.

Although there has been a growing tendency allowing individual choice of partners without state interference (in 1966, the U.S. Supreme Court, for example, declared unconstitutional laws prohibiting marriage between individuals of different races in a decision appropriately called *Loving* vs. *Virginia*), statutes continue to prohibit gay or lesbian marriages. The military also enforces its own particular form of homogamy, barring relationships and marriages between officers and enlisted personnel as "fraternizing."

The most important elements of homogamy include those listed below. These elements are strongest in first marriages and weaken in second and subsequent marriages (Glick, 1988).

RACE AND ETHNICITY. Most marriages are between members of the same race. Between 1970 and 1986, the number of interracial marriages increased 2.5 times, from 310,000 to 827,000, or about 1.5 percent of all marriages. Only 22 percent of interracial marriages were between African Americans and whites (0.3 percent of all marriages). In 75 percent of African American/white marriages, African-American men marry white women. Most interracial marriages are between whites and African Americans, Asian Americans, or Native Americans (U.S. Bureau of the Census, 1990). It is not clear whether interracial marriages are as stable or less stable than nonmixed marriages, because the few published studies are contradictory (Heer, 1974; Monahan, 1970).

The degree of intermarriage is of concern to members of ethnic groups because it affects the assimilation rate and continued ethnic identity (Stevens and Schoen, 1988). Ethnic identity continues to be important for Latinos, who tend to marry others of their own ethnic group. Among Italians, Poles, Germans, and Irish, however, only one in four in this country marries within his or her ethnic group.

Related to racial and ethnic homogamy is linguistic homogamy, which is determined by the language spoken at home by native-born Americans (Steven and Schoen, 1988). Linguistic homogamy is especially important for Latinos. There are more than 11 million native-born Spanish speakers in the United States, as well as over a million each of German, French, Italian, and Polish speakers. (African-Americans lost their native languages as a result of forced assimilation during slavery.) Linguistic homogamy allows direct transmission of cultural characteristics across generations. Among European ethnic groups whose members speak a non-English language at home, language continues to be an important factor in mate selection, especially for those with lower levels of education.

RELIGION. Until the late 1960s, religion was a significant factor affecting marital choice. Today, however, approximately 15 to 20 percent of all marriages are interfaith (Glenn, 1982). Almost half of all Catholics marry outside their faith (Maloney, 1986). Almost 25 percent of Jews choose a non-Jewish partner, up from 6 percent in the early 1960s (Gruson, 1985).

Religious groups tend to discourage interfaith marriages, believing that they may weaken individual beliefs, lead to children being reared in a different faith, or secularize the family. Such fears, however, may be overstated. Among Catholics who marry Protestants, there seems to be little secularization by those who feel themselves to be religious (Petersen, 1986). Only a few studies have looked at the effect of interfaith marriage on marital stability. These show that although divorce rates vary according to religions and denominations, in general interfaith marriages tend to have about a 10 percent higher divorce rate than marriages within the same faith (Bumpass and Sweet, 1972; also see Glenn, 1982, on marital happiness). More recently, researchers studied the effects of three types of religious homogamy—denominational affiliation, church attendance, and belief in the Bible—on marital satisfaction and stability (Heaton and Pratt, 1990). They found that denominational homogamy was the most important factor contributing to marital success. Joint church attendance had a slight impact, and similar beliefs about the Bible had little effect.

Fashionable ladies fall in love with acrobats and have to marry colonels. Shop assistants fall in love with countesses and are obliged to marry shop girls.

George Bernard Shaw

SOCIOECONOMIC CLASS. Most people marry within their own socioeconomic class because of shared values, tastes, goals, occupations, and expectations. People tend to marry those who have the same educational background as themselves, reflecting the fact that educational attainment is related to class. Even if a person marries someone from a different race or ethnic group, religion, or age group, the couple will probably be from the same socioeconomic class. Women, more than men, sometimes marry below their class, possibly as a result of women's slightly lower status.

AGE. People tend to marry others within their age group, although the man is usually slightly older than the woman. Age is important because we view ourselves as members of a generation, and each generation's experience of life leads to different values and expectations. Furthermore, different developmental and life tasks confront us at different ages. A twenty-year-old woman wants something different from marriage and from life than a sixty-year-old man does. By marrying people of similar ages, we ensure congruence for developmental tasks. (See Atkinson and Glass, 1985, for discussion of age in marriage.)

The man who marries for money earns it.

Yiddish proverb

These factors in the choice of partner interact with one another. Race, ethnicity, and socioeconomic class, for example, are often closely related because of discrimination. Many African Americans and Latinos are working class and are not as well educated as whites. Whites generally tend to be better off economically and are usually better educated. Thus a marriage that is endogamous in terms of race is also likely to be endogamous in terms of education and social class.

More recently, social scientists have been studying marital homogamy in terms of personality characteristics (Antill, 1983; Buss, 1984; Kurdeck and Smith, 1987; Lesnick-Oberstein and Cohen, 1984). They have found that people tend to choose partners who share similar characteristics. Individuals who were impulsive, accurate reasoners, quarrelsome, or extroverted chose similar partners. The researchers hypothesized that choosing partners who share similar personality characteristics provides greater communication, empathy, and understanding.

Marriages that are homogamous tend to be more stable than heterogamous ones (Burr, 1973; but see Dean and Gurak, 1978). Three possible explanations have been given for this (Udry, 1974):

1. Heterogamous couples may have considerably different values, attitudes, and behaviors, which may create a lack of understanding and conflict.

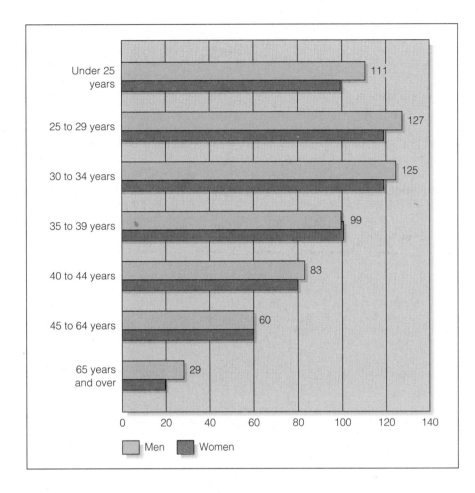

FIGURE 4.1

Ratio of Unmarried Men to Unmarried Women in 1990.

SOURCE U.S. Bureau of Census, *Marital Status and Living Arrangements: March, 1990.* Current Population Reports, 1991. Figure 9.

2. Heterogamous marriages may lack approval from parents, relatives, and friends. Couples are then cut off from important sources of support during crises.

3. Heterogamous couples are probably less conventional and therefore less likely to continue an unhappy marriage for the sake of appearances.

Marriage: Squeeze and Gradient.

The Marriage Squeeze. One of the facts of contemporary life is that more women than men are eligible for marriage. After World War II through the early 1960s, there was a significant increase in the birthrate, resulting in the "baby boom." Since women tend to marry men several years older than themselves, "baby-boom" women reached the average age for marriage two years earlier than men born the same year. The result was a "marriage squeeze" in which there were greater numbers of women than men looking for marriage partners.

The marriage squeeze has partly reversed itself in the 1990s as the smaller number of women born after the baby boom have more older men to choose from. In fact, that time has already arrived for white women under thirty, where there are as many as 25 percent more "suitable" men for every 100 "suitable" women. (Suitability is defined by educational level and age preference.) After age thirty, however, the marriage squeeze is in force again. As these women age, the marriage squeeze becomes even tighter.

THE MARRIAGE GRADIENT. "All the good ones are taken," is a common complaint of women in their thirties and beyond. (And for African-American women, it begins even earlier.) According to sociologist Jesse Bernard, their complaint may be right. Bernard (1982) wrote:

In our society, the husband is assigned a superior status. It helps if he actually *is* superior in ways—in height, for example, or age or education or occupation—for such superiority, however slight, makes it easier for both partners to conform to the structural imperatives. The [woman] wants to be able to "look up" to her husband, and he, of course, wants her to. The result is a situation known sociologically as the marriage gradient.

Men and women, as we have seen, tend to marry those with the same class and cultural background. But within this general homogamy, men tend to marry women slightly below them in age, education, and so on. This tendency creates the marriage gradient. Bernard continues:

The result is that there is no one for the men at the bottom to marry, no one to look up to them. Conversely, there is no one for the women at the top to look up to; there are no men superior to them. . . . [The] never-married men . . . tend to be "bottom-of-the-barrel" and the women. . . . "cream-of-the-crop."

Among college-educated men and women, the "cream-of-the-crop" by educational status, 93 percent of the men married but only 83 percent of the women were married. By educational status, college-educated men represented the highest proportion of males who married, while college-educated women represented the lowest proportion of females who married (Glick, 1984b).

African Americans have a lower marriage rate than whites. Comparing the rates between African Americans and whites, sociologist Robert Staples (1988) suggests that the differences can be understood best by examining them along class and gender lines. Staples argues:

Among lower-income Blacks, the structural constraints consist of the unavailability and undesirability of Black males in the eligible pool of potential mates. Due to the operational effects of institutional racism, large numbers of Black males are incarcerated, unemployed, narcotized, or fall prey to early death.

Among middle-class African Americans, significantly more women attend college than men, making it more difficult for women to find men with comparable educational backgrounds, an important element in homogamy. As a result, researchers have found that homogamy has been less important for African-American women in contrast to white women. Compared to white women, African-American women have tended to marry less educated men and men who have previously been married (Taylor et al., 1991).

The Stages of Mate Selection: Stimulus-Value-Role

Let us say that you meet someone who fits all the criteria of homogamy: same ethnic group, religion, educational level, and class background. Homogamically speaking, he is "Mr. Right," she is "Ms. Right," and your children would be "Little Rights." He or she is the person your parents dream of you marrying. And, of course, you can't stand each other. Homogamy by itself doesn't work. You need to start with "magic." Or, more precisely, according to Bernard Murstein (1976, 1987), you need to start with stimulus, the chemistry of attraction that *stimulates* you to want to have a relationship with another.

Murstein developed a three-stage theory—the stimulus-value-role theory—to explain the development of romantic relationships. This theory is based on exchange.

Each partner evaluates the other; if the exchange seems more or less equitable, the two will progress to the next stage.

❑ Stimulus refers to each person being drawn or attracted to the other before actual interaction. This attraction can be physical, mental, or social; it can be based on a person's reputation or status. The stimulus stage is, according to Murstein, most prominent on the first encounter, when one has little information with which to evaluate the other person.

❑ Value refers to partners weighing each other's basic values, trying to determine if they are compatible. Each person tries to figure out the other's philosophy of life, politics, sexual values, religious beliefs, and so on. If both highly value rap music, it is a plus for the relationship. If they disagree on religion—one is a dedicated fundamentalist and the other a militant atheist—it is a minus for the relationship. Each person adds or subtracts the pluses and minuses along value lines. Based on the outcome, the couple will either disengage or go on to the next stage. Values are usually determined between the second and seventh meetings.

❑ Role refers to behaviors, or how each person fulfills his or her roles as lover, companion, friend, worker—and potential husband or wife, mother or father. Are their behaviors consistent with marital roles? Are they emotionally stable? This aspect is evaluated in the eighth and subsequent encounters.

In this theory, all couples go through these stages in a defined sequence. Although this theory has been one of the most prominent theories explaining relationship development, it has been criticized by some scholars. Most notably, scholars ask if men and women *really* test their degree of fit (Huston et al., 1981). For example, militant fundamentalists and atheists may sometimes believe that they are compatible. They may not discuss religion; instead they might focus on the "incredible" sexual intensity of their relationship. Or they may make errors in arithmetic: they may mistakenly believe that religion is not *that* important, only to discover after they are married that religion is *very* important.

❑ ROMANTIC RELATIONSHIPS

As more and more people delay marriage, never marry, or seek to remarry after divorce or widowhood, romantic relationships, observes one scholar (Surra, 1991), "will take different shapes at different points in time, as they move in and out of marriage, friendship, romance, cohabitation, and so on." As a result, researchers are shifting from the traditional emphasis on mate selection toward the study of the formation and development of romantic relationships, such as the dynamics of heterosexual dating, cohabitation, post-divorce relationships, and gay and lesbian relationships. The field of personal relationships is developing broad focus (Kelley et al., 1983; Perlman and Duck, 1987).

Dating, going out, getting together—all such terms describe important rituals for pairing and, in many cases, for finding a marriage partner. In contemporary America, most individuals—whether they are single, divorced, widowed, or gay or lesbian—find romantic partners by some form of dating. They narrow the field through a process of getting to know the other person. Those potential partners who do not fit the general characteristics required by endogamy tend to be weeded out through peer pressure or parental veto.

The functions of dating vary with age and motivation. Initially, dating is for fun, for doing something with someone—going to the beach, having coffee, seeing a movie, going dancing, hanging out. Dating helps us learn to relate to another per-

Dreams are the touchstones of our character.

Henry David Thoreau

The physical expression of affection is an important aspect of relationships.

son. In high school or college, dating may become more involved; choosing a partner may be at stake. Is your date a potential mate? If so, will that person be a good partner? Will he or she be caring, loving, loyal, dependable, like children, work? And if one is a single parent, how will the other be as a stepparent? The rush of romantic feelings sometimes makes such considerations appear irrelevant; love will triumph over all, we like to think, as we hide our heads in the sand. Even if these issues are discussed, it may not be possible to predict how a partner will act in a marital or long-term relationship. There are some clues, however, which we will discuss later in this chapter.

Ongoing Relationships

TRADITIONAL DATING. The traditional dating pattern is formal. Each person has a role to play. The man initiates the date; the woman waits to be called. The man is anxious lest he be turned down; he may feel his stomach churn while he tries to appear calm and calls the woman or "accidentally" runs into her (after weeks of planning). The woman's problems are complementary. Because she must wait to be called and must appear demure, she can only express her interest indirectly by glances, tone of voice, body language, or playing helpless (Larkin, 1979). She may be so indirect that the man doesn't catch on. Also, she might not even be called by the person with whom she wants to go out—someone else may call instead. It may be as difficult for a woman to turn down a man as it is for some men to ask out a woman. "I don't want to hurt his feelings" is a common reason expressed by women who find themselves going out on a date with someone they don't particularly like.

The woman on a formal date is supposed to be passive, expects to have her way paid, and tries to please the man without truly giving in to sexual pressure. In accordance with the traditional female stereotype, she is expected to display less sexual interest than the man and to curtail the sexual advances of her date (Allgeier and McCormick, 1982). The relationship is an exchange of favors. This type of dating is ultimately oriented toward mate selection.

GETTING TOGETHER. Over the last decade an alternative to the traditional dating pattern has emerged, both among high school and college students (Miller and Gordon, 1986). It is often referred to as "getting together." Egalitarian gender roles, probably more than any other factor, are responsible for this emerging pattern. Getting together is based on mutuality and sharing. Equality is an important value, and to symbolize equality, each person pays his or her own way. Therefore, the feelings of obligation that accompany one person spending money are absent. The man does not expect the woman to kiss him or go to bed with him in exchange for his showing her a good time. The woman does not feel that she owes the man anything. They go out together as equals.

Traditional gender roles are deemphasized. The woman may call up the man rather than wait for his call. Honesty and intimacy are highly valued, and self-disclosure is considered an important quality. Instead of being centered around an event, getting together emphasizes spontaneity. Males and females do not necessarily get together as couples but often meet in groups. They get together informally for pizza or hamburgers, for a picnic, or to study for a class. A man and a woman may begin to spend more time together as a result of these gatherings, but often it is within the group context. Neither person has the responsibility for asking the other out. Much of the anxiety of formal dating is avoided.

Sexuality moves from an exchange of favors to mutual involvement and satisfaction. Ideally, sexual involvement reflects true feelings and desires rather than the need to prove oneself or pay a debt. Friendship, respect, and common interests serve as the basis for decisions about whether to become sexually involved (Libby, 1976).

When people get together in this fashion, the pattern of mate selection may include the following sequence of steps: (1) getting together formally, (2) living together, and/or (3) marriage. When compared to dating, however, getting together is not as oriented toward eventual mate selection.

FRIENDSHIPS. Relations between men and women who are "just friends" generally differ from those in which men and women are dating or are romantically involved (Komarovsky, 1985). Among those who are just friends, women are more likely to share expenses, to take the initiative in calling male friends, and to self-disclose more than they are in dating relationships. Because sex is not perceived as part of a friendship, many of the conflicts about sex are absent. Friendship offers many of the same advantages—such as acceptance, spontaneity, and understanding—as a romantic relationship (Davis, 1985).

Same-sex friendships tend to predominate, but male/female friendships are fairly common. In Keith Davis's (1985) study of 250 students and members of one community, 56 percent of the men and 44 percent of the women had close friends of the other sex. But close male/female friendships differed from same sex friendships. Same-sex friends tend to self-disclose more, offer practical help, have a greater sense of stability in the relationship, and show a greater willingness to give their utmost.

It is not uncommon for male/female friends to become romantically involved eventually. The development of both friendships and romantic relationships follows some of the same patterns. As friends make the transition to romantic partners, they may perceive a danger: friends tend to stay friends, but lovers may part. Because they value the stability, friends who fall in love with each other may hesitate to change their relationship. Others, however, believe that their friendship gives them a strong basis for love.

POWER IN DATING RELATIONSHIPS. Power doesn't seem to be a concern for most people in dating relationships. In fact, one study of dating couples found that both

FOCUS

Computer Dating and Homogamy

Compatibility Plus, a computer dating service, distributes this questionnaire to its clients. Complete the questionnaire and then examine it in terms of the social and personality characteristics you and your "ideal match" share. To what extent do you find homogamy operating? What do you think would be your chances of liking a person who was your "ideal match"? What other factors would be important?

❏ **Questionnaire Instructions**

Each question has two headings: "YOURSELF" and "IDEAL MATCH."

❏ For "YOURSELF" mark the box on the left that best describes you.
❏ Then, mark all the boxes on the right that best describe your "IDEAL MATCH."
❏ Please answer all the questions. If none of the choices is the exact answer you wish to give, then mark the answer that comes closest.

YOURSELF   IDEAL MATCH
1. Age _____ yrs.
2. Minimum age acceptable   _____ yrs.
   Maximum age acceptable   _____ yrs.
3. Height: ___ ft. ___ in.
4. Minimum height acceptable   ___ ft. ___ in.
5. Sex
   ❏ 1) Male ....❏
   ❏ 2) Female ....❏
6. Race
   ❏ 1) White (non-Hispanic) ....❏
   ❏ 2) Hispanic ....❏
   ❏ 3) Asian ....❏
   ❏ 4) Black ....❏
   ❏ 5) Other _____ ❏
                    (write in)
7. Body Build
   ❏ 1) Heavy...❏
   ❏ 2) Moderately heavy ....❏
   ❏ 3) Average ....❏
   ❏ 4) Moderately thin ....❏
   ❏ 5) Other_____ ❏
                    (write in)

8. Religion
   ❏ 1) Catholic..❏
   ❏ 2) Protestant...❏
   ❏ 3) Jewish...❏
   ❏ 4) Eastern Mysticism ....❏
   ❏ 5) Atheist or Agnostic..............................❏
   ❏ 6) Other_____ ❏
                    (write in)
9. Economic Bracket
   ❏ 1) Low income..❏
   ❏ 2) Average income.....................................❏
   ❏ 3) Above average ....❏
   ❏ 4) Much above average ....❏
10. Furthest Education
   ❏ 1) Grade School...❏
   ❏ 2) High School...❏
   ❏ 3) Some College ....❏
   ❏ 4) Graduated College.................................❏
   ❏ 5) Post-graduate study...............................❏
11. Diet
   ❏ 1) No restrictions ....❏
   ❏ 2) No red meat ....❏
   ❏ 3) Kosher ....❏
   ❏ 4) Macrobiotic ....❏
   ❏ 5) Vegetarian ....❏
12. Tobacco use
   ❏ 1) Non-smoker (only)..................................❏
   ❏ 2) Light smoker ....❏
   ❏ 3) Regular smoker.......................................❏
13. Children Living With You
   ❏ 1) None ....❏
   ❏ 2) One ....❏
   ❏ 3) Two ....❏
   ❏ 4) Three or more..❏
14. Political Outlook
   ❏ 1) Liberal ....❏
   ❏ 2) Moderate ....❏
   ❏ 3) Conservative ....❏
   ❏ 4) Progressive–Radical................................❏
   ❏ 5) Other _____ ❏
                    (write in)

continued on next page

men and women thought that they had about equal power in their relationships (Sprecher, 1985).

Even though most dating couples may not think about power too much, that doesn't mean that power is a nonexistent issue in dating relationships (Grauerholz,

FOCUS

15. Affection
    - ☐ 1) Very affectionate...☐
    - ☐ 2) Moderately affectionate ....☐
    - ☐ 3) Mildly affectionate..☐
    - ☐ 4) Non-demonstrative...☐
    - ☐ 5) Other _____ ☐
        (write in)

16. Sense of Humor
    - ☐ 1) Very funny or witty ....☐
    - ☐ 2) Average ....☐
    - ☐ 3) Mild ....☐

17. Assertiveness
    - ☐ 1) Very assertive ....☐
    - ☐ 2) Moderately assertive ....☐
    - ☐ 3) Mildly assertive...☐
    - ☐ 4) Non-assertive..☐

18. General Disposition
    - ☐ 1) Easy going–flexible ....☐
    - ☐ 2) Moderate ....☐
    - ☐ 3) Firm ....☐

19. Favorite Parties
    - ☐ 1) Loud and lively...☐
    - ☐ 2) Quiet and formal ....☐
    - ☐ 3) Small and intimate..☐
    - ☐ 4) None–prefer one to one...................................☐

20. Dancing
    - ☐ 1) Love it..☐
    - ☐ 2) Like it...☐
    - ☐ 3) Mild interest ....☐
    - ☐ 4) Dislike it ....☐

21. Sexual Activity
    - ☐ 1) Very important..☐
    - ☐ 2) Moderately important ....☐
    - ☐ 3) Not essential ....☐

22. Relationship Desired
    - ☐ 1) Committed one to one ....☐
    - ☐ 2) Friends and lovers...☐
    - ☐ 3) Nonsexual friendship.......................................☐
    - ☐ 4) Just sexual..☐

23. Favorite Activities and Interests
    (Check all you enjoy)
☐ swimming	☐ dancing	☐ yoga
☐ surfing	☐ walking	☐ meditation
☐ sailing	☐ partying	☐ astrology
☐ bicycling	☐ playing music	☐ photography
☐ jogging	☐ listening to music	☐ art
☐ hiking	☐ concerts	☐ cooking
☐ skiing	☐ plays	☐ politics
☐ tennis	☐ movies	☐ shopping
☐ racquetball	☐ beach	☐ reading
☐ volleyball	☐ travelling	☐ bars
☐ aerobics	☐ golf	☐ television

24. Personality Traits
    (Check all that describe you)
☐ sexy	☐ intelligent	☐ emotional
☐ spontaneous	☐ considerate	☐ possessive
☐ romantic	☐ imaginative	☐ frugal
☐ playful	☐ conventional	☐ polite
☐ positive	☐ patient	☐ decisive
☐ energetic	☐ talkative	☐ reserved
☐ inquisitive	☐ generous	☐ moody
☐ sociable	☐ sincere	☐ serious
☐ athletic	☐ tolerant	☐ anxious
☐ relaxed	☐ loyal	☐ lazy
☐ open	☐ witty	☐ demanding

25. Additional Remarks:
    _____
    _____

1987). If power does become a source of conflict, it may not become as intense an issue as in a marriage. Strong power conflicts can be avoided by dissolving the relationship in question.

In marriage, the person with the most economic resources usually has the most power. Generally, this means the man, because he is more likely to be employed and to earn more money than the woman. In dating relationships, however, economic resources do not appear to be as important a power resource for men as their ability to date other women (Sprecher, 1985). The easier men thought it would be for them to go out with other women, the more power they had in a dating relationship.

Controlling sex and the reciprocation of love is an important resource for women (Safilios-Rothschild, 1976, 1977). This seems to be true both in marriage and in dating relationships. As long as her partner is in love with her, the woman is able to use that love as a resource. One researcher (Sprecher, 1985) wrote:

Women probably have traditionally had to become skilled at controlling their emotions in heterosexual relationships in order to acquire bargaining power. Indeed, evidence has been found that men are more romantic than women. . . . It has also been found that men are the first to fall in love . . . and the last to fall out of love. . . . The evidence suggests that men may value and need the love from women more than women value and need the love from men. Often unable to have access to other desirable resources (money, status), women have had to use the control of love as a means to gain some power in a relationship.

The more men and women contributed to the affective side of the relationship relative to their partners, the less power they felt they had. For women, in fact, the less they loved their partner, the more power they felt they had.

Problems in Dating

Satisfaction in dating relationships appears to be related to whether one believes the other will make a good marital partner in the future, is approved by parents and peers, and provides sustained and positive experiences (Riffer and Chin, 1988). But dating, as we all know, whether it is a source of recreation or a means of selecting a partner, can cause problems and create stress.

DATING RITUALS IN FLUX. Dating rituals are in flux (Komarovsky, 1985). Although nontraditional women believe that the male prerogative of initiating the first date is a patriarchal holdover, few dare violate this norm. After one or two dates and in established relationships, both men and women appear equally free to initiate dates (modified by power issues or personal involvement). Mirra Komarovsky wrote:

The strongest sanction against violating the male prerogative of the first move was the male interpretation of such initiative as a sexual come-on. Men described such aggressive women as "sluts." Indignant as the women were to this inference, they hesitated to expose themselves to the risks, unless they were among the very few who did so with full knowledge of the implications.

Komarovsky recounted the experiences of one first-year college woman who was eager to share some of the new ideas she encountered in her classes:

There was this one guy in my philosophy class who was really bright. He used to make brilliant comments in class and I wanted to get to know him, so I could talk to him about philosophy. So I approached him and asked him whether he would like to go out for a cup of coffee. My intention was to talk about the lecture, but when we sat down, all he wanted to talk about was how I felt about sex, and when we could go out on a date. I kept telling him that sex wasn't the reason I asked him out. I was trying to be honest and straightforward with him, but he wouldn't believe it. He thought that the reason I asked him out for a cup of coffee was a sexual come-on. I never asked another guy out on a date.

Another problem is who pays when going out on a date. Some women in Komarovsky's study were fearful that male acquaintances would be put off if they offered to pay their share. Other women, whether traditional or egalitarian, who of-

There are two tragedies in life. One is to lose your heart's desire. The other is to gain it.

George Bernard Shaw

fered to pay found themselves mocked by their dates. Some men who allowed their dates to pay still insisted on choosing where they went, whether the women wanted to go there or not. Still others allowed their dates to pay but not publicly; instead, for example, the women secretly slipped money to their dates under the dinner table.

Divergent gender role conceptions also complicate dating in the initial stages (and sometimes beyond). Often when two people lack complementary gender role conceptions, the woman is more egalitarian and the man more traditional. The man may want the woman to be subordinate to his desires and wishes. She, however, may ask for an equal share in the decision making. In such cases, the relationship is not likely to become mutually satisfying.

Finally, it is apparent that large numbers of both men and women have sexual involvements outside dating relationships that are considered exclusive. One study of college students (Hansen, 1987) indicated that over 60 percent of the men and 40 percent of the women had been involved in erotic kissing outside the relationship; 35 percent of the men and 11 percent of the women had had sexual intercourse with someone else. Of those who knew of their partner's affair, a large majority felt that it had hurt their own relationship. When both partners had engaged in affairs, each believed that their partner's affair had harmed the relationship more than their own had. Both men and women seem to be unable to acknowledge the negative impact of their own outside relationships. It is not known whether those who tend to have outside involvement in dating relationships are also more likely to have extramarital relationships after they marry.

PROBLEMS AMONG WOMEN. In a random study of 227 college women and 107 men, nearly 25 percent of the women said that they received unwanted pressure to engage in sex, usually before the establishment of an emotional bond between the couple (Knox and Wilson, cited in Knox, 1991). (For a discussion of acquaintance rape, see Chaper 12.) Komarovsky (1985) cited male sexual pressure as a major barrier between men and women. A woman who wanted to see a man again faced a dilemma: how to encourage him to ask her out again without engaging in more sexual activity than she wanted. Men whose sexual advances were rejected by their dates often salved their hurt egos by accusing the women of having sexual hang-ups or being lesbians. Women rated places to go (23 percent) and communication (22) almost as high on their list of dating problems as sexual pressure (Knox, 1985).

PROBLEMS AMONG MEN. For men, the number-one problem, cited by 35 percent, was communicating with their dates (Knox, 1985). Men often felt that they didn't know what to say, or they felt anxious about the conversation dragging. Communication may be a particularly critical problem for men, because traditional gender roles do not encourage the development of intimacy and communication skills among males. A second problem, shared by almost identical numbers of men and women, was where to go. A third problem, named by 20 percent of the men but not mentioned by women, was shyness. Although men can take the initiative to ask for a date, they also face the possibility of rejection. For shy men, the fear of rejection is especially acute. A final problem, again one not shared by women, was money, cited by 17 percent of the men. Men apparently accept the idea that they are the ones responsible for paying for a date.

The problems of shyness and money are related to traditional conceptions of dating in which the male initiates the first date and pays the woman's expenses. It seems that a common ground exists here for change, since women find themselves limited by not being able to initiate the first date and would often be happy to share expenses.

BREAKING UP. "Most passionate affairs end simply," Hatfield and Walster (1981) noted. "The lovers find someone they love more." Love cools; it changes to indifference or hostility. This may be a simple ending, but it is also painful, because few relationships end by mutual consent (Hill et al., 1976). In Hill and his colleagues' two-year study of 231 college couples, the average couple had been going out for eight months; three-fourths were dating each other exclusively. Generally, the men fell in love more rapidly and the women fell out of love more quickly. At the end of the study, only 128 couples were still together. Fifty-one percent of the breakups were initiated by the women, 42 percent were initiated by the men, and 7 percent were mutual. (If the man initiated the breakup, the chance was greater that the couple remained friends.) For college students, breakups are more likely to occur during vacations or at the beginning or end of the school year. Such timing is related to changes in the person's daily living schedule and the greater likelihood of quickly meeting another potential partner.

Breaking up is rarely easy, whether you are initiating it or "receiving" it. Thinking about the following may help. If you initiate the breakup:

❏ *Be sure that you want to break up:* If the relationship is unsatisfactory, it may be because conflicts or problems have been avoided or have been confronted in the wrong way. Instead of being a reason to break up, conflicts or problems may be a rich source of personal development if they are worked out. Sometimes people erroneously use the threat of breaking up as a way of saying, "I want the relationship to change."

❏ *Acknowledge that your partner will be hurt.* There is nothing you can do to erase the pain your partner will feel; it is only natural. Not breaking up because you don't want to hurt your partner may actually be an excuse for not wanting to be honest with him or her, or with yourself.

❏ *Once you end the relationship, do not continue seeing your former partner as "friends" until considerable time has passed.* Being friends may be a subterfuge for continuing the relationship on terms wholly advantageous to yourself. It will only be painful for your ex-partner, since he or she may be more involved in the relationship than you. It may be best to wait to become friends until your partner is involved with someone else (and by then he or she may not care).

❏ *Don't change your mind.* Ambivalence after ending a relationship is not a sign that you made a wrong decision; neither is loneliness. Both simply indicate that the relationship was valuable for you.

If your partner breaks up with you:

❏ *The pain and loneliness you feel are natural.* Despite their intensity, they will eventually pass. They are part of the grieving process that attends the loss of an important relationship, but they are not necessarily signs of love.

❏ *You are a worthwhile person, whether you are with a partner or not.* Spend time with your friends; share your feelings with them. They care. Do things that you like; be kind to yourself.

❏ *Repeat these clichés:* No one ever died of love. (Except me.) There are other fish in the ocean. (Who wants a fish?) In other words, keep a sense of humor, it may help ease the pain.

❏ SINGLEHOOD

Almost 79 million adult Americans were unmarried in 1990. They represent a diverse group: never-married, divorced, young and old, single parents, gay men and lesbians, widows and widowers, and so on. And they live in diverse situations that

The land of marriage has this peculiarity, that strangers are desirous of inhabiting it, whilst its natural inhabitants would willingly be banished from thence.

Michel de Montaigne

affect how they experience their singleness. In 1989, almost 22 million Americans of all ages—representing 24 percent of the population—lived alone. Thirteen million unmarried adults between the ages of eighteen and twenty-four, over half that age group, lived with their parents. Almost 7.5 million adults are single parents. Over 5.6 million unmarried men and women cohabit; many hundreds of thousands more cohabit in gay and lesbian relationships (U.S. Bureau of the Census, 1991). Other men and women share housing as friends or roommates; the elderly live with their children, in senior apartments, or in rest homes; military men and women live in barracks; and so on.

As you can see, the varieties of unmarried life-styles in America are too complex to examine under any single category. Those who are regarded as singles, however, are generally young or middle-aged adults, heterosexual, not living with someone, and working rather than attending school or college. In this section, we will focus on never-married singles. Those who are not married because of the death of a spouse are generally studied in the context of widowhood; they usually do not participate in a singles life-style. Gay men and lesbians are generally studied within a context of the gay and lesbian world. For many gay men and lesbians, however, the only reason they remain unmarried is that society refuses to permit marriages between those of the same sex.

The number of single adults is rising as a result of several factors (Buunk and van Driel, 1989; Macklin, 1987):

❑ Delayed marriage, with a median age at marriage of 26 years for men and 23.8 years for women in 1990 (U.S. Bureau of Census, 1991). The longer one postpones marriage, the greater the likelihood of never marrying. It is estimated that between 8 and 9 percent of men and women now in their twenties will never marry.
❑ Expanded life-style and employment options currently open to women.
❑ Increased rates of divorce and decreased likelihood of remarriage, especially among African Americans. In 1988, 7.6 percent of the population was divorced.
❑ Increased number of women enrolled in colleges and universities.
❑ More liberal social and sexual standards, including the increasing acceptance of cohabitation.
❑ Ratio of unmarried men to unmarried women. In 1990, the sex ratio for ages 18 to 24 years is 111 men per 100 women; for ages 25 to 29 years, it is 127 men per 100 women; for ages 30 to 34, it is 125 men per 100 women.

There are significant differences in rates of singlehood between whites, African Americans, and Latinos. Among whites, never-married men and women represent 20 percent of the population; among African Americans, they represent 30 percent of the population; among Latinos, never-married individuals represent 25 percent of the population.

The rise in the number of never-married African-American women has been particularly startling (Taylor et al, 1991). Between 1975 and 1985, the proportion of married African-American women declined from 80 percent to 65 percent (compared to an 89 percent to 82 percent drop for whites). Among African Americans born in 1954, about 86 percent of the men are expected to marry by the time they reach 45 years, but only 70 percent of the women are expected to marry.

Culture and the Individual versus Marriage

Despite the importance of intimate relationships for our development as human beings, our culture is ambivalent about marriage. Paul of Tarsus (I Corinthians 7: 7–9) declared that it was best for people to remain chaste, as he himself had done. "But

T A B L E   4.1   Pushes and Pulls Toward Marriage and Singlehood

Which of these pushes and pulls are true for you? Why?

TOWARD MARRIAGE	
Pushes	*Pulls*
Cultural norms	Love and emotional security
Loneliness	Physical attraction and sex
Parental pressure	Desire for children
Economic pressure	Desire for extended family
Social stigma of singlehood	Economic security
Fear of independence	Peer example
Media images	Social status as "grown up"
Guilt over singlehood	Parental approval

TOWARD SINGLEHOOD	
Pushes	*Pulls*
Fundamental problems in marriage	Freedom to grow
Stagnant relationship with spouse	Self-sufficiency
Feelings of isolation and loneliness	Expanded friendships
Poor communication with spouse	Mobility
Unrealistic expectations of marriage	Career opportunities
Sexual problems	Sexual exploration
Media images	

SOURCE: Adapted from Peter J. Stein. "Singlehood: An Alternative to Marriage." *The Family Coordinator 24:4 (1975)*.

if they cannot," he wrote, "let them marry: For it is better to marry than to burn." In contemporary culture we find two contradictory myths about marriage, which many people hold simultaneously. Richard Udry (1974) observed:

The first myth—"and they lived happily ever after"—portrays marriage as a continuous courtship. The second myth is the picture of the domestic grind: the husband sits behind the paper, the wife moves about in the morning disarray; the husband leaves for work, the wife spends the day among dishes, diapers, and dirty little children. Although, as with most myths, no one *really* believes either one of them, they continue to affect the behavior of most people.

A continuing tension exists between the alternatives of singlehood and marriage (Stein, 1976). The singles subculture is glorified in the mass media; the marriages portrayed on television are situation comedies or soap operas abounding in extramarital affairs. Yet single persons are rarely fully satisfied with being single and may yearn for marriage. They are pulled toward the idea of marriage by their desires for intimacy, love, children, and sexual availability. They are also pushed toward marriage by parental pressure, loneliness, and fears of independence. Married persons, at the same time, are pushed toward singlehood by the limitations they feel in married life. They are attracted to singlehood by the possibility of creating a new self, having new experiences, and achieving independence. (For the pros and cons of singlehood, see Stein and Finguid, 1985, and Schumm, 1985.)

Types of Never-Married Singles

Much depends on whether a person is single by choice and whether he or she considers being single temporary or permanent (Shostak, 1987). If one is voluntarily

A woman without a man is like a fish without a bicycle.

Gloria Steinem

single, his or her sense of well-being is likely to be better than that of a person who is involuntarily single. Arthur Shostak (1981, 1987) has divided singles into four types. Singles may shift from one type to another at different times.

❒ *Ambivalents.* Ambivalents are voluntarily single and consider their singleness temporary. They are not seeking marital partners, but they are open to the idea of marriage. These are usually younger men and women who are actively pursuing education, career goals, or "having a good time." Ambivalents may be included among those who are cohabiting.

❒ *Wishfuls.* Wishfuls are involuntarily and temporarily single. They are actively seeking marital partners but have been unsuccessful so far. They consciously want to be married.

❒ *Resolveds.* Resolved individuals regard themselves as permanently single. A small percentage are priests or nuns or single parents who prefer rearing their children alone. The largest number, however, are "hardcore" singles who simply prefer the state of singlehood. Their numbers increased at five times that of the population between 1970 and 1980.

❒ *Regretfuls.* Regretful singles would prefer to marry but are resigned to their "fate." A large number of these are well-educated, high-earning women over forty who find a shortage of similar men as a result of the marriage gradient.

All but the resolveds share an important characteristic: they want to move from a single status to a romantic couple status. "The vast majority of never-married adults," wrote Shostak (1987) "work at securing and enjoying romance." Never-married singles share with married Americans "the high value they place on achieving intimacy and sharing love with a special one" (Shostak, 1987).

Singles: Myths and Realities

Cargan and Melko (1982), in a study of 400 households in Dayton, Ohio, examined various myths and realities about singlehood. They concluded the following:

MYTHS.

❒ *Singles are dependent on their parents.* Few differences exist between singles and marrieds in their perceptions of their parents and relatives. They do not differ in perceptions of parental warmth or openness and differ only slightly in the amount and nature of parental conflicts.

❒ *Singles are self-centered.* Singles value friends more than do married people. Singles are more involved in community service projects.

❒ *Singles have more money.* Fewer than half the singles interviewed made more than $10,000 a year. Married couples were better off economically than singles, in part because both partners worked.

❒ *Singles are happier.* Singles tend to believe that they are happier than marrieds, whereas marrieds believe that they are happier than singles. Single men, however, exhibited more signs of stress than single women. A national survey conducted by Robert Weiss (1981) found that 23 percent of the single men and 27 percent of the single women felt lonely; in contrast, only 6 percent of the married women and 10 percent of the married men reported feeling lonely.

❒ *Singles view singlehood as a lifetime alternative.* The majority of singles expected to be married within five years. They did not view singlehood as an alternative to marriage but as a transitional time in their lives.

Heterosexuals, gays, and lesbians cohabit. A significant difference between heterosexual and gay cohabitation is that many gay men and lesbians who would marry are prohibited from doing so by current laws.

REALITIES.

❐ *Singles don't easily fit into married society.* Singles tend to socialize with other singles. Married people think that if they invite singles to their home, they must match them up with an appropriate single member of the other sex. Married people tend to think in terms of couples.

❐ *Singles have more time.* Singles are more likely to go out twice a week and much more likely to go out three times a week compared with their married peers. Singles have more choices and more opportunities for leisure-time activities.

❐ *Singles have more fun.* Although singles tend to be less happy than marrieds, they have more "fun." Singles go out more often, engage more in sports and physical activities, and have more sexual partners than marrieds. Apparently fun and happiness are not equated.

❐ *Singles are lonely.* Singles tend to be more lonely than married people; the feeling of loneliness is more pervasive for the divorced than for the never-married.

Relationships in the Singles World

Although dating in the singles world is somewhat different from dating in high school and college, there are similarities. Like their counterparts in school, singles emphasize recreation and entertainment, sociability, and physical attractiveness. But singles have considerably more casual sexual involvements. There are few virgins in the singles world. The casualness of sex may be a source of problems. Men often desire more casual sex and fewer commitments than women; women often want greater intimacy, commitment, and emotional involvement than men.

MEETING EACH OTHER. The problem of meeting other single people is very often the central problem of the singles world. In college, students meet each other in classes or dormitories, at school events, or through friends. There are many meeting places and large numbers of eligibles. Singles have less opportunity to meet available peo-

Miss, n. *A title with which we brand unmarried women to indicate that they are in the market. Miss, Missis (Mrs.) and Mister (Mr.) are the three most distinctly disagreeable words in the language, in sound and sense. Two are corruptions of Mistress, the other of Master. In the general abolition of social titles in this country they miraculously escaped to plague us. If we must have them, let us be consistent and give one to the unmarried man. I venture to suggest Mush, abbreviated to Mh.*

Ambrose Bierce (1842–1914?)

ple. For one thing, there are fewer eligible persons. For another, singles who are not also in school or taking courses do not have access to an informal network such as school provides. As a result, a singles industry of bars, resorts, clubs, and housing makes billions of dollars by providing opportunities for singles to become doubles.

Because of this lack of structure, most singles have to rely on meeting someone through friends; the blind date and arranged dinner party are major devices for meeting others in the singles world. One single person (in Bradley et al., 1977) said:

> I will never say no when a friend says, "Hey, I'd like you to meet someone." I want to be totally open and available for any type of new meeting or encounter. Even if I'm tired, not feeling too well, doubtful, dubious, whatever, I'll usually make the effort to meet someone and consider the possibility, "This could be someone important. This could be someone wonderful."

Other frequent means of meeting singles include hobbies, work, and talking to a stranger (Barkas, 1980). Singles bars, bars, social or community functions, health clubs, and placing or answering personal ads are used less frequently. The least frequent means are video dating services, singles resorts or clubs, or introduction services (Mullan, 1984). Among those who are willing to try nontraditional means of meeting a partner, there may be less emphasis on homogamy. In a study of students who were asked to create advertisements of themselves, respondents tended to be less traditional regarding careers, ethnicity, and religion (LaBeff et al., 1989).

RELATIONSHIPS. When people form relationships within the singles world, both the man and woman tend to remain highly independent (Gagnon and Greenblat, 1978). Singles work, and, as a result, the man and woman tend to be economically independent of each other. They may also be more emotionally independent, because much of their energy may already be heavily invested in their work or careers. The relationship that forms consequently tends to emphasize autonomy and egalitarian roles. The fact that single women work is especially important. Single women tend to be more involved in their work, either from choice or necessity, but the result is the same: they are accustomed to living on their own without being supported by a man.

The emphasis on independence and autonomy blends with an increasing emphasis on self-fulfillment, which, some critics argue, makes it difficult for some to make commitments. Commitment requires sacrifice and obligation, which may conflict with ideas of "being oneself." A person under obligation can't necessarily do what he or she "wants" to do; such a person may have to do what "ought" to be done (Bellah et al., 1985; Lasch, 1977).

According to Barbara Ehrenreich (1984), men are more likely to flee commitment because they need women less than women need men. They feel oppressed by their obligation to be the family breadwinner. In the marital exchange, argues Ehrenreich, men need women less because men make more money than women and can obtain many of the "services" provided by wives, such as cooking, cleaning, intimacy, and sex, outside of marriage without being tied down by family demands and obligations. Thus, men may not have a strong incentive to commit, marry, or stay married.

□ COHABITATION

The Rise of Cohabitation

In 1990, more than 2.9 million heterosexual couples (and 1.5 million gay and lesbian couples) were living together in the United States (U.S. Bureau of the Census,

1991). In contrast, only 523,000 heterosexual couples were cohabiting in 1970. (For census purposes, heterosexuals who cohabit are called POSSLQs [pronounced *possel-kews*]—persons of the opposite sex sharing living quarters.) Cohabitation appears to be becoming part of the courtship process (Macklin, 1987; Tanfer, 1987).

Concerning cohabitation, Paul Glick and Graham Spanier (1980) noted, "Rarely does social change occur with such rapidity. Indeed, there have been few developments relating to marriage and family life which have been as dramatic as the rapid rise in unmarried cohabitation." Cohabitation is increasingly accepted at almost every level of society. By age 30, about half of all men and women will have cohabited. Currently, 4 percent are cohabiting (Bumpass and Sweet, 1988). Some scholars, in fact, believe that cohabitation is becoming institutionalized as part of the normal mate selection process (Gwartney-Gibbs, 1986). Today the only difference between those who cohabit and those who do not lies not in social adjustment, family background, or social class but in degree of religiousness. Those who have a high degree of religiosity and regular church attendance tend not to live together before marriage. For the religious, living together is still often considered "living in sin" (Newcomb, 1979). (For a discussion of cohabitation in Canada, see White, 1987).

Living together has become more widespread and accepted in recent years for several reasons. (For the pros and cons, see Gaylin, 1985, and Atwater, 1985.)

❐ *The general climate regarding sexuality is more liberal than it was a generation ago.* Sexuality is more widely considered to be an important part of a person's life, whether or not he or she is married. The moral criterion for judging sexual intercourse has shifted; love rather than marriage is now widely regarded as making a sexual act moral.

❐ *The meaning of marriage is changing.* Because of the dramatic increase in divorce over the last two decades, marriage is no longer thought of necessarily as a permanent commitment. Permanence is increasingly replaced by serial monogamy—a succession of marriages. Since the average marriage now lasts only seven years, the difference between marriage and living together is losing its sharpness.

❐ *Men and women are delaying marriage longer.* As long as children are not desired, living together offers advantages for many couples. When the couple want children, however, they will usually marry so that the child will be "legitimate."

Cohabitation does not seem to threaten marriage. Eleanor Macklin (1987), one of the major researchers in the field, noted:

Nonmarital cohabitation in the United States serves primarily as a part of the courtship process and not as an alternative to marriage. The great majority of young persons plan to marry at some point in their lives . . . and most cohabiting relationships either terminate or move into legal marriage within a year or two.

The most notable social impact of cohabitation is that it delays the age of marriage for those who live together. As a consequence, cohabitation may actually encourage more stable marriages, because the older a person is at the time of marriage, the less likely he or she is to divorce. Furthermore, a later marriage is likely to produce fewer children. Those who cohabit before marriage tend to want few or no children (Newcomb, 1979).

Types of Cohabitation

There is no single type of cohabitation, just as there is no single type of person who cohabits. At least five different types of relationships can be described, according to Macklin (1978):

❐ *Temporary casual convenience.* Two people share the same living quarters because it is expedient and convenient to do so.

❐ *Affectionate dating or going together.* Two people live together because they enjoy being with each other; they will continue living together as long as it is mutually satisfying.

❐ *Trial marriage.* This includes persons who are "engaged to be engaged" as well as couples who are trying to discover if they want to marry each other.

❐ *Temporary alternative to marriage.* Two people are committed to each other but are waiting for a better time to marry.

❐ *Permanent alternative to marriage.* Two people live together essentially as husband and wife but reject the idea of marriage.

Most college students who live together identify their cohabiting relationship as strong, affectionate, and monogamous. They share a deep attachment to each other but have not reached the point of making a long-term commitment. It is not known what proportion of older cohabiting couples fall into the various types.

Living together takes on a different quality among those who have been previously married. In 1989, about 40 percent of cohabiting relationships had at least one previously married partner, and about 30 percent of all cohabiting couples had children from earlier relationships. As a result, the motivation in these relationships is often colored by painful marital memories and the presence of children (Bumpass and Sweet, 1990). In these cases, men and women tend to be more cautious about making their commitment. They use their cohabitation as a way of testing their compatibility in marriage (Buunk and van Driel, 1989).

Cohabitation and Marriage Compared

TRANSITORY NATURE OF LIVING TOGETHER. Living together tends to be more transitory than marriage (Teachman and Polonko, 1990). A study based on national census figures indicates that 63 percent of such couples maintain a cohabiting relationship less than two years (Glick and Spanier, 1980). Either the couple split up or they get married. Those who marry after they have lived together usually do so because they want to formalize their commitment, because they want to have children, or because of pressures from parents or employers. Although cohabitation usually does not last as long as marriage, such relationships are often extremely

TABLE 4.2	Unmarried Couples, by Selected Characteristics, 1970 to 1990, and by marital Status of Partners, (in thousands)								
						MARITAL STATUS OF FEMALE			
PRESENCE OF CHILDREN AND AGE OF HOUSEHOLDER	1970	1980	1990	MARITAL STATUS OF MALE	TOTAL	NEVER MARRIED	DIVORCED	WIDOWED	HUSBAND ABSENT
Unmarried couples	523	1,589	2,856	Total 1990	2,856	1,595	963	142	157
No. of children under 15 yr.[1]	327	1,159	1,966	Never married	1,584	1,178	311	30	65
Some children under 15 yr.[1]	196	431	891	Divorced	973	285	555	60	44
Under 25 yr. old	55	411	911	Widowed	95	27	3	34	3
25–44 yr. old	103	837	1,945	Married, wife absent	204	77	40	19	46

[1]Children in unmarried-couple households are under 14 years old.

SOURCE: U.S. Bureau of the Census. *Marital Status and Living Arrangements: March 1990.* Population Reports Series, p. 20, 1991.

satisfactory. They often end not because the relationship itself is bad but because marriage satisfies new or different needs.

DIFFERENT COMMITMENTS. When a couple live together, their primary commitment is to each other. As long as they feel they love each other, they will stay together. In marriage, the couple make a commitment not only to each other but to their marriage as well. Marriage often seems to become a third party that enters the relationship between a man and a woman. Each partner will do things to save a marriage; they may give up dreams, work, ambitions, and extramarital relationships to make a marriage work. A man and a woman who are living together may not work as hard to save their relationship. Although society encourages married couples to make sacrifices to save their marriage, unmarried couples rarely receive the same support. Parents may even urge their "living together" children to split up rather than give up plans for work, school, or career. If the couple is beginning to encounter sexual difficulties, it is more likely that they will split up if they are cohabiting than if they are married. It may be easier to abandon a problematic relationship than to change it.

FINANCES. A striking difference between cohabiting and married couples is the pooling of money as a symbol of commitment (Blumstein and Schwartz, 1983). People generally assume that in marriage the couple will pool their money. This arrangement suggests a basic trust or commitment to the relationship; the individual is willing to sacrifice his or her particular interests to the interests of the relationship. Among most cohabiting couples, money is not pooled. In fact, one of the reasons couples cohabit rather than marry is to maintain a sense of financial independence. One man said, "A strong factor in the success of the relationship is the fact that we're economically independent of each other. We make no decisions that involve joint finances and that simplifies life a great deal" (Blumstein and Schwartz, 1983).

Only if the couple expect to be living together for a long time or to marry do they pool their income. As Blumstein and Schwartz point out:

Since the majority of cohabitors do not favor pooling, these facts say important things about pooling and commitment. When couples begin to pool their finances, it usually means they see a future for themselves. The more a couple pools, the greater the incentive to organize future financial dealings in the same way. As a "corporate" sense of the couple emerges, it becomes more difficult for the partners to think of themselves as unattached individuals.

WORK. Traditional marital roles call for the husband to work; it is left to the discretion of the couple whether the woman works. The husband is basically responsible for supporting his wife and family. In cohabiting relationships, the man is not expected to support his partner (Blumstein and Schwartz, 1983). If the woman is not in school, she is expected to work. If she is in school, she is nevertheless expected to support herself. Married couples may fight about the wife going to work; such fights do not generally occur among cohabiting couples.

SOCIETAL SUPPORT. Compared to marriage, cohabitation receives less social support, except from peers. It may be considered an inferior or immoral relationship—inferior to marriage because it does not symbolize lifetime commitment and immoral because it involves sexual activity without the sanction of marriage.

This lack of social reinforcement is an important factor in the greater instability of living-together relationships. Parents usually do not support cohabitation with the same enthusiasm as they would marriage. (If they do not like their son's or daughter's partner, however, they may console themselves with the thought that "at least they are not married.") Young adults often must hide the fact that they are living together for fear of parental rejection, anger, or reprisals.

Unmarried couples often find the greatest amount of social support from their friends, especially other couples who are living together. They are able to share similar problems with fellow cohabitants, such as whether to tell parents, how to handle visiting home together, difficulties in obtaining housing, and so forth. Because unmarried couples tend to have similar values, commitments, and uncertainties, they are able to give each other support in the larger noncohabiting world.

Impact of Cohabitation on Marital Success

There is no consensus on whether cohabitation significantly increases or decreases later marital stability (Teachman and Polonko, 1990). Although couples who are living together often argue that cohabitaton helps prepare them for marriage, such couples are statistically as likely to divorce as those who do not live together before marriage. In one study (Newcomb and Bentler, 1980), researchers interviewed 159 couples applying for marriage licenses. About half were living together at the time; the other half had not lived together. Four years later, the researchers were able to interview seventy-seven of these couples. Thirty-one percent had divorced. Those who had lived together were no less likely to have divorced than those who had not lived together. Among those still married, each group expressed about the same degree of marital satisfaction. Those who had lived together before argued less but had more problems with alcohol, drugs, and extramarital affairs. The differences probably had less to do with the effect of premarital cohabitation than with different personality characteristics. People who live together before marriage tend to be more liberal, more sexually experienced, and more independent than people who do not live together before marriage. Other studies have found that those who had cohabited before marriage were no more or less satisfied with their marriages than other couples (Jacques and Chason, 1979; Watson, 1983).

One study, however, noted slightly less marital satisfaction among married couples who had cohabited than among married couples who had not (DeMaris and Leslie, 1984). The researchers suggest that either cohabiting couples expect more out of marriage and are disappointed or else they are less likely to adapt well to traditional marital roles. They concluded:

The evidence accumulated to date would indicate that, while living together before marriage is increasingly becoming a common phase of courtship, cohabitation has no particular advantage over traditional practices in assuring couple compatibility in marriage.

 # SUMMARY

❑ The *marriage marketplace* refers to the selection activities of men and women when sizing someone up as a potential date or mate. In this marketplace, each person has resources, such as social class, status, age, and physical attractiveness. People tend to choose partners whose overall rating is about the same as their own.

❑ The *marital exchange* is based on gender roles. Traditionally, men offer status, economic resources, and protection; women offer nurturing, childbearing, homemaking skills, and physical attractiveness. Recent changes in women's economic status give women more bargaining power; the decline in the value of housekeeping and children and the increase of female sexual availability give men more bargaining power.

❑ Initial impressions are heavily influenced by physical attractiveness. A *halo effect* surrounds attractive people, from which we infer that they have certain traits, such as warmth, intelligence, sexiness, and strength.

❑ The *"rating and dating"* game refers to the evaluation of men and women by their appearance. Most people, however, choose equals in terms of looks, intelligence, and education. If there is an appreciable difference in looks, usually there is some kind of trade-off in which a lower-ranked trait is exchanged for a higher-ranked one.

❑ The *field of eligibles* consists of those whom our culture approves as potential partners. It is limited by the principles of *endogamy,* marriage within a particular group, and *exogamy,* marriage outside the group.

❑ The field of eligibles if further limited by *homogamy,* the tendency to choose a mate whose individual or group characteristics are similar to ours, and by *heterogamy,* the tendency to choose a mate whose individual or group characteristics are different from ours. Homogamy is especially powerful in our culture, particularly the factors of race, religion, socioeconomic class, and age.

❑ According to Murstein, romantic relationships go through a three-stage development process: *stimulus-value-role.* Stimulus is what brings people together; value refers to the compatability of each person's basic values; and role refers to behaviors in roles as lover, companion, and so on.

❑ Traditional dating emphasizes formality, traditional gender roles, male assertiveness, and female passivity. More recently, the idea of "getting together" has developed. Getting together emphasizes mutuality, spontaneity, and egalitarian gender roles. It is less oriented toward mate selection than traditional dating.

❑ Friendship offers some of the same benefits as romantic or dating relationships. In contrast to dating relationships, sex is usually not an issue in friendships. Friendships may sometimes develop into romantic relationships.

❑ Problems in dating include who initiates the first date, who pays, and complementary gender role conceptions. For women, problems include sexual pressure from men, communication, and where to go on the date. For men, problems include communication, where to go, shyness, and money.

❑ The singles world consists of men and women over the age of twenty-five who have never married or are divorced, who are working, and who do not have primary childrearing responsibilities. In the singles world, relationships tend to be casual. Meeting other unattached persons is a major difficulty for singles. Continual tension exists between the alternatives of singlehood and marriage.

❑ Singles may be classified into *ambivalents,* who are voluntarily and temporarily single; *wishfuls,* who are involuntarily and temporarily single; *resolveds,* who are permanently single by choice; and *regretfuls,* who are permanently and involuntarily single.

❑ Relationships in the singles world tend to stress independence and autonomy. The emphasis on individual self-fulfillment works against the making of commitments. The marital exchange favors men in the singles world and may also work against commitment.

❑ Cohabitation has become acceptable in society. At least five types of cohabitation have been noted: (1) temporary casual convenience, (2) affectionate dating or going together, (3) trial marriage, (4) temporary alternative to marriage, and (5) permanent alternative to marriage. Compared with marriage, cohabitation is more transitory, has different commitments, and lacks extensive social support. It does not seem to have much effect on eventual marital success. Cohabitation has become increasingly popular because of a more liberal sexual climate, the changed meaning of marriage, delayed marriage, and delayed childbearing.

PART 3

Sexuality
and Reproduction

CHAPTER 5

Understanding Our Sexuality

The sexual act is in time what the tiger is in space.

Georges Bataille

I MAGINE YOURSELF SITTING ON THE BEACH, READING. You see a man or woman walk by and feel a flash of sexual attraction to him or her. What is it that attracts you? Often we ascribe our feelings to the other person, saying that he or she has sex appeal. Actually, this sex appeal resides more in us than in the person to whom we are attracted. Our culture defines what is "sexy." Through learning we incorporate our culture's ideas of what traits, looks, body features, and so on are sexually appealing.

Beneath the apparent instinctiveness of sexuality lies a profound amount of learning that begins in childhood. We learn to whom to be attracted, when to be attracted, what to do sexually, and how to feel about what we do. All of these factors are defined by culture and learned by each individual (Cook, 1981; Simon and Gagnon, 1984).

Cultures vary in what they consider sexually attractive and arousing (Dion, 1981; Rosenblatt and Anderson, 1981). The aspects of beauty that appear universal are health and youth, both of which are linked to the reproductive aspects of sexuality. The only cultural constants of a man's sexual attractiveness are his skills, prowess, strength, and health, not his appearance per se. In contrast, a woman's sexual attractiveness tends to be perceived more in terms of physical appearance. The specifics of attractiveness vary from culture to culture. Many cultures view a woman's breasts as nonsexual; in our culture, breasts are considered to be erotic. In Victorian America, a woman's ankles were seen as being erotic; today no one pays much attention to ankles. Obesity in men was valued in Polynesia; in the United States, fitness and a trim body are the ideal.

☐ OUR SEXUAL SCRIPTS

Our gender roles are critical in learning sexuality. Gender roles tell us what behavior (including sexual behavior) is appropriate for each gender. Our sexual impulses

The only unnatural sex act is one that can't be performed.

Alfred Kinsey

In our society, intimacy is more frightening than sex. This is somewhat more of a problem for men, but it is also true for women.

Helen Singer Kaplan

Because sexual desire is in the minds of most people coupled with the idea of love, they are easily misled to conclude that they love each other when they want each other physically. . . . Sexual attraction creates, for the moment, the illusion of union, yet without love this "union" leaves strangers as far apart as they were before.

Erich Fromm, The Art of Loving

Pop culture saturates us with its erotic images. Music videos have the most sexual content of any medium, transforming Madonna into one of the leading erotic icons of the 1990s.

are organized and directed through our sexual scripts, which we learn and act out. A script is like a road map or blueprint that gives general directions; it is more like a sketch than a detailed picture of how our culture expects us to act. But even though a script is generalized, it is often more important in guiding our actions than our own experiences. Over time, we may modify or change our scripts, but we will not throw them away.

Traditional Sexual Scripts

Traditional sexual scripts are most powerful when we are young and inexperienced. These scripts vary according to gender. Male scripts tend to exaggerate sexuality, whereas female scripts tend to underrate it.

MALE SEXUAL SCRIPTS. Bernie Zilbergeld (1979) calls the male sexual script the "fantasy model" of sex. He suggests that men hold a number of myths about sexuality, which include the following:

❐ *Men should not have (or at least should not express) certain feelings.* Men should not express doubts; they should be assertive, confident, and aggressive. Tenderness and compassion are not masculine feelings.
❐ *Performance is the thing that counts.* Sex is something to be achieved, to be a winner at. Feelings only get in the way of the job to be done. Sex is not for intimacy but for orgasm.
❐ *The man is in charge.* As in other things, the man is the leader, the person who knows what is best. The man initiates sex and gives the woman her orgasm. A real man doesn't need a woman to tell him what women like; he already knows.
❐ *A man always wants sex and is ready for it.* It doesn't matter what is going on, a man wants sex; he is always able to become erect. He is a machine.
❐ *All physical contact leads to sex.* Since men are basically sexual machines, any physical contact is a sign for sex. Touching is seen as the first step toward sexual intercourse; it is not an end in itself. There is no physical pleasure except sexual pleasure.
❐ *Sex equals intercourse.* All erotic contact leads to sexual intercourse. Foreplay is just that: warming up, getting one's partner excited for penetration. Kissing, hugging, erotic touching, or oral sex are only preliminaries to intercourse.
❐ *Sexual intercourse leads to orgasm.* The orgasm is the proof of the pudding. The more orgasms, the better the sex. If a woman does not have an orgasm, she is not sexual. The man feels that he is a failure because he was not good enough to give her an orgasm. If a woman requires clitoral stimulation to have an orgasm, she has a problem.

Common to all these myths is a separation of sex from love (or any feelings). Sex is a performance.

FEMALE SEXUAL SCRIPTS. Whereas the traditional male sexual script focuses on sex over feelings, the traditional female sexual script focuses on feelings over sex, on love over passion. The traditional female sexual scripts cited by Barbach (1982) include the following:

❐ *Sex is good and bad.* Women are taught that sex is both good and bad. What makes sex good? Marriage or a committed relationship. What makes sex bad? A casual or uncommitted relationship. Sex is good, so good that a woman needs to save

---

Why is it that the people most outraged when government puts its hand in your pockets for taxes are often the people quickest to applaud when government sticks its nose into your bedroom?

The New York Times editorial

In the beginner's mind there are many possibilities, in the expert's mind there are few.

Shunryo Suzuki, Zen Mind, Beginner's Mind

He who wears his morality as his best garment were better naked.

Kahil Gibran, The Prophet

Our collective fantasies center on mayhem, cruelty, and violent death. Loving images of the human body— especially of bodies seeking pleasure or expressing love—inspire us with the urge to censor.

Barbara Ehrenreich

All men are animals, but some make good pets.

Mid Vogue

Sex, depersonalized, allows us to avoid the challenge of using our whole self, our total energies and feelings, to present and communicate ourselves to another. Sex is the victim of the fear of love.

Rosemary Reuther

Sentiments are for the most part traditional; we feel them because they were felt by those who preceded us.

William Hazlitt (1778–1830)

it for her husband (or for someone with whom she is deeply in love). Sex is bad; if it is not sanctioned by love or marriage, she'll get a bad reputation.

❒ *Sex is for men.* Men want sex, women do not. Women are sexually passive, waiting to be aroused. As a result of this script, women do not feel comfortable about asserting their sexual needs and desires.

❒ *Men should know what women want.* This script tells women that men know what they want—even if women don't tell them. Women are supposed to remain pure and sexually innocent. It is up to the man to arouse the woman, even if he doesn't know what a particular woman finds arousing. To keep her image of sexual innocence, she does not tell him what she wants.

❒ *Women shouldn't talk about sex.* Many women cannot easily talk about sex. Our language does not have many good words to describe it. We only have scientific words ("sexual intercourse"), obscene words ("fuck"), and euphemisms ("make love"); the first seems cold, the second dirty, and the third coy. Not only does the lack of words inhibit communication but so does the reluctance to admit sexual feelings and the lack of sexual assertiveness. People sometimes feel that they don't know their partners well enough to communicate their needs. Ironically, they know their partners well enough to have sex but not well enough to talk about it.

❒ *Women should look like "Playmates."* The media presents ideally attractive women as "Playmates," beautiful models with slender hips, large breasts, and long legs. They are always young, with not a pimple, wrinkle, or gray hair in sight. Ordinary women worry that they are too fat, too plain, too old. As a result of these cultural images, many women are self-conscious about their physical appearance. They often feel awkward without their clothes on to hide their imagined flaws.

❒ *Women are nurturers.* Women give, men receive. Women give themselves, their bodies, their pleasures to men. Everyone else's needs come first—his desire over hers, his orgasm over hers. Yet, if a woman always puts her partner's enjoyment first, she may be depriving herself of her own enjoyment. As Barbach (1982) points out, "If our attention is so totally riveted on another person, or on external events rather than on ourselves, it is impossible to experience the full pleasure and sensation of the sexual event."

❒ *There is only one right way to have an orgasm.* Women often learn that there is only one "right" way to have an orgasm: during sexual intercourse as a result of penile stimulation. But there are many ways to have orgasm: through oral sex; manual stimulation before, during or after intercourse; masturbation with a vibrator; and so on. For women who rarely or never have orgasm during sexual intercourse to believe this is the only legitimate way to orgasm deprives them of expressing themselves sexually in other ways.

Contemporary Sexual Scripts

Traditional sexual scripts have been challenged by more liberal and egalitarian ones. Sexual attitudes and behaviors have become increasingly liberal for both white and African-American males and females; African-American attitudes and behaviors continue to be somewhat more liberal than those of whites (Belcastro, 1985; Gutherie, 1988; Peters and Wyatt, 1988; Weinberg and Wilson, 1988; Wilson, 1986). Many college-age women have made an explicit break with the more traditional scripts, especially the good girl/bad girl dichotomy and the older belief that "nice" girls don't enjoy sex (Moffatt, 1989). Older professional single women also appear to reject the old images (Davidson and Darling, 1988). We do not know how Latino sexuality and Asian-American sexuality have changed, as there is almost no research on their sexual scripts, values, and behavior.

Contemporary sexual scripts include the following elements for *both* genders (Gagnon and Simon, 1987; Reed and Weinberg, 1984; Rubin, 1990; Seidman, 1989; Strong and DeVault, 1994 [in press]):

❐ Sexual expression is a positive good.
❐ Sexual activities are a mutual exchange of erotic pleasure.
❐ Sexuality is equally involving and both partners are equally responsible.
❐ Legitimate sexual activities are not limited to sexual intercourse but also include masturbation and oral-genital sex.
❐ Sexual activities may be initiated by either partner.
❐ Both partners have a right to experience orgasm, whether through intercourse, oral-genital sex, or manual stimulation.
❐ Nonmarital sex is acceptable within a relationship context.

These contemporary scripts give increasing recognition to female sexuality; they are increasingly relationship-centered rather than male-centered. Women, however, are still not granted full sexual equality with males (Williams and Jacoby, 1989).

The sources of these script changes may be traced to increasingly egalitarian gender roles; the replacement of the conservative sex-as-reproduction ideology with the liberal sex-as-pleasure ideology that emphasizes the pleasurable, bonding aspects of sexuality; and the recognition of female sexuality (Strong and DeVault, 1994 [in press]).

❐ SEXUAL BEHAVIOR

Sexual behavior is a complex activity, more than the simple release of tension through orgasm. Orgasm does not even have to be the goal of erotic activity. We may engage in erotic activity for its own sake, for the sheer pleasure of touch and arousal. But whether or not our erotic activities include orgasm, they involve deep feelings about ourselves and others, ranging from ecstatic delight and pleasure to guilt and shame, from love to contempt, from self-respect to self-degradation. Although our culture gives us certain meanings to associate with sex (for example, masturbation is bad, sex within marriage is sacrosanct), we ourselves are ultimately responsible for how we feel about our sexual behavior. Because we learn to be sexual, we can also unlearn those aspects of our sexuality—feelings, attitudes, or behaviors—that do not contribute to our functioning as healthy, happy human beings.

Autoeroticism

Autoeroticism refers to sexual activities that involve only the self. Autoeroticism is an intrapersonal activity rather than an interpersonal one. It may be the most diverse form of sexuality a person experiences, for it includes masturbation, sexual fantasies, and erotic dreams. Ironically, it is also the form of sexual behavior about which many people feel the greatest anxiety and guilt.

SEXUAL FANTASIES. "A fantasy is a map of desire, mastery, escape, and obscuration," wrote Nancy Friday (1980), "the navigational path we invent to steer ourselves between the reefs and shoals of anxiety, guilt, and inhibition." Erotic fantasy is probably the most universal of all sexual behaviors. Nearly everyone has experienced such fantasies, but because they may touch on feelings or desires considered personally or socially unacceptable, they are not widely discussed. Fantasies may interfere with an

Two monks, Tanzan and Ekido, were travelling down the road in a heavy rain. As they turned a bend, they came upon a beautiful young woman in a silk kimono. She was unable to pass because the rain had turned the road to mud.

Tanzan said to her, "Come on," and lifted her in his arms and carried her across the mud. Then he put her down and the monks continued their journey.

The two monks did not speak again until they reached a temple in which to spend the night. Finally, Ekido could no longer hold back his thoughts and he reprimanded Tanzan. "It is not proper for monks to go near women," he said. "Especially young and beautiful ones. It is unwise. Why did you do it?"

"I left the woman behind," replied Tanzan. "Are you still carrying her?"

Zen tale

individual's self-image, causing confusion as well as a loss of self-esteem. No necessary relationship exists, however, between a person's sexual fantasies and what he or she does in real life. Nevertheless, people often feel guilty about having sexual fantasies, believing them to be deviant, obsessive, or a sign of sexual addiction (Davidson and Hoffman, 1986). African Americans tend to be more accepting of their fantasies than whites, who often feel guilty about them (Price and Miller, 1984).

Sexual fantasies serve a number of important functions in maintaining our psychological equilibrium. First, fantasies help direct and define our erotic goals. They take our generalized sexual drives and give them concrete images and specific content. These goals are generally conservative insofar as they usually do not greatly exceed idealized models of the type of person we are attracted to; we fantasize about certain types of men or women and reinforce our attraction through fantasy involvement. Second, sexual fantasies allow us to plan or anticipate situations that may arise. They are a form of rehearsal in which we mentally practice how to act. Third, erotic fantasies provide an escape from a dull or oppressive environment. Fourth, even if our sexual lives are satisfactory, we may indulge in sexual fantasies to bring novelty and excitement into the relationship. Many people fantasize things they would not actually do in real life. Fantasy offers a safe outlet for sexual curiosity. One study (Davidson and Hoffman, 1986) found that fantasies appear to help many married women become sexually aroused and experience orgasm during sexual intercourse. Fifth, sexual fantasies have an expressive aspect in somewhat the same manner as dreams. Our sexual fantasies may offer a clue to our current interests, pleasures, anxieties, fears, or problems. Since fantasies take only a few details from the stream of reality, what we select is often meaningful, expressing feelings that lie beneath the surface of our consciousness (Sue, 1979).

EROTIC DREAMS. Although there is considerable research about sexual fantasies, research about erotic dreams is almost nonexistent. Almost all of the men and two-thirds of the women in Kinsey's (1953) study reported having had overtly sexual dreams. Like fantasies, dreams do not usually go far beyond an individual's experience. But while fantasies tend to be logical and related to ordinary reality, the images of dreams are frequently very intense. Individuals may awaken in the night to find their bodies moving as if they were making love. Both men and women may experience nocturnal orgasms.

MASTURBATION. **Masturbation** is stroking, rubbing, caressing, or otherwise stimulating the genitals to give sexual pleasure. Individuals may masturbate during particular periods of their lives or throughout their entire lives. Kinsey (1953) reported that 92 percent of the men and 58 percent of the women he interviewed said that they had masturbated. Today both the incidence and frequency of masturbation appear to have increased slightly. Male African Americans are less accepting of masturbation than whites (Cortese, 1989; Wilson, 1986). Among college women, masturbation becomes increasingly accepted as a healthy sexual activity as they progress in their education; this is especially true if they have studied sexuality. As women continue through college, greater numbers practice masturbation (Davidson and Darling, 1988). Although there is no comparable evidence for college males, based on Kinsey data (1984), it is likely that the overwhelming majority have masturbated.

Masturbation is one way in which people learn about their bodies, what pleases them sexually, how their bodies respond, and what their natural sexual rhythms are. Pioneer sex therapists William Masters and Virginia Johnson (1970) instructed their clients to masturbate as a means of overcoming specific sexual problems and discovering their sexual potential. Estimates of success range from 20 to 82 percent (Wakefield, 1987).The success rates of masturbation exercises for **preorgasmic** women (those who have not experienced orgasm) are unclear, however.

Although the frequency of masturbation often decreases significantly when a sexual partner is available, masturbation is not necessarily a substitute for intercourse. Studies of married men and women suggest that both continue to masturbate (Petersen et al., 1983; Tavris and Sadd, 1977). The majority of wives who masturbate do so when their husbands are away. In one study, 70 percent of the women did not tell their husbands about masturbating (Grosskopf, 1983).

Husbands tend to masturbate more frequently than wives; 43 percent of the husbands versus 22 percent of the wives in a *Playboy* study masturbated more than once a week (Petersen et al., 1983). Husbands' motives, however, were different from wives'. Husbands tended to masturbate as a supplement to intercourse rather than as substitute for it. Among elderly married men, about 50 percent masturbated regularly (Weizman and Hart, 1987).

We don't know the effect of masturbation on marriage, although guilt about it may be a negative factor. The fact that most husbands and wives do not tell each other about masturbation suggests that for whatever reason—guilt, embarrassment, or shame—they are not communicating about an important aspect of their sexuality.

Masturbation is an intrinsically and seriously disordered act.

Vatican Declaration Concerning Sexual Questions, 1976

Interpersonal Sexuality

Interpersonal sexuality is more complex than autoerotic sexuality because it involves two people with different scripts, moods, desires, cycles, and feelings who have to synchronize their sexuality with each other. This is true of heterosexual, gay, lesbian, and bisexual couples.

Sexual interactions may or may not include intercourse. Virginity does not necessarily make a person asexual. A man or woman may engage in numerous noncoital activities, such as pleasuring, kissing, petting, oral sex, and so on. As anyone who has ever engaged in any of these activities knows, they may be extremely erotic. Penetration is not the test of sexuality.

ORAL SEX. In recent years, oral sex has become a part of our sexual scripts (Gagnon, 1986). Psychologist Lilian Rubin (1990) reports young women today express pleasure about oral sex, in contrast to twenty years ago; a minority of middle-aged women, who earlier believed oral sex was "dirty" or immoral, continue to feel some ambivalence (Rubin, 1990). **Cunnilingus** refers to the erotic stimulation of a woman's vulva by her partner's mouth and tongue. (*Cunnilingus* is derived from the Latin *cunnus* [vulva] and *lingere* [to lick]. **Fellatio** refers to the oral stimulation of a man's penis by his partner's sucking and licking. (*Fellatio* is from the Latin *fellare* [to suck].) Cunnilingus and fellatio may be performed singly or mutually. Between 60 and 95 percent of the men and women in various studies report that they have engaged in oral sex (Delamater and MacCorquodale, 1979; Petersen et al., 1983).

Among girls of junior-high-school age, more have given or received oral sex than have engaged in sexual intercourse; among boys, more have had sexual intercourse than have given or received oral sex. For both sexes, fellatio is less common than either sexual intercourse or cunnilingus (Newcomer and Udry, 1985). A study (Moffatt, 1989) of university students of both sexes found that oral sex was regarded as an egalitarian, mutual practice. Students felt less guilty about it than sexual intercourse because oral sex was not "going all the way." Another study (Herold and Way, 1983) of female undergraduates found that 61 percent had engaged in oral sex. The best predictors of whether these women engaged in oral sex were if they

*And not yet cloy thy lips with loathed
    satiety,
But rather famish them amid their
    plenty,
Making them red and pale
    with fresh variety;
Ten kisses short as one, one long as
    twenty:
A Summer's day will seem an hour but
    short
Being wasted in such time-beguiling
    sport.*

William Shakespeare

*Safe Sex: Ten Top Obstacles (or
Excuses)*
 1. The heat of the moment
 2. Talking about safe sex
 3. Putting on a condom
 4. Buying a condom
 5. Condom as unromantic
 *6. Partner not wanting to use
condom*
 *7. Anticipating partner's objection
to condom*
 8. Rejection by partner
 9. Loss of partner
10. Unavailability of condoms

felt guilt about it, had experienced sexual intercourse, and were committed in their dating relationships. Some women feel that fellatio is more intimate than sexual intercourse, whereas others feel that it is less intimate. The overwhelming majority of men enjoy giving oral sex to their partners (Petersen et al., 1983).

Participants often express concern about whether they give oral sex "correctly" and whether their partners enjoy it. Both men and women occasionally complain about their partners' genital hygiene. For women, they key issue is whether to swallow the ejaculate; men are generally in favor of it, whereas women differ considerably and are concerned about the aesthetics of it (Moffatt, 1989).

Unless the possibility of HIV infection is completely ruled out, fellatio should be practiced only with a condom, because the virus that causes AIDS is carried in semen and may infect a person through cuts or sores in the mouth. (HIV does not infect through ingestion [swallowing].)

SEXUAL INTERCOURSE. **Sexual intercourse** is penile/vaginal penetration and stimulation. Although reproduction traditionally was the only legitimate aim of sexual intercourse (and continues to be so for the Catholic Church and some traditionalist groups), for most people reproduction is usually not their primary motive for having sexual intercourse. (In fact, at any single time, the majority of people probably fervently hope that pregnancy does not occur.) Instead, sexual intercourse is a complex interaction. As with many other types of activities, the anticipation of reward triggers a pattern of behavior. The reward may not necessarily be orgasm, however, because the meanings of sexual intercourse vary considerably at different times for different people. There are many motivations for sexual intercourse; sexual pleasure is only one. These motivations include showing love, having children, giving and receiving pleasure, gaining power, ending an argument, demonstrating commitment, seeking revenge, proving masculinity or femininity, or degrading someone (including yourself). One man said (in Hite, 1981), "Even more important than orgasm is being able to wrap your arms and legs and whatever else around another human being. It makes you feel less alone, more alive. There's nothing like it."

In contemporary American sexual practices, sexual intercourse is regarded as "real sex," whereas other sexual practices, such as fondling, petting, partner masturbation, and oral sex are not the "real thing" (Hite, 1976; Moffatt, 1989) Sexual success is equated with orgasm, frequency, techniques, variety, and emotional mastery of the sexual experience (Moffatt, 1989). The emphasis on sexual intercourse, however, limits the playfulness and diversity of eroticism. As Hite (1976) observed:

There is no reason why physical intimacy with men should always consist of "foreplay" followed by intercourse and male orgasm; and there is no reason why intercourse must always be part of heterosexual sex. Sex is intimate physical contact for pleasure, to share pleasure with another person (not just alone). You can have sex to orgasm, or not to orgasm, genital sex, or just physical intimacy—whatever seems right to you. There is never any reason to think the "goal" must be intercourse and to try to make what you feel fit into that context.

Sexual intercourse without a condom is unsafe sex unless the possibility of HIV

Now, there's something real old, but still hot news;
It's been around since Lincoln, but out of view;
You'd stuff it in your wallet so your mom can't see;
It's called the condom, baby, and you better believe;
It ain't under the shelf now, it's on display;
With all this disease going around today;
You need peace of mind when you do the wild thing;
So, a condom, brother, don't forget to bring!
Now, if what I say sounds a little bit sleazy;
If using a condom makes you feel kind of queasy;
Don't take it too hard 'cause there's no doubt, That modern diseases can take you out!
So, don't be ashamed, take one when you go dancin'
And use the condom for a little romancin,
'Cause bein' safe don't mean you're weak;
And you won't find yourself up the creek!
Protect yourself! Word! Protect yourself! Homeboy!
Protect yourself! My man, if I was you, I'd . . .
Protect yourself!

Fat Boys, "Protect Yourself"

"THIS IS INTIMACY? A CLOSE RELATIONSHIP WITH GOOD COMMUNICATION IS INTIMACY? I THOUGHT INTIMACY WAS SOMETHING PHYSICAL."

FOCUS

Preventing Sexually Transmitted Diseases and HIV/AIDS

"Do you have chlamydia, gonorrhea, herpes, syphilis, HIV, or any other sexually transmitted disease?" is hardly a question you want to ask someone on a first date. But it is a question to which you need to know the answer before you become sexually involved. Just because a person is nice is no guarantee that he or she does not have an STD. No one can tell by a person's looks, intelligence, or moral fervor whether he or she has contracted a sexually transmitted disease. And the costs are too great in this age of HIV/AIDS to become sexually involved with a person without knowing the answer to this question.

Americans are in the middle of the worst STD epidemic in our history. In 1989, more than 13 million Americans were infected by STDs. College students are as vulnerable as anyone else. Untreated chlamydia and gonorrhea have led to pelvic inflammatory disease (PID) in 1.7 million women annually, many of whom become sterile (Hilts, 1990). A 1989 survey of 17,000 college students, in fact, indicated that 0.2 percent of students were infected by HIV (Johnson, 1990). Overall, HIV has infected as many as 1.5 million Americans. By July 1990, 143,000 Americans had developed or died from AIDS. HIV and AIDS cases are increasing at a disproportionate rate for African Americans and Latinos; sexually transmitted cases among heterosexuals are increasing at a greater rate than among gay men (*Morbidity and Mortality Weekly Reports*, 1990). These figures indicate that virtually all adults in the United States will be related to, personally know, work with, or go to school with people who are infected with HIV or

know others whose friends, relatives, or associates test HIV-positive.

AIDS is particularly devastating because it is both incurable and death-dealing. AIDS is an acronym for **acquired immune deficiency syndrome.** It is called

Acquired   because people are not born with it;

Immune   because the disease relates to the immune system;

Deficiency   because of the body's lack of immunity;

Syndrome   because the symptoms occur together as a group.

Although there is no vaccine to prevent or cure HIV infection (the **human immuno deficiency** virus that causes AIDS) or the subsequent AIDS symptoms, we have considerable knowledge about the nature of the virus and how to prevent its spread.

❑ *AIDS is caused by the human immunodeficiency virus (HIV), which attacks the body's immune system.* HIV is carried in the blood, semen, and vaginal secretions of infected persons. The virus may incubate up to five years or longer. At this time, it is believed that most who carry the virus will develop the symptoms that inevitably lead to AIDS.

❑ *HIV is transmitted only in certain clearly defined circumstances: the exchange of blood (as by shared needles), sexual contact involving semen or vaginal secretions, or prenatally, from an infected woman to her fetus through the placenta.*

❑ *Heterosexuals, bisexuals, and gay men and lesbians are susceptible to the sexual transmission of HIV.* Currently four percent of AIDS cases are

attributed to heterosexual transmission. The rate of heterosexual HIV transmission, however, is rising at three times the rate of gay transmission and almost twice the rate of transmission by intravenous needles. Among women, heterosexual contact accounts for almost 30 percent of AIDS cases.

❑ *There is a definable progression of HIV infection and a range of illnesses associated with it known as AIDS.* HIV attacks the immune system. Once the immune system is impaired, AIDS symptoms occur as opportunistic diseases that the body normally resists infect the individual. The most common opportunistic diseases are *Pneumocystis carinii* pneumonia and Kaposi's sarcoma, a skin cancer. It is an opportunistic disease rather than HIV that kills the person with AIDS.

❑ *The presence of HIV can be detected through antibody testing.* To date there are no widely available tests to detect the presence of HIV itself. The Western Blot and ELISA antibodies tests are *reasonably* accurate blood tests that show whether the body has developed antibodies in response to HIV. HIV antibodies develop between one and six months after infection. Antibody testing should take place at one- and six-month intervals. The Western Blot test is more accurate but also more expensive. (Often the ELISA test is administered first and if the result is positive, the Western Blot is recommended as a follow up.) If the antibody is present, the test will be positive. That means that the person has been infected with HIV and an active virus is present. The presence of

continued on next page

infection has been absolutely ruled out. To prevent the transmission of HIV and other sexually transmitted diseases (as well as to prevent pregnancy), men and women should engage in sexual intercourse only if they use a condom.

FOCUS

HIV does not mean, however, that the person necessarily will develop AIDS symptoms in the near future.

❑ *All those with HIV (whether or not they have symptoms) are HIV carriers.* They may infect others through unsafe sexual activity or by sharing needles; if they are pregnant, they may infect the fetus.

The development of AIDS symptoms in HIV-positive individuals may be slowed by the use of AZT drug therapy. The earlier an HIV-positive person begins taking AZT, the more effective it is in retarding AIDS symptoms. Because early therapy is important, any person who believes that he or she may have been exposed to HIV should be tested—but no sooner than one month following the suspected exposure (to allow time for antibodies to appear). A sound nutritional regimen, in conjunction with the appropriate drug therapy, may help maintain health when HIV is diagnosed early. Once AIDS symptoms develop, *Pneumocystis carinii* pneumonia may also be treated with AZT.

PROTECTING YOURSELF AND OTHERS. Although some people have changed their behaviors to reduce the risk of STD and HIV infection, many continue to jeopardize their health and lives—as well as the health and lives of their partners' and loved ones—by failing to take adequate precautions. They worry about STDS and HIV but do not take the necessary steps—such as *always* using condoms—to prevent infections. One study of sexually active young adults found that 44 percent had not changed their behavior in any way to reduce the risk of HIV

infection (Cochran, Keidan, and Kalechsteir, 1989).

However difficult it may be, the key to protecting ourselves and others is talking with our partners about STDs in an open, nonjudgmental way. To prevent the transmission of STDs, there are several things an individual needs to know about a partner before becoming sexually involved.

❑ *Does he or she have an STD?* The best way of finding out is by asking. If you feel nervous about broaching the subject, you can rehearse talking about it. Write out what you want to say, engage yourself in an imaginary dialogue, or role play with a friend. It may be sufficient to ask in a light-hearted manner, "Are you as healthy as you look?" Or, because many people are uncomfortable asking about STDs, you can open up the topic by revealing your anxiety: "This is a little difficult for me to talk about because I like you and I'm embarrassed, but I'd like to know whether you have herpes, or HIV, or something like that." And if you have an STD, you can say, "Look, I like you, but we can't make love right now because I have a chlamydial infection and I don't want you to get it."

Keep in mind that even a person who believes he or she doesn't have an STD may honestly not know. Women with chlamydia and gonorrhea, for example, are generally asymptomatic. Both men and women infected with HIV may be asymptomatic for years, although they are capable of spreading the infection through sexual contact. It pays to be cautious. Either refrain from sex or use a prophylactic—a condom or the

recently developed women's condom.

❑ *Does he or she have multiple sex partners?* The more sex partners a person has, the more likely he or she is to contract an STD. A person who has multiple partners should be checked annually for STDs. A person is at higher risk for contracting HIV if he or she is or was sexually involved with a gay or bisexual male, an IV-drug user (or former user), a prostitute, or a hemophiliac (Hearst and Hulley, 1988).

❑ *Does he or she have condoms?* If you don't know whether your partner has an STD, use a condom. Even if you don't discuss STDs, condoms are simple and easy to use without much discussion. Both men and women can carry them. (About 40 percent of condom sales are now to women.) A woman can take a condom from her purse and give it to her partner; if he doesn't want to use it, she can say, "No condom, no sex."

A latex condom is an excellent prophylactic against most STDs when properly used. It is not 100 percent effective in preventing STDs, however. A conservative estimate is that condoms are about 90 percent effective (Hearst and Hulley, 1988). Spermicides with nonoxynol-9 (or condoms treated with the spermicide) give additional protection against some STDs, possibly including HIV. (See Resource Center for more detailed information on STDs and HIV/AIDS.)

ANAL INTERCOURSE. In anal intercourse the male inserts his erect penis into his partner's anus. Both heterosexuals and gay men participate in this activity. For

FIGURE 5.1

AIDS and Ethnicity, 1990

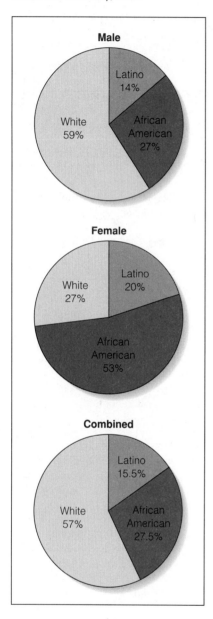

Male

Latino 14%
African American 27%
White 59%

Female

White 27%
Latino 20%
African American 53%

Combined

Latino 15.5%
White 57%
African American 27.5%

SOURCE: HIV/AIDS Surveillance Report, August, 1990

Sex contains all, bodies, souls,
Meanings, proofs, purities, delicacies,
*   results, promulgations,*
Songs, commands, health, pride, the
*   seminal milk*
All hopes, benefactions, bestowals, all
*   loves, beauties, delights of the earth,*
These are contain'd in sex as parts of
*   itself and justifications of itself.*

Walt Whitman (1819–1892)

heterosexual couples who engage in it, anal intercourse is generally an experiment or occasional activity rather than a common mode of sexual expression. A 1987 *Redbook* survey of the magazine's female readers found that 43 percent of its respondents had tried anal intercourse, but only 12 percent reported enjoying it (Rubenstein and Tavris, 1987). For many gay men, anal intercourse is an important mode of sexual interaction.

Because of AIDS, however, anal intercourse among both gay men and heterosexuals is a potentially dangerous form of sexual interaction. It is the most prevalent mode of sexually transmitting HIV because the delicate membranes lining the anus are easily torn, providing a path of entry for HIV carried in the semen. If a couple practices anal intercourse, they should engage in it *only* if both are certain that they are free from HIV *and* if they use a condom.

❏ SEXUALITY AND AGING

Our bodies and sexuality develop and change from birth through old age. During puberty we develop secondary sex characteristics and become fertile. These changes are essential for the expression of adult sexuality, which is characterized by autoerotic and interpersonal sexual behaviors. It is not until middle age that additional important body changes affecting sexuality occur.

Sexuality and Middle Age

Men and women view aging differently. As men approach their fifties, they fear the loss of their sexual capacity but not their attractiveness; in contrast, women fear the loss of their attractiveness but generally not their sexuality. As both age, purely psychological sitmuli, such as fantasies, become less effective for arousal. Physical stimulation remains effective, however.

Among American women, sexual responsiveness continues to grow from adolescence until it reaches its peak in the late thirties or early forties; it is usually maintained at more or less the same level into the sixties and beyond. Men's physical responsiveness is greatest in late adolescence or early adulthood; beginning in men's twenties, responsiveness begins to slow imperceptibly. Changes in male sexual responsiveness become apparent only when men are in their forties and fifties. As a man ages, achieving erection requires more stimulation and time and the erection may not be as firm.

Around the age of fifty, the average American woman begins **menopause,** which is marked by the cessation of the menstrual cycle. Menopause is not a sudden event. Usually, for several years preceding menopause, the menstrual cycle becomes increasingly irregular. Although menopause ends fertility, it does not end interest in sexual activities. The decrease in estrogen, however, may cause thinness and dryness in the vagina that makes intercourse painful. The use of vaginal lubricants will remedy much of the problem. A review of the literature on the effects of hormone replacement therapy (HRT) on sexual functioning indicates that estrogen therapy leads to gynecological improvement and thus improves the context for unimpaired sexual activity (Walling, Andersen, and Johnson, 1990). There is no male equivalent to menopause. Male fertility slowly declines, but men in their eighties are often fertile.

Most studies on aging and sexuality indicate a decline in sexual desire or interest as people age. But a recent longitudinal study (Hällstrom and Samuelsson, 1990), in which almost 700 middle-aged women were interviewed twice, at a six-year interval, suggests that sexual desire tends to be more stable than originally believed. Almost two-thirds of the women studied experienced no significant change in their levels of desire after six years. Twenty-seven percent experienced a decline, while 10 percent experienced an increase. What is most notable about this study is that it shows the impact of marital satisfaction and mental health on sexual desire. Desire is not related to increasing age alone. Not surprisingly, many of the women whose desire decreased over six years felt that their marriages lacked intimacy, had spouses who were alcoholic, and were themselves depressed. Such an unhappy combination is a sure antidote to desire. Those whose desire increased had initially experienced weaker desire, had troubled marriages, and had been depressed. Six years later, as their marriages improved and their mental health improved, their desire increased, moving them closer to the average.

Because of physical changes, noted Herant Katchadourian (1987), "Middle-aged couples may be misled into thinking that this change heralds a sexual decline as an accompaniment to aging." Katchadourian continued:

Sexual partners who have been together for a long time have the benefits of trust and affection. In the younger years of marriage, sex tends to be a battleground where scores are settled and peace is made, but if a couple has stuck together until middle age, sex should become a demilitarized zone. . . . They continue to enjoy the physical pleasures of sex but do not stop there . . . the sensual quality of the person, rather than the body as such, becomes the main course.

Both researchers and the general public tend to ignore the emotional and sensual qualities of the relationships of the aged.

Sexuality and the Aged

The sexuality of the aged tends to be invisible in our culture. According to Georgia Barrow (1989), there are several reasons for this. First, we associate sexuality with the young, assuming that sexual attraction exists only between those with youthful bodies. Interest in sex is considered normal and virile in twenty-five-year-old men, but in seventy-five-year-old men it is considered lechery (Corby and Zarit, 1983). Second, we associate the idea of romance and love with the young; many of us find it difficult to believe that the aged can fall in love or love intensely. Yet a fifty-seven-year-old woman said of a seventy-two-year-old man she had recently met (quoted in Barrow, 1989):

It was as if I were 17 and had never been on a date. I had never turned anybody on in my life, so far as I knew. Now, all of a sudden, it was Christmas. Believe it or not, we fell in love.

Third, we continue to associate sex with procreation, measuring a woman's femininity by her childbearing and mother role and a man's masculinity by the children he sires. Finally, the aged generally do not have as strong sexual desires as the young and they are not expressed as openly.

Sexuality is one of the least understood aspects of life in old age. Many older people continue to adhere to the standards of activity or physical attraction they held when they were young. Sexual behavior is defined by researchers and the general population alike as masturbation, sexual intercourse, or orgasm. These definitions have "overshadowed the emotional, sensual, and relationship qualities that give meaning, beyond release, to sexual expression. . . . What has been ignored are the walking hand-in-hand or arm-in-arm; the caring for one another; the touching and holding, with or without intercourse" (Weg, 1983b). A study of 200 men and women between eighty and one hundred years of age confirms the most common form of erotic activity as touching and caressing without intercourse. Masturbation was the next most frequent, followed by sexual intercourse (Bretschneider and McCoy, 1988). About half of elderly married men report masturbating regularly (Weiztman and Hart, 1987). Although masturbation may be the only significant genital outlet for an older man or woman, society disapproves of it (Pratt and Schmall, 1989).

The greatest determinants of an aged individual's sexual activity are health and the availability of a partner. A major study of older people found only 7 percent of those who were single or widowed to be sexually active, in contrast to 54 percent of those living with a partner (Verwoerdt et al., 1969). Frequency of sexual intercourse for the latter group, with an average age of seventy years, ranged from three times a week to once every two months. Those who described their sexual feelings as having been weak or moderate in their youth stated that they were without sexual feelings. Those who do not have partners may turn to masturbation as an alternative (Pratt and Schmall, 1989).

Physiologically, men are less responsive than women. The decreasing frequency of intercourse and the increasing time required to attain an erection produce anxieties in many older men about erectile dysfunctions (impotence), anxieties that may very well lead to dysfunctions. When the natural slowing down of sexual responses is interpreted as the beginning of sexual dysfunctioning, this self-diagnosis triggers a spiral of fear and even greater difficulty in having or maintaining an erection. One study (Weitzman and Hart, 1987) found that about 31 percent of elderly male respondents were unable to have an erection.

Women, who are sexually capable throughout their lives, have different concerns. They face greater social constraints than men (Robinson, 1983). Women are confronted with an unfavorable sex ratio (twenty-nine males for every one hundred females over sixty-five years), a greater likelihood of widowhood, norms against marrying (let alone cohabitating with) younger men, less probability of remarriage, the double standard of aging, and inhibiting gender roles. Grieving over the death of a partner, isolation, and depression also affect their sexuality (Rice, 1989).

After age seventy-five, a significant decrease in sexual activity takes place. This seems to be related to health problems, such as heart disease, arthritis, and diabetes. Often older people indicate that they continue to feel sexual desires; they simply lack the ability to express them because of their health (Verwoerdt et al., 1969). In a study (White, 1982) of men and women in nursing homes, whose ages averaged eighty-two years, 91 percent reported no sexual activity immediately prior to their interviews. Seventeen percent of these men and women, however, expressed a desire for sexual activity. Unfortunately, most nursing homes makes no provision for the sexuality of the aged. Instead, they actively discourage sexual expression—not only sexual intercourse but also masturbation—or try to sublimate their clients' erotic interests into crafts or television. Such manipulations, however, do little to satisfy the erotic needs of the elderly.

For some of the very old, noted Erik Erikson (1986), "memories seem to evoke an immediate, sensual reinvolvement in their earliest adulthood commitments to intimacy." Erikson related the story of one elderly woman, who vibrantly recalled meeting her husband:

I was crazy about him. We went out together for three months, but he never touched me. Finally I told him, "Something better happen tonight or else." I wouldn't explain any more. So he kissed me that night and he kissed me until the day he died.

"Reminiscing about the sensuality of early love," Erikson (1986) wrote, "enables her to view with life-span perspective the unwelcome extent to which she now remains largely apart. Perhaps, in eliciting the feelings of an earlier time, it also helps fill this current void." Many older widows do not miss the sexual aspect of their lives, however, as much as they do the social aspects of their married lives. It is the companionship, the activity, the pleasure found in their partners that these older women most acutely miss (Malatesta, Chambless, Pollack, and Cantor, 1989).

□ SEX AND PHYSICAL LIMITATIONS

A wide range of disabilities and physically limiting conditions affect human sexuality, yet the sexual needs and desires of disabled people have been generally overlooked and ignored. One physician was amazed to learn from a panel of paraplegics that "if they had their choice between getting back their walking or their normal sexual function, they'd choose sex." He went on to say, "In the hospital we put all our effort toward walking—we were doing nothing about this other problem."

In 1987, Ellen Stohl, a twenty-three-year old paraplegic, created controversy by posing seminude for an eight-page layout in *Playboy*. Some people (including some editors at *Playboy*) felt that the feature could be construed as exploitive of people with disabilities. Others, Stohl among them, felt that it would help normalize society's perception of those with disabilities. She said, "I realized I was still a woman. But the world didn't accept me as that. Here I am a senior in college and have a 3.5 average, and people treat me like I'm a 3-year-old" (quoted in Cummings, 1987).

Many people are subject to sexually-limiting conditions for some or all of their lives. These conditions may be congenital, appearing at birth, such as cerebral palsy (a neuromuscular disorder) and Down's syndrome (a developmentally disabling condition) (Cromer, et al., 1990; Rowe, 1987). They may be caused by a disease such as arthritis or cancer, or be the result of an accident, as in the case of spinal cord injuries (Rieve, 1989; Walsh and Walsh, 1989; Prigatano, 1989). As a result of such a condition, limitations may be placed on a person's ability to move freely; he or she may not experience the range of sense and sensation that is available to the able-bodied. Communication may be problematic (Peterson, 1979).

A person with a physical limitation may have various kinds of equipment and paraphernalia to deal with, such as an artifical limb (prosthesis), a brace, a wheelchair, an ostomy bag, crutches or a cane.

Changing Expectations

Educating those with physical limitations as to their sexual potential and providing counseling to build self-esteem and combat negative stereotypes are increasingly being recognized as crucial issues by the medical community (Bullard and Knight, 1981; Money et al., 1975).

To establish sexual health, the person with physical limitations must overcome previous sexual performance expectations and realign them with his or her actual sexual capacities. In cases where the spinal cord is completely severed, for example, there is no feeling in the genitals, but that does not eliminate sexual desires or put a stop to other possible sexual behaviors. Men with spinal cord damage are generally able to have erections and ejaculate, even though the orgasmic feelings accompanying ejaculation are generally absent. Women with spinal cord injuries generally do not experience orgasm although they are able to experience sensuous feelings in other parts of their bodies. People with spinal cord injuries (and anyone else, for that matter) may engage in oral or manual sex—anything, in fact, that they and their partners find pleasurable and acceptable. They may discover new erogenous areas of their bodies, such as their thighs, necks, ears, or underarms. Spinal cord injuries do not usually affect fertility. Many women with such injuries are able to have painless childbirth, although forceps delivery or cesarean section may be necessary.

OVERCOMING GUILT. An important problem for many people with disabilities is overcoming the guilt they feel because their bodies are not ideal. They often live in dread of rejection, which may or may not be realistic, depending on whom they seek as partners. Many disabled people have rich fantasy lives. This is fortuitous because imagination is a key ingredient to developing a full sexual life. Robert Lenz (Lenz and Chaves, 1981), a consultant in the field of sexuality and disability, received a quadriplegic spinal cord injury when he was sixteen. In the film *Active Partners* he says:

One thing I do know is that I'm a much better lover than I ever was before. There are a lot of reasons for that, but one of the biggest is that I'm more relaxed. I don't have a list of do's and don'ts, a timetable or a proper sequence of moves to follow, or the need to "give" my partner an orgasm every time we make love. Sex isn't just orgasm for me; it's pleasuring, playing, laughing, and sharing.

A major function of therapists working with clients with limitations is to give their clients "permission" to engage in sexual activities that are appropriate to their capacities and to suggest new activities or techniques (Kolodny et al., 1979). Clients should also be advised about the use of vibrators and artificial penises and vaginas; these devices "should be available in surgical supply stores as freely as the porno shops, where they are presently sold" (Diamond, 1974).

COMMUNICATING NEEDS. It is important to understand that sexual satisfaction is not synonymous with orgasm. Sex is a means of communicating deeply intimate and human feelings to another person. These feelings can be communicated between lovers without elaborate nightlong bouts of lovemaking or the idealized anatomy of the able-bodied, godlike figures on television and movie screens. Satisfaction really comes from good sexual communication and intimacy, fostered by trust, sensitivity, creativity, patience, and when indicated, a sense of humor. Robert Lenz again:

I learned very shortly after getting out of the rehabilitation center the difference between the proper, medical way of doing things and the practical, easy way of doing things. I've gotten very pragmatic—you might say that now she [Bernadette, his partner] drops me into bed. Now that's what I call pragmatic!

You only possess what will not be lost in a shipwreck.

El-Ghazaki

SEXUAL RIGHTS OF PEOPLE WITH DISABILITIES. Although the concerns of people with limitations are becoming more visible, there is a marked tendency on the part of the rest of humanity to put its collective head in the sand, believing that what it doesn't see does not exist. But none of us is immune to accidents or to numerous debilitating diseases and conditions. By refusing to recognize the existence and concerns of those with physical and developmental limitations, the rest of us do a profound disservice to our fellow human beings and ultimately to ourselves. Also, feminists have expressed increased concern about women with disabilities (Begum, 1992).

The sexual rights of the physically disabled include:

1. The right to sexual expression.
2. The right to privacy.
3. The right to be informed and to have access to needed services such as contraceptive counseling, medical care, genetic counseling, and sex counseling.
4. The right to choose one's marital status.
5. The right to have or not have children.
6. The right to make one's own decisions and develop to one's fullest potential.

❏ PREMARITAL SEXUALITY

Increased Legitimacy of Sex Outside of Marriage

Over the last several decades, there has been a remarkable increase in the acceptance of premarital sexual intercourse. We use the term *premarital* to refer to sexual activities between unmarried adolescents and young adults. When discussing the sexual activities of unmarried middle-aged and older single adults (whether never married, divorced, or widowed) we use the term *nonmarital* sexuality. While taking place outside of marriage, the sexual activities of unmarried older adults are not "premarital" in the same sense as those of never-married adolescents and young adults.

For adolescents and young adults, the advent of effective birth control methods, changing gender roles that permit females to be sexual, and delayed marriages have played a major part in the rise of premarital sex. For middle-aged and older adults, increasing divorce rates and longer life expectancy have created an enormous pool of once-married men and women who engage in nonmarital sex. Only extramarital sex—sex outside the marital relationship—continues to be consistently frowned upon.

The increased legitimacy of sex outside of marriage has transformed both dating and marriage. Sexual intercourse has become an acceptable part of the dating process for many couples, whereas only petting was acceptable before. Furthermore, marriage has lost some of its power as the only legitimate setting for sexual intercourse (Furstenberg, 1980). One important result is that many people no longer feel that they need to get married to express their sexuality in a relationship (Scanzoni, Polonko, Teachman, and Thompson, 1989).

The degree and kind of a person's sexuality reaches up into the ultimate pinnacle of his spirit.

Friedrich Nietzsche

Factors Leading to Premarital Sexual Involvement

What are the factors that lead men and women to have premarital intercourse? What influences the timing of sex in their relationship? Researcher Susan Sprecher (1989) identifies individual, relationship, and environmental factors affecting the decision to have premarital intercourse.

For human beings, the more powerful need is not for sex per se, but for relationship, intimacy and affirmation.

Rollo May

INDIVIDUAL FACTORS. There are a number of individual factors influencing the decision to have premarital intercourse. These include previous sexual experience, sexual attitudes, personality characteristics, and gender. The more premarital sexual experience a man or woman has had in the past, the more likely he or she is to engage in sexual activities in the present. Once the psychological barrier against premarital sex is broken, sex appears to become less taboo. This seems to be especially true if the earlier sexual experiences were rewarding in terms of pleasure and intimacy. Those with liberal sexual attitudes are more likely to engage in sexual activity than those with restrictive attitudes. In terms of personality characteristics, men and women who did not feel high levels of guilt about sexuality were more likely to engage in sex, as were those who valued erotic pleasure.

RELATIONSHIP FACTORS. Two of the most important factors determining sexual activity in a relationship are the level of intimacy in the relationship and the length of time the couple has been together. Even those who are less permissive in their sexual attitudes accept sexual involvement if the relationship is emotionally intimate and long-standing. Individuals who are less committed (or not committed) to

Abstinence sows sand all over the ruddy limbs and flaming hair.

William Blake (1757–1827)

a relationship are less likely to be sexually involved. The style of love discussed in Chapter 3 also seems to have an effect. Ludic lovers were more sexually permissive than agapic lovers. Some evidence also suggested that storgic and pragmatic lovers were less permissive. Finally, persons in equitable relationships, wherein power is shared equally, are more likely to be sexually involved than those in inequitable ones.

ENVIRONMENTAL FACTORS. In the most basic sense, the physical environment affects the opportunity for sex. Since sex is a private activity, the opportunity for it may be precluded by the presence of parents, friends, roommates, or children. The cultural environment also affects premarital sex. The values of one's parents or peers may encourage or discourage sexual involvement. A person's ethnic group also affects premarital involvement: generally, African Americans are more permissive than whites; Latinos are less permissive than Anglos. Furthermore, a person's subculture—such as the university or church environment, the divorced world, the gay and lesbian community—exerts an important influence on sexual decision making.

❑ MARITAL SEXUALITY

It is better to marry than to burn.

Corinthians 7:9

When people marry, they may discover that their sexual lives are very different than they were before marriage. Sex is now morally and socially sanctioned. It is in marriage that the great majority of heterosexual sexual activities take place. Yet if we were to judge by the media, little sex occurs within marriage. On television soaps, twenty-four times as much sex takes place between unmarried partners as between married ones. Furthermore, erotic activity is often linked with violence

Sexuality can be expressed in erotic playfulness.

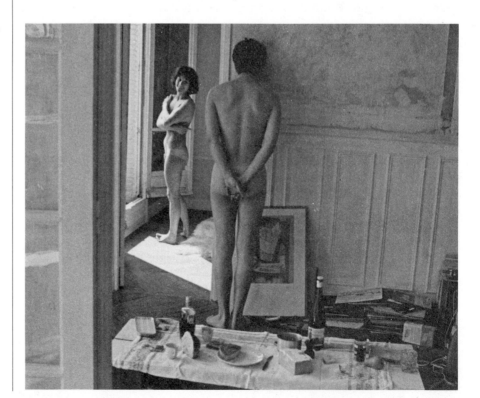

(Roberts, 1982). Sexual research is not much different from the media. There are literally hundreds of studies on adolescent sexuality, nonmarital sexuality, extramarital sexuality, gay and lesbian sexuality, and sexual variations. Almost no studies, however, exist on marital sexuality (P. MacCorquodale, 1989). Researchers probably know more about moon rocks than they do about marital sex.

Role of Sexuality

Marital sex tends to diminish in frequency the longer a couple is married. For newly married couples, the average rate of marital intercourse is about three times a week. As the partners get older, the frequency declines. In early middle age, a married couple makes love an average of one and a half to two times a week. After age fifty, the rate is about once a week or less. (These are *average* rates, individual couples may make love more or less often and still be in the normal range.) Sex also becomes more routine in marriage.

Sex is only one bond among many in marriage. It is a more important bond in cohabitation than in marriage because cohabitors don't have the security and future orientation of marriage to cement their relationship. Most married couples don't seem to feel that declining frequency is a major problem, especially if they rate their overall relationship as good. Blumstein and Schwartz (1983) found that most married people attributed the decline to lack of time or physical energy or to "being accustomed" to each other. Also, other activities and interests engage them besides sex. But if the frequency of sex is low in cohabiting relationships, discord is likely.

New Meanings to Sex

Sexuality within marriage is substantially different from premarital and nonmarital sex in at least three ways. First, sex in marriage is expected to be monogamous over a lifetime. Second, procreation is a legitimate goal. Third, sex takes place in the everyday world.

MONOGAMY. The most significant factor shaping marital sexuality is the expectation of **monogamy,** sexual exclusiveness. Before or after marriage, a person might have various sexual partners, but within marriage, all sexual interactions are expected to take place between spouses. This expectation of monogamy lasts a lifetime; a person marrying at age twenty commits himself or herself to forty to sixty years of sex with one person and no others. Within a monogamous relationship, each partner must decide how to handle fantasies, desires, and opportunities for extramarital sexuality. For example, do you tell your spouse that you have fantasies about other people? That you masturbate? Do you flirt with others? Do you have an extramarital relationship? If so, do you tell your spouse? How do you handle sexual conflicts or difficulties with your partner? How do you deal with sexual boredom or monotony?

SOCIALLY SANCTIONED REPRODUCTION. Sex also takes on a procreative aspect within marriage. Until recently, procreative sex within marriage was the only acceptable form of sex in Western culture. Now sex and reproduction can be separated by means of birth control. Although it is obviously possible to get pregnant before marriage, marriage is the only socially sanctioned setting in which to have children in our society. When a couple marry, they are confronted with the task of deciding whether or not to have children. It is one of the most crucial decisions they will make. Having children alters a person's life even more than marriage: marriages can be dissolved, but a person never stops being a parent.

The vow of fidelity is an absurd commitment, but it is the heart of marriage.

Robert Capon

Sexuality is a good gift from God and is a fundamental means of realizing life-in-community. This gift includes all that it means to be male and female and is not limited to coital behavior. All expressions of human sexuality affect the emergence of genuine personhood and should reflect a concern for personal integrity, relational fidelity and the equality of men and women.

United Methodist Church

If the couple decide to have a child, the nature of their sexual interactions may change from being simply an erotic activity to an intentionally reproductive act as well. Many parents who planned their children speak of the difference between sex as pleasure and sex as reproduction. One woman told the authors:

We wanted to have a child for a long time and when I quit taking birth control pills, we started making love to have a child. Each time we did it, we knew we might be conceiving. That made it really different from before when it just felt good or was fun. I can't explain why, just that it was really different knowing that we might be creating something.

CHANGED SEXUAL CONTEXT. The sexual context changes with marriage. Because married life takes place in a day-to-day living situation, sex must also be expressed in the day-to-day world. Before marriage, sex may have taken place only in romantic or seductive settings, at home when parents were away, or in the back seat of a car. These situations make sexual encounters highly charged with emotions ranging from intense love to anxiety and fear.

After marriage, sex must be arranged around working hours and at times when the children are at school or asleep. Sometimes one or the other partner may be tired, frustrated, or angry. The emotions associated with premarital sex may disappear. Some of the passion of romantic love eventually disappears as well, to be replaced with a love based on caring and commitment.

A primary task in marriage is to make sex meaningful in the everyday world. Sex in marriage is a powerful bond. Although we may tend to believe that good sex depends on good techniques, it really depends more on the quality of the marriage. One woman remarked to her husband, "What really turns me on is to see you doing housework." The husband, perplexed, asked why, because housework did not make him feel particularly sexy. "Because when I see you vacuuming, it gives me a warm feeling of love for you, which makes me want to make love with you." If the marriage is happy, the couple is more likely to have good sex; if it is unhappy, the unhappiness is likely to be reflected in the sexual relationship.

Sex therapists are turning increasingly to examining marital dynamics rather than the individual as the source of sexual problems (Kaplan, 1979). As Blumstein and Schwartz (1983) point out, "An unhappy sex life does not necessarily mean that a couple is sexually incompatible. Their sexual relationship may be undermined by other problems." It does not matter what the conflict is about—housework, children, money—it is likely to be carried over into the bedroom.

☐ EXTRAMARITAL SEXUALITY

Most people decry extramarital sexuality, but many engage in it. In fact, one researcher (Sponaugle, 1989) estimates that at least 52 million Americans have engaged in extramarital sex at least once during their marriages. Extramarital involvements assume many forms (see Thompson, 1983, and Sponaugle, 1990, for reviews of the research literature). These involvements may be (1) sexual but not emotional, (2) sexual and emotional, or (3) emotional but not sexual (Thompson, 1984). Very little research has been done on extramarital relationships in which both people are emotionally but not sexually involved. Thompson's study, however, found that of 378 married and cohabiting individuals, the three types of extrarelational involvement were about equally represented. Twenty-one percent had been in relationships that were primarily sexual, 19 percent in relationships that were sexual and emotional, and 18 percent in relationships that were emotional but not sexual. All told, 43 percent had been in some form of extramarital relationship.

A Frontier Guard

The bamboo leaves rustle
On this cold, frosty night.
I am wearing seven layers of clothing
But they are not as warm, not as warm
As the body of my wife.

Anonymous, 8th-Century Japanese

Adultery in your heart is committed not only when you look with concupiscence [strong or excessive sexual desire] at a woman who is not your wife. The husband must not use his wife, her femininity, to fulfill his instinctive desire. Concupiscence . . . diminishes the richness of the perennial attraction of persons for interpersonal communication. Through such a reduction, the other person becomes the mere object for satisfying a sexual need and it touches the dignity of the person.

Pope John Paul II

Why should we take advice on sex from the Pope? If he knows anything about it, he shouldn 't.

George Bernard Shaw

Extrarelational experiences are not confined to married and cohabiting couples. Couples in exclusive dating relationships are also involved in sexual activities outside the relationship. As we saw earlier in our discussion of dating, a large percentage of persons in "exclusive" dating couples are involved in various erotic activities outside the relationship. It may very well be that those who engage in sex outside of their exclusive dating relationships are also more likely to engage in extramarital sex. Up to this point, however, research has not explored the possible relationship between the two.

Models of nonexclusive marital relationships may be grouped into several types: extramarital sexuality, nonsexual extramarital relationships, open marriage, sexually open marriage, swinging, and group marriage (Weiss, 1983).

Extramarital Sex in Exclusive Marital Relationships

In marriages that assume emotional and sexual exclusivity, mutuality and sharing are emphasized. Extramarital sexual relationships are assumed to be destructive of the marriage; close friendships with members of the other sex may also be judged to be threatening. The possibility of infecting one's husband or wife with a sexually transmitted disease (STD) must also be considered. As a result of these marital assumptions, extramarital relationships almost always take place without the knowledge or permission of the other partner. If the marital assumptions are violated, we have "guidelines" on how to handle the violation. According to David Weiss (1983): "These guidelines encourage the 'adulterer' to be secretive and discreet, suggest that guilt will be a consequence, and maintain that the spouse will react with feelings of jealousy and rejection if the [extramarital sex] is discovered."

If the extramarital relationship is discovered, a marital crisis probably ensues. Many married people feel that the spouse who is unfaithful has broken a basic trust. Sexual accessibility implies emotional accessibility. When a person learns that his or her spouse is having an affair, the emotional commitment of that spouse is brought into question. How can you prove that you still have a commitment? You cannot. Commitment is assumed; it can never be proven. Furthermore, the extramarital relationship may imply to the partner (rightly or wrongly) that he or she is sexually inadequate or uninteresting.

Extramarital Sex in Nonexclusive Marital Relationships

There are several types of nonexclusive marriages (Weiss, 1983): (1) open marriage in which intimate but nonsexual friendships with others are encouraged, (2) sexually open marriages, (3) swinging, and (4) group marriage/multiple relationships. The marriage relationship is considered the primary relationship in both nonconsensual extramarital relationships (described previously) and in open marriages and swinging relationships. Only the group marriage/multiple relationships model rejects the primacy of the marital relationship. Group marriage is the equal sharing of partners, as in polygamy; it may consist of one man and two or more women, one woman and two or more men, or two or more couples.

SWINGING. Swinging (also called mate sharing or wife swapping) is a form of consensual extramarital sex in which couples engage in sexual activities with others in a social context clearly defined as recreational sex. Swinging is structured to prevent intimacy. Such social contexts include swinging parties or commercial club settings. Married couples swing together (Weiss, 1983). Forming an intimate relationship with an extramarital partner is prohibited.

It has been estimated that 2 percent of adult Americans have engaged in swinging (Weiss, 1983). Although swingers are popularly perceived to be deviant, radical, or psychologically troubled, they tend not to differ significantly from most Americans. They tend to be white, middle-class, politically conservative, and quite "normal" except for their swinging. They tend to be less religious than nonswingers (Jenks, 1985; Weiss, 1983). It is not known what impact the AIDS crisis has had on swinging, though anecdotal information suggests the epidemic has not affected it.

OPEN MARRIAGE. The partners in a sexually open marriage have mutually agreed that each may have openly acknowledged and independent sexual relationships with others. There has been little research on sexually open marriages. Blumstein and Schwartz (1983) found that 15 to 26 percent of the couples in their sample had "an understanding" that permitted extramarital relations in certain circumstances. The rules differ from couple to couple. Blumstein and Schwartz observe:

An open relationship does not mean that anything goes . . . The most important rules provide emotional safeguards—for example, never seeing the same person twice, never giving out a phone number, never having sex in a couple's bed or with a mutual friend. Sex outside the relationship is potentially very disruptive. Traditional marriages have dealt with this by ruling out nonmonogamy. Couples who engage in open relationships formulate rules to guide their behavior, to make outside sex very predictable and orderly. These rules remind the partners that their relationship comes first and anything else must take second place.

An intriguing study (Rubin and Adams, 1986) attempted to measure the impact of sexually open marriages on marital stability. The researchers matched eighty-two couples in 1978 and were able to do a follow-up study of seventy-four couples five years later. It was found that there was no significant difference in marital stability related to whether the couple was sexually open or monogamous in their marriage. Among those marriages that broke up, the reasons given were not related to extramarital sex. No appreciable differences were found in terms of marital happiness or jealousy.

Even though considerable numbers of Americans engage in extramarital sexual behavior, it does not appear that they reject the monogamous norm. Extramarital affairs will probably continue for the most part as secretive affairs.

Motivation in Extramarital Relationships

People who engage in extramarital affairs have a number of different motivations, and these affairs satisfy a number of different needs. John Gagnon (1977) described the appeal that extramarital affairs have for the people involved:

Most people find their extramarital relationships highly exciting, especially in the early stages. This is a result of psychological compression: the couple gets together; they are both very aroused (desire, guilt, expectation); they have only three hours to be together.... Another source of attraction is that the other person is always seen when he or she looks good and is on best behavior, never when feeling tired or grubby, or when taking care of children, or when cooking dinner.... Each time, all the minutes that the couple has together are special because they have been stolen from all these other relationships. The resulting combination of guilt and excitement has a heightening effect, which tends to explain why people may claim that extramarital sex and orgasms are more intense.

Most extramarital sex does not involve a love affair but is generally self-contained and more sexual than emotional (Gagnon, 1977). Affairs that are both emotional and sexual appear to detract most from the marital relationship, whereas

A cuckold is the husband of an unfaithful wife—a far nastier and more humiliating state . . . than being the wife of a philanderer, for which in fact no word exists.

Anne Fausto-Sterling, *Myths of Gender*

affairs that are only sexual or only emotional seem to detract least (Thompson, 1984). More women than men have emotional affairs; almost twice as many men as women have affairs that are only sexual. About equal percentages of men and women are involved in affairs that are both sexual and emotional.

Studies have found little significant correlation between social background characteristics and extramarital sexuality (Thompson, 1983). Personal characteristics and the quality of the marriage appear to be more important, and of the two, personal characteristics—alienation, need for intimacy, emotional independence, and egalitarian sex roles—were stronger correlates of extramarital sex than the quality of the marriage (Thompson, 1984). Nevertheless, the lower the marital satisfaction and the lower the frequency and quality of marital intercourse, the greater the likelihood of extramarital sexual relationships. Most people become involved in extramarital sex because they feel that something is missing in their marriage. Whatever the state of their marital relationship, they have not judged it defective enough to consider divorce. Extramarital relationships are a compensation or substitute for these deficiencies. They help maintain the status quo by giving emotional satisfaction to the unhappy partner.

Research by Ira Reiss and his colleagues (1980) suggested that extramarital affairs appear to be related to two variables: unhappiness of the marriage, and premarital sexual permissiveness. Generally speaking, in happy marriages a partner is less likely to seek outside sexual relationships. If a person had premarital sex, he or she is more likely to have extramarital sex. Persons who break the social prohibition against premarital sex are less likely to be restrained by prohibitions against extramarital sex. Once the first prohibition is broken, the second holds less power.

Most men and women whose marriages break up after their involvement in an extramarital affair feel that the affair was an effect rather than a cause of marital problems. But if their spouse was also involved in such an affair, they identify the spouse's infidelity as a cause of marital problems (Spanier and Margolis, 1983).

❐ GAY AND LESBIAN RELATIONSHIPS

Between 3 and 10 percent of the American population is gay or lesbian (Marmor, 1980). In discussing gay men and lesbians, like many researchers, we generally do not use the terms *homosexual* and *homosexuality*, because they continue to convey negative or pathological connotations. Instead, we use **gay** or **gay male** to refer to men and **lesbian** to refer to women. Replacing the term *homosexual* is critical in expanding our understanding of gay men and lesbians. It helps us see gay men and lesbians as whole persons by underlining the fact that sexuality is not the only aspect of their lives: their lives also include love, commitment, desire, caring, work, children, religious devotion, passion, politics, loss, and hope. Sex is important, obviously, but it is not the only significant aspect of their lives, just as it is not the only significant aspect of the lives of heterosexuals.

Those with gay or lesbian orientations have been called sinful, sick, or perverse, reflecting traditional religious, psychoanalytic and some medical approaches. Contemporary thinking in sociology and psychology has rejected these older approaches as biased and unscientific. Instead, sociologists and psychologists have focused their work on how men and women come to identify themselves as gay or lesbian, how they interact among themselves, and what impact society has on them (Heyl, 1989). Researchers reject the idea that gay men and lesbians are inherently deviant or pathological. As noted sociologist Howard Becker (1963) pointed out, "deviant behavior is behavior that people so label." Deviance is created by social groups that make rules

When you prevent me from doing anything I want to do, that is persecution; but when I prevent you from doing anything you want to do, that is law, order, and morals.

George Bernard Shaw

whose violation results in violators being labeled deviant and treated as outsiders. Gay and lesbian behavior, then, is deviant only insofar as it is called deviant.

Gay and Lesbian Identities

IDENTIFYING ONESELF AS GAY OR LESBIAN. Many researchers believe that a person's sexual interest or direction as heterosexual, gay, or lesbian is established by age four or five (Marmor, 1980). But identifying oneself as gay or lesbian takes considerable time and includes several phases, usually beginning in late childhood or early adolescence (Blumenfeld and Raymond, 1989; Troiden, 1988). Homoerotic feelings, that is, feelings of sexual attraction to members of the same sex, almost always precede gay or lesbian activity by several years (Bell et al., 1981). Various studies have indicated that the average gay male does not identify himself as gay until age nineteen to twenty-one (Troiden and Goode, 1980). The more heterosexual experiences during high school that a boy has beyond kissing, the longer it takes him to recognize that he is fundamentally gay. The significant factor is that he is less likely to enjoy his youthful heterosexual encounters (Bell et al., 1981).

The first phase in acquiring a gay or lesbian identity is marked by fear and suspicion that somehow one's desires are different. At first, the person finds it difficult to label these emotional and physical desires for the same sex. His or her initial reactions often include fear, confusion, or denial. Worse, adolescents fear their family's discovery of their homoerotic feelings. "Nowhere has the hostility to homosexuality been more frightening to large numbers of gay men and lesbians than in their own families, forcing them to feel like minority group members in their own homes" (Voeller, 1980). In the second phase, the person actually labels these feelings of attraction, love, and desire as gay. If the feelings recur often enough, a person is eventually forced to acknowledge that they are gay or lesbian feelings. The third phase includes the person's self-definition as gay. This may take considerable struggle, for it entails accepting a label that society generally calls deviant. Questions then arise about whether to tell parents or friends—whether to hide one's identity ("go into the closet") or make the identity known ("come out of the closet").

Some gay men or lesbians may go through two additional phases. One phase is to enter the gay subculture. A gay person may begin acquiring exclusively gay friends, going to gay bars and clubs, or joining gay activist groups. In the gay world, gay and lesbian identities incorporate a way of being in which sexual orientation is a major part of their identity as a person. As Michael Denneny (quoted in Altman, 1982) said: "I find my identity as a gay man as basic as any other identity I can lay claim to. Being gay is a more elemental aspect of who I am than my profession, my class, or my race."

Similarly, Pat Califia (quoted in Weeks, 1985) said: "Knowing I was a lesbian transformed the way I saw, heard, perceived the whole world. I became aware of a network of sensations and reactions that I had ignored all my life."

The final phase begins with a person's first gay or lesbian love affair. This marks the commitment to unifying sexuality and affection. Sex and love are no longer separated. Most gay men and lesbians have had such love affairs, despite the stereotypes of anonymous gay sex.

COMING OUT. Being gay or lesbian is increasingly associated with a total life-style and way of thinking (Conrad and Schneider, 1980). In making gay or lesbian orientation a life-style, **coming out** (publicly acknowledging one's gayness) has become especially important as an affirmation of one's sexuality (Richardson, 1984). Coming out is a major decision, because it may jeopardize many relationships, but it is

Something is happening to gay men, and we are suddenly no longer affiliated with family. Where do they think we came from? The cabbage patch?

Larry Kramer

It is better to be hated for what one is than loved for what one is not.

André Gide

also an important means of self-validation. By publicly acknowledging one's gay or lesbian orientation, a person begins to reject the stigma and condemnation associated with it (Friend, 1980). Generally, coming out occurs in stages, first involving family members, especially the mother and siblings and later the father. Coming out to the family often creates a crisis, but generally the family accepts the situation and gradually adjusts (Holtzen and Agresti, 1990). Misinformation about gay and lesbian sexuality, religious beliefs, and homophobia, however, often interfere with parental response, initially making adjustment difficult (Borhek, 1988; Cramer and Roach, 1987). After the family, friends may be told, and, in fewer cases, employers and co-workers.

Gay men and women are often "out" to varying degrees. Some may be out to no one, not even themselves. Some are out only to their lovers, others to close friends and lovers but not to their families, employers, associates, or fellow students. Others may be out to everyone. Because of fear of reprisal, dismissal, or public reaction, gay and lesbian school teachers, police officers, members of the military, politicians, and members of other such professions are rarely out to their employers, co-workers, or the public.

There are over a million and a half gay and lesbian couples living together in the United States. Same-sex couples often make commitments to long-term relationships or marriages in which there tends to be more sharing and equality than in many heterosexual relationships.

Gay and Lesbian Couples

In 1987, there were over 1.5 million gay or lesbian couples living together. Ninety-two thousand of these couples had children living with them (U.S. Bureau of the Census, 1987). The relationships of gay men and lesbians have been stereotyped as less committed than heterosexual couples because (1) gay men and lesbians cannot legally marry, (2) they may not appear to emphasize sexual exclusiveness, and (3) heterosexuals misperceive love between gay and lesbian couples as being somehow less "real" than love between heterosexuals. Numerous similarities exist between gay and heterosexual couples, according to Letitia Peplau (1981; 1988). Regardless of their sexual orientation, most people want a close, loving relationship with another person. For gay men, lesbians, and heterosexuals, intimate relationships provide love, satisfaction, and security. There is one important difference, however. Heterosexual couples tend to adopt a traditional marriage model, whereas gay couples tend to have a "best-friend" model. Peplau (1988) observes:

A friendship model promotes equality in love relationships. As children, we learn that the husband should be the "boss" at home, but friends "share and share alike." Same-sex friends often have similar interests, skills, and resources—in part because they are exposed to the same gender-role socialization in growing up. It is easier to share responsibilities in a relationship when both partners are equally skilled—or inept—at cooking, making money, disclosing feelings, or whatever.

With this model, tasks and chores are often shared, alternated, or done by the person who has more time. Usually, both members of the couple support themselves; rarely does one financially support the other (Peplau and Gordon, 1982).

Few gay and lesbian relationships are divided into the traditional heterosexual provider/homemaker roles. Among heterosexuals, these divisions are gender-linked as male or female. But in cases in which the couple consists of two men or two women, these traditional gender divisions make no sense. As one gay male remarked, "Whenever I am asked who is the husband and who is the wife, I say, 'We're just a couple of happily married husbands.' " Tasks are often divided pragmatically, according to considerations such as who likes cooking more (or dislikes it less) and work schedules (Marecek, Finn, and Cardell, 1988). Most gay couples are dual-worker couples; neither partner supports or depends on the other economical-

The Catholic Church says it's OK to be gay, as long as you don't practice homosexuality. I say it's OK to be Catholic as long as you don't practice Catholicism.

Bob Smith

ly. Further, since gay and lesbian couples are the same sex, the economic discrepancies based on greater male earning power are absent. One partner does not necessarily have greater power than the other based on income. Although gay couples emphasize egalitarianism, if there are differences in power, they are attributed to personality; if there is an age difference, the older partner is usually more powerful (Harry, 1988).

For both gay men and lesbians, love serves an important function in solidifying their sexual identity and connecting their sexuality with affection. One major study (Bell and Weinberg, 1978) found that virtually every gay man and lesbian who was interviewed had experienced at least one long-term relationship. Almost all the respondents reported that the relationship was important and meaningful to them. One gay man said, "I got a feeling of being loved and having my love accepted. It was a great feeling—companionship and mutual dependence." A lesbian commented about her first relationship, "I got a deeper understanding of another person's capacity for feeling."

Because they confront societal hostility, gay men and lesbians fail to receive the general social support given heterosexuals in maintaining relationships. One rarely finds parents, for example, urging their gay or lesbian children to make a commitment to a stable same-sex relationship or, if the relationship is rocky, to stick it through.

The Gay Response to HIV and AIDS

Although HIV and AIDS strikes heterosexuals as well as gay men, gays experience not only the disease itself but also the stigma attached to it by the larger society. Because there is little support from the larger world for gay men infected with HIV and those with AIDS symptoms, the gay and lesbian communities have become major advocates and sources of support (Altman, 1986). They have been instrumental in the development of research foundations, education and counseling programs, and outreach programs for those infected with HIV or diagnosed with AIDS.

Because of the HIV/AIDS crisis, gay men have altered their sexual behavior patterns considerably. As a result of their efforts, their rate of HIV infection has diminished significantly. The greatest increases in HIV infection and AIDS rates are now found among heterosexuals who contract the virus sexually and users of intravenous (IV) drugs (and their infants). The changes in gay male behavior led the national AIDS commission to indicate that the main reservoir for the transmission of HIV is no longer gay men but IV-drug users.

The urban gay subculture once viewed their sexuality as a celebration of homoeroticism and self, a response to centuries of repression. But the HIV/AIDS crisis devastated the generation of gay baby boomers. "The only social activity was going to funerals," said one gay journalist (Salholz, 1990). The HIV/AIDS crisis led to reevaluation of the role of sexuality in gay culture. Sex became associated with death. Therapist Douglas Carl (1986) wrote, "The pressure on gay men to couple has increased dramatically; at the same time, young people who have never before considered death must deal with it on a daily basis." Fear and celibacy became a way of life. Now a younger generation of gay men are seeking to present a sex-positive message, uniting an affirmation of their sexuality as the deepest expression of self with a commitment to safe sex practices.

Morality is the custom of one's country and the current feeling of one's peers. Cannibalism is moral in a cannibal country.

Samuel Butler (1612–1680)

Homophobia

The response to gay men and lesbians has varied considerably in different cultures. Among seventy-six cultures studied by Ford and Beach (1972), almost two-thirds accepted certain forms of male-to-male sexuality. Our own society's hostility toward gay men and lesbians represents a minority viewpoint. Conventional fears, anxieties, and guilt about sexuality merge with stereotypes of gay men and lesbians to create **homophobia,** the fear or hatred of gay men and lesbians. Homophobia continues to be widespread in the United States. A recent Gallup poll found that only 47 percent of all adults believe that gay and lesbian relations between consenting adults should be legal.

IMPACT OF HOMOPHOBIA. It is well established that many of the problems facing gay men and lesbians result from the social and cultural contexts in which they live (Herek, 1984, 1986). As a result of homophobia, gay men and lesbians are discriminated against in employment, military service, housing, and parental rights. Gay men and lesbians face imprisonment for engaging in the same sexual activities (such as oral-genital sex) in which heterosexuals commonly engage (*Harvard Law Review*, 1990). Medical and public health efforts against HIV (human immunodeficiency virus) infections and AIDS were inhibited at first because the disease was perceived as "the gay plague" and was considered "punishment" against gay men for their "unnatural" sexual practices (Altman, 1986).

Gay men and lesbians may experience rejection by family, friends, and peers. Such rejection may lead gay men and lesbians themselves to feel homophobic— against themselves, unable to accept their sexuality; against their partners; and against other gay men or lesbians (George and Behrendt, 1987; Sophie, 1987). If they internalize society's hostility, gay men and lesbians may become depressed and feel themselves to be perverted, evil, or sick (Warren, 1980).

Gay and lesbian African Americans face a double issue. They must deal with their own self-acceptance as gays and lesbians in an African-American culture that tends to be nonaccepting of their orientation. They must also deal with being African-Americans in a gay and lesbian subculture that is overwhelmingly white (Loiacano, 1989). Latinos also face similar cultural and identity issues. Their difficulties are compounded, however, by the Catholic church's pervasive cultural influence, which continues to negate gay sexuality (Carballo-Dieguez, 1989).

Homophobia adversely affects heterosexuals as well. First, it creates aversive emotions in heterosexuals, such as fear and hatred, that affect their own psychological functioning and well-being. Second, it alienates them from their gay or lesbian family members, friends, neighbors, or coworkers. For fear of rejection, gay and lesbian children may hide their orientation from their family. Sometimes a family discovers that a member is gay only after he has been infected with HIV or develops AIDS symptoms. Then the family must deal with both their own homophobia and the illness or death or dying of their son, brother, or father. Third, homophobia limits heterosexuals' range of feelings and behaviors, such as hugging or being emotionally intimate with same-sex friends, because of their fear that such intimacy may be gay or perceived as gay (Thompson, Grisanti, and Pleck, 1985). This may lead to exaggerated displays of masculinity or femininity.

SOURCES OF HOMOPHOBIA. Homophobia is derived from several sources (Marmor, 1980): (1) a deeply rooted insecurity about one's own sexuality and gender identity, (2) a strong fundamentalist religious orientation, and (3) ignorance about gay men and lesbians. In addition, homophobic individuals are less likely to have had personal contact with gays or lesbians, are more likely to be older and less well educated, and are more likely to express traditional, restrictive attitudes toward sex and to manifest more guilt about sex (Herek, 1984). Some research (Herek, 1986) suggests

Dear Abby

In response to a homophobic reader who launched into a bitter tirade against gay men moving into a house across the street and then asked: "How can we improve the quality of the neighborhood?"

Abigail van Buren replied: "You could move."

Sin is whatever obscures the soul.

André Gide

that the traditional heterosexual male gender role includes homophobia. Traditional male heterosexuals affirm their heterosexuality by strongly expressing whom they are *not* (that is, gay men).

Much homophobia finds justification in selected passages in the Judeo-Christian scriptures (Boswell, 1980; Bullough, 1976; see Edwards, 1989, for a critique of creationist homophobia). As historian John Boswell noted (1980), however, "Religious beliefs may cloak or incorporate intolerance. . . . Careful analysis can almost always differentiate between conscientious application of religious ethics and the use of religious precepts as justification for personal animosity or prejudice." Although both gay and lesbian sexuality were condemned in Leviticus ("Thou shalt not lie with mankind, as with womankind" [18:22]), the same book equally condemned lying and stealing ("Thou shalt not steal nor deal falsely, nor lie to one another" [19:11]). Yet neither liars nor thieves were later denounced—or burned—with the same moral vengeance as were gay men and lesbians. In the story of Sodom and Gommorah, according to the book of Ezekiel (16:49–50), Sodomites "were haughty and did abominable things." Within the Biblical context, the conventional meaning of the word *abominable* is idolatry, or the worshipping of idols (Bullough, 1976).

⬚ SEXUAL RESPONSIBILITY

Because we have so many sexual choices today, we need to understand what responsibilities our sexuality entails. Sexual responsibility includes the following:

1. *Disclosure of intentions.* Each person needs to reveal to the other whether a sexual involvement indicates love, commitment, recreation, and so on.

2. *Freely and mutually agreed-upon sexual activities.* Each individual has the right to refuse any or all sexual activities without the need to justify his or her feelings. There can be no physical or emotional coercion.

3. *Use of mutually agreed-upon contraception in sexual intercourse if pregnancy is not intended.* Both persons in a sexual relationship are *equally* responsible for preventing an unintended pregnancy in a mutually agreed-upon manner.

4. *Use of safe sex practices.* Each person is responsible for practicing safe sex unless both have been monogamous with each other for at least five years. Safe sex practices (discussed in the Resource Center) guard against sexually transmitted diseases, especially HIV/AIDS. Such practices do not transmit semen, vaginal secretions, or blood during sexual activities.

5. *Disclosure of infection from or exposure to STDs.* Each person must inform his or her partner about having or being exposed to an STD because of the serious health consequences, such as infertility or pelvic inflammatory disease, that may follow untreated infections. If you are infected, you must refrain from behaviors such as sexual intercourse, oral-genital sex, or anal intercourse, which may infect your partner. To help insure that STDs are not transmitted, use a condom.

6. *Acceptance of the consequences of your sexual behavior.* Each person needs to be aware of and accept the possible consequences of his or her sexual activities. These consequences can include emotional changes, pregnancy, and sexually transmitted diseases. Because sexual interactions often change the nature of a relationship, this means accepting responsibility for the emotional changes that may occur for both yourself and your partner. If an unintended pregnancy results, you must make a responsible decision and acknowledge or support the feelings of your partner.

Responsibility in many of these areas is facilitated when sex takes place within the context of an ongoing relationship. In that sense, sexual responsibility leads to a

Sin is geographical.

Bertrand Russell

question of values. Is responsible sex possible outside an established relationship? Are *you* able to act sexually responsible? Sexual responsibility also leads to the question of the purpose of sex in your life. Is it for intimacy, erotic pleasure, reproduction, or other purposes?

SUMMARY

❑ Traditional male sexual scripts include denial or non-expression of feelings, emphasis on performance and being in charge, belief that men always want sex and that all physical contact leads to sex, and assumptions that sex equals intercourse and that sexual intercourse always leads to orgasm. Traditional female sexual scripts suggest that sex is both good and bad (depending on the context), sex is for men, men should know what women want, women shouldn't talk about sex, women should look like beautiful models, women are nurturers, and there is only one right way to experience an orgasm.

❑ Contemporary male/female sexual scripts are more egalitarian, consisting of beliefs that sex is a positive good, involves a mutual exchange, may be initiated by either sex, and so on.

❑ *Autoeroticism* is sexual activity that involves only the self. It includes sexual fantasies, erotic dreams, and masturbation.

❑ Sexual fantasies are probably the most universal of all sexual behaviors. They are normal aspects of our sexuality. Erotic fantasies serve several functions: (1) they take our generalized sexual drives and help define and direct them, (2) they allow us to plan or anticipate erotic situations, (3) they provide a pleasurable escape from routine, and (4) they provide clues about the unconscious.

❑ *Masturbation* is an important way to learn about sexuality. People masturbate by stroking, rubbing, caressing, or otherwise stimulating their genitals. Most men and the majority of women have masturbated. People continue to masturbate during marriage, although married men tend to masturbate to supplement their sexual activities whereas women tend to masturbate as a substitute for such activities.

❑ Erotic dreams are widely experienced. People may have orgasms during their dreams.

❑ Oral sex involves *cunnilingus, fellatio,* or mutual oral stimulation. Oral sex has become widely accepted. It is practiced by heterosexuals, gay men, and lesbians.

❑ *Sexual intercourse* is penile/vaginal penetration and stimulation. It is a complex interaction, involving more than erotic pleasure or reproduction. It is a form of communication that may express a host of feelings, including love, hate, need, and contempt.

❑ Anal intercourse is practiced by heterosexuals and gay men. From a health perspective it is dangerous, because it is primarily through anal intercourse that HIV is sexually transmitted.

❑ In middle age, women tend to reach their sexual peak, which is often maintained into their sixties; they also experience *menopause,* the cessation of menstruation. The sexual responsiveness of men declines somewhat, causing men to require greater stimulation and time to become aroused. There is no male equivalent to menopause.

❑ The sexuality of the aged tends to be invisible because we associate sexuality with youth and because the elderly themselves do not have desires as strong as they did in their youth. Men fear erectile dysfunctions, whereas women may be anxious about their physical attractiveness and face greater social constraints than men. The main determinants of sexual activity in old age are the availability of a partner and a person's state of health.

❑ A wide range of disabilities and physical limitations affect people's sexuality. People with these limitations need support and education so that they may enjoy their full sexual potential. Society as a whole needs to be aware of the concerns of people with disabilities and to allow them the same sexual rights as others.

❑ In sexual decision making, loving or liking is often the most important factor determining first intercourse or intercourse with a new partner.

❑ Martial sexuality is generally expected to be *monogamous,* sexually exclusive, takes place in a day-to-day context, and includes reproduction as a socially sanctioned goal. Sex is only one bond among many in marriage. Marital sex tends to decline in frequency over time, but this does not generally signify marital deterioration.

❑ Extramarital sexual involvements assume three basic forms: primarily sexual, primarily emotional, and emotional and sexual. Women are increasingly engaging in extramarital affairs; male involvement has remained relatively high. Most people have extramarital affairs because they feel that something is lacking in their marriage. The two most important factors predicting extramarital involvement are whether the marriage is happy and whether the individual was permissive about premarital sex.

❑ Approximately 3 to 10 percent of the population is gay or lesbian. *Coming out,* identifying oneself as gay or lesbian, occurs over considerable time, usually beginning in late childhood or adolescence. The earliest phase begins with fear or suspicion that one's sexual desires are different or strange. In the second phase the person labels these feelings as gay. The last phase consists of defining oneself as gay or lesbian. Two additional phases include entering the gay subculture and having a long-term gay or lesbian relationship. As a result of the AIDS crisis, gay men are changing their sexual behaviors to diminish their risks.

❑ *Homophobia* refers to fear or hatred of gay men and lesbians. Many of the problems facing gay people, such as discrimination, are a result of homophobia.

❑ Sexual responsibility includes: disclosure of intentions, freely and mutually agreed-upon sexual activities, use of contraception, and safe sex practices, disclosure of STD infection or exposure, and acceptance of consequences of sexual behavior.

C H A P T E R   6

Pregnancy and Childbirth

O U T L I N E

All is beautiful, yes!
Now Mother Earth
And Father Sky
Join one another and meet
Forever helpmates.

Navajo Night Chant

T HE BIRTH OF A WANTED CHILD is considered by many parents to be the happiest event of their lives. Today, however, pain and controversy surround many aspects of this altogether natural process. As we struggle to balance the rights of the mother, the father, the fetus, and society itself in these matters, we find ourselves considering the quality of life as well as life's mere existence.

For most American women, pregnancy will be relatively comfortable and the outcome predictably joyful. Yet for increasing numbers of others, especially among the poor, the prospect of having children raises the spectres of drugs, disease, malnutrition, and familial chaos. Then there are those couples who have dreamed of and planned for families for years only to find that they are unable to conceive.

In this chapter we will view pregnancy and childbirth as both biological and social processes. In addition, we will consider infertility, reproductive technologies, adoption, and pregnancy loss. We will look at the emotional aspects of pregnancy and the challenges of the transition to parenthood.

❑ INFERTILITY

Infertility is generally defined as the inability to conceive a child after trying for a year or more. Until recently, the problem of infertility attracted little public attention. In the last few years, however, numerous couples, many of whom have deferred pregnancy because of career plans or later marriages, have discovered that they are unable to conceive or that the woman is unable to carry the pregnancy to live birth. Still, a recent study by the National Center for Health Statistics (Cimons, 1990) showed that overall, the fertility rate for American women is not declining. In 1988, 8.4 percent of women aged fifteen to forty-four years had an "impaired ability" to have children. This means that one out of twelve or thirteen American couples is involuntarily childless. The greatest increase in infertility is found among young couples in the twenty- to twenty-four-year-old bracket. Their infertility rate rose from 3.6 percent in 1965 to 10.6 in 1982. Infertility among young African-American couples has risen even more dramatically; it is almost twice that of white couples (Faludi, 1989). Every year well over a million American couples seek help for infertility.

Emotional Responses to Infertility

By the time a couple seek medical advice about their fertility problems, they may have already experienced a crisis in confronting the possibility of not being able to become biological parents. Many such couples feel they have lost control over a major area of their lives (Callan, 1987). A number of studies suggest that women generally are more intensely affected than men (Brand, 1989; McEwan, Costello, and Taylor, 1987; Raval et al., 1987). After seeking help, childless couples typically go through three phases, according to Miriam Mazor (1979) (also see Mazor and Simons, 1984):

The first phase revolves around the injury to the self implicit in the situation. Patients are preoccupied with the infertility study and with formulating theories about why it is happening to them, what they have done wrong, why they are so defective and bad that they are denied something the rest of the world takes for granted. The second phase occurs when treatment is unsuccessful; it involves mourning the loss of the children the partner will never bear and an intense examination of what parenthood means to them as individuals, as a couple, and as members of families and of society. Finally, in the third phase, they must come to terms with the outcome of the study: they must make some kind of decision about their future, whether to pursue plans for adoption or for donor insemination or to adjust to childlessness and go on with life.

Infertility Treatment

Almost without exception, fertility problems are physical, not emotional, despite myths to the contrary that often prevent infertile couples from seeking medical treatment. The two most popular myths are that anxiety over becoming pregnant leads to infertility and that if an infertile couple adopts a child, the couple will then be able to conceive on their own (Kolata, 1979). Neither has any basis in medical fact, although it is true that some presumably infertile couples have conceived following an adoption. (This does not mean, however, that one should adopt a child to remedy infertility.) The leading cause of infertility among women is blocked fallopian tubes, generally as a result of **pelvic inflammatory disease (PID),** an infection of the fallopian tubes or uterus that is usually sexually transmitted. Among men the primary causes of infertility are low sperm count, lack of sperm motility (ability of sperm to move spontaneously) and blocked passageways. Approximately 10 percent of cases of infertility are unexplained. In some of these cases, fertility is restored for no discernable reason; in others, the infertility remains a mystery (Jones, 1989). About 60 percent of couples with serious infertility problems will eventually achieve a pregnancy (Lord, 1987). (See Porter and Christopher, 1984, for a review of infertility, coping patterns, and treatment.)

Artificial Insemination

When childlessness is the result of male infertility (or low fertility) or a genetically transmitted disorder carried by the male, couples may try **artificial insemination.** Single women who want children but who have not found an appropriate partner or who wish to avoid emotional entanglements have also made use of this technique, as have lesbian couples. The American Fertility Society estimates that there are about 30,000 births a year from artificial insemination (Kantrowitz and Kaplan, 1990).

During ovulation, semen is deposited by syringe near the cervical opening. The semen may come from the partner; if he has a low sperm count, several collections of semen may be taken and frozen, then collectively deposited in the woman's vagina, improving the odds of conception. If the partner had a vasectomy earlier, he may have had the semen frozen and stored in a sperm bank. If the man is sterile or has a genetically transferable disorder, **therapeutic donor insemination (TDI)** (also known as artificial insemination by donor [AID]) may be used. Anonymous donors—often medical students—are paid nominal amounts for their deposits of semen which may be used at once or frozen. Artificial insemination tends to produce males rather than females; in the general population, about 51 percent of the children born are male, but this figure reaches almost 60 percent when conception is achieved artificially. Artificial insemination has a success rate of about 60 percent for infertile couples.

Most doctors inseminate women at least twice during the preovulatory phase of their menstrual cycle; on the average, women who become pregnant have received inseminations over a period of two to four months (Curie-Cohen, 1979; Scott et al., 1990).

The practices of fertility clinics and sperm banks vary widely with respect to medical and genetic screening and limitations on the number of times a particular donor may be used. In a study by the Congressional Office of Technology Assessment in 1988, more than half the physicians surveyed said they did not screen donors for HIV. The commercial sperm banks surveyed did screen for HIV, however, as well as for most other sexually transmitted diseases (Gaines, 1990). There has been one reported case in the United States of a woman contracting HIV through donated semen (Chiasson, Stoneburner, and Joseph, 1990). The American Fertility Society (1990) has issued guidelines for screening semen donors for HIV. The Society has concluded that "under present circumstances the use of fresh semen for donor insemination is no longer warranted and that all frozen specimens should be quarantined for 180 days and the donor retested and found to be seronegative for HIV before the specimen is released." Although the viability of sperm is reduced by freezing, new techniques of cryopreservation minimize the deleterious effects (Shanis, Check, and Baker, 1989). Recent studies show that TDI with frozen semen can have a success rate comparable to that with fresh semen (Byrd et al., 1990; Scott et al., 1990).

GIFT and ZIFT

Another fertilization technique, **gamete intrafallopian transfer (GIFT),** may be recommended for couples who have no known reason for their infertility. In this process, sperm and eggs are collected from the parents and deposited together in the fallopian tube. In 1988, 892 live GIFT babies were delivered, including 159 sets of twins, 34 sets of triplets, 3 sets of quadruplets, and 1 set of quintuplets (Perlman, 1990).

In **ZIFT (zygote intrafallopian transfer),** eggs and sperm are united in a petri dish and then transferred to the fallopian tube to begin cell division. In 1988 there were 98 ZIFT babies, representing a success rate of about 20 percent (Perlman, 1990).

In Vitro Fertilization

In vitro fertilization (IVF) entails combining sperm and egg in a laboratory dish and subsequently implanting the blastocyst into the uterus of the mother or a surrogate. Sometimes the blastocyst is frozen and stored, to be implanted at a later date. The egg can come from the mother or from a donor. If it is a donor ovum, the donor may be artificially inseminated with the father's sperm and, the embryo removed from the donor and transplanted in the mother-to-be's uterus.

The first birth achieved through IVF occurred in 1978 in England. Successful pregnancies from this procedure have since come to term in the United States, Australia, the Netherlands, and several other countries. The number of IVF births is increasing every year. In 1988, 3,427 IVF babies were delivered in the United States. These procedures are all quite costly and must usually be repeated a number of times before viable pregnancy results. Varying success rates—from 12 to something over 20 percent—have been reported for IVF (Jones, 1989; Yulsman, 1990).

Surrogate Motherhood

The idea of one woman bearing a child for another is not new. In the Old Testament (Genesis 16:1–15), Abraham's wife Sarah, finding herself unable to conceive, arranged for her husband to impregnate her servant Hagar. These days the procedures are considerably more complex, and the issues are definitely cloudier.

For couples in which the woman cannot conceive, or can conceive (provide an ovum) but cannot carry a child because of uterine problems, **surrogate motherhood** may seem to be a blessing from heaven. To others it is a sexist practice, tantamount to baby-selling or "wombs for rent." Both Orthodox Judaism and Roman Catholicism flatly oppose it. Others object to surrogacy on the grounds that it has racist overtones: most couples who engage surrogate mothers are white and want a child who "looks like them." It might be cheaper and less troublesome ethically to adopt a child, especially a child from a foreign country or one with "special needs"; the adopted child, however, would most likely not be white (or Anglo). Undoubtedly a number of ethical and legal issues are raised. The most important of these, according to medical law expert Lori Andrews (1984), is "whether each feels the other side will keep its promises."

Some people question the motives of surrogate mothers. There have been cases of women having babies for their friends or even for their relatives. In 1991 a South Dakota woman became the first American "surrogate granny" when she was implanted with the fertilized ova of her daughter, who had been born without a uterus (Plummer and Nelson, 1991). Some women simply extend this kind of altruism to women they don't know. One surrogate mother sent the adoptive mother a poem (quoted in Kantrowitz et al., 1987): "Roses are red/Violets are blue/We're going to have a baby/Congratulations to you, too." A study of 125 surrogate candidates found their major motivations to be money (they are usually paid $10,000 to $25,000 or more), liking to be pregnant, and unreconciled birth traumas, such as abortion or relinquishing a child for adoption (Parker, 1983). In this country, several hundred (possibly as many as 500) children each year are born to surrogate mothers (Andrews, 1984; Woodward, 1987). A number of agencies now exist to match surrogates and couples, highlighting the commercial potential of surrogacy.

Well-publicized court battles involving surrogacy point to the need for some kind of regulation. In the celebrated "Baby M" case, after numerous legal twists and turns, the New Jersey Supreme Court ruled in 1988 that contracts involving surrogate motherhood in exchange for money were illegal. It also ruled that a woman could volunteer to become a surrogate as long as no money was paid and she was allowed to revoke her decision to give up the child. "We . . . restore the surrogate as mother of the child. She is not only the natural mother, but also the legal mother," the court wrote (cited in Hanley, 1988). The baby in question was allowed to remain in the custody of her biological father and his wife, a situation previously determined to be in the child's best interests. A lower court subsequently awarded the surrogate mother six hours a week of unsupervised visitation with the child.

In 1990, however, a California Superior Court judge denied a surrogate mother parental rights. In this case, the genetic mother (who had had a hysterectomy that did not remove her ovaries) and her husband contributed the egg and sperm for in vitro fertilization. The embryo was then transplanted in the uterus of the surrogate, who had contracted with the genetic parents to carry the fetus for $10,000. In delivering his ruling, the judge declared that the surrogate had served in the role of a foster parent. "I decline to split the child emotionally between two mothers," he said. He also urged the legislature to set guidelines that take the new medical technologies into consideration (Mydans, 1990).

Although many states have laws prohibiting women from taking payment in exchange for giving a child up for adoption, most have not as yet enacted legislation specifically relating to surrogacy. Exceptions are Nevada, which has legitimized surrogacy contracts involving payment, and Arkansas, which specifies that the couple who contract with the surrogate are the legal parents. Several other states have declared such contracts unenforceable, while at least one state is considering making surrogacy for pay a felony (Budiansky, 1988). Proposed legislation in other states would require all parties to undergo counseling and the surrogate and biological father to be screened for genetic and sexually transmitted diseases (Donovan, 1986). (See Andrews, 1984, for guidelines on choosing surrogacy.)

For some people involved in surrogacy, the outcome seems to be satisfying and joyful. One couple attended the delivery of their baby. The father wrote (Shapiro, 1987):

Finally the baby's head emerged. Lynne [his wife] looked over at me, her eyes glowing. The nurses were also smiling. "One more push, Martha," the doctor said, "Here it comes . . . and it's . . . a baby girl."

I couldn't tell if she was pretty or not. . . . Her mouth . . . was definitely familiar—exactly like one of my nieces.

Lynne had moved to Martha's side and was holding her hand. Martha turned toward her and said, "Lynne, go see your baby."

Adoption

The mother that carries you in her heart is your true mother.

Heather Guffee

It is estimated that a little over 2 percent of the American population is adopted (Samuels, 1990). Adoption is the traditionally acceptable alternative to pregnancy for infertile couples. In recent years, many Americans—married and single, childless or with children—have been choosing to adopt for other reasons as well. They may have concerns about overpopulation and the number of homeless children in the world. They may wish to provide families for older or disabled children. Although tens of thousands of parents and potential parents are currently waiting to adopt, there is a shortage of available healthy babies (especially healthy *white* babies) in this country. In 1970 the number of adoptions per year peaked at 175,000. Today the number has declined, owing to more effective birth control and an increase in the number of single mothers who choose to keep their children. The National Committee for Adoption estimates that there were over 60,000 adoptions by non-relatives in 1986; precise figures are unavailable, as the federal government has not kept statistics on adoptions since 1975 (Gibbs, 1989).

For domestic adoptions arranged by agencies, the wait for a healthy infant or toddler averages one to five years (Kennedy, 1984). Because of this relatively long waiting period, many couples (and some single women) are arranging their own adoptions with birth mothers, using newspaper advertisements and the help of lawyers or agencies specializing in "open" or "cooperative" adoptions (Caplan, 1990; Gibbs, 1989; Lord, 1987). In **open adoption,** the birth mother has an active role in selecting her child's new parents. She may choose to continue to have some form of contact with her child or the adoptive parents—anything from receiving pictures and an update on the child's birthday to having some type of visitation as a family friend.

The costs of open adoption tend to run between $6,000 and $20,000 or more, depending on lawyer and agency fees and the birth mother's expenses (if the state allows these to be covered by the adoptive parents). Adoption laws vary widely from state to state; six states prohibit private adoption, whereas California and Texas have laws that are considered quite supportive of it (Gibbs, 1989; see Caplan, 1990, for an absorbing and well-researched account of open adoption).

Many adoption experts agree that some form of open adoption is usually in the best interests of both the child and the birth parents. One study of sixty-eight parents who had given up their infants in closed adoption revealed that fifty still experienced the pain of loss ten to thirty-three years later, and fifty-six (82 percent) wished that they could reunite with their children when they reached adulthood (Sorosky, Baran, and Pannor, 1978). Adopted children have been disproportionately represented in mental health clinics. Some researchers suggest that this may be due to "genealogical bewilderment," a condition that may lead to learning disabilities and social dysfunction as a result of feeling cut off from one's roots (Theroux, 1990). Several states have now enacted laws allowing adoptees to get copies of their original birth certificates. Other states have set up voluntary registries to assist adoptees and biological parents who wish to meet each other.

Some professionals in the adoption field believe that it is not in the child's best interest to tell him or her of the adoption. Psychiatrist Dennis Donovan thinks that children should be given only the information they ask for (only if they ask) and no more. He believes that telling a child he or she was loved by the birth mother but was still given up blocks the child's ability to attach (cited in "At a Glance," 1990).

In addition to open adoptions, foreign adoptions are also increasingly favored. In 1987, more than 10,000 foreign-born children were admitted to the United States as immigrant orphans (Lewin, 1990). Over half of those adoptions were from Korea, the principal source of foreign children in recent years. During the last few years, however, foreign adoptions have declined somewhat because of the Korean government's efforts to phase out its foreign adoption program. Traditionally Koreans have been unwilling to adopt unrelated children because of the culture's strong emphasis on bloodlines, but as Korean attitudes change, more and more Korean orphans will stay in their birth country (Lewin, 1990). International adoption agencies are working to expand their programs in India, the Philippines, Colombia, and a number of other Asian and Latin American countries. For foreign adoptions, the waiting period is usually around a year, although it may be longer depending on the political climate of the country in question. The costs vary widely, depending on the number and kind of agencies involved and whether or not the parents travel to pick up their child.

Families with children from other cultures face challenges in addition to those faced by other adoptive families. There is usually little information about the birth parents and no opportunity for continued contact. Older children from foreign countries must deal with the loss of their birth parents and other significant people. They must also adjust to different customs, strange food, and a baffling new language. To combat a sense of rootlessness, many parents of foreign-born children endeavor to give them an understanding of their birth country and its culture. They often participate in supportive networks with other adoptive families.

Adoptive families face unique problems and stresses. They may struggle with the physical and emotional strains of infertility; they endure uncertainty and disappointment as they wait for their child; and they may have spent all their savings and then some in the process. Still, most adopting families report feeling greatly enriched by the experience (Brodzinsky and Huffman, 1988). One mother wrote (Sylviachild, 1984):

Adoption is another way of building families; for after our child is with us, the same issues of sleeping through the night, parent exhaustion, learning to parent, coping with the first fever, bad diaper rash, ear infections, enjoying, worrying, teaching and learning with our child, and all the other wonderful and frustrating parts of being a family occur whether we have adopted or given birth to our child.

Adopted children may feel uniquely loved. Suzanne Arms (1990) recounted, "When Joss was six, he was overheard explaining to a friend how special it was to be adopted. Apparently," she added, "he made a good case for it, because when his friend got home, he told his mother he wanted to be adopted so he could be special too." (See the Resource Center for organizations to contact about adoptions.)

❑ REPRODUCTIVE TECHNOLOGY

During the last twenty years we have witnessed an explosion of scientific and technological developments in the area of reproduction. In the wake of this explosion, we are left with legal, moral, and ethical questions unlike any that humanity has had to face before. Many of these questions have no apparent answer but only beget more questions. In 1987 the Vatican addressed many of these issues in a doctrinal statement entitled "Instruction on Respect for Human Life in Its Origin and on the

Most adoptive families feel greatly enriched by the experience of adoption, as witnessed by this proud big brother and his new sister.

Life is full of unfamiliar, even unprecedented relationships, and adopted or not, part of life is adjusting, seeing that diversity is enriching, even when it's not all good.

Phyllis Theroux

Union between man and woman is a creative act and has something divine about it. . . . The object of love is a creative union with beauty on both the spiritual and physical levels.

Plato, The Symposium

Dignity of Procreation: Replies to Certain Questions of the Day." It declared its moral opposition to a wide range of birth technologies, including embryo transfer, experiments with embryos, most forms of artificial insemination, and surrogate motherhood.

Combating Infertility

If your parents didn't have any children, there's a good chance that you won't have any.

Clarence Day

The concern with infertility that has swept the United States has created opportunities for scientific research and economic opportunism. The paramount value that many of us place on fertility—equating it with maturity, creativity, productivity, accomplishment, and the essence of our maleness or femaleness—has fueled the engine of reproductive technology. The techniques and technologies developed to achieve conception include fertility drugs, artificial insemination and the establishment of sperm banks, in vitro fertilization (including embryo freezing), surrogate motherhood, and embryo transplants.

Sex preselection techniques are also a subject of much interest, although consistently reliable methods for assuring the gender of one's choice do not yet exist. Research indicates that the odds may be swayed slightly (Glass and Ericsson, 1982; Hewitt, 1987; Whelan, 1986). In addition to the desire to bear children, the desire to bear *healthy* (perfect?) children has encouraged the development of new diagnostic technologies.

Diagnosing Abnormalities of the Fetus

Ultrasound examinations use high frequency sound waves to create a picture of the fetus in *utero*. The sound waves are transmitted through a quartz crystal; when they detect a change in the density, the sound waves bounce back to the crystal. The results are interpreted on a television-like screen; the picture is called a **sonogram.** Sonograms are used to determine fetal age and the location of the placenta; when used with amniocentesis, they help determine the fetus's position so that the needle may be inserted safely. Often, it is possible to determine the fetus's sex. More extensive ultrasound techniques can be used to gain further information if there is the possibility of a problem with the fetus's development. Although no problems in humans have been noted to result from ultrasound, high levels of ultrasound have created problems in animal fetuses.

In **amniocentesis,** amniotic fluid is withdrawn from the uterus with a long, thin needle inserted through the abdominal wall. The fluid is then examined for evidence of possible birth defects such as Down's syndrome, Tay-Sachs disease, spina bifida, and other conditions caused by chromosomal abnormalities. The sex of the fetus can also be determined. Eighty to 90 percent of amniocentesis tests are performed in cases of "advanced" maternal age, usually when the mother is over thirty-five. The test is performed at about sixteen weeks of gestation.

Alpha-feto protein (AFP) screening is a test (or series of tests) done on the mother's blood after sixteen weeks of gestation. It reveals neural tube defects such as anencephaly and spina bifida. It is much simpler than amniocentesis but sometimes yields false positive results (Samuels and Samuels, 1986). If the results are positive, other tests, such as amniocentesis or ultrasound, will be performed to confirm or negate the AFP screening findings.

Amniocentesis carries a slight risk (a ½ to 2 percent chance of fetal death, depending on how early in pregnancy the test is performed) (Brandenburg et al., 1990; Hanson et al., 1990; McCormack et al., 1990). For approximately 95 percent of women who undergo prenatal testing, the results are negative. The results of amniocentesis and AFP screening can't be determined, however, until approximately

FOCUS

Ethics of Reproductive Technology

The desire to have healthy, happy, beautiful children is understandable, basic, and human. But in the face of today's reproductive technology, many of us may have to search our souls for the answers to a number of ethical questions. When faced with infertility, the possibility of birth defects, or the likelihood of a difficult labor, we need to weigh the possible benefits of a given technique against the costs and risks involved. What are your feelings about the following reproductive issues?

□ *Fetal diagnosis:* If you (or your partner) were pregnant, would you choose to have ultrasound? Should ultrasound be used routinely in all pregnancies or only in selected cases, such as when the mother is over thirty-five or there is a suspected problem? When would you consider amniocentesis appropriate? Should all fetuses be electronically monitored during birth (entailing the attachment of electrodes to the infant's scalp *in utero*), or should this technique be reserved for problem births? Would you want your child to be routinely monitored in this way?

□ *Cesarean section:* How would you determine that C-section was necessary for yourself or your partner? Should vaginal delivery be attempted first? What if it were a breech birth? What if you (or your partner) had had a previous C-section?

□ *Artificial insemination and in vitro fertilization:* Should these techniques be available to anyone who wants

them? Under what circumstances, if any, would you use these techniques? What are the rights of *all* the parties involved: parents, donors, physicians, child? What are the embryo's or fetus's rights? For example, does a frozen embryo have the "right to life" if its parents die before it is implanted in a surrogate?

□ *Surrogate motherhood:* Should a woman be allowed to "carry" a pregnancy for a couple using father-donated sperm? Does it matter if profit is involved? Should a contract involving surrogate motherhood be legally binding? Whose rights should take precedence, those of the surrogate (who is the biological mother) or of the couple (which includes the biological father)? What are the child's rights? Who decides? Can you think of a circumstance when you might wish to have the services of a surrogate mother? Could you be a surrogate or accept your partner being one?

□ For all the preceding techniques, consider the following questions: Who is profiting (scientists, physicians, business people, donors, parents, children)? Who is bearing the greatest risks? How great are the costs—monetary and psychological—and who is paying them? What are the long-range goals of this technology? Are we "playing God?" How might this technology be abused? Are there certain techniques you think should be outlawed?

□ *Abortion:* When do you think human life begins? Do we ever have the right to take human life? Under

what conditions, if any, should abortion be permitted? Whenever the pregnant woman requests it? If there is a serious birth defect? If there is a minor birth defect (such as a shortened limb)? If the fetus is the "wrong" sex? If rape or incest led to the pregnancy? Under what conditions, if any, would you have an abortion or want your partner to have one? If you had an unmarried, pregnant teenage daughter, would you encourage her to have one?

□ *Tissue donation:* Is it appropriate to use the tissues or organs of human corpses for medical purposes? Is it appropriate to use aborted fetuses for tissue donation? For research?

□ *Life and death:* Is prolonging the life of an infant always the most humane choice? What if it also prolongs suffering? Should life be prolonged whenever possible, at all costs? Who decides?

□ *Fertility and fulfillment:* Do you think your reproductive values and feelings about your own fertility (or lack of it) are congruent with reality, given the world's population problems? For you, are there viable alternatives to conceiving or bearing a child? What are they? Would adoption be one alternative? Why?

For further discussion of these issues, see Corea, 1985; Lyon, 1985; Shelp, 1986; for a thoughtful discussion of reproductive technology from a feminist viewpoint, see Rowland, 1987; for a discussion of this topic with special reference to Canada, see Eichler, 1989.

twenty weeks of pregnancy; consequently, if the pregnancy is terminated through abortion at this stage, the process is likely to be physically and emotionally difficult.

A promising alternative to amniocentesis recently introduced in the United States is **chorionic villus sampling (CVS).** This procedure involves removal through the abdomen (by needle) or through the cervix (by catheter) of tiny pieces of the membrane that encases the embryo; it can be performed between nine and eleven weeks of pregnancy. The relative safety of CVS is still under study. In 32,000 procedures, there was a 1.9 percent miscarriage rate (Kolata, 1987). Some of these miscarriages, however, would have occurred anyway. An advantage of CVS is that it can yield results sooner than amniocentesis (Kolker, 1989).

If a fetus is found to be defective, it may be carried to term, aborted, or, in rare but increasing instances, surgically treated while still in the womb (Kolata, 1990). Gene therapy, in which defective enzymes in the genes of embryos are replaced by normal ones, is considered a challenging frontier of reproductive medicine (Lyon, 1985).

During childbirth, mothers and infants are likely to be attached to various types of monitoring machines. Studies have shown that while fetal monitoring is helpful in high-risk cases, it is generally not helpful in normal (low-risk) situations. The 1988 National Commission to Prevent Infant Mortality stated that although "sophisticated technologies and great expense can save babies born at risk . . ., the lack of access to health care, the inability to pay for health care, poor nutrition, unsanitary living conditions, and unhealthy habits such as smoking, drinking and drug use all threatened unborn children" (cited in Armstrong and Feldman, 1990).

☐ BEING PREGNANT

Pregnancy Tests

Chemical tests designed to detect the presence of **human chorionic gonadotropin (HCG),** a hormone secreted by the placenta, usually determine pregnancy approximately two weeks following a missed (or spotty) menstrual period. In the **agglutination test,** a drop of the woman's urine causes a test solution to coagulate if she is not pregnant; if she is pregnant, the solution will become smooth and milky in consistency. Home pregnancy tests to detect HCG may be purchased in most drugstores. The directions must be followed closely. Blood analysis can also be used to determine if a pregnancy exists. Although such tests diagnose pregnancy with better than 95 percent accuracy, no absolute certainty exists until a fetal heartbeat and movements can be detected or ultrasound is performed.

The first reliable physical sign of pregnancy can be distinguished about four weeks after a woman misses her period. By this time, changes in her cervix and pelvis are apparent during a pelvic examination. **Hegar's sign**—a softening of the uterus just above the cervix, which can be felt through the vagina—is particularly useful to the examiner. A slight purple hue colors the labia minora; the cervix also takes on a purple color rather than its usual pink.

The Pregnant Woman and Her Partner

A woman's feelings during pregnancy will vary dramatically according to who she is, how she feels about pregnancy and motherhood, whether the pregnancy was planned, whether she has a secure home situation, and many other factors. Her feelings may be ambivalent; they will probably change over the course of the pregnancy.

A woman's first pregnancy is especially important because it has traditionally symbolized her transition to maturity. Even as social norms change and it becomes more common and "acceptable" for women to defer childbirth until they've established a career or for them to choose not to have children, the significance of first pregnancy should not be underestimated. It is a major developmental milestone in the lives of mothers—and of fathers as well (Notman and Lester, 1988; Snarey et al., 1987; for male procreative consciousness, see Marsiglio, 1991).

A couple's relationship is likely to undergo changes during pregnancy. It can be a stressful time, especially if the pregnancy was unanticipated. Communication is especially important at this time, because each partner may have preconceived ideas about what the other is feeling. Both partners may have fears about the baby's well-being, the approaching birth, their ability to parent, and the ways in which the baby will interfere with their own relationship. All of these concerns are normal. Sharing them, perhaps in the setting of a prenatal group, can deepen and strengthen the relationship (Kitzinger, 1989). If the pregnant woman's partner is not supportive or if she does not have a partner, it is important that she find other sources of support—family, friends, women's groups—and that she not be reluctant to ask for help.

A pregnant woman's relationship with her own mother may also undergo changes. In a certain sense, becoming a mother makes a woman the equal of her own mother. She can now lay claim to being treated as an adult. Women who have depended on their mothers tend to become more independent and assertive as their pregnancy progresses. Women who have been distant, hostile, or alienated from their own mothers may begin to identify with their mothers' experience of pregnancy. Even women who have delayed childbearing until their thirties may be surprised to find their relationships with their mothers changing and becoming more "adult." Working through these changing relationships is a kind of "psychological gestation" that accompanies the physiological gestation of the fetus (Silver and Campbell, 1988).

The first **trimester** (three months) of pregnancy may be difficult physically for the expectant mother. She may experience nausea, fatigue, and painful swelling of the breasts. She may also have fears that she may miscarry or that the child will not be normal. Her sexuality may undergo changes, resulting in unfamiliar needs (for more, less, or differently expressed sexual love), which may in turn cause anxiety. Education about the birth process and her own body's functioning as well as support from partner, friends, relatives, and health-care professionals are the best antidotes to fear.

During the second trimester, most of the nausea and fatigue disappear, and the pregnant woman can feel the fetus move within her. Worries about miscarriage will probably begin to diminish, too, for the riskiest part of fetal development has passed. The pregnant woman may look and feel radiantly happy. She will very likely feel proud of her accomplishment and be delighted as her pregnancy begins to show. She may feel in harmony with life's natural rhythms. One mother wrote (in Jones, 1989):

I love my body when I'm pregnant. It seems round, full, complete somehow. I find that I am emotionally on an even keel throughout; no more premenstrual depression and upsets. I love the feeling that I am never alone, yet at the same time I am my own person. If I could always be five months pregnant, life would be bliss.

Some women, however, may be concerned about their increasing size. They may fear that they are becoming unattractive. A partner's attention and reassurance will ease these fears.

The third trimester may be the time of the greatest hardships in daily living. Water retention **(edema)** is a common problem during late pregnancy. Edema may cause swelling in the face, hands, ankles, and feet, but it can often be controlled by cutting down on salt and carbohydrates in the diet. If dietary changes do not help this condition, a pregnant woman should consult her physician. Her physical abilities are limited by her size. She may be forced by her employer to stop working (many public schools, for example, do not allow women to teach after their sixth month). A family dependent on the pregnant woman's income may suffer a severe financial crunch.

The woman and her partner may become increasingly concerned about the upcoming birth. Some women experience periods of depression in the month preceding their delivery; they may feel physically awkward and sexually unattractive.

Since mother is not all there is to any woman, once she becomes a mother, how does a woman weave the mother into her adult self?

Andrea Eagan

Predicting the Date of Birth. Everyone wants to know when his or her baby's going to be born. It is fairly simple to figure out the date: add seven days to the first day of the last menstrual period. Then subtract three months and add one year. For example, if a woman's last menstrual period began on July 17, 1992, add seven days (July 24). Next subtract three months (April 24). Then add one year. This gives the expected date of birth as April 24, 1993. Few births actually occur on the date predicted, but 60 percent of babies are born within five days of the predicted time.

Man is a rational animal, but only women can have babies.

Anonymous

Expectant parents may feel that the fetus is already a member of the family.

Many feel an exhilarating sense of excitement and anticipation marked by energetic bursts of industriousness. They feel that the fetus is a member of the family (Stanton, 1985). Both parents may begin talking to the fetus and "playing" with it by patting and rubbing the mother's belly.

The principal developmental tasks for the expectant mother may be summarized as follows (Valentine, 1982; also see Notman and Lester, 1988; Silver and Campbell, 1988; and Snarey et al., 1987):

❐ Development of an emotional attachment to the fetus
❐ Differentiation of the self from the fetus
❐ Acceptance and resolution of the relationship with the woman's own mother
❐ Resolution of dependency issues (generally involving parents or husband/partner)
❐ And, increasingly, evaluation of practical/financial responsibilities

And for the expectant father:

❐ Acceptance of the pregnancy and attachment to the fetus
❐ Evaluation of practical/financial responsibilities
❐ Resolution of dependency issues (involving wife/partner)
❐ Acceptance and resolution of the relationship with the man's own father

Fetal Development

Fertilization usually occurs when the ovum is in the fallopian tube. The **zygote** (fertilized ovum) begins to develop at once. During the first week, as it makes its way toward the uterus, the zygote's cells will divide once or twice a day, creating a **blastocyst.** The blastocyst then implants itself in the uterine wall, which has spent the past three weeks preparing for its arrival. Within nine months, a single cell will become the 6,000 billion cells that constitute a human being (see Figure 6.1).

What did you look like before you were conceived?

Zen Koan (Riddle)

FIGURE 6.1

Embryo and Fetus Growth

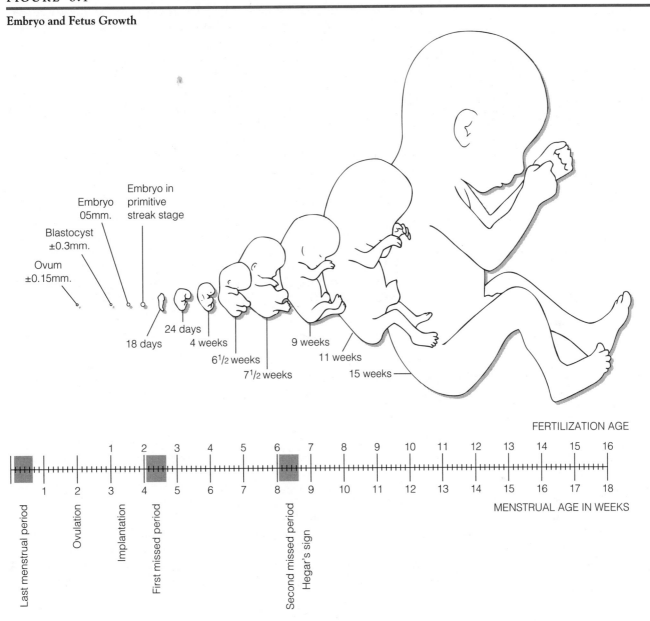

The blastocyst rapidly grows into an **embryo** (which will, in turn, become a **fetus** around the eighth week of development). During the third week of development, the first body segments and the brain begin to be formed. Heart, circulatory system, and digestive system develop in the fourth week. The fifth week sees the formation of arms and legs; the heart begins to pump blood. In the sixth week the eyes and ears form. At eight weeks the fetus is about the size of a thumb; its face and features begin to form, and its bones and internal organs develop. Arms, hands, fingers, legs, feet, toes, and eyes are almost fully developed at twelve weeks. At fifteen weeks, the fetus has a strong heartbeat, fair digestion, and active muscles. Most bones are developed by then, and the eyebrows appear. At this stage the fetus is covered with a fine, downy hair called **lanugo.**

Throughout its development, the fetus is nourished through the **placenta.** The placenta begins to develop from part of the blastocyst during the first week after fertilization. It grows larger as the fetus does, passing nutrients from the mother's bloodstream to the fetus, to which it is attached by the umbilical cord. The placenta serves as a biochemical barrier; it allows dissolved substances to pass to the fetus but blocks blood corpuscles and large molecules.

By five months, the fetus is ten to twelve inches long and weighs between one-half and one pound. The internal organs are well developed, although the lungs cannot function well outside the uterus. At six months, the fetus is eleven to fourteen inches long and weighs more than a pound. At seven months, it is thirteen to seventeen inches long, weighing about three pounds. At this point, most healthy fetuses are viable—that is, capable of surviving outside the womb (although some fetuses are viable at five or six months, they require specialized care to survive). The fetus spends the final two months of gestation growing rapidly. At term (nine months), it will be about twenty inches long and weigh about seven pounds. (Photographs on pages 158–159 show embryonic and fetal development.)

Complications of Pregnancy

Usually, pregnancy proceeds without major complications. Good nutrition is one of the most important factors in having a complication-free pregnancy. However, some women experience minor to serious complications, which we discuss here.

THE PLACENTA AND HARMFUL SUBSTANCES. Substances other than nutrients may reach the developing embryo or fetus through the placenta. Although few extensive studies have been done on the subject, toxic substances in the environment may affect the health of the fetus. Whatever a woman eats or drinks is eventually received by the embryo or fetus in some proportion. A fetus's blood-alcohol level, for example, is equal to that of the mother (Rosenthal, 1990).

Studies have linked chronic ingestion of alcohol during pregnancy to **fetal alcohol syndrome (FAS),** which can include unusual facial characteristics, small head and body size, congenital heart defects, defective joints, poor mental capabilities, and abnormal behavior patterns. Lesser amounts of alcohol may result in **fetal alcohol effect (FAE),** the most common problem of which is growth retardation (Waterson and Murray-Lyon, 1990). The Centers for Disease Control estimate that more than 8,000 alcohol-affected babies are born every year in this country (2.7 babies out of every 1,000). Some studies place the figure much higher—as high as 50,000 alcohol-affected births per year (Getlin, 1989). The Centers for Disease Control also report that FAS is six times more common in African Americans than in whites and thirty times more common in Native Americans (Rosenthal, 1990). (Studies have also found that African-American and Latina women are more likely to abstain from alcohol than white women and that a woman's level of alcohol consumption rises with her education and income [Rosenthal, 1990].) Most experts counsel pregnant women to abstain entirely from alcohol because there is no safe dosage known at this time.

Mothers who regularly use opiates (heroin, morphine, codeine, and opium) are likely to have infants who are addicted at birth. Cocaine—especially in the smokeable "crack" form—can cause devastating birth defects. A study in New York of drug-exposed infants revealed that the opiate-exposed babies showed more neuro-logical damage than the cocaine-exposed babies and that those infants exposed to polydrug abuse (both opiates and cocaine) were worse off than those exposed to any single drug in terms of gestational age at birth, birthweight, and length of hospital stay (Kaye et al., 1989). A 1989 study in Rhode Island found that 35 (7.5 percent) out of the 465 women in labor who were studied had drug traces in their urine (Centers for Disease Control, 1990). (The urine samples were provided to the Department of Health without names to protect the women's anonymity, although various demographic data were supplied.)

Cigarette smoking affects the unborn child as well. Babies born to women who smoke during pregnancy are an average of one-fourth to one-half pound lighter at birth than babies born to nonsmokers. Smoking has been implicated in sudden infant death syndrome, respiratory disorders in children, and various adverse pregnancy outcomes, but there is controversy about the extent of damage done by tobacco and the mechanisms by which it occurs (Abel, 1984; Enkin, 1984).

Prescription drugs should be used only under strict medical supervision, as some may cause serious harm to the fetus. Isotretinoin (Acutane), a popular anti-acne drug, has been implicated in over 1,000 cases of severe birth defects over the past several years (Kolata, 1988). Vitamins, aspirin, and other over-the-counter drugs, as well as large quantities of caffeine-containing food and drink (coffee, tea, colas, chocolate) should be avoided or used only under medical supervision. Vitamin A in large doses can cause serious birth defects.

INFECTIOUS DISEASES. Infectious diseases can also damage the fetus. If a woman contracts German measles (rubella) during the first three months of pregnancy, her child may be born with physical or mental disabilities. Immunization against rubella is available, but it must be done before the woman is pregnant. Sexually transmitted diseases may also damage the fetus. In 1988, the Centers for Disease Control recommended that all pregnant women be screened for hepatitis-B, a virus that can be passed to the infant at birth. If the mother tests positive, her child can be immunized immediately following birth (Moore, 1988). A woman with gonorrhea may expose her child to blindness from contact with the infected vagina; the baby will need immediate antibiotic treatment. A woman with HIV or AIDS has a 30 to 40 percent chance of passing the virus to the fetus via the placenta (Fischl et al., 1987). The number of infants with HIV is increasing as more women become infected before or during pregnancy. In 1989 there were 547 HIV-positive newborns, a 38 percent increase over the previous year (Cowley, 1990). Nationwide, more than 1,600 children have AIDS; three times that number are estimated to be infected with HIV ("AIDS and Children," 1989). Not all newborns who test positive for HIV go on to develop AIDS; some "reconvert" to negative status once their mother's blood is no longer in their system.

The increasingly widespread incidence of genital herpes may present some hazards for newborns. The herpes simplex virus may cause brain damage and is potentially life-threatening for these infants. Careful monitoring by a physician can determine whether or not a vaginal delivery should take place. Charles Prober (1987) and colleagues at the Stanford Medical School have extensively studied births to mothers with herpes. They found that a number of infants born to infected mothers had herpes antibodies in their blood; these infants did not contract herpes during vaginal delivery. Although the harmful potential of neonatal herpes should not be underestimated, if the appropriate procedures are followed by the infected mother and her physician or midwife, the chance of infection from genital lesions is minimal (Dr. Margaret Yonekura in "Neonatal Herpes . . . ," 1984). The Centers for

a

b

c

d

Disease Control estimate the incidence of neonatal herpes to be 400 to 1,000 cases
annually (Stone et al., 1989). An initial outbreak of herpes can be dangerous if the
woman is pregnant; the virus may be passed through the placenta to the fetus. In
rare cases, herpes-infected infants may be born to mothers who show no symptoms
themselves. This indicates that undiagnosed intrauterine herpes infections may be
passed to the fetus (Stone et al., 1989).

e

a. After ejaculation, several million sperm move through the cervical mucus toward the fallopian tubes; an ovum has descended into one of the tubes. En route to the ovum, millions of sperm are destroyed in the vagina, uterus, or fallopian tubes. Some go the wrong direction in the vagina and others swim into the wrong tube.

b. The ovum has divided for the first time following fertilization, the mother's and father's chromosomes have united. In subsequent cell divisions the genes will be identical. After about a week, the blastocyst will implant itself into the uterine lining.

c. The embryo is five weeks old and is two-fifths of an inch long. It floats in the embryonic sac. The major divisions of the brain can be seen as well as an eye, hands, arms, and a long tail.

d. The embryo is now seven weeks old and is almost an inch long. Its outer and inner organs are developing. It has eyes, a nose, mouth, lips, and tongue.

e. At twelve weeks, the fetus is over three inches long and weighs almost an ounce.

f. At sixteen weeks, the fetus is more than six inches long and weighs about seven ounces. All its organs have been formed. The time that follows is now one of simple growth.

f

Once the baby is born, a mother who is experiencing a herpes outbreak should wash her hands often and carefully and not permit contact between her hands, contaminated objects, and the baby's mucous membranes (inside of eyes, mouth, nose, penis, vagina, and rectum). If the father is infected, he should do likewise until the lesions have subsided.

ECTOPIC PREGNANCY. In **ectopic pregnancy** (tubal pregnancy), the incidence of which has more than quadrupled in the last twenty years, the fertilized egg implants itself in the fallopian tube. Generally this occurs because the tube is obstructed, most often as a result of pelvic inflammatory disease (Hilts, 1990a). The pregnancy will never come to term. The embryo may spontaneously abort, or the embryo and placenta will continue to expand until they rupture the fallopian tube. **Salpingectomy** (removal of the tube) and abortion of the embryo or fetus may be necessary to save the mother's life.

TOXEMIA AND ECLAMPSIA. **Toxemia,** which may appear in the twentieth to twenty-fourth week of pregnancy, is characterized by high blood pressure and edema (fluid retention and swelling). It can generally be treated through nutritional means. If untreated, toxemia can develop into **preeclampsia** after the twenty-fourth week.

Preeclampsia is characterized by increasingly high blood pressure. These conditions are also known as **gestational edema-proteinuria-hypertension complex.** If untreated they can lead to **eclampsia,** maternal convulsions that pose a serious threat to mother and child. Eclampsia is not common; it is prevented by keeping the blood pressure down through diet, rest, and sometimes medication. It is important for a pregnant woman to have her blood pressure checked regularly.

LOW BIRTH WEIGHT. Prematurity or **low birth weight (LBW)** is a major complication in the third trimester of pregnancy, affecting about 7 percent of newborns yearly (over 260,000 in 1987) in the United States (U.S. Bureau of the Census, 1990). The most fundamental problem of prematurity is that many of the infant's vital organs are insufficiently developed. An LBW baby usually weighs less than 5.5 pounds at birth. Most premature infants will grow normally, but many will experience disabilities. LBW infants are subject to various respiratory problems as well as infections. Feeding, too, is a problem because the infants may be too small to suck a breast or bottle, and their swallowing mechanisms may be too underdeveloped to permit them to drink. As premature infants get older, problems such as low intelligence, learning difficulties, poor hearing and vision, and physical awkwardness may become apparent.

Premature delivery is one of the greatest problems confronting obstetrics today. About half the cases are related to teenage pregnancy, smoking, poor nutrition, and poor health in the mother (Schneck et al, 1990); the causes of the other half are unknown. One study of LBW babies found a six-fold increase in the risk of low birthweight if the mother had financial problems during pregnancy (Binsacca et al., 1987). (A 1987 study of 1,382 women indicated that delaying childbearing until after age thirty-five does *not* increase the risk of delivering an LBW infant [Barkan and Bracken, 1987].)

Prenatal care is extremely important as a means of preventing prematurity (Rush et al., 1988). A third of all LBW births could be averted with adequate prenatal care (Scott, 1990b). For this reason, the federal government's reduction or elimination of supplemental assistance for pregnant women on welfare has created alarm among many health professionals. Marian Wright Edelman, president of the

Children's Defense Fund, blames the government for a "lack of very basic supports" (quoted in "U.S. Assailed on Infant Mortality," 1987). We need to understand that if children's needs are not met today, we will all face the consequences of their deprivation tomorrow. The social and economic costs are bound to be very high.

☐ PREGNANCY LOSS

The loss of a child through miscarriage, stillbirth, or death during early infancy is often a devastating experience that has been largely ignored in our society. The statement, "You can always have another one," may be meant as consolation, but it is particularly chilling to the ears of a grieving mother. In the past few years, however, the medical community has begun to respond to the emotional needs of parents who have lost a pregnancy or an infant.

Spontaneous Abortion

Spontaneous abortion (miscarriage) is a powerful natural selective force toward bringing healthy babies into the world. About one out of four women is aware she has miscarried at least once (Beck, 1988). Studies indicate that at least 60 percent of all miscarriages are due to chromosomal abnormalities in the fetus (Adler, 1986). Furthermore, as many as three-fourths of all fertilized eggs do not mature into viable fetuses (Beck, 1988). A recent study found that 32 percent of implanting embryos miscarry (Wilcox et al., 1988). The first sign that a pregnant woman may miscarry is vaginal bleeding ("spotting"). If a woman's symptoms of pregnancy disappear and she develops pelvic cramps, she may be miscarrying; the fetus is usually expelled by uterine contractions. Most miscarriages occur between the sixth and eighth weeks of pregnancy (Welch and Herman, 1980). Evidence is increasing that certain occupations involving exposure to chemicals increase the likelihood of spontaneous abortions (Hemminki et al., 1983).

Infant Mortality

The U.S. infant mortality rate has halted its decreasing trend and seems to be stabilized at approximately 11 deaths per 1,000 births (U.S. Bureau of the Census, 1988). Nevertheless, among developed nations, our country ranks twenty-second for low infant mortality (Hilts, 1990b). (This means that twenty-one countries have *lower* infant mortality rates than the United States.) In some inner-city areas such as Detroit, Washington, D.C., and parts of Oakland (California), the infant mortality rate approaches that of nonindustrialized countries, with more than 20 deaths per 1,000 births (Petit, 1990). Approximately 40,000 American babies less than one year old die each year. Most of these infants are victims of the poverty that often results from racial or ethnic discrimination. Up to a third of these deaths could be prevented if mothers were given adequate health care (Scott, 1990a). The infant mortality rate for African Americans is almost twice that for whites. Native Americans are also at high risk; for example, about one out of every 67 Navajo infants dies each year (Wilkerson, 1987). Since 1981, the federal government has dramatically cut pregnancy and infant care programs such as WIC (Women, Infants, and Children) programs to fund its record-breaking military budget. Medicaid and Aid to Families with Dependent Children have also been cut, leaving many families without pre- or postnatal care. On the state level also, the current trend is to cut back on medical and health care for low-income people. In countries such as

France, Sweden, and Japan, for example, all pregnant women are entitled to free prenatal care. Free health care and immunizations are also provided for infants and young children. Working Swedish mothers are guaranteed one year of paid maternal leave, and French families in need are paid regular government allowances (Scott, 1990a). Although the United States has the resources to support its mothers and children in similar ways, such programs are few and far between. We are one of the wealthiest countries in the world, but our families do not necessarily reap the benefits suggested by that wealth.

Although many infants die of poverty-related conditions, others die from **congenital** problems (conditions appearing at birth) or from infectious diseases, accidents, or other causes. Sometimes the causes of death are not apparent; in 1985, one out of every 378 infant deaths was attributed to **sudden infant death syndrome (SIDS),** a particularly perplexing phenomenon wherein an apparently healthy infant dies suddenly while sleeping.

Coping with Loss

The depth of shock and grief felt by many who lose an infant before or during birth is sometimes difficult to understand for those who have not had a similar experience. What they may not realize is that most women form a deep attachment to their children even before birth. At first, the attachment may be a "fantasy image of [the] future child" (Friedman and Gradstein, 1982). During the course of the pregnancy, the mother forms an actual acquaintance with her infant through the physical sensations she feels within her. Thus the death of the fetus can also represent the death of a dream and of a hope for the future. This loss must be acknowledged and felt before psychological healing can take place (Panuthos and Romeo, 1984).

Women (and sometimes their partners) who must face the loss of a pregnancy or a young infant generally experience similar stages in their grieving process. The feelings that are experienced are influenced by many factors: supportiveness of the partner and other family members, reaction of social networks, life circumstances at the time of the loss, circumstances of the loss itself, whether other losses have been experienced, the prognosis for future childbearing, and the woman's unique personality (Friedman and Gradstein, 1982). Physical exhaustion and, in the case of miscarriage, hormone imbalance often compound the emotional stress of the grieving mother. The initial stage of grief is often one of shocked disbelief and numbness. This stage gives way to sadness, spells of crying, preoccupation with the loss, and perhaps loss of interest in the rest of the world. Emotional pain may be accompanied by physical sensations and symptoms, such as tightness in the chest or stomach, sleeplessness, and loss of appetite. It is not unusual for parents to feel guilty as if they had somehow caused the loss, although this is rarely the case. Anger (toward the physician, perhaps, or God) is also a common emotion. (In Chapter 10, death and the grieving process are discussed at greater length.)

Experiencing the pain of loss is part of the healing process. This process takes time—months, a year, perhaps more for some. Support groups or counseling are often helpful, especially if healing does not seem to be progressing—if, for example, depression and physical symptoms don't appear to be diminishing. (See Resource Center for support groups.) Keeping active is another way to deal with the pain of loss, as long as it isn't a way to avoid facing feelings. Projects, temporary or part-time work, or travel (for those who can afford it) can be ways of renewing energy and interest in life. Planning the next pregnancy may be curative, too, keeping in mind that the body and spirit need some time to heal. It is important to have a physician's input before proceeding with another pregnancy; specific considerations

Dear Auntie will come with presents and will ask, "Where is our baby, sister?" And, Mother, you will tell her softly, "He is in the pupils of my eyes. He is in my bones and in my soul."

Rabindranath Tagore

may need to be discussed, such as a genetic condition that may be passed to the child or a physiological problem of the mother. If future pregnancies are ruled out, the parents need to take stock of their priorities and consider other options that may be open to them, such as adoption. Counselors and support groups can be invaluable at this stage.

◻ GIVING BIRTH

Labor and Delivery

Throughout a woman's pregnancy, she occasionally feels contractions of her uterus that are strong but usually not too painful. These are called **Braxton Hicks contractions.** They exercise the uterus, preparing it for labor. During labor these contractions also begin the **effacement** (thinning) and **dilation** (opening up) of the cervix. It is difficult to say exactly when labor starts, which helps explain the great differences reported in lengths of labor for different women. When the uterine contractions become regular, true labor begins. During these contractions, the lengthwise muscles of the uterus involuntarily pull open the circular muscles around the cervix. This process generally takes from two to thirty-six hours. Its duration depends on the size of the baby, the baby's position in the uterus, the size of the mother's pelvis, and the condition of the uterus. The length of labor tends to shorten after the first birth experience.

Labor can generally be divided into three stages (see Figure 6.2). The first stage is usually the longest, lasting from four to sixteen hours. An early sign of first-stage labor is the expulsion of a plug of slightly bloody mucus that has blocked the opening of the cervix during pregnancy. At the same time or later on, there is a second fluid discharge from the vagina. This discharge, referred to as the "breaking of the waters," is the **amniotic fluid,** which comes from the ruptured **amniotic membrane.** (Because the baby is subject to infection after the protective membrane breaks, the woman should receive medical attention soon thereafter, if she has not already.)

The contractions at the end of the first stage of labor, which is called **transition,** come more quickly and are much more intense. Many women report this as the most difficult part of labor. During the last part of first-stage labor, the baby's head enters the birth canal. This marks the shift from dilation of the cervical opening to expulsion of the infant. The cervix is now almost fully open, but the baby is not yet completely in position to be pushed out. Some women may feel despair, isolation, and anger at this point. Many appear to lose faith in those assisting in the birth. A woman may find that management of the contractions seems beyond her control; she may be afraid that something is wrong. At this time she needs the full support and understanding of her helpers. Transition is usually, though not always, brief (half an hour to one hour).

Second-stage labor begins when the baby's head moves into the birth canal and ends when the baby is born. During this time many women experience a great force in their bodies. Some women find this the most difficult part of labor. Others find that the contractions and bearing down bring a sense of euphoria. One father described his wife's second-stage labor (Jones, 1986):

When the urge to bear down swept through her, Jan felt as if she were one with all existence and connected with the vast primordial power that summons life forth from its watery depths.

The baby is usually born gradually. With each of the final few contractions, a new part of the infant emerges. The baby may even cry before he or she is com-

[Power] sounds in our bodies. Contractions creep up, seizing ever stronger until they make a mockery of all the work we have done on our own. Birth can silence our ego and, for the moment, we feel ourselves overcome by a larger life pounding through our own.

Penny Armstrong and Sheryl Feldman, A Wise Birth

FIGURE 6.2 (Opposite page)

Childbirth

During the last phase of pregnancy, the fetus usually settles in a head-down position. In the first stage of labor (a), Braxton Hicks contractions begin effacement and dilation of the cervix. When the cervix is fully dilated (b), the baby's head can enter the birth canal; usually the amniotic membrane has ruptured by this time. During second-stage labor (c), the baby moves through the birth canal and into the outside world. The soft bones of the head may be "molded" by pressure in the birth canal, resulting in a temporarily unusual appearance. The placenta (d), is expelled during third-stage labor.

pletely born, especially if the mother did not have medication. Sheila Kitzinger (1985) described the moment of birth as a sexual event:

. . . The whole body slips out in a rush of warm flesh, a fountain of water, a peak of overwhelming surprise and the little body is against her skin, kicking against her thighs or swimming up over her belly. She reaches out to hold her baby, firm, solid, with bright, bright eyes. A peak sexual experience, the birth passion, becomes the welcoming of a new person into life.

The baby will still be attached to the **umbilical cord** connected to the mother, which is not cut until it stops pulsating. He or she will appear wet, often covered by a milky substance called **vernix.** The head may look oddly shaped at first, from the molding of the soft plates of bone during birth. This shape is temporary, and the baby's head usually achieves a normal appearance within twenty-four hours.

After the baby has been delivered, the uterus will continue to contract, expelling the placenta (afterbirth) and completing the third and final stage of labor. The doctor or midwife will examine the placenta to make sure that it is whole. If the practitioner has any doubt that the entire placenta has been expelled, he or she may examine the uterus to make sure no parts of the placenta remain to cause adhesions or hemorrhage.

For a few days following labor (especially if it is a second or subsequent birth), the mother will probably feel strong contractions as the uterus begins to return to its prebirth size and shape. This process, called **involution,** takes about six weeks. She will also have a bloody discharge called **lochia,** which continues for several weeks.

Choices in Childbirth

HOSPITAL BIRTH. The impersonal, routine quality of hospital birth is increasingly being questioned. As Margaret Mead observed, hospital conditions have generally been designed not for the woman who is giving birth but "primarily to facilitate the ministrations of the obstetrician" (Mead, 1975). One woman described her initial feelings in the hospital (in Leifer, 1990):

When they put that tag around my wrist and put me into that hospital gown, I felt as if I had suddenly just become a number, a medical case. All of the excitement that I was feeling on the way over to the hospital began to fade away. It felt like I was waiting for an operation, not about to have my baby. I felt alone, totally alone, as if I had just become a body to be examined and not a real person.

Another woman was shocked at the impersonal treatment (in Leifer, 1990):

And then this resident gave me an internal [examination], and it was quite painful then. And I said: "Could you wait till the contraction is over?" And he said he had to do it now, and I was really upset because he didn't even say it nicely, he just said: "You'll have to get used to this, you'll have a lot of this before the baby comes."

Some hospitals are responding to the need for a family-centered childbirth. The father does not necessarily need to handcuff himself to the delivery table to be present during the birth. Indeed, fathers may often participate today. Nor do the mother and the infant always need to be separated immediately after birth. Hospitals may permit rooming-in (the baby stays with the mother rather than in the nursery) or a modified form of rooming-in. Regulations vary as to when the father and other family members and friends are allowed to visit. Some hospitals restrict visits to specific visiting hours, even if the mother and the child are in the same room.

But the norm is still all too often the impersonal birth. During one of the most profound experiences of her life, a woman may have her baby among strangers to

Before birth.

Placenta
Amniotic sac
Umbilical cord

Bladder
Cervix
Vagina

a

b

c

d

whom birth is merely routine. She will probably be given a routine enema and have her pubic hair shaved, even though surgery is not anticipated. She and her unborn child will likely be wired to beeping machines. During delivery, she will probably be given an **episiotomy** (a surgical procedure enlarging the vaginal opening by cutting through the perineum toward the anus), whether or not it is actually needed. A recent study of a large inner-city hospital revealed an episiotomy rate of 80 percent (Hetherington, 1990); yet one midwife who has assisted at over 1,200 births reported a rate of less than 1 percent (Armstrong and Feldman, 1990). Some form of anesthetic will be administered in most cases, as well as various hormones (to intensify the contractions and to shrink the uterus after delivery). The mother isn't the only recipient of the drugs, however; they go directly through the placenta to the baby, in whom they may reduce heart and respiration rates.

The baby is usually delivered on a table, against the force of gravity. He or she may be pulled from the womb with forceps. In most cultures, a woman gives birth while sitting in a birthing chair, kneeling or squatting. Until the present century, most American women used birthing chairs; the delivery table was instituted for the convenience of the physician. A few hospitals use a motorized birthing chair that can be raised, lowered, or tilted according to the physician's and the woman's needs.

Following birth, the baby is generally taken to a nursery and is diapered and clothed, his or her first lesson, observed Margaret Mead (1975), "in expecting cloth to intervene between one body and the next." If the baby has not been drugged, his or her lips are ready for sucking, seeking the breast that is not there. If the infant is a boy, the foreskin of the penis may be cut off within the next day or two (see p. 170 for discussion of circumcision). During the next two or three days, the infant will be brought to the mother at scheduled intervals for feeding and visiting. In the last few years, some hospitals have tried to comply with mothers' wishes for "demand" feeding (when the baby feels hungry, as opposed to when the hospital wants to feed the child), but because most hospital maternity wards are busy places, they often find it difficult to meet the individual needs of many infants and mothers. If the mother is breastfeeding, a rigid hospital schedule can make it difficult for her to establish a feeding routine with her child.

Childbirth does not have to be this way. Increasingly, Americans are choosing alternatives of prepared childbirth, rooming-in, birthing centers, home births, and midwives. The chief of obstetrics at a major hospital observed, "It's a major upheaval in medicine, and the conflict has tended to polarize the consumer and the care giver. The basic problem is that we have changed obstetrics with the latest medical advances and not incorporated essentially humanistic considerations" (Trafford, 1980; see Pallow-Fleury, 1983, for questions to ask about a hospital's birth policies).

CESAREAN SECTION. **Cesarean section** (C-section) is the removal of the fetus by an incision in the mother's abdominal and uterine walls. The first reported cesarean section performed on a living woman occurred in the seventeenth century, when a butcher cut open his wife's uterus to save her and their child. In 1970, 5.5 percent of American births were done by cesarean section. Today cesarean births account for about 24 percent of all births; more than 900,000 women have C-sections each year (U.S. Bureau of the Census, 1990). This represents more than a 400 percent increase in twenty years.

Although there is a decreased mortality rate for infants born by C-section, the mothers' mortality rate is higher. As with all major surgeries, there are possible complications, and recovery can be slow and difficult.

Hoping to reduce the alarming increase in C-sections, the National Institutes of Health have issued the following guidelines:

❒ Because a woman has had a previous cesarean delivery does not mean that subsequent deliveries must be C-sections; whenever possible, women should be given the option of vaginal birth.

❒ Abnormal labor does not mean that a C-section is necessary. Sleep or medication may resolve the problems. Only after other measures have been tried should a physician perform a cesarean, unless the infant is clearly in danger.

❒ Breech babies (those who enter the birth canal buttocks or feet first) do not necessarily require C-sections. A physician's experience using his or her hands to deliver the baby vaginally is crucial.

If a woman does not want a C-section unless it is absolutely necessary, she should learn about her physician's attitude and record on cesareans. It is noteworthy that the greatest number of cesareans are performed in the socioeconomic group of women with the lowest medical risk (Hursh and Summey, 1984). In a study of 245,854 births, the C-section rate for middle- and upper-income women was 22.9 percent, whereas for lower-income women it was 3.2 percent (Gould et al., 1989). Therefore, it is assumed that cesareans are often performed for reasons other than medical risk. Some of the reasons offered include threat of malpractice (although such suits are apparently rare for vaginal deliveries), lack of physician training in vaginal births, and "economic incentives" for the hospital and the physician (Cohen and Estner, 1983). A 1987 international study by the U.S. Department of Health and Human Services urged the medical community to consider the appropriateness of the continued rise in C-sections (Notzon et al., 1987).

THE MEDICALIZATION OF CHILDBIRTH. In this century, American childbirth has moved from the home to the hospital. It has, for the most part, moved from the hands of female midwives to the hands (and instruments) of male doctors. Although only 5 to 10 percent of births actually require medical procedures, we seem to assume that childbirth is an inherently dangerous process. Of course, in high-risk cases, the advances of technology can and do save lives. But the questions remain: Why do women accept unnecessary, uncomfortable, demeaning, and even dangerous intervention in the birth process? Why do they tolerate a 24 percent cesarean rate, a 61 percent episiotomy rate, the almost universal administration of drugs, and the use of intrusive fetal monitoring—not to mention routine enemas and shaving of pubic hair? Why do they allow their infant boys to have their penises surgically altered? Why do they accept, often without question, the physician's opinion over their own gut feelings?

Penny Armstrong and Sheryl Feldman (1990) suggest that society's increasing dependence on technology has hampered women's ability to view birth as a natural process for which they are naturally equipped. Women have allowed themselves to be persuaded that technology can do the job better than they can on their own. Society expects birth technology to deliver a "product"—a "perfect" baby—without understanding that nature has already equipped women to deliver that product without much outside interference in the physical process (although encouragement and emotional support are paramount). Sheila Kitzinger (1989) writes:

It is not advances in medicine but improved conditions, better food and general health which have made childbirth much safer for mothers and babies today than it was 100 years ago. The rate of stillbirths and deaths in the first week of life is directly related to a country's gross national product and to the position of the mother in the social class.

The idea that the pain of childbirth is to be avoided at all costs is a relatively new one. When Queen Victoria accepted ether during labor in 1853, she undoubtedly had little idea of the precedent she was setting. It was, in fact, the increasing use of anesthesia in the nineteenth century that brought childbirth into the hospital. While today's advocates of "natural" childbirth do not deny that there is pain involved, they do argue that it is a different pain from that of injury and that normally it is worth experiencing. This "pain with a purpose" is an intrinsic part of the birth process (Kitzinger, 1989). To obliterate it with drugs is to obliterate the mother's awareness and the baby's as well, depressing the child's breathing, heart rate, and general responsiveness in the process.

Another aspect of dependence on technology is that we get the feeling we are omnipotent and should be able to solve any problem. Thus if something goes wrong with a birth—if a child is stillborn or has a disability—we look around for something or someone to blame. We have become unwilling to accept that some aspects of life and death are beyond human control.

Prospective parents face a daunting array of decisions. The more informed they are, however, the better able they will be to decide what is right for them. According to Armstrong and Feldman (1990):

Teaching women that they have say—whether they consciously exercise it or not—is a major educational undertaking, one that requires breaking the hold obstetrical medicine has on the American imagination and helping women to rediscover their natural power at birth.

. . . in the 19th century, the possibility of eliminating "pain and travail" created a new kind of prison for women—the prison of unconsciousness, of numbed sensations, or amnesia, and complete passivity.

Adrienne Rich, Of Woman Born

Women can give birth by the action of their own bodies, as animals do. Women can enjoy the process of birth and add to their dignity by being educated to follow the example set by instinctive animals.

Dr. Robert A. Bradley

PREPARED CHILDBIRTH. **Prepared childbirth** (or natural childbirth) was popularized by Grantly Dick-Read (1972) in the first edition of his book *Childbirth Without Fear* in the 1930s. Dick-Read observed that fear causes muscles to tense, which in turn increases pain and stress in childbirth. He taught both partners about childbirth and gave them physical exercises to ease muscle tension. Encouraged by Dick-Read's ideas, women began to reject anesthetics during labor and delivery and were consequently able to take a more active role in childbirth as well as be more aware of the process.

In the 1950s, Fernand Lamaze (1956, 1970) developed a method of prepared childbirth based on knowledge of conditioned reflexes. Women learn to mentally separate the physical stimulus of uterine contractions from the conditioned response of pain. With the help of a partner, women use breathing and other exercises throughout labor and delivery. Although Lamaze did much to advance the cause of prepared childbirth, he has been criticized by other childbirth educators as too controlling or even "repressive" according to Armstrong and Feldman (1990). One does not give birth, they write, "by direction, as if it were a flight plan."

Prepared childbirth, then, is not so much a matter of controlling the birth process as of understanding it and having confidence in nature's plan. "One attends one's physiological voice," write Armstrong and Feldman (1990). "One credits the information coming from one's body and one's psyche; one follows one's impulses." Michael Odent, who heads a remarkable maternity clinic in Pithiviers, France, believes strongly that laboring mothers should be allowed freedom to give birth in their own ways. In *Birth Reborn* (1984) he writes:

We encourage women in labor to give in to the experience, to lose control, to forget all they have learned—all the cultural images, all the behavioral patterns. The less a woman has learned about the "right" way to have a child, the easier it will be for her.

Clinical studies consistently show better birth outcomes for mothers who have had prepared childbirth classes (Conway, 1980). Prepared mothers (who usually attend classes with the father or other partner) handle pain more successfully, use less medication and anesthesia, express greater satisfaction with the childbirth process, and experience less postpartum depression than women undergoing routine hospital births (Hetherington, 1990).

BIRTHING ROOMS AND CENTERS. Birth (or maternity) centers, institutions of long standing in England and other European countries (see Odent, 1984), now are being developed in the United States. In 1990 there were 132 free-standing birth centers in this country (Armstrong and Feldman, 1990). Although they vary in size, organization, and orientation, birth centers share the view that childbirth is a normal, healthy process that can be assisted by skilled practitioners (midwives or physicians) in a homelike setting. The mother (or couple) has considerable autonomy in deciding the conditions of birth—lighting, sounds, visitors, delivery position, and so on. Some of these centers can provide some kinds of emergency care; all have procedures for transfer to a hospital if necessary.

An extensive survey of 11,814 births in birth centers in 1988 concluded that "birth centers offer a safe and acceptable alternative to hospital confinement for selected pregnant women, particularly those who have previously had children, and that such care leads to relatively few cesarean sections" (Rooks et al., 1989). Another large study showed that free-standing birth centers are associated with "a low cesarean section rate, low neonatal mortality [or] no neonatal mortality" (Eakins, 1989). Some hospitals now have their own birthing centers (or rooms) that provide for labor and birth in a comfortable setting and allow the mother or couple considerable autonomy. Hospital practices vary widely, however; prospective parents should carefully determine their needs and thoroughly investigate their options.

HOME BIRTH. Home births have increased during the last two decades, although they still constitute a small fraction of total births, amounting to not quite 2 percent, according to available data. Home births tend to be safer than hospital births if they are supervised by midwives or physicians. This is, in part, the result of careful medical screening and planning that eliminate all but the lowest-risk pregnancies. A couple can create their own birth environment at home, and home births cost considerably less, usually at least one-third less, than hospital delivery. With the supervision of an experienced practitioner, a couple have little to worry about. But if a woman is at risk, she is wiser to give birth in a hospital where medical equipment is readily available.

MIDWIFERY. The United States has an increasing number of certified nurse-midwives who are trained not only as registered nurses but also in obstetrical techniques. They are well qualified for routine deliveries and minor medical emergencies. They also often operate as part of a total medical team that includes a backup physician, if needed. Their fees are generally considerably less than a doctor's. Nurse-midwives usually participate in both hospital and home births, although this may vary according to hospital policy, state law, and the midwives' preference. (Massachusetts, Alabama, South Dakota, and Wisconsin bar nurse-midwives—although not necessarily lay midwives—from attending home births ["Massachusetts Midwife . . .," 1987].)

Lay midwifery, in which the midwives are not formally trained by the medical establishment but by other experienced midwives, has also increased in popularity in the past two decades. Many satisfactory births with lay midwives in attendance have been reported, but extensive, reliable information is not available, owing to the "underground" nature of lay midwifery, which is often practiced outside of (and without the support of) the regular practice of medicine. Many midwives belong to organized groups; a number of these groups use some form of self-certification to insure that high professional standards are maintained (Butter and Kay, 1990).

If a woman decides she wants to give birth with the aid of a midwife outside a hospital setting, she should have a thorough medical screening to make sure she or her infant will not be at risk during delivery. She should learn about the midwife's training and experience, what type of backup services the midwife has in the event of complications or emergencies, and how the midwife will handle a transfer to a hospital if it becomes necessary.

The Question of Circumcision

In 1975, the American Academy of Pediatrics and the American College of Obstetricians and Gynecologists issued a statement declaring that there is "no absolute medical indication" for routine circumcision. This surgical operation, which involves slicing and removing the sleeve of skin (foreskin) that normally covers the glans penis, has been performed routinely on newborn boys in the United States since the 1930s (Romberg, 1985). Circumcision is often done without anesthesia. It is obviously painful; in some tribal societies it is performed to initiate boys into the harsh realities of manhood. It carries medical risks in 4 to 28 percent of the cases (Samuels and Samuels, 1986). The principal risks are excessive bleeding, infection, and faulty surgery. It can be life-threatening.

In spite of the fact that it is not a medical necessity, almost 60 percent of newborn boys were circumcised in 1985, according to the National Center for Health Statistics. Although this represents a substantial drop from an estimated 93 percent being circumcised in 1975, it still places the United States far ahead of other Western countries, which circumcise less than 1 percent of their newborn boys. The exception is Israel; in Judaism the ritual circumcision, the *bris*, is an important religious event. Circumcision has religious significance for Moslems as well (Bullough, 1976).

Besides religious reasons, the other reasons given by parents for circumcising their infants are "cleanliness" and "so he'll look like his dad." A circumcised penis is not necessarily any cleaner than an intact one. Infants do not require cleaning under their foreskins (Brody, 1985); adults do, but it is no more difficult to wash under one's foreskin than behind one's ears. If reasonable cleanliness is observed, an intact penis poses no more threat of disease to a man's sexual partner than a circumcised one would. As for "looking like dad," most parents can probably find ways to keep their son's self-esteem intact along with his foreskin. There is no evidence we know of to suggest that little boys are seriously traumatized if dad's penis doesn't look exactly like theirs. We know one dad (circumcised) who says to his sons (uncircumcised), "Boy, you guys are lucky. You should've seen what they did to me!"

❑ AFTER THE BIRTH

Breastfeeding

About three days after childbirth, **lactation**—the production of milk—begins. Before lactation, sometimes as early as the second trimester, a yellowish liquid called **colostrum** is secreted by the nipples. It is what nourishes the newborn infant before the mother's milk comes in. Colostrum is high in protein and contains antibodies

And you shall circumcise the flesh of your foreskin: and it shall be a token of the covenant between Me and you.

Genesis 17:9–14

It is not to diffuse you that you were born of your mother and father—it is to identify you,
It is not that you should be undecided, but that you should be decided.
Something long preparing and formless is arrived and formed in you,
You are thenceforth secure, whatever comes or goes.

Walt Whitman

that help protect a baby from infectious diseases. Hormonal changes during labor begin the changeover from colostrum to milk, but unless a mother nurses her child, her breasts will soon stop producing milk. If she chooses not to breastfeed, she is usually given an injection of estrogen soon after delivery to stop lactation. It is not certain, however, whether estrogen is actually effective; furthermore, it may cause an increased risk of blood clotting.

Breastfeeding has declined significantly over the last few years, dropping from 60% to 52% between 1984 and 1988. Nutritionists are alarmed. A mother's milk— if she is healthy and has a good diet—offers the best nutrition for the baby. In addition, her milk contains antibodies that will protect her child from infectious diseases. Finally, a breastfed baby is less likely to become constipated, contract skin diseases, or develop respiratory infections. Low birth-weight babies, similarly, do best with mother's milk rather than formula or mature milk from a donor, since "nature adapts mother's milk to meet infant's needs" (Johnson and Goldfinger, 1981). A benefit to the mother is that hormonal changes, stimulated by breastfeeding, cause the uterus to contract and help ensure its return to a normal state. The American Academy of Pediatricians endorses total breastfeeding for a baby's first six months. Breastfeeding has psychological as well as physical benefits. Nursing provides a sense of emotional well-being for both mother and child through close physical contact. A woman may feel that breastfeeding affirms her body, giving her assurance that she is plentiful, capable of nourishing, able to sustain the life of another through her milk.

American mothers may worry about whether they will be able to breastfeed "properly." But what the distinguished physician Dr. Niles Newton wrote in 1955 still applies today:

All is beautiful
All is beautiful
All is beautiful, yes!
Now Mother Earth
And Father Sky
Join one another and meet
forever helpmates
  All is beautiful
  All is beautiful
  All is beautiful, yes!
Now the night of darkness
And the dawn of light
Join one another and meet
forever helpmates
  All is beautiful
  All is beautiful
  All is beautiful, yes!
Now the white corn
And the yellow corn
Join one another and meet
forever helpmates
  All is beautiful
  All is beautiful
  All is beautiful, yes!
Life that never ends
Happiness of all things
Join one another and meet
Forever helpmates
  All is beautiful
  All is beautiful
  All is beautiful, yes!

Navajo Night Chant

Successful breast-feeding is the type of feeding that is practiced by the vast majority of mothers all over the world. It is a simple, easy process. When the baby is hungry, it is simply given a breast to suck. There is an abundance of milk, and the milk supply naturally adjusts itself to the child's growth and intake of other foods.

Many American women choose not to breastfeed. Their reasons include the inconvenience of not being able to leave the baby for more than a few hours at a time, tenderness of nipples (which generally passes within several days to two weeks), and inhibitions about nursing a baby, especially in public. If a woman works, bottle feeding may be her only practical alternative, as American companies rarely provide leaves, part-time employment, or nursing breaks for their female employees. Some women may have a physical condition that precludes breastfeeding. Some men feel jealous of the baby's intimate relationship with their partner. Others feel incompetent because they cannot contribute to nourishing their child.

Bottle feeding an infant does make it possible for the father and other caregivers to share in the nurturing process. Some mothers (and fathers) have discovered that maximum contact and closeness can be enjoyed when the infant is held against their naked breast while nursing from a bottle.

Making Adjustments

The time immediately following birth is a critical period for family adjustment. No amount of reading, classes, and expert advice can prepare expectant parents for the real thing. The three months or so following childbirth (the "fourth trimester") constitute the **postpartum period.** This time is one of physical stabilization and emotional adjustment. New mothers, who may well have lost most of their interest in sexual activity during the last weeks of pregnancy, will probably find themselves returning to prepregnancy levels of desire and coital frequency. Some women may have difficulty reestablishing their sexual lives because of fatigue, physiological problems such as continued vaginal bleeding, and worries about the infant (Reamy and White, 1987).

The postpartum period also may be a time of significant emotional upheaval. Even women who had easy and uneventful births may experience a period of "postpartum blues" characterized by alternating periods of crying, unpredictable mood changes, fatigue, irritability, and occasionally mild confusion or lapses of memory. A woman has irregular sleep patterns because of the needs of her newborn, the discomfort of childbirth, or the strangeness of the hospital environment. Some mothers may feel lonely, isolated from their familiar world. Many women blame themselves for their fluctuating moods. They may feel that they have lost control over their lives because of the dependency of their newborns. One woman commented (Boston Women's Book Health Collective, 1978):

We often feel guilty, because we think our own inadequacies are the cause of our unhappiness. We rarely question whether the roles we have are realizable. Because of social pressures surrounding motherhood, and the mystique of the maternal instinct . . . many women are unable to pinpoint their feelings of confusion and inadequacy or are unable to feel that it is legitimate to verbalize their hesitation and problems.

Biological, psychological, and social factors are all involved in postpartum depression. Biologically, during the first several days following delivery, there is an abrupt fall in certain hormone levels. The physiological stress accompanying labor, as well as dehydration, blood loss, and other physical factors, contribute to lowering the woman's stamina. Psychologically, conflicts about her ability to mother, ambiguous feelings toward or rejection of her own mother, and communication problems with the infant or partner may contribute to the new mother's feelings of depression and helplessness. Finally, the social setting into which the child is born is important, especially if the infant represents a financial or emotional burden for the family. Postpartum counseling prior to discharge from the hospital can help couples gain perspective on their situation so that they know what to expect and can evaluate their resources (Reamy and White, 1987).

Although the postpartum blues are felt by many women, they usually don't last more than a couple of weeks. Interestingly, men seem to get a form of postpartum blues as well. Dr. Martha Zaslow and her colleagues (1981) at the National Institute of Child Health observed, "It looks increasingly as if a number of the things we assumed about mothers and motherhood are really typical of parenthood." When infants arrive, many fathers do not feel prepared for their new parenting and financial responsibilities. Some men are overwhelmed by the changes that take place in their marital relationship. Fatherhood is a major transition for them, but their feelings are overlooked, because most people turn their attention to the new mother. (The transition to parenthood for mothers and fathers is discussed at greater length in Chapter 8.)

Perhaps the new father will be allowed (or expected) to have equal status with the mother as a nurturing parent and to take on an equal share of household and child-rearing duties. Then, not only will the mother be able to experience some relief from the physical drain of motherhood, but the father also may experience his family from within rather than as a burdened provider watching from the outside. Studies indicate that "parental similarities far outweigh differences, suggesting that beyond the biological advantage accorded the mother by virtue of her physiology, both parents are equally capable of caring for their young" (Belsky et al., 1984). Both traditional gender roles and our traditional work structure, which does not permit men the opportunity to be at home or to work part-time, stand in the way of fathers participating equally (or replacing mothers) as the primary nurturers. Nature does not prevent men from nurturing, but societal expectations and the social structure do.

The birth of a child is one of the most important events in many people's lives. It fills mothers and fathers alike with a deep sense of accomplishment. The experience itself is profound and totally involving. A father described his daughter's birth (in Armstrong and Feldman, 1990):

Toward the end, Kate [his wife] had her arms around my neck. I was soothing her, stroking her, and holding her. I felt so close. I even whispered to her that I wanted to make love to her—It wasn't that I would have or meant to—it's just that I felt that bound up with her.

Colleen was born while Kate was hanging from my neck. . . . I looked down and saw Mimi's [the midwife's] hands appearing and then, it seemed like all at once, the baby was in them. I had tears streaming down my face. I was laughing and crying at the same time. . . . Mimi handed her to me with all the goop on her and I never even thought about it. She was so pink. She opened her eyes for the first time in her life right there in my arms. I thought she was the most beautiful thing I had ever seen. There was something about that, holding her just the way she was. . . . I never felt anything like that in my life.

SUMMARY

❐ *Infertility* is defined as the inability to conceive a child after trying for a year or more. The primary causes of male infertility are low sperm count, blocked passageways, and lack of sperm motility. The primary causes of female infertility are blocked fallopian tubes (often the result of *pelvic inflammatory* disease), endometriosis, and hormal abnormalities.

❐ The explosion of technological developments in the reproductive field have led to new legal and ethical considerations. These technologies include *ultrasound, chorionic villus sampling, amniocentesis, fetal monitoring, artificial insemination, in vitro fertilization, embryo transfer,* and *surrogate motherhood.* Artificial insemination involves depositing sperm by syringe in a woman's vagina. It is successful about 60 percent of the time. In vitro fertilization (IVF) involves combining sperm and egg in the laboratory and implanting the resultant blastocyst in the uterus of the mother or surrogate.

❐ About 2 percent of the American population is adopted. *Open adoption,* in which the birth mother is actively involved in the process, is increasing, as are foreign adoptions.

❐ The first reliable test of pregnancy can be made two to four weeks after a woman misses her menstrual period. A chemical test called the *agglutination test* will determine the presence of *human chorionic gonadotropin* (HCG) in the urine. *Hegar's sign,* a softening of the uterus, can be detected by a trained examiner. Pregnancy is confirmed by the detection of fetal heartbeats and movements or examination by ultrasound.

❐ A woman's feelings will vary greatly during pregnancy, owing to a number of factors. It is important for her to be able to share her fears and to have support from her partner, friends, relatives, and health-care workers.

❐ *Fertilization* of the ovum by a sperm usually takes place in the fallopian tube. During the first week, the fertilized ovum *(zygote)* divides many times to form a *blastocyst,* which implants itself in the uterine wall. It becomes an *embryo,* then a *fetus,* which is nourished through the *placenta,* an organ that gathers nutrients from the mother's bloodstream and passes them to the fetus via the *umbilical cord.*

❐ Harmful substances—including cocaine, opiates, tobacco, alcohol, marijuana, barbiturates, and caffeine—may be passed to the embryo or fetus through the placenta. Infectious diseases, such as rubella, may damage the fetus. Sexually transmitted diseases may be passed to the infant through the placenta or through the birth canal during childbirth.

❐ *Ectopic pregnancies, spontaneous abortion, preeclampsia,* and *low birth weight* are the most important complications of pregnancy. Preeclampsia is characterized by increasingly high blood pressure after the twenty-fourth week of pregnancy. Premature or low-birth-weight (LBW) babies usually weigh less than 5.5 pounds at birth; often their vital organs are not sufficiently developed.

❐ About 15 percent of pregnancies end in *spontaneous abortion* (miscarriage), largely because of chromosomal abnormalities in the fetus. Infant mortality rates in the United States are high compared to those in other industrialized nations. Infants of poor families are at particularly high risk. Loss of pregnancy or death of a young infant is recognized as a serious life event; parents who suffer this loss need support during the grieving process.

❐ Throughout pregnancy a woman feels *Braxton Hicks contractions,* which exercise the uterus in preparation for labor. The Braxton Hicks contractions also begin the *effacement* (thinning) and *dilation* (opening up) of the cervix to permit delivery.

❐ Labor can be divided into three stages. First-stage labor begins when uterine contractions become regular. When the cervix has dilated approximately ten centimeters, the baby's head enters the birth canal; this is called *transition.* In second-stage labor, the baby emerges from the birth canal. In third-stage labor, the placenta (afterbirth) is expelled.

❐ *Cesarean section* is the removal of the fetus by an incision through the mother's abdomen into her uterus. A dramatic increase in C-sections in recent years has led to criticism that the procedure is used more often than necessary.

❐ *Prepared childbirth* encompasses a variety of methods that stress the importance of understanding the birth process and of relaxation and emotional support of the mother during childbirth.

❐ Hospital birth practices, which have been designed for the convenience of the hospital rather than that of the mother, child, and father have come under increasing criticism. Professionally staffed birthing centers and special birthing rooms in hospitals are providing attractive alternatives to impersonal hospital birth settings for normal births.

❐ Nurse-midwives and lay midwives are trained in obstetric techniques. Many women are now choosing midwives to deliver their babies because they want home births, cannot afford physicians, or prefer the attendance of a woman (most physicians are male, most midwives female).

❐ *Circumcision,* the surgical removal of the foreskin, has been performed routinely in this country for many years. There are no medical reasons for this painful and sometimes dangerous procedure, and the practice is being increasingly questioned. Circumcision holds religious meaning for Jews and Muslims.

❐ About 60 percent of American women breastfeed their children today. Mother's milk is more nutritious than formula or cow's milk and provides immunities to many diseases. Nursing offers emotional rewards to mother and infant.

❐ A critical adjustment period follows the birth of a child. The mother may experience feelings of depression (sometimes called "postpartum blues") that are a result of biological, psychological, and social factors. Participation of the father in nurturing the infant and performing household duties may help alleviate both the mother's and father's feelings of confusion and inadequacy.

PART 4

Development

CHAPTER 7

Family Life Cycles

OUTLINE

For everything there is a season
And a time to every purpose
under heaven.

Ecclesiastes 3:1

M ARRIAGE IS A PROCESS IN WHICH PEOPLE INTERACT WITH EACH OTHER, create families, and give each other companionship and love. Marriage is not static; it is always changing to meet new situations, new emotions, new commitments and responsibilities. The marriage process may begin informally with cohabitation or formally with engagement. Marriage itself ends with divorce or with the death of a partner. We may begin marriage thinking we know how to act within it, but we find that the reality of marriage requires us to be more flexible than we had anticipated. We need flexibility to meet our needs, our partners' needs, and the needs of the marriage. We may have periods of great happiness and great sorrow within marriage. We may find boredom, intensity, frustration, and fulfillment. Some of these may occur because of our marriage; others may occur in spite of it. But, as we shall see, marriage encompasses many possibilities.

⬚ THE DEVELOPMENTAL PERSPECTIVE

The developmental framework, one of the most influential ways of looking at families, is an interdisciplinary approach that unites sociology and related disciplines with child and human development (Duvall, 1988). It sees individual and family development as interacting with each other.

The Individual Life Cycle

Our identity, our sense of who we are, is not fixed or frozen. It changes as we mature. At different points in our lives, we are confronted with different developmental tasks. Our growth as human beings depends on the way we resolve these problems. Erik Erikson (1963) describes the human life cycle as containing eight developmental stages. At each stage we have an important developmental task to accomplish, and each stage intimately involves the family. The way we deal with these stages, which are summarized here, is strongly influenced by our families and marriages. We cannot separate our identity from either.

INFANCY: TRUST VERSUS MISTRUST. In the first year of life, children are wholly dependent on their parenting figures for survival. It is then they learn to trust by having their needs satisfied, by being loved, held, and caressed. Without loving care, the infant may develop a mistrusting attitude toward others and toward life in general.

TODDLER: AUTONOMY VERSUS SHAME AND DOUBT. Between ages one and three, children learn to walk and talk; they begin toilet training. At this stage they need to develop a sense of independence and mastery over their environment and themselves. Parents need to encourage independence and make toilet training a positive rather than shameful experience.

EARLY CHILDHOOD: INITIATIVE VERSUS GUILT. Ages four to five are years of increasing independence. The family must allow the child to develop initiative while at the same time directing the child's energy. The child must not be made to feel guilty about his or her desire to explore the world.

SCHOOL AGE: INDUSTRY VERSUS INFERIORITY. Between ages six and eleven, children begin to learn that their activities pay off, that they can be creative. The family

. . . if one advances confidently in the direction of his dreams, and endeavors to live the life which he has imagined, he will meet with a success unexpected in his common hours.

Henry David Thoreau

needs to encourage the child's sense of accomplishment. Failing to do so may lead to feelings of inferiority in the child.

ADOLESCENCE: IDENTITY VERSUS ROLE DIFFUSION. The years of puberty between ages twelve and eighteen may be a time of turmoil, when adolescents try new roles as they make the transition to adulthood. To make a successful transition, they need to develop goals, a philosophy of life, a sense of self. The family needs to be supportive as the adolescent tentatively explores adulthood. If the adolescent fails to establish a firm identity, he or she is likely to drift without purpose.

YOUNG ADULTHOOD: INTIMACY VERSUS ISOLATION. These are the years when the adolescent leaves home and begins to establish intimate ties with other people through cohabitation, marriage, or other important intimate relationships. Without making other intimate connections, the young adult may be condemned to isolation and loneliness.

ADULTHOOD: GENERATIVITY VERSUS SELF-ABSORPTION. Now the individual establishes his or her own family and finds satisfaction in family relationships. It is a time of creativity. Work becomes important as a creative act, perhaps as important as family or an alternative to it. The failure to be productive may lead to self-centeredness and a "what's-in-it-for-me" attitude toward life.

The young are slaves to dreams; the old servants of regrets. Only the middle aged have all their senses.

Hervy Allen

MATURITY: INTEGRITY VERSUS DESPAIR. In old age, the individual looks back on life to understand its meaning—to assess what has been accomplished and to gauge the meaning of his or her relationships. Those who can make a positive judgment have a feeling of wholeness about their lives. The alternative is despair.

The Family Life Cycle

Just as individuals have life cycles with specific stages, so do marriages and families. Within these stages each marriage and family has its own unique history (Aldous, 1978). The concept of the **family life cycle** uses a developmental framework to explain people's behavior in families. According to the developmental framework, families change over time in terms of both the people who are members of the family and the roles they play. At various stages in the family life cycle, the family has different developmental tasks to perform. Much of the behavior of family members can be explained in terms of the family's developmental stage. The key factor in such developmental studies is the presence of children. The family organizes itself around its childrearing responsibilities. A woman's role as wife is different when she is childless than when she has children. A man's role is different when he is the father of a one-year-old than when he is the father of a fifteen-year-old.

The family life-cycle approach gives us important insights into the complexities of family life. Not only is the family performing various tasks during its life cycle, but each family member takes on various developmental tasks during each stage of the life cycle. The task for families with adolescents, for example, is to give their children greater autonomy and independence. While the family is coping with this new developmental task, an adolescent daughter has her own individual task of trying to develop a satisfactory identity. Meanwhile, her older brother is struggling with intimacy issues, her younger sister is developing industry, her parents are dealing with issues of generativity, and her grandparents are confronting issues of integrity.

The whole world is a comedy to those who think, a tragedy to those who feel.

Horace Walpole (1717–1797)

*For everything there is a season, and a
    time to every purpose under heaven:
a time to be born and a time to die;
a time to plant, and a time to pluck up
    what is planted;
a time to kill, and a time to heal;
a time to break down, and a time to
    build up;
a time to weep, and a time to laugh;
a time to mourn, and a time to dance;
a time to cast away stones and a time to
    gather stones together;
a time to embrace, and a time to refrain
    from embracing;
a time to seek, and a time to lose;
a time to keep, and a time to cast away;
a time to rend, and a time to sew;
a time to keep silence, and a time to
    speak:
a time to love, and a time to hate;
a time for war, and a time for peace.*

Ecclesiastes 3: 1–8

STAGES OF THE FAMILY LIFE CYCLE. One of the most widely used approaches divides the family life cycle into eight stages (Duvall and Miller, 1985). The eight-stage approach reflects the model life cycle. It does not encompass the family life cycle of single-parent or remarried families.

❏ *Stage I: Beginning Families.* During this stage, the married couple has no children. In the past this stage was relatively short, because children soon followed marriage. Today, however, it may last until a couple is in their late twenties or thirties. On the average, this stage is about two or three years. In the 1980s the average age for women to have their first child was twenty-five. Most studies on marital satisfaction agree that couples experience their greatest satisfaction in this stage (Glenn, 1991).

❏ *Stage II: Childbearing Families.* Because families tend to space their children about thirty months apart, the family is still considered to be forming. By this time the average family has two children. Although mothers are deeply involved in childbearing and childrearing, about half work outside the home. Stage II lasts around two and a half years. Marital satisfaction begins to lessen and continues to decline through the stage of families with schoolchildren (IV) or those with teenagers (V).

❏ *Stage III: Families with Preschool Children.* This family's oldest child is thirty months to six years. The parents, especially the mother, are still deeply involved in childrearing. This stage lasts about three and a half years.

❏ *Stage IV: Families with Schoolchildren.* This family's oldest child is between six and thirteen years old. With the children in school and more free time, the mother has more options available to her. By now, most women have reentered the job market. This stage lasts about seven years.

❏ *Stage V: Families with Adolescents.* In a family with adolescents, the oldest child is between thirteen and twenty years old. Marital satisfaction reaches its nadir. This stage lasts about seven years.

❏ *Stage VI: Families as Launching Centers.* By this time, the first child has been launched into the adult world. This stage lasts until the last child leaves home, a period averaging about eight years. Virtually all studies show that marital satisfaction begins to rise for most couples during this stage.

❏ *Stage VII: Families in the Middle Years.* This stage lasts from the time the last child has left home to retirement. It is commonly referred to as the "empty nest" stage. It is a distinct new phase in the family life cycle (Borland, 1982). Until this century most parents continued to have children until middle age, and the childrearing and launching periods were extended into old age. The empty nest period has increased from two to thirteen years in this century; it is one of the most dramatic changes that has occurred in the family life-cycle pattern (Glick, 1977a). More recently, however, because of deferred marriage and the high cost of housing, many adult children continue to live at home or return home after being away for a number of years. This "not-so-empty nest" phase, argue some scholars, constitutes a more recent variation in the middle-years stage (Glick, 1989; Mattessich and Hill, 1987). At this time, many families begin caretaking activities for elderly relatives, especially parents and parents-in-law.

❏ *Stage VIII: Aging Families.* The working members of the aging family have retired. Usually, the husband retires before the wife, since he tends to be older. If the wife works, the husband may remain alone at home until she also retires (Keith et al., 1981). Chronic illnesses begin to take their toll. Eventually, one of the spouses dies, usually the husband. The surviving spouse may live alone, with other family members, or be cared for by them.

FAMILY LIFE-CYCLE VARIATIONS. A major limitation of the family life-cycle approach is its tendency to focus on the intact nuclear family as "the family." Paul Glick, who coined the term "family life cycle" in 1947, has noted that there are a number of social changes affecting the traditional family life cycle (Glick, 1989). Deferred marriages, the rise of cohabitation, divorce, remarriage, single parenthood, and gay and lesbian families introduce notable variations in the life course of the family. As marriages are increasingly deferred, cohabitation rates have skyrocketed. It may be useful, Glick suggests, to include a cohabitational stage that recognizes the significance of living together in family development. In addition, the family life cycle of single adults is considerably different from that of their married counterparts. For childless adults who have never married, the families of orientation may become the central family focus. Single women, for example, may be intimately connected to their parents as caregivers; these women may be tied to children as aunts (Allen and Pickett, 1987; Allen, 1989).

Scholars are also recognizing the importance for ethnicity in family life cycles. The timing of the various stages, for example, is affected by ethnicity. African Americans are less likely to marry than whites; blacks who marry often do so at a later age. Single parenthood is more prevalent among African-American families than among white ones. In 1988, for example, 59 percent of black families were headed by single parents compared to 22 percent of white families (Rawlings, 1989). African Americans are also more likely than whites or Latinos to begin their family life cycle with unmarried single-parent families.

Of all these variations, researchers are increasingly focusing on two common alternatives to the traditional intact family life cycle: the single-parent and the stepfamily life cycles. Today, nearly one out of three families is a single-parent family, formed either through divorce or births to single women.

Most single-parent families are headed by divorced women, who usually divorce between stages II and IV, during the childbearing through school-age stages. About 72 percent of recently divorced women will remarry. If they remarry, the single-parent stage generally lasts between three and six years. If these divorced women do not remarry, they continue their single parenting until their adolescent children are launched (Mattessich and Hill, 1987).

The second type of single-parent family originates with unmarried mothers. Almost one out of every four births in this country is to an unmarried mother. Currently more than half of the children born to African Americans and 17 percent of those born to whites are born to unmarried mothers (U.S. Bureau of the Census, 1991). Some of the mothers are divorced but the majority have never been married. About a third are adolescents and another third are between ages twenty and twenty-four years. They usually have become pregnant unintentionally. Their family life cycle begins with a single-parent family as its first stage. In this stage, the young mother (especially if she is adolescent) and her child often live with the child's grandmother or cohabit with the child's father. The second stage may be marriage. After marriage, the family life cycle may follow more traditional patterns or diverge back into the single-parent pattern. Families that begin with single parenthood, however, are more likely to be unstable (Mattessich and Hill, 1987).

Stepfamilies are formed when either the husband or wife has children from a previous marriage or relationship. After single parenthood, the stepfamily generally forms during the school-age and adolescent family stages (Mattessich and Hill, 1987). The parents and stepparents, who are usually aged thirty years or older, have a double developmental task: they must simultaneously enter beginning marriage and childrearing stages.

The number of marriages is greater in proportion to the ease and convenience of supporting a family. When families can be easily supported, more persons marry and earlier in life.

Benjamin Franklin

◻ BEGINNING MARRIAGES

Cohabitation, Engagement, and Weddings

The first stage of the family life cycle may begin with engagement or cohabitation followed by a wedding, the ceremony that represents the beginning of a marriage.

Courtship is as old as Adam and Eve, who got off to a fast start by being naked when they met.

Jack Smith

ENGAGEMENT. Engagement is the culmination of the formal dating process. Today, in contrast to the past, engagement has greater significance as a ritual than as a binding commitment to be married. Engagement is losing its ritualistic meaning, however, as more couples start out in the less traditional "getting together" pattern or live together. These couples are less likely to become formally engaged. Instead, they announce that they "plan to get married." Because it lacks the formality of engagement, "planning" to get married is also less socially binding.

Engagement performs several functions:

◻ Engagement signifies a commitment to marriage and helps define the goal of the relationship as marriage.

◻ Engagement prepares couples for marriage by requiring them to think about the realities of everyday married life—money, friendships, religion, in-laws. They are expected to begin making serious plans about how they will live together as a married couple.

◻ Engagement is the beginning of kinship. The future marriage partner begins to be treated as a member of the family. He or she begins to become integrated into the family system.

◻ Engagement allows the prospective partners to strengthen themselves as a couple. The engaged pair begin to experience themselves as a social unit. They leave the youth or singles culture and prepare for the world of the married, a remarkably different world.

To speak frankly, I am not in favour of long engagements. They give people the opportunity of finding out each other's character before marriage, which I think is never advisable.

Oscar Wilde, The Importance of Being Earnest

Matrimony is a process by which a grocer acquires an account the florist had.

Francis Rodman

COHABITATION. The rise of cohabitation has led to its becoming an alternative beginning of the contemporary family life cycle (Glick, 1989; Surra, 1991). A quarter of the men and women who marry, for example, are living together at the time of their marriage; 40 percent of couples who remarry live together prior to marriage (Coleman and Ganong, 1991; Glenn, 1991). They may have children.

Although cohabiting couples may be living together before marriage, their relationship is not legally recognized until the wedding. Nor is the relationship afforded the same social legitimacy. Relatives do not consider cohabitors, for example, as kin (such as sons-in-law or daughters-in-law). At the same time, however, there is some evidence that cohabitation helps prepare a couple for marriage and weeds out incompatible couples (Glenn, 1991). It also performs some of the same functions as engagement, such as preparing the couple for some of the realities of marriage and helping them think of themselves in terms of being a couple as well as individuals.

Ceremonies are the outward expression of inner feeling.

Lao-tzu (d. 531 B.C.)

THE WEDDING. Weddings are ancient rituals that symbolize a couple's commitment to each other. The word *wedding* is derived from the Anglo-Saxon *wed,* meaning "pledge" (Chesser, 1980). The exchanging of rings dates back to ancient Egypt and symbolizes trust, unity, and timelessness, since a ring has no beginning and no end. It is a powerful symbol. (When singles meet for the first time, one of their first acts may be to glance at each other's fingers to see if there is a wedding ring.) To return a ring or take it off in anger is a symbolic act. Not wearing a ring may be a symbolic statement about a marriage. Another custom, carrying the bride over the threshold, was practiced in ancient Greece and Rome. It was a symbolic abduction growing out of the belief that a daughter would not willingly leave her father's house. The eating of cake is similarly ancient, representing the offerings made to household gods; the cake made the union sacred (Coulanges, 1960). The honeymoon tradition can be traced to a pagan custom for insuring fertility: each night after the marriage ceremony, the couple drank honey wine until the moon completed a full cycle. The honeymoon was literally a time of intoxication for the newly married man and woman.

Church weddings are medieval in origin, a result of the church expanding its power over secular matters. Before that time, marriage was a family affair in which the father "gave" his daughter away in marriage. The church usurped the family's power and declared marriage a sacrament. As a divine institution, marriage could not be dissolved.

Whether a first or second (or third) marriage, the central meaning of a wedding is that it symbolizes a profound life transition. Most significantly, the man and woman take on marital roles. For young men and women entering marriage the first time, marriage signifies a major step into adulthood. Some of the apprehension felt by those planning to marry may be related to their taking on these important new roles and responsibilities. Many will have a child in the first year of marriage. (Over 20 percent of all women are pregnant when they marry.) Therefore, the wedding must be considered a major rite of passage. Before a man and a woman exchange their marriage vows, they are single, and their primary responsibilities are to themselves. Their parents may have greater claims on them than they do on each other. But with the exchange of a few words, they are transformed. When they leave the wedding scene, they leave behind singlehood. They are now responsible to each other as fully as they are to themselves and more than they are to their parents.

Establishing Marital Roles

The expectations that two people have about their own and each other's marital roles are based on gender roles and their own experience. There are four traditional

Honor—a moral cousin of manners—requires your telling the truth about yourself before the wedding.

Miss Manners

Marriage often unites for life two people who scarcely know each other.

Honoré Balzac

Married in haste, we repent at leisure.

William Congreve (1670–1729)

assumptions about husband/wife responsibilities: (1) The husband is the head of the household, (2) the husband is responsible for supporting the family, (3) the wife is responsible for domestic work, and (4) the wife is responsible for childrearing.

The traditional assumptions about marital responsibilities do not necessarily reflect marital reality, however. For example, the husband traditionally may be regarded as head of the family, but power tends to be shared. With the rise of dual-earner families, there is no longer a single provider. Both men and women contribute to the financial support of the family; in fact, women earn more than men in about 20 percent of marriages (Atkinson and Boles, 1984). Although responsibility for domestic work still tends to reside with women, men are beginning to share housework. The mother is generally still responsible for childrearing, but fathers are beginning to participate more.

Although tradition has assigned many of these responsibilities along gender lines, they do not always fit the temperament and abilities of a particular husband and wife or the needs of the family.

. . . until two people, who are married, look into each other's eyes and make a solemn commitment to each other—that they will stop at nothing, that they will face any cost, any pain, any struggle, go out of their way so that they may learn and seek in order that they may make their marriage a continuously growing experience—until two people have done that they are not in my judgement married.

David Mace and Vera Mace

MARITAL TASKS. There are a number of marital tasks that newly married couples need to begin in order to build and strengthen their marriages. The failure to successfully complete these tasks may contribute to what researchers identify as the "duration of marriage effect," the tendency for marital satisfaction to decrease over time (see Focus, "Examining Marital Satisfaction"). These tasks are primarily adjustment tasks and include the following:

□ *Establishing marital and family roles.* Discuss marital role expectations for self and partner; make appropriate adjustments to fit each other's needs and the needs of the marriage. Discuss childbearing issues; negotiate parental roles and responsibilities.

□ *Providing emotional fulfillment and support for each other.* Learn how to give and receive love and affection, support the other emotionally and fulfill one's own identity as both an individual and a partner.

□ *Adjusting personal habits.* Adjust to each other's personal ways by enjoying, accepting, tolerating, or changing personal habits, tastes, and preferences, such as differing sleep patterns, levels of personal and household cleanliness, musical tastes, and spending habits.

□ *Negotiating gender roles.* Adjust gender roles and tasks to reflect individual personalities, skills, needs, interests, and equity.

□ *Making sexual adjustments with each other.* Learn how to physically show affection and love, discover mutual pleasures and satisfactions, negotiate timing and activities, and decide on the use of birth control.

□ *Establishing family/employment priorities.* Balance employment and family goals; recognize importance of unpaid household labor as work; negotiate childcare responsibilities; decide on whose employment, if either, receives priority. Divide household responsibilities equitably.

□ *Developing communication skills.* Share intimate feelings and ideas with each other. Learn how to talk to each other about difficulties. Share moments of joy and pain. Establish communication rules, such as never threatening or walking out during a disagreement. Learn how to negotiate differences to enhance the marriage.

□ *Managing budgetary and financial matters.* Establish mutually agreed upon budget; make short-term and long-term financial goals, such as saving for vacations or home purchase. Establish rules for resolving money conflicts.

□ *Establishing kin relationships.* Participate in extended family; manage boundaries between family of marriage and family of orientation.

❑ *Participating in larger community.* Make friends; meet neighbors. Become involved in community, school, church, or political activities.

As you can see, there are numerous tasks that a newly married couple must undertake as their marriage takes form. If the tasks are undertaken in a spirit of love and cooperation, they offer the potential for marital growth, richness, and connection (Whitbourne and Ebmeyer, 1990). But if they are avoided or undertaken in a selfish or rigid manner, the result may be conflict and marital dissatisfaction.

IDENTITY BARGAINING. People carry around idealized pictures of marriage long before they meet their marriage partner. They have to adjust these preconceptions to the reality of their partner's personality and the circumstances of their marriage. The process of adjustment is called **identity bargaining** (Blumstein, 1975). The most important person in this process is the partner. Mirra Komarovsky (1987) pointed out that a spouse has a "vital stake" in getting his or her partner to fulfill certain obligations. "Hardly any aspect of marriage is exempt from mutual instruction and pressures to change," she wrote.

Identity bargaining is a three-step process:

❑ First, a person has to identify with the role he or she is performing. A man must *feel* that he is a husband and a woman must *feel* that she is a wife. The wedding ceremony acts as a catalyst for role change from the single state to the married state.
❑ Second, a person must be treated by the other as if he or she fulfills the role. The husband must treat his wife as a wife; the wife must treat her husband as a husband. The problem is that a couple rarely agrees on what actually constitutes the roles of husband and wife. This is especially true now as the traditional content of marital roles is changing.
❑ Third, the two people must negotiate changes in each other's roles. A woman may have learned that she is supposed to defer to her husband, but if he makes an unfair demand, how can she do this? A man may believe his wife is supposed to be receptive to him whenever he wishes to make love, but if she is not, how should he interpret her sexual needs? A woman may not like housework (who does?), but she may be expected to do it as part of her marital role. Does she then do all the housework or does she ask her husband to share responsibility with her? A man believes he is supposed to be strong, but sometimes he feels weak—does he reveal this to his wife? Eventually, these adjustments must be made. At first, however, there may be

Marriage is that relation between men and women in which the independence is equal, the dependence mutual and the obligation reciprocal.

L. Anspacher

Reprinted by permission of UFS, Inc.

confusion; both partners may feel inadequate because they are not fulfilling their role expectations.

Although some may fear losing their identity in the give and take of identity bargaining, the opposite may be true: one's sense of identity may actually grow in the process of establishing a relationship. A major study by Whitbourne and Ebmeyer (1990) on marriage and identity concludes:

Couples can grow as individuals and as a pair through the operation of the identity processes. . . . The attempt that couples make to accommodate each other has its benefits as the alliance between them is strengthened and solidified. . . . The relationship between identity and intimacy is reciprocal. Perhaps the greatest impetus for growth of identity is through the unique and intense bond that the intimate relationship can offer.

In the process of forming a relationship, you discover yourself. An intimate relationship requires you to define who you are.

Establishing Boundaries

When young people marry, they often have strong ties to their parents. Until the wedding, their family of orientation has greater claim to their loyalties than their spouse-to-be. Once the ceremony is completed, however, the newlyweds must establish their own family independent of their families of orientation. The couple must negotiate a different relationship with their parents, siblings, and in-laws. Loyalties must shift from their families of orientation to their newly formed family. The families of orientation must accept and support these breaks (Minuchin, 1974). Indeed, opening themselves to outsiders who have become in-laws places no small stress on families (Carter and McGoldrick, 1989).

The new family must establish its own boundaries. The couple must decide how much interaction with their families is desirable and how much influence their families of orientation may have. There are often important ties to the parents that may prevent new families from achieving their needed independence. First is the tie of habit. Parents are used to being superordinate; children are used to being subordinate. The tie between mothers and daughters is especially strong; daughters often experience greater difficulty separating themselves from their mothers than do sons. These continuing ties may cause an adult child to feel conflicting loyalties toward parents and spouse (Cohler and Geyer, 1982). Much conflict occurs when a spouse feels an in-law is exerting too much influence on his or her partner—for example, a mother-in-law insisting that her son visit each Sunday and the son accepting despite the protests of his wife, or a father-in-law warning his son-in-law to establish himself in a career or risk losing his wife. If conflict occurs, husbands and wives need to put the needs of their spouses ahead of their parents.

Another tie to the family of orientation may be money. Newly married couples often have little money or credit with which to begin their families. They may turn to parents to borrow money, cosign loans, or obtain credit. But financial dependence keeps the new family tied to the family of orientation. The parents may try to exert undue influence on their children because it is their money, not their children's money, that is being spent. They may try to influence their children's purchases; they may refuse to loan money to buy something of which they disapprove.

The critical task is to form a family that is interdependent rather than totally independent or dependent. It is a delicate balancing act as parents and their adult children begin to make adjustments to the new marriage. We need to maintain bonds with our families of orientation and to participate in the extended family network, but we cannot let those bonds turn into chains.

It is an easier thing to be a lover than a husband, for the same reason that it is more difficult to be witty everyday than now and then.

Honoré Balzac

When a young man marries, he divorces his mother.

Yiddish Proverb

Some young men and women use marriage as a means of breaking away from overpossessive parents. But marriage which is considered by the participants as part of the strategy of emancipation from parents will bring with it tremendous psychological hazards. Despite their ostensible defiance, children who seek so drastic a means of establishing their independence have by no means done so efficiently. The complexities and subtleties of this parent-child battle reflect themselves in the marriage itself. In-law problems may thus be one phase of parent-child relational problems.

Jessie Bernard

❐ YOUTHFUL MARRIAGES

Youthful marriages represent stages II through IV in the family life cycle: childbearing families (stage II), families with small children (stage III), and families with school-age children (stage IV).

Impact of Children

Husband and wife both usually work until their first child is born; about half of all working women leave the workplace for at least a short period of time to attend to childrearing responsibilities after the birth of their first child. The husband continues his job or career. Although the first child makes him a father, fatherhood generally does not radically alter his relationship with his work. The woman's life, however, traditionally changes with motherhood. If she continues her outside employment, she is usually responsible for arranging child care and juggling her employment responsibilities when her children are sick. And, if her story is like that of most employed mothers, she continues to have primary responsibility for the household and children. If she withdraws from the workplace, her contacts during most of the day are with her children and possibly other mothers. This relative isolation requires her to make considerable psychological adaptation in her transition to motherhood, leading in some cases to unhappiness or depression. Typical struggles in families with young children concern child-care responsibilities and parental roles. The woman's partner may not understand her unhappiness because he sees her fulfilling her roles as wife and mother. She herself may not fully understand the reasons for her feelings as she is performing her traditional roles. The partners may increasingly grow apart during this period. During the day they move in different worlds, the world of the workplace and the world of the home; during the night they cannot relate easily because they do not understand each other's experiences.

Individual Changes

Around the time people are in their thirties, the marital situation changes substantially. The children have probably started school and the mother, who usually has the lioness's share of duties, now begins to have more freedom from childrearing responsibilities. She evaluates her past and decides on her future. The majority of women who left jobs to rear children return to the workplace by the time their children reach adolescence. By working, women generally increase their marital power.

Husbands in this period may find that their jobs have already peaked; they can no longer look forward to promotions. They may feel stalled and become depressed as they look into the future, which they see as nothing more than the past repeated for thirty more years. Their families may provide emotional satisfaction and fulfillment, however, as a counterbalance to workplace disappointments.

❐ MIDDLE-AGED MARRIAGES

Middle-aged marriages generally represent stages V and VI in the family life cycle: families with adolescents (stage V) and families as launching centers (stage VI). Couples in these stages are usually in their forties and fifties.

Families with Adolescents

Adolescents require considerable family reorganization on the part of the parents: they stay up late, infringe upon their parents' privacy, and leave a trail of empty

Any marriage, happy or unhappy, is infinitely more interesting and significant than any romance, however passionate.

W. H. Auden

Seldom, or perhaps never, does a marriage develop into an individual relationship smoothly and without crises; there is no coming to consciousness without pain.

Carl Jung

The best way to keep children at home is to make the home atmosphere pleasant—and let the air out of the tires.

Dorothy Parker

The most dramatic change experienced by a married couple is the birth or adoption of their first child. As a result, mother/father roles are added to wife/husband roles.

pizza cartons, popcorn, dirty clothes, and spilled soft drinks in their wake. As Carter and McGoldrick (1989) pointed out:

Families with adolescents must establish qualitatively different boundaries than families with younger children. . . . Parents can no longer maintain complete authority. Adolescents can and do open the family to a whole array of new values as they bring friends and new ideas into the family arena. Families that become derailed at this stage are frequently stuck at an earlier view of their children. They may try to control every aspect of their lives at a time when, developmentally, this is impossible to do successfully. Either the adolescent withdraws from the appropriate involvements for this developmental stage or the parents become increasingly frustrated with what they perceive as their own impotence.

Increased family conflict may occur as adolescents begin to assert their autonomy and independence (Troll, 1985). Conflicts over tidiness, study habits, communication, dating and responsibility may emerge. Adolescents want rights and privileges but have difficulty accepting responsibility. Conflicts are often contained, however, by both parents and adolescents tacitly agreeing to avoid "flammable" topics such as how the teenager spends his or her time. Such tactics may be useful in maintaining

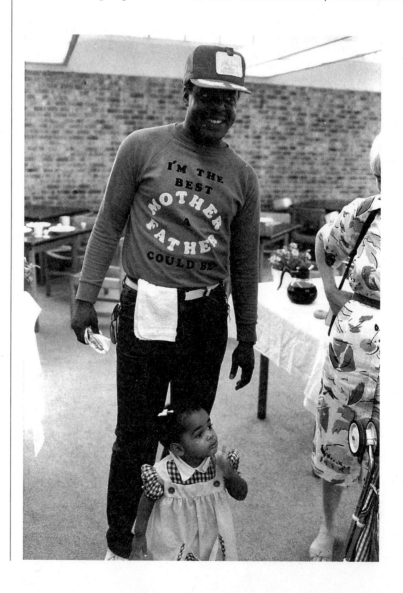

family peace, but in the extreme they can backfire by increasing family distance and inauthenticity. Despite the growing pains accompanying adolescence, parental bonds generally remain strong (Gecas and Seff, 1991).

Families as Launching Centers

Some couples may be happy or even grateful to see their children leave home, some experience difficulties with this exodus, and some continue to accommodate their adult children under the parental roof.

THE EMPTY NEST. As children are "launched" from the family (or ejected, as some parents wryly put it), the parental role becomes increasingly less important in daily life. The period following the child's exit is commonly known as the "empty nest" period. Most parents make the transition reasonably well (Anderson, 1988). In fact, marital satisfaction generally begins to rise for the first time since the first stage of marriage (Glenn, 1991). For some parents, however, the empty nest is seen as the end of the family. Children have been the focal point of much family happiness and pain—and now they are gone.

Traditionally, it has been asserted that the departure of the last child from home leads to an **empty nest syndrome** among women, characterized by depression and identity crisis. The problem with the idea of the empty nest syndrome is that there is little evidence for it being widespread. Rather, it is a myth that reinforces the traditional view that women's primary identity is found in motherhood. Once deprived of their all-encompassing identity as mothers, the myth goes, women lose all sense of purpose. In reality, however, mothers may be more likely to complain that their adult children have *not* left home.

The couple must now recreate their family minus their children. Their parental roles become less important and less stressful on a day-to-day basis (Anderson, 1988). The husband and wife must rediscover themselves as man and woman. Some couples may divorce at this point if the children were the only reason the pair remained together.

THE NOT-SO-EMPTY NEST: ADULT CHILDREN AT HOME. Just how empty homes actually are after children reach eighteen is open to question. In fact, the majority of unmarried adult children do not leave home until they are more than twenty-four years old. Adult children may live at home while attending college or working; some may have returned following divorce. Most children, however, move away from home when they marry.

The number of adult children living at home has grown over the last few decades as young adults continue to delay marriage. Skyrocketing housing costs, which amount to between 60 and 90 percent of a young adult's income, have also kept them at home (Saluter, 1989). Today, about 70 percent of never-married men and women aged eighteen to twenty-four years live at home with their parents. Although stereotypes suggest that men are more independent than women, when it comes to leaving home, men apparently exhibit more dependent behavior. Broken down by gender, about 61 percent of young men and 48 percent of young women live with their parents. Almost a third of divorced men and women return home (Saluter, 1989). Researchers note that there are important financial and emotional reasons for this trend (Mancini and Bliezner, 1991). High unemployment, housing costs, and poor wages lead to adult children returning home. High divorce rates as well as personal problems push adult children back to the parental home for social support, childcare, as well as cooking and laundry service.

The proverbial minister, priest and rabbi were debating the point at which life begins. The priest said, "Life begins at the moment of conception, when the sperm invades the egg." The minister insisted that "Life begins at birth, with that first breath of God's air." But the rabbi, older and wiser, said "You're both too young to know this, but life doesn't really begin until the kids leave home and the dog dies."

Frank Pittman

*After the kids
leave home,
    some parents
    suffer
    from the
    empty-nest syndrome;
Others—
    change the locks!*

Anonymous

FOCUS

Examining Marital Satisfaction

Because marriage and the family have moved to the very center of people's lives as a source of personal satisfaction, we now evaluate them according to how well they fulfill emotional needs. Marital satisfaction influences not only how we feel about our marriages and our partners, but it also affects how we feel about ourselves. If we have a good marriage, we tend to feel happy and fulfilled (Glenn, 1991).

Considering the various elements that make up or affect a marriage—from identity bargaining to economic status—it should not be surprising that marital satisfaction ebbs and flows. The ebb, however, begins relatively early for many couples. Researchers have found significant declines in the average level of marital satisfaction beginning in the first year of marriage (McHale and Huston, 1985). In some cases the decline in marital satisfaction during the first stage of marriage may mean that we have chosen the wrong partner. In fact, those with low satisfaction during the beginning marriage stage are four to five times as likely to divorce as those with high satisfaction (Booth et al., 1986). Satisfaction generally continues to decline during the first ten years of marriage, perhaps longer (Glenn, 1989). Studies consistently indicate that marital satisfaction changes over the family life cycle, following a U-shaped or curvilinear curve (Glenn, 1991; Suitor, 1991). Satisfaction is highest during the initial stages then begins to decline but rises again in the later years. There seems to be little difference in marital satisfaction between first marriages and remarriages (Vemer et al., 1989).

It was once thought that those couples with average or higher marital satisfaction would have stable marriages whereas those with low satisfaction would have divorce-prone marriages. Although low marital satisfaction may make a marriage more likely to end in divorce, marital dissatisfaction alone cannot predict eventual divorce (Kitson and Morgan, 1991). Many unhappy marriages continue to endure in the face of misery and discord; sometimes they outlast much happier marriages. Unhappy marriages continue if there are too many barriers to divorce (such as a potential decline in the standard of living) and if the available alternatives seem less attractive than the current marriage. And happier marriages sometimes end in divorce if there are few barriers and better alternatives (Glenn, 1991.)

DECLINE IN MARITAL SATISFACTION: WHO'S TO BLAME—CHILDREN OR TIME?

Why does marital satisfaction tend to decline soon after marriage? Two explanations for changes in marital satisfaction have been given by researchers. The first explanation ascribes the changing patterns of satisfaction to the presence of children. The second points to the effects of time on marital satisfaction.

CHILDREN AND MARITAL SATISFACTION
Traditionally, researchers have attributed decline in marital satisfaction to the arrival of the first child: children take away from time a couple spends together, are a source of stress, and cost

money. The decline reaches its lowest point when the oldest child enters adolescence (or school, according to some studies). When children begin leaving home, marital satisfaction begins to rise again.

It seems paradoxical that children cause marital satisfaction to decline. For many people, children are among the things they value most in their marriages. In fact, children may not be the monsters that some researchers believe them to be. First, attributing the decline to children creates a single-cause fallacy—that is, attributing a complex phenomenon to one factor when there are probably multiple causes. Second, the arrival of children at the same time that marital satisfaction declines may be coincidental, not causal. Other undetected factors may be at work. Although many societal factors make childrearing a difficult and sometimes painful experience for some families, it is also important to note that children create parental roles and the family in its most traditional sense. The marital relationship may be less than fulfilling with children present, but many couples may make a trade-off for fulfillment in their parental roles. In times of marital crisis, parental roles may be the glue that holds the relationship together until the crisis passes. Many couples will endure intense situational conflict, not for the sake of the marriage but for the sake of the children. If the crisis can be resolved, the marriage may be even more solid than before. We need to balance marital satisfaction with family satisfaction.

continued on next page

Better a Socrates dissatisfied than a pig satisfied.

John Stuart Mill

Young adults at home are such a common phenomenon that one of the leading family life-cycle scholars suggests a new family stage—adult children at home (Aldous, 1990). This new stage is not one that parents had anticipated. About 80 per-

FOCUS

THE DURATION OF MARRIAGE AND MARITAL SATISFACTION More recently, researchers have looked for factors besides children that might explain decline in marital satisfaction. The most persuasive alternative is the **duration-of-marriage effect.** The duration-of-marriage effect refers to the accumulation over time of various factors, such as unresolved conflicts, poor communication, grievances, role overload, heavy work schedules, and child-rearing responsibilities, that cause marital disenchantment.

The duration-of-marriage effect is most notable during the first stage of marriage rather than during the transition to parenthood that follows (White and Booth, 1985). This early decline may reflect the replacement of unrealistic expectations about marriage by more realistic ones, challenging us to be intimate and loving in the every day world. Since beginning marriage requires us to undertake numerous relational tasks, the transition from singlehood to marriage is a time filled with challenges. How we handle these challenges may set the tenor for our marriages for years to come. Those who handle them successfully have the tools with which to enhance their marriages; those who fail may see their marriages decline in satisfaction.

SOCIAL AND PSYCHOLOGICAL FACTORS IN MARITAL SATISFACTION

Social factors are important ingredients in marital satisfaction. Income level, for example, is a significant factor. Blue-collar workers have less marital satisfaction than white-collar, managerial, and professional workers because their lower income creates financial distress (Feldman and Feldman, 1975). Unemployment and economic uncertainty as sources of stress and tension also directly affect marital satisfaction. If a couple has an insufficient income or is deeply in debt, how to allocate their resources—for rent, repairing the car, buying a CD player—becomes critical, sometimes involving conflict-filled decisions.

Psychological factors also affect marital satisfaction (Richard, Wakefield, and Lewak, 1990). Although it was once believed that marital satisfaction was dependent on a partner's fulfilling complementary needs and qualities (an introvert marrying an extrovert, for example), research has failed to substantiate this assertion. Instead, success seems to depend on partners being similar in their psychological makeup and personalities. Outgoing people are happier with outgoing partners; tidy people like tidy mates. Furthermore, a high self-concept (how a person perceives himself or herself) as well as how the spouse perceives the person also contributes to marital satisfaction.

A psychological perspective may help to explain why many middle-years marriages experience low levels of satisfaction. The middle stages of the family life cycle are also when adults enter midlife, a time characterized by psychological crises and reevaluation. The causes of decreased marital satisfaction may be the result of the adults' own psychological concerns and distress. Steinberg and Silverberg (1987) suggest, "It is reasonable to assume that these feelings may provoke disenchantment in the marital relationship, regardless of changes in the adolescent or parent-adolescent relationship."

Even though much of the literature points to declines in marital satisfaction, we must remember that not all marriages suffer a significant decline. For many marriages, the decline is small or rises in satisfaction after a relatively short period. Even for those whose marriages decrease significantly in satisfaction, the decline may be offset by other satisfactions, such as pleasure in parental roles or a sense of security. Studies consistently demonstrate, for example, that the psychological and physical health of married men and women tends to be better than that of individuals who are unmarried (Gove, Styles, and Hughes, 1990).

It is important to understand that marital satisfaction is not static. It fluctuates over time, battered by stress, enlarged by love. Husband and wife continuously maneuver through myriad tasks, roles, and activities—from scrubbing floors to kissing each other—to give their marriages form. Children, who bring us both delight and frustration, constrain our lives as a couple but challenge us as mothers and fathers and enrich our lives as a family. Trials and triumphs, laughter and tears, punctuate the daily life of marriage. If we are committed to each other and to our marriage, work together in a spirit of flexibility and cooperation, find time to be alone together, and communicate with each other, we lay the groundwork for our marriages being rich and meaningful.

---

cent of the parents with children twenty-two and over had not expected the child to be living at home, according to one study (Clemens and Axelson, 1985). Almost half reported serious conflict with their children. For parents, the most frequently

Men can only be happy when they do not assume the object of life is happiness.

George Orwell

When I was young, I was told: "You'll see when you're fifty." I am fifty and I haven't seen a thing.

Erik Satie

Anyone who fails to go along with life remains suspended stiff and rigid in mid-air. That is why so many people get wooden in their old age; they look back and cling to the past with a secret fear of death in their hearts. From the middle of life onward, only he remains virtually alive who is ready to die with life, for in the secret hour of life's midday the parabola is reversed, death is born. We grant goal and purpose to the ascent of life, why not to the descent?

Carl Jung

mentioned problems were the hours of their children's coming and going and their failure to clean and maintain the house. Most wanted their children to be "up, gone, and on their own."

Reevaluation

Middle-aged people find that they must reevaluate relations with their children, who have become independent adults, and must incorporate new family members as in-laws. Some must also begin considering how to assist their own parents, who are becoming more dependent as they age. (See Mancini and Bliezner, 1991, for research review of aging parents and adult children.)

Couples in middle age tend to reexamine their aims and goals (Levinson, 1977; Rubin, 1976; Steinberg and Silverberg, 1987). On the average, husbands and wives have thirteen more years of marriage without children than they used to, and during this time their partnership may become more harmonious or more strained. The man may decide to stay at home more and not work as hard as before. The woman may commit herself more fully to her job or career or she may remain at home, enjoying her new child-free leisure. Because the woman has probably returned to the

FIGURE 7.1

This figure shows the average standard scores on marital satisfaction over eight stages of the family life cycle, as indicated by three separate studies. Note that all three record a decline in marital satisfaction around the time of the birth of children and an increase in marital satisfaction when children leave home.

SOURCE: Boyd C. Rollins and Kenneth L. Cannon, "Marital Satisfaction over the Family Life Cycle," *Journal of Marriage and the Family,* May 1974.

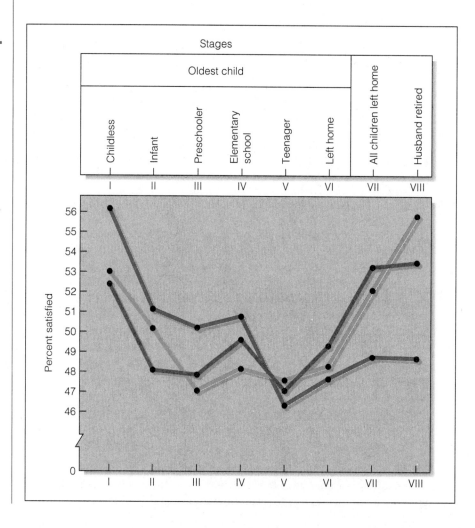

workplace, wages and salary earned during this period may represent the highest amount the couple will earn.

As people enter their fifties, they probably have advanced as far as they will ever advance in their work. They have accepted their own limits, but they also have an increased sense of their own mortality. Not only do they feel their bodies aging, but they begin to see people their own age dying. Some continue to live as if they were ageless—exercising, working hard, keeping up or even increasing the pace of their activities. Others become more reflective, retreating from the world. Some may turn outward, renewing their contacts with friends, relatives, and especially their children.

❒ LATER-LIFE MARRIAGES

Later-life marriages represent the last two stages (stages VII and VIII) of the family life cycle. A later-life marriage is one in which the children have been launched and the partners are middle-aged or older. During this period, the three most important factors affecting middle-aged and older couples are health, retirement, and widowhood (Brubaker, 1991). In addition, these women and men must often assume caretaking roles of their own aging parents or adjust to adult children who have returned home.

Later middle-aged men and women tend to enjoy good health, are firmly established in their work, and have their highest discretionary spending power, because their children are gone (Voydanoff, 1987). As they age, however, they tend to cut back on their work commitments for both personal and health reasons.

As they enter old age, men and women are better off than we have been accustomed to believe (Aldous, 1987). Beliefs that the elderly are neglected and isolated tend to reflect myth more than reality (Bengston and Robertson, 1985). A national study of the aged found that 41 percent of those with children see or talk with them daily, 21 percent twice a week, and 20 percent weekly. Over half have children within thirty minutes driving time (U.S. Bureau of the Census, 1988).

Beliefs that the elderly are a particularly poverty-stricken group are also misleading. Because of government programs benefiting the elderly, the poverty rate for the elderly declined during the 1980s while that of other groups substantially increased. The poverty rate for the general population in 1986 was 14.7 percent, but it was only 7 percent of those over sixty-five. We must not think, however, that all aged people are generally well off. The poverty rate for aged African Americans was 22.1 percent, and it was 17.3 percent for Latinos; these figures, however, were below the overall poverty rates for both groups (U.S. Bureau of the Census, 1990).

The health of the elderly also appears to be improving as they increase their longevity. Half of those between seventy-five and eighty-four years are free of health problems that require special care or limit their activities. Bernice Neugarten notes, "Even in the very oldest group, those above eighty-five, more than one-third report no limitation due to health" (Toufexis, 1988). Individuals between seventy-five and eighty gained four years in life expectancy between 1968 and 1980. More married couples are living into old age; there are fewer widows at younger ages.

The Intermittent Extended Family: Sharing and Caring

Although many later-life families contract in size as children are launched, pushed, or cajoled out of the nest, other families may expand as they come to the assistance of family members in need. Families are most likely to become an **intermittent extended family** during their later-life stage (Beck and Beck, 1989). Intermittent ex-

All the world's a stage
And all the men and women
*   merely players:*
They have their exits and their
*   entrances:*
And one man in his time plays
*   many parts,*
His acts being seven ages. At
*   first the infant,*
Mewling and puking in the
*   nurse's arms.*
Then the whining school-boy,
*   with his satchel*
And shining morning face,
*   creeping like snail*
Unwillingly to school. And
*   then the lover,*
Sighing like furnace, with a
*   woeful ballad*
Made to his mistress's eyebrow.
*   Then a soldier,*
Full of strange oaths, and
*   bearded like the pard,*
Jealous in honor, sudden and
*   quick in quarrel,*
Seeking the bubble reputation,
Even in the cannon's mouth.
*   And then the justice,*
In fair round belly with good
*   capon lined,*
With eyes severe and beard of
*   formal cut,*
Full of wise saws and modern
*   instances;*
And so he plays his part. The
*   sixth age shifts*
Into lean and slippered
*   pantaloon,*
With spectacles on nose and
*   pouch on side,*
His youthful hose, well saved,
*   a world too wide*
For his shrunk shank; and his
*   big manly voice,*
Turning again toward childish
*   treble, pipes*
And whistles in his sound.
*   Last scene of all,*
That ends this strange eventful
*   history,*
Is second childishness and
*   mere oblivion,*
Sans teeth, sans eyes, sans
*   taste, sans everything.*

William Shakespeare, As You Like It

tended families are families that take in other relatives during a time of need. These families "share and care" when younger or older relatives are in need or crisis: they help daughters who are single mothers; a sick parent, aunt, or uncle; an unemployed cousin (see Chapter 10 for a discussion of family caregiving). When the crisis passes, the dependent adult leaves and the family resumes its usual structure.

Intermittent extended families tend to be linked to ethnicity. Using national population studies, researchers estimate that the families of almost two-thirds of African-American women and a third of white women were extended for at least some part of the time during their middle age. Latino women are more likely than non-Latino women to form extended households (Tienda and Angel, 1982). Asian families are also more likely to live at some time in extended families. There are two reasons for the prevalence of extended families among certain ethnic groups. First, extended families are by cultural tradition more significant to African Americans, Latinos, and Asian Americans than to whites. Second, ethnic families are more likely to be economically disadvantaged. They share households and pool resources as a practical way to overcome short-term difficulties. In addition, there is a higher rate of single parenthood among African Americans that makes mothers and their children economically vulnerable. These women often turn to their families of orientation for emotional and economic support until they are able to get on their own feet.

Parenting and Grandparenting

PARENTING. A few years ago, a Miami Beach couple reported their son missing (Treas and Bengston, 1987):

Joseph Horowitz still doesn't understand why his mother got so upset. He wasn't "missing" from their home in Miami Beach: he had just decided to go north for the winter. Etta Horowitz, however, called authorities. Social worker, Mike Weston finally located Joseph in Monticello, N.Y., where he was visiting friends. Etta, 102, and her husband, Solomon, 96, had feared harm had befallen their son Joseph, 75.

Parenting does not end when children grow up. Most elderly parents still feel themselves to be parents, but they are parents in different ways. Their parental role is considerably less important in their daily lives. They generally have some kind of regular contact with their adult children, usually by letters or phone calls; parents and adult children also visit each other fairly frequently and often celebrate holidays or birthdays together. One study (Aldous, 1987) found that middle-class parents typically assisted their children financially or provided services. Parents made loans, gave gifts, or paid bills for their children around six times a year; they also provided child care about the same number of times. They assisted in shopping, house care, and transportation and also helped in times of illness.

Yet parents do not necessarily assist their children equally. Joan Aldous (1987) noted, "Parents were most in touch with children who, although adults, were most in need of parental attention." Parents tend to assist those whom they perceive to be in need, especially children who are single or divorced. Parents perceive their single children as being "needy" because they have not yet established themselves in occupational and family roles. These children may need financial assistance and may lack intimate ties; their parents may provide both until their children are more firmly established. Parents often assist divorced children, especially if grandchildren are involved, by providing financial and emotional support. They also provide child-care and housekeeping services. Parents generally provide the greatest assistance to their children who are single mothers.

Love seems the swiftest, but it is the slowest of all growths. No man or woman really knows what perfect love is until they have been married a quarter of a century.

Mark Twain

Many a man that cudden't direct ye to th' drug store on th' corner whin he was thirty will get a respectful hearin' whin age has further impaired his mind.

Finley Peter Dunne, Old Age

In providing assistance to their children, the parents exercised considerable control over whom they would help and how involved they would become. Despite their continued parental concern, they tended to be maritally rather than parentally oriented. They valued their independence from their children. When one woman was asked how she would feel about an adult child coming back home to live, she exclaimed, "Oh, God, I wouldn't like it. I'm tired of waiting on people" (Aldous, 1987).

In Aldous's study, adult children generally reciprocated in terms of physical energy. They helped in household chores and yard work about six times a year; they also assisted to some extent with physical care during illness.

Some elderly parents never cease being parents because they provide home care for children who are severely limited either physically or mentally. Many elderly parents, like middle-aged parents, are taking on parental roles again as divorced children return home for financial or emotional reasons. Although we don't know how elderly parents "parent," presumably they are less involved in traditional parenting roles. The presence of adult children in aging families does not seem to detract from marital quality as it does when children remain home in middle-aged families (Suitor and Pillemer, 1987). According to Aldous the major drawback was that husband/wife conflict increased if there was parent/child conflict.

GRANDPARENTING. The image of the lonely, frail grandmother in a rocking chair needs to be discarded, notes researcher Gregory Kennedy (1990). Grandparents are often not very old, nor are they very lonely. And they are certainly not absent in contemporary American family life. Grandparents are "a very present aspect of family life, not only for young children but young adults as well," writes Kennedy.

Grandparenting is expanding tremendously these days, creating new roles that relatively few Americans played a few generations back (Cherlin and Furstenberg, 1986). Three-quarters of older Americans are grandparents. The typical fifteen-year-old has more than a fifty-fifty chance of having three grandparents living. Of those Americans who are grandparents, 40 percent are also great-grandparents!

Grandparents play important emotional roles in American families; the majority appear to establish strong bonds with their grandchildren (Cherlin and Furstenberg, 1986; Kennedy, 1990). A recent study (Kennedy, 1990) found that almost half of the student respondents had at least one grandparent living in the same town; another fifth had a grandparent living within fifty miles. More than half of the students felt very close to at least one grandparent; a few identified their closest relationship as being with a stepgrandparent. Grandparents are important in helping achieve family cohesiveness by conveying family history, stories, and customs. They frequently act as a stabilizing force for their children and grandchildren when the families are divorcing and reforming as single-parent families or stepfamilies (Barranti, 1985).

Grandparents are often involved in the daily care of their grandchildren. About a fourth of preschoolers of employed mothers are cared for by their grandmothers for an average of twenty-seven hours per week (Presser, 1989). Furthermore, about 5 percent of all children live with their grandparents; of these, about one-third are cared for only by their grandparents. According to one study, 13 percent of African-American children, 5 percent of Latino children, and 3 percent of white children lived with their grandparents (Saluter, 1990). Kennedy (1990) found that African Americans more than whites expected grandparents to be authority figures, to provide childrearing assistance, and to assist with parent/child communication. He also found that students in single-parent families and stepfamilies expected grandparents to be more involved and influential than those in intact families.

1. Avoid fried meats which angry up the blood.
2. If your stomach disputes you, lie down and pacify it with cool thoughts.
3. Keep the juices flowing by jangling around gently as you move.
4. Go very lightly on the vices, such as carrying on in society. The social ramble ain't restful.
5. Avoid running at all times.
6. Don't look back. Something might be gaining on you.

Satchel Paige

Grandparenting tends to fall into three distinct styles, according to a national study of 510 grandparents by Andrew Cherlin and Frank Furstenberg (1986):

❑ *Companionate*. Most grandparents perceive their relationships with their grandchildren as companionate. The relationships are marked by affection, companionship, and play. Because these grandparents tend to live relatively close to their grandchildren, they can have regular interaction with them. Companionate grandparents do not perceive themselves as rule makers or enforcers; they rarely assume parent-like authority. Companionate grandparents accounted for 55 percent of the grandparents in the survey.
❑ *Remote*. Remote grandparents are not intimately involved in their grandchildren's lives. Their remoteness, however, is due to geographical remoteness rather than emotional remoteness. Geographical distance prevents regular visits or interaction with their grandchildren that would bind the generations together more closely. About 29 percent of the grandparents were classified as remote.
❑ *Involved*. Involved grandparents are actively involved in what have come to be regarded as parenting activities: making and enforcing rules and disciplining children. Involved grandparents (most often grandmothers) tend to emerge in times of crisis, such as when the mother is an unmarried adolescent or enters the workforce following divorce. Some involved grandparents may become "over involved," however. They may cause confusion as the family tries to determine who is the real head of the family. Involved grandparents made up 16 percent of the grandparents in the study.

What determines the amount of interaction between grandparents and grandchildren? Cherlin and Furstenberg (1986) succinctly summed up the three most important factors: "distance, distance, and distance." Other factors include age, health, employment, personality, and other responsibilities (Troll, 1985). The middle generation is usually responsible for determining how much interaction takes place between grandparents and grandchildren. If rivalry rather than cooperation ensues, the middle generation may restrict grandparent/grandchildren interaction. But most families gain from such interactions (Barranti, 1985).

Single parenting and remarriage has made grandparenthood more painful and problematic for many grandparents. Stepfamilies have created stepgrandparents, who are often confused about their grandparenting role. Are they *really* grandparents? The grandparents whose son or daughter does not have custody often express concern about their future grandparenting role (Goetting, 1990). Although research indicates that children in stepfamilies tend to do better if they continue to have contact with both sets of grandparents, it is not uncommon for the parents of the noncustodial parent to lose contact with their grandchildren (Bray and Berger, 1990).

Retirement and Widowhood

Retirement, like other life changes, has the potential for satisfactions and problems. In a time of relative prosperity for the elderly, retirement is an event to which older couples generally look forward. The key to marital satisfaction in these later years is continued good health (Brubaker, 1991).

RETIREMENT. There is a growing trend toward early retirement among financially secure men and women. Changing social mores have led many to value leisure more than increased buying power and other job benefits. In fact, today three-fourths of men and more than four-fifths of women choose to collect their social security

We have not finished thinking, imagining, acting. It is still possible to know the world; we are unfinished men and women.

Carlos Fuentes

checks before they reach sixty-five years (Dentzer, 1990). Two scholars (Treas and Bengston, 1987) note, "Together with greater prosperity, early retirement has probably reordered the preoccupations of later life toward greater concern with leisure activities—a development most compatible with the historic shift to companionate marriages." The bumper sticker "We're spending our children's inheritance" seen on campers and RVs captures this shift in sentiment.

When men reach their sixties, they usually retire from their jobs, losing a major activity through which they defined themselves. In spite of this, most men look favorably on retirement. Their role as husband becomes more important as they focus on leisure activities with their wives. In addition, many retirees are not really retired; many continue working part-time (Dentzer, 1990). Volunteer activities become more important. At home, the division of labor becomes somewhat more egalitarian; men participate in more household activities than they did when they were working (Rexroat and Shehan, 1987).

If the woman worked outside the home, she may experience some feelings of loss upon retirement, especially if she was involved in a career (Johnson and Price-Bonham, 1980). A woman who retires may not find herself facing the same identity issues as a man, however, because women often have had (or continue to have) important family roles as wife, homemaker, grandmother, and possibly mother.

If a woman has been a full-time homemaker, she probably experiences no abrupt role change in her sixties. There is no retirement for homemakers, however ironic that may be. Because "a woman's work is never done," homemakers may have the last laugh, for if they choose, they can perform their traditional role without any interruption throughout their entire lives.

The marital relationship generally continues along the same track following retirement: those who had vital, rewarding marriages will probably continue to have happy marriages, whereas those whose marriages were difficult will continue to have unsatisfying relationships (Brubaker, 1991). The retired couple experiences the highest degree of marital satisfaction since the first family stage, when they had no children (Johnson et al., 1986).

Although retirement affects marital interaction, changes in health are far more important over the long run. As long as both partners are healthy, the couple can continue their marital relationship unfettered. If one becomes ill or disabled, the other generally comes to his or her aid, providing care and nurturance. One study (Johnson, 1985) of elderly marriages in which a spouse was recuperating from hospitalization found high levels of marital adjustment; husbands and wives dealt positively with their caregiving demands. Ill spouses also receive help from other family members, including their adult children, siblings, and other relatives.

WIDOWHOOD. Marriages are finite; they do not last forever. Eventually, every marriage is broken by divorce or death. Despite high divorce rates, most marriages end with death, not divorce. "Until death do us part" is a fact for most married people.

In 1989, almost two-thirds of those between sixty-five and seventy-four years were married. Among those eighty-five years and older, however, only 4 percent were married; the remainder were widowed. Because of difference in longevity, most widowed persons are women. Among women from sixty-five to seventy-four, 51 percent lived with their husbands, but only 9 percent over age eighty-four lived with a spouse. In contrast, among men sixty-five to seventy-four years, 78 percent lived with their wives; among those over eighty-four years, 48 percent lived with a spouse (Saluter, 1990). Because of the disproportionate sex ratio of women to men, one researcher estimated that fewer than 5 percent of women widowed over age fifty-five will remarry (Hiltz, 1978). If a woman is widowed at fifty-five and dies at

Tho' much is taken, much abides; and tho'
We are not now that strength which in old days
Moved earth and heaven; that which we are, we are—
One equal temper of heroic hearts,
Made weak by time and fate, but strong in will
To strive, to seek, to find, and not to yield.

Alfred, Lord Tennyson

seventy-five, she may have spent as much time as a widow as she spent raising children.

Widowhood is often associated with a significant decline in income, plunging the grieving spouse into financial crisis and hardship in the year or so following death. This is especially true for poorer families (Smith and Zick, 1986). For both men and women among the elderly, their financial situation is related to their feelings of well-being.

Recovering from the loss of a spouse is often difficult and prolonged (Kübler-Ross, 1982). (See Chapter 10 for discussion of death and the grieving process.) The woman may experience considerable disorientation and confusion from the loss of her role as a wife and companion. Having spent much of her life as part of a couple—having mutual friends, common interests, shared goals—the widow suddenly finds herself alone. Whatever the nature of her marriage, she experiences grief, anger, distress, and loneliness. Physical health appears to be tied closely to the emotional stress of widowhood. Widowed men and women experience more health problems over the fourteen months following their spouses' death than those with spouses. Over time, however, widows appear to regain much of their physical and emotional health (Brubaker, 1991).

Eventually widows adjust to the loss. Some like their new freedom. Others believe that they are too old to remarry; still others cannot imagine living with someone other than their former husband. (Those who had good marriages think of remarrying more often than those who had poor marriages.) A large number of elderly men and women live together without remarrying. For many widows, widowhood lasts the rest of their lives.

 # SUMMARY

◻ The eight developmental stages of the life cycle described by Erik Erickson include (1) infancy: trust versus mistrust, (2) toddler: autonomy versus shame and doubt, (3) early childhood: initiative versus guilt, (4) school age: industry versus inferiority, (5) adolescence: identity versus role diffusion, (6) young adulthood: intimacy versus isolation, (7) adulthood: generativity versus self-absorption, and (8) maturity: integrity versus despair.

◻ The *family life cycle* examines developmentally how families change over time in terms of both the people who are members of the family and the roles they play. The family life cycle consists of eight stages: beginning families, childbearing families, families with preschool children, families with schoolchildren, families with teenagers, families as launching centers, families in the middle years, and aging families.

◻ Variations on the traditional life cycle include ethnic, single-parent, and stepfamily variations.

◻ Engagement is the culmination of the formal dating pattern. It prepares the couple for marriage by involving them in discussions about the realities of everyday life, it involves family members with the couple, and it strengthens the couple as a social unit. Cohabitation performs many of the same functions as engagement.

◻ A wedding is an ancient ritual that symbolizes a couple's commitment to each other. It marks a major transition in life as the man and woman take on marital roles.

◻ Marriage involves many powerful traditional role expectations, including assumptions that the husband is head of the household and is expected to support the family and that the wife is responsible for housework and childrearing.

◻ Marital tasks include establishing marital and family roles, providing emotional support for each other, adjusting personal habits, negotiating gender roles, making sexual adjustments, establishing family/employment priorities, developing communication skills, managing budgetary and financial matters, establishing kin relationships, and participating in the larger community.

◻ Couples undergo *identity bargaining* in adjusting to marital roles. This is a three-step process: a person must identify with the role, the person must be treated by the other as if he or she fulfills that role, and both people must negotiate changes in each other's roles.

◻ A critical task in early marriage is to establish boundaries separating the newly formed family from the couple's family of orientation. Ties to the families of orientation may include habits of subordination and economic dependency.

❐ In youthful marriages, about half of all working women leave the work force to attend to childrearing responsibilities.

❐ In middle-aged marriages, women may question their role as mother; men often feel disappointment with their work. Families must deal with issues of independence of their adolescent children. Most women do not suffer from the *empty nest syndrome*—that is, depression over the end of their active mother role. In fact, for many families, there is no empty nest because of the increasing presence of adult children in the home. As children leave home, parents reevaluate their relationship with each other and their life goals.

❐ In later-life marriages, no children are present. The most important factors affecting this life-cycle stage are health, retirement, and widowhood. As a group, the aged have the lowest poverty level of any group; they have good health through the early years of old age and regular contact with their children. Many, especially ethnic families, have *intermittent extended families,* in which aging parents, adult children, or other relatives periodically live with them during time of need.

❐ Parenting roles continue through old age. Elderly parents provide financial and emotional support to their children; they often take active roles in childcare and housekeeping for their daughters who are single parents. Divorced children and those with physical or mental limitations may continue living at home.

❐ Grandparenting is an important role for the middle aged and aged; it provides them with a sense of continuity. Grandparents often provide extensive childcare for grandchildren. Approximately 5 percent of American children live with their grandparents. Grandparenting can be divided into three styles: companionate, remote, and involved.

CHAPTER 8

Parents and Children

In every child who is born, under no matter what circumstances, and of no matter what parents, the potentiality of the human race is born again.

James Agee

❏ SHOULD WE OR SHOULDN'T WE? CHOOSING TO HAVE CHILDREN

PARENTHOOD MAY NOW BE CONSIDERED A MATTER OF CHOICE owing to widespread use of birth control. If men and women want to have children, they can decide when to have them. As a result, America's birthrate has fallen to an average of two children per marriage, the number deemed ideal by 56 percent of the people interviewed in a 1985 Gallup poll. A little more than twenty-five years ago, 37 percent of those interviewed wanted a large family of four or more children. Today only 11 percent want so large a family. Approximately 2 percent want no children at all, according to the 1985 poll, but that number is expected to increase (see Nock, 1987).

In some areas, "reproductive decision-making" workshops and classes are being offered to help women order their priorities about career, life-style, and childrearing. One study found that 42 percent of the women who attended such a workshop were able to make a clear reproductive choice at the program's conclusion (Daniluk and Herman, 1984).

Child-Free Marriage

In recent articles and discussions of marriages in which there are no children, the term *childless* is often replaced by **child-free.** This change in terminology reflects a shift of values in our culture. Couples who do not choose to have children need no longer be viewed as lacking something hitherto considered essential for personal fulfillment. Indeed, the use of the suffix "free" suggests liberation from the bonds of a potentially oppressive condition (see Callan, 1985). Women who choose to be child-free are generally well educated and career oriented. One woman expressed her feelings as follows (in Boston Women's Health Book Collective, 1978a).

When I see someone who's dragging along a child who's screaming and I'm on a date with a man who's saying "You're not a whole woman if you can't have my baby," then I say, "Why don't you go over to that child and listen to the screaming for a few minutes?" The reality is that there's a lot of noise. There's a lot of mess. And it's not just for a few days. It's for years.

Even when there is less familiar and societal pressure to reproduce, the decision to remain without children is not always easily made. Although the partners in some child-free marriages have never felt that they wanted to have children, for most the decision seems to have been gradual. J.E. Veevers (1980) identified four stages of this decision process:

1. The couple decides to postpone children for a definite time period (until he gets his degree, until she gets her promotion, and so on).
2. When the time period expires, they decide to postpone children indefinitely (until they "feel like it").
3. They increasingly appreciate the positive advantages of being child-free (as opposed to the disadvantages of being childless).
4. The decision is made final, generally by the sterilization of one or both partners.

Studies of child-free marriages show nine basic categories of reasons given by those who have chosen this alternative (Houseknecht, 1987). The categories in descending order of importance are as follows:

❏ Freedom from child-care responsibility and greater opportunity for self-fulfillment
❏ More satisfactory marital relationship

Aunt Tillie: Do you like children? Uncle Gus: I do if they're properly cooked.

W.C. Fields

❐ Wife's career considerations
❐ Monetary advantages
❐ Concern about population growth
❐ General dislike of children
❐ Early socialization experiences and doubts about parenting ability
❐ Concern about physical aspects of childbirth
❐ Concern for children in present world conditions

Couples usually have some idea that they will or will not have children before they marry. If the intent isn't clear from the start or if one partner's mind changes, the couple may have serious problems ahead. A New York banker, aged forty-four, whose wife had been continuing to postpone childbirth, complained in frustration, "What these intelligent women owe the world is not just what they do or who they are—they owe the world a legacy to pass on" (in Francke, 1980).

Many studies of child-free marriages indicate a higher degree of marital adjustment or satisfaction than is found among couples with children. In one study, child-free women reported more frequent exchange of stimulating ideas with their husbands, more shared projects and outside interests, and greater agreement on household tasks and career decisions (Houseknecht, 1982). These findings are not particularly surprising if we consider the great amount of time and energy that child-rearing entails. It has also been observed that divorce is more probable in child-free marriages, perhaps because, unlike some other unhappily married couples, the child-free couples do not stay together "for the sake of the children" (Glenn and McLanahan, 1982; see Houseknecht, 1987, for a review of the current literature on voluntary childlessness).

Deferred Parenthood

A report from the National Center for Health Statistics (1982) indicated that a "baby boomlet" was in progress in the early 1980s. Births to women in their thirties more than doubled between 1970 and 1979 and continued to increase in the 1980s. In 1989 the U.S. Bureau of the Census reported a "bumper crop" of 4 million babies (to women of all ages). This increase in births is attributed to the fact that women in their thirties (themselves products of the post–World War II baby boom) have postponed childbirth. Although most women still begin their families while in their twenties, demographers predict that the trend toward later parenthood will continue to grow, especially in middle- and upper-income groups (Price, 1982; Whitehead, 1990).

The average age at marriage has increased slowly and steadily since 1960. More career and life-style options are available to single women than in the past. Marriage and reproduction are no longer economic or social necessities. People may take longer to search out the "right" mate (even if it takes more than one marriage to do it), and they may wait for the right time to have children. Increasingly effective birth control (including safe, legal abortion) has also been a significant factor in the planned deferral of parenthood.

Besides giving parents a chance to complete education, build careers, and firmly establish their own relationship, delaying parenthood can also be advantageous for other reasons. Maternity and medical expenses, food, furniture and equipment, clothes, toys, baby-sitters, lessons, and summer camp are costly. In 1989 the annual cost of raising a child ranged from $4,100 to $9,770, depending on the family's income level, age of the child, and region of residence (Lino, 1990). (These costs are based on two-parent, two-child families; with three or more children, the cost per

FOCUS

Am I Parent Material?

These questions are designed to stimulate ideas that you may not have thought about. There are no right answers and no grades—your answers are right for you and may help you decide for yourself whether or not you want to be a parent. Because we all change, your answers to some of these questions may change two, five, even ten years from now. You *do* have a choice. Check out what you know and give it some thought. Then do what seems right for you.

DOES HAVING AND RAISING A CHILD FIT THE LIFE-STYLE I WANT?

1. What do I want out of life for myself? What do I think is important?
2. Could I handle a child and a job at the same time? Would I have time and energy for both?
3. Would I be ready to give up the freedom to do what I want to do, when I want to do it?
4. Would I be willing to cut back my social life and spend more time at home? Would I miss my free time and privacy?
5. Can I afford to support a child? Do I know how much it takes to raise a child?
6. Do I want to raise a child in the neighborhood where I live now? Would I be willing and able to move?
7. How would a child affect *my* growth and development?
8. Would a child change my educational plans? Do I have the energy to go to school and raise a child at the same time?
9. Am I willing to give a great part of my life—*at least eighteen years*—to being responsible for a child? And am I prepared to spend a large portion of my life being concerned about my child's well-being?

WHAT'S IN IT FOR ME?

1. Do I like doing things with children? Do I enjoy activities that children can do?
2. Would I want a child to be " like me"?
3. Would I try to pass on to my child my ideas and values? What if my child's ideas turn out to be different from mine?
4. Would I want my child to achieve things that I wish I had but didn't?
5. Would I expect my child to keep me from being lonely in my old age? Do I do that for my parents? Do my parents do that for my grandparents?
6. Do I want a boy or a girl child? What if I don't get what I want?
7. Would having a child show others how mature I am?
8. Will I prove I am a man or a woman by having a child?
9. Do I expect my child to make my life happy?

RAISING A CHILD: WHAT'S THERE TO KNOW?

1. Do I like children? When I'm around children for a while, what do I think or feel about having one around all the time?
2. Do I enjoy teaching others?
3. Is it easy for me to tell other people what I want, or need, or what I expect of them?
4. Do I want to give a child the love he or she needs? Is loving easy for me?
5. Am I patient enough to deal with the noise and the confusion and twenty-four-hour-a-day responsibility? What kind of time and space do I need for myself?
6. What do I do when I get angry or upset? Would I take things out on a child if I lost my temper?

7. What does discipline mean to me? What does freedom, or setting limits, or giving space mean? What is being too strict or not strict enough? Would I want a perfect child?
8. How do I get along with my parents? What will I do to avoid the mistakes my parents made?
9. How would I take care of my child's health and safety? How do I take care of my own?
10. What if I have a child and find out I made a wrong decision?

HAVE MY PARTNER AND I REALLY TALKED ABOUT BECOMING PARENTS?

1. Does my partner want to have a child? Have we talked about our reasons?
2. Could we give a child a good home? Is our relationship a happy and strong one?
3. Are we both ready to give our time and energy to raising a child?
4. Could we share our love with a child without jealousy?
5. What would happen if we separated after having a child, or if one of us should die?
6. Do my partner and I understand each other's feelings about religion, work, family, child raising, future goals? Do we feel pretty much the same way? Will children fit into these feelings, hopes, and plans?
7. Suppose one of us wants a child and the other doesn't? Who decides?
8. Which of these questions do we need to *really* discuss before making a decision?

SOURCE: ETR Associates/Network Publications, "Am I Parent Material?" (pamphlet).

child declines.) To raise a child through age seventeen runs from $81,810 to $160,080 in current, non-inflated dollars. Obviously, parents who have had a chance to establish themselves financially will be better able to bear the economic burdens of childrearing. Ann Goetting's (1986) review of parental satisfaction research revealed that "those who postpone parenthood until other components of their lives—especially their careers—are solidified" express enhanced degrees of satisfaction. Older parents may also be more emotionally mature and thus more capable of dealing with parenting stresses (although age isn't necessarily indicative of emotional maturity). In addition, as Jane Price (1982) wrote, "Combating the aging process is something of a national preoccupation. . . . In our society, the power of children to revitalize and refresh is part of the host of forces encouraging men and women to become parents much later than they did in the past."

◻ BECOMING A PARENT

A man and woman who become parents enter a new phase of their lives. More than marriage, parenthood signifies adulthood—the final, irreversible end of youthful roles. A person can become an ex-spouse but never an ex-parent. The irrevocable nature of parenthood may make the first-time parent doubtful and apprehensive, especially during the pregnancy. Yet people have few ways of preparing for parenting. Parenthood has to be learned experientially (although ideas can modify practices). A person may receive assistance from more experienced parents, but each new parent has to learn on his or her own. (See Goetting, 1986, and Umberson, 1989, for reviews of the literature on parental satisfaction.)

Transition: Parental Stress

The abrupt transition from a nonparent to a parent role may create considerable stress. Parents take on parental roles literally overnight, and the job goes on without relief around the clock. Many parents express concern about their ability to meet all the responsibilities of childrearing (see Klinman and Vukelich, 1985).

Many of the stresses felt by new parents closely reflect gender roles (Scott and Alwin, 1989; see Cowan and Cowan, 1988, for a study of changes in male and female roles after birth). Overall, mothers seem to experience greater stress than fathers (Harriman, 1983). Although a couple may have an egalitarian marriage before the birth of the first child, the marriage usually becomes more traditional once a child is born. The wife may give up her job to rear the child. Because her husband is usually away at work during the day, the housework becomes her full responsibility. Her world narrows, focusing increasingly on the demands of motherhood. If the mother must continue to work in addition to the father, or if the woman is single, she will have a dual role as both homemaker *and* provider. She will also probably have the responsibility for finding adequate child care, and it will probably be she who stays-home with the child when he or she is sick.

A study by Jacqueline Ventura (1987) found multiple role demands to be the greatest source of stress for mothers. Thirty-five percent of mothers were concerned about juggling a job, parenting, housekeeping, and "taking care of husband." (A "small number of fathers also described the struggle to finish take-home work or household tasks and help with child care.") A study by Judith Myers-Walls (1984) found that mothers' adjustment to fulfilling multiple roles was made easier if they used the following coping strategies: (1) holding a positive view of the situation, (2) developing a "salient" role (deciding which role should dominate when conflict

Having a family is like having a bowling alley installed in your head.

Martin Mull

Warning! The Surgeon General has determined that trying to be a good parent can be hazardous to your health.

Art Dworken

arose), (3) compartmentalizing roles, and (4) compromising standards (of household cleanliness, for example). Abner Boles and Harriet Curtis-Boles (1986) suggest that African-American families' flexibility and egalitarianism may stand them in good stead during this transition to parenthood: "Black families have repeatedly demonstrated an ability to cross the boundaries of gender-linked sex roles and perform roles as needed to insure the effective functioning of the family."

There are various other sources of parental stress. Sixty-four percent of fathers in Ventura's study described severe stress associated with their work. A number of mothers and fathers were concerned about not having enough money. Other sources of stress involve infant health and care, infant crying, interactions with the spouse (including sexual relations), interactions with other family members and friends, and general anxiety and depression (Harriman, 1983; McKim, 1987; Ventura, 1987; Wilkie and Ames, 1986).

Although the first year of childrearing is bound to be stressful, the couple experience less stress if they (1) have already developed a strong relationship, (2) are open in their communication, (3) have agreed on family planning, and (4) originally had a strong desire for the child (Russell, 1974). Psychiatrist and researcher Jerry M. Lewis and colleagues (Lewis, Owen, and Cox, 1989) stress the importance of "marital competence" in the "successful incorporation of the child into the family." Another important factor in maintaining marital quality during this time is the father's emotional and physical support (Tietjen and Bradley, 1985). Jay Belsky (1986) writes, "The more help that husbands can be induced, encouraged, or coerced to give around the home, the less dissatisfied the wife is likely to be with the union."

Ventura (1987) suggests that families can be assisted by improved health care and support in three areas: (1) *Support:* During the prenatal period, parents need help locating community resources, such as La Leche League and child-care assistance, so that they can "restore their energy" during the postpartum period. Fathers need to be encouraged in their nurturing role. Employers need to restructure schedules, develop child-care programs, and institute parental leave policies. (2) *Coordination of care:* Parents need good communication and support from practitioners following the birth. They need "concrete explanations and demonstrations." Health practitioners, child-care providers, and community professionals need to coordinate their communication with each other. (3) *Anticipatory care and problem solving:* Teaching about development, childhood illnesses, and safety should be an ongoing part of clinic and child-care services. (For discussion of the transition to parenthood, also see Belsky, 1985a, 1985b, and 1985c; and Grossman et al., 1987. For a discussion of African-American couples and transition to parenthood, see Boles and Curtis-Boles, 1986.)

Parents and the Disabled Child

The advent of disability in a family, whether through birth, illness, or accident, is a tremendous stress on the family unit, especially at first. Parents may be overwhelmed with feelings of guilt, uncertainties about their parenting abilities, and fears about the future. Mothers especially feel the effects of this stress, because they are generally responsible for the child's day-to-day care. Siblings of disabled children also experience added stress. Some studies have indicated that the marital relationship may suffer in families with a disabled child, although it is only the already shaky marriages that are seriously threatened (Harris, 1984). Another study showed couples' marital adjustment to be unaffected (Collins, 1986). Healthy marriages may actually be enhanced through the experience of rearing a "special" child (Belsky et al., 1984). (The impact of disability and chronic illness on the family is discussed in greater detail in Chapter 10.)

Schneider (1983) developed a model describing stages of grief that is applicable to all life circumstances involving significant loss, including the loss of health or ability in a child. The six stages of this model are as follows:

1. Initial awareness, often accompanied by guilt and panic. If the loss event occurs at birth, the mother is especially tired and vulnerable at this stage.
2. Strategies to overcome loss, characterized by the ambiguity of holding on and letting go simultaneously.
3. Awareness of the extent and complications of loss. Much energy is consumed in dealing with this phase, often resulting in poor physical health. The griever experiences resentment, cynicism, and anger.
4. Completions: healing, acceptance of loss, resolution. This may be a lengthy process.
5. Resolution and reformations, bringing an enhanced sense of personal power.
6. Transcending loss, being free of its power to bind and limit. New energy and growth are now possible.

All parents at times find themselves torn between wanting independence for their children and wanting to protect them from pain. Parents of disabled children probably feel this conflict even more acutely than others. One of the main challenges that these parents face is assessing their child's ability to be independent and helping him or her to gain self-sufficiency. The National Information Center for Children and Youth with Handicaps (NICHY, 1990) suggests that this poses the greatest challenge to parents of girls, who are doubly stereotyped—both as "helpless, dependent" people with a disability and as "passive, dependent" females. NICHY suggests that parents help their children become independent by first of all looking within themselves to see what their own biases and expectations are. There may be changes that the parents or siblings can make in the way in which they treat the disabled child, such as letting him or her do things with less help. "The single, most important thing parents can do," according to NICHY, "is to expect [the child] to *aspire*." Parents can also help by being involved in the child's education and knowledgeable about the child's rights and opportunities.

Children are subject to numerous disabling afflictions and conditions—Down's syndrome, autism, cerebral palsy, cystic fibrosis, blindness, physical abnormalities, growth disorders, and injuries, to name just a few. Some of these disabilities are physical, some developmental, some both. Despite the prevalence of such conditions, we tend to shy away from anyone who is not "normal." Families of disabled children report that not only strangers but also friends, neighbors, family members, and even medical and service personnel treat them and their children insensitively. Such reactions serve to remind parents that their children are not valued by society. The parents may hold themselves responsible for the child's behavior or condition. In a study of families with disabled children, almost 40 percent reported that their children were not receiving needed educational, medical, or other services (Collins, 1986). This kind of treatment not only deprives the disabled and their families of much needed support and acceptance, but it also deprives the rest of society of valuable relationships and interactions. Families with disabled members need to fight social isolation by reaching out to their friends for assistance, forming networks with similar families, and learning to use existing community resources (see Resource Center at the end of the text).

Motherhood

Many women see their destiny as motherhood. Given the choice of becoming mothers or not (made possible through birth control), most women would probably

Most mothers find fulfillment (as well as fatigue and frustration) in their motherhood roles. The overwhelming majority would choose to become mothers again if given the choice.

**Cleaning and scrubbing can wait till
   tomorrow.
For babies grow up we've learned to our
   sorrow.
So quiet down cobwebs, dust go to
   sleep.
I'm rocking my baby and babies don't
   keep.**

Anonymous

choose to become mothers at some point in their lives, and they would make this choice for very positive reasons (see Cook et al., 1982; Gallup and Newport, 1990; Genevie and Margolies, 1987). But many women make no conscious choice; they become mothers without weighing their decision or considering its effect on their own lives and the lives of their children and partners. The consequences of a non-reflective decision—bitterness, frustration, anger, or depression—may be great. Yet it is also possible that a woman's nonreflective decision will turn out to be "right" and that she will experience unique personal fulfillment as a result.

Although researchers are unable to find any instinctual motivation for having children among humans (which does not necessarily mean that such motivation does not exist), they recognize many social motives impelling women to become mothers. When a woman becomes a mother, she may feel that her identity as an adult is confirmed. Having a child of her own proves her womanliness because from her earliest years she has been trained to assume the role of mother. She has changed dolls' diapers and pretended to feed them, practicing infant care. She played house while her brother built forts. The stories a girl has heard, the games she has played, the textbooks she has read, the religion she has been taught, the television she has watched—all have socialized her for the mother role. As Jessie Bernard (1982) wrote, "An inbred desire is no less potent than an instinctive one. The pain and anguish resulting from deprivation of an acquired desire for children are as real as the pain and anguish resulting from an instinctive one." Whatever the reason, most women choose motherhood.

And most, though not all, would choose it again. Interviews with 2,000 mothers found that eight out of ten would have children if they had the chance to do it again (Genevie and Margolies, 1987). Still, there remains an ambivalence that many mothers face. Liz Koch (1987) writes:

We fear we will lose ourselves if we stay with our infants. We resist surrendering even to our newborns for fear of being swallowed up. We hear and accept both the conflicting advice that bonding with our babies is vital, and the opposite undermining message that to be a good mother, we must get away as soon and as often as possible. We hear that if we mother our own babies full time, we will have nothing to offer society, our husbands, ourselves, even our children. We fear isolation, lack of self-esteem, feelings of entrapment, of emotional and financial dependency. We fear that we will be left behind—empty arms, empty home, empty women, when our children grow away. . . . The reality is that in many ways contemporary America does not honor Mothering.

Koch observes that the "job" of mother is not valued because it is associated with "menial tasks of housekeeper, cook, laundrymaid" and so on. She writes:

If instead we looked at our mothering in and of itself, we could begin to separate the house from our role as mother. . . . It is also a way to educate our partners about the importance of caring for young children. . . . If we separate out and redefine our role as mother, it can become meaningful work, with intellectual, creative, and physical dimensions. . . . It becomes important to keep the creative juices flowing, like in any other profession, by meeting with colleagues, i.e. other mothers, and reading relevant material which can be assimilated by what feels right in our hearts.

Whether a mother is employed outside the home or works at home "full-time," her role deserves to be valued by society. Koch says of the "special state" of motherhood:

Being mothers is truly immersing ourselves in a special state, a moment to moment state of being. It is difficult to look at our day and measure success quantitatively. The day is successful when we have shared moments, built special threads of communication, looked deeply into our children's eyes and felt our hearts open. . . . It is important that we see our job as vitally important to our own growth, to our community, to society, and to world peace. Building family ties, helping healthy, loved children grow to maturity is a worthwhile pursuit. . . . The transmission of values is a significant reason to raise our own children. We are there to answer their questions and to show children, through our example, what is truly important to us.

Fatherhood

When we speak of "mothering" a child, everyone knows what we mean: nurturing, caring for, feeding, diapering, soothing, loving. Mothers generally "mother" their children almost every day of the year for at least eighteen consecutive years. The meaning of "fathering" is quite different. "Fathering" a child need take no more than a few minutes if we understand the term in its traditional sense—that is, impregnating the child's mother. Nurturant behavior by a father toward his child has not typically been referred to as "fathering." ("Mothering" doesn't seem appropriate either in this context.) The verb "to parent" has been coined to fill the need for a word that adequately describes the child-tending behaviors of both mothers and fathers (see Verzaro-Lawrence, 1981).

As we have seen, the father's traditional roles of provider and protector are instrumental; they satisfy the family's economic and physical needs. The mother's role in this traditional model is expressive; she gives emotional and psychological support for her family. However, the lines between these roles are becoming increasingly blurred because of economic pressures and new societal expectations.

From a developmental viewpoint, the father's importance to the family derives not only from his role as a representative of society, connecting his family and his culture, but also from his role as a developer of self-control and autonomy in his children. Research indicates that although mothers are inclined to view both sons and daughters as "simply children" and to apply similar standards to both sexes, fa-

It is so still in the house.
There is a calm in the house;
The snowstorm wails out there,
And the dogs are rolled up with snouts
under the tail.
My little boy is sleeping on the ledge,
On his back he lies, breathing through
his open mouth.
His little stomach is bulging round—
Is it strange if I start to cry with joy?

Eskimo mother's song

The family today emphasizes the expressive (emotional) qualities of all its members, including the father, much more than in the past.

thers tend to be differently involved with their male and female children. This may place a daughter at a disadvantage, since she has less opportunity to develop instrumental attitudes and behaviors. It may also be disadvantageous to a son, as it can limit the development of his own expressive patterns and interests (Gilbert et al., 1982). In contrast to this research, Kyle Pruett's study (1987) of "primary nurturing fathers" (fathers who provide the main day-to-day care) showed that these men treated their girl and boy children essentially equally.

In 1971, Rebelsky and Hanks found that fathers interacted an average of 37.7 seconds per day with their infant children (those between two weeks and three months of age). A more recent study found fathers averaging eight minutes per day with their children on weekdays and fourteen minutes per day on weekends (contrasted with homemaker mothers' thirty and thirty-six minutes, respectively) (Fischman, 1986). In other studies, half the preschool children questioned said that they preferred television to daddy, and one child in ten said that the person that the child feared most was his or her father (none of them named mother as most feared) (Pogrebin, 1982a). Although fathers today are participating increasingly in pregnancy and birth processes, it is not clear that this involvement predisposes the father to greater participation with his children later on.

It appears that the family today emphasizes the expressive qualities of all its members, including the father, much more than in the past (Lamb, 1986). The "emergent" perspective described by Robert Fein (1980) views men as psychologically capable of participating in virtually all parenting behaviors (except gestation and lactation). Further, such participation is beneficial to the development and well-being of both children and adults. The implicit contradiction between the terms "real man" and "good father" needs to be resolved if boys are to develop into fathers who feel their "manhood enlarged and not depleted by active, caring fatherhood" (Pogrebin, 1982a). We see this contradiction epitomized by parents' fear of allowing boys to play with dolls. When a child plays with a doll, he or she is modeling the familiar parent/child relationship. By discouraging boys from "playing house," we create "an aversion to the very activities that make a man a good father" (Pogrebin, 1982a).

In support of this emergent view of fatherhood, Dr. Benjamin Spock (1968, 1976) has made a number of changes in his *Baby and Child Care* (otherwise known as the "Baby Bible"). On the subject of father participation in childrearing, the original version (1945) said:

A man can be a warm father and a real man at the same time . . . . Of course I don't mean that the father has to give as many bottles or change just as many diapers as the mother. But it's fine for him to do these things occasionally. He might make the formula on Sunday.

The revised edition (Spock and Rothenberg, 1985) advises its fathers to take on at least half of the child management duties and participate in the housework:

When a father does his share as a matter of course . . . it does much more than simply lighten his wife's work load and give her companionship. . . . It shows that he believes this work is crucial for the welfare of the family, that it calls for judgment and skill, and that it's his responsibility as much as it is hers. . . . This is what sons and daughters need to see in action if they are to grow up without sexist attitudes.

Research into father care of infants has revealed one dramatic finding: If a man is involved in the physical care of his own or someone else's child younger than three years, the probability that he will later be involved in the abuse of any child is greatly reduced (Parker and Parker, 1984 and 1986).

In his intensive study, Kyle Pruett (1987) found that "fatherhood is changing, with fastball speed, especially compared with the languid pace of social evolution."

Don't be the man you think you should be, be the father you wish you'd had.

Letty Cottin Pogrebin

We learn from experience. A man never wakes up his second baby just to see it smile.

Grace Williams

He concluded that fathers must be encouraged to develop the nurturing quality in themselves in order to experience the "unimagined rewards" of parenthood. James A. Levine, a former vice-president of the Bank Street College of Education who now leads fatherhood seminars at major corporations, says that the new father is a man who "attempts to make childrearing an important part of his life" (quoted in Lawson, 1990). Levine lists several trends that are indicative of the father's changing role: more men are attending the births of their children and taking time off from work afterward; more men are taking children to day care or to the doctor; more men are enrolled in parenting classes; diaper-changing tables are appearing in the men's rooms of airports and train stations; and fathers with babies are becoming highly visible in advertising (Lawson, 1990). "The truth is leaking out," Pruett writes, "through the real lives of men and their children that the uninvited, uninvolved, unwelcomed, inept father is moving toward obsolescence." (See Lamb, 1986, for a collection of essays on fatherhood in today's society.)

⊓ OTHER IMPORTANT CHILD SOCIALIZERS

Child Care

Supplementary child care is a crucial issue for today's parents of young children. The number of dual-worker and single-parent families has doubled in the past decade; such families are now the rule rather than the exception. Many parents must look outside their homes for assistance in childrearing. About two million children currently receive formal, licensed day care, and another 5 million attend nursery schools. Uncounted millions are cared for by relatives or baby-sitters, and perhaps 5 million children under the age of ten have no one at all to look after them (Watson, 1984b). (See Chapter 9 for a discussion of the role of day care in maternal employment.) Day-care homes and centers, nursery schools, and preschools can relieve parents of some of their childrearing tasks and also furnish them with some valuable time of their own. Dr. Nathan Talbot (1976), professor of pediatrics at Harvard University, wrote:

With three provisos, these out-of-home experiences can so enrich a father's or mother's life that s/he is better able to serve the needs of the children than s/he would be if s/he stayed home all the time. The first proviso is that the children are well cared for. . . . The second is that at least one parent continues to be readily available to the children for a minimum of one or two hours most days. The third is that a parent . . . remain the person responsible for the upbringing of the children. . . . Supplementary child care can solidify rather than disrupt the family and can improve rather than hurt the children's chances for happy and developmentally rich lives.

What does group care have to offer children? Studies of infants and young children in group-care situations have shown that their development is stimulated or enhanced by enriched child-care environments (Belsky, 1991; Kutner, 1988). Emotional security and patterns of attachment to parents do not seem to be significantly altered by quality group-care experiences. Other studies have indicated that the overall effect of day care on intellectual development is neither beneficial nor adverse. Furthermore, in the case of disadvantaged families, high-quality child care has great positive effect (Belsky et al., 1984).

Dr. Burton White, director of Boston's Center for Parent Education, however, sees the trend toward increasing use of day care as a "disaster": "Both parents don't have to work—they both *want* to work to maintain a house and lifestyle. They are putting their desires above the welfare of the baby" (cited in Watson, 1984b). This assessment may apply to families in which one parent has a substantial income, but for many dual-earner families and most single-parent families, child care is a necessity, not a luxury. As Jay Belsky and colleagues (1984) point out, "Since it is unlikely that mothers will return in large numbers to the role of full-time homemakers, and that day care will go away, . . . the critical issue [in day care] is the condition of care."

National concern periodically is focused on day care by revelations of sexual abuse of children by their caregivers. Although these revelations have brought providers of child care under close public scrutiny and have alerted parents to potential dangers, they have also produced a backlash within the child-care profession. Some caregivers are now reluctant to have physical contact with the children; male child-care workers feel especially constrained and may find their jobs at risk (Chaze, 1984). A national study (Finkelhor, 1988), however, found that children have a far greater likelihood of being sexually abused by a father, stepfather, or other relative than by a day-care worker. In 1985 the U.S. Department of Health and Human Services announced new day-care guidelines, calling for training of staff in the prevention and detection of child abuse, thorough checks on prospective employees, and allowance of parental visits at any time. But critics believe that the government should go farther in establishing standards for day care itself. Senator Paula Hawkins (quoted in Collins, 1985) stated, "They really have to consider the quality of the care, and not just the quality of the care-givers." Government funding and assistance for day-care programs remain small to nonexistent.

What can parents do to insure quality care for their children? In addition to the obvious requirements of cleanliness, comfort, good food, a safe environment, and an attentive, trained staff, parents should look for the following (from Watson, 1984b):

❑ *A stable staff.* Children are more secure when they know who is caring for them. Ideally, the staff should be trained in child development or psychology.
❑ *Small groups.* Infants especially need close attention and stimulation. Older preschoolers can function in groups of four to eight children per adult, depending on the children's ages.
❑ *Appropriate attention.* Children need attention appropriate to their developmental stage.
❑ *Appropriate activities.* Activities should be appropriate to the children's developmental stage, reflecting their needs to learn about themselves and their environment.
❑ *Parental involvement.* Parents should be welcomed and their involvement with the child-care program encouraged.

As with a number of critical services in our society, those who most need supplementary child care are those who can least afford it. Child care done properly is a costly business (even though child-care work remains a relatively low-paying, low-status job). The United States is one of the few industrialized nations that does not have a comprehensive national day-care policy. In fact, beginning in 1981, the federal government dramatically cut federal contributions to day care; many state governments followed suit. Nathan Talbot (1976) observed that "we are shortchanging ourselves and the future of our nation by failing to invest in our children as our best and most critically important asset. . . . Child care is worthy of a position close to the top in our national hierarchy of priorities."

Television

In most American households the television is on at least seven hours each day. Starting around age four, most Americans watch an average of four hours of TV or

A body at rest tends to remain at rest.

Newton's First Law of Motion

more each day. The average American child, by the time he or she reaches eighteen, will have spent at least sixteen thousand hours watching television. No other activity except sleep occupies more time for children and adolescents (Brown, 1990; Singer, 1983). An average viewing week of thirty hours includes about four hundred commercials and provides a kaleidoscopic mix of Kix, Trix, Gummi Bears, Pound Puppies, jaded yuppies, Superman, Superboy, Super Mario Brothers, Classic Coke, practical jokes, violent crimes, cheap wine, fancy cars, fast food, Fred Flintstone, Freddy Krueger, and Peg Bundy. Thirty hours of watching television is thirty hours not spent interacting with family members, playing outside, playing creatively, reading, fantasizing, doing homework, exploring, or even napping. Besides limiting children's time for such pursuits, television has also been implicated in a number of individual, familial, and societal disorders.

Researchers have documented a variety of physiological effects produced by television, including altered brain-wave (trancelike) states and hyperactivity, impaired eye movements, and impaired hand and body use. Low levels of microwave radiation are emitted by color sets. Although the manufacturers assure us that we are in no danger, we are also cautioned not to sit too close "just in case." Television has also been observed to have deleterious effects on learning and perception, nutrition, life-style, and family and social relationships (Fabes, Wilson, and Christopher, 1989; Moody, 1980). Not all research supports the assertion that TV is detrimental to family life, however. Some studies have shown that positive feelings result when families share their viewing experience (Kubey and Csikszentmihalyi, 1990).

Much parent/child conflict revolves around eating habits. And anyone watching television, especially children's television, cannot help but be aware of the amount of junk-food advertising (for sweetened breakfast cereals, candy, sodas) directed toward children. One expert testified before Congress that "an advertisement to a child has the quality of an order, not a suggestion." Thus, responsible parents are put in the position of having to defend good nutrition against the incessant bom-

To be able to fill leisure intelligently is the last product of civilization.

Bertrand Russell

Television provides role models for children. What kind of message do you believe this African-American child is receiving from her cartoon heroine?

bardment of commercials. Advertisers count on the child's ability to influence parents' buying—where both children's and adults' products are concerned.

Because of the constant pressure to buy and the necessity of regulating their children's viewing habits, some parents choose not to have a television. Once the television is gone, it is often not missed. It may be missed more by adults who use it for their own entertainment and as a baby-sitter for their children. Children are peer oriented and have their friends to play with. The use of television as a baby-sitter underscores a dilemma for many parents: they disapprove of what their children see, but they also want to have the time to themselves that may be obtained by letting their children watch television.

Children learn about the world from watching television. Although some valuable and thought-provoking information may be gained from it (especially if the viewer is an economically or culturally "disadvantaged" child), much of television programming promotes or condones racist, sexist, agist, homophobic and other negative stereotypes. Images of women have improved in recent years, but depictions of the family still tend to be stereotypical or romanticized. Middle-class families are likely to be portrayed as "superpeople" who deal effectively with any problem, whereas working-class families (especially fathers) are more likely to be shown as inept (Fabes, Wilson, and Christopher, 1989). Researchers have expressed concern that the idealization of middle-class life presents unrealistic goals and may lead impressionable viewers to question the adequacy of their own lives.

Much television programming also promotes violence and fear (Fabes, Wilson, and Christopher, 1989). The cumulative effect of television, according to a report by the Annenberg School of Communications, is the creation of the "mean world syndrome," the belief that crime and violence are much more pervasive in the world than they actually are (Pogatchnik, 1990). A report issued by the National Institute of Mental Health stated that "overwhelming" evidence indicates that "excessive" violence on television causes aggressive behavior in children (Tooth, 1985). This conclusion was based on the results of approximately 2,500 separate studies conducted since the early 1970s. Besides encouraging aggressive behavior, television also has the effect of desensitizing viewers to observed violent acts. Children may learn to see violence as an acceptable means of problem solving and to show no moral outrage at acts of destructive aggression.

Kate Moody (1980) suggests the following criteria for helping parents to evaluate what their children watch:

1. What kind of distinction is made between reality and make-believe? If there is a transition between the two, is it clearly signaled to children?

2. Is the program geared to the child's level of understanding?

3. How are problems solved? By using others? By hitting? Revenge? Money? Magic? Cooperation?

4. What role models are offered? Are sex or race stereotypes reinforced?

5. What is the pace of the program? What special effects are used? What is the noise/confusion level?

6. How is humor used? Does a laugh track tell the child what is to be considered funny?

7. How is the world portrayed? As a dangerous and fearsome place?

8. What kind of commercials are associated with the program? Junk food? Fast cars? Personal hygiene products?

9. What is the child's response to the program? Is he or she aggressive, cooperative, excitable, calm? What kinds of play follow viewing?

10. Is the program good enough to be worth the parent's time?

. . . TV causes . . . serious and pervasive violence in normal . . . youngsters who watch TV attentively and regularly. What results from this psychic abuse is the impoverishment of personality and the trivialization of life.

Herb Kohl

We are drowning our youngsters in violence, cynicism and sadism piped into the living room and even the nursery. The grandchildren of kids who used to weep because the Little Match Girl froze to death now feel cheated if she isn't slugged, raped, and thrown into a Bessemer converter.

Jenkin Lloyd Jones

❑ CHILDREN AND ETHNICITY

A person's ethnicity is not necessarily fixed and unchanging. Researchers generally agree that ethnicity has both objective and subjective components. The objective component refers to one's ancestry, cultural heritage and, to varying degrees, physical appearance. The subjective component refers to whether one **feels** he or she is a member of a certain ethnic group, such as African American, Latino, Asian American, Native American, and so on. If both parents are from the same ethnic group, the child will probably identify as a member of that group. But if he or she has parents from different ethnic groups, ethnic identification becomes more complex. In such cases, one may identify with both groups, only one, or according to the situation—Latino when with Latino relatives and friends or Anglo when with Anglo friends and relatives. However we choose to identify ourselves, our families are the key to the transmission of ethnic identification.

Ethnicity and Child Socialization

A child's ethnic background affects how he or she is socialized. Latinos and Asian Americans, for example, stress the authority of the father in the family. In both groups, parents command considerable respect from their children, even when the children become adults. Older siblings, especially brothers, have authority over younger siblings and are expected to set a good example (Becerra, 1988; Tran, 1988; Wong, 1988). Asian Americans tend to discourage aggression in children and for discipline to rely on censure and shame rather than physical force.

Groups with minority status in the United States may be different from each other in some ways, but they also have much in common. For one thing, they em-

America's children are becoming increasingly ethnically diverse. By the year 2000, half of America's children will be from non-white or non-Anglo ethnic groups. In California, these children already represent the majority.

phasize education as the means for their children to achieve success. For another, they are often dual-worker families, so the children may have considerable exposure to television while the parents are away from home. This may be viewed as a mixed blessing: on the one hand, TV may help children who need to acquire English language skills; on the other, it can promote fear, violence, and negative stereotypes of women and minority status groups. It can discourage creativity and encourage passivity. Former world light heavyweight champion Jose Torres (1991) counsels young Latinos: "Instead of watching TV, read and write. Words are the symbols of reality, and a well-read person, skilled at decoding those symbols, is better able to comprehend and think about the real world."

Some American children are raised with a strong sense of ethnic identification, whereas others are not. Identification with a particular group gives a sense of pride, security, and belonging. At the same time, it can also give a sense of separateness from the mainstream society. Often, however, that sense of separateness is imposed by the greater society. Discrimination and prejudice shape the lives of many American children. According to Margaret Beale Spencer (1985), a minority status child's "acquisition of a healthy psyche requires an intervention between societally communicated cultural assumptions and the minority child's healthy psychological development." Nonminority status children generally do not experience this lack of congruence between society's values and healthy psychological development. Parents of ethnic minority children may try to prepare their children for the harsh realities of life beyond the family and immediate community (Peterson, 1985). One researcher (Richardson, 1981) wrote about African Americans:

Black mothers know that their children will ultimately experience racism. They believe that racism experiences can be devastating and destructive if the child has not been prepared to recognize or develop techniques and strategies for coping with these experiences. The mothers also know that black children will ultimately have to know they are black and understand what a black identity means in a racist society.

Raising Children to Be Prejudice-Free

The world in which our grandparents grew up was simpler than our own in many ways. Towns and neighborhoods stayed the same from year to year, and customs didn't change much either. People passed their prejudices on to their children, who often accepted them without question, because they had little or no experience to teach them otherwise. George Simpson and Milton Yinger (1985) explain: "If asked why he dislikes a member of a minority group, [the child] will recite the reasons taught him by his culture, by the adults around him—always assuming, of course, that they are strictly his own reasons and that they are the true reasons."

In today's fast-changing world, we cannot afford to cling complacently to the narrow-mindedness and prejudices of the past. Technological advances in communication and transportation are quickly shrinking the distances between us and other peoples of the world. At home we are becoming more diverse ethnically and linguistically. By the year 2020, it is expected that one out of every three people in the United States will be from what we now call a "minority" group (Sobol, 1990). Timothy Bergen comments: "The future will be in a culturally pluralistic nation and a rapidly shrinking world" (quoted in Fuller, 1989/1990). We must learn to live together with respect and tolerance for our ethnic, cultural, and personal differences (see Matiella, 1991).

The following guidelines are suggested to help parents foster an appreciation of cultural differences in their children.

❑ Explore your family's heritage with your children. Look at old photos and talk to grandparents and other older family members. Find out about the hopes and dreams they had and the obstacles they overcame. Learn more about your cultural background through the art, music, and literature.

❑ Examine your own attitudes and knowledge about other ethnic groups. Expand your understanding of other cultures and encourage your child's interest in new cultural experiences. Possible resources include libraries, museums, language classes, travel agents, festivals, dances, concerts, music tapes, cookbooks, ethnic markets, and restaurants. Be sure that you have an up-to-date world map or globe for reference. Consider finding pen pals in other countries or helping to support a foreign child in need through an agency (such as Child Reach or Save the Children) that encourages correspondence between participants. Think about hosting a visiting high school or university student—for a school term or just for dinner.

❑ Whenever possible, take the opportunity to celebrate diversity and contradict stereotypes. Help children develop critical thinking so that they can recognize stereotyping—for example, in TV shows that always portray "the Native American in full headdress, the black man as the villain and Hispanics with lots of children" (Wardle, 1989/1990). Get children books, posters, videos, puzzles, and dolls that honor cultural and ethnic diversity.

❑ It's important to be open to questions about race and ethnicity so that children don't get the idea that these are taboo subjects. If you don't know an answer, do some research, or talk to your child's teacher or a librarian. If your son or daughter has a conflict with someone from another ethnic group, guide the child to deal with personal issues and not to blame the other person's culture or ethnic group. If you hear children using stereotyped or derogatory terms, intervene. Let them know it's not right to put others down or tease them about their differences. And watch your own language! Call ethnic groups by the names they prefer rather than common usage terms or slang that may be offensive.

❑ Select child-care groups and schools with ethnically diverse staffs and children. Support your children's friendships with others of diverse backgrounds. Make sure that schools teach positively about diversity and that events such as holiday programs don't enforce stereotypes. For example, Native Americans should be portrayed as a diverse people with unique ways of life, legends, philosophy, and contributions and not represented merely as "guests" of the Pilgrims on Thanksgiving. In addition, schools need to be sensitive to religious differences when planning such programs. With imagination, these events can be conducted so that they include presentations from diverse cultural groups and can be both entertaining and educational for all.

❑ Take action. Don't ignore bigotry when it happens. If someone makes a racist remark, say, "Please don't talk that way around me or my children." When your children see you standing up for your beliefs, they will learn to do the same. Encourage your child to respond to put downs or aggressive teasing with a stock response such as, "Don't call me that. It's not fair" ("Talking to Children. . . .," 1989/1990).

❑ It all starts with self-esteem. If we let children know that they are valued, they are more likely to find value in others. If they are sensitive to others' feelings, they are less likely to form prejudices.

Although these guidelines have been formulated with ethnic and cultural differences in mind, many of them can be applied to or adapted for learning to appreciate and accept people with other kinds of differences—such as those who have disabilities or who are gay or lesbian. (For a more complete discussion of children and cultural diversity, see Matiella, 1991.)

❑ GAY AND LESBIAN PARENTING

There may be as many as 1.5 million lesbian mothers rearing their children in the United States (Hoeffer, 1981). The number of gay fathers is estimated to be 1 to 3 million (Bozett, 1987b). Most of these parents are or have been married. Heterosexual fears about gay and lesbian parents center around parenting abilities, fear of sexual abuse, and worry that the children will become gay or lesbian.

Lesbian Mothers

While their sexual orientation is different from heterosexual single mothers, lesbian mothers share many similarities with them. One study of lesbian and heterosexual single mothers (Kirkpatrick et al., 1981) found that their life-styles, childrearing practices, and general demographic data were strikingly similar. One of the few areas in which lesbian and heterosexual mothers differed from each other was in cohabitation, according to another study (Lewin and Lyons, 1982). Most heterosexual mothers felt no need for secrecy if they were living with a man. But many lesbian mothers felt increased vulnerability to hostility from outsiders if they were cohabiting. In particular, they feared the responses from neighbors, their children's playmates, and their own parents. As a result, lesbian mothers may feel forced to exclude their partners from school or other social activities involving their children. Lesbians also fear losing their children in custody disputes. This fear is well-founded, as only about 15 percent of lesbian mothers win custody of their children. This is an improvement, however, over the situation in 1970, when less that 1 percent gained custody (Goldstein, 1986).

When children learn that their mothers are lesbians, according to one study of families with formerly married lesbian mothers, they are initially shocked (Lewis, 1980). At first, they tend to deny any pain or anger. Generally they have more difficulty in accepting their mother's lesbian identity than their parents' divorce or separation because there is no community of support. It is much easier to talk with others about their parents divorcing than about their mother being a lesbian. In Karen Lewis's study (1980), children between nine and twelve years of age felt a deep need to keep their mother's lesbian identity a secret. As a result, these children felt a sense of isolation; they were unable to talk over their feelings with their friends. Both children and older adolescents worried that they might become gay or lesbian or that others might think they were gay or lesbian. The boys tended to become angry at their mother's partner, blaming her for their mother's sexual orientation. But whatever the children's response, all expressed a desire to accept their mothers. "Problems between the mother and children," observed Lewis, "seemed secondary to the children's respect for the difficult step she had taken." Therapist Saralie Bisnovitch Pennington (1987) wrote, "I cannot emphasize enough that children fare best in homes where the mothers are secure in both their lesbian identity and their parental role, and where they have a strong support system that includes other lesbian mothers."

Some lesbians, especially those in committed relationships, are choosing to create families through artificial insemination. To date, there are no reliable data on the number of such births, but anecdotal information indicates that it is in the thousands. There are many questions raised when a lesbian couple contemplates having a baby in this way: Who will be the birth mother? What will the relationship of the other mother be? Will the donor be known or unknown? If known, will the child have a relationship with him? Will the child have a relationship with the donor's partner? Which, if any, of the child's grandparents will have a relationship with him or her? Will there be a legal contract between the parenting parties? There are few precedents to learn from or role models to follow in these cases (see Pies, 1987). Another issue that such couples have to face is that the nonbiological parent has no legal tie to the child. Furthermore, society may not recognize her as a "real" parent, since children are expected to have only one *real* mother and one *real* father.

Gay Fathers

The reasons gay men marry are generally the same reasons heterosexuals marry (Bozett, 1987b). These might be genuine love or companionship; pressure from family, friends, or girlfriend; an attempt to "cure homosexuality"; or lack of awareness that one is gay. Most marriages of gay men appear to start off satisfactorily. Over time, however, the sexual relationship declines and the man begins to participate in clandestine same-sex liaisons. Once they have children, most gay men tend to stay married (Ross, 1972, 1978). For those whose wives accept their sexual orientation, the marriage may be fairly stable. But for most it is likely to be characterized by deceit, shame, and increasing anger. If such marriages do end in divorce, however, it is not necessarily a direct result of the homosexuality; it seems that gay men's marriages "like most other marriages, deteriorate for a variety of reasons" (Bozett, 1987b).

Studies of gay fathers indicate that "being gay is compatible with effective parenting" (Bozett, 1987c; Harris and Turner, 1986). Furthermore, it appears that gays who disclose their orientation to their children and who have a stable gay relationship tend to provide better-quality parenting than those who remain married and keep their gayness hidden. Married gay fathers may spend much of their free time seeking out sexual partners; they may also be workaholics who spend much of their time away from home (Miller, 1979). One study of gay fathers (Turner, Scadden, and Harris, 1985) concluded that (1) most gay fathers have positive relationships with their children, (2) the father's sexual orientation is relatively unimportant to

Lesbian families created through artificial insemination are a unique family form. Are such families single-parent families, stepfamilies, or a new family form?

the relationship, and (3) gay fathers endeavor to create stable home environments for their children. Another study (Harris and Turner, 1985/1986) found that there were no significant differences in the parenting of gays, lesbians, and heterosexuals except that the nongay parents apparently tried harder to provide "opposite sex" role models. Although the research on children of gay fathers is fairly limited at this time, it seems to indicate that the children's responses are similar to those of children of lesbian parents. Their primary concerns, especially at first, are about what others may think. They are embarrassed if their fathers are blatantly gay, and they worry that others will think they are too. Nevertheless, even though "children may not understand why their fathers are gay, and some may strongly disapprove, the child-father bond is maintained" (Bozett, 1987).

Fears about Gay and Lesbian Parenting

Heterosexual fears about the parenting abilities of lesbians and gays are unwarranted. Fears of the sexual abuse of children by gay parents or their partners are completely unsubstantiated. A review of the literature on the children of gay men and lesbians found that there were virtually no documented cases of sexual abuse by gay parents or their lovers; such exploitation appears to be committed disproportionately by heterosexuals (Cramer, 1986).

Fears about gay parents rejecting children of the other sex also seem unfounded. Such fears reflect the popular misconception that being gay or lesbian is a rejection of members of the other sex. Many gay and lesbian parents go out of their way to make sure that their children have role models of both sexes. Many also say that they hope their children will develop heterosexual identities in order to be spared the pain of growing up gay in a homophobic society. One study (Green, 1978) of thirty-seven children of lesbians found that all developed heterosexual identities. Another study (Hoeffer, 1981) of the children of lesbians and single heterosexual mothers found a lack of notable differences between the children. Both groups of children preferred toys associated with traditional gender roles. Peers rather than parents seem to have the greatest influence on a child's gender-role behavior (Green et al., 1986; Hoeffer, 1981).

As Brenda Maddox (1982) observed, "Gay people, once they are parents, are no more theoretical than straight parents. They have produced the children. They love them."

❑ STYLES AND STRATEGIES OF CHILDREARING

A parent's approach to training, teaching, nurturing, and helping a child will vary according to cultural influences, the parent's personality, the parent's basic attitude toward children and childrearing, and the role model that the parent presents to the child.

Authoritarian, Permissive, and Authoritative Parents

The three basic styles of childrearing may be termed *authoritarian*, *permissive*, and *authoritative* (Baumrind, 1971, 1983).

Authoritarian parents typically require absolute obedience. The parents' maintaining control is of first importance. "Because I said so," is a typical response to a child's questioning of parental authority, and physical force may be used to assure obedience. Working-class families tend to be more authoritarian than middle-class

Because it's good for you. Reason given to make child eat food it does not want.

Miss Manners

families. Diana Baumrind found that children of authoritarian parents tend to be less cheerful than other children and correspondingly more moody, passively hostile, and vulnerable to stress (see Belsky et al., 1984).

Permissive attitudes are more popular in middle-class families than in working-class families. The child's freedom of expression and autonomy are valued. Permissive parents rely on reasoning and explanations. Yet permissive parents may find themselves resorting to manipulation and justification. The child is free from external restraints but not from internal ones. The child is supposedly free because he or she conforms "willingly," but such freedom is not authentic. This form of socialization creates a bind: "Do what we tell you to do because *you* want to do it." Two psychologists commented on internalized control as a means of socialization as follows (Sluzki and Eliseo, 1971):

"If you do not obey, we shall be angry with you, but if you obey only because we are telling you, we shall also be angry, because you should be independent." (That is, *want* to do whatever one *should* do of one's own will.) This injunction creates an untenable situation, because it demands that an external source be confused with an internal one.

Baumrind (1983) found that although children of permissive parents are generally cheerful, they exhibit low levels of self-reliance and self-control.

Parents with **authoritative** attitudes toward childrearing rely on positive reinforcement and infrequent use of punishment. They direct the child in a manner that shows awareness of his or her feelings and capabilities. Parents encourage the development of the child's autonomy within reasonable limits and foster an atmosphere of give and take in parent/child communications. Parental support is a crucial ingredient in child socialization. It is positively related to cognitive development, self-control, self-esteem, moral behavior, conformity to adult standards, and academic achievement (Gecas and Seff, 1991). Control is exercised in conjunction with support by authoritative parents. Children raised by authoritative parents tend to approach novel or stressful situations with curiosity and show high levels of self-reliance, self-control, cheerfulness, and friendliness (Baumrind, 1983). The childrearing strategies discussed later in this chapter may be used by parents who take an authoritative approach to childrearing.

How to Raise Your Child: The Needs of Parents and Children

About 150 years ago, Americans began turning to books to learn how to act and live rather than turning to each other. They began to lose confidence in their own abilities to make appropriate judgments. The vacuum that formed when traditional ways broke down under the impact of industrialization was filled by the so-called "expert." The old values and ways had been handed down from parents to child in an unending cycle; men and women had learned how to be mothers and fathers from their own parents. But with increasing mobility, the continuity of generations ceased. A woman's mother was often not physically present to help her with her first child. New mothers were not able to turn to their more experienced kin for help. Instead, they enlisted the aid of new authorities—the experts who through education and training supposedly knew what to do. If your baby was colicky, for example, the experts recommended a drop of laudanum in the baby's bottle. (The laudanum would put the baby to sleep, but it would also make him or her a heroin addict by the end of a year.)

Contemporary parents may still follow experts' advice even if it conflicts with their own beliefs. Yet if an expert's advice counters their own understanding, parents should carefully examine that advice as well as their own beliefs. All parents

The secret of dealing successfully with a child is not to be its parent.

Mell Lazarus

The perniciousness of so much of the advice from experts that pervades the media is that it undermines the confidence of parents in their own abilities and values, overemphasizes the significance of specific child-rearing techniques, and grossly misrepresents the contribution the expert in psychiatry or education can make to the conduct of ordinary family life.

Rita Kramer

should take an expert's advice with at least a grain of salt. It is the parents' responsibility to raise their children, not the expert's.

CHILDREN'S DEVELOPMENTAL NEEDS. Although the relative effects of physiology and environment on human development are much debated by today's experts, it is clear that both nature and nurture play important roles. Jerome Kagan (1984) has presented a strong case for the role of biology in early development. He holds that the growth of the central nervous system in infants and young children ensures that such motor and cognitive abilities as walking, talking, using symbols, and becoming self-aware will occur "as long as children are growing in any reasonably varied environment where minimal nutritional needs are met and [they] can exercise emerging abilities." Furthermore, according to Kagan, children are biologically equipped for understanding the meaning of right and wrong by the age of two; but although biology may be responsible for the development of conscience, social factors can encourage its decline.

In addition to physiological maturation, important factors affecting early development are (1) the acquisition of knowledge, (2) the formation of attachments (especially maternal), and (3) individual temperamental differences (such as inhibited/restrained/watchful or uninhibited/energetic/spontaneous) (Kagan, 1984). Development in later childhood can also be profoundly affected by social forces.

Parents often want to know what they can do to raise healthy children. Are there specific parental behaviors or amounts of behaviors (say, twelve hugs a day?) that all children need to grow up healthy? Apart from saying that basic physical needs must be met (adequate food, shelter, clothing, and so on) along with some basic psychological ones, experts cannot give us detailed instructions. Jerome Kagan (1976) wrote:

Children do not require any specific actions from adults to develop optimally. There is no good evidence that children must have a certain amount or schedule of cuddling, kissing, spanking, holding, or deprivation of privileges in order to become gratified and productive adults. The child does have some psychologic needs, but there is no fixed list of parental behaviors that can be counted on to fill those requirements. The psychological needs of children vary with age and the context of their growth.

According to Kagan, in our society a child needs to:

1. Feel valued by parents and a few special adults (such as a teacher, aunt, or grandparent).
2. Develop autonomy in attitudes and behaviors.
3. Develop and perfect talents that are desirable in society.
4. Develop successfully in a sexual context and be able to love and be loved.

Kagan also observed that because our values tend to derive from our profit-oriented economic system, crowded urban conditions, and competitive institutions, in general they tend to emphasize self-interest, competitiveness, and narcissism. More humanistic values would foster intimacy, cooperation, and altruism.

Children have more strength, resiliency, and resourcefulness than people may ordinarily think. They can adapt to and overcome many difficult situations. Parents do not have to be overly concerned that their every action will overwhelmingly influence their child's life. A mother can lose her temper and scream at her child and the child will most likely survive, especially if the mother later apologizes and shares her feelings with the child. A father can turn his child away with a grunt because he is too tired to listen and the child will not necessarily grow up neurotic, especially if the father spends some "special time" with the child later on. (Also see Bronfenbrenner, 1985, for a discussion of children's needs in modern society.)

We can expect a conscience of every child. We don't have to build it in. All we have to do is arrange the environment so they don't lose it.

Jerome Kagan

As we grow up, we need to get different strokes from different folks in different settings to become sentient, capable, competent, and compassionate human beings.

Urie Bronfenbrenner

Psychosexual Development in the Family Context

Within the context of our overall growth, and perhaps central to it, our sexual selves develop. Within the family we learn how we "should" feel about our bodies, whether we should be ashamed, embarrassed, proud, or indifferent. Some families are comfortable with nudity in a variety of situations: swimming, bathing, sunbathing, dressing or undressing. Others are comfortable with partial nudity from time to time: when sharing the bathroom, changing clothes, and so on. Still others are more modest and carefully guard their privacy. Most researchers and therapists would allow that all these styles can be compatible with the development of sexually well-adjusted children as long as some basic needs are met:

1. The child's body (and nudity) is accepted and respected.
2. The child is not punished or humiliated for seeing the parent naked, going to the toilet, or making love.
3. The child's needs for privacy are respected.

Families also vary in the amount and type of physical contact in which they participate. Some families hug and kiss, give back rubs, sit and lean on each other, and generally maintain a high degree of physical closeness. Some parents extend this closeness into their sleeping habits, allowing their infants and small children in their beds each night. (In many cultures, this is the rule rather than the exception.) Other families limit their contact to hugs and tickles. Variations of this kind are normal. Concerning children's needs for physical contact, we can make the following generalizations:

1. All children (and adults) need a certain amount of freely given physical affection from those they love. Although there is no prescription for the right amount or form of such expression, its quantity and quality both affect children's emotional well-being and the emotional and sexual health of the adults they will become (see Kagan, 1976).
2. Children should be told, in a nonthreatening way, what kind of touching by adults is "good" and what is "bad." They need to feel that they are in charge of their own bodies, that parts of their bodies are private property, and that no adult has the right to touch them with sexual intent. It is not necessary to frighten a child by going into great detail about the kinds of things that might happen. A better strategy is to instill a sense of self-worth and confidence in children so that they will not allow themselves to be victimized (Pogrebin, 1983). We also should learn to listen to children and to trust them. They need to know that if they are sexually abused, it is not their fault. They need to feel that they can tell about it and still be worthy of love. (See Strong and DeVault, 1988, for detailed information on psychosexual development throughout life.)

> *Conscience is the inner voice which warns us that someone may be looking.*
>
> H. L. Mencken

SELF-ESTEEM. High self-esteem, what Erik Erikson called "an optimal sense of identity," is essential for growth in relationships, creativity, and productivity in the world at large. Low self-esteem is a disability that afflicts children (and the adults they grow up to be) with feelings of powerlessness, poor ability to cope, low tolerance for differences and difficulties, inability to accept responsibility, and impaired emotional responsiveness. Self-esteem has been shown to be more significant than intelligence in predicting scholastic performance.

A recent study of 3,000 children found that adolescent girls had lower self-images, lower expectations from life, and less self-confidence than boys (Daley, 1991). At age nine, most of the girls felt positive and confident, but by the time

> *We are born princes and the civilizing process makes us frogs.*
>
> Eric Berne

The Meaning of Being Me

Who am I? Who am I?
Growing up isn't easy, no matter what
*   you think.*
No. No. It's hard. It's hard.
It's standing on the brink
*   of a mountain that*
*   you're afraid of.*
*   Sometimes I ask you who I am, but*
*   you don't tell me.*
*   Sometimes I ask myself who I am. . . .*
Still a kid?
Soon a grown-up person. (Will it be
*   better then?*
Can you tell me that . . . can I believe
*   it?)*
I hear a certain song and I get
*   tears in my eyes . . .*
I see a person and I get so angry—and
*   he never even said a word . . .*
It's hard growing up . . . it's so hard.
*   Why must it be so hard . . .*
The littlest rough spot and there I
*   go—crying,*
angry . . . up to my room to break
*   down—to kick—to have bad*
*   dreams—*
I hurt you, and you, and you,
*   sometimes—but I hurt me more*
*   times.*
I don't want to hurt you and I don't
*   want to hurt me—*
But it hurts so much not to know
*   how to answer,*
Who am I?

Susan, age 11. From Carole Klein, The Myth of
the Happy Child

I take my children everywhere, but they
always find their way back home.

Robert Orhen

they entered high school, only 29 percent said they felt "happy" the way they were. The boys also lost some sense of self-worth, but not nearly as much as the girls. Ethnicity was an important factor in this study. African-American girls reported a much higher rate of self-confidence in high school than did white or Latina girls. Two reasons were suggested for this discrepancy: first, African-American girls often have strong female role models at home and in their communities; African-American women are more likely than others to have a full-time job and run a household. Second, many African-American parents specifically teach their children that "there is nothing wrong with them, only with the way the world treats them" (Daley, 1991). According to professor Carol Gilligan, this survey "makes it impossible to say that what happens to girls is simply a matter of hormones. . . . [It] raises all kinds of issues about cultural contributions, and it raises questions about the role of the schools, both in the drop of self-esteem and in the potential for intervention" (quoted in Daley, 1991).

Clemes and Bean (1983) describe four conditions necessary for developing and maintaining high self-esteem. (As you read the following, think about how families, schools, and other institutions could increase children's self-esteem.) The first condition is a sense of connectedness, of being an important part of a family, class, team, or other group and of being connected ("in touch") with our bodies. The second condition is a sense of uniqueness, a feeling that our specialness and differentness are supported and approved by others. Third is a sense of power, the belief that we have the capability to influence others, solve problems, complete tasks, make our own decisions, and satisfy our needs. Children develop a sense of power through sharing duties and responsibilities in the home and having clear limits and rules set for them. The fourth condition for the development of self-esteem is a sense of models. Human, philosophical, and operational models (mental constructs and images derived from experience) help us establish meaningful values and goals and clarify our own standards.

A study of 655 adolescents suggested that family support is "crucial for the development and maintenance of self-esteem among high-school-aged adolescents" (Hoelter and Harper, 1987; also see Gecas and Seff, 1991). Parents can foster high self-esteem in their children by (1) having high self-esteem themselves, (2) accepting their children as they are, (3) enforcing clearly defined limits, and (4) respecting individuality within the limits that have been set.

It's also important to single out the child's behavior—not the whole child—for comment (Kutner, 1988). Children (and adults as well) can benefit from specific information about how well they've performed a task. "You did a lousy job" not only makes us feel bad, but it also gives us no useful information about what would constitute a good job. Furthermore, "acknowledging your own needs and accepting them," according to Clemes and Bean, "can help you have patience and compassion for [children's] efforts to realize high self-esteem." (See Demo et al., 1987, for a discussion of self-esteem and the reciprocal character of parent/adolescent socialization.)

PARENTS' NEEDS. Although some parents' needs are met by their children, parents have other needs as well. Important needs of parents during the childrearing years are personal developmental needs (such as social contacts, privacy, and outside interests) and the need to maintain marital satisfaction. Yet so much is expected of parents that they often neglect these needs. Parents may feel a deep sense of guilt if their child is not happy or has some defect, an unpleasant personality, or even a runny nose. The burden is especially heavy for mothers, because their success is often measured by how perfect their children are. Children have their own independent personalities, however, and many forces affect a child's development and behavior. Nevertheless, as Philip Slater (1971) wrote, "Deep in their hearts most middle-class Spock-taught mothers believed that if they did their job well enough, all their children would be creative, intelligent, kind, generous, happy, brave, spontaneous, and good—each, of course in his or her own special way."

Accepting our limitations as parents (and as human beings) and accepting our lives as they are (even if they haven't turned out exactly as planned) can help us cope with the many stresses of childrearing in an already stressful world. Contemporary parents need to guard against the "burnout syndrome" of emotional and physical overload. Parents' careers and children's school activities, organized sports, scouts, and music, art, or dance lessons compete for the parents' energy and rob them of the unstructured (and energizing) time that should be spent with others, with their children, or simply alone. Learning to prioritize activities—deciding which are essential and which can be eliminated or postponed—is a valuable parenting skill.

Childrearing Strategies

One of the most challenging aspects of childrearing is knowing how to change, stop, encourage, or otherwise influence children's behavior. We can request, reason, explain, command, cajole, compromise, yell and scream, or threaten with physical punishment or the suspension of privileges; or we can just get down on our knees and beg. Some of these approaches may be appropriate at certain times; others clearly are never appropriate. Some may prove effective some of the time, some may never work very well, and no technique will work every time.

The techniques of childrearing currently taught or endorsed by educators, psychologists, and others involved with child development are included in programs such as Parent Effectiveness, Assertive Discipline, Positive Discipline, and numerous others. Although these approaches differ somewhat in their emphasis, they share most of the tenets that follow. (Also see Chapter 15 for a discussion of the traits of psychologically healthy families.)

RESPECT. Mutual respect between children and parents must be fostered in order for growth and change to occur. One important way to teach respect is by modeling—treating the child and others respectfully. Child psychologist Rudolph Dreikurs stressed the importance of treating children with kindness *and* firmness simultaneously. Counselor Jane Nelsen (1987) writes, "Kindness is important in order to show respect for the child. Firmness is important in order to show respect for ourselves and the situation."

CONSISTENCY AND CLARITY. Consistency is crucial in childrearing. Without it, children become hopelessly confused and parents become hopelessly frustrated. Patience and teamwork (a united front) on the parents' part help insure consistency. Because consistency means following through with what we say, parents should beware of making promises or threats they won't be able to keep. Clarity is important for the same reason. A child needs to know the rules and the consequences for breaking them. This eliminates the possibilities of the child being unjustly disciplined or wiggling out through loopholes. ("But, Mom, I didn't know you meant not to walk on *this* clean carpet with my muddy shoes!")

Cleaning your house with the kids still around is like shoveling the walk before it stops snowing.

Phyllis Diller

Before I got married, I had six theories about bringing up children. Now I have six children and no theories.

John Wilmot, Earl of Rochester

You can learn things from children—how much patience you have, for instance.

Franklin P. Jones

Parents are the bones on which children sharpen their teeth.

Peter Ustinov

LOGICAL CONSEQUENCES. One of the most effective ways we learn is by experiencing the logical consequences of our actions. Some of these consequences occur naturally—we forget our umbrella, we get wet. Sometimes parents need to devise consequences that are appropriate to their child's misbehavior. Dreikurs and Soltz (1964) distinguished between logical consequences and punishment. The "Three R's" of logical consequences dictate that the solution must be Related to the problem behavior, Respectful (no humiliation), and Reasonable (designed to teach, not to induce suffering). (See Nelsen, 1987, for specific examples of the application of natural or logical consequences.)

OPEN COMMUNICATION. The lines of communication between parents and children must be kept open. Numerous techniques exist for fostering communication. Among these are *active listening* and the use of *I-messages,* important components of Thomas Gordon's (1978) Parent Effectiveness program. In active listening, the parent verbally feeds back the child's communciations in order to understand the child and help him or her understand the nature of the problem. I-messages are important because they impart facts without placing blame and are less likely to promote rebellion in children than are you-messages. (Communication techniques are discussed in greater detail in Chapter 11.)

 Family meetings are another important way in which families can communicate. Regular weekly meetings provide an opportunity for being together and a forum for airing gripes, solving problems, and planning activities. Decisions are best reached by consensus rather than majority vote, as majority rule can lead to a "tyranny of the majority" in which the minority is consistently oppressed. If consensus can't be reached, the problem can be put on the next meeting's agenda, allowing time for family members to come up with alternative solutions (Nelson, 1987).

NO PHYSICAL PUNISHMENT. The American Psychological Association notes that "physical violence imprinted at an early age, and the modeling of violent behavior by punishing adults, induces habitual violence in children" (cited in Haferd, 1986). The American Medical Association also opposes physical punishment of children. While such punishment may "work" in the short run by stopping undesirable behavior, its long-range results—anger, resentment, fear, hatred—are appalling (Dodson, 1987). Besides, it often makes parents feel confused, miserable, and degraded, right along with their kids.

 More effective types of discipline use some form of behavior modification. Rewards (hugs, stickers, special activities) are given for good behavior and privileges are taken away when misbehavior is involved. Good behavior can be kept track of on a simple chart listing one or several of the desired behaviors. Undesirable behavior may be met with the revocation of TV privileges or the curtailment of other activities. *Time-outs*—sending the child to his or her room or to a "boring" place for a short time or until the misbehavior stops—are useful for particularly disruptive behavior. They also give the parent an opportunity to cool off (Dodson, 1987; also see Canter and Canter, 1985).

 Although no childrearing technique is guaranteed to be 100 percent successful all the time, it is important for families to keep seeking ways to improve their communication and satisfaction. It is also important for parents to develop and maintain confidence in their own parenting skills, their common sense, and especially their love for their children.

SUMMARY

❒ Parenthood may now be considered a matter of choice owing to effective methods of birth control. *Child-free marriage* and *deferred parenthood* are alternatives that are growing in popularity.

❒ Parental roles are acquired virtually overnight and can create considerable stress. The main sources of stress for women involve traditional gender roles and multiple role demands (parent, spouse, provider). Other sources of stress for mothers and fathers are associated with work, not having enough money, worries about infant care and health, and interactions with spouse, family, and friends.

❒ Many women find considerable satisfaction and fulfillment in motherhood. Although there is no concrete evidence of a biological maternal drive, it is clear that socialization for motherhood does exist.

❒ The role of the father in his children's development is currently being reexamined. The traditional instrumental roles are being supplemented, and perhaps supplanted, by expressive ones.

❒ Supplementary child care outside the home is a necessity for many families. The development and maintenance of quality day-care programs should be a national priority.

❒ Television has recently been implicated in a number of individual, familial, and societal disorders. Commercials generally encourage poor nutritional habits and generate conflict between parent and child. Violence on television has been demonstrated to cause aggressive behavior in children. Families are often portrayed in a stereotypical or romanticized manner, and women and members of minority status groups may be presented negatively.

❒ Ethnicity profoundly influences the way children are socialized. Identification with a group gives a sense of pride and belonging. Minority status parents may try to give their children special skills for dealing with prejudice and discrimination.

❒ Lesbian mothers share many similarities with heterosexual mothers. Most gay fathers are married. Studies indicate that children of both lesbians and gay men fare best when the parents are secure in their sexual orientation and are open about it with their children. Although the children of gay and lesbian parents may have difficulty accepting their parents' gayness at first, they generally maintain close relationships with their parents and develop the same sexual orientations and gender roles as children of heterosexuals.

❒ Basic attitudes toward childrearing can be classified as *authoritarian, permissive,* and *authoritative.*

❒ Expert advice is often relied on by today's parents. It needs to be tempered by parents' confidence in their own parenting abilities and in their children's strength and resourcefulness.

❒ Children's basic psychological needs are to (1) feel valued by parents and a few special adults, (2) develop autonomy, (3) develop and perfect talents that are desirable in society, and (4) be successful at loving and being loved.

❒ Psychosexual development begins in infancy. Infants and children learn from their parents how they should feel about themselves as sexual beings.

❒ High self-esteem is essential for growth in relationships, creativity, and productivity. Adolescent girls, especially nonblacks, are likely to be low in self-esteem. Parents can foster high self-esteem in their children by encouraging development of a sense of connectedness, uniqueness, power, and models.

❒ Contemporary strategies for childrearing include the elements of mutual respect, consistency and clarity, logical consequences, open communication, and behavior modification in place of physical punishment.

CHAPTER 9

Marriage, Work, and Economics

*A man's work is from sun
   to sun,
But woman's work is never
   done.*

Folk saying

Hᴇʀᴇ ᴀʀᴇ ᴛʜʀᴇᴇ ʙʀɪᴇꜰ ᴇxᴄʜᴀɴɢᴇꜱ ᴏᴠᴇʀʜᴇᴀʀᴅ ᴀᴛ ᴀ ᴘᴀʀᴛʏ. Identify what is wrong with each of them.

❐ Exchange number one: "Do you work?" the man asks. "No, I'm a mother," the woman replies.

❐ Exchange number two: "What do you do?" the first woman inquires politely as she is introduced to another woman. "Nothing. I'm a housewife," the second responds. "Oh, that's nice," the first replies, losing interest.

❐ Exchange number three: "What do you do?" the man asks. "I'm a doctor," the woman responds as she picks up her child, who is impatiently tugging at her. "And I'm an architect," her husband says while nursing their second child with a bottle.

In the first exchange, the woman ignores that as a mother she works. In the second exchange, both women ignore the fact that as a homemaker, the second woman works. They also devalue such unpaid work in comparison to paid work. In the third exchange, the woman identifies herself as a physician without acknowledging that she is also a mother. Her husband makes the same mistake as he identifies himself as an architect without also noting that he is a father participating in the care of his infant. As husband and wife, father and mother, both the architect and physician are unpaid family workers making important—but generally unrecognized—contributions to the family's economy.

These examples point to a curious fact: when we think of work, we tend to recognize only paid work. Family work, such as caregiving activities or household duties, is not regarded as "real" work. Because it is unpaid, family work is ignored as being somehow inferior to paid work, regardless of how difficult, time-consuming, creative, rewarding, and important it is for our lives and future as human beings. This is not surprising, for in the United States employment takes precedence over family.

The role of work in families requires many of us to rethink the meaning of family. We ordinarily think of families in terms of relationships and feelings—the family as an emotional unit. But families are also economic units bound together by emotional ties (Ross, Mirowsky, and Goldsteen, 1991). Paid work and unpaid family work as well as the economy itself profoundly affect the way we live as families. Our most intimate relationships vary according to how husbands and wives participate in paid work and family responsibilities (Voydanoff, 1987).

There are two types of work in which families participate: family work and paid work. Family work is the work we perform in the home without pay: it includes housekeeping, household maintenance, and caring for children, the ill, and the aged. Women do the overwhelming majority of family work. Paid work is the work we do for salary or wages. Traditionally men have been responsible for paid work, but currently the vast majority of women—whether single or married, with children or without—are employed. Women either support themselves or make significant contributions to family income.

Our paid work helps shape the quality of family life: it affects time, roles, incomes, spending, leisure, even individual identities. Within our families, the time we have for each other, for fun, for our children, and even for sex is the time that is not taken up by paid work. The main characteristic of our paid work in relation to the family is its inflexibility. Work regulates the family. And for most families, as in the past, a woman's work molds itself to *her* family, whereas a man's family molds itself to *his* work (Degler, 1980; Ross, Mirowsky, and Goldsteen, 1991). We must constantly balance work roles and family roles.

❐ WORKPLACE/FAMILY LINKAGES

Outside of sleeping, probably the single activity to which the majority of employed men and women devote the most time is their jobs. And we know from our own experiences that our work or studies affect our personal relationships. Work/family conflict, especially relating to work schedules and demands and to children at home, is often a painful source of stress (Menaghan and Parcel, 1991). To date, however, most research has been devoted to descriptions of home life or work life, not to how the two interact with each other. Only recently have scholars begun to look at how our jobs affect our family life, causing moodiness, fatigue, irritability, and so on (Small and Riley, 1990; see review by Bronfenbrenner and Crouter, 1982).

Work is the refuge of people who have nothing better to do.

Oscar Wilde

Work Spillover

Common sense (in addition to our own fatigue) suggests that **work spillover,** the effect of work on other aspects of our lives, is important in family life. Work spillover affects individuals and families by absorbing their time and energy and impinging on their psychological states. It links our homelife to our workplace (Piotrkowski, 1979; Small and Riley, 1990). Work is as much a part of marriage as love. What happens at work—frustration or worry, a rude customer, an unreasonable boss—affects our moods, making us irritable or depressed. We take these moods home with us, affecting the emotional quality of our relationships.

If you don't want to work you have to work to earn enough money so that you won't have to work.

Ogden Nash

Work spillover especially affects women. While for men excessive work time is the major cause of conflict between work and family, for married women it is fatigue and irritability. Joseph Pleck and his colleagues (1980) noted:

The greater family responsibilities for women may be the reason for higher reports that the physical and psychological consequences of work caused family problems. Fatigue and irritability brought home from work often makes performing family tasks more difficult. . . . Husbands generally spend longer hours on the job but perform fewer household tasks. Having the opportunity to rest after work may help make fatigue and irritability less of a problem for husbands.

As a result of work spillover, an employed woman's leisure is rarely spontaneous: it is fitted in or planned around her household work and paid work (Firestone and Shelton, 1988). The stress a husband experiences at his work can also diminish his wife's emotional health (Dooley and Catalano, 1991).

The family is very much alive as a work unit in which all members participate in tasks from house repairs to laundry, gardening and doing dishes. As homemakers, women are the primary workers in such family work. Since family work is unpaid (except sometimes for children's allowances for doing chores), it generally goes unrecognized.

Role Strain: Role Overload and Inter-Role Conflict

For families in which both partners are employed, work-related problems are more severe for parents than for nonparents. Being a working parent means performing three roles simultaneously: worker, parent, and spouse (Voydanoff and Donnelly, 1989). Because the time, energy, and commitment needed to carry out these roles are interdependent, individuals may experience difficulties such as depression, fatigue, and irritability (Gruelzow et al., 1991; Voydanoff and Donnelly, 1989; Menaghan and Parcel, 1991). Such difficulties are referred to as **role strain.** Role-strain is the most pressing problem for working families (Hansen, 1991).

Two types of role strain are especially likely to occur among working parents: **role overload** and **inter-role conflict** (interference). Overload occurs when the total prescribed activities for one or more roles are greater than an individual can comfortably or adequately handle. In role overload—what might be called the "too-many-hats" syndrome—a person can easily feel overwhelmed with the multiple responsibilities of parent/spouse/worker: she or he must care for children, be intimate with a spouse, work twelve hours a day, shop, clean house, take children to school, and so on. Inter-role conflict exists when responsibilities from the parent/spouse/worker roles conflict. In inter-role conflict, the expectations of the parent/spouse/worker roles may be contradictory or may require an individual to do two things at the same time. In this "too-many-balls-to-juggle" syndrome, for example, a parent may be expected to be in two places at once, such as at the job *and* at home caring for a sick child. Individuals high in self-esteem, however, seem to feel less inter-role conflict than those with low self-esteem (Mertensmeyer and Coleman, 1987). Women with high self-esteem, for example, accept lower housekeeping standards as realistic adjustments to their multiple roles rather than as signs of inadequacy.

Married women employed full-time often prefer working fewer hours as a means of reducing role strain (Moen and Dempster-McLain, 1987). Not surprisingly, because they have less role strain, single women (including those who are divorced) are often more advanced in their careers than married women (Houseknecht et al., 1987). They are more likely to be employed full-time and have higher occupational status and incomes. They are also more highly represented in the professions and hold higher academic positions.

⬚ THE FAMILY'S DIVISION OF LABOR

The Traditional Division of Labor: The Complementary Model

In the traditional division of labor in the family, work roles are complementary: the husband is expected to work outside the home for wages; the wife is expected to re-

To reduce the wife's role overload ("too many hats") and inter-role conflict ("too many balls to juggle"), the husband may increase his participation in household work and child care. Most husbands, however, view their increased role as "helping" rather than sharing responsibilities.

main at home caring for children and maintaining the household. (We discussed the childrearing aspect of family work in the previous chapter.) In what Berardo and colleagues (1987) refer to as "a residue of tradition," women—whether or not they are employed outside the home—remain primarily responsible for household tasks. The division of family roles along stereotypical gender lines is more characteristic of white families than African-American families. African-American women, for example, are less likely than white women to be exclusively responsible for household tasks (Broman, 1988; Maret and Finlay, 1984; Taylor et al., 1991).

MEN'S FAMILY WORK. Men's work traditionally takes place outside the home, where men fulfill their primary economic role as provider. The husband's role as provider is probably the male's most fundamental role in marriage (Menaghan and Parcel, 1991; Rubin, 1983). The basic equation is that if the male is a good provider, he is a good husband and a good father. This core concept seems to endure despite trends toward more egalitarian and androgynous gender roles.

Men are traditionally expected to contribute to family work by providing household maintenance. Such maintenance consists primarily of repairs, light construction, mowing the lawn, and other activities that are consistent with instrumental male norms. Men often contribute to housework and child care, although their contribution may not be notable in terms of the total amount of work to be done. Most studies find that women do twice as much family work as men (Spitze, 1991). Men tend to see their role in housekeeping or child care as "helping" their partner, not as assuming equal responsibility for such work. The more husbands define themselves as the provider, regardless of whether their wives are employed, the fewer household tasks husbands perform (Perry-Jenkins, 1988).

WOMEN'S FAMILY WORK. Women's family work is considerably more diverse than men's. Women's work permeates every aspect of the family. It ranges from housekeeping to child care, kin-keeping to organizing recreation, socializing children to caring for aged parents and in-laws, cooking to managing the family finances, to name but a few of the tasks. Ironically, family work is often invisible to the women who do most of it (DeVault, 1987). As Thompson and Walker (1991) observe, "Family work is unseen and unacknowledged because it is private, unpaid, commonplace, done by women, and mingled with love and leisure."

Although most women do paid work, contributing about 30 percent to the family's income, neither women nor their partners regard employment as a woman's fundamental role. Women are not duty-bound to provide; they are duty-bound to perform household tasks (Thompson and Walker, 1991). Even the law assumes that the wife is responsible for domestic work and childrearing (Weitzman, 1981). No matter what kind of work the woman does outside the home or how nontraditional she and her husband may consider themselves to be, there is seldom much equality when it comes to housework.

The greatest determinant of the amount of time a woman spends on housework is her employment status. Women spend less time on housework if they are employed (Berardo et al., 1987). Men may help their partners with washing dishes, vacuuming, or doing the laundry, but as long as they "help," household responsibility continues to fall on women.

The Homemaker Role

A woman's work may consist of unpaid family work as homemaker and paid work outside the home as employee or professional. Her work as homemaker has been

One man eats very little and is always full. But another man constantly eats and is always hungry. Why is that?

Zen riddle

I hate to be called a homemaker; I prefer "domestic goddess."

Roseanne Arnold

traditionally considered to be her primary role. Because this work is performed by women and is unpaid, however, it has been denigrated as "women's work"—inconsequential and unproductive.

Women's work contribution to the family has not always been devalued. The role of homemaker or housewife was a nineteenth-century invention, created when industrialization removed many of women's productive tasks from the home and placed them in the factory (Degler, 1980). Even then, although women made fewer things at home, they nevertheless continued their service and childrearing roles: cooking, cleaning, sewing, raising children, and nurturing the family. With the rise of a money economy in which only paid work was recognized as real work, women's work in the home went unrecognized as necessary and important labor (Andre, 1981; Bernard, 1982). (If homemakers today were paid the going rate for their work, they would earn over $50,000 annually.) Even when women work for wages, their contribution to the family income is often underrated (Bird and Bird, 1985).

Sociologist Ann Oakley (1985) described four aspects of the homemakers' role:

❏ Exclusive allocation to women, rather than to adults of both sexes
❏ Association with economic dependence
❏ Status as nonwork, or its opposition to "real," economically productive work that is paid
❏ Primacy to women—that is, its priority over other roles

Although women's attitudes toward homemaking often reflect class differences, few women find the work itself satisfying. As Komarovsky (1987) wrote, "The esteem [homemakers] attach to their roles does not . . . ensure their contentment in it." Both working-class and middle-class women tend to feel tied down by their duties as wives and mothers.

Homemaking consists primarily of household work and, if children are present, childbearing tasks. It includes the following characteristics (Hochschild, 1989; Oakley, 1985):

1. Housework tends to isolate a woman at home. She cleans alone, cooks alone, launders alone, cares for children alone. Loneliness is a common complaint.
2. Housework is unstructured, monotonous, and repetitive. A homemaker never feels that her work is done. There is always more dust, more dishes, more dirty laundry.
3. The full-time homemaker role is restricted. For a woman who is not also employed outside the home, homemaking (which may also include childrearing) is essentially her only role. By contrast, a man's role is dual—employed worker and husband/father. If the man finds one role to be unsatisfactory, he may feel satisfaction in the other. It is much more difficult for a woman to separate the satisfaction she may get from being a mother from the dissatisfaction of household work.
4. Housework is autonomous. This is one of the most well-liked aspects of the homemaker role. Being her own boss allows a woman to direct a large part of her own life. In contrast to employment, this is a definite plus.
5. Homemakers work long days and nights. This is especially true for employed mothers. For employed women, there is a "second shift" of work that awaits them at home, requiring anywhere from fifty to one hundred or more hours a week.
6. Homemaking can involve childrearing. For many homemakers, this is their most important and rewarding work. They enjoy the interactions with their infants and children. Although they can also feel overwhelmed and exhausted by the demands of childrearing, relatively few would choose not to have children.
7. Homemaking often involves role strain, especially for employed mothers as they try to perform their various obligations as parent/spouse/worker.

Many women find satisfaction in the homemaker role, even in housework. Young women, for example, may find increasing pleasure as they experience a sense of mastery over cooking, entertaining, or rearing happy children.

If homemakers have formed a network among other women—friends, neighbors, relatives—they may share many of their responsibilities. They discuss ideas and feelings and give each other support. They may share tasks as well as problems.

☐ WOMEN IN THE LABOR FORCE

Women have always worked outside the home. Single women have traditionally been members of the work force since the early nineteenth century. And there have always been large numbers of working mothers, especially among African Americans and many other poor ethnic groups (Broman, 1988; Jones, 1985). What has changed significantly is the emergence since the 1960s of a predominant family form in which both husbands and wives/mothers work outside the home (Piotrkowski et al., 1987). Until the 1970s, nonemployed wives and mothers were viewed as the norm. Recent research indicates that women's employment tends to have positive rather than negative effects on marriage. (See Spitze, 1991, for a review of the literature on women's employment and family relations; also see Menaghan and Parcel, 1991).

Why Women Enter the Labor Force

Economic necessity is a driving force for many women in the labor force. Among women in the work force in 1989, 26 percent were single, 15.6 percent were divorced or widowed, and 20 percent had husbands whose income was less than $15,000 (U.S. Bureau of the Census, 1990). Many married women and mothers entered the labor force or increased their working hours to compensate for their husband's loss in earning power (Menaghan and Parcel, 1991).

There are psychological reasons for employment as well. Employment may raise a woman's self-esteem and sense of control. Employed women are less depressed and anxious than nonemployed homemakers; they are also physically healthier (Gecas and Seff, 1989; Ross, Mirowsky, and Goldsteen, 1991). A thirty-one-year-old worker, the mother of five children, told how she felt about working in a factory (quoted in Rubin, 1976):

I really love going to work. I guess it's because it gets me away from home. It's not that I don't love my home; I do. But you get awfully tired of just keeping house. . . .

You know, when I was home, I was getting in real trouble. I had that old housewife's syndrome, where you either crawl in bed after the kids go to school or sit and watch TV by the hour. I was just dying of boredom.

There are two reasons that employment improves women's emotional and physical well-being (Ross, Mirowsky, and Goldsteen, 1991). First, employment decreases economic hardship, alleviating stress and concern not only for the woman herself but for other family members as well. For a single parent, her earnings may constitute her entire family's income. Second, an employed woman receives greater domestic support from her partner. The more a woman earns in contrast to her partner, the more likely he is to share housework and child care.

Participation in the Labor Force

In 1988, 59 million women and 67 million men were employed; women made up 47 percent of the work force (U.S. Bureau of the Census, 1990). Between 1970 and

Women constitute half the world's population, perform nearly two-thirds of its work hours, receive one-tenth of the world's income, and own less than one-hundredth of the world's property.

United Nations Report, 1985

Ah, the little troubles, Mr. Oliver, they ruin a woman's life. It's the devil, I do believe, as sends us the toothache and the east wind and tax on beer. As for your grand sorrows . . . it's almost a pleasure to grieve, all hung in weeds, like a weeping willow. But the price of eggs, Mr. Oliver, the price of eggs.

George Santayana, The Last Puritan

Doonesbury

BY GARRY TRUDEAU

Doonesbury; copyright 1987 Universal Press Syndicate. Reprinted with permission. All rights reserved.

1988, the number of married women in the labor force almost doubled. The numbers of employed women between twenty-four and thirty-four years of age (the ages during which they are most likely to bear children) rose from 39 percent to 64 percent. In 39 percent of dual-worker families, however, both husband and wife preferred that the woman not work (Ross, Mirowsky, and Goldsteen, 1991).

Almost 4 million of the employed women are single mothers; more than a quarter have preschool children (U.S. Bureau of the Census, 1990). More than half of all mothers with young children are currently in the work force. Among mothers with preschool children, one out of six works full-time in shift work—that is, during afternoons, evenings, nights, or early morning; one out of five works part-time in shift work (Presser, 1986).

Women's Employment Patterns

The employment of women has generally followed a pattern that reflects their family and child-care responsibilities. Because of these demands, women must consider the number of hours they can work and what time of day to work. When family demands increase, wives, not husbands, tend to cut back on their job time (Berk, 1985; Pleck, 1985). As a result of family considerations, women's employment rates follow an M-shaped curve. Women's entry into the job market rises from age sixteen to twenty-four; at age twenty-five, their participation drops as they begin engaging in homemaking and child-care activities. Then, after thirty-five, the rates go up again, falling toward zero as women near retirement. This M-shaped pattern, may be changing, however, as more than half of the mothers with small children are employed. Nevertheless, women face considerable barriers in their access to well-paying status jobs (Bergen, 1991).

Because of family responsibilities, women tend to interrupt their job and career lives considerably more than men. Employment interruptions have an important impact on wages: the more or longer the interruptions, the lower the wages. A study by the Bureau of the Census ("Work Interruptions and Earnings," 1985) found that one-fourth of the men but three-fourths of the women had employment interruptions lasting six months or longer. Sixty-seven percent of women's work interruptions were for

You can say this about ready-mixes—the next generation isn't going to have any trouble making pies exactly like mother used to make.

Earl Wilson

family reasons; only 2 percent of men's employment interruptions were for family reasons. Similar differences are found when comparing women who have been married (with children) to women who have never been married (without children). Among women age twenty-one to twenty-nine years, 21 percent of the never-married women had work interruptions but 81 percent of the married women have had work interruptions.

Researchers have found that a woman's decision to remain in the work force or to withdraw from it during her childbearing and early childbearing years is critical for her later work-force activities (Rexroad, 1985). If a woman chooses to work at home caring for her children, she is less likely to be employed later. If she later returns to the work force, she will probably earn substantially less than women who have remained in the work force (Rexroad, 1985; Velsor and O'Rand, 1984).

□ DUAL-EARNER MARRIAGES

Even though half of all married women held jobs in 1992, the great majority of these women were employed in low-paying, low-status jobs—secretaries, clerks, nurses, factory workers, and the like. Rising prices and declining wages pushed most of them into the job market. Employed mothers generally do not seek personal fulfillment in their work as much as they do additional family income. Their families remain their top priorities.

Dual-career families are a subcategory of dual-earner families. They differ from other dual-earner families insofar as both husband and wife have high achievement orientations, greater emphasis on gender equality, and a stronger desire to exercise their capabilities (Berardo et al., 1987). Unfortunately, they may find it difficult to achieve both their professional and family goals (Kilpatrick, 1982). Often they have to compromise one goal to achieve the other, because the work world generally is not structured to meet the family needs of its employees. As one study pointed out (Berardo et al., 1987):

The traditional "male" model of career involvement makes it extremely difficult for both spouses to pursue careers to the fullest extent possible, since men's success in careers has generally been made possible by their wives' assuming total responsibility for the family life, thus allowing them to experience the rewards of family life but exempting them from this competing set of responsibilities.

Division of Household Labor

Whether or not women are employed seems to have little impact on the division of household work. Studies suggest that employed women do twice as much housework as men (Benin and Agostinelli, 1988; Spitze, 1986). Men tend to shop rather than mop floors, clean toilets, iron, or wash dirty diapers. If the homemaker is employed thirty hours or more a week, she spends about five hours a day on housework instead of the eight hours that full-time homemakers spend. The husband's contribution to household work does not significantly increase if his spouse is employed. A study of employed wives, for example, found that 39 percent had sole responsibility for child care (compared with 56 percent of nonemployed wives); 42 percent of employed wives were solely responsible for housework (compared with 57 percent of nonemployed wives); and 34 percent of employed wives were solely responsible for washing dishes (compared with 49 percent of nonemployed wives) (Maret and Finlay, 1984). A study of African-American families found that women were twice as

A man's work is from sun to sun,
But woman's work is never done.

Folk saying

Cleaning ... should be done from the top down—starting with the ceiling, which is ridiculous. Gravity takes care of that. If there were any dirt on the ceiling, it would fall off and land on the floor. The same goes for walls. Dirt falls right off them and lands on the floor. And you shouldn't fool around with the dirt on the floor, because it will get all over the walls and ceiling.

P. J. O'Rourke

likely as men to feel overworked (Broman, 1988). Men, moreover, tend to perceive that they do more housework than they actually do (Condron and Bode, 1982).

Various factors seem to affect men's participation in housework. Men tend to contribute more to household tasks when they have the fewest time demands from their jobs—that is, early in their employment careers and after retirement (Rexroat and Shehan, 1987). Gender-role orientation also seems to affect sharing in household tasks. In one study (Bird et al., 1984), men who believed in egalitarian roles accepted more responsibility for child care, meal preparation, and cleaning. Husbands' sharing of household work was also related to their wives being employed, especially if their wives were career-oriented. As wives' income rose, they reported more participation by husbands in household tasks; increased income and job status motivate women to secure their husbands' sharing of tasks. Another study found that the more expressive and mastery-oriented the wife, the more assistance she obtained from her husband (Nyquist et al., 1985). Men who were relatively expressive helped their wives more than men who were relatively aggressive, dominant, and emotionally "tough." Husbands in one study (Benin and Agostinelli, 1988) felt most satisfied in the division of household labor if tasks were divided equally, especially if their total time spent on chores was small. Women appeared to be more satisfied if their husbands shared traditional women's chores rather than limiting their participation to traditional male tasks (such as mowing the lawn). But even men who contribute many hours to household labor do traditional male tasks (Blair and Lichter, 1991). Children appear to be less sex-segregated with their household work than their parents (Simons and Whitbeck, 1991). African Americans are less likely to divide household tasks along gender lines than whites (Maret and Finley, 1984).

Husbands and wives generally agree that if both work outside the home, household tasks should be divided equally (Huber and Spitze, 1983). Few couples do so, however. Some wives prefer the traditional division of labor or believe that higher-earning husbands should have fewer household responsibilities. In fact, most studies find that the majority of husbands and wives believe their family's division of labor is fair (Spitze, 1991). Studies increasingly show the importance of satisfaction with the division of labor and marital satisfaction (Suitor, 1991).

Childrearing Responsibilities

Men increasingly believe that they should be more involved fathers than men have been in the past (Pleck, 1985). Yet the shift in attitudes has not greatly altered men's behavior. A recent study (Darling-Fisher and Tiedje, 1990) found that the father's time involved in child care is greatest when the mother is employed full time (fathers responsible for 30 percent of the care compared to mothers' 60 percent), less when she is employed part-time (fathers 25 percent versus 75 percent for mothers), and least when she is a full-time homemaker (fathers 20 percent versus 80 percent for mothers).

A review of studies (Lamb, 1987) on parental involvement in two-parent families concluded the following:

❐ Mothers spend from three to five hours of active involvement for every hour fathers spend, depending on whether the women are employed.
❐ Mothers' involvement is oriented toward practical daily activities, such as feeding, bathing, and dressing. Fathers' time is generally spent in play.
❐ Mothers are almost entirely responsible for child care: planning, organizing, scheduling, supervising, and delegating.
❐ Women are the primary caretakers; men are secondary.

Marital Power

An important consequence of women working is a shift in the decision-making patterns in a marriage. Although decision-making power in a family is not based solely on economic resources (personalities, for instance, also play a part), economics is a major factor. A number of studies suggest that employed wives exert greater power in the home than nonemployed wives (Ferber, 1982; Ybarra, 1982, but see Sexton and Perlman, 1989). Marital decision-making power is greater among women who are employed full-time than among those who are employed part time. Wives have the greatest power when they are employed in prestigious work, are committed to it, and have greater income than their husbands.

Some researchers are puzzled about why many employed wives, if they do have more power, do not demand greater participation in household work on the part of their husbands. Joseph Pleck (1985) suggests several reasons for women's apparent reluctance to insist on their husbands' equal participation in housework. These include:

❐ Cultural norms that housework is the woman's responsibility
❐ Fears that demands for increased participation will lead to conflict
❐ Belief that husbands are not competent

Glenna Spitze (1991) believes that the division of housework will become an issue in relationships as women begin to react to the lack of equity. This may lead to increased divorce as "more women come to believe that a husband who divides labor equitably is a truly possible alternative."

Marital Satisfaction

How does employment affect marital satisfaction? Traditionally, this question was asked only of wives, not husbands; and even then, it was rarely asked of African-American wives, who had a significantly higher employment rate. In the past, married women's employment, especially maternal employment, was viewed as a problem. It was seen as taking away from a woman's time, energy, and commitment for her children and family. In contrast, *nonemployment* or *unemployment* was seen as the problem for men. But it is possible that the husband's work may *increase* marital and family problems by preventing him from adequately fulfilling his role as a husband or father: he may be too tired, too busy, or never there. It is also possible that a mother *not* being employed may affect the family adversely: her income may be needed to move the family out of poverty, and she may feel depressed from lack of stimulation (Menaghan and Parcel, 1991).

How does a woman's employment affect marital satisfaction? There does not seem to be any straightforward answer when comparing dual-earner and single-earner families (Piotrkowski et al., 1987). In part, this may be because there are trade-offs: a woman's income allows a family a higher standard of living, which compensates for the lack of status a man may feel for not being the "sole" provider. While men may adjust (or have already adjusted) to giving up their sole-provider ideal, women find current arrangements less than satisfactory. After all, women are bringing home additional income but are still expected to do the overwhelming majority of household work. Role strain is a constant factor for women, and in general, women make greater adjustments than men in dual-earner marriages. Wives are more likely to feel satisfied if their husbands do their share of household work. Wives who believe that their husbands do not do their share tend to be more critical. What appears to be important is not the number of hours that a husband puts in, but whether his wife believes he is doing his fair share of family work. The issue, then, is one of eq-

Money is a source of power that supports male dominance in the family. . . . Money belongs to him who earns it, not to her who spends it, since he who earns it may withhold it.

Reuben Hill and Howard Becker

What shall it profit a man, if he shall gain the whole world, and lose his own soul?

Mark 8:36

▉ TABLE 9.1	Percent of Family Members Reporting Common Types of Work—Family Conflicts		▉
GROUP	EXCESSIVE WORK TIME	SCHEDULE INCOMPATABILITY	FATIGUE AND IRRITABILITY
All family members*	50	28	15
Employed husbands with employed wives	63	22	11
Employed wives with employed husbands	39	39	27
Employed women in one-parent families	10	50	15

*Total sample size is 372; percentages based on weighted sample of those experiencing moderate or severe conflict.

NOTE: Figures may not add up due to rounding.

SOURCE: Joseph H. Pleck, Graham L. Staines, and Linda Lang, "Conflicts between work and family life," *Monthly Labor Review* 103(3):29–32, U.S. Department of Labor, Bureau of Labor Statistics, 1980.

uity (Gaesser and Whitbourne, 1985; Benin and Nienstadt, 1985; Pleck, 1985; Thompson and Walker, 1991).

Studies of the effect of women's employment on the likelihood of divorce are not conclusive, but they do suggest a relationship (Spitze, 1991; White, 1991). Many studies suggest that employed women are more likely to divorce. Employed women are less likely to conform to traditional gender roles, which potentially causes tension and conflict in the marriage. They are also more likely to be economically independent and do not have to tolerate unsatisfactory marriages for economic reasons. Other studies suggest that the only significant factor in employment is the number of hours the wife works. Hours worked may be important because full-time work for both partners makes it more difficult for spouses to share time together. Numerous hours may also contribute to role overload on the part of the wife (Greenstein, 1990; South and Spitze, 1986; Spitze and South, 1985).

African-American women, however, are not more likely to divorce if they are employed. This may be because of their historically high employment levels and their husbands' traditional acceptance of such employment (Taylor et al., 1991).

Overall, despite an increased divorce rate, in recent years the overall effect of wives' employment on marital satisfaction has shifted from a negative impact to no impact or even a positive impact. If there are negative effects, they generally result from specific aspects of a woman's job, such as long hours or work stress (Spitze, 1991).

Coping with Dual-Earner Marriages

Dual-earner marriages are here to stay. They are particularly stressful today because society has not pursued ways to alleviate the work/family conflict. The three greatest social needs in dual-earner marriages are (1) redefining gender roles to eliminate role overload for women, (2) providing adequate child-care facilities for working parents, and (3) restructuring the workplace to recognize the special needs of parents and families (see Boken and Viveros-Long, 1981; Regan and Roland, 1985).

Coping strategies include reorganizing the family system and reevaluating household expectations. Husbands may do more housework. Children may take on more household tasks than before (Coggle and Tasker, 1982). Household standards—such as a meticulously clean house, complicated meal preparation, and washing dishes after every meal—may be changed. Careful allocation of time and flexibility assist in coping. Home economist Kathryn Walker (1982) suggested that the best way to organize is to ask fundamental life questions: "One begins any such process by asking: What do I want to get out of home life? Until we determine what is important and identify values and goals, we cannot really plan time." Dual-earner couples often hire outside help, especially for child care, which is usually a major expense for most couples. One of the partners may reduce his or her hours of employment. Or both partners may work different shifts to facilitate child care (but this usually reduces marital satisfaction as a result) (White and Keith, 1990).

The goal for most dual-earner families is to manage their family relationships and their paid work to achieve a reasonable balance that allows their families to thrive rather than merely survive. Achieving such balance will continue to be a struggle until society and the workplace adapt to the needs of dual-earner marriages and families. (For a literature and resource review on balancing work and family, see Hansen, 1991.)

❐ FAMILY ISSUES IN THE WORKPLACE

Discrimination against Women

Because of the significant impact that women's earnings have on family well-being (whether a woman is a major contributor to a dual-earner family or the sole provider in single-parent family) women's issues are also important family issues.

ECONOMIC DISCRIMINATION. The effects of economic discrimination can be devastating for women. In 1989, women in the United States made 70 cents for every dollar that men earned (Pear, 1990). (In Sweden, women make 90 cents for every dollar made by men.) Because of the great difference in women's and men's wages, many women are condemned to poverty and are forced to accept welfare and its accompanying stigma. Wage differentials are especially important to single women. Women head 89 percent of all single-parent families and generally have to support these families. Thirty-six percent of female single-parent families live beneath the poverty level, compared with 13 percent for single-parent families headed by men (Weinberg, 1985).

Employment and pay discrimination is prohibited by Title VII of the 1964 Civil Rights Act. This law did not end the pay discrepancy between men and women, however. Much of the earnings gap is the result of occupational differences, gender segregation, and women's tendency to interrupt their employment for family reasons and to take jobs that do not interfere extensively with their family life (Beller, 1984). Earnings are about 30 to 50 percent higher in traditionally male occupations, such as truck driver or corporate executive, than in predominantly female or integrated occupations, such as secretary or school teacher (Beller, 1982). The more an occupation is dominated by women, the less it pays.

In recent years, the idea of *comparable worth* has been proposed as a means of closing the gap between men's and women's wages. Many believe that jobs held mostly by women pay less than jobs held mostly by men because they are seen as "women's

There is a simple way to define a woman's job. Whatever the duties are—and they vary from place to place and from time to time—a woman's job is anything that pays less than a man will accept for comparable work.

Caroline Bird

work" and are consequently devalued. Supporters of comparable worth argue that secretaries, nurses, and clerks should earn as much as truck drivers, mechanics, and construction workers according to measurements of the inherent worth of such jobs in terms of experience, knowledge and skills, mental demands, accountability, and working conditions. Opponents to comparable worth, however, argue that occupational wage differentials are the result of social norms, market forces, and women's own choices of putting family ahead of work. They argue that "inherent worth" is a subjective judgment and that wages should be set by the marketplace.

SEXUAL HARASSMENT. Sexuality exists in the workplace: individuals are attracted to each other, become romantically involved, engage in sexual humor, and reveal aspects of their sexual lives to each other (Gutek, 1985; Gutek et al., 1980). Sexuality becomes a problem, however, when it is used to harass another person. Women are particularly vulnerable to sexual harassment. Harassment may occur on several different levels. A woman may discover that a job, continued employment, advancement, or other benefits are dependent on being sexually available to her employer. Harassment can also come from a fellow employee who makes unwelcomed sexual advances, innuendoes, and suggestions. In fact, harassment by co-workers is more frequent than harassment by employers. Sexual harassment, like rape, is often impelled by power motives, not sexual ones. Harassment is used to dominate or humiliate another person.

Sexual harassment can have a variety of consequences. One study of workers who reported being sexually harassed (Gutek, 1985) found that 9.1 percent of the women and 1 percent of the men quit their jobs because of harassment. Almost 7 percent of the women and 2 percent of the men thought that they had been dismissed from their jobs as part of the harassment.

Economic Status of Ethnic Families

OCCUPATIONAL STRATIFICATION AMONG MEN. It is generally accepted by labor economists that the relative success of native-born whites in contrast to African Americans and Latinos is due to whites' having greater access to quality education and job training and the political leverage to protect their social and economic advantages. In addition, members of some ethnic groups lack proficiency in standard English, a critical skill, which prohibits them from employment in high-paying jobs (Bean and Tienda, 1987). Occupational differences exist along ethnic lines, which, in turn, affect the economic well-being of families (Billingsley, 1988; Malveaux, 1988). Although almost one-third of African Americans work in middle-class or professional occupations, the remainder are typically employed in declining industries or the lowest-paying jobs. Among African-American men, for example, the majority are employed in manufacturing and service jobs. Technological changes and foreign competition, especially in the automobile, steel, and industrial machines industries, have decimated American manufacturing, where African-Americans once were employed in well-paying jobs. The economic basis of the male African American worker has been dramatically undercut, causing black unemployment rates to almost double, from 9 percent in 1950 to 17 percent in 1990. After the 1950s, African Americans experienced unemployment rates twice as high or more as that of whites (Billingsley, 1988).

Occupational stratification also has an important effect on the potential earnings of Latinos. About 17 percent of native-born Latinos are in professional or managerial jobs, in contrast to 29 percent of Anglos. This number drops to 6 percent if the

Inequality is as dear to the American heart as liberty itself.

William Dean Howells

Latinos were foreign-born. With the notable exception of Cuban Americans, Latinos tend to be concentrated in blue-collar or service work. Among immigrants, farm laborers account for 12 percent of the employed (Bean and Tienda, 1987).

OCCUPATIONAL STRATIFICATION AMONG WOMEN. Employed women tend to be concentrated in relatively low-paying clerical and service occupations. At first glance, there do not appear to be major differences in the job distribution between white and African-American women, but African-American women tend to be employed in the lower-paying levels of these low-paying jobs. Writes Julianne Malveaux (1988): "In addition to being employed in jobs that are 'typically female,' Black women are also employed in jobs that are 'typically' or disproportionately Black female." For example, 41 percent of African-American women in the service industry work as chambermaids, welfare service aides, cleaners, and nurse's aides (three or four times their number overrepresented). Among the forty-eight types of clerical occupations, African-Americans are four times overrepresented in six categories: file clerks, typists, teacher aides, keypunch operators, calculating machine operators, and social welfare clerical assistants. These are among the lowest-paying clerical jobs (Malveaux, 1988).

The experience of Latinas is similar in many ways. Cuban-American and Puerto Rican women both have traditionally worked in large numbers; only in the last two decades have Mexican-American women significantly increased their rates of employment. Puerto Ricans and Mexican Americans tend to be concentrated in the lower-paying jobs. Mexican immigrant women enter agricultural jobs in large numbers. All are important in the low-paying service industries.

The overall result is that African-American, Mexican-American, and Puerto Rican families have lower incomes than whites/Anglos. Cuban Americans do well economically because of the influx of upper- and middle-class refugees who fled the Castro regime in the early 1960s. Native-born Asian Americans usually have higher median incomes than non-Asians.

The lack of affirmative action and job training programs forces many ethnic group members into unemployment, underemployment, poverty, or welfare. Others turn to the military. Said one high school counselor (Harris, 1991), "The kids whose parents have set aside money for school, they're going on to school. But the other kids, they figure they can get training and skills and a chance for college in the military." As a result, in 1990, 38 percent of the Army was composed of minority-status group members, of which 29 percent were African Americans; 7 percent of the officers were from ethnic groups.

Lack of Adequate Child Care

As mothers enter the work force in ever-increasing numbers, high-quality, affordable child care has become even more important. Currently there are 29 million children under age fifteen years whose mothers are employed (U.S. Bureau of the Census, 1990). By 1995, researchers estimate that two-thirds of all preschool children and three-quarters of all school-age children will have mothers in the work force (Hofferth and Phillips, 1987).

INADEQUATE CHILD-CARE OPTIONS. For about 70 percent of employed mothers with children five to fourteen years, school attendance is their primary day-care solution. Women with preschool children, however, do not have that option; in-home care by a relative is their most important resource. As more mothers with preschool children become employed, families are struggling to find suitable child-care arrangements. This may involve constantly switching arrangements, depending on who or what is available and the age of the child or children (Floge, 1985). Relatives, especially fathers and grandparents, are important in caring for their family's children, tending to the needs of almost 40 percent of the children. About 14 percent of the children are cared for by their fathers, 18 percent by their grandparents, and 8 percent by other relatives, such as older brothers and sisters or aunts. The younger the child, the more likely he or she is to be cared for by the grandmother (Presser, 1989). Twenty-four percent of children are cared for in family day-care homes, 14 percent in day-care centers, and 7 percent in preschools (U.S. Bureau of the Census, 1990). Women often use three or four different arrangements—the child's father, relatives living in or outside the household, day-care, or a combination of these—before a child reaches school age. For African-American and Latina single mothers, living in an extended family in which they are likely to have other adults to care for their children is an especially important factor allowing them to find jobs (Rexroat, 1990; Tienda and Glass, 1985).

Frustration is one of the most common experiences in finding or maintaining day care. Changing family situations, such as unemployed fathers finding work or grandparents becoming ill or over-burdened, may lead to these relatives being unable to care for the children. Family day-care homes and child-care centers often close because of low wages or lack of funding. Furthermore, day-care expenses, which run an average of $50 weekly, may prove to be too expensive for many families (U.S. Bureau of the Census, 1990). In fact, the high cost of child care is a major force keeping mothers on welfare from working (Joesch, 1991).

As the incidence of day care inside the child's home by relatives or baby-sitters continues to decrease, over half the children of employed parents are cared for outside their own homes, mostly in family day-care settings. This shift from parent-care at home to day care outside the home may have profound effects on how children are socialized (see Chapter 8). It certainly disturbs many parents, who wonder whether they are, in fact, good parents. Many parents express concern about their children being cared for outside their own family environment. Concerns about their children's development tends to negatively affect parental well-being and their feelings about work (Greenberger and O'Neil, 1990).

Those parents who accept the home-as-haven belief—that the home provides love and nurturing—prefer placing their children in family day-care homes. They believe that a home-like atmosphere is more likely to exist in family day-care than in preschool or children's centers, where greater emphasis is placed on education (Rapp and Lloyd, 1989). But we know relatively little about family day care: it is the most widely used and least researched form of American child care (Goelman, Shapiro, and Pence, 1990).

IMPACT OF CHILD CARE ON EMPLOYMENT OPPORTUNITIES. For women, lack of child care or inadequate child care is one of the major barriers to equal employment opportunity (U.S. Commission on Civil Rights, 1981). Many women who want to work are unable to find adequate child care or afford it. This is especially true for young, unmarried, and poor mothers. Although child-care expenses amount to 22 percent of a poor person's weekly income and 10 percent of a single parent's, government tax credits for child care do little to help those in the most need (U.S. Bureau of the Census, 1990). In 1988, about half of the benefits went to the wealthiest third of families, while the poorest third received only 3 percent (Samuelson, 1988).

In a survey of working women, 29 percent of the clerical, service, factory, and plant workers cited child care as a major problem. Among professional, managerial, and technical workers, the figure rose to 36 percent (cited in U.S. Commission on Civil Rights, 1981). Almost 6 percent of employed mothers using child care reported time lost by themselves or their husbands because of difficulties with child-care arrangements (U.S. Bureau of the Census, 1987). It is estimated that only 2,500 out of the 44,000 largest corporations in the country offer any kind of day-care for their employees (Bowen, 1988).

Childrearing responsibilities make it more difficult for women to compete equally with men in the workplaces. One unemployed mother explained (U.S. Commission on Civil Rights, 1981):

You got children to take care of. And a man does not have that hanging around his neck. You have to be a superwoman in order to get the same job that the man would very easily fall into because he doesn't have to worry about the children going to the doctor; he doesn't have to worry about the children getting sick.

In a report issued by the U.S. House of Representatives' Select Committee on Children, Youth, and Families (1985), the committee found that more than 25 percent of unemployed parents said they would work if they could find child care. The committee also reported that in nearly 25 percent of all households with young children, one or more adults had to give up work, was unable to take a job, or had to discontinue education or training because of lack of child care.

IMPACT ON EDUCATIONAL OPPORTUNITIES. Child care is an important consideration for students with children. At the University of Michigan, 20 to 25 percent of such students would seek more employment or education if child-care services were available. Forty percent of colleges and universities—approximately 1,000—provide day-care facilities for students, and waiting lists are long. One student testified before the Select Committee (1985) about her child-care difficulties:

For a year I had to drive 40 miles a day to take my infant son to a Title XX [child care for low- and moderate-income families] licensed child-care provider. Several times I was nearly forced to terminate my schooling because I had no infant care. I have often missed exams and have had to take incomplete grades because of a sick child.

For some, child care determines the pace of their academic career; for others, it determines whether additional education can be pursued.

The U.S. Commission on Civil Rights (1981) concluded that the lack of child care or inadequate child care has the following consequences:

❏ Prevents women from taking paid jobs
❏ Keeps women in part-time jobs, most often with low pay and little career mobility
❏ Keeps women in jobs for which they are overqualified and prevents them from seeking or taking job promotions or the training necessary for advancement
❏ Conflicts sometimes with women's ability to perform their work
❏ Restricts women from participating in education programs

In 1990, the federal government passed its first child-care funding legislation, providing a block grant of $4 billion to the states for child-care subsidies over the next five years (DeWitt, 1991). Even though the funds are meager compared to child-care needs, the legislation is an important milestone. For the first time in American history, the federal government has recognized the importance of child care for contemporary families.

CHILDREN'S SELF-CARE. Almost 5 percent of children between ages five and fourteen years care for themselves after school while their parents are at their jobs. Because of the lack of adequate after-school programs or prohibitive costs, children's **self-care** has quickly become a major form of child care (Koblinsky and Todd, 1989). Self-care has increased 40 percent since the early 1980s (U.S. Bureau of the Census, 1990). It is a rapidly growing phenomenon, largely the result of inadequate or costly child care and the increasing numbers of married and single mothers who work outside the home (Cole and Rodman, 1987). Self-care exists in families of all socioeconomic classes. One study (Vandell and Corasaniti, 1985) of over 300 children in a well-to-do suburb near Dallas found that 23 percent cared for themselves after school.

The popular image of self-care arrangements is negative; such children are known pejoratively as "latchkey children." Research on self-care arrangements has been sketchy and often contradictory. Some studies find no differences in levels of achievement, fear, and self-esteem between children in day-care and self-care arrangements. Other studies do find such differences. Some children are frightened, others get into mischief, and still others enjoy their independence. These differences may result from the child's own readiness to care for himself or herself, the family's readiness, and community's suitability (Cole and Rodman, 1987). Rather than rejecting self-care altogether, researchers suggest that it may be appropriate for some children and not for others. Children who are mature physically, emotionally, and mentally, whose families are able to maintain contact, and who live in safe neighborhoods, for example, may have no problems in self-care. But if children are immature or live in unsafe neighborhoods, they may find themselves overwhelmed by anxiety and fear. Each child is an individual case. Parents need to evaluate whether self-care is appropriate for their children (see Cole and Rodman, 1987, for suggested guidelines). Because of the rise in self-care, educators are developing programs to teach children and their parents such self-care skills as basic safety, time management, and other self-reliance skills (see Koblinsky and Todd, 1989, for research review).

Inflexible Work Environment

The chief value of money lies in the fact that one lives in a world in which it is overestimated.

H. L. Mencken

The workplace has failed to recognize that the family has radically altered during the last fifty years. Most businesses are run as if every worker were male with a full-time wife at home to attend to his and his children's needs. But the reality is that women make up a significant part of the work force, and *they* don't have wives at home. Allowances are not made in the American workplace for flexibility in work schedules, day-care, emergency time off to look after sick children, and so on. Many parents would reduce their work schedules to minimize work/family conflict (Moen and Dempster-McClain, 1987). Unfortunately, many don't have that option.

Carol Mertensmeyer and Marilyn Coleman (1987) note that our society provides little evidence that it esteems parenting. This seems to be especially true in the workplace, where corporate needs are placed high above family needs. Mertensmeyer and Coleman continue:

Family policymakers should encourage employers to be more responsive in providing parents with alternatives that alleviate forced choices that are incongruent with parents' values. For example, corporate-sponsored child care may offset the conflict a mother feels because she is not at home with her child. Flextime and paid maternal and paternal leaves are additional benefits that employers could provide employees. These benefits would help parents fulfill self and family expectations and would give parents evidence that our nation views parenting as a valuable role.

A model corporation would provide family-oriented policies that would benefit both its employees and itself, such as flexible work schedules, job-sharing alternatives, extended maternity and/or paternity leaves and benefits, and child-care programs or subsidies (Bowen, 1988; Raabe and Gessner, 1988). Such policies would increase employee satisfaction, morale, and commitment; they are not especially widespread, however (Orthner and Pittman, 1986).

In 1990, after decades of argument, Congress finally passed the Family and Medical Leave Act, which required employers to provide eighteen weeks of *unpaid* leave for mothers or fathers following birth or adoption or for the care of seriously ill children. Although most European countries provide *paid* leave, the President vetoed the legislation as unwarranted governmental intrusion into employment practices. (For a Senate voting model on parental leave, see Monroe and Garland, 1991; for a refutation of family leave policies based on the Connecticut experience, see Trzcinski and Finn-Stevenson, 1991.)

❐ POVERTY AND UNEMPLOYMENT

Although poverty and unemployment may appear to be only economic issues, they are not. The family and economy are intimately connected to each other. And economic inequality directly affects the well-being of America's disadvantaged families. Poverty drives families into homelessness. Poverty is consistently associated with marital and family stress, increased divorce rates, low birth weight and infant deaths, poor health, depression, lowered life-expectancy, and feelings of hopelessness and despair. Catherine Ross and her colleagues (Ross, Mirowsky, and Goldsteen, 1991) suggest the connection:

It is in the household that the larger social and economic order impinges on individuals, exposing them to varying degrees of hardship, frustration, and struggle. The struggle to pay the bills and to feed and clothe the family on an inadequate budget takes its toll in feeling rundown, tired, and having no energy, feeling that everything is an effort, that the future is hopeless, that you can't shake the blues, that nagging worries make for restless sleep, and that there isn't much to enjoy in life.

Poverty

DEMOGRAPHICS. Poverty has been increasing since 1981, primarily as a result of sharp swings in employment, an increase in single-parent families, and government cutbacks in assistance to low-income families. In 1989, more than 31.5 million Americans—over 12.8 percent of the population—lived in poverty, the lowest figure since 1980 but still higher than any time during the 1970s (Pear, 1990). If we include those who live in near-poverty (earning $14,000 or less for a family of four), the numbers increase to almost one out of every five American families. Although we tend to think of poverty as primarily an urban phenomenon, over 9 million poor live in America's rural areas. In some Iowa counties, poverty rates approach 30 percent. It is particularly ironical that hunger is a common problem in America's farming heartland (Davidson, 1990).

Poverty levels differ according to certain characteristics. In 1988, a time of economic prosperity, the percentage of those living in poverty was 10 percent for whites, 33 percent for African Americans, 28 percent for Latinos, 12 percent for Asians, and 25 percent for Native Americans (U.S. Bureau of the Census, 1990). By family type, 19 percent of two-parent families with children are poor compared to 55 percent of single-parent families (U.S. Bureau of the Census, 1990). The recession that began in 1990, coupled with cuts in public assistance, drove the poverty level up, especially among African Americans and Latinos.

Therefore I tell you, do not be anxious about your life, what you shall eat or what you shall drink, nor about your body, what you shall put on. Is not life more than food, and the body more than clothing? Look at the birds of the air; they neither sow nor reap nor gather into barns, and yet your Heavenly Father feeds them. Are you not of more value than they? And which of you by being anxious can add one cubit to his span of life? And why are you anxious about clothing? Consider the lilies of the field. How they grow; they neither toil nor spin; yet I tell you, even Solomon in all his glory was not arrayed like one of these.

Matthew 6:25–29

The rich get richer and the poor get poorer.

Miguel de Cervantes (1547–1616)

FOCUS

Hungry and Homeless in America

"I don't know how I could express hunger," a mother said. "It was not to the point where I'd pass out. The children always ate. Maybe I didn't. Maybe not for two or three nights. Maybe some juice during the day, but that's not eating." The woman had lost her job because of a difficult pregnancy; welfare benefits arrived too late to prevent eviction. For a while she stayed with relatives, but then she was shunted from one welfare hotel to another; finally, after over a year of living in welfare hotels in New York City, she was moved to a city-renovated apartment. She was lucky, for there are few such apartments available, and the waiting period for low-income public housing is about eighteen years (Kozol, 1988; Roberts, 1988).

Others are not as lucky. They sleep in parks, on steps, in abandoned buildings. They are society's outcasts. A middle-aged, homeless artist, who used to sleep beneath the outstretched arms of Jesus at the front of St. Patrick's Cathedral in New York, moved to the south side of the cathedral "because the Fifth Avenue Association says I'm bad for the tourists." He now occupies a "cardboard condominium." "It's not bad," he says. "With your body heat you won't freeze to death, even if you cut a couple of holes to breathe" (Hevesi, 1986). One researcher (Rivlin, 1990) described homelessness:

Picture a day when you cannot be certain where you will sleep, how you will clean yourself, how you will find food, how you will hang on to your belongings. . . , how you will be safe, how you will dress properly to get to work (for many homeless persons do, indeed, work), and for some, how you will fill up the long hours of a day and do so in a place that will not tolerate your presence. Ordinary activities become major struggles: finding places to wash hair or clothing, locating toilets when needed, surfaces on which to raise swollen feet, or finding food, places to keep warm in cold weather and to escape the rain, snow or summer heat.

On any given night, 735,000 Americans are homeless; between 1.3 and 2 million Americans were homeless at least one night during 1987. At least 100,000 were children, according to a major study by the National Academy of Science (1988). Probably more than 3 million Americans go hungry at least occasionally (Marin, 1987).

The face of hunger and homelessness has changed since the 1970s. Then the homeless were most often single individuals who were drug addicts, alcoholics, or mentally ill persons forced into the streets with the closing of many mental health facilities. Today, however, more than 25 percent of the homeless are families; they represent the fastest-growing sec-

tor of the homeless (Kozol, 1988). Most homeless families consist of single mothers with two or three children, most of whom are preschoolers (Bassuk et al., 1986). In some metropolitan areas, as many as three-fourths of the homeless are single mothers (Axelson and Dail, 1988). The families became homeless when the mother lost a job, separated or divorced, became physically disabled or ill, was unable to get welfare, was cut from welfare or had benefits reduced, or was unable to make ends meet on a fixed income. Without the ability to pay their rent or mortgages, they were unable to find housing or were forced to leave their homes. For many, it is a downward spiral.

About half the mothers heading homeless families are between the ages of seventeen and twenty-five years; they are equally distributed between whites and African Americans; about 7 percent are Latinas or Asians. Only 10 percent are currently married. More than half are high school graduates and one-fifth have had some college. The majority of women became homeless because they fled a relationship rather than because of eviction or job loss. Frequently, a violent incident was the precipitating cause of their homelessness, as they escaped with

continued on next page

The law, in its majesty equality, forbids the rich as well as the poor to sleep under bridges, to beg in the streets, and to steal bread.

Anatole France (1844–1924)

SPELLS OF POVERTY. Few people choose to live on welfare. Most are forced into it by circumstances. And because circumstances change, the majority of welfare recipients tend to be in poverty for spells of time rather than permanently (Bane and Ellwood, 1986). About a quarter of the American population, in fact, requires welfare assistance at one time or another during their lives because of changes in families caused by divorce, unemployment, illness, disability or death (Duncan et al., 1984). About half of our children are vulnerable to poverty spells at least once during their childhood (Duncan and Rodgers, 1988). Many families receiving welfare are in the early stages of recovery from an economic crisis caused by the death, separation, divorce, or disability of the family's major wage earner. Many who accept government their children. Homeless mothers report a lack of ongoing family, social, and emotional support. The overwhelming majority say their children are the most important source of support. Twenty-five percent of homeless mothers suffer severe depression or substance abuse, but it is not clear whether these are reactions to homelessness or causes of it (Axelson and Dail, 1988).

As a makeshift response to housing needs, some cities provide emergency shelters, usually barrack-style warehouses or single-occupancy hostels. Many shelters permit only women and children, requiring husbands and fathers in intact families to separate. Unless time limits are imposed, emergency shelters tend to become permanent residences. The shelters, however, are generally located in dangerous neighborhoods inhabited by transients, drug abusers, petty criminals, and prostitutes.

Shelters are often frightening environments for families. A twelve-year-old girl paints a desperate picture of life in a residential hotel (quoted in Edelman, 1989):

I don't like the hotel because there is always a lot of trouble there. I don't go down into the street because there is no place to play. . . . The streets are dangerous, with all kinds of sick people who

are on drugs or crazy. My mother is afraid to let me go downstairs. Only this Saturday, my friend, the security guard at the hotel, Mr. Santiago, was killed on my floor. The blood is still on the walls and on the floor.

Under such conditions, children suffer developmental delays, severe depression and anxiety, and learning difficulties. They also suffer from malnutrition. One study (Bassuk and Rubin, 1987) found that as many as half of the school-age children in their sample were in need of psychiatric evaluation; they displayed symptoms of depression, including suicide attempts. Although most of the mothers are intensely concerned about their children's well-being and future, the women feel helpless to prevent the same misfortunes from befalling their own children (Axelson and Dail, 1988).

How did this crisis in hunger and homelessness originate? The two major factors were the lack of adequate income and lack of affordable housing (Edelman and Mihaly, 1989). First, poverty increased dramatically in the early and mid-1980s, tapered off, and then substantially increased again in 1991 with a new recession. Second, a housing crisis was slowly growing. While housing prices skyrocketed, low-income rentals decreased at the

rate of 125,000 apartments a year (Whitman, 1987). Today there are more than twice as many poor households as there is affordable housing. The monthly AFDC housing allowance pays less than half the actual cost of rent. As Axelson and Dail (1988) note:

The underlying causes show every indication of persisting, and the dimensions of the problems are increasing as they become more tightly interwoven into issues of unemployment, housing scarcity, domestic violence and abuse, and cutbacks in a wide range of social services.

We like to find moral fault in the individual, attributing homelessness to character defects or drugs, rather than seeking solutions. A commitment to ending homelessness would include the following: (1) the development of low-cost housing and housing subsidy programs, (2) establishment of child-care programs that will allow homeless single mothers to work, (3) provision of mental health support to deal with psychological problems, and (4) initiation of job training and education programs to develop employable skills. As homeless families continue to live and sleep in the streets, in abandoned cars, and in rat-infested shelters, we are confronted with a basic question: Is this the best America can do for its most vulnerable families?

assistance return to self-sufficiency within a year or two. Only about 2 percent of the population depend heavily on welfare for more than seven out of ten years. Most of the children in these families do not receive welfare after they leave home.

There are two major factors related to the beginning and ending of spells of poverty: changes in income and changes in family composition. Thirty-eight percent of poverty spells begin with a decline in earnings of the head of the household, such as a job loss or a cut in work hours. Other causes include a decline in earnings of other family members (11 percent), the transition to single parenting (11 percent), the birth of a child to a single mother (9 percent), and the move of a youth to his or her own household (15 percent). One study of AFDC recipients found that

We hold the moral obligation of providing for old age, helpless infancy, and poverty far superior to that of supplying the wants of courtly extravagance.

Thomas Paine

Homeless families represent about a quarter of all the homeless population and are the fastest-growing segment of that population. Homeless children suffer depression, anxiety, and malnutrition. What would your life have been like if you had been raised without a home?

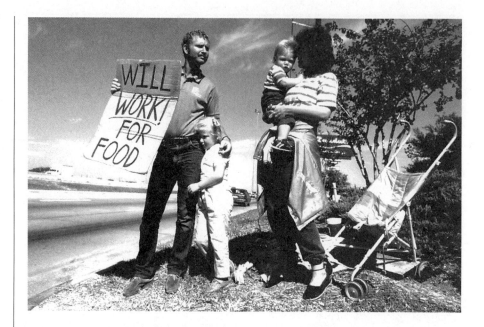

most women required assistance as a result of changes in their family situation—45 percent after separation or divorce, 30 percent after becoming unmarried mothers. One-third of the women left the program within a year, half at the end of two years, and two-thirds within four years. About a third left the program because their income had increased, another third when they remarried or reconciled with their mate, and 14 percent when their children left home or grew up.

Poverty spells are shorter if they begin with a decline in income than if they begin with transition to single parenthood or the birth of a child to a single mother. Half of poverty spells end with an increase in the earnings of the head of household and 23 percent with an increase in earnings to other family members. Fifteen percent end when the family receives public assistance, and 10 percent end when a single mother marries.

The Christian ethic is incompatible with a primary or exclusive focus on maximization of profit. . . . Decisions must be judged in light of what they do for the poor, what they do to the poor, and what they enable the poor to do for themselves. The fundamental moral criterion for all economic decisions, policies, and institutions is this: They must be at the service of all people, especially the poor.

National Conference of Catholic Bishops, Pastoral Letter, 1986

INCOME AND WEALTH. There are vast disparities in income and wealth between white, African American, Latino, and other ethnic groups. In fact, in 1990 the U.S. Census Bureau reported that over the last two decades there has been a "growing inequality of income distribution" (Pear, 1990). In 1989, for example, the median income for whites was $30,406, which was almost 60 percent greater than the $18,083 of African Americans (Pear, 1990). During the 1980s, the income disparity grew enormously, with the wealthiest 20 percent receiving a substantially higher share at the expense of the middle class and poor. Between 1979 and 1989, for example, the most affluent 5 percent of American families increased their median income from $120,253 to $148,438, while the income of the poorest 20 percent of families decreased from $9,990 to $9,431. At the same time, changes in the federal tax burden decreased the share of income that the wealthiest paid in taxes and increased the share paid by the poorest. Between 1980 and 1990, the percentage of income paid by the poorest 20 percent increased by 16.1 percent while the share paid by the wealthiest 5 percent decreased by 9.5 percent ("Shifting the Burden," 1990).

The disparity in wealth was even greater than income. (Wealth is a person's net worth, which represents decades of differences in income, investment, and the inheritance of property.) This disparity grew significantly during the 1980s (Pear, 1991). The net worth of whites is ten times that of African Americans and eight times that of Latinos. The median net worth for whites was $43,280, for African Americans, $4,170, and for Latinos, $5,520.

THE PLIGHT OF YOUNG FAMILIES. Families headed by men and women younger than thirty years are experiencing "a frightening cycle of plummeting earnings and family incomes, declining marriage rates, rising out-of-wedlock birth rates, increasing numbers of single-parent families, and skyrocketing poverty rates," wrote Marian Wright Edelman (1988). The findings of a study on young families (Johnson, Sum, and Weill, 1988) bear out Edelman's statements. Consider the following:

❐ The median income of families with young children fell 26 percent between 1973 and 1986. As a result, the poverty rate for young families soared from 12 percent to 22 percent. At the same time, the percentage of children living in poverty in young families rose from 21 to 35 percent.

❐ Young African-American and Latino families have suffered especially severe income losses. The median income of the heads of young African-American families has plummeted by half; for Latinos, the loss is one-third. Even among young African-American college graduates who head families, their median earnings have dropped 31 percent.

❐ Home ownership is beyond the reach of most young families. In 1973, it took one-fifth of a young family's median income to carry a mortgage; in 1986, it required 51 percent.

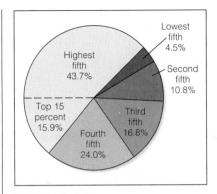

FIGURE 9.1

Money Income of Families, 1989

The distribution of family income is subject to great inequalities in the United States. The wealthiest 20 percent of families receive over 9 times as much income as the poorest 20 percent of families. The wealthiest 5 percent receive 13 times as much income as the poorest 20 percent.

SOURCE: U.S. Bureau of the Census. *Statistical Abstract of the United States, 1990.* Washington, D.C.: Government Printing Office, 1990.

FIGURE 9.2

Individuals and Children Below Poverty Level, 1989

SOURCE: U.S. Bureau of the Census. *Statistical Abstract of the United States, 1990.* Washington, D.C.: Government Printing Office, 1990.

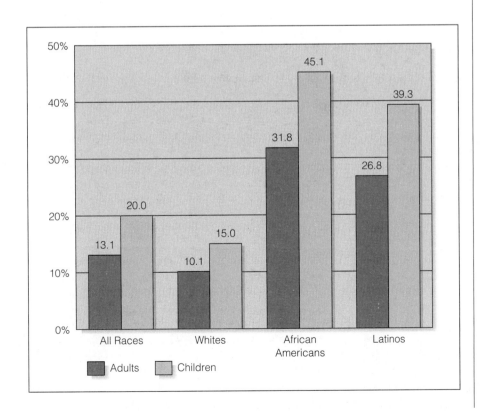

A Puerto Rican who didn't speak English came to the United States. He went along the streets of New York and came upon an expensive house. He went up to it and asked the butler in Spanish, "Who does this house belong to?"

The butler replied, "What did you say?"

The Puerto Rican misunderstood the butler, thinking he had said "Juan José."

The Puerto Rican went on and saw a beautiful car. He asked the man standing next to it, "Whose car is this?"

"What did you say?" asked the man.

"Dios mio!" exclaimed the Puerto Rican. "It belongs to Juan José."

Then he saw a prosperous clothing store. "Who owns this store?" asked the Puerto Rican.

"What did you say," was the reply.

Again the Puerto Rican thought the man had said Juan José.

The Puerto Rican saw a group of people surrounding two men fighting. "Who is fighting?" he asked.

"What did you say," replied the man.

"Juan José is fighting," the Puerto Rican said to himself.

Shortly afterward he came upon a funeral procession. "Whose funeral is this?" he asked.

"What did you say," a mourner asked.

"Oh, Juan José had died," the Puerto Rican murmured to himself.

Then the Puerto Rican saw a friend and said to him in Spanish, "Juan José has died. He was the richest man in all the United States. He wanted everything and would even fight to get it. And now he is dead. Poor Juan José that he didn't know better."

Puerto Rican folktale. (Originally West African Ananse [spider] tale brought to the Americas by enslaved blacks and modified over time to changed conditions.)

THE WORKING POOR. Since 1979, the largest increase in the numbers of poor has been among the working poor, because of low wages, occupational segregation, and the dramatic rise in single-parent families (Ellwood, 1988). Over 16 million poor men and women are "working poor." Although they work or are looking for work, they can not earn enough to raise themselves out of poverty. Almost 4 million worked full-time but remained poor (Chilman, 1991). A man or woman working full-time at minimum wage earns only 78 percent of the poverty-line income for a family of three. Almost half of two-parent working poor families had at least one adult working full-time. Four out of five poor, two-parent families are poor because of problems in the economic structure—low wages, job insecurity, or lack of available jobs. (See Chilman, 1991, for literature review.)

WOMEN, CHILDREN, AND POVERTY. The **feminization of poverty** is a painful fact. It has resulted primarily from high rates of divorce and increasing numbers of unmarried women with children (Hill, 1985). When women with children divorce, their income falls dramatically. In 1986, the median income of single-parent working women was $13,600 (U.S. Bureau of the Census, 1988).

Almost 40 percent of all children are poor; their poverty rate is the highest of any group. Like their parents, they move in and out of spells of poverty, depending on major changes in family structure, employment status of family members, or the disability status of the family head (Duncan and Rodgers, 1988). These variables, such as employment status, affect ethnic groups differently, accounting for differences in poverty rates. African Americans, for example, have significantly higher unemployment rates and numbers of never-married single mothers than other groups. As a result, their childhood poverty rates are markedly higher. Half of all African-American children under six years are poor; 40 percent of Latino children are poor, and 16 percent of white/Anglo children are poor (Pear, 1990). Being poor puts the most ordinary needs—from health care to housing—out of reach, jeopardizes the children's schooling, and undermines their sense of self (Edelman, 1989).

THE UNDERCLASS. In the last ten years, the underclass and homeless have become deeply disturbing features of American life, destroying cherished images of wealth and economic mobility. (For information about homelessness, see Focus, "Hungry and Homeless in America." We must go back to the Great Depression of the 1930s when, in the words of President Franklin Delano Roosevelt, "one third of the nation was ill-fed, ill-clad, and ill-housed" to find greater despair. One commentator (DeParle, 1991) observed why many find the underclass and homeless so disturbing:

They suggest a second, separate America, a nation within a nation whose health, welfare, and social mobility evoke the Third World. Indeed visitors startled by rows of homeless lying in Grand Central Terminal in New York strain for analogies and produce the word "Calcutta."

It is not clear exactly what the underclass is (Auletta, 1982; Wilson 1989). It comprises not simply the poor, who have always existed in great numbers in America. The underclass is primarily a phenomenon of decaying cities, where poor African Americans and Latinos are overrepresented. The underclass feel excluded from society; indeed, it is often rejected by a society that neither understands nor empathizes with its plight (Appelbome, 1991). It is not a culture of poverty, however; the underclass's behaviors, actions, and problems are often a response to lack of opportunity, urban neglect, and inadequate housing and schooling.

With the flight of manufacturing, few job opportunities exist in the inner cities; the jobs that do exist are usually service jobs that fail to pay their workers sufficient wages to allow them to rise above poverty. Schools are substandard. Without adequate medical care, the infant death rate approaches that of Third World countries. HIV infection and AIDS are epidemic. The housing projects are infested with crime and drug abuse, turning them into kingdoms of despair. Gunfire punctuates the night. A woman addicted to crack explained, "I feel like I'm a different person when I'm not here. I feel good. I feel I don't need drugs. But being in here, you just feel like you're drowning. It's like being in jail. I hate the projects. I hate this rat hole" (DePerle, 1991).

Within the inner city, its residents struggle to maintain their dignity against surging hopelessness. They live day to day, fighting the forces that threaten to engulf them. A mother waiting for her child to return home from school said: "Mostly, you try to keep them away from the drugs and violence, but it's hard. I tell my oldest boy I don't want him hanging out with the boys who are getting in trouble, and he says, 'Aw, mama, ain't nobody else for me to be with'" (DePerle, 1991).

PUBLIC ASSISTANCE PROGRAMS. What is welfare? Welfare's most basic meaning refers to health, happiness, and well-being; the word itself is derived from the Old English *wel faren*, "to fare well." Over the last generation, however, driven by conservative beliefs, welfare has taken on a bad name. We no longer wish our poor *wel faren*. The war on poverty in the 1960s became the war on welfare in the 1980s. Instead of viewing poverty as a structural feature of our economy—caused by the shift from an industrial to service economy, the lack of opportunity, and discrimination—we blame the victim. Poverty is viewed as the result of individual character flaws—or even worse, as something inherently racial (Katz, 1990; Piven and Cloward, 1972).

While poverty has increased, welfare benefits have not. In fact, the value of welfare benefits has decreased by over one-third since 1970, and fewer and fewer poor families are eligible for assistance (Kozol, 1988). The budget cutting of the 1990s is making a bad situation worse. Like many other states, for example, California cut the number of recipients of its Special Supplemental Food Program for Women, Infants and Children (WIC) program. One pregnant single parent with two children, a one-year-old and two-year-old, said (Mydans 1990): "It's going to be hard. The program helps a whole, whole lot. Sometimes you don't have the money to buy milk." To make up for the cuts, she will have to share some of the food she and her one-year-old receive from the program with her two-year-old, who is no longer eligible because of his age. And the high cost of child care keeps many AFDC mothers from working (Joesch, 1991).

In 1988, 6.1 percent of the population received public assistance; 3.8 million families, more than 11 million people, received AFDC (Aid to Families with Dependent Children) benefits, averaging $379 a month for a family with two children (U.S. Bureau of the Census, 1990). Seventy percent of single-parent families headed by women received government assistance, most often Medicaid or school lunches. Almost 40 percent of the poor, however, receive no assistance.

Despite the fact that 13 percent of the population currently lives in poverty, the number of people receiving government assistance has decreased from 6.5 percent of the population to 6.2 percent (U.S. Bureau of the Census, 1988). The number of people receiving foods stamps declined from 22 million in 1980 to 19.1 million in 1986 (U.S. Bureau of the Census, 1988). (And one does not live high on food stamps. The average food-stamp recipient receives 48 cents per meal per person; the highest amount received is 70 cents [Press, 1985]).

The true test of civilization is a decent provision for the poor.

Samuel Johnson

American "means-tested" programs do indeed debilitate and demoralize. It is not receiving benefits that is damaging but rather the benefits are so low as to ensure physical misery and an outcast social status.

Fred Block

Unemployment

Unemployment is a structural part of the American economy; it is there in good times and bad times. In the best of times, there has been a 4 percent unemployment rate. In 1992, as many as 7.5 percent were officially unemployed, though the actual numbers were probably substantially higher. During the recession that began in 1990, only one-third of unemployed men and women received unemployment benefits. Despite high unemployment, the proportion of those receiving unemployment insurance did not increase significantly, because the federal government and states gutted their unemployment insurance systems rather than raise taxes (Rosenbaum, 1990). In 1990, 2.3 million jobless men and women used up their unemployment benefits.

The human cost of these cutbacks is high. A common public policy assumption is that unemployment is primarily an economic problem. Yet joblessness also seriously affects health and the family's well-being (Liem and Rayman, 1982; Riegle, 1982). Two psychologists have called for "radically reshaping our sense of unemployment as not simply a problem in economics but as a factor in human and social welfare" (Liem and Rayman, 1982). (The psychological dimension of unemployment is discussed in Chapter 10.) The night before her unemployed husband left the state to take a temporary one-week job at one-fourth his former wage, for example, a woman let out her frustration, her eyes blazing with anger: "I'm holding down the fort. I'm paying his child support. I'm keeping things together. I'm pregnant. I'm tired, and I can't do it all" (Holmes, 1991). Her husband had been unemployed more than twenty-six weeks, the maximum period allowed for benefits by forty-eight states. Seventy-five percent of the unemployed had not found work four weeks after their benefits expired; ten weeks later, 60 percent were still unemployed (Holmes, 1991).

The types of families hardest hit by unemployment are single-parent families headed by women, African-American and Latino families, and young families. African-American, Latino, and female-headed single-parent families tend to remain unemployed longer than other types of families. Because of discrimination and the resultant poverty, they may not have important education and employment skills. Young families with preschool children often lack the seniority, experience, and skills to quickly regain employment. "Since the parents of preschoolers are also the ones most likely to lose their jobs," observed Moen (1983), "the largest toll in an economic downturn is paid by families in the early years of childbearing and child-rearing."

Related to unemployment is underemployment. **Underemployment** has been defined in several different ways: inability to work as many hours as one would like, employment at lower pay than in previous work, or working in a job below one's qualifications. Underemployment particularly affects the working poor, workers whose plants have closed, and rural Americans. (About half of rural Americans are underemployed [Zvonkovic et al., 1988].) The underemployed include men and women who work part-time making pizza deliveries while they would like to work full-time; a $5-an-hour day laborer who made $15 an hour as a foundry worker prior to the steel plant's closing; a college graduate forced to work as a sales clerk because there are no managerial jobs available. Underemployment dramatically affects a family's income and raises stress levels. As many as 10 to 15 percent of employed persons may be underemployed; a quarter of all part-time workers desire full-time work (U.S. Bureau of Labor Statistics, 1988).

Prosperity doth best discover vice; but adversity doth best discover virtue.

Francis Bacon (1561–1626)

Money is a terrible master but an excellent servant.

P. T. Barnum

Economic Discrimination against People with Disabilities

Over 14 million working-age Americans have physical or mental disabilities. Although 8 million are severely limited and need assistance in eating and dressing, many can perform limited work. Over 6 million, however, are more easily employable. Various studies indicate that workers with disabilities are at least as effective as able-bodied workers (Kilborn, 1992). A study by Du Pont corporation, for example, found that its workers with disabilities (ranging from mild to severe) performed well above its other workers in terms of attendance, were on par regarding safety, and were only slightly below in terms of job performance. But the employment of persons with disabilities has been severely limited because of bias. As a result, only 30 percent of workers with disabilities worked in 1989, mostly at part-time or irregular jobs. Because of such discrimination, 23 percent of the disabled are poor, three times the general population.

The 1990 Americans with Disabilities Act attempts to change the general social and economic conditions of those with disabilities. The act prohibits businesses from discriminating against people who are otherwise capable except for physical or mental impairments that may substantially limit a major life activity. These activities may include walking, seeing, breathing, and cognition. Except where it causes "undue hardship" on the employer, companies must provide "reasonable accommodations" to assist their workers in coping with their limitations. Such accommodation includes such things as scheduling hours to permit doctor appointments, widening restroom stalls for people in wheelchairs, or providing special tools. The average cost of these accommodations is usually less than $500. And because workers with disabilities have better attendance records and are less likely to change jobs than other workers, these costs are quickly recovered by businesses in increased productivity.

It is expected that billions of dollars in social welfare costs will be saved as a result of the employment of persons with disabililties. More importantly, however, Americans with disabilities will find their lives enriched by becoming productive members of a society that has treated them previously as "handicapped," a word whose origin can be traced back to medieval England, when mendicants placed a "hand in cap," begging for alms.

☐ FAMILY POLICY

As we examine America's priorities, it is clear that we have had an implicit family policy that directs our national goals. Although it has never been articulated, it is very powerful in determining government and corporate policies. The policy is very simple: Families are not a national priority. And its corollary is equally simple: Neither are women and children. As we enter the mid-1990s, we have the opportunity to redress this painful neglect.

Rising Interest and Obstacles

Over the years, a confusing combination of laws affecting families has been passed by state and federal governments. These laws include policies relating to family planning, abortion, sex education, foster care, maternal and child health, child support, AFDC, food stamps, and Medicare (Zimmerman and Owens, 1989). The issues underlying some of these laws, such as abortion, are controversial; others, such

Money talks.

Folk saying

Money doesn't talk.
It swears.

Bob Dylan

The stealth bomber is aptly named, for like a thief it steals from our nation's families, schools, and cities. Each stealth bomber represents fifty elementary schools, a thousand day-care centers, or 30,000 full four-year scholarships to a university.

Floyd Zimmerman

as child support, are not. But none of the family support programs that require substantial monies, such as AFDC and WIC, are adequately funded.

Since the late 1970s, interest has been rising in systematic, family-oriented legislation. A systematic approach to family policy may be defined as a set of objectives concerning family well-being and specific measures initiated by government to achieve them (Aldous and Dumon, 1991). Interest has been increasing for several reasons (Aldous and Dumon, 1991; Wisensale and Allison, 1989): (1) there has been a major increase in female-headed families because of the rise in divorce rates and births to single mothers; (2) women, especially mothers, have entered the labor force in unprecedented numbers; (3) problems confronting families, ranging from poverty to abuse, homelessness to inadequate child care, are increasingly viewed as social rather than individual problems; and (4) "the family" as symbol has become an ideological battlefield for liberals and conservatives.

With these various changes, why have we failed to develop supportive family policies? There are several reasons. First, there is strong political opposition based on different views of American families. Conservatives believe that the traditional family is the basis of society (Aldous and Dumon, 1991). Conservatives often oppose policies supporting families that do not conform to the ideal of the traditional two-parent family in which the father is the breadwinner and the mother is a housewife. This mythical, problem-free family of the past, where father knew best and mother baked cookies, is a powerful symbol. It stands at the center of resistance to legislation that assists single-parent and dual-earner families. Conservatives believe that AFDC benefits assisting single parents encourage unmarried women to bear children. According to conservatives, welfare benefits undermine the individual's desire to work. Furthermore, conservatives assert that welfare leads to family breakup. To end poverty, conservatives urge the elimination of welfare programs such as AFDC, food stamps, and housing subsidies. They believe that many of the poor are simply unwilling to work and that eliminating welfare would force them to work in order to survive. Private charities and local governments would care for the "truly needy" (Murray, 1984).

Liberals, in contrast, believe that America can be best served by recognizing the existence of diverse family forms. Many of America's families are vulnerable to poverty because of changes in the economy and family structures, especially the rise of divorce and single-parent families. Studies indicate that government welfare policies have had little to do with the rise of divorce, single-parent families, and births to single mothers. Instead, these are the result of broader social and economic changes (Aldous and Dumon, 1991; Danzinger and Plotknick, 1986). In contemporary society, most families become poor as a result of these larger changes. Welfare programs enable people to escape poverty rather than lure them into it. Liberals urge social policies to encourage self-sufficiency and to provide a decent standard of living for the poor. According to liberal thinkers, AFDC benefits provide protection for poor families until they get on their feet again (Cherlin, 1988; Ellwood, 1988). Indeed, welfare benefits help stabilize families, as those states with the most generous welfare benefits also have the lowest divorce rates (Zimmerman, 1991).

Second, there are philosophical differences about the role of government in the family (Wisensale, 1990; Zimmerman, 1988). According to conservative thinking, the state is an intruder in the family. The family is the last bastion of privacy, and it should remain inviolable. "A man's home is his castle," is the conservative credo. For liberals and feminists, in contrast, the state is an enabler. It can protect women and children from abuse, assist families in rising above poverty through welfare benefits and training programs, provide publicly funded child care, and encourage corporations to be responsive to families through legislation and taxes. Most Americans, however, fall in the middle in their thinking.

Third, there is the question of the cost. In a conservative social climate burdened by enormous deficits from decades of unrestrained military spending, there is little political will to raise the necessary taxes to fund family programs. Instead, politicians "talk" family—but as we all know, talk is cheap. Until America makes a commitment to its families, our nation's families will continue to struggle and endure in a climate of neglect.

Elements of Family Policy

Let us assume, however, that the day has arrived when we have come to agree on the importance of our families. Imagine that family health and well-being have become a national priority. Here are some of the policies that might be instituted by government and business in the areas of education, health care, work, and social services (see Edelman, 1989; Macchiarola and Gartner, 1989; for suggestions on how to influence family legislation see Monroe, 1991; for discussion of think tanks involved in family policy, see Wisensale, 1991).

HEALTH CARE

1. Guaranteed adequate medical care for every citizen, with a national health-care policy such as the kind that exists in Canada.
2. Prenatal and infant care for all mothers; adequate nutrition, immunizations, and "well baby" clinics to monitor infant health.
3. Medical and physical care of the aged and the disabled, including support for family caregivers.
4. Education for young people about sexuality and pregnancy prevention; implementation of comprehensive and realistic programs that address the economic and social realities of youth.
5. Education for all Americans about the realities of STDs, HIV, and AIDS. Guaranteed access to treatment.
6. Drug and alcohol rehabilitation programs available to all who want them.

SOCIAL WELFARE

1. Tax credits or income maintenance programs for families.
2. Child allowances to ensure a basic standard of living.
3. Child care for working or disabled parents; temporary respite child care when parents are ill or unable to care for their children; training of neighborhood day-care providers.
4. Advocacy for children, the aged, the disabled, and others who may not be able to speak up for themselves.
5. Attention given to problems of the homeless, such as food, shelter, medical and psychiatric care.
6. Regulation of children's television to promote literacy, good nutrition, humane values, and critical thinking.

EDUCATION

1. Implementation of preschool programs such as Head Start wherever needed.
2. Stress on the teaching of basic skills; use of innovative programs to reach *all* students, including out reach programs for adult literacy.

The stoical scheme of supplying our wants by lopping off our desires is like cutting off our feet when we want shoes.

Jonathan Swift (1667–1745)

The question is not whether or not government will intervene. It will. The question is will it intervene for enhancement and prevention or respond to breakdown, problems, and deviance.

Alfred Kahn and Sheila Kamerman

I was hungry—and a new committee was formed to study the causes of hunger.
I was sick—and legislators met again with new ideas for Medicare.
I was cold—and fuel bills were raised for more money to study the situation.
I was not safe in my home—and lawyers began to debate the reasons behind crime and what can be done about it.
I was lonely—and friends went into their churches to pray for me, and closed the door.
I am still hungry, sick, and lonely.

Anonymous, The Congressional Record

A modern nation's honor is not the honor of a warrior; it is the honor of a father providing for his children, it is the honor of a mother providing for her children .

E. L. Doctorow

3. Work exposure for students who wish to work through programs such as Job Corps.

4. Guarantees that *all* Americans receive the benefits of education through the implementation of bilingual and multicultural programs, special education for the developmentally disabled, and adult education.

WORKPLACE

1. Paid parental leave for pregnancy and sick children; paid personal days for child and family responsibilities.

2. Flexible work schedules for parents whenever possible; job-sharing alternatives.

3. Increased minimum wage so that workers can support their families.

4. Policies to ensure fair employment for all, regardless of race, ethnicity, gender, sexual preference, or disability.

5. Pay equity between men and women for same or comparable jobs; affirmative action programs for women and ethnic groups.

6. Corporate child-care programs or subsidies for families.

7. Individual and family counseling services; provision of flexible benefit programs.

At the 1990 United Nations World Summit on Children the United States refused to sign The Declaration on the Rights of Children because the Declaration prohibits the execution of children under age 18 and does not prohibit abortion. The only other countries besides the United States that refused to sign the Declaration on the Rights of Children were Iraq, Iran, Libya, Cambodia, and China. We are not in good company. We need to do better for our families and children. They are our national strength, our treasure, and our future.

 SUMMARY

❏ Families may be examined as economic units bound together by emotional ties. Families are involved in two types of work: paid work at the workplace and unpaid work in the household.

❏ *Workplace/family linkages* are the ways in which employment affects family life. *Work spillover* is the effect that employment has on time, energy, and psychological functioning of workers and their families at home. *Role strain* refers to the difficulties that individuals have in carrying out multiple roles. Two types of role strain are *role overload,* which occurs when total prescribed activities for one or more roles are greater than an individual can handle, and *inter-role conflict,* which occurs when roles conflict with each other.

❏ The traditional division of labor in the family follows a complementary pattern: the husband works outside the home for wages and the wife works inside the home without wages. Men's participation in household work is traditionally limited to repairs, construction, and yard work. Women's primary responsibility for household work and childrearing is part of the traditional marriage contract.

❏ Four aspects of the homemaker role are (1) its exclusive allocation to women, (2) its association with economic dependence, (3) its status as nonwork, and its (4) priority over other roles for women. Status accorded to homemakers depends on class. Working-class families accord homemakers greater status than do middle-class families.

❏ Characteristics of housework are that it (1) isolates the person at home, (2) is unstructured, monotonous, and repetitive, (3) is often a restricted, full-time role, (4) is autonomous, (5) is "never done," (6) may involve childrearing, and (7) often involves role strain.

❏ In 1988, 59 million women were employed, making up 47 percent of the work force. Women enter the work force for economic reasons and to raise their self-esteem. Employed women tend to have better physical and emotional health than nonemployed women. Women's employment tends to follow an M-shaped pattern; their labor-force participation is interrupted for family reasons over thirty times as often as it is for men.

❏ More than half of all women are in dual-earner marriages. Such women are more independent than nonemployed women and have increased power in decision making. Husbands generally do not significantly increase their share of household duties when their wives are employed. Employed mothers remain primarily responsible for childrearing. Women's employment has little or a slightly positive impact on marital satisfaction; there does seem to be a slightly greater likelihood of divorce.

❑ Family issues in the workplace include economic discrimination against women; sexual harrassment; occupational stratification for members of ethnic groups, especially women, placing them in lowest levels; lack of adequate child care; and an inflexible work environment.

❑ Almost 13 percent of the population of the United States live in poverty. Ten percent of whites, 33 percent of African Americans, 28 percent of Latinos, 12 percent of Asian Americans, and 25 percent of Native Americans are poor. The majority of poor people are women and children. Forty percent of all children are poor, representing the highest poverty rate of any group. There are significant differences between whites and members of ethnic groups in terms of income and wealth. The disparity increased dramatically during the 1980s.

❑ As many as 25 percent of Americans go through *spells of poverty,* during which time they need welfare assistance. Poverty spells generally occur because of divorce, the birth of a child to an unmarried mother, unemployment, illness, disability, or death of the head of household. Young families are particularly vulnerable to poverty. The *underclass* are urban poor, disproportionately African-American and Latino, who have little economic or social opportunity and are stigmatized by the larger society.

❑ Although most welfare recipients receive public assistance for less than two years, welfare is stigmatized. Welfare benefits have been cut, and fewer people receive welfare today increasing poverty.

❑ Unemployment most frequently affects female-headed single-parent families, African American, and Latino families, and young families. Unemployment increased during the 1990/1991 recession. Unemployment insurance, however, inadequately protects workers. *Underemployment* particularly affects the working poor, workers whose plants have closed, and rural Americans.

❑ The 1990 Americans with Disabilities Act prohibits discrimination by employers against persons with physical or mental limitations provided they are otherwise capable of performing their work. People with disabilities tend to have better safety and attendance records than other workers; their job performance is only marginally less.

❑ *Family policy* is a set of objectives concerning family well-being and the specific government measures designed to achieve those objectives. Family policy has been controversial because of conflicting viewpoints between conservatives and liberals about how best to help families, philosophical differences about the role of government, and the costs involved in its implementation. Family policy would contain provisions affecting health care, social welfare, education, and the workplace.

PART 5

Interiors

CHAPTER 10

Families and Health: Social and Psychological Perspectives

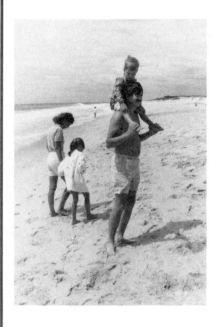

If you're afraid of the dark, remember the night rainbow. If you lose the key to your house, throw away the house. And if it's the last dance, you better dance backwards.

Cooper Edens

WHEN A PARENT BRINGS YOU SOUP as you lie sick in bed, when stress at work leaves you too tired to play with your children or enjoy your partner, when your spouse urges you to stop drinking, when a chronically ill child or aging parent requires constant attention, or when a family member dies—we are reminded that families consist of individuals with bodies. Our physical and emotional health are critical elements of family life. Until very recently, researchers ignored this aspect of family life. But during the last fifteen years, research has burgeoned on the relationship between families and health.

In this chapter we will focus on the social and psychological dimensions of families and health, for, as William Doherty and Thomas Campbell (1988) observe, "The family affects the individual's health and the individual's health affects the family." To understand the interactions between the two, we will first examine how marriage may encourage mental and physical health among men and women. We will explore the health care crisis and the various crises and stresses that affect our health and well-being as families, such as economic distress. Then we will examine family caregiving for the disabled, the chronically ill, and the elderly. Next we will explore death and grieving. Finally, we will look at alcohol and substance abuse, which may insidiously destroy individuals and families.

❑ MARRIAGE, HEALTH, AND WELL-BEING

Health is a state of physical and mental well-being, not solely the absence of disease. **Physical well-being** consists of feeling fit and able; for the disabled or chronically ill, it refers to the ability to function within their limits. **Emotional well-being** refers to feelings of happiness, hope, energy, and the zest for life (Ross, Mirowsky, and Goldsteen, 1991). Such positive definitions of health and well-being focus on the physical and emotional quality of life rather than on illness and disease. Positive definitions empower individuals to strive for wellness rather than passively accept sickness.

Marriage is good for your health, at least if you are happily married. As a whole, married men and women tend to be healthier and happier than their unmarried peers; they live longer, are less depressed, and have a higher general sense of well-being. An important study found that those who reported themselves to be very happily married had better emotional health than unmarried men and women. Those who were "pretty happy" in their marriages reported about the same levels of emotional well-being as those who were unmarried. Those who were unhappily married were *more* emotionally distressed than unmarried men and women (Gove, Hughes, and Style, 1983).

Researchers do not know at this time, however, how long-term heterosexual, gay, or lesbian cohabitation affects health. Most likely, long-term cohabitation produces many of the same positive health effects as does marriage. But because cohabiting relationships do not receive the same level of societal support as marriage, the effects may not be as strong.

There are two hypotheses as to why married individuals tend to be healthier than unmarried men and women: the *self-selecting hypothesis* and the *enabling hypothesis*. According to the self-selection hypothesis, married people tend to be healthier than single individuals because they are healthier to begin with rather than because of any benefits that marriage itself confers (Turner and Gartrell, 1978; Verbrugge, 1979). Advocates of self-selection argue that healthy people select other healthy people to marry, whereas unhealthy people are unable to find mates because they are undesirable. Close analysis of data fails to confirm this hypothesis.

Health and good estate of body are above all good.

Ecclesiastes 30:15

Life is not merely living but living in health.

Martial (A.D. 40–104)

Most researchers suggest that marriage *enables* people to be healthy (Gove, Style, and Hughes, 1990). How is it that marriage encourages health and well-being? There appear to be three contributing factors (Ross, Mirowsky, and Goldsteen, 1991): (1) living with a partner, (2) social support, and (3) economic well-being.

LIVING WITH A PARTNER. Initially, researchers believed that the major health difference between married and single men and women resulted from the presence of another person, whether it was a roommate, friend, or spouse. More recently, it has been shown that not just anyone will do. It is the person's marital partner who is critical to his or her health—a spouse who will sustain the other in time of need, make chicken soup when the partner is sick, and dance with him or her when happy. Many of these same benefits may accrue to cohabiting partners as well, though there is no research available.

SOCIAL SUPPORT. Only a spouse is committed and involved enough to provide sufficient social support to improve a partner's health. Social support consists of both instrumental and emotional elements. Instrumental support includes such things as cooking for the other, doing favors, and providing economic security. But as far as health and well-being are concerned, emotional support—the sense of being loved and cared about, esteemed and valued—appears to be more important. When spouses are not supportive, are authoritarian, divide labor unfairly, or are degrading or demeaning, their partners are often demoralized, depressed, or unhappy.

A partner's social support improves physical health in several ways (Ross, Mirowsky, and Goldsteen, 1991). Social support (1) increases psychological well-being, (2) encourages and reinforces protective health behaviors, (3) provides secondary prevention, and (4) assists recovery. First, a partner who listens and cares

Health is the state of physical and emotional well-being. Happily married individuals tend to be healthier than single men and women.

helps reduce depression, anxiety, and other psychological problems. With improvement of a person's emotional well-being, his or her physical health and survival ability increase dramatically.

Second, a partner encourages and reinforces protective health behaviors. Compared to their unmarried peers, husbands and wives have better diets and are less likely to smoke, drink heavily, drive too fast, or take risks that increase the likelihood of accidents or injuries. Because women generally have healthier life-styles than men, when they marry, men's health behaviors and survival improve more significantly than women's (Ross, Mirowsky, and Goldsteen, 1991; Umberson, 1987).

Third, a partner provides secondary prevention by helping to identify or treat an illness or disease early. A woman expresses concern about her partner's continuing cough and fever and insists that he see a physician, who diagnoses viral pneumonia, a potential killer; a man notices a discoloration on his wife's back, which turns out to be a treatable skin cancer. Another makes a sneezing, wheezing partner rest instead of going to work or school, thereby speeding recovery and building resistance to other infections.

Finally, social support aids a partner's recovery. The love and care of a partner, his or her gestures of intimacy, small acts of thoughtfulness, a familiar hand soothing a feverish forehead or softly caressing the face—all assist in the psychological recovery following an illness. It is well-documented, for example, that intimacy encourages emotional recovery following a heart attack. A husband's high level of support and caring significantly reduces the depression and anxiety that a woman experiences as she lives with breast cancer.

ECONOMIC WELL-BEING. Married men and women have higher household incomes than unmarried people: an average of $33,500 for married couples compared to $28,600 for single men and $21,500 for single women. With higher incomes and economics of scale, married men and women are more likely to visit physicians and have health insurance. They are also less likely to experience high levels of stress occasioned by the daily grind of poverty. Poverty is associated with decreased life expectancy, higher infant mortality, and higher rates of infectious diseases, disability, and mortality. The poor are more likely to get sick; if they do get sick, they are less likely to survive. Because of the close tie between race or ethnicity and income, African Americans and Latinos are especially vulnerable to higher disease and mortality rates.

❐ THE HEALTH CARE CRISIS

Imagine that you are riding your bicycle to class. You are late, so you are pedaling especially fast, but you hit a rock, causing you to flip off your bicycle. You spin through the air and tumble against the concrete curb. You hear a crunching sound. You get up; you are dizzy and nauseous and your shoulder is in intense pain. You may have suffered a concussion and you think your shoulder might be broken. Across the street is a private hospital called Mount Profit which will take care of you immediately; ten miles away is the county hospital which will examine you in its emergency room, though you will probably have to wait two to six hours while the more serious gunshot and accident victims are treated. Which hospital will you choose? (Hint: it probably depends on whether you have medical insurance.)

America's health care system is a strange paradox. Health costs account for 12 percent of the United States' gross national product. We spend $2354 per capita on health care, four times as much as Germany and eight times as much as Canada. But despite our vast outlay of money and our ever-expanding medical technology, our infant death rate is among the highest in the industrialized world. The health status of many of our African-American communities is that of third-world countries; a young black male in Detroit has a shorter life expectancy than his counterpart in Bangladesh. Almost half the poor are frozen out of the medical system, and the uninsured middle-class are petrified of losing their homes to medical bills. We are in crisis. And it is getting worse.

Health insurance has become one of the prime determinants of an individual's or family's access to medical care. The spiraling costs of medical care—up to thousands of dollars a day for hospital care—have made visits to the doctor or hospital out of the reach of most Americans without medical insurance. And yet, 33 million Americans—13 percent of the population—are uninsured. The figure rises to 22 percent for those between 16 and 24 years of age. Eighteen percent of whites, 30 percent of African Americans, and 41 percent of Latinos are uninsured (Friedman, 1991; Lewin, 1991).

Most insured people are covered either through their employment, through Medicare if they are very poor (only 40 percent of the poor are covered) or through Medicaid if they are elderly. Health insurance is closely tied to the workplace, through an employer's benefit program, usually a group insurance plan. An employee pays part or all of the insurance through his or her employer; the amount may be nominal or run into thousands of dollars per year. Because of the increasing insurance costs, employers are trying to curtail their coverage. Furthermore, employee group plans are usually not extended to part-time or temporary workers. Millions in low-paying service, retail, or agricultural jobs receive no benefits. And employees who lose their jobs often lose their coverage as well.

The connection of insurance benefits with employment may affect work decisions. A 1990 poll found that 15 percent of its respondents or their family members had changed jobs or remained on the same job because of health insurance benefits (Lewin, 1991). "Job lock" decribes the fear of changing jobs because of benefits loss. One woman, for example, wanted to change to part-time work to be with her young daughters but couldn't because she was once treated for breast cancer and would not be able to get insurance elsewhere. "The one thing I can't do now is quit because I have insurance here and I'm uninsurable if I leave," she said (Lewin, 1991).

It is often prohibitively expensive to purchase individual health insurance, costing thousands or even tens of thousands of dollars in yearly premiums. Often the insurance, despite its costs, exempts certain health categories if the individual has had any problems in the area. Other times the insurance company will exclude an individual altogether.

The effects of the insurance crisis are three fold. First, it forces the uninsured to live in constant dread of a major medical expense that can destroy their savings or force them to sell their home. Second, it leads to deteriorating health, since the uninsured do not seek timely medical attention. For the uninsured, health problems require a triage approach. In one family, for example, the oldest child needs a tooth filled, the mother has abdominal pain that requires ultrasound, and the father has a sprained ankle he keeps on ice, hoping to avoid the cost of an X-ray. They put off treatment as long as possible. Finally, they decide to seek treatment for one member. On what basis? The basis of pain. The member with the most pressing pain—the father, in this case—sees a doctor. Yet the mother's abdominal pain may indicate a life-threatening tumor. The third effect of the insurance crisis is its impact on the ability of our public hospitals to function. Because so many Americans are uninsured, they turn to inexpensive or free public hospitals for medical treatment. As a result of budget cutbacks and growing numbers of uninsured, waits in public hospitals for nonemergency visits are routinely three to six months. Physicians and nurses are over-burdened by the numbers of patients. Over the last ten years, patient visits have increased between 70 to 100 percent while funding and staff have been dramatically cut because of conservative spending priorities and budget deficits.

As the medical insurance crisis continues, the most attractive alternative to the current job-linked or welfare-linked system appears to be that modeled by the Canadian "universal insurance system," which insures all its citizens and provides them with the choice of their own private physician (Erkholm, 1991). Because it is administered through one nonprofit agency instead of numerous for-profit insurance companies, it reduces net costs by approximately 20 percent. This cost reduction allows the government to cover at no greater expense individuals and families that would not ordinarily be insured in the U.S. system. Naturally, insurance companies fight such reform tooth and nail.

❑ STRESS AND THE FAMILY

Don't trouble trouble till trouble troubles you.

Traditional African-American proverb

Life involves constant change to which both the individual and the family must adjust (Bell et al., 1980). Change brings **stress**—psychological or emotional distress or disruption. It does not matter whether the change is for the better or the worse; stress is produced in either case. **Family stress** may be defined as "an upset in the steady state of the family" (Boss, 1987). Since all families undergo periods of stress, the ability to cope successfully is seen as an important factor in measuring family health.

Family Stress and Coping

Marriage, no less than life in general, is just one damned thing after another.

Frank Pittman

Families constantly face stress, tension resulting from real or perceived demands that require the family system to adjust or adapt its behavior. When a family is under stress, its members may experience **distress,** psychological and physical tension, such as intense upset, mood changes, headaches, and muscular tension. While both individuals and families must adapt to stressful events, they must also maintain their equilibrium. They must keep their identities intact. As a result, individuals and families are involved in a delicate balancing act to adapt to changing situations while maintaining their integrity. They respond to stress in many different ways. How we cope with stressful demands determines whether or not we experience a crisis.

VARIABLES AFFECTING FAMILY'S RESPONSE TO STRESSORS. There are six variables involved in a family's response to stress:

❑ *Stressor:* a life event, such as birth, departure of a family member, illness, or unemployment, that affects the family at a certain point in time and produces change in the family system.
❑ *Family hardship*: difficulties specifically associated with the stressor, such as loss of income in the case of unemployment.
❑ *Strains:* the tensions lingering from previous stressors or the tensions inherent in family roles, such as being a parent or spouse. Strains include the emotional scars from bitter or unresolved fights or the fatigue of parenting.
❑ *Resources:* the material, psychological, or social assets that can be used by the family to influence others or to cope with stress, such as money, emotional support, or friends.

❐ *Meaning:* how the family defines the event, such as perceiving it as a stressful but manageable problem or as "the end of the world."

❐ *Coping:* the process of using the resources the family has at its disposal. The family that copes well experiences much less stress than the family that copes poorly.

Families that are unable to cope find themselves moving from a state of stress into crisis (Boss, 1987). In crisis, the family system becomes immobilized and the family can no longer perform its functions.

STRESSORS. Stressors are the provoking event in family stress, so we will examine them in some detail. Stressors may be: (1) normative or nonnormative, (2) external or internal, (3) short-term or long-term, and (4) with norms or normless.

NORMATIVE AND NONNORMATIVE STRESSORS. Certain events are common in all families across the life cycle—birth, marriage, retirement, death of elderly members, and so on. These normative stressors are typical. Other family stressors are nonnormative or atypical for all families, such as accidental death, conflict over family roles, sudden loss of income, caring for a disabled or elderly family member. Although still stressful, normative stressors can be anticipated and some of their consequences alleviated.

EXTERNAL AND INTERNAL STRESSORS. In dealing with stress, it is important whether the stressor originates from inside or outside the family. External stressors can foster family unity if they are not so constant or overwhelming that they destroy the family. Natural disasters such as floods and hurricanes encourage family cooperation. Families tend to meet these kinds of events head on. Wars and persecution have similar effects.

But internal stressors can break the family apart. Severe illness, role strain, alcoholism, unemployment, extramarital affairs, or unexpected death may destroy the same family that heroically withstood a natural disaster or persecution. The family may search for a scapegoat, fight among themselves as to whom to blame, or take sides.

SHORT-TERM AND LONG-TERM STRESSORS. A short-term stressor, such as a broken leg or temporary unemployment, creates stress for a limited time. Such stress can be extremely painful, but the family may return to its normal pattern of interactions once the short-term stressor is eliminated. Long-term stressors, however, are generally more disruptive and require considerable family adjustment. A broken leg soon mends and the family may return to its usual mode of operation, but an amputated limb requires permanent change in the way the family works, such as other family members performing some of the responsibilities of the disabled member.

STRESSORS WITH AND WITHOUT NORMS. Society often provides us with norms or guidelines that assist us in coping with stressors. If we give birth to a child under typical circumstances, our society validates us and provides us with guidelines as to how to feel and behave as the parents of a newborn, easing some of the stress associated with becoming a parent. Because we have fewer (or no) norms assisting us in the transition to parenthood if we are adoptive parents or gay or lesbian parents, however, we may experience a more stressful transition. Society is supportive of "normal" parenthood but often negative or hostile toward nonnormative parenthood.

THE DOUBLE ABC-X MODEL OF FAMILY STRESS. The most widely used model to explain family stress is the double ABC-X model (Olsen and McCubbin, 1983). A key

*When sorrows come, they come not
single spies,
But in battalions.*

William Shakespeare, Hamlet

concept in this model is the idea of **stressor pile up.** According to the double ABC-X model, during stress or crisis the family responds not only to a current stressor but also to family hardships and strains. Stressors, family hardships, and strains combine to create stressor pile up. Stressor pile up magnifies the impact of the stressor event, transforming a relatively minor stressor, such as going on a family vacation, into a catastrophic event. The stress of planning, packing, and leaving on a trip may bring other simmering problems to the surface. These problems may include lack of communication ("I thought you made the reservations"), inequitable distribution of power ("you always decide where we're going"), financial difficulties ("we can't afford this trip"), parental role issues ("why don't you ever help with the kids?") (Olsen and McCubbin, 1983; Patterson and McCubbin, 1983).

In the double ABC-X model:

Aa represents stressor pile up (the combination of the current stressor, family hardship, and strain),
B   represents the family's coping resources,
C   represents the family's *perception* of the stressor pile up, and
X   represents the outcome of the situation, which includes the coping strategies that the family brings into play as well as any disruption that may occur if the family fails to cope adequately.

There are many kinds of resources (the "B factor") that a family or an individual can draw upon. These assets may be material, psychological, emotional or social. They include money, time, health, intelligence, information, job skills, relationships with others, and support from social networks. Lack of economic resources is a significant component in stress and crisis. For the poor, everyday life is stressful as they try to make ends meet. While a crisis such as illness or unemployment may be difficult but manageable for the middle-class family with savings and health insurance, for a poor family such a crisis can be overwhelming.

The mere possession of resources is no guarantee that they will be used, however. The double ABC-X model of family stress views the actual use of resources (coping) as both a process among the B, C, and X factors and an outcome (part of X). How the family views a particular stressful event (the "C factor") is a significant variable in determining the eventual outcome. Viewing a stressful event as a crisis may very well lead to a crisis, as will utterly ignoring a situation that requires attention.

Recent research (McCubbin and McCubbin, 1987, 1989) suggests that strong families are much more successful in adapting to stress than weak families. Strong families tend to work together to resolve problems, are more democratic in their problem solving, delegate responsibilities, have considerable respect and affection for each other, and share values. These factors encourage family cohesion and support during times of stress. (See Chapter 15 for a discussion of coping mechanisms in strong families.) Weak families, however, tend to blame each other in stressful situations, are unwilling to ask for assistance or help from family members, are hesitant to shift or share burdens, and are reluctant to compromise. As a result, they have less flexibility and fewer family resources to deal effectively with stress and are more likely to have unfavorable outcomes.

Economic Distress

Economic distress refers to those aspects of economic life that are potential stressors for individuals and families (Voydanoff, 1991). Major economic stressors include unemployment, poverty, and economic strain (such as financial concerns and worry, adjustments to changes in income, and feelings of economic insecurity).

*One woe doth tread upon another's heel,
So fast they follow.*

William Shakespeare, Hamlet

What's the worst that can happen? The storm picks up our house and plants it in a better neighborhood.

Roseanne Arnold

FIGURE 10.1   The Double ABC-X Model

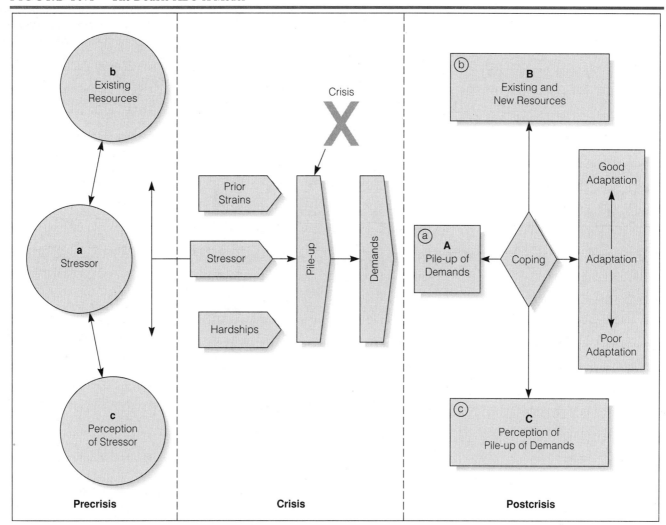

IMPACT ON MARRIAGES AND FAMILIES. In times of hardship, economic strain increases and the rates of infant mortality, alcoholism, family abuse, homicide, suicide, and admissions to psychiatric institutions and prisons also sharply increase (Liem and Rayman, 1982). Patricia Voydanoff (1991), one of the leading researchers in family/economy interactions, notes:

A minimum level of income and employment stability is necessary for family stability and co-hesion. Without it many are unable to form families through marriage and others find them-selves subject to separation and divorce. In addition, those experiencing unemployment or income loss make other adjustments in family composition such as postponing childbearing, moving in with relatives, and having relatives or boarders join the household.

Further, economic strain is related to lower levels of marital satisfaction as a result of financial conflict, the husband's psychological instability, and marital tensions.

Unemployment is a major stressor for individuals, with consequences spilling over into their families (Voydanoff, 1991). The families of the unemployed experi-ence considerably more stress than those of the employed (see Gnezda, 1984, for a review of the effects of unemployment on family functioning). The most extensive work on the effects of unemployment has been done in the Boston area. Reports by Leim and colleagues (cited in Gnezda, 1984) indicate that in the first few months of unemployment, mood and behavior changes cause stress and strain in family relations. As families adapt to unemployment, family roles and routines change. The family spends more time together, but wives often complain of their husband's "getting in the way" and not contributing to household tasks. Wives may assume a greater role in family finances by seeking employment if they are not already employed. After the first few months of unemployment, wives of the unemployed begin to feel emotional strain, depression, anxiety, and sensitiveness in marital interactions. The children of the unemployed are more likely to avoid social interactions and tend to be more distrustful; they report more problems at home than children in families with employed fathers. Families seem to achieve stable patterns around new roles and responsibilities after six or seven months. If unemployment persists beyond a year, the family becomes highly vulnerable to marital separation and divorce; family violence may begin or increase at this time.

COPING WITH ECONOMIC DISTRESS. Economic distress does not necessarily lead to family disruption. In the face of unemployment, some families experience increased cohesion (Gnezda, 1984). Families with serious problems may disintegrate. Individuals and families use a number of coping resources and behaviors to deal with economic distress (Voydanoff, 1991). Coping resources include an individual's psychological disposition, such as optimism, a strong sense of self-esteem, and a feeling of mastery. Family coping resources include a family system that encourages adaptation and cohesion in the face of problems and flexible family roles that encourage problem solving. In addition, social networks of friends and family may provide important support, such as financial assistance, understanding, and a willingness to listen.

There are several important coping behaviors that assist families in economic distress. These include:

❏ *Defining the meaning of the problem.* Unemployment means not only joblessness. It can also mean diminished self-esteem if the person feels the job loss was his or her fault. If a worker is unemployed because of layoffs or plant closings, the individual and family need to define the unemployment in terms of market failure, not personal failure.

❏ *Problem solving.* An unemployed person needs to attack the problem by beginning the search for another job; dealing with the consequences of unemployment, such as by seeking unemployment insurance and cutting expenses; or improving the situation, such as by changing occupations or seeking job training or more schooling. Spouses and adolescents can assist by increasing their paid work effort. Studies suggest that about a fifth of spouses or other family members find employment after a plant closing.

❏ *Managing emotions.* Individuals and families need to understand that stress may create roller-coaster emotions, anger, self-pity, and depression. They need to talk with each other about their feelings; they need to support and encourage each other. They need to seek out individual or family counseling services to cope with problems before they get out of hand.

❏ FAMILY CAREGIVING

Caregiving for the Chronically Ill and Disabled

We have all experienced illness and accidents that have laid us low for a few days or longer. Illnesses and accidents affect us not only bodily but also psychologically.

When we are sick or incapacitated, we are more prone to depression and mood swings. Illnesses are also stressful because they affect daily living patterns. A bout of the flu, for example, may put a student out of commission during finals week. A sprained ankle constrains mobility; a cold affects not only a sick child but also the parent who must stay home from work or school. Minor illnesses temporarily disrupt the structures of our lives and families.

Acute illnesses, such as appendicitis, require hospitalization but are of relatively short duration. Chronic illnesses, such as cystic fibrosis, diabetes, heart disease, arthritis, cerebral palsy, and asthma, never go away. A chronically ill person may be better sometimes, worse other times, but he or she remains ill. Similarly, physical limitations (such as impaired speech or movement, deafness, and blindness) and developmental impairments (such as Down's syndrome or autism) are lifelong. The care of those who are chronically ill, physically limited, or developmentally impaired is usually given at home by the family. Thus, the life course of the chronically ill or disabled, their caregivers, and their families is radically affected.

In many cases, the family must shape itself around the needs, limits, and potential of the ill or disabled family member. The magnitude of the problem for families can be imagined once we realize that as many as 2.4 million children under age seventeen have some degree of chronic activity limitation (Fitzgerald, 1987). (This represents over 5 percent of all American children.) In addition to these children, disabled, chronically ill, and aged adults must be cared for by their families. A conservative estimate would place between 6 and 10 percent of all American families caring for disabled, chronically ill, or aging family members.

Some of the problems faced by families who have members with disabilities revolve around physical access to businesses, colleges and universities, concert halls, restaurants, and other facilities open to the general public. Without such access, people with disabilities become confined and isolated in their own homes, increasing their separation from the world at large. The 1990 Americans with Disabilities Act seeks to facilitate the integration of disabled people with the able-bodied population as a whole. The act provides that buildings and businessess must make good-faith efforts to make their premises accessible to men, women, and children with disabilities. New buildings built after January 1993 must be built so that they are accessible. Telephone companies must provide as far as possible services allowing hearing- or voice-impaired people to place and receive calls from ordinary telephones. New buses, trains, and subway cars must be wheelchair-accessible. Employment discrimination is also prohibited (see Chapter 9). Advocates for people with disabilities hail the bipartisan act as an "emancipation proclamation."

FAMILY OUTCOMES. Most studies suggest that chronic illnesses have negative effects on the family. Family disruption and decreased marital satisfaction, for example, are common consequences (Hafstorm and Schram, 1984). Other studies find positive or inconsequential effects (Master et al., 1983; Shapiro, 1983). Mark Peyrot and his colleagues (1988), found that the ultimate outcome of chronic illness is not necessarily bad. They found that after a period of disruption, some families resolved the crisis in a positive manner. Such families perceive the crisis as manageable and find the personal and social resources to create a favorable outcome. Several persons reported increased cohesiveness because they were compelled to spend more time with their families. Said one diabetic (Peyrot et al., 1988):

I'm closer to my family than I was. Prior to this [onset of diabetes] I was working eighty hours a week. I spend more hours at home than I did. For the first ten years my daughter never knew me because I was never at home.

It's not easy being green.

Kermit the Frog

Other families find hidden strengths and make their priorities more clear. Another respondent said (Peyrot et al., 1988), "The traumatic experiences that we've been through pulled us closer together, made our marriage stronger. It's pointed out the more important things."

Rosalyn Darling (1987) reported similar experiences in her examination of the consequences of disability on the family. Parents experienced sorrow over their children's disability and also a genuine love and joy for them. Many families thought themselves to be stronger as a result of dealing with a family member's disability (Darling and Darling, 1982). A sister explained her bond with a developmentally disabled brother:

My experiences with Steve have been . . . the most positive experiences in my life. . . . We are very close, and my relationship with Steve is very important to me. . . . If Steve could be normal, . . . I don't know what choice I'd make. . . . I think we'd be losing something very special. . . . It's pulled our whole family together.

SOURCES OF STRESS. Families with chronically ill or disabled members are subject to various types of stresses, depending on the nature and severity of the illness or disability and whether the chronically ill or disabled person is a child, spouse or aged parent. While the care of the chronically ill or disabled child or spouse is regarded as an unpredictable stress, care of aging parents is considered a normative or predictable family stress (E. Brody, 1985; Matthews and Rosner, 1988). The general stresses experienced by families caring for ill or disabled members include the following (Darling, 1987; Patterson and McCubbin, 1983; Yura, 1987):

❏ *Strained family relationships*, including resentment by the caregiver or other family members; competition for time between the ill or disabled person, the caregiver, and family members; overt or covert rejection of the ill or disabled family member; and coalitions between the ill or disabled person and the primary caregiver that leave other family members out. Overprotection may be especially prominent in families with disabled children.

❏ *Modifications in family activities and goals*, such as reduced leisure, travel, or vacation time; change in personal or work goals (especially by the primary caregiver); and concern over having additional children if the illness or disability is genetic.

❏ *Increased tasks and time commitments*, such as the provision of special diets, daily therapy, or treatment; appointments and transportation to medical facilities; and possible need for constant attendance.

❏ *Increased financial costs* resulting from medication, therapy, medical consultation and treatment, special equipment needs, and so on. Babysitting is the largest single out-of-pocket expense for families with physically disabled children.

❏ *Special housing requirements*, such as a close proximity to medical facilities, optimal climate conditions, and special housing features (such as wheelchair ramps).

❏ *Social isolation*, resulting from the reactions of friends and relatives, individual or family embarrassment, limited mobility, fear of exposure to infections or conditions that might exacerbate the illness, inability to predict behavior, or lack of available time for social interactions.

❏ *Medical concerns*, such as the individual's willingness or ability to follow prescribed treatment, obtain competent medical care, or minimize pain and discomfort; and uncertainty of the medical prognosis.

❏ *Grieving* over disabilities and limitations, restricted life opportunities, and, for some, anticipation of early or painful death.

COPING STRATEGIES. Families who use dysfunctional coping techniques experience the most difficulty in handling chronic illnesses (Patterson and McCubbin, 1983).

Children infected with HIV have many special needs. In addition to possible health problems, they may face stigmatization at day-care centers, schools, and even from friends and family members. Their mothers may be too ill to care for them or may have died. Here, a woman and her foster daughters, who are HIV positive, share a special moment.

These dysfunctional techniques include coalitions of the ill person and the primary caretaker excluding other family members, denial of the problem, withdrawal from social involvements, inability (or refusal) to find outside help, or hostility—blaming the chronically ill person or other family members for the condition.

Functional coping techniques include "normalizing" the chronically ill or disabled person's life, aggressively seeking proper services, and working for societal changes that would be more supportive of the ill or disabled. Additional techniques include maintaining attitudes of optimism, faith, and courage and seeking social support in the community for the ill or disabled family member (Patterson and McCubbin, 1983; see Shapiro and Tittle, 1990, for discussion of adaptation patterns among Latinos). Hamilton McCubbin and his colleagues (1979) found three important successful coping patterns for families with chronically ill children. These patterns also may be applied to families with older chronically ill or disabled members:

❒ *Maintaining family integration, cooperation, and an optimistic definition of the situation.* Such families emphasize doing things together as a family, strengthening family relationships, and developing an overall optimistic attitude toward life, especially with the ill or disabled family member.

❒ *Maintaining social support, self-esteem, and psychological stability.* Spouses and parents maintain their own sense of well-being by being actively involved in outside social relationships and activities that enhance their self-esteem. They develop techniques for handling psychological tensions and strains, such as taking breaks from the situation, seeking counseling, and finding additional help.

❒ *Understanding the medical situation through communication with similar families and medical consultations.* Such families develop relationships with families that have similar problems; they share information and provide support for each other. They try to understand and master necessary medical information. They feel competent in operating home medical equipment. (See Resource Center for sources of support for the disabled and their families.)

Caregiving for the Aged

Although most elderly men and women are healthy and live independently, almost 85 percent of the 25.5 million elderly have at least one chronic illness. About 2 million elders need assistance with such daily living activities as bathing, dressing, eating, shopping, and managing money (Blieszner and Alley, 1990). At least 5 million American men and women care for an aged parent.

Even though elder care is often done with love, it can be the source of profound stress (Gelman et al., 1985):

There is a welter of conflicts, anxiety about their parents' needs colliding with the needs of their own families, the guilty longing for freedom rubbing up against the guilty conviction that they are not doing enough. For some, the ironic role reversal in becoming a parent to the parent is unsettling at a deep psychic level. The sudden or growing helplessness of people who were the authority figures in a child's life can be overwhelming.

Most elder care is provided by women, generally daughters or daughters-in-law (Mancini and Blieszner, 1991). Men, however, provide a substantial proportion of care for their aging parents or parents-in-law (Brubaker, 1991). Elder caregiving seems to affect husbands and wives differently. Women report greater distress and depression from caregiving than do men (Fitting et al., 1986). In part, this may be because men approach their daily caregiving activities in a more detached, instrumental way. Another factor may be that women frequently are not only mothers

Illnesses and disabilities may bring out hidden strength in a family.

but also workers; an infirm parent can sometimes be an overwhelming responsibility to an already burdened woman. Fortunately, most adult children in a given family participate in parental caregiving in some fashion, whether it involves doing routine caregiving, providing backup, or giving limited or occasional care (Mancini and Blieszner, 1991).

Caregivers often experience conflicting feelings about caring for an elderly relative. The caregiver/parent relationship is strongly influenced by the history of the earlier parent/child relationship. The history of these interactions either facilitates or hinders caregiving (Horowitz and Shindelman, 1983). Women are initially more involved emotionally but tend to become more stoic and detached when a few years have passed; their responses become similar to male responses (Zarit, Todd, and Zarit, 1986). Many caregivers receive satisfaction from the affection they give to and receive from a beloved parent or relative; they often receive satisfaction from the very act of nurturing. These positive feelings help balance the negative aspects involved with primary caregiving (Sheehan and Nuttall, 1988; Walker, Shin, and Bird, 1990). The conflicts experienced by primary caregivers include the following (Springer and Brubaker, 1984):

❑ Earlier unresolved antagonisms and conflicts.
❑ The caregiver's inability to accept the relative's increasing dependence.
❑ Conflicting loyalties between spousal or childrearing responsibilities and caring for the elderly relative.
❑ Resentment toward the older relative for disrupting family routines and patterns.
❑ Resentment by the primary caregiver for lack of involvement by other family members.
❑ Anger or hostility toward an elderly relative who tries to manipulate others.
❑ Conflicts over money or inheritance.

Affection certainly eases the burdens, but it does not necessarily decrease the strains of caregiving that relatives experience (Sheehan and Nuttall, 1988). Elders are especially vulnerable to abuse by their children, (see Chapter 12). Caregiver education and training programs, self-help groups, caregiver services, and family therapy provide assistance in dealing with the problems encountered by caregivers. Of these, family therapy appears to be the most effective for dealing with the emotional aspects of caregiving (Sheehan and Nuttall, 1988). In addition, elders receiving Medicaid may be eligible for respite care and homemaker/housework assistance. (See Resource Center for elder-care referral services and organizations; also see Blieszner and Alley, 1990, for an overview of elder-care resources.)

Because elder care involves complex emotions raised by issues of dependency, adult children and their parents often postpone discussions until a crisis occurs. A recent study (Hansson et al., 1990) tried to identify the normative patterns of adult children's involvement in elder care. The researchers made three points: First, a threshold needed to be crossed at which time it became clear that the aging parent needed assistance. The threshold usually involved a health crisis, a gradual awareness of the risks associated with the parents' aging, or the death or illness of the spouse. One woman wrote (Levin, 1987):

The need for more involvement in our parents' care dawned slowly as they retired, became widowed, took ill. Initially we were sympathetic but took little direct action. Our participation increased when we began to see our parents having trouble managing not only their immediate financial affairs, but also *their* responsibilities towards their own very old parents and aging siblings.

Second, the developing pattern of involvement was conservative and followed an orderly procession. Adult children began monitoring their parents' health and logistical needs more closely. Third, children began to intervene in task-oriented areas, such as home maintenance, transportation, and dealing with the bureaucracy. The children's general goal was to help their parents maintain their independence as long as possible. Only after they had exhausted other alternatives were they likely to bring the parent to live with them or to place him or her in a retirement or convalescent home.

The best way for adult children to deal with elder care is to plan ahead with their siblings and with their aging parents, if they are willing. The major tasks include (Levin, 1987): (1) planning for legal and financial incapacities; (2) managing income and expenses; (3) arranging for long-term care; (4) assessing capabilities of the whole family unit; (5) dividing responsibilities among parents, siblings, adult children, friends, and neighbors; and (6) determining community back-up services, such as meals-on-wheels programs, visiting nurses, and housekeeping services.

□ DEATH AND DYING IN AMERICA

Everyone who reads this (not to mention those who wrote it!) will die. And even though on a cognitive level we know that death comes to us all, when we actually confront death or dying, we are likely to be surprised, shocked, or at a loss about what to do.

Attitudes toward Death

The nature and extent of our feelings and fears about death have to do with who we are—our age, sex, personality, spiritual beliefs, and so on. Our feelings also have to do with the person who has died—whether he or she was young or old, whether or not the death was expected, and what our relationship was.

CULTURAL CONTEXT. Our cultural context is important in determining our response to death. Although Americans today seem somewhat more willing to talk and act realistically about death than they were a decade or two ago, as a society we remain quite ambivalent about the subject. Our responses to death and dying fall into three categories: denial, exploitation, and romanticization (Rando, 1987).

DENIAL. Although the existence of death is not specifically denied, there are practices in our culture that make it hard to view death as the real part of life it actually is. The removal of old or dying people from the home to the hospital has encouraged the belief that death is unnatural, frightening, or even disgusting. In a way, we treat death like sex: we try to shield children from it, and we use euphemisms when we speak of it ("Aunt Helen passed away," "Fluffy was put to sleep").

EXPLOITATION. At the opposite extreme of denial is the exploitation of death. Therese Rando (1987) writes:

While there has been a decline in the average individual's personal contact with death and dying, due to sociological changes and advances in technology, there has been an increase in exposure to violence and death through television, movies, and the print media. . . . Acts of murder, war, violence, terrorism, abuse, rape, crime, natural disasters, and so forth are exploited and sensationalized in the name of the public's right to know. Financial gains for the media and its sponsors are the obvious results.

The effects can be damaging. We may become overwhelmed by images of death and suffer from "annihilation anxiety." We may overcompensate and become aggressive

No man is an island, entire of itself; every man is a piece of the continent, a part of the main; if a clod be washed away by the sea, Europe is the less, as well as if a promontory were, as well as if a manor of thy friends or of thine own were. Any man's death diminishes me, because I am involved in mankind. And therefore never send to know for whom the bell tolls. It tolls for thee.

John Donne

I'm not afraid to die. I just don't want to be there when it happens.

Woody Allen

Death be not proud, though some have called thee
Mighty and dreadful, for thou art not so.
For those whom thou thinks't thou dost overthrow,
Die not, poor death, nor yet canst thou kill me.

John Donne, Holy Sonnets IX

We don't know life: how can we know death?

Confucius (551–479 B.C.)

FOCUS

HIV, AIDS and the Family

In contemporary America, those who are terminally ill are often stigmatized because they are dying. People feel uncomfortable in their presence and often avoid them. It is as if being with a dying person forces us to confront our own mortality and triggers irrational fears of somehow "catching" the death (De Spelder and Strickland, 1990). Those with HIV or AIDS suffer a double stigmatization: first, they are presumably dying; and second, they are presumably members of one of two highly stigmatized groups—gay men or IV-drug users. They are not AIDS victims or sufferers, but people *living* with AIDS.

Families are affected by HIV and AIDS in numerous ways. The following are real-life examples of how HIV and AIDS affect families and other intimate relationships (Macklin, 1988, 1989; Shilts, 1987):

❐ Parents reject their gay son because of his sexual orientation and reconcile with him only as he is dying.
❐ A grandmother whose daughter has died from AIDS now cares for her two orphaned HIV-positive grandchildren.
❐ A young executive who experimented with IV drugs five years earlier discovers he is HIV positive after he infects his wife, who in turn infects their two children neonatally; in three years, the entire family is dead.
❐ A mother discovers she is HIV-positive only after the birth of her infected son. She worries about who will care for her children if she dies.
❐ A woman's husband has AIDS and she fears that she is infected although she repeatedly tests HIV-negative.
❐ A married woman finds a notice in her lover's desk informing him that he is HIV-positive but is afraid of confronting him because she was snooping; she is afraid to talk with her husband because he believes she is monogamous.

The family system is disrupted when the family learns that one of its members has HIV or AIDS (Carter, 1989; Cates et al., 1990). The family may unite to support its infected member, or old issues may resurrect, renewing conflict between family members, especially if members focus on how the HIV was transmitted. HIV and AIDS not only transform the life of the infected individual but also the lives of those emotionally involved with him or her: lovers (past and present), partners or spouses, children, parents, brothers and sisters, friends, and caregivers. Furthermore, when people test HIV-positive or have AIDS, their partners may have been unaware of their drug use or sexual activities outside of their primary relationship. Both the infected and uninfected partners may have to confront a variety of issues (Carter, 1989). A wife may be unaware of her husband's bisexual orientation and his extramarital involvement with other men or women. She must deal simultaneously with his infection, his sexual orientation, and his extramarital involvement.

PROBLEMS EXPERIENCED BY PEOPLE WITH AIDS AND THEIR FAMILIES

The problems that both the person with HIV or AIDS and his or her family and friends may experience include social stigma and isolation, fear of contagion, fear of infection, fear of abandonment, guilt, anger, grief, and economic hardship (Macklin, 1988). (For a discussion of children's understanding of AIDS from a developmental perspective, see Schvaneveldt, Lindauer, and Young, 1990).

SOCIAL STIGMA AND ISOLATION. Unlike other terminally ill individuals, most of those with HIV or AIDS must deal with personal and societal hostility because of their sexual orientation or drug use. (Even those who are infected through blood transfusions, heterosexual intercourse, or prenatal exposure suffer stigmatization.) Some view AIDS as divine retribution for violating religious teachings against homosexuality; others believe that those with AIDS deserve the affliction because of their gay or drug activities. Some people with HIV or AIDS are fired from their jobs, evicted from their apartments, rejected by their lovers, or refused admission to school. Some families support their child through the illness but do not tell others that their son or daughter has AIDS (Cleveland et al., 1988).

FEAR OF CONTAGION. Almost everyone who has a family member with HIV or AIDS experiences some fear of becoming infected themselves, even when they know there is no rational basis for the fear. Partners may hesitate to share the same bed, relatives may be reluctant to visit or dine together, or grandparents may be fearful of babysitting for an infected child. Relationships are often severely tested. Many relatives and friends feel unable to talk openly about their anxieties.

FEAR OF INFECTION. Anxieties are high among members of high-risk groups. They may be reluctant to become involved in relationships for fear of transmitting the virus or becoming infected themselves. They may fear being tested lest they discover that they are infected. If they are tested, they fear learning the results. And if they are HIV-positive, they wonder how long they have before AIDS symptoms occur.

continued on next page

FOCUS

FEAR OF ABANDONMENT. Many with HIV or AIDS face rejection by their families not only because of their infection but also because of their sexual orientation. For many gay men, their families learn that they are gay at the same time they learn that they have AIDS. Some families are unable to cope with the needs of their dying child or sibling and consequently pull away. Others, however, stand by with increased resolve and love (Cleveland et al., 1988).

GUILT. The person with HIV or AIDS may feel guilty for being gay or an IV-drug user. He or she may feel somehow "deserving" of the infection because of "immorality," "stupidity," or lack of awareness. Families that once rejected a dying family member because he was gay may feel guilt over their earlier rejection. Or they may feel guilty because they are unable to accept or care for their ill member.

ANGER. Guilt and anger may alternate. At one time a person feels angry for being infected; at other times he or she may feel guilty about it. He or she may feel angry at family, friends, associates, and society for not being more supportive. Family members may feel angry at the person with HIV or AIDS for "getting" infected because of sexual orientation or drug behavior.

GRIEF. There is no cure for HIV or AIDS. Also, researchers increasingly believe that most people infected with HIV will develop AIDS. Those with HIV and AIDS and their family and friends feel grief for the impending loss of health, potential, and life. The grief is compounded for partners, because some may be infected themselves. Because those with AIDS tend to be young adults, the feelings of grief and loss tend to be more intense. (In New York City, AIDS is the leading cause of death among men aged twenty-one to twenty-four years.)

ECONOMIC HARDSHIP. AIDS is a costly disease. Medical and hospital expenses may run between $50,000 and $100,000. The loss of earning power, the cost of treatment, and the lack of adequate financial assistance spell financial ruin for many individuals and families. Those without health insurance face even greater hardships.

One consequence of these costs and the increasing lack of sufficient numbers of treatment facilities is a movement toward home care of persons with AIDS. More and more programs are experimenting with ways of assisting individuals to remain in their homes with the combined care of family, partners and professional caregivers. Hospice care—whose goal is to maximize the quality of life for the terminally ill—is also becoming a major alternative for persons in the last stages of AIDS (Magno, 1991).

SUPPORTING FRIENDS AND RELATIVES WITH AIDS

If you have a friend or relative with HIV or AIDS, you can provide needed support without fear of contracting the infection yourself. Some things that you can do to show your caring are described below (Martelli et al., 1987; Moffat et al., 1987):

❑ Show your caring by visiting and keeping in contact.
❑ Touch your friend or relative; touch communicates love, warmth, and hope. Don't hesitate or be afraid to touch, despite whatever apprehension you might at first have.
❑ Call before visiting to make sure that your friend or relative feels like having a visitor at a particular time.

❑ Offer to talk about HIV or AIDS and its prognosis if the other person wants to express his or her feelings about them. Find HIV or AIDS support groups for your friend or relative.
❑ Take your friend or relative out to dinner, a movie, the park or beach, or a favorite spot if his or her health permits.
❑ Offer to shop or do household chores, banking, pet care, or other tasks. Provide transportation when needed.
❑ Organize your own support group to assist or be on call for your friend or relative. In this manner, you can create a network for sharing tasks and feelings.
❑ Be available. Encourage your friend or relative to reach out when he or she needs help.

In coping with AIDS, we must attempt to reduce the stigma and discrimination associated with it, work against homophobia, recognize the impact of the illness on the family, and encourage social, health, and economic programs that support persons with AIDS. For those with AIDS, we must focus on enhancing the quality of life, remembering that they are *living* with AIDS. We are all living until we die.

or may withdraw and become desensitized to human pain. We may end up denying the realities of death altogether.

ROMANTICISM. Sometimes our images of death are glamorized and glorified. Although some deaths are in fact peaceful and "beautiful," many are not. Those who have been led to expect a beautiful death (their own or another's) may be shocked and feel betrayed to discover the messy, frustrating, or ugly aspects of dying.

FEAR OF DEATH AND DYING. There are a number of fears and anxieties that many of us share regarding the dying process and death itself. When we think about dying, we may worry about being unable to care for ourselves and becoming a burden on those we love. We may worry about pain or physical impairment. We may fear isolation, loneliness, and separation from people who are dear to us. The finality of death is often fearsome; it implies the loss of relationships, the abandonment of goals, and an end to pleasure. For some, contemplating the possibilities of an unknown afterlife or the idea of eternal nothingness may be frightening. Others may be concerned about how their bodies will look after death and what will happen to them. One of the greatest fears aroused by the thought of death is the fear of losing control: the world will go on, but we will no longer have any effect on what happens in it.

Thanatologists (those who study death and dying) tell us that a certain amount of fear of death is a good thing (Rando, 1987). It certainly helps keep us alive. A certain amount of denial is healthy, too, for it prevents us from dwelling morbidly on the subject of death. What we need to develop is a realistic, honest view of death as part of life. Acknowledging that death exists can enrich our lives greatly. It can show us the importance of getting on with the "business of living," ordering our priorities, and appreciating what is around us. "The immediacy of death," writes Rando, "will lead to honesty with yourself, leading to the recognition that you have no choice but to be resigned to death and to focus all your energies on the creative reconstruction of the only existence you have."

The Process of Dying

Unless death comes very quickly and unexpectedly, the person who is dying will undergo a number of emotional changes in addition to physical ones. These changes are often referred to as "stages," although they do not necessarily happen in a particular order. Indeed, some of them may not be experienced at all, or a person may return again and again to a particular part of the process.

STAGES OF DYING. The stages of dying, discussed below, are similar to the stages of adaptation to other stressful situations (Leming and Dickinson, 1985; also see Kübler-Ross, 1969, 1982).

❑ *Anticipation.* At some time prior to our death, we begin to prepare for it by thinking about it, feeling anxious, or being actively involved in the dying processes of others. We may begin to mobilize our personal resources.

❑ *Onset of Stressful Event.* When we become acutely ill or are forcefully reminded of our mortality in some way, we begin to face the reality that death is actually approaching. We may use denial to shield ourselves from the implications of what is happening, but sooner or later we will probably acknowledge our death.

❑ *Disorganization.* Face to face with our life's ending, we may simply fall apart. Our symptoms may worsen (perhaps temporarily), and we may become quite emotional

---

Of all the wonders that I yet have heard,
It seems to me most strange that men should fear,
Seeing that death, a necessary end,
Will come when it will come.

William Shakespeare, Julius Caesar

Death is our eternal companion. . . . It has always been watching you. It will always until the day it taps you. . . .

Death is the only wise advisor that we have. Whenever you feel . . . that everything is going wrong and you're about to be annihilated, turn to your death and ask if it is so. Your death will tell you that you're wrong; that nothing really matters outside its touch. Your death will tell you, "I haven't touched you yet."

This, whatever you're doing right now, may be your last act on earth. There is no power which could guarantee that you are going to live one minute more.

Carlos Castañeda

It is not death that a man should fear, but he should fear never beginning to live.

Marcus Aurelius (121–180)

This is what youth must figure out:
Girls, love, and living.
The having, the not having,
The spending and giving,
And the melancholy time of not knowing.

This is what age must learn about:
The ABC of dying.
The going, yet not going,
The loving and leaving.
And the unbearable knowing and not knowing.

E. B. White

and find ourselves unable to think rationally. These are signs that our adaptation is progressing. This is the beginning of grieving, a process that can restore us to psychological wholeness.

□ *Organization.* Disorganization is followed by organization, a return to more normal functioning and planning. At this point we look around and try to figure out what we need to do and who can help us. During this phase and the next, we may make our actual preparations for death.

□ *Resolution.* Ideally, when we have found our own way through this uncertain and often painful process, we will feel a sense of mastery and achievement. If we have the energy and the support of others, we may feel a sense of exhilaration. If we have not already done so, we may plan for the future by dealing with property issues, wills, insurance, and so on. We may put renewed energy into relationships, "mend fences," or spend more time sharing memories with loved ones. We may put our spiritual house in order, and we may plan our funeral and burial or cremation.

NEEDS OF THE DYING. Robert Kavanaugh (1972) wrote:

No matter how we measure [one's] worth, a dying human being deserves more than efficient care from strangers, more than machines and antiseptic hands, more than a mouthful of pills, arms full of tubes and a rump full of needles. . . . More than furtive eyes, reluctant hugs, medical jargon, ritual sacraments or tired Bible quotes, more than all the phony promises for a tomorrow that will never come.

Aside from basic physical care and perhaps relief from pain, what a dying person needs can be summed up very succinctly: *to be treated as a human being.* Our society's own ambivalence and fear of death is all too often evident in the attitudes and actions of its doctors, nurses, and other medical personnel. In response to the impersonality that has generally characterized death and dying in the hospital setting, the hospice movement has gained momentum in the last two decades. A **hospice** may be an actual place where terminally ill people can be cared for with respect for their dignity. But it is also much more than that. It is a medical program that emphasizes both patient care (including management of pain and symptoms) *and* family support. The hospice provides education, grief counseling, financial counseling, and various types of practical assistance for home care of the dying person.

Bereavement

Bereavement is our response to the death of a loved one. It includes the customs and rituals that we practice within our culture or subculture. It also includes the emotional responses and expressions of feeling that we call the grieving process.

MOURNING RITUALS. Our culture, religion, and personal beliefs all influence the type of rituals we participate in after someone dies. By prescribing a specific set of formalized behaviors, bereavement rituals can give us security and comfort; we don't have to think "What do I do now?" Social rituals such as funerals and wakes give us the opportunity to share our sorrow, to console and be consoled. A funeral also clearly marks the end of a life. Because we must face up to the fact that an important person in our life is gone, we can begin to move ahead to our "new" life. Religious rituals affirm a spiritual relationship for those who believe in them; for those who don't, they may be a source of tension or embarrassment.

For some Americans, rituals having to do with the dead consist basically of a funeral service followed by burial, entombment, or cremation. For others, there are

*your hair is falling out, and
you are not so beautiful;
your eyes have dark shadows
your body is bloated; arms covered
with bruises and needlemarks;
legs swollen and useless . . .
your body and spirit
are weakened with toxic chemicals
urine smells like antibiotics,
even the sweat
that bathes your whole body
in the early hours of morning
reeks of dicloxacillin and
methotrexate.*

*you are nauseous all the time
i am afraid to move on the bed
for fear of waking you to moan
and lean over the edge
vomiting into the bag*

*i curl up fetally
withdraw into my dreams
with a frightened back to you . . .
and i'm scared
and i'm hiding
but i love you so much;
this truth does not change . . .
years ago,
when i met you, as we were falling in
love,
your beauty attracted me:
long golden-brown hair
clear and peaceful green eyes
high cheekbones and long smooth
muscles
but you know—and this is true—
i fell in love with your soul
the real essence of you
and this cannot grow less beautiful . . .
sometimes these days
even your soul is cloudy
i still recognize you*

*we may be frightened
be hiding our sorrow
it may take a little longer
to acknowledge the truth,
but i would not want to be anywhere
else
i am here with you
you can grow less beautiful to the world
you are safe
i will always love you.*

Christine Longaker

Mourning rituals, such as funerals, help us in the healing process by recognizing the significance of a person in our lives and the reality of his or her death.

Every shut eye ain't sleep and every good-bye ain't gone.

Traditional African-American proverb

Once again I wasn't. Then I was. Now I ain't again.

Epitaph of Arthur C. Hormans

Happy is he who dies before his children.

Yoruba proverb

The believer, not the belief, brings peace.

Robert Kavanaugh

important practices to be observed long after the burial (or cremation). Under Jewish law, for example, there are three successive periods of mourning. The first of these, *shiva,* is a seven-day period during which the immediate family undergoes certain austerities, such as refraining from haircutting, shaving, and using cosmetics; going to work, or engaging in sexual relations. During the second period, *shloshim,* the prohibitions become less strict, and the final period, *avelut,* applies only if one's mother or father has died. During this eleven-month period, sons are to say *kaddish* (a form of prayer) for the parent daily. When the year of mourning is over, it is forbidden to continue practices that demonstrate grief (Kearl, 1989).

Among Latinos, *el Dia de los Muertos* (the Day of the Dead), an ancient ritual with Indian and Catholic roots that is observed on November first, is making a comeback (Garcia, 1990). In Mexico and other Latin American countries, the dead are honored with prayers, gifts of food, and a night-long graveside vigil; in the United States parades and special exhibits not only commemorate the dead but also celebrate the cultural heritage of the participants. At home, altars may be set up with pictures of those who have died, religious figures or pictures, candles, orange marigolds (the Aztec flower of death), offerings of the honored one's favorite food or drink, and perhaps cartoons or darkly humorous verses that "laugh in the face of death."

GRIEF AS A HEALING PROCESS. Like dying, grieving is a process. Thanatologists have variously described the stages of the grieving process (Kavanaugh, 1972; Kübler-Ross, 1982; Tallmer, 1987). There are also certain emotions or psychological states that may commonly be expected. Among these are shock, denial, depression, anger, loneliness, and feelings of relief. Guilt is also usually experienced as part of the grieving process (Tallmer, 1987). If we felt resentment or anger toward the dead person, we feel guilty when he or she dies, as if we somehow caused the death. If we are spared and another dies—in an accident, for example—we feel guilty for surviving. And if the deceased was a burden to us while alive, we feel compelled to shoulder a load of guilt now that the burden has been lifted.

One model looks at grieving as a four-stage process (Bowlby, 1980; Tallmer, 1987). (Remember that these stages, like those of dying, are not rigidly fixed; they may be experienced in varying sequences, simultaneously, or repeatedly.)

❑ *Numbness.* At the first news of death, we may feel stunned. Our actions may have a mechanical, robotlike quality. We may return to this stage periodically throughout mourning.

❑ *Separation Anxiety.* In this phase we "search" for our "lost" loved one. This stage is characterized by crying, outbursts of anger, pining, and calling out for the person who has died.

❑ *Despair.* Depression may set in when we realize that the person for whom we are mourning really is not going to come back. Behavior may become erratic and disorganized. Apathy may set in.

❑ *Acquisition of New Roles.* As depression diminishes, the grieving person finds that old roles and ways of relating are being replaced by new ones. At this point we may "internalize" the person we loved, making him or her "part of our inner life" (Viorst, 1986). We may even take on aspects of the person who has died. Consider the woman "who took up gardening after her brother, a passionate gardener, had died" or the "rather dull woman who acquired a gift for repartee after her husband, the witty one, had died" (Lily Pincus, cited in Viorst, 1986).

For some, most of the grieving process will be over in a matter of weeks or months. For others, it will occupy a year or two or maybe more. The first year will undoubtedly be the most difficult as holidays, birthdays, and anniversaries are experienced without the loved person. Grieving may occur sporadically for years to come, touched off by memories evoked by a particular date or by a special piece of music or a beautiful view that can no longer be shared. Healing, which is the goal of grieving, does not appear suddenly as the reward for all our suffering. Rather, it comes little by little as we work through grief (and around it and over it and under it and back through again), until we look at ourselves one day and find we are whole.

CONSOLING THE BEREAVED. When a friend or relative is bereaved, we may feel awkward or embarrassed. We may want to avoid the family of the person who has died because we "just don't know what to say."

That's okay. We really don't have to say much, except "I'm so sorry" and, perhaps, "How can I help?" Here are some suggestions for helping someone who is grieving.

❑ Listen, listen, listen. This may be the most helpful thing you can do.

❑ Express your own sadness about the death and your caring for the bereaved person, but don't say "I know how you feel" unless you really do—that is, unless you've experienced a similar loss.

❑ Talk about the person who has died. Recall special qualities he or she possessed and the good times you may have experienced. If the bereaved person begins to speak of the one who has died, don't change the subject.

❑ Give practical support: help with household tasks, do shopping or other errands, cook a meal, help with child care.

❑ If there are children, involve them in remembering. Support their grieving process (it will be different than an adult's).

❑ Don't avoid the bereaved person because *you* are uncomfortable, worry about mentioning the dead person, or attempt to point out the "bright side."

Being able to share one's grief with others is a crucial part of healing. By "just" being around and "just" listening, we can be a positive part of the process.

All goes onward and outward,
Nothing collapses
And to die is different from
What anyone supposes
And luckier.

Walt Whitman

Flesh is merely a lesson.
We learn it & pass on.
Erica Jong

The bridge between the known and the unknown is always love.

Stephen Levine

Thus shall you think of all this fleeting world: a star at dawn, a bubble in a stream, a flash of lightning in a summer cloud, a flickering lamp, a phantom, and a dream.

Diamond Sutra

On the whole I'd rather be in Philadelphia.

Epitaph suggested by W.C. Fields

	TABLE 10.1	The Signs of Alcoholism

YES	NO	QUESTIONS
____	____	1. Do you occasionally drink heavily after a disappointment, a quarrel, or when the boss gives you a hard time?
____	____	2. When you have trouble or feel under pressure, do you always drink more heavily than usual?
____	____	3. Have you noticed that you are able to handle more liquor than you did when you were first drinking?
____	____	4. Did you ever wake up on the "morning after" and discover that you could not remember part of the evening before, even though your friends tell you that you did not "pass out"?
____	____	5. When drinking with other people, do you try to have a few extra drinks when others will not know it?
____	____	6. Are there certain occasions when you feel uncomfortable if alcohol is not available?
____	____	7. Have you recently noticed that when you begin drinking you are in more of a hurry to get the first drink than you used to be?
____	____	8. Do you sometimes feel a little guilty about your drinking?
____	____	9. Are you secretly irritated when your family or friends discuss your drinking?
____	____	10. Have you recently noticed an increase in the frequency of your memory "blackouts"?
____	____	11. Do you often find that you wish to continue drinking after your friends say they have had enough?
____	____	12. Do you usually have a reason for the occasions when you drink heavily?
____	____	13. When you are sober, do you often regret things you have done or said while drinking?
____	____	14. Have you tried switching brands or following different plans for controlling your drinking?

❑ ALCOHOL, DRUG ABUSE, AND FAMILIES

America is currently facing a drug crisis in which the alcoholic or addict and his or her family are reciprocally involved. Dysfunctional families, in fact, often contribute to the development of alcoholism and drug addiction. As Robert Lewis (1989) noted:

Not only do dysfunctional families often produce addictive behavior in their members, but these addictions, in turn, then may affect the qualify of life, negatively impacting the behavior of family members and devitalizing and fracturing family relationships. The most demoralizing aspect of this reciprocity . . . is that addictions are often passed from one generation to later generations, unless there is successful intervention.

T A B L E 10.1		**The Signs of Alcoholism (cont.)**

YES	NO	QUESTIONS
____	____	15. Have you often failed to keep the promises you have made to yourself about controlling or cutting down on your drinking?
____	____	16. Have you ever tried to control your drinking by making a change in jobs, or moving to a new location?
____	____	17. Do you try to avoid family or close friends while you are drinking?
____	____	18. Are you having an increasing number of financial and work problems?
____	____	19. Do more people seem to be treating you unfairly without good reason?
____	____	20. Do you eat very little or irregularly when you are drinking?
____	____	21. Do you sometimes have the "shakes" in the morning and find that it helps to have a little drink?
____	____	22. Have you recently noticed that you cannot drink as much as you once did?
____	____	23. Do you sometimes stay drunk for several days at a time?
____	____	24. Do you sometimes feel very depressed and wonder whether life is worth living?
____	____	25. Sometimes after periods of drinking, do you see or hear things that aren't there?
____	____	26. Do you get terribly frightened after you have been drinking heavily?

If you have answered "yes" to any of these questions, you have some of the symptoms that may indicate alcoholism.

Questions 1–8 relate to the early stages of alcoholism.
Questions 9–21 relate to the middle stage.
Questions 22–26 mark the beginning of the final stage.

Signs of Alcoholism is published by the National Council on Alcoholism

For example, authoritarian parents in a dysfunctional family may belittle and humiliate their children, shaming them into obedience. The children, however, may internalize this shame and develop a deep sense of inferiority. Lowered self-esteem may lead to addictive behaviors. The addiction becomes a defense against shame, a means of masking feelings of powerlessness and self-contempt, a way of medicating against the pain.

Over the past decade, family systems intervention has become one of the most important means of treating substance abuse. Family "love bonds" are utilized to work *for* the abuser rather than *against* the abuser; strong family feelings are focused on breaking the abuse rather than denying it or sustaining it.

Alcohol Abuse and Families

Alcohol is a drug. Many people, however, do not think of alcohol as a drug; instead, it is regarded as "a drink," a beer, a glass of wine, a rum and Coke. Yet, like certain illegal drugs such as marijuana and cocaine, alcohol alters an individual's mood and perceptions. The altered state produced by alcohol is a "high"; its more extreme manifestation is drunkenness. Because alcohol is a culturally accepted drug, the current antidrug climate largely excludes alcohol from national concern.

Consider the following statistics (Lord et al., 1987; Taylor, 1988; U.S. Bureau of the Census, 1990):

☐ Over 10 million men, women, *and* children are alcoholics. Nearly 18 million adults are problem drinkers.

☐ Between 1977 and 1987, more than 1 million Americans died from alcohol-related problems or accidents. The economic costs have exceeded a billion dollars.

☐ Alcohol-related death is the leading cause of death for persons between the ages of sixteen and twenty-four. Alcoholism is the fourth-ranked cause of death in the country. Alcohol is a factor in nearly half of America's murders, suicides, and accidental deaths. Drunk drivers are responsible for half of all driving fatalities.

☐ Twenty-four percent of the families responding to a recent Gallup poll reported family problems related to alcohol, twice the level reported ten years earlier (Gallup, 1987). Seven million children live in alcoholic families. An additional 21 million are adult children of alcoholics (Lord et al., 1987).

☐ Alcohol abuse by prospective mothers (and fathers) can cause serious fetal damage, resulting in fetal alcohol syndrome, low birth weight, and other impairments (see Chapter 6 for discussion of birth complications).

These are not abstract facts about alcohol. They affect millions of American families. Alcohol abuse undermines families, relationships, and hopes. Yet the popularly perceived image of the alcoholic as a "bum in the gutter" prevails because families tend to deny their alcoholism. (See Table 10.1 for signs of alcoholism.)

The abuse of alcohol can be seen as a symptom of a disorder that is both physical *and* emotional. Health professionals view alcoholism as a disease rather than a personal shortcoming. The American Medical Association (Lord et al., 1987) defines alcoholism as follows:

Alcoholism is an illness characterized by preoccupation with alcohol and loss of control over its consumption such as to lead usually to intoxication if drinking is begun, by chronicity, by progression, and by tendency toward relapse.

Although physiological and genetic factors may predispose a person to alcoholism (Blakeslee, 1984), it appears that problem drinking, like ordinary drinking, is a learned behavior. Most people in the United States learn to drink during adolescence; most adolescents have their first drink at home but do most of their drinking away from home, with their friends. The drinking behavior that children observe at home will greatly influence their own behavior. Many alcoholics have at least one alcoholic parent. Others drink as a means of coping with stress, anxiety, or low self-esteem.

Even though we drink substantially less distilled liquor than in the past, we still consume vast quantities of beer and increasing amounts of wine. Although the percentage of alcohol in beer and wine is lower than that in distilled liquor, drinkers often don't take into account the fact that distilled liquor is generally served diluted in mixed drinks. A five-ounce glass of wine contains as much alcohol as a standard highball; a can of beer is equal in alcohol content to a rum and Coke.

The heaviest drinkers are men between eighteen and twenty-five years. Adults drink 40.1 gallons of alcoholic drinks per capita; this includes 34.4 gallons of beer, 3.5 gallons of wine, and 2.4 gallons of distilled spirits, such as whiskey and vodka (U.S. Bureau of the Census, 1991). Because this is the average rate for *all* Americans of drinking age, when you adjust for the nondrinkers and very light drinkers, you can see that the annual rate of consumption for drinkers is much higher. In fact, 10 percent of the nation's drinkers consume over half its alcohol (Lord et al., 1987).

Drinkers who are not alcoholics may also pose a danger to themselves and society. The social and economic costs of alcohol abuse are enormous. One of the heaviest costs in the devastation caused by drunk driving. Drivers in the eighteen to twenty-year-old age group are twice as likely as other drivers to be involved in alcohol-related accidents; 50 percent of all drivers killed in automobile accidents had been drinking (Givens, 1985; U.S. Bureau of the Census, 1991).

ALCOHOLISM AND THE FAMILY. Alcoholism is sometimes called a "family disease" because it involves all members of the family in a "complex interactional system" (Krimmel, 1973). The principle of homeostasis—the tendency toward stability in a system—operates in alcoholic families, maintaining established behavior patterns and strengthening resistance to change. Many alcoholic families do not progress through the normal family life-cycle stages but remain in an unhealthy (yet stable) cycling between "sober and intoxicated interactional states" (Steinglass, 1983). Krimmel (1973) described the "pathological complementary relationship" between an alcoholic husband and his wife on the morning after a drinking bout:

[The] wife responds to her husband's plea of physical illness, shame, guilt or remorse with either sympathy and forgiveness or anger and punishment. . . . If the wife is forgiving the husband has learned that forgiveness for being drunk can be obtained, provided he is appropriately remorseful and very sick. If she punishes him. . . . his guilt and shame are relieved. . . . In either case, the pattern cannot be understood except in terms of the total sequence, as if it were designed to produce forgiveness or punishment or comfortable emotional distance. . . . The spouse may derive considerable gratification from the opportunity to be the forgiver or the punisher.

TREATMENT. In one sense alcoholism is not curable. Alcoholics must stay sober to stay well. For most alcoholics this means no more drinking, ever. Although recovery is possible, a major stumbling block exists to motivating the alcoholic to pursue it. *Denial* is used by the alcoholic and his or her family and friends. "I can quit any time," says the alcoholic, or "It's not my drinking that's the problem, it's . . . (anything else)." The spouse, parent, or lover colludes in maintaining the alcoholism by denying it: "Jane is not *really* like this. She's a wonderful person when she's sober." People often deny the fact of alcoholism because of the social stigma attached to the term *alcoholic*.

Treatment for alcoholism is generally not considered possible until the alcoholic makes the conscious choice to become well. Many must first "hit bottom" before they are willing to admit that they are alcoholics. But because families are often organized around protecting the alcoholic from the consequences of his or her alcoholism, the alcoholic is able to deny his or her alcoholism. Although adolescent alcoholics also deny their problems, research indicates that they are likely to perceive their need for help if they experience serious physiological consequences of their drinking, experience serious personal problems, or have another substance abuser in the family (Lorch and Dukes, 1989).

An educated public and an enlightened approach by professionals are essential to achieve progress in freeing millions from the destructive grip of alcoholism. Family support is very important; the best results seem to be obtained when the whole family is treated (Nace et al., 1982). Indeed, for many families it is imperative that the family be treated as a unit, because its structure and stability may be organized

Alcoholism isn't a spectator sport. Eventually the whole family gets to play.

Joyce Rebeta-Burditt

around the alcoholism (Steinglass, 1983). Self-help groups such as Alcoholics Anonymous and Al-Anon (for the families of alcoholics) have had good success rates. Organizations such as Adult Children of Alcoholics offer self-help for children of alcoholic families. (See Resource Center for more information.)

Drug Abuse and Families

Although alcohol is the most commonly used and misused mind-altering substance in the United States, a number of other drugs have achieved popularity among many Americans.

We are never deceived: we deceive ourselves.

Johann Goethe

Cigarettes kill more people each year than AIDS, heroin, crack, cocaine, alcohol, car accidents, fire, and murder combined.

Iris Shannon

DRUGS AND DRUG USE. There are many kinds of *psychoactive* ("mind-affecting") drugs and many reasons for using them. After alcohol, the most commonly used psychoactive drugs include marijuana, hallucinogens (such as LSD, mescaline, and psilocybin), cocaine (and "crack," its smokable form), phencyclidine (PCP), *narcotics* ("sleep-inducing" drugs, principally heroin; also other opiates such as morphine and codeine), and inhalants (such as toluene in spray paints and nitrous oxide, or "laughing gas"). *Psychotherapeutic* ("mind-healing") drugs such as antidepressants, stimulants, and sedatives are widely used; among the most commonly abused drugs in this group are amphetamines ("speed") and the sedative-hypnotics such as methaqualone (Quaaludes), barbituates (such as secobarbital [Seconal] or "reds"), and diazepam (Valium). Drug use is prevalent in virtually all socioeconomic, sociocultural, and age groups (beginning with preteens). What varies is the drug of choice and the usage pattern.

Overall drug use seems to be declining since the peak years of the late 1970s. In fact, many experts suggest that America is in the midst of its third temperance movement (Kolata, 1991). Only the use of heroin and crack continues to maintain a steady level. These drugs continue to ravage Americans, especially poor Americans. There are numerous consequences, including the birth of "crack babies" (discussed in Chapter 6) and the spread of HIV to drug users, their sexual partners, and their children. Users of intravenously administered (IV) drugs represent the fastest growing segment of HIV infection and AIDS cases. The vast majority of those infected through IV drug use are the inner-city poor. As national drug use declines, warns Mitchell Rosenthal, the chairperson of the New York State Advisory Council on Drug Abuse, "the danger is that we will have a shrinking political interest in the problem, and the most vulnerable and high-risk populations will not get the kind of services they need" (quoted in Kolata, 1991).

Within the family, parents, adolescents, or both may be drug users. Adolescents (or adults, for that matter) may use drugs to resolve conflicts, escape stressful situations, express defiance of authority, or elicit sympathy. Emerging research suggests that survivors of sexual abuse are significantly more likely to abuse drugs and alcohol as a form of self-medication and as a way to escape family problems (Harrison, Hoffman, and Edwall, 1989). Drug use may also be a symptom of serious disturbance and a threat to health or life. Teenage drug use is of particular concern to many families.

THE FAMILY'S ROLE IN DRUG ABUSE. Researchers are increasingly recognizing the role of the family in beginning, continuing, stopping, and preventing drug use by its members (Needle et al., 1983; Sorenson and Bernal, 1987; Textor, 1987). Some researchers (Stanton, 1979) believe that parents with marital problems use their adolescent's drug abuse as a means of avoiding their own problems. These families often

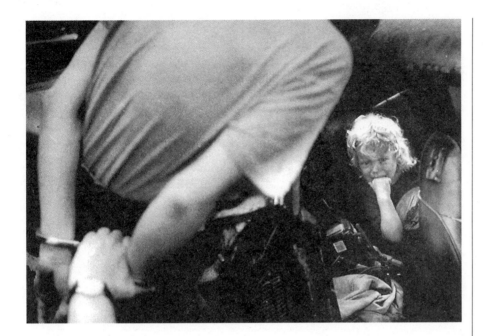

Drugs destroy not only individuals, but families as well.

deny the drug abuse and sometimes encourage it by providing money. In order to solicit care and attention from their parents, abusers engage in antisocial or self-destructive behavior. If the addict improves, however, the family suffers a crisis of its own: members become depressed, parents threaten divorce, siblings act out. Family members may sabotage the treatment of addicted members. These crises dissipate as soon as the drug user returns to his or her addiction. These families "need" their drug-abusing member to maintain their cohesiveness. The center of the problem is the family. In such cases, drug abuse is merely a symptom of family pathology.

THE ADDICT. Drug abuse often begins as an adolescent problem; it may be tied to normal adolescent experimentation (Textor, 1987). Adolescents must deal with issues of family loyalty, separation and identity, and new ways of relating with their parents. Future addicts fail at most of these tasks. Early in life they may be identified as problem children; they are viewed as weak, immature, and needing help. Because they are limited in their development, they do not have sufficient coping skills; they are nonassertive and feel that they have little control over their lives. They often fail at school, are unable to find suitable work, and refuse to accept social responsibilities. They develop negative self-images. As Martin Textor (1987) observed:

Future drug addicts are usually alienated from their peers and socially isolated. They lack real relationships, experience few romantic episodes, and expect rejection by others. Therefore, they often use drugs as a means of coping with the absence of intimacy and as a source of relief from loneliness, despair, and frustration.

Drug abusers remain intimately involved with their families. They rarely achieve real independence. Because they feel trapped, addicts may attempt to rebel against their parents or punish them for not allowing them to be free of their emotional bondage.

FAMILY LIFE. Family life for drug abusers is usually dull, shallow, and without emotion (Textor, 1987). Family members feel alienated, lonely, and unaccepted. They feel anxious, depressed, guilty, and enraged. Communication is poor: it involves unclear messages, vague information-giving, lack of direct talk, avoidance of eye contact. There is little direct expression of positive or negative emotions, because family members are intensely concerned about controlling feelings.

Such families defend against their emptiness and anger "by heavy alcohol consumption, self-medication, or overeating, all which serve as anesthetics, tranquilizers, antidepressants" (Textor, 1987). Only by "getting high" can the addict experience and express strong emotions. The parents not only rationalize their own misuse of legal drugs, such as alcohol or tranquilizers, but often deny their child's substance abuse. If they do recognize the child's abuse, neither they nor the addict accepts responsibility for the abuse. They blame each other or outside influences. The parents may excuse the addict because his or her dependency absolves them from responsibility.

The parents usually have a poor marital relationship, experience emotional distance, lack intimacy, and are dissatisfied with their sex life. They have a vital stake in maintaining their child's addiction as a means of avoiding their own problems. Their child's addiction is their way of "solving" their marital problems. In order to change the addict, the family must change. Because of family involvement, drug-abuse programs often involve intensive family therapy.

 # SUMMARY

❐ *Health* is a state of physical and mental well-being, not solely the absence of disease. *Physical well-being* consists of feeling fit and able. *Emotional well-being* consists of feelings of happiness, hope, energy, and zest for life.

❐ Happily married people tend to have better health than unmarried individuals. Marriage encourages health and well-being through (1) living with a partner, (2) social support, and (3) economic well-being. Social support improves physical health by (1) increasing psychological well-being, (2) encouraging and reinforcing protective health behaviors, (3) providing secondary prevention, and (4) aiding recovery.

❐ America is undergoing a severe health care crisis. Because of the high cost of medical care, the possession of health insurance has become a prime determinant of access to such care. Today, 13 percent of Americans do not possess health insurance; among African Americans and Latinos the percentage is significantly higher. Most health insurance is linked to employment. Unemployed, part-time, and low-paid workers in service industries are usually not covered. Only 40 percent of the poor are covered. The most promising insurance reform may follow the Canadian model of universal health insurance coverage.

❐ *Stress,* psychological distress or disruption, occurs as a result of change. Both families and individuals attempt to maintain equilibrium in the face of stress. *Family stress* is "an upset of the steady state of the family." *Stress pile up*—prior strains and hardships converging with new stressors—is important in determining stress outcome.

Normative stress, such as death of elderly members, is predictable and common to all families. *Nonnormative stress,* such as drug abuse, is neither predictable nor common to all families.

❐ The *double ABC-X* model is the most widely used model describing stress. **Aa** represents *stressor pile up,* the combination of stressors, family hardships and strains, **B** represents family coping resources, **C** represents perception of the stressor pile up, and **X** represents outcome.

❐ *Economic distress* refers to aspects of a family's economic life that may cause stress, including unemployment, poverty, and economic strain. Unemployment causes family roles to change; families spend more time together, but wives complain that husbands don't participate in housework. After about six months, a stable family pattern emerges. If unemployment continues beyond a year, families are vulnerable to divorce. Coping resources include family members' psychological disposition, an adaptive family system, and flexible family roles. Coping behaviors consist of defining the problem in a positive manner, problem solving, and managing emotions.

❐ Disabilities and chronic illnesses create many forms of stress, including strained family relationships, modifications in family activities and goals, increased tasks and time commitments, increased financial costs, special housing requirements, social isolation, medical concerns, and grieving. Functional coping patterns include maintaining family integration, social support, self-esteem, and psychological stability, as well as understanding the medical situation.

❐ Family caregiving activities often begin in middle-aged marriages when an aged parent becomes infirm or dependent. Caregivers tend to be women. Although they often experience stress, caregivers may also feel positively about helping a beloved parent or relative.

❐ Cultural influences on our perception of death cause us to respond with denial, exploitation, and romanticization. *Thanatologists,* people who study death and dying, tell us that the stages of dying are likely to include anticipation, onset of a stressful event, disorganization, organization, and resolution. Apart from physical care and relief from pain, the most important need of a dying person is to be treated as a human being. *Hospices* care for terminally ill individuals, emphasizing both patient care and family support.

❐ *Bereavement* is the response to the death of a loved one, including customs and rituals and the grieving process (emotional responses and expressions of feeling). Mourning rituals include the funeral service and burial or cremation. For Jews, there are three successive periods of mourning—*shiva, shloshim,* and *avelut;* among Latinos, *el Dia de los Muertos* (the Day of the Dead) is celebrated on November first. The grieving process may include numbness, separation anxiety, despair, and the acquisition of new roles.

❐ Alcoholism is primarily a learned behavior; it often begins as a means of coping with stress, anxiety, and low self-esteem. Alcoholism is regarded as a disease over which the alcoholic has no control. Family members unconsciously may help maintain the alcoholic's drinking. Alcoholism can be cured only if the alcoholic stops drinking permanently.

❐ Overall drug use is declining in this country. The family is often deeply implicated in sustaining drug abuse and addiction. Family members often use the abuser as a scapegoat to avoid dealing with their own problems, especially marital problems.

CHAPTER 11

Communication and Conflict Resolution

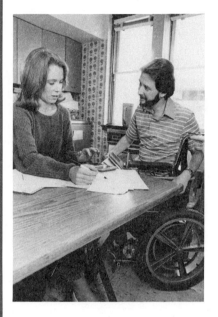

When in doubt, tell the truth.

Mark Twain

INTIMACY AND COMMUNICATION ARE INEXTRICABLY CONNECTED. When we speak of communication, we mean more than just the ability to discuss problems and resolve conflicts. We mean communication for its own sake: the pleasure of being in each other's company, the excitement of conversation, the exchange of touches and smiles, the loving silences. Through communication we disclose who we are, and from this self-disclosure intimacy grows.

One of the most common complaints of married partners, especially unhappy partners, is "We don't communicate." But it is impossible *not* to communicate—a cold look may communicate anger as effectively as a fierce outburst of words. What these unhappy partners mean by not communicating is that their communication drives them apart rather than brings them together, feeds conflict rather than resolves it. Communication patterns are strongly associated with marital satisfaction (Noller and Fitzpatrick, 1991).

In this chapter we explore how communication brings people together: how to develop communication skills, how to self-disclose, how to give feedback and affirm your partner. We also discuss the relationship between conflict and intimacy, exploring the types of conflict and the role of power in marital relationships. We look at common conflicts about sex and money. Finally, we explore some ways of resolving conflicts.

❑ COMMUNICATION PATTERNS IN MARRIAGE

There has been an explosion of research on marital communication in the last decade. Researchers are finding significant correlations between the nature of marital communication and satisfaction, as well as differences in male/female communication patterns in marriage.

Communication Patterns and Satisfaction

Researchers have found a number of patterns that distinguish the communication patterns in satisfied marriages in contrast to dissatisfied marriages (Hendrick, 1981; Noller and Fitzpatrick, 1991; Schaap, Buunk, and Kerkstra, 1988). Couples in satisfied marriages tend to have the following characteristics.

❑ *Willingness to accept conflict but to engage in conflict in nondestructive ways.*
❑ *Less frequent conflict and less time spent in conflict.* Both groups, however, experience conflicts about the same topics, especially about communication, sex, and personality characteristics.
❑ *The ability to disclose or reveal private thoughts and feelings, especially positive ones, to one's partner.* Dissatisfied spouses tend to disclose mostly negative thoughts to their partners.
❑ *Expression by both partners of more or less equal levels of affective disclosures,* such as tenderness, words of love, touch.
❑ *More time spent talking, discussing personal topics, and expressing feelings in positive ways.* One study (Kirchler, 1989) found that satisfied couples spend more time together (seven hours per day) in contrast to five hours per day for distressed couples.

The ability to accurately **encode** *(send) verbal and nonverbal messages and accurately* **decode** *(understand) such messages from their spouses.* This is especially important for husbands. Unhappy partners may actually decode the messages of strangers more accurately than those from their partners.

Whenever a feeling is voiced with truth and frankness . . . a mysterious and far-reaching influence is exerted. At first it acts on those who are inwardly receptive. But the circle grows larger and larger. . . . The effect is but the reflection of something that emanates from one's own heart.

I Ching

Married couples who love each other tell each other a thousand things without talking.

Chinese proverb

A little sincerity is a dangerous thing, and a great deal of it is absolutely fatal.

Oscar Wilde

Husband/Wife Differences in Marital Communication

For some time, researchers have been aware of gender differences in general communication patterns. More recently, they have discovered specific gender differences in marital communication (Noller and Fitzpatrick, 1991; Thompson and Walker, 1989).

First, wives send clearer messages to their husbands than their husbands send to them. Wives tend to be more sensitive and responsive to their husbands' messages, both during conversation *and* during conflict. They are more likely to reply to either positive messages ("You look great") or negative messages ("You look awful") than are their husbands, who may not reply at all.

Second, husbands more than wives tend to give neutral messages, such as, "It doesn't matter to me." Wives give more positive or negative messages. Because women tend to smile or laugh when they send messages, however, they send fewer clearly neutral messages. Husband's neutral responses make it more difficult for wives to decode what their partners really are trying to say. If a wife asks her husband if they should go to dinner or see a movie and he gives a neutral response, such as, "Whatever," does he *really* not care, or is he pretending he doesn't to avoid possible conflict?

Third, although communication differences in arguments between husbands and wives are usually small, they nevertheless follow a typical pattern. Wives tend to set the emotional tone of an argument. They escalate conflict with negative verbal and nonverbal messages ("Don't give me *that!*") or deescalate arguments by setting an atmosphere of agreement ("I understand your feelings"). Husbands' inputs are less important in setting the climate for resolving or escalating conflicts. Wives tend to use emotional appeals and threats more than husbands, who tend to reason, seek conciliation, and try to postpone or end an argument. A wife is more likely to say, "Don't you love me?" while a husband is more likely to say, "Be reasonable."

Studies suggest that poor communication skills precede the outset of marital problems (Markman, 1981; Markman et al., 1987). The material that follows will assist you in understanding and developing good communication skills.

❑ NONVERBAL COMMUNICATION

There is no such thing as not communicating. Even when you are not talking, you are communicating by your silence (an awkward silence, a hostile silence, a tender silence). You are communicating by the way you position your body and tilt your head, through your facial expressions, your physical distance from another person, and so on. Look around you. How are the people in your presence communicating nonverbally?

Much of our communication of feeling is nonverbal. We radiate our moods: a happy mood invites companionship; a solemn mood pushes people away. Joy infects; depression distances—all without a word being said. Nonverbal expressions of love are particularly effective—a gentle touch, a loving glance, or a flower.

One of the problems with nonverbal communication, however, is the imprecision of its messages. Is a person frowning or squinting? Does the smile indicate friendliness or nervousness? A person may be in reflective silence, but we may interpret the silence as disapproval or distance.

Functions of Nonverbal Communication

An important study of nonverbal communication and marital interaction found that nonverbal communication has three important functions in marriage (Noller,

It is human nature to think wisely and act foolishly.

Anatole France (1844–1924)

Silence is the one great art of conversation.

William Hazlitt (1778–1830)

The cruelest lies are often told in silence.

Robert Louis Stevenson (1850–1890)

Do you hide a spear within a smile?

Dogen, A Primer of Soto Zen

It was fortunate that love did not need words, or else it would be full of misunderstandings and foolishness.

Herman Hesse, Narcissus and Goldmund

1984): (1) conveying interpersonal attitudes, (2) expressing emotion, and (3) handling the ongoing interaction.

CONVEYING INTERPERSONAL ATTITUDES. Nonverbal messages are used to convey attitudes. Gregory Bateson described nonverbal communication as revealing "the nuances and intricacies of how two people are getting along" (quoted in Noller, 1984). Holding hands can suggest intimacy; sitting on opposite sides of the couch can suggest distance. Not looking at each other in conversation can suggest awkwardness or a lack of intimacy.

EXPRESSING EMOTIONS. Our emotional states are expressed through our bodies. A depressed person walks slowly, a happy person walks with a spring. Smiles, frowns, furrowed brows, tight jaws, tapping fingers—all express emotion. Expressing emotion is important because it lets our partner know how we are feeling so that he or she can respond appropriately. It also allows our partner to share our feeling, to laugh or weep with us.

HANDLING THE ONGOING INTERACTION. Nonverbal communications help us handle the ongoing interaction by indicating interest and attention. An intent look indicates our interest in the conversation; a yawn indicates boredom. Posture and eye contact are especially important. Are we leaning toward the person with interest or slumping back, thinking about something else? Do we look at the person who is talking or are we distracted, glancing at other people as they walk by, watching the clock?

Relationship between Verbal and Nonverbal Communication

The messages that we send and receive contain a verbal and a nonverbal component. The verbal part expresses the basic content of the message, whereas the nonverbal part expresses what is known as the *relationship* or *command* part of the message. The relationship part of the message tells the attitude of the speaker (friendly, neutral, hostile) and indicates how the words are to be interpreted (as a joke, request, or command). The full content of any message has to be understood according to both the verbal and nonverbal parts.

For a message to be most effective, both the verbal and nonverbal components must be in agreement. If you are angry and say, "I am angry," and your facial expression and voice both show anger, the message is clear. But if you say, "I am angry," in a neutral tone of voice and smile, your message is ambiguous. If you say, "I'm not angry," but clench your teeth and use an angry voice, your message is also unclear.

Eye Contact and Touching

Two of the most important forms of nonverbal communication are eye contact and touch.

EYE CONTACT. Much can be discovered about a relationship by watching how people look at each other. Making eye contact with another person, if only for a split second longer than usual, is a signal of interest. If the look is returned twice, it is an invitation to be approached. When you can't take your eyes off another person, you probably have a strong attraction to him or her. In fact, you can easily distinguish

*No matter how grouchy you're feeling
You'll find the smile more or less
  healing:
It grows a wreath all around the front
  teeth,
Thus preserving the face from
  congealing.*

Anthony Euwer

*Words must be supported by one's
entire conduct. If words and conduct
are not in accord and not consistent,
they will have no effect.*

I Ching

Touch and eye contact are important forms of communication even during disagreements for they demonstrate continued caring.

people in love by their prolonged looking into each other's eyes. In addition to eye contact, dilated pupils may be an indication of sexual interest (or poor lighting).

Research suggests that the amount of eye contact between a couple in conversation can distinguish between those who have high levels of conflict and those who don't. Those with the greatest degree of agreement have the greatest eye contact with each other (Beier and Sternberg, 1977). Those in conflict tend to avoid eye contact (unless it is a daggerlike stare).

Sociologist Georg Simmel (1950) described interactions based on mutual glances or eye contact. For him, eye contact was "the purest and most direct reciprocity that exists anywhere." He wrote:

So tenacious and subtle is this union that it can only be maintained by the shortest and straightest of line between the eyes . . . the slightest deviation from it, the slightest glance aside, completely destroys the unique character of this union.

TOUCHING. It is difficult to overestimate the significance of touch. Touch is a life-giving force for infants. If they are not touched, they may fail to thrive and may even die (Montagu, 1986). We hold hands with small children and those we love. When we are moved by someone or something, we speak of being "touched." Gathering in a circle for the "laying on of hands" has a spiritual significance that may go beyond our everyday "worldly" experience.

As with eye contact, touching is a form of communication. The amount of contact, from almost imperceptible touches to "hanging all over" each other, helps differentiate lovers from strangers. How and where a person is touched can suggest friendship, intimacy, love, or sexual interest.

Growing research on touch indicates that it often signals intimacy, immediacy, and emotional closeness (Thayer, 1986). In fact, touch may very well be the closest form of nonverbal communication. One researcher (Thayer, 1986) wrote: "If intimacy is proximity, then nothing comes closer than touch, the most intimate knowledge of another." And touching seems to go "hand in hand" with self-disclosure. Those who touch seem to self-disclose more; in fact, touch seems to be an impor-

The union and interaction of individuals is based upon mutual glances. This is perhaps the purest and most direct reciprocity that exists anywhere. . . . So tenacious and subtle is this union that it can only be maintained by the shortest and straightest line between the eyes, and the smallest deviation from it, the slightest glance aside, completely destroys the unique character of this union.

Georg Simmel

The imaginations which people have of one another are the solid facts of human life.

Charles Cooley

FOCUS

Ten Rules for Avoiding Intimacy

If you want to avoid intimacy, here are ten rules that have proved effective in nationwide testing with lovers, husbands and wives, parents and children. Follow these guidelines and you'll never have an intimate relationship.

1.   *Don't talk.* This is the basic rule for avoiding intimacy. If you follow this one rule, you will never have to worry about being intimate again. Sometimes, however, you may be forced to talk. But don't talk about anything meaningful. Talk about the weather, baseball, class, the stock market—anything but feelings.

2.   *Never show your feelings.* Showing your feelings is almost as bad as talking, because feelings are ways of communicating. If you cry or show anger, sadness, or joy, you are giving yourself away. You might as well talk, and if you talk you could become intimate. So the best thing to do is remain expressionless (which, we admit, is a form of communication, but at least it is giving the message that you don't want to be intimate).

3.   *Always be pleasant.* Always smile, always be friendly, especially if something's bothering you. You'll be surprised at how effective hiding negative feelings from your partner is in preventing intimacy. It may even fool your partner into believing that everything's okay in your relationship.

4.   *Always win.* If you can't be pleasant, try this one. Never compromise, never admit that your partner's point of view may be as good as yours. If you start compromising, that's an admission that you care about your partner's feelings, which is a dangerous step toward intimacy.

5.   *Always keep busy.* Keeping busy at school or work will take you away from your partner, and you won't have to be intimate. Your partner may never figure out that you're using work to avoid intimacy. Because our culture values hard work, he or she will feel unjustified in complaining. Incidentally, devoting yourself to your work will also give your partner the message that he or she is not as important as your work. You can make your partner feel unimportant in your life without even talking!

6.   *Always be right.* There is nothing worse than being wrong, because it is an indication that you are human. If you admit you're wrong, you might have to admit your partner's right, and that will make him or her as good as you. If he or she is as good as you, then you might have to consider your partner, and before you know it, you will be intimate!

7.   *Never argue.* If you can't always be right, don't argue at all. If you argue, you might discover that you and your partner are different. If you're different, you may have to talk about the differences so that you can make adjustments. And if you begin making adjustments, you may have to tell your partner who you *really* are, what you *really* feel. Naturally, these revelations may lead to intimacy.

8.   *Make your partner guess what you want.* Never tell your partner what you want. That way, when your partner tries to guess and is wrong (as he or she often will be), you can tell your partner that he or she doesn't really understand or love you. If your partner did love you, he or she would know what you want without asking. Not

only will this prevent intimacy but it will drive your partner crazy as well.

9.   *Always look out for number one.* Remember, you are number one. All relationships exist to fulfill *your* needs, no one else's. Whatever you feel like doing is just fine. You're okay—your partner's not okay. If your partner can't satisfy your needs, he or she is narcissistic; after all, you are the one making all the sacrifices in the relationship.

10.   *Keep the television on.* Keep the television turned on at all times, during dinner, while you're reading, when you're in bed, and while you're talking (especially if you're talking about something important). This rule may seem petty compared with the others, but it is good preventive action. Watching television keeps you and your partner from talking to each other. Best of all, it will keep you both from even noticing that you don't communicate. If you're cornered and have to talk, you can both be distracted by a commercial, a seduction scene, or the sound of gunfire. And when you actually think about it, wouldn't you rather be watching "The Simpsons" or "A Different World" anyway?

We want to caution students that this list is not complete. Everyone knows additional ways for avoiding intimacy. These may be your own inventions or techniques that you have learned from your boyfriend or girlfriend, friends, or parents. To round out this compilation, list additional rules for avoiding intimacy on a separate sheet of paper. The person with the best list wins—and never has to be intimate again.

tant factor in prompting others to talk more about themselves (Heslin and Alper, 1983; Norton, 1983).

Despite stereotypes of women touching and men avoiding touch, studies suggest that there are no consistent differences between the sexes in the amount of overall touching (Andersen et al., 1987). Men do not seem to initiate touch with women any more than women do with men. Women are markedly unenthusiastic about receiving touches from strangers, however, and express greater concern about being touched. For women, there is greater touch avoidance unless there is a relational context with the man (Heslin and Alper, 1983). However, in situations with sexual overtones, men, regardless of their marital status initiate more touching than women (Blumstein and Schwartz, 1983).

▢ DEVELOPING COMMUNICATION SKILLS

Why People Don't Communicate

We can learn to communicate, but it is not always easy. Male gender roles, for example, work against the idea of expressing feelings. The traditional male gender role calls for men to be strong and silent, to ride off into the sunset alone. If men talk, they talk about things—cars, politics, sports, work, money—but not about feelings. Also, people may have personal reasons for not expressing their feelings. They may have strong feelings of inadequacy: "If you *really* knew what I was like, you wouldn't like me." They may feel ashamed of or guilty about their feelings: "Sometimes I feel attracted to other people, and it makes me feel guilty because I *should* only be attracted to you." They may feel vulnerable: "If I told you my real feelings, you might hurt me." They may be frightened of their feelings: "If I expressed my anger, it would destroy you." Finally, people may not communicate because they are fearful that their real feelings and desires will create conflict: "If I told you how I felt, you would get angry" (also see Cole and Cole, 1985).

Obstacles to Self-Awareness

Before we can communicate with others, we must first know how we ourselves feel. Yet we often place obstacles in the way. First, we suppress "unacceptable" feelings, especially feelings such as anger, hurt, and jealousy. After a while, we don't even consciously experience them. Second, we deny our feelings. If we are feeling hurt and our partner looks at our pained expression and asks us what we're feeling, we may reply, "Nothing." We may actually feel nothing because we have anesthetized our feelings. Third, we displace our feelings. Instead of recognizing that we are jealous, we may accuse our partner of being jealous; instead of feeling hurt, we may say our partner is hurt.

Becoming aware of ourselves requires us to become aware of our feelings. Perhaps the first step toward this self-awareness is realizing that feelings are simply emotional states—they are neither good nor bad in themselves. As feelings, however, they need to be *felt*, whether they are warm or cold, pleasurable or painful. They do not necessarily need to be acted out or expressed. It is the acting out that holds the potential for problems or hurt.

Feelings as Guides for Actions

Feelings are valuable guides for actions. If we feel irritated at a partner, the irritation is a signal that something is wrong and we can work toward change. But if we suppress or deny our feeling, perhaps because we are fearful of conflict, we do not have the impetus for change. The cause remains and the irritation increases until it is

Speech is civilization itself.... It is silence which isolates.

Thomas Mann (1875–1955)

Nothing is so much to be feared as fear.

Henry David Thoreau

Words are given to man to enable him to conceal his true feelings.

Voltaire (1694–1778)

blown out of proportion; a minor annoyance becomes a major source of anger. If we are bothered by our partner leaving dirty dishes scattered around the house, we can say so and he or she has the option to change. But if we suppress or deny our irritation, the piles of dirty dishes may grow to towering heights, green mold may invade the house, and we may feel alienated from our partner without giving him or her the opportunity to change. Finally, when we become aware of our feelings, it may have grown to such intensity that we fly into a rage when we see one dirty plate, crash the dish to the floor, slam the door, and walk out.

Self-Disclosure

Through communication we reveal ourselves to others. This is called **self-disclosure.** We live much of our lives playing roles—as student, worker, husband, wife, son, or daughter. We live and act these roles conventionally. They do not necessarily reflect our deepest selves. If we pretend that we are only these roles and ignore our deepest selves, we have taken the path toward loneliness, isolation, and despair. We may reach a point at which we no longer know who we are. Almost 150 years ago Nathaniel Hawthorne cautioned, "No man, for any considerable period, can wear one face to himself, and another to the multitude, without finally getting bewildered as to which may be true." In the process of revealing ourselves to others, we discover who we are. In the process of our sharing, others share themselves with us. Self-disclosure is reciprocal.

She generally gave herself very good advice (though she seldom followed it).

Lewis Carroll

If we had no faults, we should not take so much pleasure in noting them in others.

François de La Rochefoucauld

If you don't risk anything, you risk even more.

Erica Jong

There is no greater lie than a truth misunderstood.

William James

A monk asked: "How does one get emancipated?" The master said: "Who has ever put you in bondage?"

D. T. Suzuki (1870–1966), Zen Flesh, Zen Bones

KEEPING CLOSED. If I do not disclose myself, I receive no feedback from my partner. Our relationship remains closed. We are isolated, untouched by each other. If I do not disclose myself, neither will my partner. My silence obliges him or her to remain silent. If I do not disclose myself, I will remain ignorant of myself, for my partner will not speak to me truthfully. My partner will tell me only what he or she believes I want to hear. But my partner does not truly know who I am, because I am afraid to reveal myself.

Men are less likely than women to disclose intimate things about themselves. Having been taught to be strong, they are more reluctant to express feelings of weakness or tenderness. Women find it easier to disclose their feelings, perhaps because from earliest childhood they are encouraged to express them (see Notarius and Johnson, 1982). These differences can drive wedges between men and women. One sex does not understand the other. One man complained of his wife: "Yakketty-yakkers, that's what girls are. Well, I don't know; guys talk too. But, you know, there's a difference, isn't there? Guys talk about things and girls talk about feelings" (Rubin, 1976). The differences may plague a marriage until neither partner knows what the other wants; sometimes partners don't even know what they want for themselves. In one woman's words (quoted in Rubin, 1976):

I'm not sure what I want. I keep talking to him about communication, and he says, "Okay, so we're talking; now what do you want?" And I don't know what to say then, but I know it's not what I mean. I sometimes get worried because I think maybe I want too much. He's a good husband; he works hard; he takes care of me and the kids. He could go out and find another woman who would be very happy to have a man like that, and who wouldn't be all the time complaining at him because he doesn't feel things and get close.

What is missing is the intimacy that comes from self-disclosure. People live together, or are married, but they feel lonely. There is no contact. And the loneliest loneliness is to feel alone with someone with whom we want to feel close.

How Much Openness? Can too much openness and honesty be injurious to a relationship? How much should intimates reveal to each other? Some studies suggest that less marital satisfaction results if partners have too little or too much disclosure; a happy medium offers security, stability, and safety. But a review of studies on the relationship between communication and marital satisfaction finds that a linear model of communication is more closely related to marital satisfaction than the too-little/too-much curvilinear model (Boland and Follingstad, 1987). In the linear model of communication, the greater the self-disclosure, the greater the marital satisfaction, provided that the couple is highly committed to the relationship and willing to take the risks of high levels of intimacy. Two researchers who tried to test the two approaches empirically found evidence to support only the linear model (Jorgensen and Gaudy, 1980). They cautioned, nevertheless, that couples unskilled or not used to high levels of self-disclosure might need to understand its significance before embarking on such a highly charged undertaking. Furthermore, more recent studies suggest that high levels of negativity are related to marital distress (Noller and Fitzpatrick, 1991). It is not clear whether the negativity reflects the marital distress or causes it. Most likely, the two interact and compound each other's effects.

Giving Feedback

Self-disclosure is reciprocal. If we self-disclose, we expect our partner to self-disclose as well. As we self-disclose, we build trust; as we withhold self-disclosure, we erode trust. To withhold ourselves is to imply that we don't trust the other person, and if we don't, he or she will not trust us.

A critical element in communication is feedback. If someone self-discloses to us, we need to respond to his or her self-disclosure. This response is called **feedback.** The purpose of feedback is to provide constructive information to increase another's self-awareness of the consequences of his or her behavior toward you.

I hope you have not been leading a double life, pretending to be wicked and being really good all the time. That would be hypocrisy.

Oscar Wilde

A sound marriage is not based on complete frankness; it is based on sensible reticence.

Morris L. Ernst

To say what we think to our superiors would be inexpedient; to say what we think to our equals would be ill-mannered; to say what we think to our inferiors is unkind. Good manners occupy the terrain between fear and pity.

Quentin Crisp

Reprinted with special permission of North America Syndicate, Inc.

Excuses are always mixed with lies.

Arabic proverb

A half truth is a whole lie.

Yiddish proverb

It is a luxury to be understood.

Ralph Waldo Emerson (1803–1892)

If your partner discloses to you his or her doubts about your relationship, you can respond in a number of ways. Among these are remaining silent, venting anger, expressing indifference, or giving helpful feedback. Of these responses, feedback is the most constructive and the most likely to encourage change.

First, you can remain silent. Silence, however, is generally a negative response, perhaps as powerful as saying outright that you do not want your partner to self-disclose this type of information. Second, you can respond angrily, which may convey the message to your partner that self-disclosing will lead to arguments rather than understanding and possible change. Third, you can remain indifferent, responding neither negatively nor positively to your partner's self-disclosure. Fourth, you can acknowledge your partner's feelings as valid (rather than right or wrong) and disclose how you feel in response to his or her statement. This acknowledgment and response is constructive feedback. It may or may not remove your partner's doubts, but it opens up the possibility for change, whereas silence, anger, and indifference do not.

Some guidelines (developed by David Johnston for the Minnesota Peer Program) will help you engage in dialogue and feedback with your partner:

1. *Focus on "I" statements.* An "I" statement is a statement about your feelings: "I feel annoyed when you leave your dirty dishes on the living-room floor." "You" statements tell another person how *he* or *she* is, feels, or thinks: "You are such a slob. You're always leaving your dirty dishes on the living-room floor." "You" statements are often blaming or accusatory. Because "I" messages don't carry blame, the recipient is less likely to be defensive or resentful.

2. *Focus on behavior rather than on the person.* If you focus on a person's behavior rather than on the person, you are more likely to secure change. A person can change behaviors but not himself or herself. If you want your partner to wash his or her dirty dishes, say, "I would like you to wash your dirty dishes; it bothers me when I see them gathering mold on the living-room floor." This statement focuses on behavior that can be changed. If you say, "You are such a slob; you never clean up after yourself," then you are attacking the person, and he or she is likely to respond defensively. "I am not a slob. Talk about slobs, how about when you left your clothes lying in the bathroom for a week?"

3. *Focus feedback on observations rather than on inferences or judgments.* Focus your feedback on what you actually observe rather than what you think the behavior means. "There is a towering pile of your dishes in the living room" is an observation. "You don't really care about how I feel because you are always leaving your dirty dishes around the house" is an inference that a partner's dirty dishes indicate a lack of regard. The inference moves the discussion from the dishes to the partner's caring. The question "What kind of person would leave dirty dishes for me to clean up?" implies a judgment: only a morally depraved person would leave dirty dishes around.

4. *Focus feedback on observations based on a more-or-less continuum.* Behaviors fall on a continuum. Your partner doesn't always do a particular thing. When you say that he or she does something sometimes or even most of the time, you are actually measuring behavior. If you say that your partner always does something, you are distorting reality. For example, there were probably times (however rare) when your partner picked up the dirty dishes. "Last week I picked up your dirty dishes three times" is a measured statement. "I always pick up your dirty dishes" is an exaggeration that will probably provoke a hostile response.

5. *Focus feedback on sharing ideas or offering alternatives rather than giving advice. No one likes being told what to do.* Unsolicited advice often produces anger or resentment because advice implies that you know more about what a person needs to do than

the other person does. Advice implies a lack of freedom or respect. By sharing ideas and offering alternatives, however, you give the other person the freedom to decide based on his or her own perceptions and goals. "You need to put away your dishes immediately after you are done with them" is advice. "Having to step around your dirty dishes bothers me. What are the alternatives other than my watching my step? Maybe you could put them away after you finish eating, clean them up before I get home, or eat in the kitchen? What do you think?" is offering alternatives.

6. *Focus feedback according to its value for the recipient.* If your partner says something that upsets you, your initial response may be to lash back. A cathartic response may make you feel better for the time being, but it may not be useful for your partner. For example, your partner admits lying to you. You can respond with rage and accusations, or you can express your hurt and try to find out why he or she didn't tell you the truth.

7. *Focus feedback on the amount the recipient can process.* Don't overload your partner with your response. Your partner's disclosure may touch deep, pent-up feelings in you, but he or she may not be able to comprehend all that you say. If you respond to your partner's revelation of doubts with a listing of all the doubts you have ever experienced about yourself, your relationship, and relationships in general, you may overwhelm your partner.

8. *Focus feedback at the appropriate time and place.* When you discuss anything of importance, choose an appropriate time and place. Choose a time when you are not likely to be interrupted. Turn the television off and take the phone off the hook. Also, choose a time that is relatively stress free. Talking about something of great importance just before an exam or a business meeting is likely to sabotage any attempt at communication. Finally, choose a place that will provide privacy; don't start an important conversation if you are worried about people overhearing or interrupting you. A dormitory lounge during the soaps, Grand Central Station, a kitchen filled with kids, or a car full of friends are inappropriate places.

Mutual Affirmation

Good communication in an intimate relationship includes three elements: (1) mutual acceptance, (2) liking each other, and (3) expressing liking in both words and actions. Mutual acceptance consists of people accepting each other as they are, not as they would like each other to be. People are who they are, and they are not likely to change in fundamental ways without a tremendous amount of effort, as well as a considerable passage of time. The belief that an insensitive partner will somehow magically become sensitive after marriage, for example, is an invitation to disappointment and divorce.

If you accept people as they are, you can like them for their unique qualities. Liking someone is somewhat different from being romantically in love. It is not rare for people to dislike those whom they romantically love.

Mutual affirmation entails people telling their partners that they like them for who they are, that they appreciate the little things as well as the big things that they do. Think about how often you say to your partner, your parents, or your children, "I like you," or, "I love you," "I appreciate your doing the dishes," "I like your smile." Affirmations are often most frequent during dating or the early stages of marriage or living together. As you get to know a person better, you may begin noting things that annoy you or are different from you. Acceptance turns into negation and criticism: "You're selfish," "Why don't you clean up after yourself," "Stop bugging me," "You talk too much."

If you have a lot of negatives in your interactions, don't feel too bad. Many of our negations are habitual. When we were children, our parents were probably often

Consider what life would be like if everyone could lie perfectly or if no one could lie at all. . . . If we could never know how someone really felt, and if we knew that we couldn't know, life would be more tenuous. Certain in the knowledge that every show of emotion might be a mere display put on to please, manipulate, or mislead, individuals would be more adrift, attachments less firm. And if we could never lie, if a smile was reliable, never absent when pleasure was felt, and never present without pleasure, life would be rougher than it is, many relationships harder to maintain. Politeness, attempts to smooth matters over, to conceal feelings one wished one didn't feel–all that would be gone. There would be no way not to be known, no opportunity to sulk or lick one's wounds except alone.

Paul Eckman, Telling Lies

The facts are always friendly. Every bit of evidence one can acquire, in any area, leads one that much closer to what is true.

Carl Rodgers, On Becoming Partners

APOLOGIZE, v.i. To lay the foundation for a future offense.

Ambrose Bierce, The Devil's Dictionary

It happens often enough that the lie begun in self-defense slips into self-deception.

Jean-Paul Sartre

Argument is the worst sort of conversation.

Jonathan Swift (1667–1745)

The only way to speak the truth is to speak lovingly.

Henry David Thoreau

Kindness in words creates confidence. Kindness in thinking creates profoundness. Kindness in giving creates love.

Lao-Tze

Pass no judgement, and you will not be judged; do not condemn, and you will not be condemned; acquit, and you will be acquitted; give and gifts will be given to you . . . for whatever measure you deal out to others will be dealt to you in return.

Luke 6:37–38

All intimacies are based on differences.

Henry James (1843–1910)

A number of porcupines huddled together for warmth on a cold day in winter; but because they began to prick each other with their quills, they were obliged to disperse. However, the cold drove them together again, when just the same thing happened. At last, after many turns of huddling and dispersing, they discovered that they would be best off by remaining at a little distance from each other.

Arthur Schoepenhauer

The greatest thing in family life is to take a hint when a hint is intended—and not to take a hint when a hint isn't intended.

Robert Frost (1874–1963)

We are always willing to fancy ourselves within a little of happiness and when, with repeated efforts we cannot reach it, persuade ourselves that it is intercepted by an ill-paired mate since, if we could find any other obstacle, it would be our own fault that it was not removed.

Samuel Johnson

negating: "Don't leave the door open," "Don't leave your clothes piled in the bathroom," "Don't chew with your mouth open." How often did they affirm? Once you become aware that negations are often automatic, you can change them. Because negative communication is a learned behavior, you can unlearn it. One way is to consciously make the decision to affirm what you like; too often we take the good for granted and feel compelled to point out only the bad.

❑ CONFLICT AND INTIMACY: TYPES OF CONFLICT

Conflict between people who love each other seems to be a mystery. The coexistence of conflict and love has puzzled human beings for centuries. An ancient Sanskrit poem reflected this dichotomy:

In the old days we both agreed
That I was you and you were me.
But now what has happened
That makes you, you
And me, me?

We expect love to unify us, but sometimes it doesn't. Two people do not become one when they love each other, although at first they may have this feeling. Their love may not be an illusion, but their sense of ultimate oneness is. In reality, they retain their individual identities, needs, wants, and pasts while loving each other—and it is a paradox that the more intimate two people become, the more likely they may be to experience conflict. But it is not conflict itself that is dangerous to intimate relationships; it is the manner in which the conflict is handled. Conflict is natural in intimate relationships. If this is understood, the meaning of conflict changes, and it will not necessarily represent a crisis in the relationship. David and Vera Mace (1979), prominent marriage counselors, observed that on the day of marriage, people have three kinds of raw material with which to work:

First, there are the things you have in common, the things you both like. Second are the things in which you are different, but the differences are complementary. . . . Third, unfortunately, are the differences between us which are not at all complementary, and cause us to meet head-on with a big bang. In every relationship between two people, there is a great deal of those kinds of differences. So when we move closer together to each other, those differences become disagreements.

The presence of conflict within a marriage or family does not necessarily indicate that love is going or gone. It may mean just the opposite.

Basic versus Nonbasic Conflicts

If conflict unites marriages, what tears marriages apart? Paradoxically, it is also conflict. Two types of conflict—basic and nonbasic—affect the stability of a relationship. Basic conflicts challenge the fundamental assumptions or rules of a relationship, whereas nonbasic conflicts do not.

BASIC CONFLICTS. Basic conflicts revolve around carrying out marital roles and the functions of marriage and the family, such as providing companionship, working, and rearing children. It is assumed, for example, that a husband and wife will have sexual relations with each other. But if one partner converts to a religious sect that forbids sexual interaction, a basic conflict is likely to occur because the other spouse considers sexual interaction part of the marital premise. No room for compromise exists in such a matter. If one partner cannot convince the other to change his or her belief, the conflict is likely to destroy the relationship. Similarly, despite recent changes in family roles, it is still expected that the man will work to provide for the family. If he decides to quit work altogether and not function as a provider in any way, he is challenging a basic assumption of marriage. His partner is likely to feel that his behavior is unfair. Conflict ensues. If he does not return to work, she is likely to leave him.

NONBASIC CONFLICTS. Nonbasic conflicts do not strike at the heart of a relationship. The husband wants to change jobs and move to a different city, but the wife may not want to move. This may be a major conflict, but it is not a basic one. The husband is not unilaterally rejecting his role as a provider. If a couple disagree about the frequency of sex, the conflict is serious but not basic, because both agree on the desirability of sex in the relationship. In both of these cases, resolution is possible.

Situational versus Personality Conflicts

Some conflicts occur because of a situation and others occur because of the personality of one (or both) of the partners.

SITUATIONAL CONFLICTS. Situational conflicts occur when at least one partner needs to make changes in a relationship. Such conflicts are also known as *realistic* conflicts. They are based on specific demands, like putting the cap on the toothpaste, dividing housework fifty-fifty, sharing child-care responsibilities, and so on. Conflict arises when one person tries to change the situation about the toothpaste cap, housework, or child care.

PERSONALITY CONFLICTS. Personality conflicts arise not because of situations that need to be changed but because of personality, such as needs to vent aggression or to dominate. Such conflicts are essentially unrealistic. They are not directed toward making changes in the relationship but simply toward releasing pent-up tensions. Often this takes the form of violence: slapping, hitting, pushing, and shoving. Whereas situational conflicts can be resolved through compromise, bargaining, or mediation, personality conflicts often require a therapeutic approach. Such personality conflicts may pit a compulsive-type individual against a free spirit or a fastidious personality against a sloppy one.

Power Conflicts

The politics of family life—who has the power, who makes the decisions, who does what—can be every bit as complex and explosive as politics at the national level. **Power** is the ability or potential ability to influence another person or group (Scanzoni, 1979). Most of the time we are not aware of the power aspects of our relationships. One reason for this is that we tend to believe that intimate relationships are based on love alone. Another reason is that the exercise of power is often subtle. When we think of power, we tend to think of coercion or force; as we shall see, marital power takes many forms. A final reason is that power is not constantly exercised. It comes into play only when an issue is important to both people and they have conflicting goals.

There is perhaps no phenomenon which contains so much destructive feeling as moral indignation, which permits envy or hate to be acted out under the guise of virtue.

Erich Fromm

Where he makes a jest, a problem lies. . . . Sometimes the jest brings the solution of the problem to light as well.

Sigmund Freud, Wit and Its Relation to the Unconscious

*Lady Astor: If you were my husband, Winston, I'd put poison in your tea.
Winston Churchill: If I were your husband, Nancy, I'd drink it.*

Deep-seated preferences cannot be argued about—you cannot argue a man into liking a glass of beer.

Oliver Wendell Holmes, Jr. (1841–1935)

Against all the evidence of his senses the man in love declares that he and his beloved are one, and is prepared to behave as if it were a fact.

Sigmund Freud

CHANGING SOURCES OF MARITAL POWER. Traditionally, husbands have held ultimate authority over their wives. In Christianity, the subordination of wives to their husbands has its basis in the New Testament. Paul (Colossians 3:18–19) states:

Wives, submit yourselves unto your husbands, as unto the Lord. For the husband is the head of the wife, even as Christ is the head of the Church: and he is the savior of the body. Therefore, as the Church is subject unto Christ, so let the wives be to their own husbands in everything.

Such teachings reflected the dominant themes of ancient Greece and Rome. Western society continued to support wifely subordination to husbands. English common law stated: "The husband and wife are as one and that one is the husband." A woman assumed her husband's identity, taking his last name on marriage and living in his house.

The courts have institutionalized these power relationships. The law, for example, supports the traditional division of labor in most states, making the husband legally responsible for supporting the family and the wife legally responsible for maintaining the house and rearing the children. She is legally required to follow her husband if he moves; if she does not, she is considered to have deserted him. But if she moves and her husband refuses to move with her, she is also considered to have deserted him (Weitzman, 1981).

Absolute control of the family by the husband has substantially declined since the 1920s, however, and an egalitarian standard for sharing power in families has taken much of its place (Sennett, 1980). The wife who works has especially gained more power in the family. She has greater influence in deciding family size and how money is to be spent. Her status has risen to that of "junior partner"; relatively few women achieve absolute equality with their husbands in power, resources, and authority (Scanzoni, 1979). With the commitment to egalitarian relationships, however, men exercise their power differently and more subtly. Tension may exist between ideology and reality. Sociologist William Goode (1963) observed, "One partial resolution of the . . . tension is to be found in the frequent assertion from families of professional men that they should not make demands which would interfere with his work: he takes preference as a professional, not as a family head or as a male."

The formal and legal structure of marriage makes the male dominant, but the reality of marriage may be quite different. Sociologist Jessie Bernard (1982) made an important distinction between authority and power in marriage. Authority is based in law, but power is based in personality. A strong, dominant woman is likely to exercise power over a weak, passive man simply by the force of her personality and temperament. Bernard wrote:

Power, or the ability to coerce or to veto, is widely distributed in both sexes, among women as well as among men. And whatever the theoretical or conceptual picture may have been, the actual day-to-day relationships between husbands and wives have been determined by the men and women themselves. . . . Thus, keeping women in their place has been a universal problem, in spite of the fact that almost without exception institutional patterns give men positions of authority over them.

If we want to see how power really works in marriage, we must look beneath the stereotypes. Women have considerable power in marriage, although they often feel that they have less than they actually do. They may fail to recognize their power because cultural norms theoretically put power in the hands of their husbands, and the women look at norms rather than their own behavior. A woman may decide to work, even against her husband's wishes, and she may determine how to discipline the children. Yet she may feel that her husband holds the power in the relationship

For neither man nor angel can discern Hypocrisy, the only evil that walks Invisible....

John Milton (1608–1674)

Some people are proud of their handful of justice and commit outrages against all things for its sake, till the world is drowned in their injustice.

Fredrich Nietzsche

*When my love swears that she is made of truth
I do believe her, though I know she lies.*

William Shakespeare, Sonnet CXXXVIII

Power corrupts and absolute power corrupts absolutely.

Lord Acton (1834–1902)

Habit is the enemy of truth. Lies deny truth but habit ignores it.

Floyd Zimmerman

because he is supposed to be dominant. Similarly, husbands often believe that they have more power in a relationship than they actually do, because they see only traditional norms and expectations.

BASES OF MARITAL POWER.   Power is not a simple phenomenon. It is generally agreed among researchers that family power is a dynamic, multidimensional process (Szinovacz, 1987). Generally speaking, no single individual is always the most powerful person in every aspect of the family. Nor is power necessarily always based on gender, age, or relationship. Power often shifts from person to person, depending on the issue. According to J. P. French and Bertram Raven (1959), there are six bases of marital power: (1) *coercive power*, based on the fear that the partner will punish the other; (2) *reward power*, based on the belief that the other person will do something in return for agreement; (3) *expert power*, based on the belief that the other has greater knowledge; (4) *legitimate power*, based on acceptance of roles giving the other person the right to demand compliance; (5) *referent power*, based on identifying with the partner and receiving satisfaction by acting similarly; and (6) *informational power*, based on the partner's persuasive explanation.

Raven and his colleagues (1975) studied 746 men and women in Los Angeles to see how common these various sources of power were. Coercion and reward were not particularly significant. Wives described the source of their husbands' power as expert (37 percent), referent (36 percent), and legitimate (18 percent). Husbands described the source of their partners' power as referent (48 percent), legitimate (22 percent), and expert (21 percent). Women tended to attribute the source of their husbands' power to expertness and identification. In contrast, men tended to attribute referent power to their wives.

The basis of power varied according to the domain. Decisions to visit a friend or relative tended to be based on legitimate (43 percent) or referent (27 percent) power. Cleaning or repairing something in the house tended to be based on legitimate (35 percent) or expert (28 percent) power. Significantly, the basis of a spouse's power also varied according to marital satisfaction. Among highly satisfied couples, 49 percent attributed their spouses' power to referent power and 2 percent to coercion. Among those couples who were not satisfied at all, only 21 percent said their spouses' power was referent, whereas 42 percent believed their spouses' power lay in coercion (see also Bell et al., 1981).

RELATIVE LOVE AND NEED THEORY.   Another way of looking at the sources of marital power is through the **relative love and need theory,** which explains power in terms of the individual's involvement and needs in the relationship. Each partner brings certain resources, feelings, and needs to a relationship. Each may be seen as exchanging love, companionship, money, help, and status with the other. What each gives and receives, however, may not be equal. One partner may be gaining more from the relationship than the other. The person gaining the most from the relationship is the one who is most dependent. Constantina Safilios-Rothschild (1970) observed:

The relative degree to which the one spouse loves and needs the other may be the most crucial variable in explaining the total power structure. The spouse who has relatively less feeling for the other may be the one in the best position to control and manipulate all the 'resources' that he has in his command in order to effectively influence the outcome of decisions.

Love is a major power resource in a relationship. Those who love equally are likely to share power equally (Safilios-Rothschild, 1976). Such couples are likely to make decisions according to referent, expert, and legitimate power.

PRINCIPLE OF LEAST INTEREST. Akin to relative love and need as a way of looking at power is the **principle of least interest.** Sociologist Willard Waller (Waller and Hill, 1951) coined this term to describe the curious (and often unpleasant) situation in which the partner with the least interest in continuing a relationship has the most power in it. At its most extreme form, it is the stuff of melodrama. "I will do anything you want, Charles," Laura says pleadingly, throwing herself at his feet. "Just don't leave me." "Anything, Laura?" he replies with a leer. "Then give me the deed to your mother's house." Quarreling couples may unconsciously use the principle of least interest to their advantage. The less-involved partner may threaten to leave as leverage in an argument: "All right, if you don't do it my way, I'm going." The threat may be extremely powerful in coercing a dependent partner, while it may have little effect if it comes *from* the dependent partner, because he or she has too much to lose to be persuasive. The less-involved partner can easily call the bluff.

RETHINKING FAMILY POWER. Even though women have considerable power in marriages and families, it would be a serious mistake to overlook the inequalities between husbands and wives. As feminist scholars have pointed out, major aspects of contemporary marriage, such as the continued female responsibility for housework, inequities in sexual gratification (sex is often over when the male has *his* orgasm), the extent of violence against wives, and the sexual exploitation of children, point to important areas where women are clearly subordinate to men.

Feminist scholars suggest several areas that require further consideration (Szinovacz, 1987). First, they believe that too much emphasis has been placed on the marital relationship as the unit of analysis. Instead, they believe that researchers should explore the influence of the larger society on power in marriage—specifically, the relationship between the social structure and women's position in marriage. Researchers could examine, for example, the relationship of women's socioeconomic disadvantages, such as lower pay and fewer economic opportunities than men, to female power in marriage.

Second, these scholars argue that many of the decisions that researchers study are trivial or insignificant in measuring "real" family power. Researchers cannot conclude that marriages are becoming more egalitarian on the basis of joint-decision making about such things as where a couple goes for vacation, whether to buy a new car or appliance, or which movie to see. The critical decisions that measure power are such issues as how housework is to be divided, who stays home with the children, and whose job or career takes precedence.

Some scholars suggest we shift the focus from marital power to family power. Researcher Marion Kranichfeld (1987) calls for a rethinking of power in a family context. Even if women's marital power may not be equal to men's, a different picture of women in families may emerge if we examine power within the entire family structure, including power in relation to children. The family power literature has traditionally focused on marriage and marital decision making. Kranichfeld, however, feels that such a focus narrows our perception of women's power. Marriage is not family, she argues, and it is in the larger family matrix that women exert considerable power. Their power may not be the same as male power, which tends to be primarily economic, political, or religious. But if power is defined as the ability to intentionally change the behavior of others, "women in fact have a great deal of power, of a very fundamental and pervasive nature so pervasive, in fact, that it is easily overlooked," according to Kranichfeld (1987). She further observes:

Women's power is rooted in their role as nurturers and kinkeepers, and flows out of their capacity to support and direct the growth of others around them through their life course.

For a marriage to be peaceful the husband should be deaf and the wife blind.

Spanish proverb

The awareness of sameness is friendship; the awareness of difference is love.

W. H. Auden

When a thing is funny, search it for a hidden truth.

George Bernard Shaw

"When I want to look at the world I see it the way you do. Then when I want to see it I look at the way I know and I perceive in a different way."
"Do things look consistently the same every time you see them?"
"Things don't change. You change your way of looking, that's all."

Carlos Castañeda, A Separate Reality

Marriage is one long conversation, chequered by disputes.

Robert Louis Stevenson

Women's power may have low visibility from a nonfamily perspective, but women are the lynchpins of family cohesion and socialization.

From a family perspective, women exercise power through much of their adult lives. As nurturers, they bear and rear children, instruct them in values, and help form their personalities. In addition they may care for their own aging and dependent parents. As kinkeepers, they maintain family cohesion by planning get-togethers with the extended family and writing or calling faraway relatives.

POWER VERSUS INTIMACY. The problem with power imbalances or the blatant use of power is the negative effect on intimacy. As Ronald Sampson (1966) observed in his study of the psychology of power, "To the extent that power is the prevailing force in a relationship—whether between husband and wife or parent and child, between friends or between colleagues—to that extent love is diminished." If partners are not equal, self-disclosure may be inhibited, especially if the powerful person believes his or her power will be lessened by sharing feelings (Glazer-Malbin, 1975). Genuine intimacy appears to require equality in power relationships. Decision making in the happiest marriages seems to be based not on coercion or tit for tat but on caring, mutuality, and respect for the other person. Women who feel vulnerable to their mates may withhold feelings or pretend to feel what they do not. Unequal power in marriage may encourage power politics. Each partner may struggle with the other to keep or gain power.

It is not easy to change unequal power relationships after they become embedded in the overall structure of a relationship, yet they can be changed. Talking, understanding, and negotiating are the best approaches. Still, in attempting changes, a person may risk estrangement or the breakup of a relationship. He or she must weigh the possible gains against the possible losses in deciding whether change is worth the risk.

◻ CONFLICT RESOLUTION

Dealing with Anger

Differences can lead to anger, and anger transforms differences into fights, creating tension, division, distrust, and fear. Most people have learned to handle anger by either venting or suppressing it. David and Vera Mace (1980) suggest that most couples go though a love-anger cycle. When a couple comes close to each other, they may experience conflict and they recoil in horror, angry at each other because just at the moment they were feeling close, their intimacy was destroyed. Each backs off; gradually they move closer again until another fight erupts, driving them away from each other. After a while, each learns to make a compromise between closeness and distance to avoid conflict. They learn what they can reveal about themselves and what they cannot. Because closeness brings conflict, they stop being close, and their relationship becomes empty and meaningless.

Another way of dealing with anger is suppressing it. Suppressed anger is dangerous because it is always there, simmering beneath the surface. Ultimately, it leads to resentment, that brooding, low-level hostility that poisons both the individual and the relationship.

Anger can be dealt with in a third way: recognizing it as a symptom of something that needs to be changed. If we see anger as a symptom, we realize that what is important is not venting or suppressing the anger but finding its source and eliminating it. David and Vera Mace (1980) wrote:

We are all inclined to judge ourselves by our ideals; others by their acts.

Harold Nicholson

It is possible for a man to wholly disappear and be merged in his manners.

Henry David Thoreau

Love can be angry . . . with a kind of anger in which there is no gall, like the dove's and not the raven's.

Augustine of Hippo

Anger causes a man to be far from the truth.

Hasidic saying

Epitaph on His Wife

Here lies my wife; here let her lie! Now she's at rest. And so am I.

John Dryden (1631–1700)

When your disagreements become conflict, the only thing to do is to take anger out of it, because when you are angry you cannot resolve a conflict. You cannot really hear the other person because you are just waiting to fire your shot. You cannot be understanding; you cannot be empathetic when you are angry. So you have to take the anger out, and then when you have taken the anger out, you are back again with a disagreement. The disagreement is still there, and it can cause another disagreement and more anger unless you clear it up. The way to take the anger out of disagreements is through negotiation.

Conflict Resolution and Marital Satisfaction

The way in which a couple deals with conflict resolution both reflects and perhaps contributes to their marital happiness (Boland and Follingstad, 1987). Happy couples tend to act in positive ways to resolve conflicts, such as changing behaviors (putting the cap on the toothpaste rather than denying responsibility) and presenting reasonable alternatives (purchasing toothpaste in a dispenser). Unhappy or distressed couples, in contrast, use more negative strategies in attempting to resolve conflicts (if the cap off the toothpaste bothers you, then *you* put it on). A study of happily and unhappily married couples found distinctive communication traits as these couples tried to resolve their conflicts (Ting-Toomey, 1983). The communication behaviors of happily married couples displayed the following traits:

❑ *Summarizing*. Each person summarized what the other said. "Let me see if I can repeat the different points you were making."
❑ *Paraphrasing*. Each put what the other said into his or her own words. "What you are saying is that you feel badly when I don't acknowledge your feelings."
❑ *Validation*. Each affirmed the other's feelings. "I can understand how you feel."
❑ *Clarification*. Each asked for further information to make sure that he or she understood what the other was saying. "Can you explain what you mean a little bit more to make sure that I understand you?"

In contrast, unhappily married couples displayed the following reciprocal patterns:

❑ *Confrontation*. Each member of the couple confronted. "You're wrong!" "Not me, buddy. It's you who's wrong."
❑ *Confrontation and defensiveness*. One confronted while the other defended himself or herself. "You're wrong!" "I only did what I was supposed to do."
❑ *Complaining and defensiveness*. One complained while the other was defensive. "I work so hard each day to come home to this!" "This is the best I can do with no help."

Fighting about Sex and Money

Even if, as the Russian writer Leo Tolstoy suggested, every unhappy family is unhappy in its own way, marital conflicts still tend to center around certain issues, especially communication, children, sex, money, personality differences, how to spend leisure, in-laws, infidelity, housekeeping, and physical abuse. In this section, we focus on two areas: sex and money. Then we discuss general ways of resolving conflicts.

FIGHTING ABOUT SEX. Fighting and sex can be intertwined in several different ways (Strong and DeVault, 1994 [in press]). A couple can have a specific disagreement about sex that leads to a fight. One person wants to have sexual intercourse and the

The family is a court of justice which never shuts down for day or night.

Malcolm de Chazal

If you are afraid of loneliness, don't marry.

Anton Chekhov (1860–1904)

Ninety-nine lies may save you, but the hundredth will give you away.

West African proverb

If I speak in the tongues of men and of angels, but have not love, I am as a noisy gong or a clanging cymbal.

I Corinthians 13:1

other does not, so they fight. A couple can have an indirect fight about sex. The woman does not have an orgasm, and after intercourse her partner rolls over and starts to snore. She lies in bed feeling angry and frustrated. In the morning she begins to fight with her partner because he never does his share of the housework. The housework issues obscures why she is really angry. Sex can also be used as a scapegoat for nonsexual problems. A man is angry that his wife calls him a lousy provider. He takes it out on her sexually by calling her a lousy lover. They fight about their lovemaking rather than the issue of his provider role. A couple can fight about the wrong sexual issue. A woman may berate her partner for being too quick in sex, but what she is really frustrated about is that he is not interested in oral sex with her. She, however, feels ambivalent about oral sex ("Maybe I smell bad"), so she cannot confront her partner with the real issue. Finally, a fight can be a cover-up. If a man feels sexually inadequate and does not want to have sex as often as his partner, he may pick a fight and make his partner so angry that the last thing she would want to do is to have sex with him.

In power struggles, sexuality can be used as a weapon, but this is generally a destructive tactic (Szinovacz, 1987). A classic strategy for the weaker person in a relationship is to withhold something that the more powerful one wants. In male/female struggles, this is often sex. By withholding sex, a woman gains a certain degree of power (Kaplan, 1979). Men also use sex in its most violent form: they use rape (including date rape and marital rape) to overpower and subordinate women. In rape, aggressive motivations displace sexual ones.

It is hard to tell during a fight if there are deeper causes than the one about which a couple is currently fighting. Are you and your partner fighting because you want sex now and your partner doesn't? Or are there deeper reasons involving power, control, fear, or inadequacy? If you repeatedly fight about sexual issues without getting anywhere, the ostensible cause may not be the real one. If fighting does not clear the air and make intimacy possible again, you should look for other reasons for the fights. It may be useful to talk with your partner about why the fights do not seem to accomplish anything. Step back and look at the circumstances of the fight, what patterns occur, and how each of you feels before, during, and after a fight.

MONEY CONFLICTS. An old Yiddish proverb addresses the problem of managing money quite well: "Husband and wife are of the same flesh but they have different purses." Money is a major source of marital conflict. Intimates differ about spending money probably as much as or more than any other single issue.

WHY PEOPLE FIGHT ABOUT MONEY. Couples disagree or fight over money for a number of reasons. One of the most important reasons is power. Earning wages has traditionally given men power in families. A woman's work in the home has not been rewarded by wages. As a result, full-time homemakers have been placed in the position of having to depend on their husbands for money. In such an arrangement, if there are disagreements, the woman is at a disadvantage. If she is deferred to, the old cliché, "I make the money but she spends it," has a bitter ring to it. As women increasingly participate in the work force, however, power relations within families are shifting. Studies indicate that women's influence in financial and other decisions increases if they are employed outside the home.

Another major source of conflict is allocation of the family's income. Not only does this involve decisions about who makes the decision, but it also includes setting priorities. Is it more important to pay a past-due bill or to buy a new television set to replace the broken one? Is a dishwasher a necessity or a luxury? Should money

---

Keep thy eyes wide open before marriage, and half shut afterwards.

Benjamin Franklin (1706–1790), Poor Richard's Almanac

Those who warp the truth must inevitably be warped and corrupted themselves.

Arthur Miller

Nothing is so firmly believed as that which is least known.

Francis Jeffrey (1773–1850)

It is almost as important to know what is not serious as to know what is.

John Kenneth Galbraith

An eye for an eye makes the whole world blind.

Mohandas K. Gandhi (1869–1948)

In love it is enough to please each other by loveable qualities and attractions; but to be happy in marriage it is necessary to love each other's faults, or at least to adjust to them.

Nicholas Chamfort (1740–1794)

be put aside for long-range goals, or should immediate needs (perhaps those your partner calls "whims") be satisfied? Setting financial priorities plays on each person's values and temperament; it is affected by basic aspects of an individual's personality. A miser probably cannot be happily married to a spendthrift. Yet we know so little of our partner's attitudes toward money before marriage that a miser might very well marry a spendthrift.

Dating relationships are a poor indicator of how a couple will deal with money matters in marriage. Dating has clearly defined rules about money: either the man pays, both pay separately, or each pays alternatively. In dating situations, each partner is financially independent of the other. Money is not pooled as it usually is in marriage, and power issues do not necessarily enter spending decisions, since each person has his or her own money. Differences can be smoothed out fairly easily. Both individuals are financially independent before marriage but financially interdependent after marriage. Even cohabitation may not be an accurate guide to how a couple would deal with money in marriage as cohabitors generally do not pool all (or even part) of their income. It is the working out of financial interdependence in marriage that is often so difficult.

Talking about Money. Talking about money matters is difficult. People are very secretive about money. It is considered poor taste to ask people how much money they make. Children often do not know how much money is earned in their family; sometimes spouses don't know either. One woman recently remarked that it is easier to talk with a partner about sexual issues than money matters: "Money is the last taboo," she said. But, as with sex, our society is obsessed with money.

We find it difficult to talk about money for several reasons. First of all, we don't want to appear to be unromantic or selfish. If a couple is about to marry, a discussion of attitudes toward money may lead to disagreements, shattering the illusion of unity or selflessness. Second, gender roles make it difficult for women to express their feelings about money, since they are traditionally supposed to defer to men in financial matters. Third, because men tend to make more money than women, women feel their right to disagree about financial matters is limited. This is especially true if the woman is a homemaker and does not make a financial contribution, devaluing her child care and housework contributions.

Resolving Conflicts

There are a number of ways to end conflicts. You can give in, but unless you believe that the conflict ended fairly, you are likely to feel resentful. You can try to impose your will through the use of power, force, or the threat of force. But using power to end conflict leaves your partner with the bitter taste of injustice. Finally, you can end the conflict through negotiation. In negotiations, both partners sit down and work out their differences until they can come to a mutually acceptable agreement.

Conflicts can be solved through negotiation in three major ways: (1) agreement as a gift, (2) bargaining, and (3) coexistence.

Agreement as a Gift. If you and your partner disagree on an issue, you can freely agree with your partner as a gift. If you want to go to the Caribbean for a vacation and your partner wants to go backpacking in Alaska, you can freely agree to go to Alaska. An agreement as a gift is different from giving in. When you give in, you do something you don't want to do. When you agree without coercion or threats, the agreement is a gift of love. As in all exchanges of gifts, there will be reciprocation.

The mind is its own place, and in itself can make a heaven of Hell, a hell of Heaven.

John Milton

. . . if differences that lie beyond money cannot be discussed then money is a likely battleground.

Paul Bohannan

*Be to her virtues very kind,
Be to her faults a little blind.*

Matthew Prior (1664–1721)

Always forgive your enemies—nothing annoys them so much.

Oscar Wilde

Without forgiveness life is governed by . . . an endless cycle of resentment and retaliation.

Robert Assagioli

Your partner will be more likely to give you a gift of agreement. This gift of agreement is based on referent power, discussed earlier.

BARGAINING. Bargaining means making compromises. But bargaining in relationships is different from bargaining in the marketplace or in politics. In relationships you don't want to get the best deal for yourself but the most equitable deal for both of you. At all points during the bargaining process, you need to keep in mind what is best for the relationship as well as for yourself and trust your partner to do the same. In a marriage, both partners need to win. The purpose of conflict in a marriage is to solidify the relationship, not make one partner the winner and the other the loser. To achieve your end by exercising coercive power or withholding love, affection, or sex is a destructive form of bargaining. If you get what you want, how will that affect your partner and the relationship? Will your partner feel you are being unfair and become resentful? A solution has to be fair to both, or it won't enhance the relationship.

COEXISTENCE. Sometimes differences can't be resolved but they can be lived with. If a relationship is sound, differences can be absorbed without undermining the basic ties. All too often we regard a difference as a threat rather than as the unique expression of two personalities. Rather than being driven mad by the cap left off the toothpaste, perhaps we can learn to live with it.

 SUMMARY

❐ Research indicates that happily married couples (1) are willing to engage in conflict in nondestructive ways, (2) have less frequent conflict and spend less time in conflict, (3) disclose private thoughts and feelings to partners, (4) express equal levels of affective disclosure, (5) spend more time together, and (6) accurately encode and decode messages.

❐ There are gender differences in marital communication. Wives send clearer messages; husbands tend to give neutral messages whereas wives tend to give more positive or negative messages; and wives tend to set the emotional tone and escalate arguments more than husbands.

❐ Communication includes both *verbal* and *nonverbal communication.* The functions of nonverbal communication are to convey interpersonal attitudes, express emotion, and handle the ongoing interaction. For communication to be unambiguous, verbal and nonverbal messages must agree. Silence can be a particularly destructive form of nonverbal communication.

❐ Barriers to communication are the traditional male gender role (because it discourages the expression of emotion), personal reasons such as feelings of inadequacy, and the fear of conflict.

❐ To express yourself, you need to be aware of your own feelings. We prevent *self-awareness* through *suppressing, denial,* and *displacement.* A first step toward self-awareness is realizing that our feelings are neither good nor bad but simply emotional states.

❐ *Self-disclosure* is the revelation of yourself to another. Without self-disclosure, a relationship remains closed. Men are less likely to self-disclose than women.

❐ According to some researchers, both low and high levels of self-disclosure are related to low marital satisfaction (curvilinear model). Other researchers maintain that a high level of self-disclosure is related to a high level of marital satisfaction, although it entails greater risks (linear model).

❐ *Feedback* is a constructive response to another's self-disclosure. Giving constructive feedback includes (1) focusing on "I" statements, (2) focusing on behavior rather than the person, (3) focusing feedback on observations rather than on inferences or judgments, (4) focusing feedback on the observed incidence of behavior, (5) focusing feedback on sharing ideas or offering alternatives rather than giving advice, (6) focusing feedback according to its value to the recipient, (7) focusing feedback on the amount the recipient can process, and (8) focusing feedback at an appropriate time and place.

❐ *Mutual affirmation* includes mutual acceptance, mutual liking, and expressing liking in words and actions.

❐ Conflict is natural in intimate relationships. Types of conflict include *basic* versus *nonbasic* conflicts and *situational* versus *personality* conflicts. Basic conflicts may threaten the foundation of a marriage because they challenge fundamental roles; nonbasic conflicts do not threaten basic assumptions and may be negotiable. Situational conflicts are realistic conflicts based on specific issues; personality conflicts are unrealistic conflicts based on the need of the partner or partners to release pent-up feelings or on their fundamental personality differences.

❏ *Power* is the ability or potential ability to influence another person or group. Traditionally, legal as well as de facto power rested in the hands of the husband. Recently, wives have been gaining more actual power in relationships, although the power distribution still remains unequal.

❏ The six bases of marital power are c*oercive, reward, expert, legitimate, referent,* and *informational.* These bases of power shift in different domains. Other theories of power include the *relative love and need theory,* and the *principle of least interest.*

❏ People usually handle anger in relationships by suppressing or venting it. Anger, however, makes negotiation difficult. When anger arises, it is useful to think of it as a signal that change is necessary.

❏ Major sources of conflict include sex and money. Conflicts about sex can be specific disagreements about sex, indirect disagreements in which a partner feels frustrated or angry and takes it out in sexual ways, arguments that are ostensibly about sex but that are really about nonsexual issues, or disagreements about the wrong sexual issue. Money conflicts occur because of power issues, disagreements over the allocation of resources, or differences in values.

❏ *Conflict resolution* may be achieved through negotiation in three ways: a*greement as a freely given gift, bargaining,* or *coexistence.*

CHAPTER 12

Family Violence and Sexual Abuse

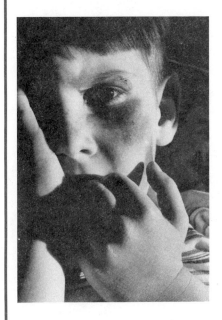

OUTLINE

When we want to read of the deeds that are done for love, whither do we turn? To the murder column?

George Bernard Shaw

I T IS AN UNHAPPY FACT that intimacy or relatedness in any form can increase the likelihood of violence or sexual abuse. Although this may seem odd at first, think about whom our society "permits" us to shove, hit, or kick. It is not a stranger, fellow student, co-worker, or employer, for if we assaulted any of them, we would run great risk of being arrested. It is with our intimates that we are allowed to do such things. Dating, loving, or being related seems to give us permission to be violent when we are angry. Those nearest and dearest are also those most likely to be slapped, punched, kicked, bitten, burned, stabbed, and shot (Gelles and Cornell, 1990; Gelles and Straus, 1988). For some boyfriends, husbands, or parents, intimacy seems to confer a right to be physically or sexually abusive. Only war zones and urban riot scenes are more dangerous places than families.

If this seems to be an exaggeration, consider the following points:

❑ Every thirty seconds, a woman is beaten by her boyfriend or husband.
❑ Thirty to 40 percent of college students in various studies report violence in dating relationships.
❑ At least a million American children are physically abused by their parents each year.
❑ Almost a million parents are physically assaulted by their adolescent or youthful children every year.
❑ As many as 27 percent of American women and 16 percent of men have been the victims of childhood sexual abuse, much of it in their own families.

Until the 1970s, Americans believed that when they locked their homes at night, they locked violence out; sadly, they also locked violence in (Walker, 1986). There is a note of hope, however. Due to the diligence of certain social scientists, physicians, mental health professionals, and concerned activists, family violence and sexual abuse are now matters of national concern. But even though these problems have been identified, there is much to be done toward reducing or eliminating them.

Researchers have not been in complete agreement about what constitutes violence. For the purposes of this book, we use Richard Gelles and Claire Pedrick Cornell's (1990) definition of **violence:** "an act carried out with the intention or perceived intention of causing physical pain or injury to another person." There are other prevalent forms of abuse, of course, such as neglect and emotional abuse, but the focus of this chapter is *physical* violence and sexual abuse. Violence may be seen as a continuum, with "normal" abuse (such as spanking) at one end and abusive violence (acts with high potential for causing injury) at the other extreme. We must look at the continuum as a whole to be concerned with "families who shoot and stab each other as well as those who spank and shove, . . . [as] one cannot be understood without considering the other" (Straus, Gelles and Steinmetz, 1980). (For a review of literature on domestic violence and sexual abuse of children, see Gelles and Conte, 1991.)

❑ THE MYTHOLOGY OF FAMILY VIOLENCE AND SEXUAL ABUSE

The understanding of family violence is often obscured by the different mythologies surrounding such violence. Here are twelve popular myths about family violence and sexual abuse in our society. Some of these myths may apply to some cases, but as generalizations they are not accurate. Many of these myths are accepted by the victims of family violence, as well as by the perpetrators themselves. As you look at

Despite fears to the contrary, it is not a stranger but a so-called loved one who is most likely to assault, rape, or murder us.

Russell and R. Emerson Dobash

the following myths, which ones do you believe (or have you believed)? What was the basis or source of your beliefs? If you no longer believe a particular myth, what changed your mind?

☐ Family violence is extremely rare.
☐ Family violence is restricted to families with low levels of education and low socioeconomic status.
☐ Most family violence is caused by alcohol or drug abuse.
☐ Violent spouses or parents have psychopathic personalities.
☐ Violent families are not loving families.
☐ Battered women cause their own battering because they are masochistic or crazy.
☐ A battered woman can always leave home.
☐ Most child sexual abuse is perpetrated by strangers.
☐ Sexual abuse in families is a fairly rare occurrence.
☐ Abused children will grow up to abuse their own children.
☐ The police give adequate protection to battered women.
☐ Most of society does not condone domestic violence.

These myths function to hide the extent of physical and sexual abuse that actually takes place inside a painfully large number of American families. Belief in these myths makes it possible to avoid some of the unhappy realities.

☐ MODELS OF FAMILY VIOLENCE

To better understand violence within the family, we must look at its place in the larger sociocultural environment (for the sociocultural roots, see Gil, 1986; Levine, 1986). Aggression is a trait that our society labels as generally desirable, especially for males. Getting ahead at work, asserting ourselves in relationships, and winning at sports are all culturally approved actions. But does aggression necessarily lead to violence? All families have their ups and downs, and all family members at times experience anger toward one another. How do we explain that violence erupts more frequently and with more severe consequences in some families than in others? The principal models used in understanding family violence are discussed in the following sections.

You can always kill a relative with a gun that isn't loaded.

Mark Twain

THE PSYCHIATRIC MODEL. The psychiatric model finds the source of family violence within the personality of the abuser. It assumes that he or she is violent as a result of mental or emotional illness, psychopathology, or perhaps alcohol or drug misuse. Although research indicates that fewer than 10 percent of family violence cases are attributable to psychiatric causes, the idea that people are violent because they are crazy or drunk is widely held (Gelles and Cornell, 1990; Steele, 1980). Gelles and Cornell (1990) suggest that this model is compelling *because* "if we can persist in believing that violence and abuse are the products of aberrations or sickness, and, therefore, believe ourselves to be well, then our acts cannot be hurtful or abusive."

THE ECOLOGICAL MODEL. The ecological perspective looks at the child's development within the family environment and the family's development within the community. Psychologist James Garbarino (1977, 1982) has suggested that cultural support for physical force against children combines with lack of family support in the community to increase the risk of intrafamily violence. Under this model, a child who doesn't "match" well with the parents (such as child with emotional or develwho doesn't "match" well with the parents (such as child with emotional or developmental disabilities) and a family that is under stress (from, for example, unemployment or poor health) and that has little community support (such as child care or medical care) is at increased risk for child abuse.

> *Men are but children of a larger growth.*
>
> John Dryden

THE PATRIARCHY MODEL. The patriarchy (male-dominance) model of family violence draws its conclusions from a historical perspective. It holds that most social systems have traditionally placed women in a subordinate position to men, thus condoning or supporting the institution of male violence (Dobash and Dobash, 1979; Martin, 1981). There is no doubt that violence against women and children, and indeed violence in general, has had an integral place in most societies throughout history. Taken alone, however, this theory does not adequately explain the variations in degrees of violence among families in the same society.

> *By our readiness to allow arms to be purchased at will and fired at whim, we have created an atmosphere in which violence and hatred have become popular pastimes.*
>
> Martin Luther King, Jr.

SOCIAL SITUATIONAL AND SOCIAL LEARNING MODELS. The social models are related to the ecological and patriarchy models in that they view the sources of violence as originating in the social structure. The social situational model views family violence as arising from two main factors: structural stress (such as low income or illness) and cultural norms (such as the "spare the rod and spoil the child" ethic) (Gelles and Cornell, 1990). In this model, groups with few resources, such as the poor, are seen to be at greater risk for family violence than those who are well-off. The social learning model holds that people learn to be violent from society at large and from their families. Although it is true that many perpetrators of family violence were themselves abused as children, it is also true that many victims of childhood violence do *not* become violent parents. These theories do not account for this discrepancy.

RESOURCE MODEL. William Goode's (1971) resource theory can be applied to family violence. This model assumes that social systems are based on force or the threat of force. A person acquires power by mustering personal, social, and economic resources. Thus, according to Goode, the person with the most resources is the least likely to resort to overt force. Gelles and Cornell (1990) explain, "A husband who wants to be the dominant person in the family but has little education, has a job low in prestige and income, and lacks interpersonal skills may choose to use violence to maintain the dominant position."

> *People hit and abuse family members because they can.*
>
> Richard Gelles

AN EXCHANGE/SOCIAL CONTROL MODEL. Gelles and Cornell (1990) posit a two-part theory of family violence. The first part, exchange theory, holds that in our interactions we constantly weigh the perceived rewards against the costs. When Gelles and Cornell say "people hit and abuse family members because they can," they are applying exchange theory. The expectation is that "people will only use violence toward family members when the costs of being violent do not outweigh the rewards." (The possible rewards of violence might be getting one's own way, exerting superiority, working off anger or stress, or exacting revenge. Costs could include being hit back, being arrested, being jailed, losing social status, or dissolving the family.)

Social control raises the costs of violent behavior through such means as arrest, imprisonment, loss of status, or loss of income. Three characteristics of families that may reduce social control—and thus make violence more likely—are the following:

1. *Inequality.* Men are stronger than women and often have more economic power and social status. Adults are more powerful than children.

2. *The Private Nature of the Family.* People are reluctant to look outside the family for help, and outsiders (the police or neighbors, for example) may hesitate to intervene in private matters. The likelihood of family violence goes down as the number of nearby friends and relatives increases (Gelles and Cornell, 1990; Nye, 1976).

3. *"Real Man" Image.* In some American subcultures, aggressive male behavior brings approval. The violent man in these groups may actually gain status among his peers for asserting his "authority."

The exchange/social control model is useful for looking at treatment and prevention strategies for family violence, which we will discuss later on in this chapter.

❑ BATTERED WOMEN

No one knows for certain how many battered women there are in the United States, but government figures indicate that battering is one of the most common and underreported crimes in the country. Here are some figures concerning violence against women in the United States (Gelles and Cornell, 1990; Gelles and Straus, 1988):

❑ About one woman in twenty-two is the victim of abusive violence each year.

❑ About half of battered women are beaten at least three times a year.

❑ One-third of murdered women were killed by their husbands or lovers.

❑ In a national survey, about one in four wives and one in three husbands said that slapping a partner was "at least somewhat necessary, normal, or good."

Battering, as used in the literature of family violence, is a catchall term that includes, but is not limited to, slapping, punching, knocking down, choking, kicking, hitting with objects, threatening with weapons, stabbing, and shooting. The use of physical force against women is certainly not a new phenomenon. It may be thought of as a time-honored tradition in our culture. The commonly used term *rule of thumb* derives from the legally sanctioned (until the nineteenth century) practice of "disciplining" one's wife with a switch or rod—provided it was no wider than the disciplinarian's thumb (a good example of the basis for the patriarchy model).

In recent years the subject of wife battering has gained public notoriety. It remains, however, subordinate in the public mind to the physical and sexual abuse of children. In part, this may be because historically and culturally, women are considered "appropriate" victims of domestic violence (Gelles and Cornell, 1990). Many expect, understand, and accept the idea that women sometimes need to be "put in their place" by men. Such misogynistic ideas provide the cultural basis for the physical and sexual abuse of women.

Battered Women and Battering Men

Battering occurs at all levels of society. It occurs most frequently among those under thirty years of age (Straus, Gelles, and Steinmetz, 1980), and it is apparently twice as prevalent among black couples as among white couples. It should be noted, however, that the rate of violence against black women by their partners appears to have dropped considerably in recent years. A 1985 survey showed a 43 percent decrease in such abuse since 1975 (Hampton, Gelles, and Harrop, 1989). (Possible reasons for this decline will be discussed later on.) Although no social class is immune to it, most studies find that marital violence is more likely to occur in low-income, low-status families (Gelles and Cornell, 1990; see Hampton, 1991, for a collection of essays on African-American family violence).

CHARACTERISTICS OF BATTERED WOMEN. Although early studies of battering relationships seemed to indicate a cluster of personality characteristics constituting a typical battered woman, more recent studies have not borne out this viewpoint. Factors such as self-esteem or childhood experiences of violence do not appear to be necessarily associated with a woman's being in an assaultive relationship (Hotaling and Sugarman, 1990). There are two characteristics, however, that do appear to be highly correlated with wife assault: low socioeconomic status and a high degree of marital conflict. A number of studies have found that wife abuse is both more common and more severe in families of lower socioeconomic status (Gelles and Straus, 1988; Hotaling and Sugarman, 1986, 1990). Marital conflict—and the apparent inability to resolve it through negotiation and compromise—is also a factor in many battering relationships. Hotaling and Sugarman (1990) found that conflicts in these marriages often were associated with a difference in expectations about the division of labor in the family, frequent drinking by the husband, and the wife's having attained a higher educational level than the husband. These researchers concluded that it is not useful to focus "primarily on the victim in the assessment of risk to wife assault."

CHARACTERISTICS OF BATTERERS. A man who systematically inflicts violence on his wife or lover is likely to have some or all of the following traits (Edelson et al., 1985; Gelles and Cornell, 1990; Goldstein and Rosenbaum, 1985; Margolin, Sibner, and Gleberman, 1988; Walker, 1979, 1984).

❐ He believes the common myths about battering.
❐ He believes in the traditional home, family, and gender-role stereotypes.
❐ He has low self-esteem and may use violence as a means of demonstrating power or adequacy.
❐ He may be sadistic, pathologically jealous, or passive-aggressive.
❐ He may have a "Dr. Jekyll and Mr. Hyde" personality, being capable at times of great charm.
❐ He may use sex as an act of aggression.
❐ He believes in the moral rightness of his violent behavior (even though he may "accidentally" go too far).

Leonore Walker (1984) believes that a man's battering is not the result of his interactions with his partner or any kind of provocative personality traits of the partner. She wrote:

The best prediction of future violence was a history of past violent behavior. This included witnessing, receiving, and committing violent acts in [the] childhood home; violent acts toward pets, inanimate objects, or other people; previous criminal record; longer time in the military service; and previous expression of violent behavior toward women. If these items are added to a history of temper tantrums, insecurity, need to keep the environment stable, easily threatened by minor upsets, jealousy, possessiveness, and the ability to be charming, manipulative, and seductive to get what he wants, and hostile, nasty and mean when he doesn't succeed—then the risk for battering becomes very high. If alcohol abuse problems are included, the pattern becomes classic.

Sociologist Norman Denzin (1984) defined the violence of batterers as "the attempt to regain, through the use of emotional and physical force, something that has been lost." (Here we see resource theory at work.) Denzin wrote:

One murder makes a villain, millions a hero.

Bishop Beilby Porteus (1731–1808)

The goal of the violent act eludes the man of violence. He is drawn over and over again into the cycle of violence. He can never succeed in establishing his dominance and will over the will of the other. In this sense his violent actions are doomed to failure, yet his very failure destroys the relationship with the one he wishes to control.

BATTERED HUSBANDS. There have been speculations about the prevalence of battered husbands. We have, after all, the cartoon image of Blondie chasing Dagwood with a rolling pin. (We don't see Dagwood chasing Blondie with a gun or knife, however, which is a much more realistic depiction of family violence.) Although it is undoubtedly true that some men are injured in attacks by wives or lovers, "husband battering" is probably a misleading term. The overwhelming majority of victims of adult family violence are women; men are rarely the victims of battery (Berk, Newton, and Berk, 1983). In one study (Saunders, 1986) investigating "husband abuse," the overwhelming majority of women reported that they acted in self-defense; they did not initiate the violence. Their actions did not cause noticeable injury. Indeed, a woman may attempt to inflict damage on a man in self-defense or retaliation, but most women have no hope of prevailing in hand-to-hand combat with a man. A woman may be severely injured simply trying to defend herself. As Gelles and Cornell (1990) observed, although there may be similar rates in hitting, "when injury is considered, marital violence is primarily a problem of victimized women." While male violence dramatically overshadows female violence, female violence does exist. Suzanne Steinmetz (1987) suggests that some scholars "deemphasize the importance of women's use of violence." As such, there is a "conspiracy of silence [which] fails to recognize that family violence is never inconsequential."

The Cycle of Violence

Lenore Walker's (1979) research has revealed a three-phase battering cycle. The duration of each phase may vary, but the cycle goes on . . . and on.

❑ Phase One: *Tension Building.* Tension is in the air. She tries to do her job well, to be conciliatory. Minor battering incidents may occur. She denies her own rising anger. Tension continues to build.
❑ Phase Two: *The Explosion.* He loses control. Sometimes she will precipitate the incident to "get it over with." He generally sets out to "teach her a lesson" and goes on from there. This is the shortest phase, usually lasting several hours but sometimes continuing for two or three days or longer.
❑ Phase Three: *"In Love" Again.* Tension has now been released and the batterer is contrite, begs forgiveness, and sincerely promises never to do it again. She chooses to believe him and forgives him. This "symbiotic bonding" (interdependence) makes intervention, help, or change unlikely during this phase.

Often the battered woman is surprised by what has touched off the battering incident. It may have been something outside the home—at the husband's job, for example. He may have come home drunk or he may have been drinking steadily at home. Alcohol is implicated in many battering incidents, possibly the majority. Results of studies of alcohol and battering vary widely; alcohol problems were reported for assaultive husbands in between 35 and 93 percent of cases, depending on the study (Leonard and Jacob, 1988; see Edelson et al., 1985, for a review of conflicting studies about battering and alcohol use.) In a battering relationship, the woman may not only suffer physical damage but also may be seriously harmed emotionally by a constant sense of danger and the expectation of violence that weaves a "web of terror" about her (Edelson et al., 1985).

When we want to read of the deeds that are done for love, whither do we turn? To the murder column.

George Bernard Shaw

Marital Rape

Marital rape represents a form of battering. Studies have reported that at least one-third of battered women have also been sexually assaulted by their partners (Finkelhor and Yllo, 1983; O'Reilly, 1983). According to David Finkelhor and Kersti Yllo (1985), "a marriage license is [considered] a license to rape." Although far too many husbands apparently agree with this statement, most states—beginning in the late 1970s—have enacted legislation to make at least some forms of marital rape illegal. As of 1990, forty-two states and the District of Columbia had enacted marital rape laws that prohibit husbands from forcing wives to engage in sex without their consent. In twenty-six of those states, husbands may be exempted from charges in some cases—for example, if they rape their wives by force but without imposing additional violence, such as threatening with a weapon, or if the woman is asleep, drugged, or ill (Russell, 1990). (When California adopted its marital rape law, state senator Bob Wilson protested, "If you can't rape your wife, who can you rape?" [O'Reilly, 1983].)

In Kentucky, Missouri, New Mexico, North Carolina, Oklahoma, South Carolina, South Dakota, and Utah, husbands can be prosecuted for marital rape only if they are living apart from their wives or if divorce proceedings have been started (Russell, 1990). And even though marital rape is now considered a crime in most states, there still remains the problem of enforcing the law. Many people discount rape in marriage as a "marital tiff" that has little to do with "real" rape (Finkelhor and Yllo, 1985). Many victims themselves have difficulty acknowledging that their husbands' sexual violence is indeed rape. And all too often, judges seem more in sympathy with the perpetrator than with the victim, especially if he is very intelligent, successful, and well-educated (Faidley, 1989). There is also the "notion that the male breadwinner should be the beneficiary of some special immunity because of his family's dependence on him" (Russell, 1990). Diana Russell goes on to say:

On the basis of such an argument, it follows that it would be a violation of the principle of equity to incarcerate men who beat up and/or rape women who are *not* their wives. Specifically, it would not be fair to the wives and children of employed stranger rapists, acquaintance rapists, date rapists, lover rapists, authority figure rapists, or rapists who rape their friends. Why should these families have to endure the loss of their breadwinners if the families of husbands of rapists are spared this hardship?

Because these kinds of attitudes are so entrenched in the American psyche, marital rape remains mostly unpublicized and underreported.

In Russell's landmark study (1982, rev. 1990) on marital rape, 930 randomly selected women in San Francisco were interviewed. Eighty-seven out of the 644 who had ever been married (about 13 percent) had been raped by their husbands. Russell found that force was used in 84 percent of the rapes and the threat of force in 9 percent. (The remaining victims were asleep, intoxicated, or surprised and not able to resist.) Thirty-one percent of the wives reported their rapes as isolated events that occurred only once. But another 31 percent reported that they had been raped more than twenty times. Other studies of wives who had been raped by their husbands (cited in Russell, 1984) reported that between 59 and 87 percent were raped multiple times.

Marital rape victims experience betrayal, anger, humiliation, and guilt. Following their rapes, many wives feel intense anger toward their husbands. One woman said, "So, he says, 'You're my wife and you're gonna. . . I just laid there thinking 'I hate him, I hate him so much.' " Another expressed her humiliation and sense of "dirtiness" by taking a shower: "I tried to wash it away, but you can't. I felt like a sexual garbage can" (Finkelhor and Yllo, 1985). Some feel guilt and blame themselves for not being better wives. And some develop negative self-images and view their lack of sexual desire as a reflection of their own inadequacies rather than as a consequence of abuse.

Dating Violence and Rape

In the last decade or so, researchers have become increasingly aware that violence and sexual assault can take place in all forms of intimate relationships. Violence between intimates is not restricted to family members. Even casual or dating relationships can be marred by violence or rape. (See *Family Relations* 40:1 [Jan. 1991] for a collection of articles on courtship aggression.)

DATING VIOLENCE. There is an alarming incidence of physical violence in dating relationships. Evidence suggests that it approaches the level of marital violence (Lane and Gwartney-Gibbs, 1985). Recent studies indicate that both men and women engage in violent behavior in dating relationships (Makepeace, 1987). One sample of 325 college students indicated that 40 percent of the women and 30 percent of the men had inflicted or received violence in their dating relationships (Lane and Gwartney-Gibbs, 1985). Another study suggested that 30 percent of the women and 25 percent of the men were the recipients of dating violence (McKinney, 1986). Even though both sexes may be involved in dating violence, greater injury is almost always inflicted on women, and unlike men, they are also sexually assaulted (Makepeace, 1986; Sugarman and Hotaling, 1989).

Violence is not usually an isolated, one-time event. One study showed that the mean number of incidents for those involved in violent dating relationships was 9.6 (Roscoe and Benaske, 1985). Although it may seem logical to assume that dating violence leads to marital violence, little actual research has been done in this area. It does appear, however, that the issues involved in dating violence are different than those generally involved in spousal violence. While marital violence may erupt over domestic issues such as housekeeping and childrearing (Hotaling and Sugarman, 1990; Walker, 1984), dating violence is far more likely to be precipitated by jealousy or rejection (Lloyd and Emery, 1990; Makepeace, 1989). One woman recounted the following incident (Lloyd and Emery, 1990):

I was waiting for him to pick me up in front of school. I was befriended by some guys and we struck up a conversation. When my boyfriend picked me up he didn't say anything. When we got home, physical violence occurred for the first time in our relationship. I had no idea it was coming. He caught me on the jaw, and hit me up against the wall. I couldn't cry or scream or anything—all I could do was look at him. He picked me up and threw me against the wall and then started yelling and screaming at me that he didn't want me talking to other guys. . . .

Lloyd and Emery found the other themes of dating violence involved the man's use of alcohol or drugs, "unpredictable" reasons, and intense anger.

Although many women will leave a dating relationship after one violent incident, others will stay through repeated episodes. Women with "modern" gender-role attitudes are more likely to leave than those with traditional attitudes (Flynn, 1990). Women who leave violent partners cite the following factors in making the decision to break up: a series of broken promises that the man will end the violence, an improved self-image ("I deserve better"), escalation of the violence, and physical and emotional help from family and friends (Lloyd and Emery, 1990). Apparently, counselors, physicians, and law enforcement agencies are not widely used in these situations (Pirog-Good and Stets, 1989; see Lloyd, 1991, for implications for intervention in courtship violence.)

ACQUAINTANCE RAPE. Although the majority of rapes *reported* to the police are stranger rapes, rapists may be acquaintances, dates, husbands, fathers, or other family members, as well as strangers. As many as half or more of all rapes involve someone whom the victim knows or with whom she is acquainted (Russell, 1984). Because many people accept the myth that rapes are committed by strangers, many **acquaintance rape** victims do not perceive themselves as having been raped since the rapist is a date, boyfriend, or cohabitor (Finkelhor and Yllo, 1980; Russell, 1984). Nor do the men who sexually assault their dates, friends, or partners perceive themselves as rapists, because they, too, believe that rapists are strangers. These men also believe that as the woman's date, boyfriend or partner, they have the "right" to have sex with her. They may believe that women are sexually passive and that when they say "no," they really mean "yes" or "make me" (Lewin, 1985). In one study, 22.5 percent of the males surveyed thought that "forced sex" was acceptable under certain conditions. These men interpreted a woman asking a man out, going to his apartment, or allowing him to pay for the date as signs that she wanted sex, and they thought that rape could be justified if she refused (Muehlenhard, 1989).

One study (Koss, 1989) on sexual aggression in college (in which thirty-two schools and 6,159 students participated) indicated the following:

❏ Almost 54 percent of the women surveyed had been sexually victimized in some way.
❏ Fifteen percent of the women had been raped, and 12 percent had experienced attempted rape; almost 90 percent knew their assailants.
❏ Forty-seven percent of the rapes were by first dates, casual dates, or romantic acquaintances.
❏ Twenty-five percent of the men had perpetrated sexual aggression. Three percent had attempted rape and 4 percent had actually raped.
❏ Almost three-quarters of the raped women did not identify their experiences as rapes.

Acquaintance rape is difficult for many women to recognize since it does not meet stereotypical images of rape. As one rape crisis advocate (Sherman, 1985) noted, "Women are hesitant to think that someone they met in an English class or at a fraternity party might assault them. We tend to visualize rapists as wearing stocking masks and jumping out at a woman from dark alleys."

Why Women Stay in Violent Relationships

Violence in relationships generally develops a continuing pattern of abuse over time. We know from systems theory that all relationships have some degree of mutual dependence, and battering relationships are certainly no different. Women stay in or return to violent situations for many reasons. Some common ones are the following:

❏ *Economic dependence.* Even if a woman is financially secure, she may not perceive herself as being able to cope with economic matters.
❏ *Religious pressure.* She may feel that the teachings of her religion require her to keep the family together at all costs, to submit to her husband's will, and to try harder.
❏ *"The children need a father."* She may sincerely believe that even a father who beats the mother is better than no father at all. If the abusing husband also assaults the children, this may be the factor that motivates the woman to seek help (but not always).

❐ *Fear of being alone.* She may have no meaningful relationships outside her marriage. Her husband may have systematically cut off her ties to other family members, friends, and potential support sources. She has nowhere to go and no way to get any real perspective on her situation.

❐ *Belief in the American dream.* This woman has accepted without question the "cult of domesticity and beliefs of family harmony and bliss" (Dobash and Dobash, 1979). Even though her existence belies this myth, she continues to believe that it is how it should (and can) be.

❐ *Pity.* She puts her husband's needs ahead of her own.

❐ *Guilt and shame.* She feels that it is her own fault if her marriage isn't working and that if she left, everyone would know she is a failure, or her husband might kill himself.

❐ *Duty and responsibility.* She feels she must keep her marriage vows "till death us do part."

❐ *Fear for her life.* She believes she may be killed if she tries to escape.

❐ *Love.* She loves him; he loves her. On her husband's death, one elderly woman (a university professor) spoke of her fifty-three years in a battering relationship (Walker, 1979): "We did everything together. . . . I loved him; you know, even when he was brutal and mean. . . . I'm sorry he's dead, although there were days when I wished he would die. . . . He was my best friend. . . . He beat me right up to the end. . . . It was a good life and I really do miss him."

Leonore Walker (1979) theorizes that women stay in battering relationships as a result of "learned helplessness." According to Walker, women who are repeatedly battered develop much lower self-concepts than women in nonbattering relationships. They begin to feel that they cannot control the battering or the events that surround them. Through a process of behavioral reinforcement, they learn to become helpless. As Walker noted, "Women are systematically taught that their personal wants, survival, and anatomy do not depend on effective and creative responses to life situations, but rather on their physical beauty to men. They learn that they have no direct control over the circumstances of their lives." If violence is used against them, women may even become desensitized to the accompanying pain and fear. The more it happens, the more helpless they feel and the less they are able to see alternative possibilities.

There are other reasons why women remain in or return to these relationships. They may have limited education or job skills and hence be economically dependent. Or they may think that they can stop the husband's violence. Lee Bowker (1983) reported that women used a variety of strategies to stop their husbands' abusiveness. These ranged from passive defense techniques (covering their bodies with arms or hands) to seeking informal help (friends) or formal help (counseling through a social service agency). The particular strategy was not important in stopping the violence, however. What made the crucial difference appeared to be the woman's determination that the violence *must* cease.

Gelles and Straus (1979) found that women who left abusive marriages were often those who had received the most severe abuse. They also found that the age of the children in the family was significant. The older the children, the more likely they were to be involved in the parents' disputes. Many women left after their teenage children had been injured while trying to protect them.

Alternatives: Police Intervention, Shelters, and Abuser Programs

Professionals who deal with domestic violence have long debated the relative merits of *compassion* versus *control* as intervention strategies (Mederer and Gelles, 1989; Rosenfeld and Newberger, 1977). Although more understanding of the dynamics of abusive relationships and the deterrence process is clearly needed, we can see that both approaches have their place. Controlling measures (which raise the "costs" of violent behavior), such as arrest, prosecution, and imprisonment, and compassionate measures, such as shelters, education, counseling, and support groups, have been shown to be successful to varying degrees under varying conditions. Used together, these interventions may be quite effective. Mederer and Gelles (1989) suggest that control measures may be used to "motivate violent offenders to participate in treatment programs."

BATTERED WOMEN AND THE LAW. As a result of family violence studies and feminist pressure, there has been a movement toward an implementation of stricter policies for dealing with domestic offenders. In Minneapolis, a study (Sherman and Berk, 1984) determined that arrest was the most effective deterrent to repeated abuse; arrests in domestic violence cases there have tripled. If an officer believes that violence has occurred within four hours before the police arrived on the scene, he or she may make a *presumptive arrest* even if the battered spouse does not wish to press charges. The Minneapolis researchers discovered that arrest was almost twice as effective as counseling or ordering the assailant off the property in preventing a recurrent assault against a woman. Researcher Lawrence Sherman (1984) suggested that arrest is a powerful deterrent because generally "the power balance is distorted in favor of the one who has the bigger muscles. When they call the police, women involve the police muscles and even up the power balance."

A more recent study, however, questioned the accuracy of the Minneapolis study's conclusions. A replicated study in Omaha indicated that although arrest did not increase the level of later violence to the woman, neither did it reduce the amount of violence (Dunford, Huizinga, and Elliot, 1989). The study did find reduced levels of violence, however, if the assailant was not present when the police arrived and an arrest warrant was issued. Thus it appears that the *threat* of arrest (which lowers one's social status) may be a better deterrent than actual arrest (Gelles and Cornell, 1990; Mederer and Cornell, 1989). Today, nearly a third of the largest police forces in the nation are instructed to arrest the assailants, although the jury is still out as to whether mandatory arrest is actually effective.

There is a general perception that domestic disputes are the most dangerous form of police work, but this assumption has been challenged. Desmond Ellis (1987) suggests that instead of being a leading cause of police deaths, domestic disturbances accounted nationally for only 5.4 percent of police fatalities over a ten-year period. Deaths associated with traffic pursuits and stops, in contrast, accounted for over 12 percent of police fatalities.

BATTERED WOMEN'S SHELTERS. At the point when a woman finds that she can leave an abusive relationship, even temporarily, she may have any of a number of serious needs. If she is fleeing an attack, she may need immediate medical attention and physical protection. She will need accommodation for herself and possibly her children. She will certainly need access to support, counseling, and various types of assistance—money, food stamps, or other basic survival items for herself and her children. She will need to deal with informed, compassionate professionals such as police, doctors, and social workers.

In the late 1970s, the shelter movement developed to meet the needs of many battered women. The shelter movement has grown slowly, hampered by lack of funding and mixed reaction from the public. There are an estimated 1,000 shelters throughout the United States, a vast improvement over the estimated *five or six* shelters in existence in 1976 (Gelles and Cornell, 1990). Besides offering immediate safe shelter (the locations of safe houses are usually known only to the residents and shelter workers), these refuges let battered women realize that they are not alone in their misery and help them form supportive networks with one another. They also provide many other services for battered women who call, such as information, advice, or referrals. Walker's (1979) research indicated that about 50 percent of women who stay longer than a week in shelters will not return to their battering relationships. She further noted that

the percentage rises dramatically if the safe house remains open to those women who return home and then want to come back to the refuge. . . . The back and forth process may occur as often as five times before the battered woman is able to leave home permanently.

Those women who seem to benefit most from shelter stays are those who have decided to "take charge of their lives," according to one study (Berk, Newton, and Berk, 1986). Hampton, Gelles, and Harrop (1989) suggest that the dramatic drop in wife abuse among African Americans may be the result of black women's "increased status" coupled with their apparent willingness to make use of shelters and other programs.

ABUSER PROGRAMS. Programs for battering men appear to be helpful in some cases, but not all. Psychotherapy, group discussion, stress management, or communication skills classes may be available through mental health agencies, women's crisis programs, or various self-help groups. One study (Gondolf, 1988) looked at fifty-one men in a program for batterers and fifty-four men who had contacted the program but did not participate. The researchers found that the participants and nonparticipants had very different views on how to stop their violence. The participants felt that the social aspects of the program—friendship and group interaction—were useful. Nonparticipants "appeared more transient, resistant to help, and more evasive." Most men in both groups seemed to rely more on "willful self-restraint to stop their violence rather than on personal and social change." Gondolf suggests that anger control is not any more successful than any other technique for stopping violence and that it "may in fact divert abusers from developing more substantial stopping

In the United States we spend more money on shelters for dogs and cats than for human beings. If we have effective animal rescue shelters for abused dogs, cats, and bunny rabbits we should be able to spare something for people as well.

Murray Straus et al.

strategies." The extent to which attending such groups actually changes abusing men's violent behavior is difficult to measure (Gelles and Conte, 1991). Gondolf's studies of men who have completed voluntary programs (1987, 1988) showed that two-thirds to three-quarters of these men were subsequently nonviolent. Gondolf also confirmed the conclusion of a number of studies of women who are successful in stopping abuse: battered women play a crucial role in stopping the violence against them. Women's insistence on their partners' getting help (the "woman factor") apparently can influence men to "learn more or try harder" to change.

❐ VIOLENCE AGAINST CHILDREN

The history of children is not a particularly happy one. At various times and places, children have been abandoned to die of exposure in deserts, in forests, and on mountainsides or have simply been murdered at birth if they were deemed too sickly, ugly, of the wrong sex, or just impractical. Male children have been subjected to castration to make them fit for guarding harems or singing soprano in church choirs. (Of course, we are more "civilized" today. Imagine, however, taking a baby boy, tying him down, and cutting off his foreskin, causing him excruciating pain and possibly putting his life at risk. The practice of circumcision is routine in contemporary America [but not in Europe]. Still, there is no compelling medical reason for circumcision, only tradition [Kempe and Helfer, 1980].) These practices (and many

Children are the least protected members of our society. Much physical abuse is camouflaged as disciplining or the parent "losing" his or her temper.

others) have all been socially condoned in their time. In the societies in which they existed, they would not be recognized as abusive. In our society, some degree of physical force against children, such as spanking, is generally accepted as "normal." Most childrearing experts currently suggest that parents use alternative disciplinary measures.

Child abuse was not recognized as a serious problem in this country until the 1960s, with the work of C. H. Kempe and his colleagues, who coined the term *battered-baby syndrome*. It is now known that *at least* a million American children are physically abused by their parents each year (Gelles and Cornell, 1990); undoubtedly many cases go unnoticed or unreported. Parental violence is among the five leading causes of death for children between the ages of one and eighteen. In 1988, 1,225 children's deaths were directly attributable to their parents (Mitchell, 1989).

Families at Risk

Research suggests that there are three sets of factors that put families at risk for child abuse and neglect: parental characteristics, child characteristics, and the family ecosystem—that is, the family system's interaction with the larger environment (Burgess and Youngblood, 1987; Vasta, 1982). The characteristics described in the next sections are likely to be present in abusive families (Straus, Gelles, and Steinmetz, 1980; Turner and Avison, 1985).

PARENTAL CHARACTERISTICS. Some or all of the following characteristics are likely to be present in parents who abuse their children:

❑ The abusing father was physically punished by his parents, and his father physically abused his mother.
❑ The parents believe in corporal discipline of children and wives.
❑ The marital relationship itself may not be valued by the parents. There may be interspousal violence.
❑ The parents believe that the father should be the dominant authority figure.
❑ The parents are low in self-esteem.
❑ The parents have unrealistic expectations for the child.
❑ There is persistent role reversal in which the parents use the child to gratify their own needs, rather than vice versa.
❑ The parents appear unconcerned about the seriousness of a child's injury, responding with "Oh, well, accidents happen."

CHILD CHARACTERISTICS. Who are the battered children? Are they any different from other children? Surprisingly, the answer is often yes; they are different in some way or at least are perceived by their parents to be so. Brandt Steele (1980) noted that children who are abused are often labeled by their parents as "unsatisfactory." Unsatisfactory may include any of the following:

❑ A "normal" child who is the product of a difficult or unplanned pregnancy, is of the "wrong" sex, or is born outside of marriage.
❑ An "abnormal" child—premature or of low birth weight, possibly with congenital defects or illness.
❑ A "difficult" child—fussy, hyperactive, and so on.

Steele also notes that all too often a child's perceived difficulties are a *result* of abuse and neglect rather than a cause.

America has sometimes been described as child-centered; however, any unbiased observer of child life in this nation will find that many millions of children are living and growing up under circumstances of severe social and economic deprivation. . . . Many of these children lack adequate nutrition, medical and dental care, and educational and vocational opportunities. . . . However high the prevalence of physical abuse of individual children within their families and homes may be, the abuse inflicted upon children collectively by society as a whole is far larger in scope and far more serious in its consequences.

David Gil, Violence against Children

Parents are the last people on earth who ought to have children.

Samuel Butler

Do not withhold correction from the child: For if you beat him with the rod, he will not die. Beat him with the rod and deliver him from hell.

Proverbs 23:13–14

FOCUS

The Epidemic of Missing Children: Myth or Reality

In the morning, as they eat their cereal, children in homes throughout America look at milk cartons with photographs of "missing children." The faces stare from the cartons as if warning the children that they, too, may become missing if they are not careful. The photographs on milk cartons, grocery bags, billboards, and television give us the impression, observed pediatrician Benjamin Spock, that "children are being abducted all the time and that this child might be next" (Kilzer, 1985).

To protect their children, parents fingerprint them in massive identification programs. They buy books warning against strangers and have dentists implant computer identification chips in their children's teeth. Schools also often stress the threat posed by strangers.

A 1990 study commissioned by the Justice Department (Finkelhor, Hotaling, and Sedlak, 1990) has helped to put the missing children "problem" into perspective. Based on interviews conducted from July 1988 to January 1989, the research-ers estimated that around 1,369,000 children are miss-

ing at some time during a given year in the United States.

Of this number, about 350,000 are abducted by a family member as a result of a custody dispute between parents. The researchers found that most of these children were back home within two days. All but 10 percent were home within a month. In 83 percent of the cases, the parent from whom the child was taken knew where the child was. Other major categories of missing children (in terms of numbers of children affected) include runaways (about 450,700 annually) and "thrownaways"—children who are forced by their parents to leave home (about 127,000). Another large category includes children who are lost, injured, or unable to return home for some other reason. This category, consisting of about 438,000 children annually, also includes a large number of "misplaced" children—those who forget or misunderstand where they are supposed to be. Most of these children return home within a day, but the fact that they are included in many estimates of missing children obscures the

number that are actually missing.

A very small percentage of missing children are abducted by strangers. The researchers estimated the number to be between 200 and 300 annually. An additional 3,200 to 4,400 are "lured away," often in conjunction with a sexual assault; they are not kidnapped, however. In another study, based on data collected from six different sources, including the National Center for Missing and Exploited Children and various police records, Hotaling and Finkelhor (1990) estimated that between 52 and 158 children are murdered yearly in stranger abductions. In contrast, 1,100 children die yearly from parental abuse or neglect. (The United States leads the world in homicides for one to four year olds, most of whom are killed by a family member.) About 2,000 children are victims of suicide every year and about 7,000 die in auto accidents.

Contrary to media claims, there is no upsurge in stranger abductions or in murders related to these abductions. Furthermore there is far greater risk to

continued on next page

There was an old woman who lived in a shoe,
She had so many children she didn't know what to do.
She gave them some broth without any bread,
And whipped them all soundly and sent them to bed.

Mother Goose rhyme

FAMILY ECOSYSTEM. As discussed earlier in this chapter, the community and the family's relation to it may be relevant to the existence of domestic violence (Garbarino, 1977). The following characteristics may be found in families that experience child abuse:

❏ The family experiences unemployment.
❏ The family is socially isolated, with few or no close contacts with relatives, friends, and groups.
❏ The family has a low level of income, which creates economic stress.
❏ The family lives in an unsafe neighborhood, which is characterized by higher-than-average levels of violence.
❏ The home is crowded, hazardous, dirty, or unhealthy.
❏ The family is a single-parent family in which the mother works and is consequently overstressed and overburdened.
❏ There are family health problems.

The likelihood of child abuse increases with family size. Parents of two children have a 50 percent higher abuse rate than do parents of a single child. The rate of

FOCUS

teenagers than to young children. Hotaling and Finkelhor (1990) write, "Runaways or children who are considered to be possible runaways are not regarded with the same solicitude as kidnap victims. Still, the data suggest that if the public is concerned about abducted and murdered children, it will have to broaden its concern to include the adolescent, who appears to be the child at highest risk."

If the epidemic of missing children is a myth, the public reaction to it is not. The myth has touched a very profound fear. In part, this fear may reflect anxieties about changing patterns of parenting and childrearing. With increasing numbers of mothers working, more children are being placed in child care than ever before. One psychologist suggests that "not being home may be tapping into hidden guilt" (Kilzer and Griego, 1985). For some, this fear may reflect anxieties concerning minorities and may touch on xenophobia, as many stories involve specific ethnic groups or foreigners. One man recalled hearing of Mexicans abducting blonde, blue-eyed children to sell to

childless couples. "They were also abducted and shipped to Africa or to Arabian harems; there were those who were forced into prostitution by Mafia pimps" (Schneider, 1987).

Whatever the source, the myth of missing children has severe consequences. First of all, it instills fear in children. Psychologist Lee Salk warns, "We are terrifying our children to the point where they are going to be afraid to talk to strangers" (Kantrowitz, 1986). Such fear makes it difficult to instill a basic sense of trust; it makes children anxious toward people they don't know and fearful of new situations. It makes them suspicious of foreigners and people who are different from themselves. Second, it affects our parenting style. It makes us afraid to let our children out of our sight. It creates anxiety in us when we are not at home or they are gone. Finally, it allows us to continue to believe that all families are happy and nurturing. It makes it easier to deny that families can be abusive, violent, or incestuous. Sexual abuse, a far more common problem than kidnapping, is much less often discussed by parents with their children. In

one study, Finkelhor (1984) found that 84 percent of parents had discussed kidnapping, but only 29 percent had talked about sexual abuse with their children.

Children need to be taught to keep themselves safe at home and at the homes of friends, neighbors, and relatives as well as on the street. But it is not necessary to terrify them in the process. If they are allowed to develop their own good judgment skills and have high self-esteem, they will feel secure, competent, and in control of their own bodies and have the tools to help them stay out of risky situations. Parents need to look at where the most plausible dangers lie. They need to acknowledge the violence and sexual abuse within families that lead children to become runaways and suicides. Or they might become involved in promoting motor-vehicle safety (see Resource Center for information on Mothers Against Drunk Driving). As Hotaling and Finkelhor (1990) write, "Children being killed by strangers who abduct them are terrible and properly feared tragedies, but they are a small portion of children who die in tragic and preventable circumstances."

---

abuse peaks at five children and declines thereafter. The overall child-abuse rate by mothers has been found to be 75 percent higher than that by fathers (Straus, Gelles, and Steinmetz, 1980). The responsibilities and tensions of mothering and the enforced closeness of mother and child may lead to situations in which women are likely to abuse their children. But, as David Finkelhor (1983) and others have pointed out, if we "calculate [child] vulnerability to abuse as a function of the amount of time spent in contact with a potential abuser, . . . we . . . see that men and fathers are more likely to abuse."

Single parents—both mothers and fathers—are at especially high risk of abusing their children (Gelles, 1989). According to Gelles, "the high rate of abusive violence among single mothers appears to be a function of the poverty that characterizes mother-only families." He states that programs must be developed that are "aimed at ameliorating the devastating consequences of poverty among single parents. . . ." Single fathers, who show a higher abuse rate than single mothers, "need more than economic support to avoid using abusive violence toward their children."

There is no crime of which one cannot imagine oneself to be the author.

Johann Goethe

We have too many high-sounding words, and too few actions that correspond with them.

Abigail Adams (1744–1818)

A society which is mobilized to keep child molesters, kidnappers, and Satanists away from innocent children is not necessarily prepared to protect children from ignorance, poverty, and ill health.

Joel Best

Intervention

The goals of intervention in domestic violence are principally to protect the victims and assist and strengthen their families. In dealing with child abuse, professionals and government agencies may be called on to provide medical care, counseling, and services such as day-care, child-care education, telephone crisis lines, and temporary foster care. Many of these services are costly, and many of those who require them cannot afford to pay. Between 1981 and 1993, government support for such services was drastically reduced by federal budget cuts. Our system does not currently provide the human and financial resources necessary to deal with these socially destructive problems.

The first step in treating child abuse is locating the children who are threatened. With heightened public awareness in recent years and mandatory reporting of suspected child abuse required of certain professionals (such as teachers, doctors, and counselors) in all fifty states, identifying these children is much easier now than it was two decades ago. Reported incidents of child abuse have increased greatly during this time, but the actual number of incidents appears to have decreased. This is good news as far as it goes. Still, there are unacceptably high levels of violence against children and not nearly enough resources to assist them. Child welfare workers are notoriously overburdened with cases, and adequate foster placement is often difficult to find (Gelles and Cornell, 1990).

Much intervention in child abuse appears to be equivalent to putting a Band-Aid on a huge malignant tumor. One survey of a number of treatment programs concluded that they were "in general . . . not very successful" (Daro and Cohn, 1988). Programs that stress education and early intervention may offer more hope. One such program, in which home visits were made by nurses to high-risk first-time mothers (teenagers, unmarried women, and women of low socioeconomic status) showed encouraging results. Those who were visited had fewer verified incidents of child abuse during their child's first two years. These mothers were also observed to punish their children less often and to provide "more appropriate play materials." Also, their children were seen less for accidents or poisoning than those in the comparison group (Olds, Henderson, Chamberlin, and Tatelbaum, 1986).

An innovative program called Project 12-Ways takes an "ecobehavioral" approach, working with both parents and the larger family ecosystem. Project 12-Ways teaches stress reduction and offers training in self-control, job-finding skills money management, and problem-solving skills. Parents are given social support, provided with counseling on how to find and use leisure time, and referred to alcohol or drug abuse programs. The program gives both parent and child basic skills training and provides education in home safety and cleanliness. Compared to foster placement, which was evaluated as being effective in reducing recurring incidences of child abuse in between 40 and 70 percent of cases, Project 12-Ways was found to be effective in 80 to 90 percent of the cases studied (Lutzer and Rice, 1984, 1986). Self-help groups such as Parents Anonymous offer nonjudgmental support and prove to be effective for parents committed to changing their behavior. (See Resource Center for information on Parents Anonymous.)

❑ THE HIDDEN VICTIMS OF FAMILY VIOLENCE

Most studies of family violence have focused on violence between spouses and parental violence toward children. There is, however, considerable violence between siblings, teenage children and their parents, and adult children and their aging parents. These are the "hidden victims" of family violence (Gelles and Cornell, 1990).

Sibling Violence

Violence between siblings is by far the most common form of family violence (Straus, Gelles, and Steinmetz, 1980). Most of this type of sibling interaction is simply taken for granted by our culture—"You know how kids are!" Straus and his associates, in a survey that included 733 families with two or more children, found that 82 percent of the children had used some sort of violence against a sibling in the preceding year. The National Association of Child Abuse estimated that 29 million siblings physically harm each other annually (Tiede, 1983). Straus and his colleagues reported these additional findings:

◻ The rate of sibling violence goes down with the increasing age of the child.
◻ Boys of all ages are more violent than girls. The highest rates of sibling violence occur in families with only male children.
◻ Violence between children often reflects what they see their parents doing to each other and to the children themselves.

The full scope and implications of sibling violence have not been rigorously explored. However, Straus, Gelles, and Steinmetz concluded that

conflicts and disputes between children in a family are an inevitable part of life. . . . But the use of physical force as a tactic for resolving their conflicts is by no means inevitable. . . . Human beings learn to be violent. It is possible to provide children with an environment in which nonviolent methods of solving conflicts can be learned. . . . If violence, like charity, begins at home, so does nonviolence.

Teenage Violence toward Parents

Most of us find it difficult to imagine children attacking their parents, because it so profoundly violates our image of parent/child relations. Parents possess the authority and power in the family hierarchy. Furthermore, there is greater social disapproval of a child striking a parent than of a parent striking a child; it is the parent who has the "right" to hit. Finally, parents rarely discuss such incidents because they are ashamed of their own victimization; they fear that others will blame them for the children's violent behavior (Gelles and Cornell, 1990).

Although we know fairly little about adolescent violence against parents, scattered studies indicate that it is almost as prevalent as spousal violence (Gelles and Cornell, 1990; Straus, 1980; Straus, Gelles, and Steinmetz, 1980). Gelles and Cornell suggest that 2.5 million parents are struck annually by their adolescent children. They report that about 900,000 parents are kicked, punched, bitten, beaten up, or have a gun or knife used on them by their teenage children each year.

The majority of youthful children who attack parents are between the ages of thirteen and twenty-four. Sons are slightly more likely to be abusive than daughters, and the rate of severe male violence tends to increase with age while that of females decreases. Boys apparently take advantage of their increasing size and the cultural expectation of male aggression. Girls, in contrast, may become less violent because society views female aggression more negatively. Most researchers believe that mothers are the primary targets of violence and abuse because they may lack physical strength or social resources and because women are "acceptable" targets for abuse (Gelles and Cornell, 1990).

Abuse of the Elderly

Of all the forms of hidden family violence, only the abuse of elderly parents by their grown children (or in some cases, grandchildren) has received considerable public attention. It is estimated that approximately 500,000 elderly are physically abused annually. An additional 2 million are thought to be emotionally abused or neglected. Much abuse of the elderly goes unnoticed, unrecognized, and unreported. Old people generally don't get out much and are often confined to bed or a wheelchair. Many do not report their mistreatment out of fear of institutionalization or other reprisal. Although some research indicates that the abused in many cases were, in fact, abusing parents, more knowledge must be gained before we can draw firm conclusions about the causes of elder abuse (Gelles and Cornell, 1990).

The most likely victims of elder abuse are the very elderly—in the majority of cases women—who are suffering from physical or mental impairments. Their advanced age renders them dependent on their caregivers for many if not all of their daily needs. It may be their dependency that increases their likelihood of being abused. Other research indicates that many abusers are financially dependent on their elderly parents; they may resort to violence out of feelings of powerlessness. Earlier research on elder abuse suggested that most abusers were the middle-aged daughters of the abused, but more recent studies show that sons are somewhat more likely to abuse (Pillemer, 1985).

While researchers are sorting out the whys and wherefores of elder abuse, battered old people have a number of crying needs. Pillemer and Suitor (1988) recommend the following services for elders and their caregiving families:

❐ Housing services, including temporary respite care to give caregivers a break and permanent housing such as rest homes, group housing, and nursing homes.
❐ Health services, including home health care, adult day-care centers, and occupational, physical, and speech therapy.
❐ Housekeeping services, including shopping and meal preparation.
❐ Support services, such as visitor programs and recreation.
❐ Guardianship and financial management.

❐ REDUCING FAMILY VIOLENCE

Based on the foregoing evidence, you may by now have concluded that the American family is well on its way to extinction as we bash, thrash, cut, shoot, and otherwise wipe ourselves out of existence. Statistically, the safest family homes are those with one or no children in which the husband and wife experience little life stress and in which decisions are made democratically (Straus, Gelles, and Steinmetz, 1980). By this definition, most of us probably do not live in homes that are particularly safe. What can we do to protect ourselves (and our posterity) from ourselves?

Prevention strategies usually take one of two paths: eliminating social stress or strengthening families (Swift, 1986). Family-violence experts make the following general recommendations (Straus, Gelles, and Steinmetz, 1980):

❐ Reduce societal sources of stress, such as poverty, racism and inequality, unemployment, and inadequate health care.
❐ Eliminate sexism. Furnish adequate day care. Promote educational and employment opportunities equally for men and women. Promote sex education and family planning to prevent unplanned and unwanted pregnancies.
❐ End social isolation. Explore means of establishing supportive networks that include relatives, friends, and community.

A . . . society which promotes the ownership of firearms, women and children; which makes homes men's castles; and which sanctions societal and interpersonal violence in the forms of wars, athletic contests, and mass media fiction (and news) should not be surprised to find violence in its homes.

Norman Denzin

❒ Break the family cycle of violence. Eliminate corporal punishment and promote education about disciplinary alternatives. Support parent education classes to deal with inevitable parent/child conflict.

❒ Eliminate cultural norms that legitimize and glorify violence. Legislate gun control, eliminate capital punishment, and reduce media violence.

❒ SEXUAL ABUSE IN FAMILIES

The incest taboo, nearly universal in human societies, prohibits sexual activities between closely related individuals. There are only a few exceptions, and these concern brother/sister marriages in the royal families of ancient Egypt, Peru, and Hawaii. **Incest** is generally defined as sexual intercourse between persons too closely related to legally marry (usually interpreted to mean father/daughter, mother/son, or brother/sister). Sexual abuse or sexual victimization in families may include incest, but it can also involve family members such as uncles, grandparents, and stepparents. Sexual activities including but not limited to intercourse are considered abusive when an adult or adolescent engages in them with a child or younger adolescent. It does not matter if the younger person is perceived by the older one as freely participating in the activity. A minor child cannot give **informed consent,** so the activity is considered self-serving for the adult or older adolescent.

Until the late 1960s, it was generally assumed that sexual abuse in families was a rare phenomenon. When such abuse became reportable under child abuse laws, however, the various protective care agencies were shocked and alarmed by the large numbers of cases that surfaced. At the same time, psychiatrists became increasingly aware of childhood sexual abuse among their clients (Rosenfeld, 1977). A recent national survey found that 27 percent of the women and 16 percent of the men surveyed had experienced sexual abuse as children (Finkelhor et al., 1990). Child sexual victimization can be divided into two categories: sexual activities between family members (intrafamilial abuse) or those activities between nonfamily members (extrafamilial abuse). The trend in current research is to look at child sexual abuse in general (Finkelhor, 1984). In doing so, researchers have found that intrafamilial and extrafamilial sexual abuse share many common elements. Because there are so many variables—such as the age and sex of the victims and perpetrators, their relationship, the type of acts involved, and whether there was force—one cannot automatically say that abuse within the family is more harmful than extrafamilial abuse.

Forms of Intrafamilial Sexual Abuse

It is not clear what type of sexual victimization is the most frequent (Peters et al., 1986; Russell, 1986). Some researchers believe that father/daughter (including stepfather/daughter) abuse is the most common; others think that brother/sister abuse is most common. Still other researchers believe that incest committed by uncles is the most common (Russell, 1986). Mother/son sexual relations are considered to be rare (or are underreported).

FATHER/DAUGHTER ABUSE. There is general agreement that the most traumatic form of sexual victimization is father/daughter abuse, including that committed by stepfathers. One study (Russell, 1986) indicated that 54 percent of the girls sexually abused by their fathers were extremely upset. In contrast, 25 percent who were

Lot went out of Zo'ar, and dwelled in the hills with his two daughters, for he was afraid to dwell in Zo'ar. So he dwelled in a cave with his two daughters. Then the first-born said to the other, "Our father is old, and there is not a man on earth to come into us in the manner of men. Let us make our father drink wine and we will lie with him that we may have offspring through our father." So they made their father drink wine that night and his older daughter went in and lay with her father. He did not know when she lay down or when she arose. And then on the next day, the older daughter said to the younger one, "Behold, I lay last night with our father. Let us make him drink wine again tonight, then you go in and lie with him that we may have children by our father." So they gave their father wine that night, and the younger daughter slept with him. He did not know when she lay down or when she arose. Thus both Lot's daughters became great with child by their father.

Genesis 19:30–36

abused by other family members reported the same degree of upset. Over twice as many abused daughters reported serious long-term consequences. Some factors contributing to the severity of father/daughter sexual relations include the following:

❐ Fathers were more likely to have engaged in penile/vaginal penetration than other relatives (18 percent versus 6 percent).
❐ Fathers sexually abused their daughters more frequently than other perpetrators abused their victims (38 percent of the fathers sexually abused their daughters eleven or more times, compared to a 12 percent abuse rate for other abusing relatives).
❐ Fathers were more likely to use force or violence than others (although the numbers for both fathers and others were extremely low).

In the past, many have discounted the seriousness of sexual abuse by a stepfather, because incest is generally defined legally as sexual activity between two biologically related persons. The emotional consequences are just as serious, however. Sexual abuse by a stepfather still represents a violation of the basic parent/child relationship. As Judith Herman (1981) noted, psychologically it does not matter if the father and child are related by blood. "What matters is the relationship that exists by virtue of the adult's parental power and the child's dependency." In fact, sexual abuse committed by stepfathers often is greater in severity. Forty-one percent of the abusing stepfathers in Russell's study (1986) abused their daughters more than twenty times. Only 17 percent of biological fathers abused their daughters that frequently. In 47 percent of the cases involving stepfathers, the abuse continued for a year or more. In contrast, 28 percent of incest committed by biological fathers continued that long.

BROTHER/SISTER SEXUAL VICTIMIZATION. There are contrasting views concerning the consequences of brother/sister incest. Researchers generally have expressed little interest in it. Most have tended to view it as harmless sex play or sexual exploration between mutually involved siblings. The research, however, has generally failed to distinguish between exploitative and nonexploitative brother/sister sexual activity. Russell (1986) suggests that the idea that brother/sister incest is usually harmless and mutual may be a myth. In her study, the average age difference between the brother (age 17.9 years) and sister (10.7 years) is so great that the siblings can hardly be considered peers. The age difference represents a significant power difference. Furthermore, not all brother/sister sexual activity is "consenting"; considerable physical force may be involved. Russell wrote:

So strong is the myth of mutuality that many victims themselves internalize the discounting of their experiences, particularly if their brothers did not use force, if they themselves did not forcefully resist the abuse at the time, if they still continued to care about their brothers, or if they did not consider it abuse when it occurred. And sisters are even more likely than daughters to be seen as responsible for their own abuse.

Russell discovered that 2 percent of the women in her random sample had at least one sexually abusive experience with a brother.

UNCLE/NIECE VICTIMIZATION. Both Alfred Kinsey (1953) and Diane Russell (1986) found the most common form of intrafamilial sexual abuse to involve uncles and nieces. Russell reported that almost 5 percent of the women in her study had been molested by their uncles, slightly more than the percentage abused by their fathers. The level of severity of the abuse was generally less in terms of the type of sexual acts and the use of force. Although such abuse does not take place within the nuclear family, many victims found it quite upsetting. A quarter of the respondents indicated long-term emotional effects (Russell, 1986).

The Abusers and the Abused

Despite the high rates of intrafamily sexual victimization, when we think of **pedophilia**—sexual attraction to or sexual use of children—we tend to think in terms of strangers. But like so many of our images of deviant individuals, our image of sex offenders is more imagination than reality (see Finkelhor, 1984, for public perceptions concerning pedophilia). In the majority of instances, the sexual abuser is known to the victim: he is a father, brother, uncle, neighbor, friend, or acquaintance. Russell (1984) found that in extrafamilial sexual abuse, 41 percent of the perpetrators were intimately connected to the victim (friend, family friend, and so on), and 42 percent were acquaintances. Another common misconception is that most sexual abusers are gay men; instead, most are heterosexual men. Even males who sexually abuse boys are not necessarily gay, note researchers (Groth and Gray, 1982). The child's age more than sex appears to be important for most male pedophiles.

The most dangerous stereotype, however, is that the offender is responding to the sexual advances of a precocious child. In this stereotype, "the offender himself is the victim of a provocative and seductive child, for here the victim is blamed for being abused, and the actual offender is not held fully responsible for his behavior" (Groth and Birnbaum, 1978; Groth, 1980). The Biblical story of Lot gives religious sanction to this myth. Other misconceptions include that the sexual abuser is an old man, someone who is insane or developmentally disabled, an alcoholic or drug addict, or a sexually frustrated or oversexed individual.

CHILDREN AT RISK. Not all children are equally at risk for sexual abuse. Although any child can be sexually abused, some groups of children are more likely to be victimized than others. A review (Finkelhor and Baron, 1986) of the literature indicates that those children at higher risk for sexual abuse are the following:

❐ Female children
❐ Preadolescent children
❐ Children with absent or unavailable parents
❐ Children whose relationships with parents are poor
❐ Children whose parents are in conflict
❐ Children who live with a stepfather

The majority of sexually abused children are girls (Finkelhor, 1984), but boys are also victims. The ratio of girls to boys appears to be between 2.5 and 4 to 1 (Finkelhor and Baron, 1986). We have only recently recognized the sexual abuse of boys; this neglect has been part of the more general neglect of all sexual victimization of males (Russell, 1984). Finkelhor (1979) speculates that males tend to underreport sexual abuse because they experience greater shame; they feel that their masculinity has been undermined. Boys tend to be blamed more than girls for their victimization, especially if they did not forcibly resist: "A real boy would never let someone do that without fighting back" (Rogers and Terry, 1984).

Most sexually abused children are between eight and twelve years of age when the abuse first takes place. Children between ten and twelve years appear to be the most vulnerable, while those under ages six and seven seem to be less vulnerable

This drawing was made by an adolescent who was impregnated by her father. According to psychologists, it expresses her inability to deal with body images, especially genitalia, and her rejection of her body's violation.

(Finkelhor and Baron, 1986). Children who have poor relationships with their parents (especially mothers) or whose parents are absent or unavailable and have high levels of marital conflict appear to be at higher risk. A child in such a family may be less well supervised and, as a result, more vulnerable to manipulation and exploitation by an adult. In this type of family, the child may be unhappy, deprived, or emotionally needy; the child may be more responsive to the offers of friendship, time, and material rewards promised by the abuser.

Finally, children with stepfathers are at greater risk for sexual abuse. Russell (1986) found that only 2.3 percent of the daughters studied were sexually abused by their biological fathers. In contrast, 17 percent were abused by their stepfathers. The higher risk may result from the incest taboos not being as strong in step-relationships and because stepfathers have not built up inhibitions resulting from parent/child bonding beginning from infancy. As a result, stepfathers may be more likely to view the child sexually. In addition, stepparents may also bring into the family step-relatives—their own parents, siblings, or children—who may feel no incest-related prohibition about becoming sexually involved with stepchildren.

THE FAMILY CLIMATE. Although traditionally we have viewed the sexual abuse of children as the result of some kind of character disorder or personality type, it now appears that it is a symptom of severe family dysfunction. To explain the dynamics of such behavior, researchers generally use a family systems model (discussed in Chapter 3). In this model, each family member has different needs and plays different roles.

The role of mothers in their daughters' abuse has been much debated (Finkelhor, 1979; Herman, 1981). It has been suggested that some mothers may unconsciously "collude" in their husband's exploitive acts (Justice and Justice, 1979). These women have sexually withdrawn from their husbands and may talk themselves out of suspicions about their husbands' behavior. But it is important not to blame the victims' mothers for the abuse, as it would misdirect the responsibility from the offender. To blame mothers for the exploitation of their daughters, Russell (1986) points out, assumes that "daughters must be chaperoned in their own homes to be safe." The role of mothers in *protecting* their daughters (and sons) from sexual aggression is well-substantiated, however (Gelles and Conte, 1991).

Justice and Justice (1979) noted several factors that appeared to be prevalent in homes where father/daughter incest occurs. It should be noted that these characteristics need not be present for abuse to occur; they are *not* causes of sexual abuse.

❏ The father is under severe stress (from job or family changes, moving, and so on). He may increase his drinking.
❏ Sex ceases between the father and the mother.
❏ The mother leaves her husband and daughter alone (for example, by working nights or being sick).
❏ The daughter is hungry for affection.
❏ The family's sexual climate is either very lax or very repressive.

Effects of Sexual Victimization

There are numerous well-documented consequences of child sexual abuse that hold true for both intrafamilial and extrafamilial abuse (see Browne and Finkelhor, 1986, for a review of the literature). These include both initial and long-term consequences.

INITIAL EFFECTS OF SEXUAL ABUSE. The initial consequences, those occurring within the first two years, include those in the following list. The proportion of victimized children who experience these disturbances ranges from a quarter to almost two-thirds, depending on the study. To date, however, the empirical literature remains sketchy (Browne and Finkelhor, 1986).

❐ *Emotional disturbances*, including fear, anger and hostility, guilt and shame.
❐ *Physical consequences*, including difficulty in sleeping, changes in eating patterns, and pregnancy.
❐ *Sexual disturbances*, including significantly higher rates of open masturbation, sexual preoccupation, and exposure of the genitals.
❐ *Social disturbances*, including difficulties at school, truancy, running away from home, and early marriages by abused adolescents.

LONG-TERM EFFECTS OF SEXUAL ABUSE. Although there can be some healing of the initial effects, child sexual abuse may leave lasting scars on the adult survivor. These adults often have significantly higher incidences of psychological, physical, and sexual problems than the general population. These problems include the following (Browne and Finkelhor, 1986):

❐ *Depression*, the most frequently reported symptom of adults sexually abused as children.
❐ Self-destructive tendencies, including suicide attempts and thoughts of suicide.
❐ *Somatic disturbances and dissociation*, including anxiety and nervousness, eating disorders (anorexia and bulimia), feelings of "spaciness," out-of-body experiences, and feelings that things are "unreal."
❐ *Negative self-concept*, including feelings of low-self esteem, isolation, and alienation.
❐ *Interpersonal relationship difficulties*, including difficulties in relating to both sexes, parental conflict, problems in responding to their own children, and difficulty in trusting others.
❐ *Revictimization*, in which women abused as children are more vulnerable to rape and marital violence.
❐ *Sexual problems*, in which survivors find it difficult to relax and enjoy sexual activities, or avoid sex and experience hypoactive (inhibited) sexual desire and lack of orgasm.

A MODEL OF SEXUAL ABUSE TRAUMA. As we have seen, there are numerous initial and long-term consequences of childhood sexual abuse. Together, these consequences create a traumatic dynamic that affects the child's ability to deal with the world. Finkelhor and Browne (1986) suggest a model of sexual abuse that contains four components: traumatic sexualization, betrayal, powerlessness, and stigmatization. When these factors converge as a result of sexual abuse, they affect the child's cognitive and emotional orientation to the world. They create trauma by distorting a child's self-concept, world view, and affective abilities. These consequences affect abuse survivors not only as children but also as adults.

TRAUMATIC SEXUALIZATION. Traumatic sexualization refers to the process in which the sexually abused child's sexuality developed inappropriately and becomes interpersonally dysfunctional. Finkelhor and Browne note:

It occurs through the exchange of affection, attention, privileges, and gifts for sexual behavior, so that the child learns sexual behavior as a strategy for manipulating others to get his or her other developmentally appropriate needs met. It occurs when certain parts of the child's anatomy are fetishized and given distorted importance and meaning. It occurs through the misconceptions and confusions about sexual behavior and morality that are transmitted to the child from the offender. And it occurs when very frightening memories and events become associated in the child's mind with sexual activity.

Sexually traumatized children learn inappropriate sexual behaviors (such as manipulating an adult's genitals for affection), are confused about their sexuality, and inappropriately associate certain emotions—such as loving and caring—with sexual activities.

As adults, sexual issues may become especially important. Survivors may suffer flashbacks, sexual dysfunctions, and negative feelings about their bodies. They may also be confused about sexual norms and standards. A fairly common confusion is the belief that sex may be traded for affection. Some women label themselves as "promiscuous," but this label may be more a result of their negative self-image than their actual behavior. There seems to be a history of childhood sexual abuse among many prostitutes.

BETRAYAL. Children feel betrayed when they discover that someone on whom they have been dependent has manipulated, used, or harmed them. Children may also feel betrayed by other family members, especially mothers, for not protecting them from abuse.

As adults, survivors may experience depression as a manifestation, in part, of extended grief over the loss of trusted figures. Some may find it difficult to trust others. Other survivors may feel a deep need to regain a sense of trust and become extremely dependent. Distrust may manifest itself in hostility and anger. In adolescents, antisocial or delinquent behavior may be a means of protecting themselves from further betrayal. Anger may express a need for revenge or retaliation. Other times, distrust may manifest itself in social isolation and avoidance of intimate relationships.

POWERLESSNESS. Children experience a basic kind of powerlessness when their bodies and personal space are invaded against their will. A child's powerlessness is reinforced as the abuse is repeated.

In adulthood, powerlessness may be experienced as fear or anxiety; a person feels unable to control events. Adult survivors often believe that they have impaired coping abilities. This feeling of ineffectiveness may be related to the high incidence of depression and despair among survivors. Powerlessness may also be related to increased vulnerability or revictimization by rape or marital violence; survivors feel unable to prevent subsequent victimization. Other survivors, however, may attempt to cope with their earlier powerlessness by an excessive need to control or dominate others.

STIGMATIZATION. Stigmatization refers to ideas of badness, guilt, and shame about sexual abuse that are transmitted to abused children and then internalized by them. Stigmatization is communicated in numerous ways. The abuser conveys it by blaming the child or, through his secrecy, communicates a sense of shame. If the abuser pressures the child for secrecy, the child may also internalize feelings of shame and guilt. Children's prior knowledge that their family or community consider such activities deviant may contribute to their feelings of stigmatization.

As adults, survivors may feel extreme guilt or shame about having been sexually abused. They may have low self-esteem because they feel that the abuse had made them "spoiled merchandise." They also feel different from others, because they mistakenly believe that they alone have been abused.

Abuse leaves children feeling broken and alone.

Treatment Programs

There is a growing trend toward dealing with child sexual abuse, especially father/daughter incest, through therapy programs working in conjunction with the judicial system rather than breaking up the family by removing the child or the offender (Nadelson and Sauzier, 1986). Because the offender is often also the breadwinner, incarcerating him may greatly increase the family's emotional distress. The district attorney's office may work with clinicians in evaluating the existing threat to the child and deciding whether to prosecute or refer the offender to therapy (or both). The goal is not simply to punish the offender but to try to assist the victim and the family in coming to terms with the abuse.

Many of these clinical programs work on several levels at once: they treat the individual, the father/daughter relationship, the mother/daughter relationship, and the family as a whole. They work on developing self-esteem and improving the family and marital relationships. If appropriate, they refer individuals to alcohol- or drug-abuse treatment programs.

A crucial ingredient to many treatment programs is individual and family attendance at self-help group meetings. These self-help groups are composed of incest survivors, offenders, mothers, and other family members. Self-help groups such as Parents United and Daughters and Sons United assist the offender in acknowledging his responsibility and in understanding the impact of the incest on all involved. "No matter the extenuating circumstances . . . , his action betrayed his child and wife and their reliance on him as father and husband," wrote Henry Giarretto (1976), director of one of the most longstanding treatment programs. (See Resource Center for information on treatment programs for sexual abuse.)

Preventing Sexual Abuse

The idea of preventing sexual abuse is relatively new. Prevention programs began about a decade ago, a few years after programs were started to identify and help child or adult survivors of sexual abuse. Such prevention programs have been hindered, however, by three factors (Finkelhor, 1986a, 1986b):

❐ Sexual abuse is complicated by different concepts of appropriate sexual behavior and appropriate partners, which are not easily understood by children.
❐ Sexual abuse, especially incest, is a difficult and scary topic for adults to discuss with children. Children who are frightened by their parents, however, may be less able to resist abuse than those who are given strategies of resistance.
❐ Sex education is controversial. Even where it is taught, instruction often does not go beyond physiology and reproduction. The topic of incest is especially opposed.

In confronting these problems, child abuse prevention (CAP) programs have been very creative. These programs typically aim at three audiences: children, parents, and professionals, especially teachers. CAP programs aimed at children include plays, puppet shows, filmstrips, videotapes, books, and comic books to teach children that they have rights. Children have the right to control their own bodies and genitals and to feel "safe," and they have the right not to be touched in ways that feel confusing or wrong. The CAP programs stress that the child is not at fault when such abuse does occur. They also try to give children possible courses of action if someone tries to sexually abuse them. In particular, children are advised to tell someone they trust (and to keep telling until they are believed).

We are healthy only to the degree that our ideas are humane.

Kurt Vonnegut, Jr.

Other programs focus on educating parents who, it is hoped, will in turn educate their children. These programs aim at helping parents discover abuse or abusers by identifying warning signs. The programs assume that the participants are not abusers or potential abusers. Parents seem reluctant, however, to deal with sexual abuse issues with their children, according to David Finkelhor (1986a). First, many do not feel that their children are at risk. Second, parents are fearful of unnecessarily frightening their children. Third, parents feel uncomfortable about talking with their children about sex in general, much less such tabooed subjects as incest. In addition, parents may not believe their own children or may feel uncomfortable confronting a suspected abuser, who may be a partner, uncle, friend, or neighbor.

Child abuse prevention programs have also directed attention to professionals, especially teachers, physicians, mental health professionals, and police officers. Because of their close contact with children and their role in teaching children about the world, teachers are especially important. Professionals are encouraged to be watchful for signs of sexual abuse and to investigate children's reports of such abuse. A number of schools have instituted programs to educate students and their parents as well.

 SUMMARY

❐ Any form of intimacy or relatedness increases the likelihood of violence or abuse. The mythology of family violence, however, obscures many of its real features. *Violence* is defined as "an act carried out with the intention or perceived intention of causing physical pain or injury to another person."

❐ The principal models used to study sources of family violence are: the *psychiatric model,* which finds the source of violence within the personality of the abuser; the *ecological model,* which looks at both the child's development in the family context and the family's development within the community; the *patriarchy model,* which finds violence to be inherent in male-dominated societies; the *social learning model,* in which violence is seen as a behavior learned within the family and larger society; the *social-situational model,* which views family violence as arising from a combination of structural stress and cultural norms; the *resource model,* which assumes that force is used to compensate for the lack of personal, social, and economic resources; and the *exchange/social control model,* which holds that people weigh the costs versus the rewards in all their actions and that they will use violence if the social controls (costs) are not strong enough. Three factors that may reduce social control are inequality of power in the family, the private nature of the family, and the "real man" image.

❐ *Battering* is the use of physical force against another person; it includes slapping, punching, knocking down, choking, kicking, hitting with objects, threatening with weapons, stabbing, and shooting. Wife battering is one of

the most common and most underreported crimes in the United States.

❐ Although there does not appear to be a "typical" battered woman, there are two characteristics that correlate highly with wife assault: low socioeconomic status and a high degree of marital conflict.

❐ A man who batters probably has some or all of the following characteristics: low self-esteem, belief in common myths about battering, traditional beliefs about the family, pathological personality characteristics, use of sex as aggression, and a belief in the moral rightness of his aggression.

❐ The three-phase *cycle of violence* in battering relationships includes (1) the tension-building phase, (2) the explosive phase, and (3) the resolution (love) phase.

❐ Marital rape is a form of battering. Many people, including victims themselves, have difficulty acknowledging that forced sex in marriage is rape, just as it is outside of marriage.

❐ The prevalence of violence and sexual assault in dating relationships is alarming. Violence is often precipitated by jealousy or rejection. Acquaintance rape may not be recognized by either the assailant or the victim, because they think that rape is done by strangers.

❐ Women may stay in or return to battering relationships for a number of reasons, including economic dependency, religious pressure or beliefs, the perceived children's need for a father, pity, guilt, a sense of duty, fear, and love. They may also be paralyzed by "learned helplessness." Women may leave violent relationships when the level of violence increases or their children become threatened. Women may also try to stop their husbands' violence. The most important factor in stopping abuse appears to be the woman's own determination that it must stop.

❒ The issue of compassion versus control is significant in domestic violence intervention. Arrest, prosecution, and imprisonment are examples of control; shelters and support groups (including abuser programs) are examples of compassionate intervention.

❒ At least a million children are physically abused by their parents each year. Many abuse cases are unreported. Parental violence is one of the five leading causes of childhood death.

❒ Families at risk for child abuse often have specific parental, child, and family ecosystem characteristics. Parental characteristics include a physically abused father, belief in corporal punishment, a devalued marital relationship and interspousal violence, low self-esteem, father dominance, unrealistic expectation for the child, parent/child role reversal, and lack of parental concern about the child's injury. Child characteristics include a "normal" child who is the product of a difficult or unplanned pregnancy, is the wrong sex, or is born outside of marriage; an "abnormal" child with physical or medical problems; or a "difficult" child. The family ecosystem includes the general social and economic environment in which the family lives; characteristics in families at risk include such conditions as poverty, unemployment, unsafe neighborhoods, and social isolation.

❒ Mandatory reporting of suspected child abuse may be helping to decrease the number of abused children. However, social workers are still overburdened, and services such as foster care are in short supply. Early intervention and education may be successful in reducing abuse, but there is a shortage of government funds for these and other programs to assist the victims of family violence.

❒ The hidden victims of family violence include siblings (who have the highest rate of violent interaction), parents assaulted by their adolescent or youthful children, and elders assaulted by their middle-aged children.

❒ Some recommendations for reducing violence include: (1) reducing sources of societal stress, such as racism and poverty; (2) eliminating sexism; (3) establishing supportive networks; (4) breaking the family cycle of violence; and (5) eliminating the legitimization and glorification of violence.

❒ *Incest* is defined as "sexual intercourse between persons too closely related to marry." Sexual victimization of children may include incest, but it can also involve other family members and other sexual activities. Child sexual victimization can be extrafamilial or intrafamilial.

❒ The most serious form of child sexual abuse is probably father/daughter (or stepfather/daughter) incest. Stepfathers abuse their daughters at significantly higher rates than do biological fathers. Brother/sister incest is often serious if it is exploitative or abusive.

❒ *Pedophilia* is sexual attraction to or sexual use of children. Most sexual abusers are known to their victims. Children at risk for sexual abuse include females, preadolescents, children with absent or unavailable parents, children with poor parental relationships, children with parents in conflict, and children living with a stepfather.

❒ A family systems model is useful for understanding child sexual abuse. Characteristics of homes in which such abuse occurs may include a father under severe stress, cessation of sexual relations between the father and mother, a father and daughter left alone regularly, an affection-deprived daughter, and a sexual climate that is either very lax or very repressive.

❒ There are both initial and long-term effects of child sexual abuse. The initial effects include emotional disturbances, physical consequences, and sexual and social disturbances. The long-term effects include depression, self-destructive tendencies, somatic disturbances and dissociation, negative self-concept, interpersonal relationship difficulties, revictimization, and sexual difficulties.

❒ The survivors of sexual abuse frequently suffer from sexual abuse trauma, characterized by traumatic sexualization, stigmatization, betrayal, and powerlessness.

❒ Offenders are increasingly being sent into treatment programs in an attempt to assist the incest survivor and family in coping with the crisis that incest creates. Self-help groups are important for many survivors of sexual abuse.

PART 6

Changes

CHAPTER 13

Coming Apart: Separation and Divorce

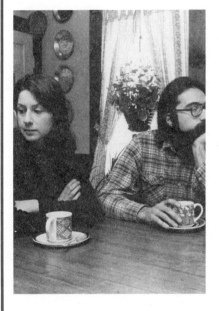

Love, the quest; marriage, the conquest; divorce, the inquest.

Helen Rowland

A MERICANS' FEELINGS ABOUT MARRIAGE AND DIVORCE SEEM STRANGELY PARA-
DOXICAL. Consider the following (Coleman and Ganong, 1991; White, 1991):

☐ *Americans like marriage:* They have one of the highest marriage rates in the industrialized world.
☐ *Americans don't like marriage:* They have one of the highest divorce rates in the
world.
☐ *Americans like marriage:* They have one of the highest remarriage rates in the
world.

What sense can we make from the fact that we are one of the most marrying, divorcing, and remarrying nations in the world? What does our high divorce rate actually tell us about how we feel about marriage?

Scholars suggest that divorce does not represent a devaluation of marriage but,
oddly enough, an idealization of it. We would not divorce if we did not have so
much hope about marriage fulfilling our various needs (Furstenberg and Spanier,
1987). In fact, divorce may very well be a critical part of our contemporary marriage
system, which emphasizes emotional fulfillment and satisfaction. Frank Furstenberg
and Graham Spanier (1987) note:

Divorce can be seen as an intrinsic part of a cultural system that values individual discretion
and emotional gratification. Divorce is a social invention for promoting these cultural ideals.
Ironically, the more divorce is used, the more exacting the standards become for those who
marry. . . . Divorce . . . serves not so much as an escape hatch from married life but as a
recycling mechanism permitting individuals a second (and sometimes third and fourth
chance) to upgrade their marital situation.

Our high divorce rate also tells us that we may no longer believe in the permanence of marriage. Norval Glenn (1991) suggests that there is a "decline in the
ideal of marital permanence and . . . in the expectation that marriages will last
until one of the spouses dies." Instead, marriages disintegrate when love goes or a
potentially better partner comes along. Divorce is a persistent fact of American
marital and family life and one of the most important forces affecting and changing
American lives today (Furstenberg and Cherlin, 1991).

Before 1974 "until death do us part" reflected reality. Then a surge in divorce
rates occurred in the mid-1960s that did not level off until the 1990s. In 1974, a wa-
tershed in American history was reached when more marriages ended by divorce
than by death. Today between 50 to 60 percent of all new marriages are likely to
end in divorce (Martin and Bumpass, 1989).

Not only does divorce end marriages and break up families, it also creates new
forms from the old ones. It creates remarriages (which are very different from first
marriages). It gives birth to single-parent families and stepfamilies. Today about one
out of every five American families is a single-parent family; more than half of all
children will become stepchildren by the year 2000 (Glick, 1989). (In contrast,
only 13 percent of Canadian families are "lone-parent" families [Statistics Canada,
1990].) And about half of current marriages include at least one spouse who is remarried (Bumpass, Sweet, and Martin, 1990). Within the singles subculture is an
immense pool of divorced men and women (most of whom are on their way to remarriage). But divorce does not create these new forms easily. It gives birth to them
in pain and travail.

Research traditionally looked on divorce from a deviance perspective (Coleman
and Ganong, 1991). It was assumed that normal, healthy individuals married and
remained married. Those who divorced were considered abnormal, immature, nar-

*Experience is the name everyone gives
to their mistakes.*

Oscar Wilde

*A man should not marry a woman with
the mental reservation that, after all, he
can divorce her.*

Talmud: Yebamoth

cissistic, or unhealthy in some manner. Social scientists, however, are increasingly viewing divorce as one path in the normal family life cycle. Those who divorce are not necessarily different from those who remain married. If we begin to regard divorce in this light, social scientists reason, part of the pain accompanying divorce may be diminished, as those involved will no longer regard themselves as "abnormal" (Raschke, 1987).

Social scientists express their greatest concern about the effects of divorce on children (Aldous, 1987; Wallerstein and Blakeslee, 1989). But even in studies of the children of divorce, the research may be distorted by traditional assumptions about divorce being deviant (Amato, 1991). For example, problems that children experience may be attributed to divorce rather than to other causes, such as personality traits or parental abuse. Although some effects are caused by the disruption of the family itself, others may be linked to the new social environment—most notably poverty and parental stress—into which children are thrust (McLanahan and Booth, 1991; Raschke, 1987).

In this chapter we look at marital separation, the changes an individual undergoes when he or she separates, no-fault divorce, custody, and the impact of divorce on children. In the next chapter we will examine how people put their lives back together after divorce and how, in doing so, they create new family structures.

❒ MARITAL SEPARATION

One of the most notable changes in recent divorce research is the recognition that divorce is not a single act but a process (Kitson and Morgan, 1991). The crucial event in a marital breakdown is the act of separation. Divorce is a legal consequence that follows the emotional fact of separation (Melichar and Chiriboga, 1988).

Although separation generally precedes divorce, not all separations lead to divorce. As many as one couple out of every six that remains married is likely to have separated for at least two days (Kitson, 1985). The majority of separated women are between fifteen and forty-five years old; a greater proportion of African Americans than whites are separated. A high proportion of women who are poor (and even more who are poor and have children) are separated (Norton and Moorman, 1987).

One study found that of those who separated, 40 percent reconciled at least once; 18 percent reconciled twice or more (Bumpass, Martin, and Sweet, 1991). Unfortunately, we don't know much about marital separation. We don't know, for example, which separations are likely to lead to reconciliations, divorce, or long-term separation (Morgan, 1988; South and Spitz, 1986). Those who reconcile may have separated in order to dramatize their complaints, create emotional distance, or dissipate their anger (Kitson, 1985). Almost all who reconciled did so within a year; 45 percent reconciled within a month. Of those who reconciled, about two-fifths were together at the time they were interviewed (Bumpass et al., 1991).

Uncoupling: The Process of Separation

The trends in divorce are fairly clear, but the causes are not. Sociologists can describe societal, demographic, and family factors that appear to be associated with divorce. Unfortunately, such variables tell us only about groups rather than individuals. Similarly, divorced men and women can tell us what they *believe* were the causes of their divorces. But human beings do not always know the reasons for their own actions. They can deceive themselves, blame others, or remain ignorant of the

It's one thing marrying the wrong person for the wrong reasons: it's another sticking it out with them.

Philip Roth, Letting Go

Divorces are made in heaven.

Oscar Wilde

Marriage is the chief cause of divorce.

Groucho Marx

Things You Told Me

I am a lousy housekeeper
I don't wash the dishes often enough
When I do wash the dishes, I run the
*   water too much*
When I clean up, I do it in the wrong
*   order*
The mustard is on the wrong shelf in the
*   refrigerator*
I arrange our refrigerator wrong
My inconsiderate children step on the
*   papers you have left neatly stacked on*
*   the living room floor*
I raise my children wrong
My little boy doesn't wash his dish
He washes his dish wrong
We make too much noise
I cut wrapping paper wrong
I massage you wrong
I touch wrong
I kiss wrong
I make love wrong
I am too sexual
My hugs are too sexual
I lay with my arm across the wrong part
*   of your body (which hurts your*
*   stomach or makes you itch)*
I pull your hair when I embrace you
I take too long to come
Or sometimes (and this is worse) I don't
*   come at all*
I sleep too close
I don't sleep close enough
I express my feelings wrong
I handle your anger wrong

(continued on next page)

*Because divorce has become part of
contemporary marital norms, it is part of the
normal life cycle for many marriages.*

causes (Burns, 1984). Sometimes marital complaints are culled from long-term marital problems as a justification for the split-up. Gay Kitson and Marvin Sussman (1982) observed that the study of marital complaints as causes of divorce is merely the study of people's perceptions: "It is perhaps an impossibility to determine what 'really' broke up the marriage." Robert Weiss (1975) used the term "account" to describe the individual's personal perception of the breakup. These accounts focus on a few dramatic events or factors in the marriage. Because accounts are personal perceptions, each spouse's account is often very different; what is important to one partner may not be important to the other. Sometimes the accounts of ex-spouses seem to describe entirely different marriages.

People do not suddenly separate or divorce. Instead, they gradually move apart through a set of fairly predictable stages. Sociologist Diane Vaughan (1986) calls this process "uncoupling." The process appears to be the same for married or unmarried couples and for gay, lesbian, and heterosexual relationships. The length of time together does not seem to affect the process. Uncoupling begins," Vaughan observes, "as a quiet, unilateral process." Usually one person, the initiator, is unhappy or dissatisfied but keeps such feelings to himself or herself. The initiator often ponders fundamental questions about his or her identity: "Who am I? Who am I in this relationship? What do I want out of my life? Can I find it in this relationship?" The dissatisfied partner may attempt to make changes in the relationship, but these are often unsuccessful, as he or she may not really know what the problem is.

Because the dissatisfied partner is unable to find satisfaction within the relationship, he or she begins turning elsewhere. This is not a malicious or intentional turning away; it is done to find self-validation without leaving the relationship. In doing so, however, the dissatisfied partner "creates a small territory independent of the coupled identity." This creates a division within the relationship. Gradually, the dissatisfied partner voices more and more complaints, which make the relationship and partner increasingly undesirable. The initiator begins thinking about alternatives to the relationship and comparing the costs and benefits of these alternatives. Meanwhile, both the initiator and his or her partner try to cover up the seriousness of the dissatisfaction, submerging it in the little problems of everyday living.

Eventually the initiator decides that he or she can no longer go on. There are several strategies for ending the relationship. One way is simply to tell the partner that the relationship is over. Another way is to consciously or unconsciously break a fundamental rule in the relationship, such as by having an extramarital affair.

Uncoupling does not end when the end of a relationship is announced, or even when the couple physically separate. Acknowledging that the relationship cannot be saved represents the beginning of the last stage of uncoupling. Vaughan (1986) wrote:

Partners begin to put the relationship behind them. They acknowledge that the relationship is unsaveable. Through the process of mourning they, too, eventually arrive at an account that explains this unexpected denouement. "Getting over" a relationship does not mean relinquishing that part of our life that we shared with another, but rather coming to some conclusion that allows us to accept and understand its altered significance. Once we develop such an account, we can incorporate it into our lives and go on.

Separation Distress

Our married self becomes part of our deepest self. Therefore, when people separate or divorce, many feel as if they have "lost an arm or a leg." This analogy, as well as the traditional marriage rite in which a man and a woman are pronounced "one," reveals an important truth of marriage: the constant association of both partners makes each almost a physical part of the other. This dynamic is true even if two people are locked in conflict; they, too, are attached to each other (Masheter, 1991).

Marital roles, however, end with separation and divorce: the man is no longer a husband and the woman is no longer a wife. If these former partners are also parents, their parental roles alter as well. In most cases, a woman becomes *more* a mother and a man becomes *less* a father. A woman's parent role becomes more significant and all-encompassing while a man's becomes less so. An important task for those who separate is to create new identities that reflect their new status (or nonstatus, as some feel).

Most newly separated people do not know what to expect. There are no divorce ceremonies or rituals to mark this major turning point. Yet people need to understand divorce to alleviate some of its pain and burden. Except for the death of a spouse, divorce is the greatest stress-producing event in life (Holmes and Rahe, 1967). The changes that take place during separation are crucial, because at this point a person's emotions are rawest and most profound. Men and women react differently during this period, although both are more depressed than their married or divorced counterparts. Men have a generally lower sense of well-being than women, yet women undergo greater emotional upheaval (Gove et al., 1990; Raschke, 1987).

Researchers have considerable knowledge about the negative consequences accompanying marital separation, some of which we will discuss in the sections that follow. In looking at this negative impact, however, we need to keep in mind Helen Raschke's (1987) caution: "The psychological and emotional consequences of separation and divorce have been more distorted than any of the other consequences as a result of the deviance perspective." The negative aspects of separation are balanced sooner or later, notes Raschke, by positive aspects, such as the possibility of finding a more compatible partner, constructing a better (or different) life, developing new dimensions of the self, enhancing self-esteem, and marrying a better parent for one's children. These positive consequences may follow or be intertwined with separation distress. In the pain of separation, we may forget that a new self will eventually emerge.

Things You Told Me (cont.)
I communicate wrong
I don't always like the things you like and I say so–this is wrong
I share my enthusiasm wrong
I'm wrong to be upset by your disrespect for me
I buy you the wrong presents
I take the wrong routes when I drive from one place to another
I drive too slow
I am too hesitant when I drive
I shift too late or too early
I drive in the wrong gear
I don't pass the slow cars when I should
I drive in the wrong lane
I ask too much of you
I relate to people wrong
I forget things because I pay attention wrong
I don't always understand what you are trying to say because I listen wrong
I'm illogical
I complain too much
I have bad manners
I'm inconsiderate
My children are untogether
I'm sick too often
I'm too serious
I take too much aspirin
I hurt your feelings
I am insensitive to your vulnerability

S.B.R.

Don't leave in a huff. Leave in a minute and a huff. If you can't leave in a minute and a huff, leave in a taxi.

Groucho Marx

. . . rather bear those ills we have Than fly to others we know not of.

William Shakespeare

FOCUS

Marital Cohesiveness

Whatever the demographic or personal reasons we may find for divorce, the ultimate reasons may escape us. Another way to understand divorce, however, is to examine marital cohesiveness, the factors that help maintain a marriage. According to George Levinger (1979), people remain married because of (1) sources of attraction, (2) barriers against leaving, and (3) sources of alternate attraction. In this model, *attraction* refers to positive forces that keep people in a relationship, *barriers* are restraining forces that keep people from leaving a relationship, and *alternative attractions* are other persons, relationships, or activities that compete with the marital relationship. The importance of each factor changes during people's lives (White and Booth, 1991).

Although Levinger's model is not romantic, it may be realistic. For those who have been ambivalent about ending a long-term relationship, these three factors may seem all too familiar.

ATTRACTIONS

Attractions include caring for one's partner, the desire for companionship, sexual pleasure, and other affectionate aspects of the relationship. They also included a good standard of living (such as home ownership or family income), similar social values, and educational and occupational status. It is not uncommon for people to stay together because they love their house more than each other.

BARRIERS

Barriers to breaking up include feelings of obligation, moral proscriptions, and external pressures. One of the strongest restraints is a couple's (especially the mother's) deep sense of love for and moral obligation to their dependent children (Levinger, 1979). One study, for example, has shown that women with children are significantly less liberal toward divorce than women without children (Jorgensen and Johnson, 1980). The presence of children, however, has little effect on men's attitudes toward divorce. The couple may also feel an obligation to the marriage itself, even if they have ceased loving each other. They may also believe that they are morally obliged by their religion not to divorce. Finally, they may feel exter-

nal pressures not to divorce. (What will our parents say? What will our friends say?) Family and community pressures have been powerful constraints on divorce in the past, but such constraints have weakened in recent years. (For the significance of commitment, see Sabatelli and Cecil-Pigo, 1985; Swenson and Trahaug, 1985; also see Heaton and Albrecht, 1991).

ALTERNATIVES

The alternatives to marriage may include singlehood and greater independence and self-direction, especially for women who may have felt their potential curtailed in marriage. Also, a person may find (or believe that he or she may find) greater happiness with another partner.

Because of the ease with which divorce may be obtained, we are living in a marriage system in which everyone is permanently available as a spouse and is continually comparing his or her current marriage with other potential marriages or with singlehood. As a result, they may not fully commit

continued on next page

As for infidelity, which has been blamed for so many divorces, that doesn't seem to be the real issue. It might be closer to the truth to say that people divorce not because one or both partners have been unfaithful, but because they are faithful—not to each other, but to themselves.

Anatole Broyard

Almost everyone suffers separation distress when a marriage breaks up. The distress is real but, fortunately, not everlasting (although it may seem so). It is situational and is modified by numerous external factors. About the only men and women who do not experience distress are those whose marriages were riddled by high levels of conflict. In these cases, one or both partners may view the separation with relief (Raschke, 1987).

During separation distress, almost all attention is centered on the missing partner and is accompanied by apprehensiveness, anxiety, fear, and often panic. "What am I going to do?" "What is he or she doing?" "I need him . . . I need her . . . I hate him . . . I love him . . . I hate her . . . I love her. . . ." Sometimes, however, the immediate effect of separation is not distress but euphoria. This usually results from feeling that the former spouse is not necessary, that one can get along better without him or her, that the old fights and the spouse's criticism are gone forever, and that life will now be full of possibilities and excitement. That feeling is soon gone. Almost everyone falls back into separation anxiety (Weiss, 1975).

FOCUS

(Glenn, 1991). If a person's present marital relationship appears strikingly less favorable than the alternatives and if the barriers to leaving the marriage do not cancel out the value of the alternatives, then the marriage is more likely to dissolve. Richard Udry (1981) found that marriages in which many marriage alternatives were available to both spouses had high divorce rates. What is striking, moreover, is that marital alternatives are a better predictor of divorce than marital satisfaction. People often stay in unhappy marriages if they believe that they do not have good alternatives. They may also leave relatively satisfactory marriages if they think that their alternatives are better. In a society in which everyone is available, whether married or not, people may tend to see the grass as being greener on the other side of the fence. If the fence (barrier) is not too high, people may abandon their familiar turf for the greener pastures on the other side. Unfortunately, that grass on the other side may prove to be only Astroturf.

Levels of attraction, like barriers and alternatives, change over the course of an individual's life (White and Booth, 1991). This may account for the greater likelihood of divorce occurring in the first years of marriage instead of in longer-lasting marriages. Two researchers note (White and Booth, 1991), "Because barriers are few and alternatives high, people in short marriages get divorced even when their marriages are not very unhappy." Rather than accept an unfulfilling marriage, men and women in their youth are more likely to divorce, as they may be childless, not own a house, and feel that they could do much better than their current spouse. Things change as the marriage continues and the partners grow older. In long marriages, there are more barriers, such as children or home ownership, and fewer alternatives, such as a dearth of attractive, unattached potential partners. The level of marital unhappiness needs to be much higher to lead to divorce in such marriages.

This model of marital cohesiveness may be useful for examining the cohesiveness of your own relationship. Take two sheets of paper; entitle one "Myself" and the other "My Partner."

Divide each sheet into three columns. Label the first column "Attractions," the second one "Barriers," and the third one "Alternatives." Then list the various attractions, barriers, and alternatives in your current relationship (or a previous one if you are no longer in a relationship) for both you and your partner. Based on the attractions, barriers, and alternatives for both you and your partner, how cohesive do you think your relationship is? For you, which element is the most important for maintaining your relationship? For your partner? Are there things you can do (or not do) to make it more cohesive?

FACTORS AFFECTING DISTRESS. Separation distress affects people in a variety of ways. An unexpected separation is probably most painful for the partner who is left. Other factors affecting distress include the length of time married, who takes the initiative in leaving, whether someone new is found, the quality of the postmarital relationship, and personal resources.

LENGTH OF TIME MARRIED. Separations that take place during the first two years of marriage are less difficult for the husband and wife to weather. Those couples who separate after two years find separation more difficult, since it seems to take about two years for people to become emotionally and socially integrated into marriage and their marital roles (Weiss, 1975). After that point, additional years of marriage seem to make little difference. Generally, a person married for two years will suffer distress over the loss of marital roles as much as one married ten years.

Nothing proves better the necessity of an indissoluble marriage than the instability of passion.

Honoré de Balzac (1799–1850)

THE LEAVER AND THE LEFT. Considerable research has focused on finding out whether being the initiator makes a difference in separation distress (Buehler, 1987). It appears that the initiator has a greater sense of personal control over his or her life (Petit and Bloom, 1984). Noninitiators feel powerless, because they are unable to prevent the leaving. All they can do is stand by and watch their lives disintegrate. Initiators frequently feel a strong sense of guilt about hurting their partners and may worry about their own capacity to make emotional commitment (Weiss, 1975). Noninitiators often have a more difficult time accepting the divorce, experience more loneliness, and miss their former spouse more than they are missed (Spanier and Thompson, 1983, 1984). Who leaves whom does not seem to make much difference in the length or intensity of separation distress, but it does affect the character of the distress.

FINDING SOMEONE NEW. A new relationship reduces much of the distress caused by separation and almost entirely prevents the loneliness caused by emotional isolation. It also reinforces a person's sense of self-worth. But it does not entirely eliminate separation distress. It does not end the disruption of intimate personal relations with the former partner, children, friends, and relatives (Weiss, 1975). If the newly separated person was involved extramaritally with someone prior to the separation, the involvement may have provided needed emotional support and intimacy as the marriage unraveled. Such an extramarital relationship rarely ends in marriage; following divorce, however, the nature of the affair may change.

QUALITY OF THE POSTMARITAL RELATIONSHIP. After separation, husbands and wives may treat each other in ways that range from friendly consideration and care to outright hostility and warfare. Civilized divorces are certainly to be desired, especially if children are involved, but they are not easy to achieve. It usually takes considerable time for emotions to cool and wounds to heal. It may also require substantial effort and insight for the ex-partners to get beyond blame, hurt, and anger. If former partners do achieve friendly relations, they may feel reassured that the years they spent together were not meaningless. For some people, however, the quality of their former marriage may have been so poor that it isn't worth the effort to maintain contact.

RESOURCES. The more resources a person has, the better he or she may handle the separation crisis. These resources may be emotional as well as social and financial. Too often people blame themselves for not adjusting well to a marital breakup; they feel depressed and are angry with themselves for feeling depressed. People who are more resilient and have greater energy and imagination tend to do better than others. Those who have a tendency to withdraw, whose self-confidence is usually low, and who panic or get depressed easily have a harder time recovering. A person who becomes socially isolated following a breakup tends to be susceptible to an emotional or health breakdown (Pilisuk, 1982).

For a newly separated person, the old social world breaks up and must be recreated separate from the former partner (Milardo, 1987). Parents become an important resource for their divorcing adult children (Johnson, 1988). They provide economic assistance and emotional support; they are also important for their grandchildren in easing the divorce transition. Relatives of the former spouse often become unavailable, distant, or hostile. One study found that 70 percent of in-laws disapproved of the former spouse (Spanier and Thompson, 1987). Friends may splinter, some remaining friendly to both partners, others being friends only with one or championing one over the other. But the emotional support of friends often proves to be stronger than that of family (Spanier and Thompson, 1987). Friends thus become especially important in overcoming the isolation and loneliness that generally accompanies a separation. One woman, as she planned to leave her husband, made a determined effort to establish a network of friends to help cushion the shock. Eventually the distress wanes and life returns to a more stable pattern. The ups and downs associated with the separation disappear.

LONELINESS. As the separation continues, separation distress slowly gives way to loneliness. Eventually, loneliness becomes the most prominent feature of the broken relationship. Old friends can sometimes help provide stability for a person experiencing a marital breakup, but those who give comfort need to be able to tolerate the other person's loneliness. One man told the authors that he counts as true friends only those who listened to him being miserable day after day. However, separated people often consider themselves a burden and will turn away from old friends who seem happy and content. In fact, married friends are generally supportive during the first two months, but then their contacts with the separated person rapidly decline, perhaps in part because they related to the person as part of a couple rather than as an individual in his or her own right (Hetherington et al., 1977).

Beginning group therapy with other recently divorced people may help. Within such a group, separated or divorced people discover that their loneliness is not unusual and that they are not going crazy; on the contrary, their response is quite normal under the circumstances.

ESTABLISHING A POSTDIVORCE IDENTITY. A person goes through two distinct phases in establishing a new identity following marital separation: transition and recovery (Weiss, 1975). The *transition period* begins with the separation and is characterized by separation distress and then loneliness. In this period's later stages, most people begin functioning in an orderly way again, although they still may experience bouts of upset and turmoil. The transition period generally ends within the first year. During this time, individuals have already begun making decisions that provide the framework for new selves. They have entered the role of single parent or non-custodial parent, have found a new place to live, have made important career and financial decisions, and have begun to date. Their new lives are taking shape.

The *recovery period* usually begins in the second year and lasts between one and three years. By this time the separated or divorced individual has already created a reasonably stable pattern of life. The marriage is becoming more of a distant memory, and the former spouse does not arouse the intense passions he or she once did. Mood swings are not as extreme and depressed periods are fewer. Yet the individual still has self-doubts that lie just beneath the surface. A sudden reversal, a bad time with the kids, doubts about a romantic involvement can suddenly destroy a divorced person's confidence. By the end of the recovery period, the distress has passed. Those who have a strong sense of well-being are more likely to remarry within a few years (Spanier and Furstenberg, 1982).

It takes some people longer than others to recover, because each person experiences the process in his or her own way. But most are surprised by how long the recovery takes—they forget that they are undergoing a major discontinuity in their lives. Weiss (1975) estimates that it takes between two and four years after the initial separation for a divorced person to establish a new identity, to feel strong and confident. It is probably closer to four years for most. By anyone's reckoning, that is a long time, especially because it is a time marked by mood swings, uncertainty, and questioning.

One must first have chaos in oneself to give birth to a dancing star.

Friedrich Nietzsche

To free oneself is nothing; it's being free that is hard.

André Gide

Excuses

Are you leaving because you are hungry?
Aha! Is your stomach your master?

Are you leaving me to cover yourself?
Have I not a blanket on my bed?

Are you leaving me because you are thirsty?
Then take my breast, it flows over for you.

Traditional African poem

Sometimes I wonder if men and women really suit each other. Perhaps they should live next door and just visit now and then.

Katharine Hepburn

The problem of a satisfactory marriage remains incapable of purely private solutions.

C. Wright Mills

Dating Again

A first date after years of marriage and subsequent months of singlehood evokes some of the same emotions felt by inexperienced adolescents. Separated or divorced men and women who are beginning to date again may be excited, nervous, worry about how they look, and wonder whether or not it is okay to hold hands, kiss, or make love. They may feel that dating is incongruous with their former selves or be annoyed with themselves for feeling excited and awkward. Furthermore, they have little idea of the norms of postmarital dating (Spanier and Thompson, 1987).

For many divorced men and women, the greatest problem is how to meet other unmarried people. They believe that marriage has put them "out of circulation" and many are not sure how to get back in. Because of the marriage squeeze, separated and divorced women in their thirties or older are at a particular disadvantage: considerably fewer men are available than women. The problem of meeting others is most acute for single mothers who are full-time parents in the home, since they lack opportunities to meet potential partners. Divorced men, having fewer child-care responsibilities and more income than divorced women, tend to have more active social lives.

Dating fulfills several important functions for separated and divorced people. First, it is a statement to both the former spouse and the world at large that the individual is available to become someone else's partner (Vaughan, 1986). Second, dating is an opportunity to enhance one's self-esteem (Spanier and Thompson, 1987). Free from the stress of an unhappy marriage, dating may lead people to discover, for example, that they are more interesting and charming than either they or (especially) their former spouses had imagined. Third, dating initiates individuals into the singles subculture where they can experiment with the freedom about which they may have fantasized when they were married. Interestingly, Spanier and Thompson (1987) found no relationship between dating experience and well-being following separation.

Several features of dating following separation and divorce differ from premarital dating. First, dating does not seem to be a leisurely matter. Divorced people "are too pressed for time, too desperately in search of the 'right' person to waste time on a first date that might not go well" (Hunt and Hunt, 1977). Second, dating may be less spontaneous if the divorced woman or man has primary responsibility for children. The parent must make arrangements about child care; he or she may wish not to involve the children in dating. Third, finances may be strained; divorced mothers may have income only from low-paying or part-time jobs or AFDC benefits while having many child-care expenses. In some cases a father's finances may be strained by paying alimony or child support. Finally, separated and divorced men and women often have a changed sexual ethic based on the simple fact that there are few (if any) divorced virgins (Spanier and Thompson, 1987).

Sexual activity is an important component in the lives of separated and divorced men and women. Engaging in sexual relations for the first time following separation assists people in accepting their newly acquired single status. Because sexual fidelity is usually an important element in marriage, becoming sexually active with someone other than one's spouse is a dramatic symbol that the old marriage vows are no longer valid (Spanier and Thompson, 1987). Men initially tend to enjoy their sexual freedom following divorce, but women generally do not find it as meaningful. For men, sexual experience following separation is linked with their well-being. Sex seems to reassure men and bolster their self-confidence. Sexual activity is not as strongly connected to women's well-being (Spanier and Thompson, 1987). After a while, sex becomes a secondary consideration in dating as people look for a deeper, more intimate relationship (Kohen et al., 1979).

◻ DIVORCE CONSEQUENCES

Most divorces are not contested; between 85 and 90 percent are settled out of court through negotiations between spouses or their lawyers. But divorce, whether it is amicable or not, is a complex legal process, involving highly charged feelings about custody, property, and children (who are sometimes treated by angry partners as property to be fought over).

No-Fault Divorce

Since 1970, beginning with California's Family Law Act, forty-eight states have adopted no-fault divorce (while still providing for "legal grounds" divorce when applicable).

BASIC ASPECTS OF NO-FAULT DIVORCE. No-fault divorce has changed four basic aspects of divorce (Weitzman and Dixon, 1980; Weiztman, 1985), described below. Although no-fault has had no effect on divorce rates, it has decreased the time involved in the legal process (Kitson and Morgan, 1991).

1. No-fault divorce has eliminated the idea of fault-based grounds. Under no-fault divorce, no one is accused of desertion, cruelty, adultery, impotence, crime, insanity, or the host of other melodramatic acts or omissions. Neither party is found guilty of anything; rather, the marriage is declared unworkable and is dissolved. Husband and wife must agree that they have irreconcilable differences (which they need not describe) and that they believe it is impossible for their marriage to survive the differences.

2. No-fault divorce eliminates the adversary process. The stress and strain of the courtroom are eliminated under the new procedure. There is little research, however, to document whether no-fault divorce has been successful in lowering the distress level or conflict among divorcing couples (Kitson and Morgan, 1991).

3. The bases for no-fault divorce settlements are equity, equality, and need rather than fault or gender. "Virtue" is no longer financially rewarded, nor is it assumed that women need to be supported by men. Community property is to be divided equally, reflecting the belief that marriage is a partnership with each partner contributing equally, if differently. The criteria for child custody are based on a sex-neutral standard of the "best interests of the child" rather than a preference for the mother.

4. No-fault divorce laws are intended to promote gender equality by redefining the responsibilities of husbands and wives. The husband is no longer considered head of the household but is an equal partner with his wife. The husband is no longer solely responsible for support, nor the wife for the care of the children. The limitations placed on alimony assume that a woman will work.

UNANTICIPATED CONSEQUENCES OF NO-FAULT DIVORCE. When California passed the first no-fault divorce law, reformers were optimistic about its results. No-fault has been successful in eliminating much of the sham and acrimony that resulted from traditional divorce law. However, sociologist Lenore Weitzman argued in her landmark work, *The Divorce Revolution* (1985), that no-fault divorce's gender-neutral rules, designed to treat men and women equally, have placed older homemakers and mothers of young children at a disadvantage:

Since a woman's ability to support herself is likely to be impaired during marriage, especially if she is a full-time homemaker and mother, she may not be "equal" to her former husband at the point of divorce. Rules that treat her as if she is equal simply serve to deprive her of the financial support she needs.

Husbands typically enhance their earning capacity during marriage. In contrast, wives typically decrease their earning capacity because earlier they had quit or limited their participation in the work force to fulfill family roles. This withdrawal from full participation limits their earning capacity when they reenter the work force. Divorced homemakers may have out-dated experience, few skills, and no seniority. Furthermore, they continue to have the major responsibility and burden of childrearing.

Probably the most damaging unintended consequence of the no-fault divorce laws is that they systematically impoverish divorced women and their children. When women divorce, they are often left in great economic hardship. A single mother's income is about 67 percent of her predivorce income, while the income of a divorced man is about 90 percent of his predivorce income (Duncan and Hoffman, 1985). Because over half of the children born today will live in a single-parent family at some point during their childhood, through no-fault divorce rules "we are sentencing a significant proportion of the next generation of American children to periods of financial hardship" (Weitzman, 1985).

Economic Consequences

One of the most striking differences between two-parent and single-parent families is poverty. One out of every two single mothers lives below the poverty level, whereas only one out of ten two-parent families is poor (McLanahan and Booth, 1991). The overwhelming majority of single mothers have become poor as a result of their marital disruption. They became poor because of (1) the low-earning capacity of the mother, (2) lack of child support, and (3) inadequate welfare benefits (discussed in Chapter 9).

EMPLOYMENT. Separation and divorce dramatically change many mothers' employment patterns. If a mother was not employed prior to separation, she is likely to seek a job following her split-up. The reason is simple: If she and her children relied on alimony and child support alone, they would soon find themselves on the street. One study found that the proportion of mothers employed 1,000 hours or more a year increased from 51 percent to 73 percent following divorce (Duncan and Hoffman, 1985). Most employed single mothers are still on the verge of financial disaster, however. On the average, they earn only a third as much as married fathers. This is partly because women tend to earn less than men and partly because they work fewer hours, primarily because of child-care responsibilities (Garfinkel and McLanahan, 1986). The general problems of women's lower earnings capacity and lack of adequate child care are particularly severe for single mothers. Sex discrimination in employment and lack of societal support for child care condemn millions of single-mother families to poverty.

ALIMONY AND CHILD SUPPORT. Alimony and child support payments do little to alleviate the financial struggles of single-parent families. Most women and children experience dramatic downward mobility following divorce. For many women, their source of income changes from primarily joint wages earned during marriage to their own wages, private transfers (child support payments, alimony, and help from relatives), and welfare. Private transfers account for 35 percent of the annual income for lower-income women, 55 percent for middle-income women, and 73 percent for upper-income women. Welfare and food stamps account for 60 percent of the income of lower-income women, 37 percent of middle-income women, and 26 percent of upper-income women. ("Lower-," "middle-," and "upper" income classifications denote the woman's economic status prior to divorce.)

When the legal system treats men and women equally at the point of divorce, it ignores very real economic inequalities between men and women in our society, inequalities that marriage itself creates.

Lenore Weitzman, The Divorce Revolution

In 1989 less than 14 percent of divorcing women received alimony. Child support was awarded to 67 percent of white women, 33.7 percent of African-American women, and 40.9 percent of Latina women. About 58 percent of single mothers were awarded child support, but only 50 percent received full payment, 26 percent received partial payment, and 24 percent received none (U.S. Bureau of the Census, 1990). Federal law provides that by 1994, all child support payments will be automatically withheld from parental paychecks (Hinds, 1989). But even when fathers pay support, the amount is generally low. It generally depends more on the father's circumstances than the needs of the mother and children (Teachman, 1991). Alimony and child support payments make up only about 10 percent ($1,246) of the income of white single mothers and 3.5 percent ($322) of the income of African-American single mothers (McLanahan and Booth, 1991). Studies indicate that fathers are generally able to pay about twice the amount they currently pay (Garfinkel and Oellerich, 1989). Although some argue that divorced and remarried fathers cannot pay additional support without pushing themselves and their new families into poverty, evidence indicates that this is not true in the majority of cases (Duncan and Hoffman, 1985).

While there is general approval, at least in principal, of child support, alimony is more controversial. In the past, alimony represented the continuation of the husband's responsibility to support his wife. Today, however, the objectives of alimony are not clear (Oster, 1987). Currently, laws suggest that alimony should be awarded on the basis of need to those women who would otherwise be indigent. At the same time, there is a strong countermovement in which alimony represents the return of a woman's "investment" in marriage (Oster, 1987; Weitzman, 1985). Weitzman argues that a woman's homemaking and child-care activities must be considered important contributions to her husband's present and future earnings. If divorce rules don't give a wife a share of her husband's enhanced earning capacity, then the "investment" she made in her spouse's future earnings is discounted. According to Weitzman, alimony and child support awards should be made to divorced women in recognition of the wife's primary child-care responsibilities and her contribution to her husband's work or career. Such awards will help raise divorced women and children above the level of poverty to which they have been cast as a result of no-fault divorce's specious equality. A recent landmark court decision, in fact, upheld the "investment" doctrine by ruling that a woman who supported her husband during his medical education was entitled to a portion of his potential lifetime earnings as a physician (Oster, 1987).

❑ CHILDREN AND DIVORCE

A traditional nuclear family, merely because it is intact, does not necessarily offer an advantage to children over a single-parent family or stepfamily. A traditional family racked with spousal violence, sexual or physical abuse of children, alcoholism, neglect, severe conflict, or psychopathology creates a destructive environment that is likely to inhibit children's healthy development. As Anne Goetting (1981) observed in her review of the research literature on divorce, marital conflict in a two-parent family is more harmful to children than living in a tranquil single-parent family or stepfamily. One study (Hess and Camara, 1979) comparing the behavior of children from traditional nuclear and divorced families found that relationships among family members were more important influences on behavior than marital status. Children living in happy two-parent families appear to be the best adjusted and those from conflict-ridden two-parent families appear to be the worst adjusted. Children from single-parent families are in the middle. The key to

When I can no longer bear to think of the victims of broken homes, I begin to think of the victims of intact ones.

Peter DeVries

children's adjustment following divorce is a lack of conflict between divorced parents (Kline, Johnston, and Tschann, 1991).

Telling children that their parents are separating is one of the most difficult and unhappy events in life. Whether or not the parents are relieved about the separation, they often feel extremely guilty about their children. Children are generally aware of parental discord and are upset by the separation, although their distress may not be apparent. However, parental separation and divorce may not be equally disturbing for all children. Several studies (Kurdek et al., 1981; Kurdek and Siesky, 1980) suggest that divorce is not necessarily perceived by children as an overly distressing experience. Other studies found that about 25 percent of children of divorced parents were extremely depressed five years following the divorce (Wallerstein and Blakeslee, 1989). A recent study utilized a **meta-analysis** approach (combining statistical data from previous studies and reanalyzing it) of earlier divorce studies on the impact of parental divorce of the well-being of their children in adulthood (Amato and Keith, 1991) and found very little difference in the well-being of children from divorced families and intact families.

The Three Stages of Divorce for Children

Growing numbers of studies have appeared on the impact of divorce on children, but these studies frequently contradict one another. Part of the problem is a failure to recognize divorce as a process for children as opposed to a single event. Divorce is a series of events and changes in life circumstances. Many studies focus on only one part of the process and identify that part with divorce itself. Yet at different points in the process, children are confronted with different tasks and adopt different coping strategies. Furthermore, the diversity of children's responses to divorce is the result, in part, of differences in temperament, sex, age, and past experiences (Hetherington, Cox, and Cox, 1979).

Children experience divorce as a three-stage process, according to Wallerstein and Kelly (1980b). Studying sixty California families during a five-year period, these researchers found that for children divorce consisted of initial, transition, and restabilized stages.

❐ *Initial Stage*. The initial stage, following the decision to separate, was extremely stressful; conflict escalated and unhappiness was endemic. The children's aggressive responses were magnified by the parents' inability to cope because of the crisis in their own lives.

❐ *Transition Stage*. The transition stage began about a year after the separation, when the extreme emotional responses of the children had diminished or disappeared. The period was characterized by restructuring of the family and by economic and social changes: living with only one parent and visiting the other, moving, making new friends and losing old ones, financial stress, and so on. The transition period lasted between two and three years for half the families in the study.

❐ *Restabilization Stage*. Finally came the restabilized stage, which the families had reached by the end of five years. Economic and social changes had been incorporated into daily living. The postdivorce family, usually a single-parent or stepfamily, had been formed.

Children's Responses to Divorce

Younger and older children respond differently to divorce, mainly in the way in which they express—or do not express—their feelings.

Why is happiness such a precious thing? What have we done with our lives so that everywhere we turn, no matter how hard we try not to, we cause other people sorrow?

William Styron

YOUNGER CHILDREN. Younger children react to the initial news of a parental breakup in many different ways. Feelings range from guilt to anger and from sorrow to relief, often vacillating among all of these. The most significant factor affecting children's responses to the separation is their age. Preadolescent children, who seem to experience a deep sadness and anxiety about the future, are usually the most upset. Some may regress to immature behavior, wetting their beds or becoming excessively possessive. Most children, regardless of their age, are angry because of the separation. Very young children tend to have more temper tantrums. In one three-year study of forty-eight preschoolers, the play patterns regressed both cognitively and socially shortly after divorce (Hetherington et al., 1979). A year following the divorce, the children showed high rates of dependency, acting out, seeking help, and behaving noncompliantly. Slightly older children become aggressive in their play, games, and fantasies—for example, pretending to hit one of their parents.

Children of school age may blame one parent and direct their anger toward him or her, believing the other one innocent. But even here the reactions are varied. If the father moves out of the house, the children may blame the mother for making him go or they may be angry at him for abandoning them, regardless of reality. Younger schoolchildren who blame their mother often mix anger with placating behavior, fearing she will leave them. Preschool children often blame themselves, feeling that they drove their parents apart by being naughty or messy. They beg their parents to stay, promising to be better. It is heartbreaking to hear a child say, "Mommy, tell Daddy I'll be good. Tell him to come back. I'll be good. He won't be mad at me any more."

Problems seem to be compounded when there are children of various ages. The parents must deal with a range of responses that can be almost overwhelming. One woman (quoted in Hunt and Hunt, 1977) said:

My fourteen-year-old son was mortified and went to elaborate lengths to keep anyone from knowing. My twelve-year-old daughter had seen it coming; she cried a lot, but in the main she seemed vastly relieved. The eight-year-old blamed herself for all our quarrels and threw up regularly for weeks. The seven-year-old told his father, "We'll get it all fixed up so you can come back, Dad," but he had tantrums, played with matches in his room, and stole money from my purse.

When parents separate, children want to know with whom they are going to live. Feeling strong bonds with the parent who left, they want to know when they can see him or her. If they have brothers or sisters, they want to know if they will remain with their siblings. They especially want to know what will happen to them if the parent they are living with dies. Will they go to their grandparents, their other parent, an aunt or uncle, or a foster home? These are practical questions, and children have a right to answers. They need to know what lies ahead for them amidst the turmoil of a family split-up so that they can prepare for the changes ahead. Some parents report that their children seemed to do better psychologically than they themselves did prior to a split-up. Children often have more strength and inner resources than parents realize. Yet in a study in which 560 divorced parents were asked to assess the impact of their divorce on their children two years after it had occurred, the majority felt that their children had been affected negatively (Fulton, 1979).

The outcome of separation for children, Weiss (1975) observed, depends on several factors related to the children's age. Young children need a competent and loving parent to take care of them; they tend to do poorly when a parenting adult becomes enmeshed in constant turmoil, depression, and worry. With older, preadolescent children, the presence of brothers and sisters help, because the children have others to play with and rely on in addition to the single parent. If they have good friends or do well in school, this contributes to their self-esteem. Regardless of the child's age, it is important that the absent parent continue to play a role in his or her life. The children need to know that they have not been abandoned and that the absent parent still cares (Wallerstein and Kelly, 1980b). They need continuity and security even if the old parental relationship has radically changed.

The financial effect of divorce appears to have some impact on a child's later adjustment. Economic stress is particularly acute in divorced families. One study of twenty-five seven- to thirteen-year-olds found that all who were maladjusted came from families that had experienced a 50 percent drop in income (De Simone-Luis et al., 1979). Another study found limited financial resources an important variable in determining stress among children of divorce (Hodges et al., 1979).

ADOLESCENTS. Family life before separation seems to affect how adolescents respond to their parent's divorce. In one study, 76 percent of the adolescents reported that there had been conflict in the marriage before separation (McLoughlin and Whitfield, 1984). Sixty percent of the conflict was verbal, but 38 percent was both verbal and physical. In spite of the reported conflict, almost half of these adolescents were surprised that their parents had split up. They had come to view conflict as a normal part of marital life.

Adolescents also find parental separation traumatic. About half the adolescents studied felt relieved that their parents had separated; the other half were troubled. Those who were glad came from homes that had considerable conflict; after the divorce, they tended to believe that their parents' divorce was a good idea. Only about 40 percent of the adolescents continued contact with the noncustodial parent; of these, 68 percent saw the parent once a month or more. The 60 percent who did not see their noncustodial parent usually chose not to do so. This was especially true of daughters whose fathers had been involved in an extramarital relationship (McLoughlin and Whitfield, 1984).

Adolescents tend to protect themselves from the conflict preceding separation by distancing themselves. Although they usually experience immense turmoil within, they may outwardly appear cool and detached. Unlike younger children, they rarely blame themselves. Rather, they are likely to be angry with both parents, blaming them for upsetting their lives. Adolescents may be particularly bothered by their parents' beginning to date again. Some are shocked to realize that their parents are sexual beings, especially when they see a separated parent kiss someone or bring someone home for the night. The situation may add greater confusion to the adolescents' emerging sexual life. Some may take the attitude that if their mother or father sleeps with a date, why can't they? Others may condemn their parents for acting "immorally."

HELPING CHILDREN ADJUST. Helen Raschke's (1987) review of the literature of children's adjustment after divorce found that the following factors were important:

❑ Prior to separation, open discussion with the children of the forthcoming separation and divorce and problems associated with them.
❑ The child's continued involvement with the noncustodial parent, including frequent visits and unrestricted access.
❑ Lack of hostility between the divorced parents.
❑ Good emotional and psychological adjustment to the divorce on the part of the custodial parent.
❑ Good parenting skills and the maintenance of an orderly and stable living situation for the children.

Children as Pawns

Continued involvement with the children by both parents is important for the children's adjustment. The greatest danger is that children may be used as pawns by their parents after a divorce. The recently divorced often suffer from a lack of self-esteem and a sense of failure. One means of dealing with the feelings caused by divorce is to blame the other person. To prevent further hurt or to get revenge, divorced parents may try to control each other through their children. Myron Harris (1972) wrote:

The need to find oneself loved and reassured as to being adequate or exceptional as a parent becomes particularly strong when all else is taken away. Thus, the opportunity for utilizing other individuals in this security-pursuing endeavor beckons most strongly—in fact, more strongly to the unconscious parts of ourselves than to the conscious, for the former are desperate, painfully needful, crying, and often panicked, while the latter have managed somehow to be more reasonable and socially restrained. It is obvious that the presence of children makes them an easily available commodity for use.

Harris suggested that divorced parents who use their children may employ one or more of the following tactics:

1. *Alienating children's affection.* Because one parent feels deprived of the former spouse's affection, he or she may try to deprive the other parent of the children's affection. If, say, the wife had an affair during the time of the split up, the husband may try to have the wife declared an unfit mother as revenge. She may be a wholly competent, trustworthy mother, but in his rage the husband does not see that. He is so wounded that he wants to hurt his wife as he has been hurt. The children, of course, are torn by divided loyalties.

2. *Using children to maintain bonds.* Children are sometimes used to continue the attachment between divorced spouses. On the pretext of asking for advice or assistance, a man may call his former spouse. "What shall I do about Sonia being sick all the time? Do you think it's serious? Do you think I should send her to summer school?" Although such questions may be legitimate, they can be used to hold on to an ex-spouse, keeping him or her tied to the intimate workings of the family. Some may hope that if they hold on long enough, there will be a reconciliation. Here again the child is being manipulated.

3. *Demanding total allegiance.* Each parent may demand the children's total allegiance. The mother may attack the father in front of the children or denigrate him in his absence; the father may similarly attack the mother, telling the children that she is a bad person and parent. Harris described one case in which each divorced partner attempted to turn the children against the other:

The effort to force them into the position of hostages, held in emotional bondage to the parent with whom they were spending time, was so persisting and unrelenting that the children were forced to alternately deny love to the opposing parent and avow loyalty only to the parent with whom they were currently spending time.

The children in this case were four and five years old. It is not difficult to imagine their stress and confusion.

4. *Holding children hostage.* Children may be used directly as hostages for money, emotional support, or services. In one divorce agreement, the woman spelled out rigid visitation privileges, and whenever her former husband was late with support payments, was late in picking up the child, or had to cancel a visit, she would refuse to allow him to see the child next time.

When Jason and the Argonauts returned from their search for the Golden Fleece, he had taken a new wife. His wife Medea was enraged with grief, anger, and jealousy. A sorceress, she wove a golden cloth which she gave to Jason's bride. When she wore it, it turned to flames and burned her to death. Then Medea killed her two children to take revenge upon the unfaithful Jason and fled the palace in a chariot pulled by dragons.

Greek myth

Types of Custody

Of all the issues surrounding separation and divorce, custody issues are generating the "greatest attention and controversy" among researchers (Kitson and Morgan, 1991). When the court awards custody to one parent, the decision is generally based on one of two standards: the best interests of the child or the least detrimental of the available alternatives (Musetto, 1981). In practice, however, custody of the children is usually awarded to the mother. Three reasons can be given for this: (1) women usually prefer custody and men do not, (2) custody to the mother is traditional, and (3) the law reflects a bias that assumes women are naturally better able to care for children.

The major types of custody are sole, joint, and split. In **sole custody,** the child lives with one parent, who has sole responsibility for physically raising the child and making all decisions regarding his or her upbringing. There are two forms of **joint custody:** legal and physical. In joint legal custody, the children live primarily with one parent, but both share jointly in decisions about their children's education, religious training, and general upbringing. In joint physical custody, the children live with both parents, dividing time more or less equally between the two households. Under **split custody,** the children are divided between the two parents, the mother usually taking the girls and the father the boys. About 5 percent of children from divorced families are shared in split custody arrangements (Spanier and Furstenberg, 1987).

Sole custody has been the prevailing practice in the United States; about 70 percent of all custody is sole custody. Since women have traditionally been responsible for childrearing, sole custody by mothers has seemed the closest approximation to the traditional family, especially if the father is given free access (Awad and Parry, 1980). Furthermore, many men have not had the day-to-day responsibilities of childrearing and do not feel (or are not perceived to be) competent in that role.

In recent years, increasing numbers of fathers have been gaining custody of their children following divorce (Pearson et al., 1982). Thirteen percent of single families were headed by men in 1990. A child's adjustment to the father as a single parent, according to one study, appears to depend on how well the father parents (Santrock and Warsack, 1979). Although parenting has been primarily the mother's task, increasing numbers of men may have joint or sole custody of their children as new parenting roles evolve.

SOLE CUSTODY. Sole custody does not mean that the noncustodial parent is prohibited from seeing his or her children. Wallerstein and Kelly (1980b) believe that if one parent is prohibited from sharing important aspects of the children's lives, he or she will withdraw from the children in frustration and grief. Children experience such withdrawal as a rejection and suffer as a result. Generally, it is considered in the best interests of the child for him or her to have easy access to the noncustodial parent. If it is the father, his relationship with his child often changes in a positive manner as a result of the divorce, since he has increased opportunity to interact with his child in a conflict-free atmosphere (Friedman, 1980). The relationship between the visiting parent and child may change in unexpected ways. One study showed that the changes for better or worse in the relationship were related to the difficulties and psychological conflicts arising from visitation and divorce, the father's ability to deal with the limitations of his visiting relationship, and the age and sex of the child (Wallerstein and Kelly, 1980a).

JOINT CUSTODY. Joint custody, in which both parents continue to share legal rights and responsibilities as parents, is becoming increasingly widespread. Thirty-three

"Best interests of the child." . . . It makes me want to laugh, to see it stated so baldly, as if it were a simple thing. It is almost all there is to being a good parent: best interests of the child, assessed incessantly, in everything from toilet training to religious education. But it is simple only when the issue at hand is putting fingers in a fire or going barefoot in the snow. The rest of the time it means separating what is good for the child from what is good for you. In that sense, it feels as if you are doing the impossible.

Anna Quindlen

states now have joint custody laws (Freed and Walker, 1988). Wallerstein and Kelly (1980b) argue that such arrangements may work out for the best interests of the child. Joint custody does not necessarily mean that the child's time is evenly divided between the parents but that "two committed parents, in two separate homes [care] for their youngsters in a postdivorce atmosphere of civilized, respectful exchange."

A number of advantages accrue to joint custody. First, it allows both parents to continue their parenting roles. Second, it avoids a sudden termination of a child's relationship with one of his or her parents. Joint custody fathers tend to be more involved with their children, spending time with them and sharing responsibility and decision making (Bowman and Ahrons, 1985). Third, by dividing the labor, it lessens many of the burdens of constant child care experienced by most single parents. Joint custody, however, requires considerable energy from the parents in working out both the logistics of the arrangement and their feelings about each other (see "The Binuclear Family" in Chapter 14). Many parents with joint custody find it difficult, but they nevertheless feel that it is satisfactory. The children do not always like joint custody as much as the parents do. About a third of the children in one study valued the arrangement because it gave them access to both parents, but they felt overburdened by the demands of two households (Steinman, 1981).

Inevitably, there are benefits and drawbacks to any custody arrangement. Joint custody should be available as an alternative but not automatically awarded. Sometimes, although it may be in the best interests of the parents for each of them to continue parenting roles, it may not necessarily be in the best interests of the child. Derdeyn and Scott (1984) noted, "There is a marked disparity between the power of the joint custody movement and the sufficiency of evidence that joint custody can accomplish what we expect of it." For parents who choose joint custody, it appears to be satisfactory. But when joint custody is mandated by the courts over the opposition of one or both parents, it may be problematic at best. Joint custody may force two parents to interact ("cooperate" is too benign a word) in instances in which they would rather never see each other again, and the resulting conflict and ill-will may end up being detrimental to the children.

CUSTODY DISPUTES AND CHILD STEALING. The "best-interests" and "least detrimental alternative" standards by which parents are awarded custody are vague. This may encourage custody fights because it makes the outcome of custody hearings uncertain and increases hostility; any derogatory evidence or suspicions, ranging from dirty faces to child abuse, may be considered relevant (Mnookin, 1975). As a result, child custody disputes are fairly common in the courts. As many as one-third of all postdivorce legal cases involve children (Emery and Wyer, 1987).

As discussed in Chapter 12, about 350,000 children are abducted each year by family members in child custody disputes. Most are returned in two days to a week, and generally the parent from whom the child was taken knows the child's whereabouts (Hotaling, Finkelhor, and Sedlack, 1990; Finkelhor, Hotaling, and Sedlak, 1991). According to researcher David Finkelhor, the number of family abductions could be reduced significantly. Under the present system, courts don't respond to people's needs and fears in bitter custody disputes. "For many people, going into court for custody is too risky, too expensive, and too time-consuming," Finkelhor notes (quoted in Barden, 1990), "so they grab the child." Finkelhor suggests that much child stealing could be prevented by the court assigning a mediator to whom the distressed parents could turn in times of crisis. Mediation would ease parental anxiety and offer an alternative to legal proceedings, which tend to inflame the situation.

There is no denying that separation or divorce is filled with pain for everyone involved—husband, wife, and children. But it is not only an end, it is also a beginning of a new life for each person. This new life includes new relationships and possibilities, new families with unique relationships: the single-parent family and the stepfamily. We will explore these family forms in the next chapter.

 # SUMMARY

❑ *Divorce* is an integral part of the contemporary American marriage system, which values individualism and emotional gratification. Divorce serves as a recycling mechanism, giving people a chance to improve their marital situation by marrying again. Researchers are increasingly viewing divorce as a normal part of the family life cycle rather than as a form of deviance.

❑ Divorce creates the single-parent family, remarriage and the stepfamily. The divorce rate increased significantly in the 1960s but leveled off in the early 1990s. About half of all current marriages end in divorce.

❑ *Uncoupling* is the process by which couples drift apart in predictable stages. Initially, uncoupling is unilateral; the initiator begins to turn elsewhere for satisfactions, creating an identity independent of the couple. The initiator voices more complaints and begins to think of alternatives. Eventually the initiator ends the relationship. Uncoupling ends when both partners acknowledge that the relationship cannot be saved.

❑ In establishing a new identity, newly separated people go through transition and recovery. Transition begins with the separation and is characterized by *separation distress,* a condition of general stress, anxiety, and anger. Separation distress is usually followed by loneliness. Separation distress is affected by (1) whether the person had any forewarning, (2) length of time married, (3) who took the initiative in leaving, (4) whether someone new is found, and (5) available resources. The more personal, social and financial resources a person has at the time of separation, the easier the separation generally will be. Women generally experience dramatic downward mobility.

❑ Dating again is important for separated or divorced people. Their greatest social problem is meeting other unmarried people. Dating is a formal statement of the end of a marriage; it also permits individuals to enhance their self-esteem.

❑ *No-fault divorce* has revolutionized divorce by eliminating fault-finding and the adversarial process and by treating husbands and wives as equals. The most damaging unintended consequence of no-fault divorce is the growing poverty of divorced women with children.

❑ The economic consequences of divorce include impoverishment of women, changed female employment patterns, and very limited child support and alimony.

❑ Children in the divorce process go through three stages: (1) the initial stage, lasting about a year, when turmoil is greatest; (2) the transition stage, lasting up to several years, in which adjustments are being made to new family arrangements, living and economic conditions, friends, and social environment; and (3) the restabilized stage, when the changes have been integrated into the children's lives.

❑ A very significant factor affecting the responses of children to divorce is their age. Young children tend to act out and blame themselves, whereas adolescents tend to remain aloof and angry at both parents for disrupting their lives. Adolescents may be bothered by their parent's dating again.

❑ The outcome of divorce for children depends on several factors, including their own inner resources, contact with the noncustodial parent, economic stability, and, for younger children especially, a nurturing, competent parent.

❑ Divorced parents may use their children against each other. Such parents may attempt to (1) deprive the other parent of the children's affection, (2) use the children to maintain bonds with the divorced spouse, (3) demand the children's total allegiance, and (4) use the children directly as hostages for money, emotional support, or services.

❑ The major types of custody are *sole, joint,* and *split.* Custody is generally based on one of two standards: the best interests of the child or the least detrimental of the available alternatives. Custody is generally awarded to the mother. Recently, however, more fathers have been gaining custody; the child's adjustment to living with the father depends on the father's parenting capabilities, not his gender. Joint custody has become more popular because men are becoming increasingly involved in parenting.

❑ As a result of custody disputes, as many as 350,000 children are stolen from custodial parents each year. Most are returned home within a week. Court-assigned mediation would help ease parental anxiety and present alternatives to custody-related abductions.

CHAPTER 14

New Lives, New Families

Marriage is made in Heaven,
but second marriages are
arranged by people.

Yiddish proverb

T HE 1990S MARK THE DEFINITIVE SHIFT from a traditional marriage and family system to a pluralistic one. The traditional family system, based on lifetime marriage and the intact nuclear family as its norm, is giving way to a pluralistic one created by divorce, remarriage, and births to single women. This new pluralistic family system consists of three major types of families: (1) intact nuclear families, (2) single-parent families, and (3) stepfamilies. The dominance of the new system is attested to by the following facts (Bumpass, Sweet, and Martin, 1990; Coleman and Ganong, 1991; Demo and Acock, 1991; Gongla and Thompson, 1987):

❏ The chances are more than two out of three that an individual will divorce, re-marry, or live in a single-parent family or stepfamily as a child or parent sometime during his or her life.

❏ Remarriage is as common as first marriage. Half of all recent marriages involve at least one previously married partner.

❏ Over one-fifth of all families are currently single-parent families. Single-parent families are growing faster in number than any other family form. Approximately half of all children born in the 1990s will live in single-parent families sometime during their childhoods.

❏ Over 2.3 million households have stepchildren living with them; the number of noncustodial stepfamilies without children living with them is significantly higher. One-sixth of all children, almost 10 million, are currently members of stepfamilies. Over a third of all children can expect to live in a stepfamily at sometime during their childhood.

Because of this shift to a pluralistic family system, researchers are beginning to reevaluate single-parent families and stepfamilies and to view them as typical rather than deviant family forms (Coleman and Ganong, 1991; Pasley and Ihinger-Tallman, 1987). It is useful to see these families as different structures pursuing the same goals as traditional nuclear families: the provision of intimacy, economic cooperation, the socialization of children, and the assignment of social roles and status.

The binuclear family is the postdivorce family consisting of two nuclear families, the nuclear family that includes the mother (or ex-wife) and that which includes the father (or ex-husband). The creation of the binuclear family presents both rewards and challenges for its members.

If we shift our perspective from structure to functions, the important question is no longer whether a particular family form is deviant. (If prevalence of a family form determines deviance, logic tells us that the traditional nuclear family may soon become deviant.) The important question becomes whether a specific family—regardless of whether it is a traditional, single-parent, or stepfamily—succeeds in performing its functions (Ahrons and Rodgers, 1987; Gongla and Thompson, 1987). In a practical sense, as long as a family is fulfilling its functions, it is a *normal* family. As Bert Adams (1985) observes, ". . . whether we see today's changes as problems or solutions depends to a great extent on what we value most."

The dramatic rise in single-parent families and stepfamilies over the last twenty years is the result of shifting social values and trends rather than individual shortcoming or pathologies. Single-parent families and stepfamilies have become a natural part of the contemporary American marriage system. As such, they are not problems in themselves. Instead, to a great extent, many of their problems lie in the stigma attached to them and their lack of support by the larger society (Ahrons and Rodgers, 1987; Gongla and Thompson, 1987). If we are going to strengthen these families, note Constance Ahrons and Roy Rodgers (1987), "we must unambiguously acknowledge and support them as normal, prevalent family types that have resulted from major societal trends and changes."

☐ THE BINUCLEAR FAMILY

One of the most unique, complex, and ambiguous relationships in contemporary America is what some researchers are beginning to call the binuclear family (Ahrons and Rodgers, 1987). The binuclear family is a postdivorce family system with children. It is the original nuclear family divided in two. The binuclear family consists of *two* nuclear families—the maternal nuclear family headed by the mother (the ex-wife) and the paternal one headed by the father (the ex-husband). Both single-parent families and stepfamilies are forms of binuclear families.

Divorce ends a marriage but not a family. It dissolves the husband/wife relationship but not the father/mother, mother/child, or father/child relationship. The family reorganizes itself into a binuclear family. In this new family, ex-husbands and ex-wives may continue to relate to each other and to their children, although in substantially altered ways. The significance of the maternal and paternal components of the binuclear family varies. In families with joint physical custody, the maternal and paternal families may be equally important to their children. In single-parent families headed by women, the paternal family component may be minimal.

Complexity of the Binuclear Family

The binuclear family system may be the most complex in America today. Consider the family history of two children, Paige and Daniel Brickman. (See Figure 14.1 for a diagram of their binuclear family.)

When Paige was six and Daniel eight, their parents separated and divorced. The children continued to live with their mother, Sophia, in a single-parent household while spending weekends and holidays with their father, David. After a year, David began living with Jane, a single mother, who had a five-year-old daughter, Lisa.

Three years after the divorce, Sophia married John, who had joint physical custody of his two daughters, Sally and Mary, aged seven and nine. Paige and Daniel continued living with their mother while their stepfather's children lived with them every other week. After two years of marriage, Sophia and John had a son, Joshua. About the same time, David and Jane split up; they continued to maintain close ties because of the bonds formed between David and Lisa. A year later, David married Julie, who had physical custody of two children, Sally and Gabriel; the next year, they had a son, David, Jr. Lisa visits every few weeks.

Although Paige and Daniel's binuclear family is not at all unusual, don't be surprised if it's hard to figure out who's related to whom. As Ahrons and Rodgers (1987) point out, "The variations in family structure that result from remarriage in binuclear families almost defy categorization." Ten years after their parents divorced, Paige's and Daniel's family consists of the following family members: two biological parents, two stepparents, three stepsisters, one stepbrother, and two half brothers. In addition, they had a "cohabiting" stepmother and stepsister with whom they continued to have close ties. Their extended family includes two sets of biological grandparents and stepgrandparents, and a large array of biological and step aunts, uncles, and cousins. Paige and Daniel continue to have two households to which they belong as children.

Subsystems in the Binuclear Family

To clarify the different relationships, researchers divided the binuclear family into five subsystems (Ahrons and Rodgers, 1987):

❐ Former spouse subsystem
❐ Remarried couple subsystem
❐ Parent/child subsystem
❐ Sibling subsystems: step- and half-siblings
❐ Mother/stepmother—father/stepfather subsystems

FORMER SPOUSE SUBSYSTEM. Although divorce severs the husband/wife relationship, the mother/father relationship endures as former spouses continue their parenting responsibilities. While the degree of involvement for the noncustodial parent varies, children generally benefit from the continued involvement of both parents. The former spouses, however, must deal with a number of issues. These include the following:

❐ Anger and hostility toward each other as a result of their previous marriage and separation.
❐ Conflict regarding child custody, parenting styles, values, and aspirations concerning their children.
❐ Shifting roles and relationships between former spouses when one or both remarry.
❐ The ability to incorporate others as stepparents, stepsiblings, and stepgrandparents into the family system when one or both former spouses remarry.

As long as former spouses are able to separate parenting from personal issues involving each other, they may form effective coparenting relationships. Ahrons and Wallisch (1987) indicated that about half of the former spouses in their study are able to work well with each other; another quarter interact, but with substantial conflict. About a quarter are unable to coparent because of the high degree of conflict.

REMARRIED COUPLE SUBSYSTEM. Remarried couples are generally unprepared for the complexities of remarried life. If they have physical custody of children from the first marriage, they must provide access between the children and the noncustodial parents. Both custodial and noncustodial parents must facilitate the exchange of children, money, decision-making power, and time. This may often be difficult.

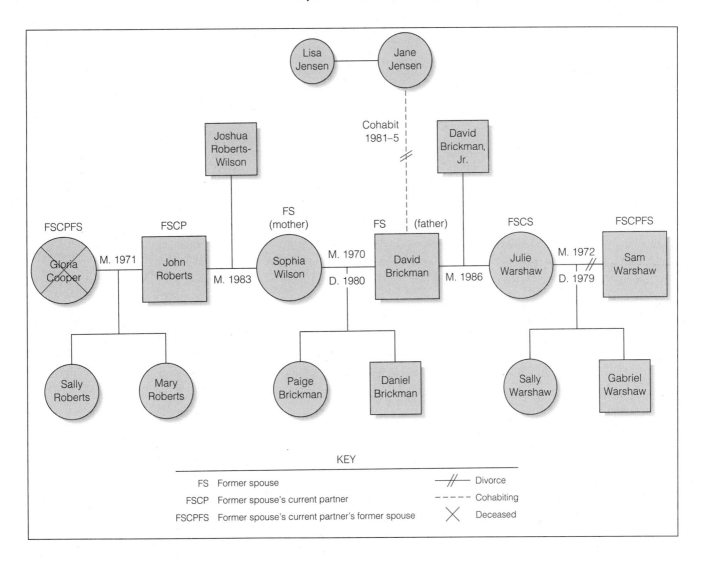

KEY

FS	Former spouse	—//—	Divorce
FSCP	Former spouse's current partner	- - - - -	Cohabiting
FSCPFS	Former spouse's current partner's former spouse	✕	Deceased

Typical marital issues such as power and intimacy may become magnified, as they frequently involve not only the remarried couple but the former spouse as well. Because of custody arrangements, for example, the former spouse may exercise veto power over the remarried couple's plan to take a family vacation because it conflicts with visitation.

PARENT-CHILD SUBSYSTEMS. Remarriage is probably more difficult for children than parents. While parents are caught in the excitement of romance, their children may be reacting with anxiety and distress. Their parents are making choices that affect the children but over which the children themselves have little or no control. Furthermore, remarriage destroys the children's fantasies that their parents will reunite. Children may not want the stepparent to function as a parent for various reasons. The children may feel, for example, that the stepparent is usurping the role of the absent biological parent. Or they may resent the stepparent's intrusion into their restructured single-parent family.

Both the biological parent and stepparent must make adjustments. Former single parents, for example, must adjust to the presence of a second parent in decision-

FIGURE 17.1

Diagram of Binuclear Family

The binuclear family consists of five subsytems: former spouse, remarried couple, parent/child, sibling (biological, step, and half), and mother-stepmother/father-stepfather subsystems. Identify these subsystems in the diagram above.

FOCUS

Strengthening Binuclear Families

Because binuclear families are becoming a family norm, it is important for us to strengthen rather than stigmatize them. We can do much as individuals and as a society to assist these families. Some of the strategies that those involved in binuclear families can use are described in the following paragraphs.

DIVORCE MEDIATION AND THERAPY

Divorce mediation and therapy strive to minimize the pain and acrimony involved in divorce, as the quality of coparenting relationships is significantly affected by the emotional terms on which husbands and wives divorce (Ahrons and Rodgers, 1987). No-fault divorce eliminates some of the blaming that accompanies divorce, but property, support, custody, and visitation issues are often characterized by bitter conflict and recriminations. Mediation encourages divorcing spouses to try to resolve their differences through negotiation and compromise with the help of a trained mediator.

Divorce therapy helps individuals and families come to terms with the end of their marriages. In particular, divorce therapy assists individuals in resolving their feelings of failure and their anger toward their former spouses. For children, divorce therapy aids in the avoidance of self-blame and assists the transition to single-parent families or stepfamilies.

NORMALIZING BINUCLEAR FAMILIES

Cultural stereotypes depict single-parent families, stepfamilies, and stepchildren as deviant or abnormal (Coleman and Ganong, 1987). Such stereotypes are unrealistic and damaging, however; they distort the actual picture of these families. We need to recognize that there is nothing deviant or pathological about single-parent families or stepfamilies. Binuclear families have become normal families in the contemporary American family system. Stepfamilies, indeed, may not be especially different from traditional nuclear families. Children and parents face similar issues in all types of families. Parents and stepparents alike, for example, are likely to experience difficulties with favoritism, discipline, and child care (Ihinger-Tallman and Pasley, 1987).

USE OF THERAPY IN MANAGING BINUCLEAR FAMILY DYNAMICS

Individuals and families need to recognize that they undergo immense stress as they move from nuclear families to single-parent families or stepfamilies. Rather than waiting until problems become uncontrollable, individuals and families should seek assistance while the problems still remain manageable. Ihinger-Tallman and Pasley (1987) suggest that families use therapeutic interventions to explore the following issues:

❑ Grief resolution following the end of the first marriage
❑ Creation of an environment that will assist custodial and noncustodial parents in dealing with coparenting issues
❑ Right of parents to consider their needs as being as important as those of their children

❑ Development of problem-solving and negotiation skills
❑ Exploration of alternative roles, rules, and rituals in both single-parent families and stepfamilies
❑ Identification of stepparent behaviors that enhance the relationship between stepparent and stepchild
❑ Consolidation of parental and stepparental authority

SOCIETAL RECOGNITION

Societal institutions need to recognize both the normality and widespread existence of binuclear families. Most social institutions, such as schools, religious groups, health-care organizations, and government agencies, ignore the needs of these families. Instead, they are geared toward serving traditional nuclear families. Schools, for example, often fail to inform noncustodial parents of parent/teacher meetings. Or they may schedule such meetings for times when working single-parents are unable to attend. Teachers sometimes assume that simply because a child is a member of a single-parent family or stepfamily, he or she will have emotional problems or learning difficulties.

The challenge before us as individuals and as a society is to recognize that binuclear families are normal families. It is our responsibility to strengthen these families in every way we can.

making and childrearing practices. Stepparents, however, have the greatest adjustment to make. Because remarried families tend to model themselves after traditional nuclear families, stepparents often expect that the stepparent role will be similar to the parent role. Stepfathers who have their own children may feel conflict because they are "more" a father to their stepchildren than to their biological ones. Stepmothers, however, seem to experience greater stress than stepfathers. The stress may result from stepmothers' relatively high degree of involvement in child-care and nurturing activities, which are not adequately acknowledged or appreciated by stepchildren.

Following remarriage, the level of contact between children and nonresidential parents changes significantly. The average level of weekly contact for a single father is double that of a remarried father. If both parents remarry, the level of contact drops 300 percent (Furstenberg and Nord, 1982).

SIBLING SUBSYSTEMS: STEPSIBLINGS AND HALF-SIBLINGS. When parents remarry, their children may acquire "instant" brothers or sisters who may differ considerably in age and temperament. The sibling relationships may be especially complex in binuclear families. Consider Paige and Daniel's stepsibling and half-sibling relationships. In their mother's family the two children had to adjust to a half-brother and two stepsisters who lived with them half-time. In their father's family, they adjusted to a "cohabiting" sibling who was "like" a sister. When their father remarried, they gained two stepsiblings and a little later a half-brother. To make matters more complex, biological relationships do not guarantee emotional closeness. Paige feels closest, for example, to her "cohabitant sibling" Lisa and her stepsister Sally, neither of whom lived with her. Daniel, however, feels closest to Mary, his stepsister, and Joshua, his half-brother.

All things being equal, stepsiblings are predisposed to bond with each other because family norms require affection between family members (Pasley, 1987). Bonding will occur most rapidly when siblings are of similar age and sex, have similar experiences and values, are interdependent, and perceive greater rewards than costs in their relationships.

Stepsiblings and siblings contend with each other for parental affection, toys, attention, physical space, and dominance. Sharing a parent with a new stepparent is often difficult enough, but to share the parent with a stepsibling can be overwhelming. Visiting biological children compete with stepchildren who are living with the visiting children's biological parent.

MOTHER/STEPMOTHER—FATHER/STEPFATHER SUBSYSTEMS. The relationship between new spouses and former spouses often influences the remarried family. The former spouse can be an intruder in the new marriage, a source of conflict between the remarried couple. Other times the former spouse is a handy scapegoat for displacing problems. Much of the current spouse/former spouse interaction depends on how the ex-spouses themselves feel about each other. Ahrons and Rodgers (1987) found that about half of current spouses felt somewhat detached from the former spouse; they felt as if they were "acquaintances." About a quarter liked the former spouse, and the remaining quarter reported feeling competitive or jealous.

☐ SINGLE PARENTING

Single-parent families are the fastest growing family form in the United States. No other family type has increased in number as rapidly. Between 1960 and 1989, the percentage of single-parent families almost tripled, from 9 percent to 24 percent. During the last few years, however, the rate of increase has slowed, especially for African-American families (Saluter, 1990). As many as 64 percent of white children and 89 percent of African-American children born in 1980 will spend part of their childhood in a single-parent family (Hofferth, 1985). The single-parent family, more than the dual-worker family or stepfamily, is a radical departure from the traditional nuclear family. Both the dual-worker family and the stepfamily are two-parent families; the single-parent family is not.

In previous generations, the life pattern most women experienced was (1) marriage, (2) motherhood, and (3) widowhood. Single-parent families existed in the past, but they were formed by widowhood rather than divorce or births to unmarried women; significant numbers were headed by men. But a new marriage and family pattern has taken root. Its greatest impact has been on women and their children. The life pattern many women now experience is (1) marriage, (2) motherhood, (3) divorce, (4) single parenting, (5) remarriage, and (6) widowhood. Divorce is a key factor creating today's single-parent family. For those who are not married at the time of their child's birth, the pattern may be (1) motherhood, (2) single parenting, (3) marriage, and (4) widowhood.

Single parenting is difficult, but for many single parents the problems are manageable in comparison to the misery and hopelessness of unhappy or abusive marriages. Although most studies emphasize the stress of single parenting, some studies view it as building strength and confidence in many women. Miller (1982) observed:

A significant number of the single women studied have solved many extraordinary problems in the face of formidable obstacles. Their single parenthood has led to personal growth for many. In adulthood they have made major revisions in their roles in life and in their self- and object-representations. Many have become contributors to their community, and their children are often a source of strength rather than difficulty.

Characteristics of Single-Parent Families

Single-parent families share a number of characteristics, including the following: (1) creation by divorce or births to unmarried women, (2) usually female-headed households, (3) significance of ethnicity, (4) poverty, (5) diversity, and (6) transitional character.

CREATION BY DIVORCE OR BIRTHS TO UNMARRIED WOMEN. Single-parent families tend to be created by marital separation, divorce, or births to unmarried women rather than by widowhood. In fact, in less than twenty years, births to unmarried women have increased fourfold: from 7 percent in 1970 to 29 percent in 1988 of all births (Rawlings, 1989).

In contrast to single parenting by widows, parenting by divorced or unmarried mothers receives less social support. A divorced mother usually receives less assistance from her own kin and considerably less (or none) from her former partner's relatives. Widowed mothers, however, often receive social support from their husband's relatives. Our culture is still ambivalent about divorce and considers single-parent families deviant. (See Leslie and Grady, 1985.)

FEMALE-HEADED HOUSEHOLDS. Eighty-seven percent of single-parent families are headed by women. This has important economic ramifications because of sex discrimination in wages and job opportunities as discussed in Chapter 9.

SIGNIFICANCE OF ETHNICITY. Ethnicity is an important demographic factor in single-parent families (Saluter, 1990). In 1989, among white children, 19 percent lived in single-parent families; among African Americans, 55 percent lived in such families; among Latinos, 31 percent lived in single-parent families. Four times as many whites lived in two-parent families as in single-parent families; in African-American families, about a third more children lived in single-parent families than in two-parent families (Saluter, 1990). White single mothers were more likely to be divorced than their African-American or Latina counterparts, who were likely to be unmarried at the time of the birth or widowed. Of single parents, 50 percent of white mothers, 24 percent of African-American mothers and 30 percent of the Latina mothers were divorced (Johnson, 1980). African-American and Latino families are more likely to live below the poverty level, both as single-parent and two-parent families.

POVERTY. Married women usually experience a sharp drop in their income when they separate or divorce (as discussed in Chapter 13). Among unmarried single mothers, poverty and motherhood go hand in hand. Because they are women, because they are often young, and because they are frequently from ethnic minorities, they have few financial resources. Single mothers are under constant economic stress trying to make ends meet (McLanahan and Booth, 1991). They work at low wages or endure welfare or both. They are unable to plan because of their constant financial uncertainty. They move more frequently than two-parent families as economic and living situations change, uprooting themselves and their children. They may accept material support from kin, but often at the price of receiving unsolicited "free advice," especially from their mothers.

DIVERSITY OF LIVING ARRANGEMENTS. There are many different kinds of single-parent households. Single-parent families show great flexibility in managing child care and housing with limited resources. In doing so, they rely on a variety of household arrangements. Only about 56 percent of single-parent households consist of just a single parent and his or her children (Payton, 1982). Forty-four percent of single parents head other types of family structures. Some rent out rooms. A third live in modified extended families consisting of their own children and another adult who is a relative, a boarder, or a cohabitant. Many adolescent and young African-American mothers live with their own mothers in a three-generation setting.

TRANSITIONAL FORM. Single parenting is usually a transitional state. A single mother has strong motivation to marry or remarry because of cultural expectations, economic stress, role overload, and a need for emotional security and intimacy. For many, however, especially single women in their thirties and forties, single parenting has become a more intentional and less transitional life-style (Gongla and Thompson, 1987). Some older women choose unmarried single parenting because they have not found a suitable partner and are concerned about declining fertility. Others choose single parenting because they do not want their lives and careers encumbered by the compromises necessary in marriage. And still others choose it because they don't want a husband or because they are lesbian and are not co-parenting with a partner.

Children in a Single-Parent Family

More than 60 percent of people who divorce have children living at home. One study indicated that children remain in single-parent homes an average of about 6 years for whites and 7.5 years for African Americans (Hofferth, 1985). Of children born in 1980 who will live in a single-parent family, white children can expect to spend about 31 percent of their childhood in single-parent families, African-American children about 59 percent.

STABILITY AND LONELINESS. After a divorce, the single parent is usually glad to have the children with him or her (Weiss, 1979). Everything else seems to have fallen apart, but as long as divorced parents have their children, they retain their parental function. Their children's need for them reassures them of their own importance. The mother's success as a parent becomes even more important to counteract the feelings of low self-esteem that result from divorce. Feeling depressed, the mother knows she must bounce back for the children. Yet after a short period, she comes to realize that her children do not fill the void left by her divorce. The children are a chore as well as a pleasure, and she may resent being constantly tied down by their needs. Thus minor incidents with the children—a child's refusal to eat or a temper tantrum—may get blown out of proportion.

A major disappointment for many new single parents is the discovery that they are still lonely. It seems almost paradoxical. How can a person be lonely amid all the noise and bustle that accompany children? However, children do not ordinarily function as attachment figures; they can never be potential partners. The attempt to make them so is harmful to parent and child. Yet children remain the central figures in the lives of single parents. This situation leads to a second paradox: although children do not completely fulfill a person, they rank higher in most single mothers' priorities than anything else (Weiss, 1975).

CHANGED FAMILY STRUCTURE. A single-parent family is not the same as a two-parent family with one parent temporarily absent (Weiss, 1976, 1979). The permanent absence of one parent dramatically changes the way in which the parenting adult relates to the children. Generally, the mother becomes closer and more responsive to her children. Her authority role changes, too. A greater distinction between parents and children exists in two-parent homes. Rules are developed by both mothers and fathers. Parents generally have an implicit understanding to back each other up in childrearing matters and to enforce mutually agreed-on rules. In the single-parent family no other partner is available to help maintain such agreements; as a result, the children may find themselves in a much more egalitarian situation. Consequently, they have more power to negotiate rules. They can badger a single parent into getting their way about staying up late, watching television, or going out. They can be more stubborn, cry more often and louder, whine, pout, and throw temper tantrums. Any parent who has tried to get children to do something they do not want to do knows how soon he or she can be worn down. So single parents are more willing to compromise: "Okay, you can have a *small* box of Cocoa Puffs. Put that large one back and promise you won't fuss like this anymore." In this way, children acquire considerable decision-making power in single-parent homes. They gain it through default—the single parent finds it too difficult to argue with them all the time.

Children in single-parent homes may also learn more responsibility. They may learn to help with kitchen chores, to clean up their messes, or to be more considerate. In the single-parent setting, the children are encouraged to recognize the work their mother does and the importance of cooperation. One woman related how her husband had always washed the dishes when they were still living together. At that time it had been difficult to get the children to help around the house, particularly with the dishes. Now, she said, the children always do the dishes—and they do the vacuuming and keep their own rooms straightened up, too (also see Greif, 1985).

LONG-TERM CONSEQUENCES. Throughout the 1970s, most research examining the impact of single-parent families on children was positive. These studies focused on the strengths of single-parent families, celebrating the ingenuity and energy of single mothers. In part, this was a reaction to the earlier pathological view of single parenting. While single parents continue to demonstrate love and creativity in the face of adversity, more recent research on their children has not been as optimistic as it once was. A review (McLanahan and Booth, 1991) of the relevant studies found that young children from mother-only families tended not to do as well academically as those from two-parent families. In adolescence and young adulthood, children from single-parent families had fewer years of education and were more likely to drop out of high school. They had lower earnings and were more likely to be poor. They were more likely to marry young, have children early (whether married or single), and divorce. These conclusions are consistent for whites, African Americans, Latinos, and Asian Americans.

It is not entirely clear whether these results are due to the nature of the family structure or to the debilitating effects of poverty. The reviewers note that socioeconomic status accounts for some, but not all, of the effects. Some of the effects are attributed to family structure. But Harriet Pipes McAdoo (1988) traces the cause to poverty. She notes that African-American families are able to meet their children's needs in a variety of structures. "The major problem arising from female-headed families is poverty," she wrote. "The impoverishment of Black families has been more detrimental than the actual structural arrangement."

◻ NONCUSTODIAL PARENTS

Researchers know very little about noncustodial or nonresidential fathers (Depner and Bray, 1990). They know even less about noncustodial mothers, who account for about 13 percent of noncustodial parents (Christensen, Dahl, and Rettig, 1990).

The single-parent family is the fastest growing family form in the United States. Eighty-seven percent are headed by women. Over half of all African-American children live in single-parent families.

What we do know about men, however, tells us that they often suffer grievously from the disruption or disappearance of their father role following divorce. They feel depressed, anxious, guilt-ridden; they feel a lack of self-esteem (Arditti, 1990). The change in status from full-time father to noncustodial parent leaves fathers bewildered about how they are to act: there are no norms for an involved noncustodial parent. This lack of norms makes it especially difficult if the relationship between the former spouses is bitter. Without adequate norms, fathers may become "Disneyland Dads," interacting with their children during weekends, taking them to movies, out for pizza; or they may become "Disappearing Dads," absenting themselves from any contact at all with their children. For many concerned noncustodial fathers, the question is simple but painful: "How can I be a father if I'm not a father anymore?"

Many fathers are not successful in being noncustodial fathers and abandon the role altogether. Children tend to have little contact with the nonresidential parent. A national survey of children ages eleven to sixteen years with divorced parents found that less than half had seen their father in the previous year (Furstenberg, Morgan, and Allison, 1986). In a study by Frank Furstenberg and Christine Nord (1982), only 16 percent of the children saw their nonresident father as much as once a week; almost 40 percent of the children had had no contact with their father in five years or even knew where he was living.

The reduced contact between nonresidential fathers and children seems to weaken the bonds of affection. One study of college students found that children in single-mother families tend to feel less close to their fathers than those in two-parent families. Seventeen percent of the students from single-mother families reported feeling close to their fathers, in contrast to 38 percent of those from two-parent families (White, Brinkerhoff, and Booth, 1985). Many years later, when the divorced fathers are middle-aged or elderly, they continue to have less contact with their adult children than married fathers. Divorced fathers are less likely to consider their children as sources of support in times of need (Cooney and Uhlenberg, 1990). Furstenberg and Nord (1982) concluded that "marital dissolution involves either a complete cessation of contact between the nonresidential parent and child or a relationship that is tantamount to a ritual form of parenthood."

❐ REMARRIAGE

Marriage is made in Heaven, but second marriages are arranged by people.

Yiddish proverb

Samuel Johnson described remarriage as "the triumph of hope over experience." And Americans are a hopeful people. About half of all divorced women remarry within seven years of separation. Among those who remarry between twenty-four and thirty-four years of age, the time between divorce and remarriage is about three years (Bumpass, Sweet, and Martin, 1990).

For the younger age groups, this quickness to remarry is somewhat paradoxical. Many newly divorced men and women express great wariness about marrying again. Yet at the same time they are actively searching for mates. Women often view their divorced time as important for their development as individuals, whereas men, who often complain that they were pressured into marriage before they were ready, become restless as "born-again bachelors" (Furstenberg, 1980).

Remarriage Rates

Over half of all marriages in the United States are marriages in which at least one partner has been previously married (Bumpass, Sweet, and Martin, 1990). Remarriage is more or less standard for divorced persons, but the rates have been declining, especially for African Americans and women under age twenty-five years. In addition to age and ethnicity, the presence of children may also affect remarriage.

AGE. A man's or woman's age at the time of separation is the greatest individual factor affecting remarriage. As with the "marriage market" in first marriages, as a person ages, the number of potential partners declines; at the same time one's own "marketability" decreases with increasing age. For women, the highest remarriage rate takes place in their twenties; it declines by a quarter in their thirties and by two-thirds in their forties. As we saw in Chapter 2, the double standard of aging affects women more negatively than men.

Remarriage rates for younger women have been declining. Their remarriage rates, in fact, have dropped by almost half since 1965. The decrease may be related to women choosing to cohabit rather than remarry.

ETHNICITY. Ethnicity also affects remarriage rates. About 55 percent of white women and 42 percent of African-American women remarry. Latinas are less likely to remarry than either whites or African Americans. The remarriage rates have been declining for African Americans, although first-marriage rates have also been declining.

PRESENCE OF CHILDREN. Although children from earlier marriages traditionally have been thought to decrease the likelihood of remarriage, the evidence is mixed. A review of the literature found that the presence of children decreases the rate of marriage by about one-quarter (Bumpass, Sweet, and Martin, 1990). The effects are

1. Bride 2. Groom 3. Groom's daughter from first marriage 4. Bride's mother 5. Bride's mother's current lover 6. Bride's sperm donor father 7.&8. Sperm donor's parents who sued for visitation rights to bride 9. Bride's mother's lover at time of bride's birth 10. Groom's mother 11. Groom's mother's boyfriend 12. Groom's father 13. Groom's stepmother 14. Groom's father's third wife 15. Groom's grandfather 16. Groom's grandfather's lover 17 Groom's first wife

most marked when a woman has three or more children. Most of the research, however, is ten to fifteen years old, and the increased prevalence of single-parent families and stepfamilies may have decreased some of the negative impact of children.

Courtship

The norms governing courtship prior to first marriage are fairly well defined. As courtship progresses, individuals spend more time together; at the same time, family and friends limit their time and energy demands because "they're in love." Courtship norms for second marriages, however, are not especially clear (Rodgers and Conrad, 1986). For example, when is it acceptable for formerly married (and presumably sexually experienced) men and women to become sexually involved? What type of commitment validates "premarital" sex among postmarital men and women? How long should courtship last before a commitment to marriage is made? Without clear norms, courtship following divorce can be plagued by uncertainty about what to expect.

One clear difference, however, appears to be in terms of cohabitation. Although 15 to 25 percent of people marrying for the first time may be living together at the time of marriage, 40 percent of those remarrying are cohabiting (Coleman and Ganong, 1991). This larger percentage may reflect the desire to test their compatibility in a "trial marriage" to prevent later marital regrets (Buunk and van Driel, 1989).

If neither partner has children, courtship for remarriage may resemble courtship before the first marriage, with one major exception: the memory of the earlier marriage exists as a model for the second marriage. It may trigger old fears, regrets, habits of relating, wounds, or doubts. At the same time, having experienced the day-to-day living of marriage, the partners have more realistic expectations. Their courtship may be complicated if one or both are noncustodial parents. In that event, visiting children present an additional element.

Courtship differs considerably from that preceding a first marriage if one or both members in the dating relationship is a custodial parent. Single parents are not often a part of the singles world, because such participation requires leisure and money, which single parents generally lack. Children rapidly consume both of these resources.

Although single parents may wish to find a new partner, their children usually remain the central figures in their lives. This creates a number of new problems. First, the single parent's decision to go out at night may lead to guilt feelings about the children. If a single mother works and her children are in day care, should she go out in the evening or stay at home with them? Second, a single parent must look at a potential partner as a potential parent as well. A person may be a good companion and confidant and be fun to be with, but if he or she does not want to assume parental responsibilities, the relationship will often stagnate or be broken off. Too, a single parent's new companion may be interested in assuming parental responsibilities, but the children may regard him or her as an intruder and try to sabotage the new relationship.

A single parent may also have to decide whether to permit a lover to spend the night when the children are in the home. This is often an important symbolic act. For one thing, it brings the children into the parent's new relationship. If the couple have no commitment, the parent may fear the consequences of the children's emotional involvement with the lover; if they break up, the children may be adversely affected. Single parents are often hesitant to expose their children again to the distress of separation; the memory of the initial parental separation and divorce is often still painful. For another thing, having a lover spend the night reveals to the children that their parent is a sexual being. This may make some single parents feel uncomfortable and may also make the parent vulnerable to moral judgment by his or her children. Single parents are often fearful that their children will lose respect for them under such circumstances. Sometimes children do judge their parents harshly, especially their mothers. Parents are often deeply disturbed at being condemned by children who do not understand their need for love, companionship, and sexual intimacy. Finally, having someone sleep over may trigger the resentment and anger that the children feel toward their parents for splitting up. They may view the lover as a parental replacement and feel deeply threatened.

Characteristics of Remarriage

Remarriage is considerably different from first marriage in a number of ways. First, the new partners get to know each other during a time of significant changes in life relationships, confusion, guilt, stress, and mixed feelings about the past (Keshet, 1980). They have great hope that they will not repeat past mistakes, but there is usually some fear that the hurts of the previous marriage will recur (McGoldrick and Carter, 1989). The past is still part of the present. A Talmudic scholar once commented, "When a divorced man marries a divorced woman, four go to bed."

Remarriages occur later than first marriages. People are at different stages in their life cycles and may have different goals (Furstenberg, 1980). A woman who already has had children may enter a second marriage with strong career goals. In her first marriage, raising children may have been more important (see Teachman and Heckert, 1985).

Divorced people have different expectations of their new marriages. In a study of second marriages in Pennsylvania, Furstenberg (1980) discovered that three-fourths of the couples had a different conception of love than couples in their first marriages. Two-thirds thought they were less likely to stay in an unhappy marriage; they had already survived one divorce and knew they could make it through another. Four out of five believed their ideas of marriage had changed. One woman said:

I think second marriages are less idealistic and a little more realistic. You realize that it's going to be tough sometimes but you also know that you have to work them out. You come into a second marriage with a whole new set of responsibilities. It's like coming into a ballgame with the bases loaded. You've got to come through with a hit. Likewise, there's too much riding on the relationship; you've got to make it work and you realize it more after you've been divorced before. You just have to keep working out the rules of the game.

Finally, the majority of remarriages create stepfamilies. Sixty percent of remarriages include a parent with physical custody of one or more children. Another 20 percent include a noncustodial parent (Weingarten, 1980). A single-parent family is generally a transition family leading to a stepfamily, which has its own unique structure, satisfactions, and problems.

Marital Satisfaction and Stability

According to various studies, remarried people are about as satisfied or happy in their second marriages as they were in their first marriage. As in first marriages, marital satisfaction appears to decline with the passage of time (Coleman and Ganong, 1991). Yet despite the fact that marital happiness and satisfaction are more or less the same in first and second marriages, remarried couples are more likely to divorce. How do we account for this paradox? Researchers have suggested several reasons for

A person who has been married many years knows more about marriage than one who has been married many times.

Anonymous

the higher divorce rate in remarriage. First, persons who remarry after divorce are more likely to use divorce as a way of resolving an unhappy marriage. Furstenberg and Spanier (1987) noted that they were continually struck by the willingness of remarried individuals to dissolve unhappy marriages: "Regardless of how unattractive they thought this eventuality, the great majority indicated that after having endured a first marriage to the breaking point they were unwilling to be miserable again simply for the sake of preserving the union."

Second, remarriage is an "incomplete institution" (Cherlin, 1978, 1981). Society has not evolved norms, customs, and traditions to guide couples in their second marriages. As Andrew Cherlin (1978) observed:

Problems are created by a complex family structure which cannot occur in first marriages. Because of the lack of social regulation, each family must devise its own solutions to these problems. The work of establishing rules increases the potential for conflict among family members, and the increased conflict, in turn, increases the likelihood of divorce.

There are no rules, for example, defining a stepfather's responsibility to a child: Is he a friend, a father, a sort of uncle, or what? Nor are there rules establishing the relationship between an individual's former spouse and his or her present partner: are they friends, acquaintances, rivals, or strangers? Remarriages don't receive the same family and kin support as do first marriages.

Third, remarriages are subject to stresses that are not present in first marriages. Perhaps the most important stress is stepparenting. Children can make the formation of the husband/wife relationship more difficult because they compete for their parents' love, energy, and attention. In such families, time together alone becomes a precious and all-to-rare commodity. Furthermore, although children have little influence in selecting their parent's new husband or wife, they have immense power in "deselecting" them. Children have "incredible power" in maintaining or destroying a marriage, observed Marilyn Ihinger-Tallman and Kay Pasley (1987):

Children can create divisiveness between spouses and siblings by acting in ways that accentuate differences between them. Children have the power to set parent against stepparent, siblings against parents, and stepsiblings against siblings.

❑ THE STEPFAMILY

Remarriages that include children are very different from those that do not. The families that emerge from remarriage with children are known as stepfamilies, but they are also called *blended, reconstituted,* or *restructured families* by social scientists, names that emphasize their structural differences from other families. Satirist Art Buchwald, however, calls them "tangled families." He may be close to the truth in some cases. Nevertheless, by the year 2000, there may be more stepfamilies in America than any other family form (Pill, 1990). If we care about families, we need to understand and support stepfamilies.

Stepfamilies: A Different Kind of Family

When we enter a stepfamily, many of us expect to recreate a family identical to an intact family. The intact nuclear family becomes the model against which we judge our successes and failures. But researchers believe that stepfamilies are significantly different from intact families (Coleman and Ganong, 1991; Pill, 1990). If we try to make our feelings and relationships in a stepfamily identical to those of an intact family, we are bound to fail. But if we recognize that the stepfamily works differently and provides different satisfactions and challenges, we can appreciate the richness it brings us and have a successful stepfamily.

STRUCTURAL DIFFERENCES. Six structural characteristics make the stepfamily different from the traditional first-marriage family (Visher and Visher, 1979). Each one is laden with potential difficulties.

1. In stepfamilies, almost all members have lost an important primary relationship. The children may mourn the loss of their parent or parents and the spouses the loss of their former mates. Anger and hostility may be displaced onto the new stepparent.

2. One biological parent lives outside the current family. He or she may either support or interfere with the new family. Power struggles may occur between the absent parent and the custodial parent, and there may be jealously between the absent parent and the stepparent.

3. The relationship between a parent and his or her children predates the relationship between the new partners. Children have often spent considerable time in a single-parent family structure. They have formed close and different bonds with their parent. A new husband or wife may seem to be an interloper in the children's special relationship with their parent. A new stepparent may find that he or she must compete with the children for their parent's attention. The stepparent may even be excluded from the parent-child system.

4. Stepparent roles are ill-defined. No one knows quite what he or she is supposed to do as a stepparent. Most stepparents try role after role until they find one that fits.

5. Many children in stepfamilies are also members of the noncustodial parent's household (as discussed earlier in "The Binuclear Family"). Each home may have differing rules and expectations. When conflict arises, children may try to play one household against the other. Furthermore, as Visher and Visher (1979) observed:

The lack of clear role definition, the conflict of loyalties that such children experience, the emotional reaction to the altered family pattern, and the loss of closeness with their parent who is now married to another person create inner turmoil and confused and unpredictable outward behavior in many children.

6. Children in stepfamilies have at least one extra pair of grandparents. Children get a new set of stepgrandparents, but the role these new grandparents are to play is usually not clear. A study by Spanier and Furstenberg (1980) found that grandparents were usually quick to accept their "instant" grandchildren.

Before we examine the stepfamily, we would do well to keep in mind that when Ganong and Coleman (1984) reviewed the empirical literature comparing stepfamilies to traditional nuclear families, they found no significant differences in relationships with stepfathers as compared to fathers, perceptions of parental happiness, degree of family conflict, and positive family relationships. Only the clinical literature tends to uphold the image of stepfamilies beset by conflict and traumas (Ganong and Coleman, 1986). One researcher (Chilman, 1986) pointed out:

Clinicians particularly tend to view this family form as traumatic because they see the selected group of troubled people who come for counseling. They do not see those who are making a relatively trouble-free adjustment to their marriage.

It may well be that stepfamilies are not very different from traditional nuclear families. We perceive them as being different because we use a "deficit model" in examining them (Coleman and Ganong, 1991). Thus we look for deficiencies and exaggerate problems or differences.

DIFFERENCES IN COHESION AND ADAPTABILITY. When examining stepfamilies, we need to understand the balance between emotional involvement and individual autonomy. Do healthy stepfamilies handle issues of cohesion and adaptability differently than members of healthy intact families? This is especially important if children are active members of a binuclear family. How do they manage being members of *two* nuclear families? Do stepfamilies have less cohesion than intact families? Do they have more adaptability?

According to Cynthia Pill (1990), healthy stepfamilies may differ from healthy intact families on both dimensions: Healthy stepfamilies are less cohesive and more adaptable than healthy intact families. Pill found that healthy stepfamilies demonstrated "remarkable capacity to allow for differences among family members and to permit looser, more flexible family relationships." Stepfamilies did not demand family unity at the price of individuality. Pill found that many healthy stepfamilies, for example, allowed their children to decide whether to come on the family vacation together or to spend time with their other birth parent. She also found that the closest emotional relationships generally were formed between biologically related family members. This meant that the stepparent was not necessarily as emotionally close as he or she might have been if the children were biologically related. Yet the stepparents noted this in a matter-of-fact manner, observing that it was understandable. Pill wrote:

While many stepparents wished that they might have been a part of the children's lives at an earlier stage, both because of the influence they would have had in the formation of the children's values and also because of the bonding that would have occurred, most were accepting of the limitations that entering children's lives later in their development brings.

Because stepfamilies had to continually adapt to the coming and going of family members, stepfamilies needed to be more adaptable than intact families: they needed to adjust expectations, define and redefine roles (such as redefining the father role to fit the stepfather), and create a meaningful definition of "family" for stepfamilies.

The overwhelming majority of stepfamilies felt they had become "family." When asked how they thought they had become a family, the family members replied that they had developed a sense of connectedness and a mutual feeling of caring and support among family members. Sharing major life events, such as birth or death, and living their mundane, everyday life together were the major factors giving them a sense of family identity and helping to solidify family feelings. Such experiences might include eating spaghetti together when wild noodles, dripping with tomato sauce, flapped against Mom's white dress. Or they might include common occurrences such as holding hands in prayer, dancing to favorite music, Dad's "stupid" but endearing jokes, or stories about dating disasters. Stepfamilies collect trivia, record odd events in the family's collective unconscious, recall revealing incidents, and weave these diverse strands together to create a family story or mythology. In creating family stories, stepfamilies begin to see themselves as uniquely different from all other families. And in doing so, stepfamilies become families in the deepest, most profound sense.

Problems of Women and Men in Stepfamilies

Most people go into stepfamily relationships expecting to recreate the traditional nuclear family found on "The Cosby Show" or "Family Ties"; they are full of love, hope, and energy. Perhaps the hardest adjustment they have to make is realizing that stepfamilies are different from traditional nuclear families—and that being different does not make stepfamilies inferior. A nuclear family is neither morally superior to the stepfamily nor a guarantor of happiness.

WOMEN IN STEPFAMILIES. Stepmothers tend to experience more problematic family relationships than stepfathers (Santrock and Sitterle, 1987). To various degrees, women enter stepfamilies with certain feelings and hopes. Stepmothers generally expect to do the following (Visher and Visher, 1979):

❑ Make up to the children for the divorce.
❑ Create a happy, close-knit family and a new nuclear family.
❑ Keep everyone happy.
❑ Prove that they are not wicked stepmothers.
❑ Love their stepchild instantly and as much as their own biological children.
❑ Receive instant love from their stepchildren.

Needless to say, most women are disappointed. Expectations of total love, happiness, and the like would be unrealistic in any kind of family, traditional as well as stepfamily. The warmer a woman is to her stepchildren, the more hostile they may become to her because they feel she is trying to replace their "real" mother. If a stepmother tries to meet everyone's needs—especially her stepchildren's, which are often contradictory, excessive, and distancing—she is likely to exhaust herself emotionally and physically. It takes time for her and her children to become emotionally integrated as a family.

The most serious problems full-time stepmothers experience may be due to the differences between families with stepfathers and those with stepmothers (Furstenberg and Nord, 1985). Bitter custody fights may leave the children emotionally troubled and hostile to stepmothers, whom they perceive as "forcibly" replacing their mothers. In other instances, children, especially adolescents, may move from their mother's home to their father's because their mother can no longer handle them. In either case, the stepmother may be required to parent children who have special needs or problems. Stepmothers may find these relationships especially difficult. Typically, stepmother/stepdaughter relationships are the most problematic (Clingempeel et al., 1984). Relationships become even more difficult when the stepmothers never intended to become full-time stepparents.

MEN IN STEPFAMILIES. Different stepfamily expectations are placed on men. Because men are generally less involved in childrearing, they usually have no "cruel stepparent" myths to counter. Nevertheless, men entering stepparenting roles may find certain areas particularly difficult at first (Visher and Visher, 1979). A critical factor in a man's stepparenting is whether he has children of his own. If he does, they are more likely to live with his ex-wife. In this case, the stepfather may experience guilt and confusion in his stepparenting, because he feels he should be parenting his own children. When his children visit, he may try to be "superdad," spending all his time with them and taking them to special places. His wife and stepchildren may feel excluded and angry.

A stepfather usually joins an already established single-parent family. He may find himself having to squeeze into it. The longer a single-parent family has been functioning, the more difficult it usually is to reorganize it; the children may resent his "interfering" with their relationship with their mother (Wallerstein and Kelly, 1980). His ways of handling the children may be different from his wife's, resulting in conflict.

Working out rules of family behavior is often the area in which a stepfamily encounters its first real difficulties. Although the mother usually wants help with disci-

Queen: No, be assur'd you shall not find me, daughter,
After the slander of most stepmothers,
Evil-ey'd unto you.
Imogen: Dissembling courtesy! How fine this tyrant
Can tickle where she wounds.

Shakespeare, Cymbeline

pline, she often feels protective if the stepfather's style is different from hers. To allow a stepparent to discipline a child requires trust from the biological parent and a willingness to let go. Disciplining often elicits a child's testing response: "You're not my real father. I don't have to do what you tell me." Disciplining establishes legitimacy because only a parent or parent-figure is expected to discipline in our culture. Disciplining, however, may be the first step toward family integration, because it establishes the stepparent's presence and authority in the family.

The new stepfather's expectations are important. Often, however, they are exceedingly unrealistic. "The usual situation," Visher and Visher (1979) noted, "is that he is blind to the complexity of the situation." He believes that "love will conquer all" and that the problems can be easily resolved—usually by his wife. The researchers continued:

Very often, as tension develops in the stepfamily, the husband looks to his wife to improve the situation. He considers that she is the one responsible for the daily functioning of the family and therefore it is her mismanagement that is causing the upset. Frequently, the wife has the same expectations of herself and tries harder and harder to cope with and alter the situation. The harder she tries the worse things get, and the relationship between the couple usually suffers. The expectation that the wife is responsible for the emotional relationships within the family is unrealistic, for no single person can unravel the complicated stepfamily situation.

Conflict in Stepfamilies

Achieving family solidarity in the stepfamily is a complex task. When a new parent enters the former single-parent family, the family system is thrown off balance. Where equilibrium once existed, there is now disequilibrium. A period of tension and conflict usually marks the entry of new people into the family system. Questions arise about them: Who are they? What are their rights and their limits? Rules change. The mother may have relied on television as a baby-sitter, for example, permitting the children unrestricted viewing in the afternoon. The new stepfather, however, may want to limit the children's afternoon viewing, creating tension. To the children, everything seemed fine until this stepfather came along. He has disrupted their old pattern. Chaos and confusion will be the norm until a new pattern is established, but it takes time for people to adjust to new roles, demands, limits, and rules.

Conflict takes place in all families—traditional nuclear families, single-parent families, and stepfamilies. If some family members do not like each other, they will bicker, argue, tease, and fight. Sometimes they have no better reason for disruptive behavior than that they are bored or frustrated and want to take it out on someone. These are fundamentally personal conflicts. Other conflicts are about definite issues: dating, use of the car, manners, television, friends. These can be between partners, between parents and children, or among the children themselves. There are certain types of stepfamily conflicts, however, whose frequency, intensity, or nature distinguish them from conflicts in traditional nuclear families. These conflicts are about favoritism, divided loyalties, and material goods and services.

FAVORITISM. Favoritism exists in families of first marriages as well as in stepfamilies. In stepfamilies, however, the favoritism often takes a very different form. Whereas a parent may favor a child in a biological family on the basis of age, sex, or personality, in stepfamilies favoritism tends to run along kinship lines. A child is favored by one or the other parent because he or she is the parent's biological child; or if a new child is born to the remarried couple, they may favor him or her as a child of their joint love. In American culture, where parents are expected to treat children equally, favoritism based on kinship seems particularly unfair.

DIVIDED LOYALTY. "How can you stand that lousy, low-down, sneaky, dirty mother [or father] of yours?" asks (or more accurately, demands) a hostile parent. It is one of the most painful questions children can confront, for it forces them to take sides against someone they love. One study (Lutz, 1983) found that about half of the adolescents studied confronted situations in which one divorced parent talked negatively about the other. Almost half of the adolescents felt themselves "caught in the middle." Three-quarters found such talk stressful.

Divided loyalties put children in no-win situations, forcing them not only to choose between parents but to reject new stepparents. Children feel disloyal to one parent for loving the other parent or stepparent. But divided loyalties, like favoritism, can exist in traditional nuclear families as well. This is especially true of conflict-ridden families in which warring parents seek their children as allies.

DISCIPLINE. Researchers generally agree that discipline issues are among the most important causes of conflict among remarried families (Ihinger-Tallman and Pasley, 1987; Knaub et al., 1984; Messinger, 1976). Discipline is especially difficult to deal with if the child is not the person's biological child. Disciplining a stepchild often gives rise to conflicting feelings within the stepparent. Stepparents may feel that they are overreacting to the child's behavior, that their feelings are out of control, and that they are being censured by the child's biological parent. Compensating for fears of unfairness, the stepparent may become overly tolerant.

The specific discipline problems vary from family to family, but a common problem is interference by the biological parent with the stepparent (Mills, 1984). The biological parent may feel resentful or overreact to the stepparent's disciplining if he or she has been reluctant to give the stepparent authority. As one biological mother who believed she had a good remarriage stated (quoted in Ihinger-Tallman and Pasley, 1987):

Sometimes I feel he is too harsh in disciplining, or he doesn't have the patience to explain why he is punishing and to carry through in a calm manner, which causes me to have to step into the matter (which I probably shouldn't do). . . . I do realize that it was probably hard for my husband to enter marriage and the responsibility of a family instantly . . . but this has remained a problem.

As a result of interference, the biological parent implies that the stepparent is wrong and undermines his or her status in the family. Over time, the stepparent may decrease his or her involvement in the family as a parent figure.

MONEY, GOODS, AND SERVICES. Problems of allocating money, goods, and services exist in all families, but they can be especially difficult in stepfamilies. In first marriages, husbands and wives form an economic unit in which one or both may produce income for the family; husband and wife are interdependent. Following divorce, the binuclear family consists of two economic units, the custodial family and the noncustodial family. Both must provide separate housing, which dramatically increases their basic expenses. Despite their separation, the two households may nevertheless continue to be extremely interdependent. The mother in the custodial single-parent family, for example, probably has reduced income. She may be employed but still dependent on child-support payments or AFDC. She may have to rely more extensively on child care, which may drain her resources dramatically. The father in the noncustodial family may make child-support payments or contribute to medical or school expenses, which depletes his income. Both households have to deal with financial instability. Custodial parents can't count on always receiving their child-support payments, which makes it difficult to undertake financial planning. The rate of noncompliance in making child-support payments increases over time. By the third year after divorce, noncompliance increases to 60 percent; by the fifth year, it is as high as 80 percent (Kressel, 1985).

When one or both of the former partners remarry, their financial situation may alter significantly. Upon remarriage, the mother receives less income from her former partner or welfare benefits. Instead, her new partner becomes an important contributor to family income. At this point, a major problem in stepfamilies arises. What responsibility does the stepfather have in supporting his stepchildren? Should he or the biological father provide financial support? Because there are no norms, each family must work out its own solution.

Stepfamilies typically have resolved the problem of distributing their economic resources by using a *one-pot* or *two-pot* pattern (Fishman, 1983). In the one-pot pattern, families pool their resources and distribute them according to need rather than biological relationship. It doesn't matter whether the child is a biological child or stepchild. One-pot families typically have relatively limited resources and consistently fail to receive child support from the noncustodial biological parent. By sharing their resources, one-pot families increase the likelihood of family cohesion.

In two-pot families, resources are distributed by biological relationship; need is secondary. These families tend to have a higher income and one or (usually) both parents have former spouses who regularly contribute to the support of their biological children. Expenses relating to children are generally handled separately; usually there are no shared checking or savings accounts. Two-pot families maintain strong bonds between members of the first family. For these families, a major problem is achieving cohesion in the stepfamily while maintaining separate checking accounts.

Just as economic resources need to be redistributed following divorce and remarriage, so do goods and services (not to mention affection). While a two-bedroom home or apartment may have provided plenty of space for a single-parent family with two children, a stepfamily with additional residing or visiting stepsiblings can experience instant overcrowding. Rooms, bicycles, and toys, for example, need to be shared; larger quarters may have to be found.

Time becomes a precious commodity for harried parents and stepparents in a stepfamily. When visiting stepchildren arrive, duties are doubled. Stepchildren compete with parents and other children for time and affection.

It may appear that remarried families are confronted with many difficulties, but traditional nuclear families also face financial, loyalty, and discipline problems. We need to put these problems in perspective. (After all, half of all current marriages end in divorce, which suggests that first marriages are not problem-free.) When all is said and done, the problems that remarried families face may not be any more overwhelming than those faced by traditional nuclear families (Ihinger-Tallman and Pasley, 1987).

Stepfamily Strengths

Because we have traditionally viewed stepfamilies as deviant, we have often ignored their strengths. Instead, we have only seen their problems. Let us end this chapter, then, by focusing on the strengths of stepfamilies.

FAMILY FUNCTIONING. While traditional nuclear families may be structurally less complicated than stepfamilies, stepfamilies are nevertheless able to fulfill traditional family functions. A binuclear single-parent, custodial, or noncustodial family may provide more companionship, love, and security than the particular traditional nuclear family it replaces. If the traditional nuclear family was ravaged by conflict, violence, sexual abuse, or alcoholism, for example, the single-parent family or stepfamily that replaces it may be considerably better. There may not be as much emotional closeness as in first families, but second families generally experience less trauma and crisis (Ihinger-Tallman and Pasley, 1987).

New partners may have greater objectivity regarding old problems or relationships (Ihinger-Tallman and Pasley, 1987). First, new partners can accelerate emotional disengagement between former spouses. Such disengagement leads to the dampening of conflicts. Second, once an individual is involved in a new marriage, he or she may feel less of a need to hold onto bitterness and enmity (Furstenberg and Spanier, 1987). Third, new partners are sometimes able to intervene between former spouses to resolve longstanding disagreements, such as custody or child-care arrangements.

IMPACT ON CHILDREN. Stepfamilies potentially offer children a number of benefits that can compensate for the negative consequences of divorce.

❒ Children gain multiple role models from which to choose. Instead of having only one mother or father after whom to model themselves, children may have two mothers or fathers, the biological parents and the stepparents.
❒ Children gain greater flexibility. They may be introduced to new ideas, different values, alternative politics. For example, while biological parents may be unable to encourage certain interests, such as music or model airplanes, because they lack training or interest, a stepparent may play the piano or be a diehard modeler. In such cases, that stepparent can assist his or her stepchildren in pursuing their development. In addition, children often have alternative living arrangements that enlarge their perspectives.
❒ Stepparents may act as a sounding board for their children's concerns. They may be a source of support or information in areas in which the biological parents feel unknowledgeable or uncomfortable.
❒ Children may gain additional siblings, either as stepsiblings or half-siblings.
❒ Children gain an additional extended kin network, which may become as important and loving (or more) as their original kin network.
❒ Finally, children may gain parents who are happily married. Most research indicates that children are significantly better adjusted in happily remarried families than in conflict-ridden traditional nuclear families.

As we near the twenty-first century, it is clear that the American family is no longer what it was at the beginning of the twentieth century. The single-parent family or stepfamily, however, does not imply an end to the American family. Rather, these forms provide different paths that contemporary American families take as they strive to fulfill the hopes, needs, and desires of their members. And they are becoming as Amercian as Beaver Cleaver's family and apple pie.

SUMMARY

❑ The *binuclear family* is a postdivorce family system with children. It consists of two nuclear families, the mother-headed family and the father-headed family, and children. Both single-parent families and stepfamilies are forms of binuclear families.

❑ The binuclear family consists of five subsystems: former spouse, remarried couple, parent/child, sibling, and mother/stepmother–father/stepfather subsystems.

❑ Single parenting is an increasingly significant family form in America. Single-parent families tend to be created by divorce or births to single women, are generally headed by women, are usually poor, involve a wide variety of household types, are predominantly African-American or Latino, and are usually a transitional stage.

❑ Relations between the parent and his or her children change after divorce: the single parent generally tends to be emotionally closer but to have less authority. Most single parents work; child care is a constant problem. Dating poses unique problems for single parents: they may feel guilty for going out, they must look at potential partners as potential parents, and they must deal with their children's judgments or hostility.

❑ Courtship for second marriage does not have clear norms. Individuals seem to take about as long in second marriage courtship as in first marriage courtship. If children are not involved from the earlier marriage, the only major difference between first and second marriage courtship is that the first marriage exists as a model. Courtship is complicated by the presence of children, for remarriage involves the formation of a stepfamily.

❑ Remarriage differs from first marriage in several ways: partners get to know each other in the midst of major changes, they remarry latter in life, they have different marital expectations, and their marriage often creates a stepfamily.

❑ Marital happiness appears to be about the same in first and second marriages. Remarried men are more likely to express greater marital satisfaction. Remarried couples are slightly more likely to divorce than couples in their first marriages. This may be accounted for either by their will-ingness to use divorce as a means of resolving an unhappy marriage or because remarriage is an "incomplete institution." Stresses accompanying stepfamily formation may also contribute.

❑ Traditionally scholars have viewed stepfamilies from a "deficit" perspective. As a result, they assumed that step-families were very different from traditional nuclear families. More recently, scholars have begun to view stepfamilies as normal families; they have found few significant differences in levels of satisfaction and functioning between stepfamilies and traditional nuclear families. Only clinical research continues to find significant difficulties; such findings, however, may be attributed to the clinical method's traditional focus on pathology.

❑ The *stepfamily* differs from the original family because (1) almost all members have lost an important primary relationship, (2) one biological parent lives outside the current family, (3) the relationship between a parent and his or her children predates the new marital relationship, (4) stepparent roles are ill-defined, (5) often children are members of the noncustodial parent's household, and (6) children have at least one extra pair of grandparents.

❑ Stepmothers tend to experience greater stress in step-families than stepfathers. In part this may be because their families are more likely to have been subject to custody disputes or have children with troubled family history.

❑ Stepfathers tend not to be as involved as stepmothers. They often experience difficulty in being integrated into the family.

❑ A key issue for stepfamilies is family solidarity—the feeling of oneness with the family. Healthy stepfamilies may have less cohesion but greater adaptability than intact families. Conflict in stepfamilies is often over favoritism, divided loyalty, discipline, and money, goods, and services.

❑ Stepfamily strengths may include improved family functioning and reduced conflict between former spouses. Children may gain multiple role models, more flexibility, concerned stepparents, additional siblings, additional kin, and happily-married parents.

PART 7

Strengths

CHAPTER 15

Marriage and Family Strengths

The tree of love gives shade to all.

African-American proverb

IF WE DEFINE THE FAMILY AS SIMPLY A PEOPLE-PRODUCING FACTORY, we will call all families that produce offspring "successful." Yet we know that a family has other important functions. As you will recall from Chapter 1, the basic tasks of the family are (1) reproduction and socialization, (2) economic cooperation, (3) assignment of status and social roles, and (4) intimacy. How well a family is able to accomplish these tasks appears to depend on a number of characteristics and abilities. In this chapter we discuss the particular characteristics that seem to make marriages and families strong. We explore how culture and ethnicity can contribute to family success, and we examine how the relationships with the extended family, with friends, and with fictive kin (friends who are like family) help sustain the family unit. Finally, we look at the ecology of the family—that is, how the family interacts with the community.

❑ MARITAL STRENGTHS

Marriage may be seen as a forum for negotiating the balance between the desire for intimacy and the need to maintain a separate identity. To negotiate this balance successfully, we need to develop what sociologist Nelson Foote (1955) called "interpersonal competence," the ability to share and develop an intimate, growing relationship with another.

Marital Strengths versus Family Strengths

Many of the traits of healthy marriages are also found in healthy families, discussed later in this chapter. Indeed, marital competence can be viewed as a necessary basis for family success (Epstein et al., 1982; Lewis et al., 1976). It might seem ideal if couples could perfect their interpersonal skills before the arrival of children. Child-free couples generally have more time for each other and substantially less psychological, economic, and physical stress. In reality, however, many of our marital skills probably develop alongside our family skills. Thus, as we improve communication with our spouses, for example, our communication with our children also improves.

There have been hundreds of studies on marital happiness and very few (and those only in the last decade or so) on *family* happiness. Still, an argument can be made that certain kinds of strengths accrue only to families with children. The relationships of couples with children generally have greater stability than those of childless couples, because the emotional cost of a breakup is much greater when children are present. Also, the relationships of parents to their children are rewarding in and of themselves and fulfill much of the need for intimacy. Sometimes the bonds between the individual parent and the children or between the children themselves can sustain a family during times of marital stress. Furthermore, the growing acceptance of singlehood and child-free marriages notwithstanding, society expects its adults to be parents and rewards the attainment of the parental role with approval and respect.

Essential Marital Strengths

Therapist-researcher David Mace (1980) cites the essential aspects of successful marriage as commitment, communication, and the creative use of conflict. Recent research indicates that the strongest predictor of marital success may be the effectiveness of communication experienced by the couple before marriage (Goleman, 1985). Numerous studies show that there is a strong correlation between a couple's

A good marriage is that in which each appoints the other guardian of his individuality.

Rainer Maria Rilke (1875–1926)

A Marriage Ring

*The ring so worn as you behold
So thin, so pale, is yet of gold;
The passion such it was to prove:
Worn with life's cares, love yet
was love.*

George Crabbe (1754–1832)

communication patterns and marital satisfaction (Noller and Fitzpatrick, 1991). Classes and workshops are being developed in many communities to help teach these vital marital skills to couples before they commit themselves to marriage. Communication and conflict resolution were discussed in Chapter 11.

Mace defines commitment in terms of the relationship's potential for growth. He wrote, "There must be a commitment on the part of the couple to ongoing growth in their relationship. . . . There is tremendous potential for loving, for caring, for warmth, for understanding, for support, for affirmation; yet, in so many marriages of today it never gets developed." Commitment to any endeavor—and marriage is certainly no exception—requires the willingness and ability to *work*. In their study of strong families, Nick Stinnett and John DeFrain (1985) quoted one-half of a married couple:

You know the stereotypical story of the couple who have the lavish wedding, expensive rings, and exotic honeymoon and then settle down. The work is over. She gets dumpy and nags; he gets sloppy and never again brings flowers. We were like that until one day when we examined our life together and found it lacked something. Then we decided that the wedding, rings, and honeymoon marked the beginning, *not* the end. We had to renew the marriage all along.

Commitment to the sexual relationship within marriage appears to be an important aspect of marital strength (Stinnett and DeFrain, 1985). All the families in the Stinnett and DeFrain study recommended sexual fidelity. An extramarital relationship does not mean the end of a strong marriage, however. Sometimes an affair can be a "catalyst for growth" (Stinnett and DeFrain, 1985). A couple may not realize how far they have drifted apart, how much their communication has deteriorated, or how important the marital relationship is until the extramarital relationship brings things into clearer focus. When spouses who love each other have sexual liaisons outside their marriage, it is almost certainly a sign that their relationship is in trouble. Yet they can then take the painful lessons they've learned and use them to forge a stronger and better marriage.

Another aspect of commitment is sacrifice. Often people give up things—work demands, social activities, or material goods—for those they love without thinking twice about it. Sometimes difficult choices must be made. Within a committed relationship, there is give-and-take so that neither partner ends up in the "martyr" role (see Stinnett and DeFrain, 1985). When spouses give up something in order to be together, they nurture the marriage relationship, which in turn supports and strengthens the individual.

A study (Bell, Daly, and Gonzales, 1987) of 109 married women revealed key strategies perceived to maintain marital closeness. They included:

❑ Honesty
❑ Listening
❑ Openness
❑ Physical and verbal affection
❑ Physical attractiveness
❑ Sensitivity
❑ Supportiveness

The study also showed that the participating women believed themselves to be "more responsible than their husbands for the maintenance of their marriages." Whether or not the women were more responsible could not be determined by the research. The researchers did point out, however, that "individuals within close relationships tend to perceive themselves as more responsible than their partners for its positive aspects."

The great secret of successful marriage is to treat all disasters as incidents and none of the incidents as disasters.

Harold Nicholson

We can look at marriage as a kind of task to be performed (albeit willingly and joyfully) or as a growing thing to be nurtured. Whatever metaphor we choose, we see that the relationship requires time, energy, patience, thoughtfulness, planning, and perhaps a little more patience in order to grow and prosper. Commitment to this success (and the sacrifices that commitment may entail) is an essential component in the formation of strong marriages and strong families as well.

❑ FAMILY STRENGTHS

Of course, it's not really possible to make a family happy and healthy by merely prescribing a dose of good communication or a shot of trust. Researchers do observe, however, that certain characteristics tend to exist in the families that they view as successful.

Family as Process

As the saying goes, "nobody's perfect," and neither is any family. Perfection in families, as in most other aspects of life, exists as an ideal, not as a reality. Family quality can be seen as a continuum, with a few very healthy or unhealthy families at either end and the rest somewhere in between. Also, family quality varies over the family life cycle. Generally, families experience increased stress during the childbearing and teenager phases of the cycle. The overall cohesiveness of the family is severely tested at these times, and although families often emerge stronger, they may have experienced periods of distrust, disorder, and unhappiness.

Families also are idiosyncratic: each is different from all the others. Some may function optimally when the children are very young and not so well when they become teenagers, whereas the reverse may be true for other families. Some families may possess great strengths in certain areas and weaknesses in others. But all families constantly change and grow. The family is a process.

Communication

The role of communication in establishing family strength is paramount. Whatever their differences, all researchers seem to agree that good communication skills are the bedrock of family success. Through communication, the family fulfills its roles, especially as a socializer of children and provider of intimacy; through communication, other important qualities of family success are generated.

The aspects of healthy communication were discussed in Chapter 11. The communication and conflict–resolution skills discussed there apply not only to parents' relationships with each other but also to parent/child and child/child relationships. Among the most significant things a family can teach its children are the value of expressing their feelings effectively and the importance of truly listening to the expressions of others.

Affirmation, Respect, and Trust

AFFIRMATION. For most of us, the phrase that we like best to hear in the world consists of three little words. "I love you" may be a short sentence, but it can go a long way toward soothing a hurt, drying a tear, restoring a crumbling sense of self-worth, and maintaining a feeling of satisfaction and well-being. Supporting others in our family—letting them know we're interested in their projects, problems, feelings, and

Our family is not yet so good as to be degenerating.

Kurt Ewald

opinions—and being supported and affirmed in return is essential to family health (Gecas and Seff, 1991).

RESPECT. Another way we show that we care about our family members, friends, and fellow human beings is by according them respect for their uniqueness and differences, even if we may not necessarily understand or agree with them. Healthy families encourage the development of individuality in their members, though it may lead to difficulties when the children's views begin to diverge widely from those of their parents—on such subjects, for example, as religion, premarital sex, consumerism, patriotism, and childrearing. Criticism, ridicule, and rejection undermine self-esteem and severely restrict individual growth. Families that hamper the expression of their children's attitudes and beliefs tend to send into society children who are unable to respect differences in others. In addition to exhibiting respect for others, a healthy family member also insists on being respected in return.

TRUST. The establishment of trust, you will recall, is a child's first developmental stage acording to Erik Erikson. Not only must an infant develop trust in his or her parents but a growing child must also continue to feel that other family members can be relied on absolutely. In turn, children learn to act in ways that make their parents trust them. Children in healthy families are allowed to earn trust as deemed appropriate by the parents. Children who know they are trusted are then able to develop self-confidence and a sense of responsibility for themselves and others.

Although family strengths may vary over the life cycle, researchers observe certain characteristics, such as affirmation, respect and common spiritual ground, in healthy families.

It is not only children who need to "earn" the right to be called trustworthy; parents do, too. It's important for parents to be realistic in their promises to children and honest about their own mistakes and shortcomings. It's also important for children to see that their parents trust each other.

The family you come from isn't as important as the family you're going to have.

Ring Lardner (1885–1933)

ROLE MODELING. Many researchers agree that parental role modeling is a crucial factor in the development of qualities that ensure personal psychological health and growth (Epstein et al., 1982; Lewis et al., 1976). A loving relationship between parents, observed a family program administrator, "seems to breed security in the children, and, in turn, fosters the ability to take risks, to reach out to others, to search for their own answers, become independent, and develop a good self-image" (quoted in Curran, 1983). The more children observe their elders in situations that demonstrate mutual trust, respect, and care, the more they are encouraged to incorporate these successful and satisfying behaviors into their own lives. In divorced families, a continued positive relationship between the parents (if possible) is crucially important to the developing child (Goldsmith, 1982).

Responsibility, Morality, and Spiritual Wellness

One of the family's principal socializing tasks is to teach the responsibility of the individual for his or her own actions. Fostering morality, a code of ethics for dealing with our fellow human beings, is also essential.

RESPONSIBILITY AND MORALITY. The acquisition of responsibility is rooted in self-respect and an appreciation of the interdependence of people. When we as children develop a sense of our own self-worth, we begin to understand how much difference our own acts can make in the lives of others; this feeling of "making a difference" aids the further growth of self-esteem.

Successful families realize the importance of delegating responsibility (participating in household chores, sharing in family decisions, and so on) and of developing responsible behavior (completing homework, remembering appointments, keeping our word, cleaning up our own mess). Sometimes children may have to accept more responsibility than they want, as when their dual worker or single parents rely on them for assistance. Although these situations may be detrimental for children in families already suffering severe economic (or other) hardships, in many families children have come to benefit from the added responsibility; they feel a sense of accomplishment and worthiness. Parental acknowledgment for a job well done goes a long way toward building responsibility.

Healthy families also know the importance of allowing children to make their own mistakes and face the consequences. These lessons can be very painful at times, but they are stepping stones to growth and success. Along with a sense of responsibility, healthy families help develop their children's ability to discriminate between right and wrong. This morality may be grounded in specific religious principles but need not be; it is, however, based on a firm conviction that the world and its people must be valued and respected. Harvard psychologists Robert Coles and Jerome Kagan believe that children are naturally equipped with a basic moral sense; parents need to recognize and nurture that sense from early on. Besides helping children resolve their moral dilemmas, healthy parents take care to be responsible for their own behavior. Parental hypocrisy sets the stage for disrespect, disappointment, and rebellion.

SPIRITUAL WELLNESS. The families in Stinnett and DeFrain's study (1985) described the "spiritual dimension" in various ways: "faith in God, faith in humanity, ethical behavior, unity with all living things, concern for others, or religion." It's necessary to have a broad definition of spirituality because the experience is entirely subjective; it means different things to different people. Yet strong families share common spiritual ground. In these families, spiritual wellness is a "unifying force, a caring center within each person that promotes sharing, love, and compassion for others. It is a force that helps a person transcend self and become part of something larger" (Stinnett and DeFrain, 1985).

Spirituality gives meaning, purpose, and hope. In the case of formal religions, it provides a sense of community and support (Abbott, Berry, and Meredith, 1990). In times of adversity, families tap their spiritual resources to gain the strength that they need to sustain themselves. Stinnett and DeFrain (1985) suggest seven ways to help spirituality work in families:

1. Set aside time each day for meditation, prayer, or contemplation. Try to get outdoors to enjoy the beauty of nature.
2. Join (or help form) a discussion group to consider religious or philosophical issues.
3. Examine your own values. Try keeping a journal of your thoughts.
4. Help your children to clarify their values.
5. Identify three of your strengths. Work on developing them more fully. Identify three of your weaknesses. Decide how you can improve in these areas.
6. Have regular family devotionals. "Read . . . inspirational material, pray, sing, count your blessings, reaffirm your love and commitment to each other."
7. Volunteer time, energy, and money to a cause that helps others.

Spiritual wellness, it should be noted, is not necessarily the same as religiosity. Rigid religious doctrines "that promote traditional sex roles or negative approaches to family planning" have been found by some researchers to be "detrimental to family life" (Abbott, Berry, and Meredith, 1990; Brigman, 1984). "There is a gray area between moral refraction and spiritual reflection as people look for life's purpose," Robert Coles says. "Religion has no monopoly on spirituality" (quoted in Mehren, 1990; see Coles, 1990, for a study of spirituality in children's lives).

Traditions and Family History

TRADITION AND RITUAL. Through tradition and ritual, families find a link to the past and consequently a hope for the future. Traditions, especially those rooted in our cultural background, help give us a sense of who we are as a family and as a community. We have such strong feelings about our holiday rituals that sometimes our families suffer particular stresses during holiday times if expectations of family unity are not met.

There are many varieties of traditions and rituals, from elaborate holiday celebrations to daily or weekly routines. Children's bedtime rituals with blankets, books, bears, or prayers give security and comfort, as do Sunday morning rituals that find the family together in church or in bed with the funny papers. Large and small rituals, if not passed down from preceding generations, can be freshly created and passed *forward*. Therapist Mary Whiteside (1989) advises that stepfamilies may benefit particularly from the creation of new rituals, which can "generate a feeling of closeness" and "provide fuel for weathering the more difficult times." She adds, "As these experiments . . . succeed enough to recur and to emerge as customs, the stepfamily unit begins to feel as if it has a life of its own."

There are only two lasting bequests we can hope to give our children. One is roots; the other, wings.

Hodding Carter

Prune Cake

Cream: 1 c. brown sugar
1/2 c. shortening

Add: 1 egg
3/4 c. combined orange and prune juice
a little grated orange rind
1 tsp. soda
1 tsp. cinnamon
1/2 tsp. allspice
salt
2 c. flour

Beat and add 1 c. prunes cut in pieces; add nuts if desired. Bake at 350 for 35 min. or until done. [Grandma Mimi's note at bottom follows.] "Found this old recipe. It's the one I used during the Depression–made and sold for profit."

We can only hold to the name of family when we actively celebrate ourselves, tell each other stories, and pass the sense of oneness on to our children–the way we pass on a taste for chestnut stuffing or cranberry relish with orange. It is the traditions that we constantly create that become the special glue to hold us together over time and distance.

Ellen Goodman

*Cuando cuentas cuentos,
cuenta cuantos cuentos cuentas
cuando cuentas cuentos.
(When you tell stories
count how many stories you tell
when you tell stories.)*

Spanish tongue twister

FAMILY HISTORY. Strong families often have a strong sense of family history. Like family traditions, family memorabilia—scrapbooks, photos, letters, recipes, and mementos—are a satisfying link to the past. When we recall such family tales as the one in which "Grandma was seventeen, and she lost her bloomers on the dance floor," we not only have a good laugh on Grandma but we also identify with her chagrin and her resourcefulness (she kicked them behind a sofa), and perhaps we add to the story an account of an embarrassing moment of our own. Family stories may also bring up recurring themes unique to our particular family's experience (Martin, Hagestad, and Didrick, 1988).

Ethnicity and the Family

Ethnicity, writes Monica McGoldrick (1982), "is more than race, religion, and national or geographic origin. . . . It involves conscious and unconscious processes that fulfill a deep psychological need for identity and a sense of historical continuity. It is transmitted by an emotional language within the family and reinforced by the surrounding community."

In the "melting pot" of American society, ethnicity is a complicated and ever-changing phenomenon. Although some ethnic groups intermarry with and adapt rapidly to mainstream society, others, by choice or by pressure from without, have retained many of their traditions and values. In this sense, the United States can be seen more as a cauldron of very complex stew than as a homogenized melting pot.

An ethnic group may possess particular strengths that help its families to survive in a larger society that is often less than welcoming and sometimes overtly hostile. During slavery and in its aftermath, for example, amid racism and discrimination, African Americans needed to rely on their own families and community strengths. Strong kinship networks have been a major resource of black families during times of trouble (Chatters, Taylor, and Neighbors, 1989; McGoldrick, 1982); these kinship patterns have their roots in the family forms of West Africa (Allen, 1978; Gutman, 1976). Family values such as unconditional love for children, respect for self and others, and the "assumed natural goodness of the child" are other strengths of

"Coming of age" rituals, such as bar mitzvahs and bat mitzvahs, give young people a sense of continuity and identity within their culture or ethnic group.

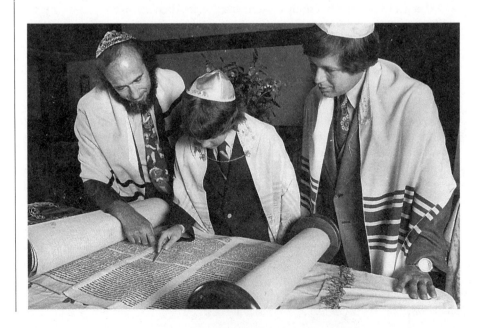

the African-American family (Nobles, 1988). Robert Taylor (1990) and his colleagues noted that a distinctive task of African-American parents is to attempt to prepare their children for the "realities of being black in America." (Also see Hill, 1972; Nobles, 1988; Staples, 1976.)

Urban anthropologist John Price (1981) studied the ways in which Native Americans in Los Angeles adjusted to an urbanized life. He found that although some traditional family patterns (such as multifamily residences) have declined, kinship networks remain "strong and supportive." Indians from over 100 different tribes have found ways to share their pride in their common heritage through Native American sports leagues and dance groups, powwows, and traditional crafts. Many also "commute" frequently to the home reservation to renew their family and cultural ties.

Families in every American ethnic group, whether newly arrived, long settled, or Native American, have a richness of tradition and insight to add to society. Even those whose ancestors came here one or two or three hundred years ago and who consider themselves "mongrels" of no specific pedigree are likely to preserve some ethnic flavor within their families—in their holiday celebrations, traditional recipes, names, verbal expressions, or ties to the old world. A significant challenge to today's society is to preserve and protect the uniqueness of all the ethnic groups of which it is composed while allowing the fulfillment of the promise of "liberty and justice for all."

Play and Leisure Time

"Lack of time . . . might be the most pervasive enemy the healthy family has" (Curran, 1983). Stress management, role overload, and executive burnout are concepts that would have been considered strange fifty or so years ago, yet now they are major themes in everyday life. The fast pace and complex activities of our lives threaten a crucial resource—time. Without time, families lack the opportunity to nurture the basic qualities, like communication, that ensure their health and growth. Without time, families lack the opportunity to simply be. Healthy families realize that they need to get away from work and responsibilities and simply enjoy one another and life in general. Quality time together need not be spent on lengthy or expensive vacations; a relaxed meal or a game in which everyone participates can serve the same purpose a lot more often.

The capacity to enjoy our family, with humor and playfulness and without strict scheduling, seems to come more easily to some than to others. Parents may have difficulty learning to leave a messy desk at work or a sticky kitchen floor at home in order to relax with each other or with their children. They may feel a moral obligation to be a "good provider" or a "perfect housekeeper," which precludes their closing the door on disorder and going for a walk in the park. Yet time taken to play and relax with our loved ones pays off in ways that clean desks and shiny floors never can. When we are realistic, we see that the papers will never stop flowing onto the desk and the jam will never stop dripping onto the floor, but our children and our mates will not be as they are now ever again. If we don't take the time now to enjoy our families, we've lost an opportunity forever. Healthy families know this and give play and leisure time high priority.

Coping with Stress

Among the resources a healthy family possesses are the coping strategies that it brings into play during stressful times. These strategies can be seen as part of a "pool of resources" that the family has available to draw from when the going gets tough

*If you don't know your past
You don't know your future.*

Ziggy Marley

If you cannot get rid of the family skeleton, you may as well make it dance.

George Bernard Shaw

FOCUS

Tradition and Ritual in Modern American Life

If we think about all the rituals and holidays that we take for granted in our lives, we may be forced to conclude that humans are just naturally "party animals." Our lives are measured with life-cycle rituals, mainly surrounding birth, the transition to adulthood, marriage, and death. Our years are punctuated with holidays and celebrations, both religious and secular. Weddings and funerals have their own unique characteristics among different ethnic groups, as do "baby-welcoming" rituals such as baptism among Christians and *bris* (circumcision) among Jews. Many ethnic and cultural groups also celebrate the child's transition to adult status—with *bar* or *bat mitzvahs*, church confirmations, or "coming-out" parties. Other rituals, such as family reunions or tribal gatherings (powwows), may be associated with a particular holiday or convened when the family or community feels the need.

In addition to "traditional" holidays celebrated in the United States, such as Christmas, Passover, and Thanksgiving, holidays introduced by more recent immigrants enrich our culture. *Yuan Tan* (Chinese New Year), *Tet* (Vietnamese New Year), *Hana Matsuri* (the Japanese observance of the Buddha's birthday), *Ramadan* (the Islamic month of fasting), and *el Dia de los Muertos* (the Latino Day of the Dead) are just a few examples of holidays currently celebrated by American families. Among African Americans, Juneteenth, a celebration of emancipation, is being revived in many parts of the country.

Although many holidays commemorate historic events, their origins may well lie in ancient rites having to do with the movements of the sun and moon, the cycle of the seasons, or other natural events, such as the flooding of a river or the ripening of acorns. The impulses that brought our ancestors together to celebrate the beginnings of new life or give thanks for a successful harvest may have since taken on different meanings, but the observances often retain their ancient symbols—fertile bunnies and decorated eggs, for example, or displays of scarecrows along with harvested grains, fruits, and nuts.

Besides giving people a way of expressing their unity with nature, ritual celebrations also bring them together in a common purpose and strengthen their bonds to each other and to the community. Some ceremonies, such as marriage, formally (we might say "legally") create new relationships (in-laws) with attendant duties and privileges. Rituals, such as coming-of-age ceremonies, also strengthen the ties of the individual to the group. Some elements common to many diverse rituals are the use of food and drink; costumes; music and dance; ritual objects such as candles, flowers, and feathers; representations of people or deities; and special words (prayers, chants, incantations, blessings, vows).

A brief sampling of current holidays and rituals practiced in the United States follows. The holidays are listed in the order they occur through the year.

❑ **Yuan Tan** Chinese New Year begins on the first day of the lunar year, at the first new moon when the sun is in the constellation known to Westerners as Aquarius (typically between January 10 and February 19). It is celebrated for fourteen days, until the full moon, culminating in a nighttime parade accompanied by fireworks and featuring a huge, bejeweled dragon with a papier-maché head, a long, red, fabric body, and the legs of many humans underneath. The dragon represents fertility and prosperity.

❑ **Tet** The Vietnamese New Year, *Tet Nguyen Dan,* also coincides with the start of the lunar year, although the celebration begins days earlier. Traditionally, Vietnamese families make new clothes and many new purchases in preparation for the coming year. The father or grandfather lights candles on the ancestral altar, and symbolic objects and many kinds of foods are offered. At midnight on the first day of the year, the ancestral spirits are welcomed. This day is considered portentious, so families carefully monitor their words and actions to insure a year of harmony and good fortune.

❑ **Hana Matsuri** On April 8, Japanese Buddhists commemorate the birthday of Siddhartha Gautama, the Buddha (*Shakyamuni,* in Japanese). Traditionally, images of the infant Buddha are bathed with hydrangea tea, and flowers, incense, and chanting are offered at Buddhist shrines and temples. *Hana*

continued on next page

(Stinnett and DeFrain, 1985). (The effects of stress on the family were discussed in Chapter 10.)

POSITIVE ATTITUDE. An optimistic outlook and a tendency to look on the bright side of things characterize strong families. This doesn't mean that they don't recog-

FOCUS

Matsuri is also known as the Flower Festival.

❑ **Pesach** The Feast of the Passover is a Jewish festival that begins after the first full moon of spring (Nisan 15 on the Hebrew calendar). It commemorates the flight of the Jews from Egypt under the leadership of Moses. *Pesach* has been celebrated for more than 3,000 years. Associated with Passover is the *Seder*, a family service and meal in remembrance of the ancestors' hardships. Traditional foods include matzohs (unleavened bread) and lamb (a holdover from the ancient sacrificial rite).

❑ **Juneteenth** The African-American holiday Juneteenth originated in Texas following the Civil War. Although the Emancipation Proclamation became law in January 1863, the last slaves were not freed until June 19, 1865, when Union troops rode into Galveston, Texas. Traditionally, Juneteenth (along with other Jubilee or Freedom Days) included such events as barbecues, baseball games, speeches, parades, concerts, and dances. As African Americans moved northward, the holidays moved with them, but during World War II such celebrations were considered unpatriotic as they emphasized a separate history from the white majority. Renewed interest in black history has sparked the revival of Juneteenth in communities across the United States.

❑ **Ramadan** The Islamic Fast of *Ramadan* begins with the new moon of the tenth lunar month and lasts until the next new moon. During *Ramadan,* the faithful fast daily between daybreak and dusk and spend as much time as possible in the mosque (place of worship) or at prayer. A mosque may be brilliantly lit to commemorate Mohammed's illumination on the Night of Power. The Koran (the Muslim holy book) is read in its entirety over the course of the month. On the twenty-ninth night the fast is broken, and the feast of *Eid Ui Fitr* begins. There are special foods, confections, and presents for the children.

❑ **Christmas** Although the exact date of Jesus's birth is not known, it has been celebrated by Christians since the fourth century on December 25—around the time of the winter solstice, the Roman holiday Saturnalia, and the Jewish Chanukah. Over time Christmas has taken on many quasi-religious and nonreligious aspects, including feasts, the exchange of gifts, decorations (such as evergreen trees and branches, which symbolize eternal life), and rituals. The tradition of visits by Santa Claus (St. Nicholas) was brought to the New World by early Dutch immigrants. The cartoonist Thomas Nast first gave Santa his sleigh and reindeer to take presents to soldiers in the Civil War. Music and pageantry are important to many people's Christmas celebrations, and a variety of traditions are practiced all over America by different ethnic and cultural groups.

❑ **La Quinceañera** On their fifteenth birthdays, young women of Latin American descent may be "introduced" into society in a ritual celebration known as the *quinceañera* (fifteenth-year celebration). A great deal of preparation usually goes into the event, which begins with a special Catholic mass involving the girl's family and godparents and proceeds to a dance and feast that is generally as lavish as the parents can afford. There may be both a dance band and a *mariachi* band; the guest of honor and her attendants, in their matching formal dresses, open the party with a specially choreographed waltz.

❑ **Powwows** Powwows—large gatherings of various Native American groups—involve demonstrations and contests of singing, dancing, and drumming. Powwows are secular in nature, unlike tribal religious ceremonies, which are usually carried out solemnly in private. Some performers at powwows are professionals who travel the "powwow circuit," keeping the traditions of their particular tribe alive. But anyone can participate, even small children, learning the steps their people have done for hundreds of years in dances portraying different animals, hunting techniques, or historical events. Traditional songs may be augmented with modern verses—to honor veterans of Korea and Vietnam, for example (Pareles, 1990). Powwows help keep Native American culture alive. A Mohawk singer expressed his feelings (quoted in Pareles, 1990): "I didn't learn anything about my culture when I was younger. But the more I find out, the more I've been seeing the logic of it and how beautiful and natural it was."

nize and deal with their problems, but they choose to dwell on the positive rather than the negative. Stinnett and DeFrain (1985) quoted one of their respondents:

I don't recommend that you burn the house to learn the lesson, but we did stand on our front lawn one frosty fall morning and looked at the pile of ashes that had been our home. And then we all looked at each other and suddenly we were hugging and crying with joy because we were OK.

Everything comes of itself at the appointed time. This is the meaning of heaven and earth.

I Ching

Tradition and ritual are central to our lives. Among Catholics, a child's first communion is an important milestone.

If you're afraid of the dark, remember the night rainbow. If you lose the key to your house, throw away the house. And if it's the last dance, you better dance backwards.

Cooper Edens

Experience is not what happens to a man; it is what a man does with what happens to him.

Aldous Huxley (1894–1963)

ADAPTABILITY. Strong families often need to bend in order to avoid breaking. Under stress, family members may be required to change their routines or plans or to take on unfamiliar roles. If families are inflexible in their standards, expectations, or behavior, they may find themselves on a collision course with crisis.

UNITED FRONT. Healthy families support each other so that no individual has to bear a burden all alone. Family members can help each other by lending emotional or physical support. They offer a cheery word or a shoulder to cry on. They wash the dishes, take the kids on an outing, share belongings, lend money, or assist in a thousand other big and little ways.

SPIRITUAL RESOURCES. Faith, prayer, and a sense of greater purpose provide strength, comfort, and hope to many in times of hardship. The spiritual dimension of healthy families was discussed earlier in this chapter.

COMMUNICATION. The importance of good communication cannot be overstated. Not only does communication help us get through stressful times, but it can also prevent many potentially stressful events from occurring. Chapter 11 deals exclusively with this vital quality of healthy families.

GETTING HELP. Healthy families are not problem-free; they may even have as many problems as unhealthy families. What distinguishes them from their less-successful counterparts is their willingness to face problems head on and to get help when it's needed. Problems—large and small—beset all of us. Sometimes we don't recognize small problems until they've grown too big to ignore, but healthy families recognize a problem when they see one and are able to take responsibility for it. They know that for many kinds of family problems, they need to look at the entire family system to find solutions. Healthy families accept problems as they come along and

FIGURE 15.1

Family Strengths Inventory

The Family Strengths Inventory was developed by Nick Stinnett and John DeFrain to identify areas of strengths and weaknesses in families. Complete the inventory and then compute the score by adding the numbers you have circled. (You might also have other family members complete it independently to get a sense of their perceptions of your family.) The score will fall between 13 and 65.

What does the score mean, according to the researchers? A score below 39 is below average. It indicates that there are areas in your family relationships that need improving. Look at the areas in which you scored low to help you target where you need work. Scores from 39 to 52 are average. Scores above 52 indicate strong families. Consider discussing the inventory results with your family.

FAMILY STRENGTHS INVENTORY

Circle on a five-point scale (with 1 representing the least degree and 5 representing the greatest degree) the degree to which your family possesses each one of the following.

Spending time together and doing things with each other

| 1 | 2 | 3 | 4 | 5 |

Commitment to each other

| 1 | 2 | 3 | 4 | 5 |

Good communication (talking with each other often, listening well, sharing feelings with each other)

| 1 | 2 | 3 | 4 | 5 |

Dealing with crises in positive manner

| 1 | 2 | 3 | 4 | 5 |

Expressing appreciation to each other

| 1 | 2 | 3 | 4 | 5 |

Spiritual wellness

| 1 | 2 | 3 | 4 | 5 |

Circle the degree of closeness of your relationship with your spouse on a five-point scale (with 1 representing the least degree and 5 representing the greatest degree).

| 1 | 2 | 3 | 4 | 5 |

Circle the degree of closeness of your relationship with your children on a five-point scale (with 1 representing the least degree and 5 representing the greatest degree).

| 1 | 2 | 3 | 4 | 5 |

Circle the degree of happiness of your relationship with your spouse on a five-point scale (with 1 representing the least degree and 5 representing the greatest degree).

| 1 | 2 | 3 | 4 | 5 |

Circle the degree of happiness of your relationship with your children on a five-point scale (with 1 representing the least degree and 5 representing the greatest degree).

| 1 | 2 | 3 | 4 | 5 |

Some people make us feel good about ourselves. That is, they make us feel self-confident, worthy, competent, and happy about ourselves. What is the degree to which your spouse makes you feel good about yourself? Indicate on the following five-point scale (with 1 representing the least degree and 5 representing the greatest degree).

| 1 | 2 | 3 | 4 | 5 |

Indicate on the following five-point scale the degree to which you think you make your spouse feel good about himself/herself (with 1 representing the least degree and 5 representing the greatest degree).

| 1 | 2 | 3 | 4 | 5 |

Indicate on the following five-point scale the degree to which you think you make your children feel good about themselves (with 1 representing the least degree and 5 representing the greatest degree).

| 1 | 2 | 3 | 4 | 5 |

---

have developed techniques for dealing with the smaller ones; when the large problems—the true crises—occur, the healthy family knows where to turn for help.

Although some family resources (such as private counseling) can be costly, many low-cost or free services are available. Preventive programs such as parent education classes and marriage enrichment workshops are designed to keep strong families strong. Other resources include support groups that deal with specific problems such as alcoholism, physical disabilities, or loss and grief; family counseling programs; and other programs, workshops, and classes offered by schools, churches, hospitals, and community health agencies.

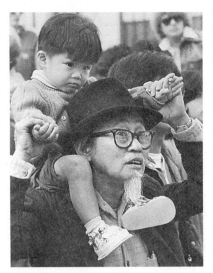

Grandparents and grandchildren provide love and meaning for each other.

The more hands that are offered, the lighter the burden.

Haitian proverb

Families today create their own relatives as needed.

Barbara Settles

❏ KIN AND COMMUNITY

Intimacy Needs

Whether we are married or single, we need relationships in which we can be intimate. Neither couples nor individuals can function well in isolation. Robert Weiss (1969) noted that people have needs that can be met only in relationships with other people. These needs can be summarized as follows:

1. *Nurturing others.* This need is filled through caring for a partner, children, or other intimates both physically and emotionally.
2. *Social integration.* We need to be actively involved in some form of community; if we are not, we feel isolated and bored. We meet this need through knowing others who share our interests and participating in community or school projects.
3. *Assistance.* We need to know that if something happens to us, there are people we can depend on for help. Without such relationships, we feel anxious and vulnerable.
4. *Intimacy.* We need people who will listen to us and care about us; if such people are not available, we feel emotionally isolated and lonely.
5. *Reassurance.* We need people to respect our skills as persons, workers, parents, and partners. Without such reassurance, we lose our self-esteem.

The Extended Family: Helping Kin

Few aspects of family life exist to which relatives (especially parents and siblings) do not make a contribution (Schneider, 1980).

Among African-American families, grandparents are often a valuable resource for child care and child socialization (Flaherty, Facteau, and Garver, 1990; Kennedy, 1990). Adult siblings are also important sources of help in times of need, especially among African Americans (Chatters, Taylor, and Neighbors, 1989). Another way the black extended family takes care of its members is through the process of "absorption" or "informal adoption." Adults who are ill or aged or children whose parents are unable to care for them are absorbed into the homes of relatives who have the resources to support them. Children incorporated into the family in this way are treated as equals to the children already in the household (Martin and Martin, 1978).

In many families parents loan money to their adult children at low or no interest. They may give or loan them the down payment for a home, for example. The obligations that these loans and gifts entail differ according to a person's age and marital status. If the children are young and single, parents may still expect to exercise considerable control over their children's behavior in return for their support. But if the children are older or—more important—married, there are fewer obligations.

Even when extended families are separated geographically, they continue to provide emotional support (Anderson, 1982). Contacts with kin are especially important in the lives of the aged. As we saw earlier, the elderly tend to have frequent contact with their kin. A recent national study found that almost two-thirds had seen a child within the previous week (U.S. Bureau of the Census, 1988).

Fictive Kin

In addition to kinship networks, many families have extensive networks of **fictive kin** (also called *pseudokin*). As discussed in Chapter 1, people in these relationships treat each other as family even though they are not related by blood. Both financial and emotional support may be given in these networks; there is usually the expectation of reciprocity, the understanding that favors will be returned.

An important component in Latino family life is *compadrazgo*. In this relationship, a child's godparents *(padrinos)*, who sponsor the child at baptism, become "companion parents" (Fitzpatrick, 1981). Also, witnesses at a marriage may become the *compadres* of the married couple. *Compadres* feel "a deep sense of obligation to each other for economic assistance, support, encouragement, and even personal correction" (Fitzpatrick, 1981).

Friendship

Families today find close friends, casual acquaintances, and temporary support within a complex and changing social network. Traditional sources of community support, such as church groups, are augmented by other sources. Parents meet one another and form friendships in groups that center around their children—parent-teacher groups, scouts, athletic groups. Peer support groups and self-help groups are available to fill a variety of short- or long-term needs; lasting friendships are often formed within such contexts. People may join political groups to work with others for change in society; they join hobby groups, crafts clubs, or dance classes in order to share their special interests with others. Some networks of support provide specific information or services for dealing with specific needs, whereas others provide more general help (Cooke et al., 1988). Social networks enrich our day-to-day lives and provide vital assistance in times of stress and crisis. One study of social support found that the sources most often mentioned were relatives (other than spouse or children), close friends, special groups, and co-workers (Cooke et al., 1988).

The Family in the Community

FAMILY ECOLOGY. Urie Bronfenbrenner (1979) has proposed that we look at the family in an "ecological environment." He suggests that we think of this environment in terms of a set of nested Russian dolls. The developing child is the tiny innermost doll, contained inside the various systems—such as home or school—that influence him or her. The interplay among the many systems profoundly affects the child in their midst. Furthermore, the influences of external factors—such as the flexibility of the parents' job schedules or the availability of good health care—also play a critical role.

Raising children isn't an individual act. It is a social and communal enterprise, involving kin, neighbors, other parents, friends, and many other unrelated adults.

Barbara Dafoe Whitehead

SUPPORT FOR THE FAMILY. The well-being of the family depends not solely on its own resources, then, but also on the support it receives from the community in which it is embedded (Unger and Sussman, 1990). This community includes extended family, friends, schools, employers, health-care providers, and government agencies at local, state, and federal levels. As discussed in Chapter 9, the United States is far behind most industrialized nations in terms of the support it gives families in the areas of health, education, social welfare, and workplace policy. The need for creativity and energy in these areas is great and presents challenges and opportunities for those who wish to work with the families of today and tomorrow.

If you have built castles in the air, your work need not be lost; that is where they should be. Now put the foundations under them.

Henry David Thoreau

Here is the test to find whether your mission on earth is finished: If you're alive, it isn't.

Richard Bach, Illusions

The family, in all its forms, is a resource that needs to be nurtured, strengthened, and protected.

Despite the complexities of modern life, the families that love and shelter and teach us remain America's greatest national resource. They deserve to be nurtured, strengthened, and protected.

 SUMMARY

❑ Marital success requires the development of *interpersonal competence*. Commitment (including sexual fidelity and the willingness to sacrifice), communication, and the creative use of conflict are essential aspects of success in marriage.

❑ The family should be seen as a process; family health may change over the course of the family life cycle.

❑ Healthy families (1) develop communication skills; (2) give affirmation, respect, and trust; (3) teach responsibility and morality; (4) promote spiritual wellness; (5) preserve tradition and family history; (6) share play and leisure time; and (7) cope with stress by having a positive attitude, being adaptable, presenting a united front, using spiritual resources and good communication, and getting help when needed.

❑ A sense of ethnicity or cultural heritage is an important source of strength for many American families. Often an ethnic group possesses particular strengths that help its families survive in an indifferent or unwelcoming larger society.

❑ We all have needs that can be met only in close relationships with others. These needs are to nurture others, to be socially integrated in some form of community, to have assistance we can rely on, to be intimate with others, and to be reassured about our skills. Kin, friends (including *fictive kin*), neighbors, and a variety of social networks all contribute to our well-being. They provide assistance and emotional support that give our families added strength.

❑ The family exists in the environment of community and is influenced directly and indirectly by many systems existing outside of itself. The well-being of the family depends not only on its own resources but also on the support of the larger community. For this reason, policies supportive of the family are crucial to its survival.

❒   Self-Help Resource Directory   ❒

The information resources that follow include information centers and counseling centers, as well as support groups, prerecorded tape services, and crisis centers. Use them, share the questions that led you to call, and discover new information on numerous topics.

The directory is easy to use. Each resource is located under a general subject heading. You'll find a description of the service, its hours, and its location by city and state. To call a resource, follow the code found by its telephone number:

❒ LD—Long-distance. Many important resources must be dialed at your expense. Dial direct, if you can, and remember the difference in time.

❒ TF—Toll-free. Some organizations have toll-free numbers. The 800 prefix designates that convenience. Telephone these resources at no charge.

Need information on a topic that isn't included? Check your telephone directory for important local resources. If you can't find the information you need, check at the reference desk of your local public, college, or university library.

Adoption

ALMA Society
P.O. Box 154
Washington Bridge Station
New York, NY 10033
LD 212-581-1568

The Adoptees' Liberty Movement Association is a non-profit organization with chapters throughout the U.S. ALMA believes in the right of adult adoptees and the biological parents of adoptees to locate one another. It supports and assists biologically related people searching for each other. Call or write for membership information, newsletter, or chapter list.

International Concerns Committee for Children
911 Cypress Drive
Boulder, CO 80303
LD 303-494-8333
Monday–Friday   9 AM–4 PM

This organization provides information about ways to help homeless children, including foster parenting and adoption. It publishes the annual *Report on Foreign Adoption* (with frequent updates) containing current information on many aspects of adoption. It also maintains a listing service of children in urgent need of homes. In addition, it publishes a newsletter and provides information and counseling to adoptive families. Nominal cost for publications. Write or call for brochure. Leave a message and your call will be returned collect.

North American Council on Adoptable Children
1821 University Ave., Suite N-498
St. Paul, MN 55104
LD 612-644-3036
Monday–Friday   9 AM–5 PM

The council provides a wealth of information and support services to adoption agencies and parents. Call or write for publications.

Adoptive Families of America, Inc.
3333 Hwy. 100 North
Minneapolis, MN 55422
LD 612-535-4829

AFA is a private, nonprofit membership organization that provides problem-solving assistance and information to adoptive and prospective adoptive individuals and families. U.S. membership is $24 yearly and includes a subscription to *OURS Magazine*.

You can also contact the appropriate local government agency for adoption information. Check your telephone directory for your city or county's social services, family services, public welfare, child welfare, or social welfare department. Check the Yellow Pages under "Adoption."

AIDS and HIV

Good Samaritan Project Teen Hotline
Kansas City, MO
TF 800-234-TEEN (234-8336)
Monday–Saturday   4 PM–8 PM

Staffed by trained high school students, this hotline gives accurate information to teens and their parents.

San Francisco AIDS Foundation
25 Van Ness Ave.
San Francisco, CA 94103
TF 800-FOR-AIDS (800-367-2437)
LD (Tagalog) 415-864-5855 X 2087
LD (Spanish) 415-864-5855 X 2079
Monday–Friday   9 AM–9 PM
Saturday and Sunday   11 AM–5 PM

The foundation promotes AIDS education and provides information and referrals to people with AIDS and their families. Support services provided in San Francisco area. Publications available.

National HIV and AIDS Information Service
TF 800-342-2437 (342-AIDS)
24 hours

The hotline can give you general information on HIV and AIDS and refer you to doctors, clinics, testing services, legal services, or counselors in your area. Spanish-speaking operators are available. Free brochures in a number of languages are available on request. For brochures in Spanish, call 800-344-SIDA; for others, call above number.

Alcohol and Drug Abuse Prevention

Al-Anon Family Groups
1372 Broadway
New York, NY 10018
TF 800-356-9996
Monday–Friday   8 AM–5 PM

Al-Anon is a worldwide fellowship for relatives and friends of alcoholics who "share their experience, strength and hope in order to solve their common problems and to help others do the same." There are over 25,000 Al-Anon groups, including 3,500 Alateen groups for teenagers. They publish numerous pamphlets, books, newsletters, and a magazine. Material is available in 24 languages as well as in Braille and on tape. Check your telephone directory for local listings or call above toll-free number for information.

Alcoholics Anonymous (AA)
P.O. Box 459, Grand Central Station
New York, NY 10163
LD 212-686-1100
Monday–Friday   9 AM–5 PM

AA is a voluntary worldwide fellowship of men and women who meet together to attain and maintain sobriety. There are no dues or fees for membership; the only requirement is a desire to stop drinking. There are over 87,000 groups and more than 1,790,000 members in 134 countries. Information on AA and chapter locations worldwide is available at the telephone number listed above. Check your telephone directory for local listings.

There are a growing number of alternative groups to AA. These groups emphasize personal responsibility and reject some of AA's views. SOS (Secular Organization for Sobriety), RR (Rational Recovery), and WFS (Women for Sobriety) are among the groups

with increasing numbers of local chapters. Check your telephone directory or dial information.

Mothers Against Drunk Driving (MADD)
669 Airport Fwy., Suite 310
Hurst, TX 76053
LD 817-268-6233
FAX 817-268-6827

MADD's membership is made up of drunk-driving victims and concerned citizens. Its concerns are to speak on behalf of victims, to reform drunk-driving laws, and to educate the public. It assists victims with the legal process, conducts research, and sponsors workshops. Local chapters throughout the United States. Publications available. Write or call for program and membership information.

National Clearinghouse for Alcohol and Drug Information (NCADI)
P.O. Box 2345
Rockville, MD 20852
TF 800-729-6689
Monday–Friday   9 AM–7 PM

NCADI provides a referral service, answering inquiries on alcohol- and drug-related subjects by telephone or mail. The clearinghouse also gathers and disseminates current information (including books, curriculum guides, directories, and posters) free of charge.

Phoenix House Foundation
164 W. 74th Street
New York, NY 10023
LD 212-595-5810
Monday–Friday   9AM–5 PM

Phoenix House is a multiservice drug abuse agency offering residential treatment in New York City and Southern California. It has numerous educational and treatment programs for youth and adults. Information and referrals are available on request.

Breastfeeding (SEE Infant Care)

Child Abuse

Clearinghouse on Child Abuse and Neglect Information
P.O. Box 1182
Washington, DC 20013
LD 703-821-2086
Monday–Friday   9 AM–5 PM

The clearinghouse provides information for professionals and concerned citizens interested in child maltreatment issues. A database of resources for professionals is available; the staff also performs searches for specific topics. Numerous publications, including bibliographies and research reviews, are available. Write or call for free catalog.

National Child Abuse Hotline

TF 800-422-4453

24 hours

Provides general information and referrals.

National Committee for Prevention of Child Abuse

332 S. Michigan Ave., Suite 950

Chicago, IL 60604-4357

LD 312-663-3520

NCPCA is a volunteer-based organization dedicated to reducing child abuse. It offers educational programs and materials and support and self-help groups for parents. There are numerous local chapters. Write or call for information and chapter list.

Parents Anonymous (PA)

7120 Franklin Ave.

Los Angeles, CA 90046

TF 800-421-0353

TF (California) 800-352-0386

Monday–Friday   9 AM–5 PM

Parents Anonymous has over 1,200 local chapters that provide support for parents who abuse or fear they may abuse their children. Parents Anonymous also publishes materials on child abuse; send SASE. Call toll-free number for information and crisis counseling.

Conflict Resolution

Children's Creative Response to Conflict (CCRC)

Box 271

Nyack, NY 10960

LD 914-358-4601

FAX 914-358-4924

CCRC's trained facilitators conduct workshops for students, teachers, and parents to learn cooperation and conflict-resolution skills. Teacher's handbook (in English or Spanish), newsletter, and other publications available. Write or call for brochure and list of local branches.

Consumer Services

Consumer Information Center

P.O. Box 100

Pueblo, CO 81002

LD 719-948-3334

Numerous booklets on a variety of topics—careers, children, health, housing, money, and many others—are available. Booklets are free or in 50¢–$3.00 range. Write or call for catalog.

Consumer Product Safety Commission (CPSC)

5401 Westbard Ave.

Bethesda, MD 20207

LD 301-492-6580

Monday–Friday   9 AM–4:30 PM

TF (Automated machine) 800-638-2772

TTY for the deaf 800-492-8140

The CPSC is involved in the evaluation of the safety of products sold to the public. Commission staff members will answer questions and provide free printed materials on different aspects of consumer product safety, such as the safety of children's toys or household appliances. The commission does not answer questions from consumers on automobiles, cosmetics, drugs, prescriptions, warranties, advertising, repairs, or maintenance.

FDA Consumer Affairs Office

5600 Fishers Lane

Rockville, MD 20857

LD 301-443-5006

Monday–Friday   9 AM–5 PM

The Consumer Affairs offices provides information and referrals on food products, pharmaceutical drugs, and cosmetics.

Occupational Safety and Health Administration (OSHA)

200 Constitution Ave.

Washington, DC 20210

LD 202-523-8017

Monday–Friday   9 AM–5 PM

The OSHA Office of Information provides a referral service and basic information on job safety and the dangers posed by toxic substances in the workplace. There is no charge for pamphlets and booklets and a nominal charge for a catalog.

Disabled

Mainstream

1030 15th St., NW, Suite 1010

Washington, DC 20005

LD 202-898-1400 (Voice/TDD)

Monday–Friday   9 AM–5 PM

Mainstream provides information on affirmative action for the disabled and will make referrals to agencies or state offices. In Washington, D.C., and Dallas, Texas, Project LINK places workers with disabilities, free of charge. Workshops, publications, newsletter available. Write or call for information.

National Information Center for Children and Youth with Disabilities (NICHCY)

P.O. Box 1492

Washington, DC 20013

TF 800-999-5599

LD 703-893-6061

Monday–Friday   9 AM–5 PM

NICHCY is a national clearinghouse and referral source for parents of disabled children and professionals who work with them. Publications, including an informative newsletter and extensive resource list, provided free of charge.

Parents Helping Parents
535 Race St., Suite 220
San Jose, CA 95126
LD 408-288-5010

Parents Helping Parents is a support group for parents of children who are physically and/or mentally disabled. The group provides telephone counseling, and in-home visits if possible, information, and referrals to local agencies and support groups. Brochure available.

Drug Abuse (SEE Alcohol and Drug Abuse Prevention)

Environment

Conservation and Renewable Energy Inquiry and Referral Service (CAREIRS)
P.O. Box 8900
Silver Springs, MD 20907
TF 800-523-2929
TF (AK and HI) 800-233-3071

CAREIRS provides general and specific information on renewable energy technologies and energy conservation techniques for residential and commercial needs. CAREIRS offers more than 150 publications, fact sheets, bibliographies, and 500 computerized letter units free of charge.

Earthworks Press
1400 Shattuck Ave., Box 25
Berkeley, CA 94704
LD 415-841-5866

Earthworks publishes material for those concerned with protecting the environment. Check your local bookstore or write for such titles as *50 Simple Things You Can Do to Save the Earth* ($4.95), *30 Simple Energy Things You Can Do to Save the Earth* ($3.95), *The Recycler's Handbook* ($4.95), and *The Next Step: 50 More Things You Can Do to Save the Earth* ($5.95). Include $1.00 postage per book. Bulk rates available.

Family Planning

Planned Parenthood Federation of America
810 Seventh Ave.
New York, NY 10019
LD 212-541-7800

Most cities have a Planned Parenthood organization listed in the telephone directory. Planned Parenthood provides information, counseling, and medical services related to reproduction and sexual health to *anyone* who wants them. No one is denied because of age, social group, or inability to pay. Information can also be obtained through the national office, listed above.

Zero Population Growth
1400 16th St., NW, Suite 320
Washington, DC 20036
LD 202-332-2200
Monday–Friday   9 AM–5 PM

ZPG is a national, nonprofit membership organization that works to achieve a sustainable balance between the earth's population and its environment and resources. Teaching materials, numerous publications, and newsletter available. There is a charge for multiple copies.

Public Health Departments

Counties throughout the United States, regardless of size, have county health clinics that will provide low-cost family planning services. Some cities also have public health clinics. To locate them look up the city or county in the telephone directory, then check under headings such as:

Department of Health
Family Planning
Family Services
Health
Public Health Department
(City or County's name) Health (or Medical) Clinic

Fatherhood

The Fatherhood Project
c/o James Levine
330 7th Ave.
New York, NY 10001
LD 212-268-4846

"A national research, demonstration, and dissemination project designed to encourage wider options for male involvement in child-rearing." Pamphlets available on various subjects related to families and work.

Gay and Lesbian Resources

National Federation of Parents FLAG
P.O. Box 27605
Washington, DC 27605
LD 202-638-4200

Parents FLAG (Parents and Friends of Lesbians and Gays) provides information and support for those who care about gay and lesbian individuals. Write or call for number of a parent contact in your area or check phone directory for regional offices. Publications available.

National Gay and Lesbian Task Force
1734 14th St. NW
Washington, DC 20009
LD 202-332-6483
Monday–Friday   9 AM–5 PM

The National Gay and Lesbian Task Force provides information and referrals on gay and lesbian issues and rights.

National Lesbian and Gay Lifeline
TF 800-LIFE-661 (800-543-3661)
6 PM–12 midnight

Counseling line provides support in various areas and referrals to groups such as gay and lesbian Alcoholics Anonymous.

Health Information

Alzheimer's Disease and Related Disorders Association
70 East Lake Street, Suite 600
Chicago, IL 60601
LD 312-853-3060

Supports family members of those affected by Alzheimer's disease and related disorders. Promotes research and education. Represents patients' continuing care needs to health-care agencies, government, business, and communities. Newsletter.

American Institute for Preventative Medicine
24450 Evergreen Rd., Suite 200
Southfield, MI 48075
LD 313-352-7666

For $2.00, the AIPM will send you a directory of toll-free numbers to call for advice and referrals on numerous health-related issues such as alcohol abuse or cancer.

Centers for Disease Control (CDC)
1600 Clifton Rd. NE
Atlanta, GA 30333
LD 404-639-3286
Monday–Friday   9 AM–5 PM

Inquiries from the public on topics such as preventative medicine, health education, immunization, and communicable diseases can be directed to the Office of Information at the CDC. The office will also answer questions on occupational safety and health issues, family planning, and public health problems such as lead-based paint and rodent control. Inquiries are answered directly or referred to an appropriate resource.

Family Caregivers of the Aging (see National Council on the Aging under "Seniors" heading)

Home Care Hotline
TF 800-847-8480
TF (NY) 800-422-4546

Sponsored by the National League of Nursing, the hotline provides information on the availability of home care resources and the location of accredited agencies.

Medicaid/Medicare
Department of Health and Human Services

Washington, DC
LD 202-245-7000
Monday–Friday   9 AM–5 PM

This consumer inquiry office answers questions on child health, social security, and all aspects of Medicaid and Medicare. The office also provides a referral service that includes listings of local welfare offices.

National Cancer Institute
9000 Rockville Pike, Rm. 340
Bethesda, MD 20892
TF 800-4-CANCER (422-6237)
HI 800-524-1234
Monday–Friday   9 AM–4:30 PM

Hotline counselors answer questions and give referrals to local doctors and support groups. For free brochures and other information, call or write.

National Health Information Center (NHIC)
P.O. Box 1133
Washington, DC 20013-1133
LD 301-565-4167
TF 800-336-4797 (referral database)

The NHIC is a central clearinghouse designed to refer consumers to health information resources. The clearinghouse has identified many groups and organizations that provide health information to the public. All health-related questions are welcomed, although the NHIC is unable to respond to questions requiring medical advice or diagnosis. A variety of publications is available.

TEL-MED
952 S. Mount Vernon
Colton, CA 92324
LD 714-825-6034
Monday–Friday   9 AM–5 PM

TEL-MED is a tape library of recorded medical messages. There are over 600 tapes, 3 to 7 minutes long, on different medical subjects. Titles include "Accidents in the Home," "Heart Attack," "Sleep," "Where Did I Come From, Mama?" and many others.

Infant Care

La Leche League International
P.O. Box 1209
Franklin Park, IL 60131-8209
LD 708-455-7730
LD 708-830-8087 (24 hour counseling hotline)

La Leche League provides advice and support for nursing mothers. Write for brochure or catalog of numerous publications. For local groups, check telephone directory or call the above number.

National Organization of Circumcision Information
Resource Centers (NOCIRC)
P.O. Box 2512

San Anselmo, CA 94979
LD 415-488-9883
Monday–Friday   9 AM–5 PM

NOCIRC is a nonprofit health resource center that provides medical and legal information of the subject of circumcision and female genital mutilation. It is against routine hospital circumcision of newborns. Pamphlets, newsletters, and referrals to physicians and lawyers are available. Send SASE with 2 oz. postage. Videotape for rent or purchase also available. Biannual international symposium.

Infertility

The American Fertility Society
2140 Eleventh Ave. South, Suite 200
Birmingham, AL 35205-2800
LD 205-933-8494
Monday–Friday   8:30 AM–4:30 PM

The American Fertility Society provides up-to-date information on all aspects of infertility, reproductive endocrinology, conception control, and reproductive biology. Booklets, pamphlets, selected reading list, resource lists, a medical journal, and postgraduate courses are available. Also available: ethical guidelines for new reproductive technologies, position paper on insurance for infertility services, and revised procedures for semen donation. Write or call for further information.

Resolve, Inc.
5 Water St.
Arlington, MA 02174
LD 617-643-2424
Monday–Friday   9 AM–4 PM

Resolve, a national nonprofit organization focusing on the problem of infertility, refers callers to chapters across the nation, provides fact sheets on male and female infertility, and publishes a newsletter and a directory of infertility resources. Phone counseling is also offered. There is a small charge for publications.

Marriage Enhancement

The Association for Couples in Marriage Enrichment
P.O. Box 10596
Winston-Salem, NC 26108
TF 800-634-8325
Monday–Friday   8:30 AM–5 PM

Established by David and Vera Mace, ACME is a nonprofit, nonsectarian organization that promotes activities to strengthen marriage. It offers weekend retreats, local chapter meetings, workshops, and conferences throughout the U.S. and Canada. Members may purchase books, tapes, and other materials at a discount. Write for brochures and resource list.

Worldwide Marriage Encounter
1908 E. Highland Ave., #A

San Bernardino, CA 92404
LD 714-881-3456
Monday–Friday   8:30 AM–5 PM

Although Marriage Encounter retreats are designed with Catholic couples in mind, spaces are also reserved for couples of other faiths. Encounter weekends are offered in many parts of the country to enhance communication in marriage. A donation is asked but not required. Call or write for brochure and application.

Peace

Beyond War
222 High St.
Palo Alto, CA 94301-1097
LD 415-328-7756
FAX 415-328-7785

A nonprofit, nonpartisan educational foundation of volunteers in more than 40 states and 6 countries dedicated to "living in concert with the planet and with each other and contributing to the continuity of life."

The Friendship Force
Suite 575 South Tower
One CNN Center
Atlanta, GA 30303
LD 404-522-9490
FAX 404-688-6148

A nonprofit, nonpolitical organization designed to bring people of many countries together through international exchanges of "Citizen Ambassadors." There are over 100 chapters nationwide. Quarterly magazine is $5.00 per year.

Sane/Freeze: Campaign for Global Security
1819 H. St., NW, Suite 1000
Washington, DC 20006
LD 202-862-9740

Sane/Freeze seeks a comprehensive U.S.-Soviet nuclear test ban treaty, a bilateral halt to the nuclear arms race, deep reductions in nuclear weapons, and an end to U.S. military intervention abroad. Publications available.

20/20 Vision
695 Pleasant St., Suite 203
Amherst, MA 01002
TF 800-669-1782

For $20 a year, 20/20 Vision sends a monthly postcard with local and national military, environmental, and economic justice issues, including all information needed to write or call legislators. Local chapters are in more than 30 states.

Pregnancy (ALSO SEE **Family Planning, Infant Care**)

American College of Nurse-Midwives
1522 K St., NW, Suite 1000

Washington, DC 20005
LD 202-289-0171

Write or call the college for a directory of certified nurse-midwives in your area or to get information on accredited university-affiliated nurse-midwifery education programs.

Birthright

686 N. Broad St.
Woodbury, NJ 08096
TF 800-848-5683
Monday–Friday   9:30 AM–12:30 PM
                   7 PM–9 PM

Birthright is an assistance and counseling service for pregnant women. Services include telephone counseling in any aspect of pregnancy and referral to Birthright chapters and clinics throughout the U.S. and Canada. Birthright counsels against abortion and does not give out information concerning birth control.

National Abortion Rights Action League (NARAL)

1101 14th St., NW
Washington, DC 20005
LD 202-408-4600
Monday–Friday   9 AM–5:30 PM

A political organization concerned with family planning issues and dedicated to making abortion "safe, legal, and accessible" for all women. Affiliated with many state and local organizations. Newsletter and brochures available.

Teratogen Registry

TF 800-532-3749
Monday–Friday   9 AM–5 PM

When you're living for two, that means being twice as careful. Pregnant women and health-care professionals seeking the latest information about the effects of drugs and medications on unborn babies may use this free and confidential service. Pregnant women who have been exposed to suspected teratogens (substances harmful to the fetus) can also participate in a free follow-up program after birth.

Pregnancy Loss and Infant Death

Sudden Infant Death Syndrome Alliance

10500 Little Patuxent Pkwy., Suite 420
Columbia, MD 21044
TF 800-221-SIDS
LD 301-964-8000 (Maryland)

The National SIDS Alliance provides emotional support to families who have lost a child to sudden infant death syndrome. It has chapters throughout the U.S. and provides free crisis counseling, referrals, and information. It also supports research into SIDS. Free literature on request.

SHARE

St. Elizabeth's Hospital
211 South Third St.

Belleville, IL 62222
LD 618-234-2415
Monday–Friday   8 AM–4:30 PM

SHARE and its affiliate groups offer support for parents who have experienced miscarriage, stillbirth, or the death of a baby. They offer a manual on starting your own SHARE group, a national listing of groups and parent contacts, selected bibliography, resource manual on farewell rituals, children's books, and a newsletter. Check your local directory for groups, which may also be listed under "Sharing Parents," "Hoping and Sharing," "HAND," or a similar heading.

Rape

National Clearinghouse on Marital and Date Rape

2325 Oak
Berkeley, CA 94708
LD 415-548-1770
24 hours (message tape)

The clearinghouse provides information, referrals, seminars, and speakers covering numerous aspects of marital and date rape. There is a nominal charge for publications and consultation services. Calls returned collect.

Check your telephone directory for "Rape Crisis Center" or a similar listing to find the local crisis center nearest you; the service is available in almost all cities.

Runaways

National Runaway Switchboard

TF 800-621-3230

The National Runaway Switchboard provides toll-free telephone services for young people who have run away from home, those considering leaving home, and parents. The service helps young people define their problems, determines if an emergency exists, and refers callers to programs that provide free or low-cost help. Complete confidentiality is guaranteed. If the caller wants to reestablish communication with his or her family, a message can be taken for delivery within 24 hours.

Runaway and Homeless Youth Program

P.O. Box 1182
Washington, DC 20013

This program funds the preceding hotline and other services such as temporary shelters, counseling, and outreach programs. Write for brochure and other information.

Self-Help

National Self-Help Clearinghouse

25 W. 43rd St., Rm. 620
New York, NY 10036
LD 212-642-2944

The clearinghouse maintains a databank and referral service to provide information on thousands of self-help groups throughout the United States. They publish manuals and a newsletter on self-help. Write or call for information; send SASE if you want a list of local clearinghouse throughout the country.

The Consumer Information Center, part of the U.S. General Services Administration, offers numerous booklets on a variety of useful subjects. See "Consumer Services" section of Self-Help Resource Directory.

Seniors

Gray Panthers Project Fund
1424 16th St., NW, Suite 602
Washington, DC 20036
LD 202-387-3111
Monday–Friday   9 AM–5 PM

A multigenerational, intergenerational organization formed for education and advocacy, working to bring about an affordable, quality national health system protecting all ages. Works against all forms of discrimination to ensure economic justice. Promotes negotiation and other peaceful means of conflict resolution to replace war. Annual dues of $15.00 include quarterly newsletter.

National Council on the Aging
600 Maryland Ave., SW
Washington, DC 20024
LD 202-479-1200

Promotes the concerns of older Americans in many areas and develops methods and resources for meeting their needs. Consultations, speakers, meetings, programs, and many publications available. Family Caregivers of the Aging, part of the NCA, provides information and support for those caring for aging parents.

Sex Education and Sex Therapy

Sex Information and Education Council of the United States (SIECUS)
130 W. 42nd St., Suite 2500
New York, NY 10036
LD 212-819-9770

SIECUS is a nonprofit educational organization that promotes "healthy sexuality as an integral part of human life." It provides information or referrals to *anyone* who requests it. It maintains an extensive library and computer database. Publications include sex education guides for parents (in English and Spanish) and a comprehensive bimonthly journal, *SIECUS Report*. Memberships available.

American Association of Sex Educators, Counselors, and Therapists (AASECT)
435 N. Michigan Ave., Suite 1717
Chicago, IL 60611
LD 312-644-8557

FAX 312-644-0828
Monday–Friday   9 AM–5 PM

AASECT is a nonprofit educational association of physicians, counselors, social workers, educators, and so on. Its objectives are "to provide training and education in human sexuality and standards for sex education, counseling, and therapy programs." It publishes a newsletter and the *Journal of Sex Education and Therapy*.

Sexual Abuse

Parents United
P.O. Box 952
San Jose, CA 95108
LD 408-453-7616
TF 800-422-4453 (Crisis counseling)
Monday–Friday   9 AM–5 PM

Parents United and its related groups Daughters and Sons United and Adults Molested as Children United are self-help groups for all family members affected by incest and child sexual abuse. They provide referrals to treatment programs and self-help groups throughout the country. A number of informative publications are available, including a bimonthly newsletter. Write or call for literature list. The Giarretto Institute—at the above address and phone—is a separate nonprofit organization that provides treatment and therapist training.

Sexually Transmitted Diseases (ALSO SEE AIDS and HIV AND Health Information)

Herpes Resource Center
P.O. Box 13827
RTT Park, NC 27709
LD 919-361-8488
Monday–Friday   9 AM–7 PM

Provides referrals for people who are infected with herpes virus or who think that they may be. Confidential.

STD Hotline (American Social Health Association)
TF 800-227-8922
Monday–Friday   8 AM–11 PM

The STD Hotline provides information on all aspects of sexually transmitted diseases. It will describe symptoms but cannot provide diagnosis. It provides referrals for testing and further information. Confidentiality is maintained.

Single Parents

Parents Without Partners
8807 Colesville Rd.
Silver Springs, MD 20910
LD 301-588-9354
Monday–Friday   9 AM–5 PM

Parents Without Partners is a mutual support group for single parents and their children. It has numerous local groups with more than 115,000 members. It offers educational programs and literature, including *The Single Parent* magazine. It also offers low-cost recreation and member benefits such as insurance, credit card, auto club, discount travel, and scholarships for PWP children.

Single Mothers by Choice
P.O. Box 1642
New York, NY 10028
LD 212-988-0993

SMC is a national group that supports single mothers and single women who are considering motherhood. It offers workshops, support groups, a newsletter, a bibliography, and information about artificial insemination and adoption. Although based in New York City, it has members throughout the U.S. and Canada.

Suicide Prevention

The Samaritans
500 Commonwealth Ave.
Boston, MA 02215
LD 617-247-0220
24 hours

The Samaritans is a worldwide nonreligious organization of trained volunteers who talk with, and listen to, anyone who is suicidal, lonely, or depressed. The confidential service is dedicated to the prevention of suicide and the alleviation of loneliness and depression. Although the service is based in Massachusetts, staffers will help anyone in any area of the country. Brochures and pamphlets are available. Check your telephone directory white pages under "Suicide Prevention" for local listings.

Samariteen
LD 617-247-8050
3 PM–9 PM

Same as above but staffed by trained 16- to 19-year olds.

Surrogate Parenting

The Center for Surrogate Parenting, Inc.
8383 Wilshire Blvd., Suite 750
Beverly Hills, CA 90211
LD 213-655-1974 (collect accepted)
TF (CA only) 800-696-4664
Monday–Friday   9 AM–5 PM

The Center for Surrogate Parenting is a private organization that matches prospective parents and surrogates for a fee. Extensive screening is involved. Write or call for further information.

Terminal Illness

National Hospice Organization
1901 N. Moore St., Suite 901
Arlington, VA 22209
LD 703-243-5900
TF 800-658-8598 (Referrals only)
Monday–Friday   9 AM–5 PM

Hospices provide support and care for people in the final phase of terminal disease. There are over 1,700 hospice programs in the U.S., many of which are NHO members. The hospice "team" provides personalized care to minister to the physical, spiritual, and emotional needs of the patient and family. Call or write for literature and referral information.

Women

National Organization for Women (NOW)
1000 16th St., NW, Suite 700
Washington, DC 20036
LD 202-331-0066

NOW is an organization of women and men who support "full equality for women in truly equal partnership with men." NOW promotes social change through research, litigation, and political pressure. Newspaper and other publications available. Many cities have local chapters of NOW. Membership dues vary.

Work and Family

Families and Work Institute
330 7th Ave.
New York, NY 10001
LD 212-465-2044
FAX 212-465-8637

"A nonprofit research and planning organization committed to developing new approaches for balancing the changing needs of America's families with the continuing need for workplace productivity." The institute conducts research, disseminates information, and participates in planning and management training with businesses and organizations.

❑ Sexual Life—Taking Care of our Bodies* ❑

❑ CHOOSING A METHOD OF BIRTH CONTROL

Taking Risks

Most people know they are taking a chance when they don't use contraception. The more frequently a person engages in unprotected intercourse without a resultant pregnancy, however, the more likely he or she is to take chances again. A subtle psychology develops: somehow, apparently by will power, good vibes, or the gods' kindly intervention, the woman will not get pregnant. Eventually, the woman or couple will feel almost magically invulnerable to pregnancy. Each time they are lucky, their risk taking is reinforced.

The consequences of an unintended pregnancy—economic hardships, interruption of education, adoption, or abortion—may be overwhelming. Why, then, do people take chances in the first place? Part of the reason is faulty knowledge. People often underestimate how easy it is to get pregnant. Also, they may not know how to use a contraceptive method correctly, especially if they use the calendar (rhythm) method (which is not too reliable to begin with). Finally, Kristin Luker (1975) suggests that we can look at contraceptive use in terms of a cost/benefit analysis. She observes, "The decision to take a contraceptive risk is typically based on the *immediate* costs of contraception and the *anticipated* benefits of pregnancy." But the anticipated benefits usually prove illusory. "The potential benefits of pregnancy seldom become real; they vanish with the verdict of a positive pregnancy test or [are] later outweighed by the actual costs of the pregnancy." Some of the costs are acknowledging sexuality; planning, obtaining, and continuing contraception; and lack of spontaneity.

ACKNOWLEDGING SEXUALITY. On the surface, it may seem fairly simple to acknowledge that we are sexual beings, especially if we have conscious sexual desires and engage in sexual intercourse. Yet acknowledging our sexuality is not necessarily easy, for sexuality may be surrounded by feelings of guilt, conflict, and shame. The younger or less experienced we are, the more difficult it is to acknowledge our sexuality.

PLANNING CONTRACEPTION. Planning contraception requires us to admit not only that we are sexual but also that we plan to be sexually active. Without such planning, men and women can pretend that their sexual intercourse "just happens" in a moment of passion, when they have been drinking, or when the moon is full—even though it happens frequently.

Developments in the past generation have shifted contraceptive responsibility from the man to the woman, requiring women to more consciously define themselves as sexual. To do so, they have had to abandon traditional, passive sexual roles. Many women are reluctant to plan contraceptive use because they fear they will be regarded as sexually aggressive or promiscuous.

Since it is women who get pregnant, men tend to be unaware of their responsibility or to downplay their role in conception and pregnancy. Males, especially adolescents, lack the awareness that supports contraceptive planning. Yet males are more fertile than females. The average male is fertile twenty-four hours a day for fifty or more years. Females, in contrast, are fertile only a few days of the month for thirty-five years or so.

OBTAINING CONTRACEPTION. Difficulty in obtaining contraception may be a deterrent to using it. It is often embarrassing for sexually inexperienced persons. Buying condoms, foam, or sponges at the local drugstore is a public announcement that a person is sexual. Who knows if your mother, teacher, or minister might be down the aisle buying toothpaste (or contraceptives, for that matter) and might see you? Adolescent girls may be too embarrassed to undergo the pelvic examination necessary for obtaining birth control pills.

CONTINUING CONTRACEPTION. Many people, especially women using pills, practice contraception consistently and effectively within a steady relationship but give up their contraceptive practices if the relationship breaks up. They define themselves as sexual only within the context of a relationship. When men or women begin a new relationship, they may not use contraception because the relationship has not yet become long term; they do not expect to have sexual intercourse or to have it often. They are willing to take chances.

LACK OF SPONTANEITY. Using contraceptive devices such as condoms or a diaphragm may destroy the feeling of spontaneity in sex. For those who justify their sexual behavior with romantic impulsiveness, using these devices seems cold and mechanical. Others do not use them because it would mean untangling bodies and limbs, interrupting the passion of the moment.

ANTICIPATED "BENEFITS." Many men and women fantasize that even an "accidental" pregnancy might be beneficial. These anticipated benefits include (1) proving womanhood or manhood, (2) proving fertility, (3) defining a commitment, and (4) defining or redefining a person's relationship to his or her parents. Unfortunately, once a woman becomes pregnant, the anticipated benefits often fail to materialize.

Men and Contraception

Because women bear children and have most of the responsibility for raising them, they may have a greater interest than their partners in controlling their fertility. Nevertheless, it is unfair to assume, as people generally do in our society, that the total responsi-

---

* See Bryan Strong and Christine DeVault, Understanding Our Sexuality (2d ed.), St. Paul, MN: West Publishing Co., 1988, for a more detailed discussion of birth control, sexually transmitted disease, and sexual health.

bility for contraception should be the woman's. Men may participate in contraception by using condoms, which are quite effective when used properly, especially in combination with a spermicide. Condoms have the additional advantage of being effective in helping prevent the spread of STDs, including HIV. They are also known as prophylatics because they protect against disease.

In addition to using a condom, there are other ways a man can help take contraceptive responsibility. These include the following:

❏ Explore ways of making love without intercourse.
❏ Help pay doctor or clinic bills and share the cost of pills or other contraceptive supplies.
❏ Check on supplies, help keep track of the menstrual cycle, and help his partner with supplies.
❏ In a long-term relationship, if no (or no more) children are wanted, he can have a vasectomy.

In order to be fully responsible in using birth control, a person must know the options available, how reliable these methods are, and the advantages and disadvantages (including possible side effects) of each method. Choosing the best form of birth control for yourself and your partner, especially if you have not been practicing contraception, is not easy. But knowing the facts about the methods gives you a solid basis from which to make decisions and more security once a decision is reached. If you need to choose a birth control method for yourself, remember that *the best method is the one you will use consistently.* When you are having intercourse, a condom left in a purse or wallet, a diaphragm in the bedside drawer, or a forgotten pill in its packet on the other side of town is not an effective means of birth control.

The following material is written in sufficient detail to serve as a reference guide for those who are seeking a birth control method or who have questions about their current method. Of course, a person with painful or unusual symptoms or with questions not dealt with here should seek professional advice from a physician or family planning clinic.

In the following text, where we discuss method effectiveness, *theoretical effectiveness* implies perfectly consistent and correct use; *user effectiveness* refers to *actual* use (and misuse) based on studies by health care organizations, medical practitioners, academic researchers, and pharmaceutical companies. User effectiveness is sometimes significantly lower than theoretical effectiveness because of factors that keep people from using a method properly or consistently. These factors may be inherent in the method or may be the result of a variety of influences on the user.

Hormonal Methods: The Pill and Implants

BIRTH CONTROL PILLS. "The pill" is actually a series of pills (20, 21, or 28 to a package) containing the synthetic hormones estrogen and progestin, which regulate egg production and the menstrual cycle. When taken for birth control they accomplish some or all of the following: inhibit ovulation, thicken cervical mucus (preventing sperm entry), inhibit implantation of the blastocyst, or promote early spontaneous abortion of the blastocyst. The pill produces basically the same chemical conditions that would exist in a woman's body if she were pregnant.

Oral contraceptives must be prescribed by a physician or family planning clinic. There are a number of brands available that contain varying amounts of hormones. Most commonly prescribed are the combination pills, which contain a fairly standard amount of estrogen and differing doses of progestin according to the pill type. In the triphasic pill, the amount of progestin is altered during the cycle, purportedly to approximate the "normal" hormonal pattern. There is also a minipill containing progestin only, but it is generally prescribed only in cases where the woman should not take estrogen. It is considered slightly less effective than the combined pill, and it must be taken with precise and unfailing regularity to be effective.

With the 20- and 21-day pills, one pill is taken each day until they are all used. Two to five days later the woman should begin her menstrual flow. Commonly, it is quite light. (If the flow does not begin, the woman should start the next series of pills seven days after the end of the last series. If she repeatedly has no flow, she should talk to her health practitioner.) On the fifth day of her menstrual flow the woman should start the next series of pills.

The 28-day pills are taken continuously. Seven of the pills have no hormones. They are there simply to avoid breaks in the routine; some women prefer them because they find them easier to remember.

Along with the new contraceptive implants, the pill is considered the most effective birth control method available (except for sterilization) when used correctly. It is not effective when used carelessly. The pill must be taken every day, as close as possible to the same time each day. If one is missed, it should be taken as soon as the woman remembers and the next one taken on schedule. If two are missed, the method cannot be relied on and an additional form of contraception should be used for the rest of the cycle.

It should be remembered that the pill in no way protects against sexually transmitted diseases. Women on the pill should consider the additional use of a condom to reduce the risk of STDs.

EFFECTIVENESS. The pill is more than 99.5 percent effective theoretically. User effectiveness (the rate shown by actual studies) is between 95 and 98 percent.

ADVANTAGES. Pills are easy to take. They are dependable. No applications or interruptions are necessary before or during intercourse. Some women experience side effects that please them, such as more regular or reduced menstrual flow or enlarged breasts.

POSSIBLE PROBLEMS. There are many possible side effects, which may or may not bother the user, that can occur from taking the pill. Those most often reported are:

❏ change (usually decrease) in menstrual flow
❏ breast tenderness
❏ nausea or vomiting
❏ weight gain or loss

Some others are:

❏ spotty darkening of the skin
❏ nervousness, dizziness

❑ loss of scalp hair
❑ change in appetite
❑ change (most commonly, decrease) in sex drive
❑ increase of body hair
❑ increase in vaginal discharge and yeast infections

These side effects can sometimes be eliminated by changing the prescription, but not always. Certain women react unfavorably to the pill because of existing health factors or extra sensitivity to female hormones. Women with heart or kidney diseases, asthma, high blood pressure, diabetes, epilepsy, gall bladder diseases, sickle-cell anemia, or those prone to migraine headaches or mental depression are usually considered poor candidates for the pill.

The pill also creates health risks, but to what extent is a matter of controversy. Women taking the pill stand a greater chance of problems with circulatory diseases, blood clotting, heart attack, and certain kinds of liver tumors. There is also an increased risk of contracting chlamydia. The health risks are low for the young (about half the number of risks encountered in childbirth), but they increase with age. The risk for smokers, women over 35, and those with certain other health disorders is about four times as great as childbirth. For women over 40 the risks are considered high. Current literature on the pill especially emphasizes the risks for women who smoke. Definite risks of cardiovascular complications and various forms of cancer exist due to the synergistic action of the ingredients of cigarettes and oral contraceptives.

A number of studies have linked pill use with certain types of cancer, but they have not been conclusive. The risk of some types of cancer, such as ovarian and endometrial, appears to be significantly *reduced* by pill use. On the other hand, a link between cervical cancer and long-term pill use has been suggested by several studies. Regular Pap smears are recommended as an excellent defense against cervical cancer, for pill users and nonusers alike.

Certain other factors may need to be taken into account in determining if oral contraception is appropriate. Young girls who have not matured physically may have their development slowed by early pill use. Nursing mothers cannot use pills containing estrogen because the hormone inhibits milk production. Some lactating women use the minipill successfully.

Millions of women (approximately 10 million in the U.S.) use the pill with moderate to high degrees of satisfaction. For many women, if personal health or family history does not contraindicate it, oral contraception is both effective and safe.

IMPLANTS. In December of 1990, the FDA approved a new contraceptive—thin, matchstick-sized capsules containing progestin that are implanted under a woman's skin. Over a period of up to five years, the hormone is slowly released. When the implants are removed, fertility is restored. A set of soft tubes is surgically implanted under the skin of the upper arm in a simple doctor's-office procedure with local anesthesia. Once implanted, the capsules are not visible but may be felt under the skin. The implants, under the tradename Norplant, are currently on the market in more than fourteen countries. The cost may run as high as several hundred dollars, but it is probably less expensive than a five-year supply of birth control pills.

EFFECTIVENESS. Although Norplant has not been observed or tested to the degree that other contraceptives have, initial reports indicate a failure rate one-tenth to one-twentieth that of the pill. It may be the most effective contraceptive ever marketed.

ADVANTAGES. Convenience is clearly a big advantage of the implant. Once the implant is in, there's nothing to remember, buy, do, or take care of.

POSSIBLE PROBLEMS. The chief side effect, experienced by about half of implant users, is a change in the pattern of menstrual bleeding, such as lengthened periods or spotting between periods. Norplant should not be used by women with acute liver disease, breast cancer, blood clots, or unexplained vaginal bleeding. Possible long-term negative effects are not known at this time.

Barrier Methods: Condom, Diaphragm, Cervical Cap, Sponge, and Women's Condom

Barrier methods are designed to keep sperm and egg from getting together. Barrier methods available to women are the diaphragm, the cervical cap, the contraceptive sponge (which also contains a sperm-killing chemical) and the women's condom. The barrier device used by men is the condom. The effectiveness of all barrier methods is increased by use with spermicides (sperm-killing chemicals).

CONDOMS. A condom is a thin sheath of rubber (or processed sheep's intestine) that fits over the erect penis and thus prevents semen from being transmitted. Condoms are available in a variety of sizes, shapes, and colors. Some are lubricated and some are treated with spermicides. They are easily obtainable from drug stores, and most kinds are relatively inexpensive. Condoms are the third most widely used form of birth control in the United States. In 1980, it was estimated that they were used by 40 million couples throughout the world.

Condoms not only provide effective contraception when properly used, they also guard against the transmission of a number of sexually transmitted diseases such as chlamydia, gonorrhea, genital herpes, and AIDS if they are made of latex rather than sheep's intestine. Due to increased publicity regarding the transmissibility of the AIDS virus (HIV), both heterosexuals and gay men are increasingly using latex condoms as prophylactic (disease-preventing) devices. Condom use does not guarantee *total* safety from STDs, however, as sexual partners may also transmit certain diseases by hand, mouth, and external genitalia other than the penis; also, condoms may occasionally tear or leak.

Today an estimated 40 percent of condoms are purchased by women, and condom advertising and packaging increasingly reflect this trend. Even if a women regularly uses another form of birth control, such as the pill or IUD, she may want to have the added protection provided by a condom, especially if it has been treated with spermicide (which provides further protection against disease organisms). Contraceptive aerosol foam and contraceptive film (a thin, translucent square of tissue that dissolves into a gel) are the most convenient spermicidal preparations to use with condoms.

EFFECTIVENESS. Condoms are 98 to 99 percent effective theoretically. User effectiveness is 90 percent. Failures sometimes occur from mishandling the condom, but they are usually the result of not putting it on until after some semen has leaked into the vagina, or simply not putting it on at all.

ADVANTAGES. Condoms are easy to obtain. They are easy for men and women to carry in a wallet or purse. They help protect against STDs, including herpes and HIV.

POSSIBLE PROBLEMS. The chief drawback to a condom is that it must be put on after the man has been aroused but before he enters his partner. This interruption is the major reason for users neglecting or "forgetting" to put them on. Some men complain that sensation is dulled, and (very rarely) cases of allergy to rubber are reported. Both problems can be remedied by the use of animal tissue condoms. These are thinner and conduct heat better. *Animal tissue condoms, however, should not be used for prophylaxis; viral STDs such as genital herpes and HIV may easily penetrate them.* The condom user must take care to hold the sheath at the base of his penis when he withdraws, in order to avoid leakage.

HINTS ON CONDOM USE.

❑ Use condoms every time you have sexual intercourse; this is the key to successful contraception and disease prevention.
❑ Use a spermicide with the condom. Foam and film are both easy to apply. Spermicide helps protect against pregnancy and STDs, including chlamydia, gonorrhea, herpes, and HIV.
❑ Do not put a condomless penis into the vagina! Even if the man has great "control," there is *always* the possibility of pre-ejaculatory leakage.
❑ Leave about a half-inch of space at the condom tip, and roll the condom all the way down to the base of the penis.
❑ *Soon* after the ejaculation, the penis should be withdrawn. Make sure someone holds the base of the condom firmly against the penis as it is withdrawn.
❑ After use, check the condom for possible torn spots. If you are not using a spermicide (you should be!) and you find a tear or hole, *immediately* insert foam or jelly into the vagina. This may reduce the chance of pregnancy. If torn condoms are a persistent problem, use a water-based lubricant such as K-Y jelly or a spermicide to reduce friction.
❑ Do not reuse condoms.
❑ Keep condoms in a cool, dry and *convenient* place.
❑ To protect against HIV and other organisms, use a latex condom, *not* one made of animal tissue.

If you or your partner are uncomfortable with condom use, consider the following:

❑ Communication is crucial. It may seem "unromantic," but planning your contraception strategy *before* you are sexually entangled is essential. Giving or getting a disease or worrying about pregnancy is about as *unromantic* as you can get. Consider visiting a family planning clinic for counseling—together. Neither partner should be forced to use a form of birth control he or she is truly unhappy with. But the issue of protection must be dealt with—by both of you.
❑ Don't forget your sense of humor and playfulness. Condoms can actually provide lots of laughs, and laughter and sex go well together. Fancy condoms—colored, ribbed, glow-in-the-dark, etc.—are popular for their entertainment value.

Stand your ground. (This is mainly for women, as it is generally men who object to condoms.) Unless you want to be pregnant and are sure your partner is free of STDs, you need protection during sex. If he says no to condoms, you can say no to him. If he cares about you, he will work with you to find birth control and "safe sex" methods that suit you both.

DIAPHRAGM. The diaphragm is a rubber cup with a flexible rim. It is placed in the vagina, blocking the cervix, to prevent sperm from entering the uterus and fallopian tubes. Different women require different sizes, and a woman may change sizes, especially after a pregnancy; the size must be determined by an experienced practitioner. Diaphragms are available by prescription from doctors and family planning clinics. Somewhat effective by itself, the diaphragm is highly effective when used with a spermicidal cream or jelly. (Creams and jellies are considered more effective than foam for use with a diaphragm.) Diaphragm users should be sure to use an adequate amount of spermicide and to follow their practitioner's instructions with care.

The diaphragm can be put in place up to two hours before intercourse. It should be left in place six to eight hours afterward. A woman should not dislodge it or douche before it is time to remove it. If intercourse is repeated within six hours, the diaphragm should be left in place but more chemical contraceptive should be inserted with an applicator. However, a diaphragm should not be left in place longer than 24 hours.

Diaphragms need to be replaced about once a year because the rubber deteriorates, losing elasticity and increasing the chance of splitting. Any change in the way the diaphragm feels, as well as any dramatic gain or loss of weight, calls for a visit to doctor or clinic to check the fit.

EFFECTIVENESS. When properly used, *with spermicide*, diaphragms are 98 percent effective. Numerous studies of diaphragm effectiveness have yielded varying results. Typical user effectiveness (actual statistical effectiveness) is in the 81 to 83 percent range. The lowest effectiveness ratings appear among young diaphragm users and inconsistent users.

ADVANTAGES. The diaphragm can be placed well before the time of intercourse. For most women, there are few health problems associated with its use. It helps protect against diseases of the cervix and PID.

POSSIBLE PROBLEMS. Some women dislike handling or placing diaphragms, or the mess or smell of the chemical contraceptives used with them. Some men complain of rubbing or other discomfort caused by the diaphragm. Occasionally a woman is allergic to rubber. Some women become more prone to urinary tract infections. As there is a small risk of toxic shock syndrome (TSS) associated with its use, a woman should not use a diaphragm under the following conditions:

❑ during menstruation or other bleeding
❑ following childbirth (for several months)
❑ during abnormal vaginal discharge
❑ if she has had TSS or if *Staphylococcus aureus* bacteria are present

She should also:

❑ never wear the diaphragm for more than 24 hours.
❑ learn to watch for the warning signs of TSS:
    Fever (101° or higher)
    Diarrhea
    Vomiting
    Muscle aches
    Sunburnlike rash

CERVICAL CAP. The cervical cap is a small rubber barrier device that fits snugly over the cervix; it can be filled with spermicidal cream or jelly. Cervical caps come in different sizes and shapes; proper fit is extremely important, and not everyone can be fitted. Fitting must be done by a physician or at a health clinic.

EFFECTIVENESS. There is a limited amount of research data in this country regarding the cervical cap's effectiveness. Reported user effectiveness ranges from 73 to 92 percent.

ADVANTAGES. The cervical cap may be more comfortable and convenient than the diaphragm for some women. It does not interfere with the body physically or hormonally.

POSSIBLE PROBLEMS. Some users are bothered by an odor that develops from the interaction of the cap's rubber and either vaginal secretions or the spermicide. There is some concern that the cap may contribute to erosion of the cervix. If a woman's partner's penis touches the rim of the cap, it can become displaced during intercourse. Theoretically the same risk of TSS exists for the cervical cap as for the diaphragm. The precautions discussed in the section on diaphragms also apply.

CONTRACEPTIVE SPONGE. In 1983 the FDA approved the contraceptive sponge for over-the-counter sales. When inserted into the vagina, the polyurethane sponge blocks the opening of cervix and releases a spermicide. It must be left in place for at least six hours (or as long as 24 hours) following intercourse and then disposed of.

EFFECTIVENESS. The sponge has a theoretical effectiveness rate of about 87 to 90 percent. It has a user-effectiveness rate of about 83 percent. The lowest observed effectiveness rate is 72 percent.

Higher failure rates seem to appear among women who have previously given birth.

ADVANTAGES. The sponge's advantages include convenience, safety, effectiveness, and possible prevention of some sexually transmitted diseases. It is easy to obtain.

POSSIBLE PROBLEMS. No long-term studies of the sponge's safety have been completed. It is recommended that the sponge *not* be used during menstruation because of the risk of toxic shock syndrome at that time. The precautions discussed in the section on diaphragms also apply to the contraceptive sponge. Some women report an unpleasant odor from the sponge; some report allergic reactions; others report inadvertently expelling the sponge during a bowel movement.

WOMEN'S CONDOM. The women's condom is a disposable, soft, loose-fitting polyurethane sheath with a diaphragm-like ring at each end. One ring is inside the sheath and is used to insert and anchor the condom next to the cervix. The larger outer ring remains outside the vagina and acts as a barrier, protecting the vulva and the base of the penis.

Because of the newness of this product, its effectiveness is not known at this time, although clinical tests have indicated that it is less likely to leak than men's latex condoms. In laboratory trials, the women's condom was not permeated by HIV or cytomegalovirus, indicating that it may be a promising alternative for both contraception and the control of STDs.

Spermicides

A spermicide is a substance that is toxic to sperm. The most commonly used spermicide in products sold in the United States is the chemical nonoxynol-9.

Spermicidal preparations are available in a variety of forms: foam, film, jelly, cream, tablets, and suppositories. Contraceptive sponges and some condoms are also treated with spermicides. Spermicidal preparations are considered most effective when used in combination with a barrier method.

A further benefit of spermicides is that they significantly reduce STD risk. Nonoxynol-9 has been demonstrated to have a toxic effect on a number of disease agents, including HIV. Of course, use of spermicides, although it lowers the risk of contracting an STD, does not entirely eliminate it.

CONTRACEPTIVE FOAM. Contraceptive foam is a chemical spermicide sold in aerosol containers. Methods of application vary with each brand, but usually foam is released deep in the vagina either directly from the container or with an applicator. It forms a barrier to the uterus and inactivates sperm in the vagina. It is most effective if inserted no more than half an hour before intercourse. Shaking the container before applying the foam increases its foaminess so that it spreads farther. The foam begins to go flat after about 30 minutes. It must be reapplied when intercourse is repeated.

EFFECTIVENESS. Foam has a theoretical effectiveness rate of 98.5 percent. User failure brings its effectiveness down to as low as 71 percent. User failures tend to come from not applying the foam every single time the couple has intercourse, from relying on foam inserted hours before intercourse, or from relying on foam placed hurriedly or not placed deep enough. If used properly and consistently, however, it is quite reliable. Used with a condom, it is highly effective.

ADVANTAGES. There are almost no medical problems associated with the use of foam. Foam helps provide protection against certain sexually transmitted diseases.

POSSIBLE PROBLEMS. Some women dislike applying foam. Some complain of messiness, leakage, odors, or stinging sensations. Occasionally, a woman or man may have an allergic reaction to it.

CONTRACEPTIVE FILM. Contraceptive film is a relatively new spermicidal preparation. It is sold in packets of small (2" square), translucent tissues. This thin tissue contains the spermicide nonoxynol-9; it dissolves into a sticky gel when inserted into the vagina. It should be inserted directly over the cervix, not less than five minutes or more than one-and-a-half hours before intercourse. It remains effective for two hours after insertion. Contraceptive film works effectively in conjunction with the condom.

EFFECTIVENESS. Extensive research has not been done on the effectiveness of film, due to its relative newness on the market. The highest effectiveness rates reported are from 82 to 90 percent. Of course, proper and consistent use with a condom highly increases the effectiveness.

ADVANTAGES. Film is easy to use for many women. It is easily obtained from a drugstore. It is easy to carry in a purse, wallet, or pocket.

POSSIBLE PROBLEMS. Some women may not like inserting the film into the vagina. Some women may be allergic to it. Increased vaginal discharge and temporary pain while urinating after using contraceptive film have been reported.

CREAMS AND JELLIES. These chemical spermicides come in tubes and are inserted with applicators or placed inside diaphragms or cervical caps. They can be bought without prescription at most drugstores. They work in a manner similar to foams but are considered less effective when used alone. Like foam, jellies and creams seem to provide some protection against venereal diseases. This factor makes their use with a diaphragm even more attractive.

SUPPOSITORIES AND TABLETS. These chemical spermicides are inserted into the vagina before intercourse. Body heat and fluids dissolve the ingredients, which will inactivate sperm in the vagina after ejaculation. They must be inserted early enough to dissolve completely before intercourse.

EFFECTIVENESS. Reports on these methods vary widely. It is suspected that the variations are connected with each user's technique of application. Directions for use that come with these contraceptives are not always clear. Jellies, creams, vaginal tablets, and suppositories should be used in conjunction with a barrier method for maximum effectiveness.

ADVANTAGES. The methods are simple and easily obtainable, with virtually no medical problems. They *help* protect against STDs, including chlamydia, trichomonas, gonorrhea, genital herpes, and HIV.

POSSIBLE PROBLEMS. Some people have allergic reactions to the spermicides. Some women dislike the messiness, smells, or necessity of touching their own genitalia. Others experience irritation or inflammation, especially if they use the method frequently. A few women lack the vaginal lubrication to dissolve the tablets in a reasonable amount of time. And a few women complain of having anxiety about the method's effectiveness during intercourse.

The IUD (Intrauterine Device)

The IUD is a tiny plastic or metal device that is inserted into the uterus through the cervical opening. The particular type of device determines how long it may be left in place—one year to indefinitely.

Although most IUDs have been withdrawn from the U.S. market because of the proliferation of lawsuits against their manufacturers in recent years, they are still considered a major birth control method. There clearly are some risks involved with the IUD, especially for certain women. Nevertheless, it remains the birth control method of about 70 million women throughout the world, including 40–45 million women in China.

Strictly speaking, the IUD is not a contraceptive. It is a birth control device that works principally by preventing the blastocyst from implanting in the uterine wall or by disrupting a blastocyst that has already implanted. The IUD may also serve to immobilize sperm and (in the case of progestin-bearing IUDs) induce thickened cervical mucus. IUDs must be inserted and removed by a trained practitioner.

EFFECTIVENESS. IUDS are 97 to 99 percent effective theoretically. User effectiveness is 90 to 96 percent.

ADVANTAGES. Once inserted, IUDs require little care. They don't interfere with spontaneity during intercourse.

POSSIBLE PROBLEMS. Insertion is often painful. Heavy cramping usually follows and sometimes persists. Menstrual flow usually increases. Up to one-third of users, especially women who have never been pregnant, expel the device within the first year. This usually happens during menstruation. The IUD can be reinserted, however, and many women retain it the second time.

The IUD is associated with increased risk of pelvic inflammatory disease (PID). Because of the risk of sterility induced by PID, many physicians recommend that women planning to have children use alternative methods. Women who have had PID or who have multiple sex partners should be aware that an IUD will place them at significantly greater risk of PID, STDs, and other infections.

The IUD cannot be inserted in some women due to unusual uterine shape or position. Until recently the IUD was considered difficult to insert and less effective for teenage girls. But newer, smaller IUDs have been found to provide good protection even for young teenagers.

Occasionally the device perforates the cervix. This usually happens at the time of insertion, if it happens at all. Removal sometimes requires surgery.

Sometimes pregnancy occurs and is complicated by the presence of the IUD. If the IUD is not removed, there is a 50 percent chance of spontaneous abortion; if it is removed, the chance is 25 percent. Furthermore, spontaneous abortions that occur when an IUD is left in place are likely to be septic (infection-bearing) and possibly life-threatening.

Fertility Awareness Methods

Fertility awareness methods of contraception require substantial education, training, and planning. They are based on a woman's knowledge of her body's reproductive cycle. These methods require high motivation and self-control; they are not for everyone.

Fertility awareness is also referred to as "natural family planning." Some people make the following distinction between the two. With fertility awareness, the couple may use an alternate method (such as diaphragm with jelly or condom with foam) during the fertile part of the woman's cycle. Natural family planning does not include the use of any contraceptive device and is thus considered more "natural"; it is approved by the Roman Catholic church.

Fertility awareness methods include the rhythm (calendar) method, the basal body temperature (BBT) method, the mucus (also called the Billings or ovulation) method, and the sympto-thermal method, which combines the latter two. These methods are not recommended for women who have irregular menstrual cycles, including postpartum and lactating mothers.

All women can benefit from learning to recognize their fertility signs. It is useful to know when the time of greatest likelihood of pregnancy occurs, both for women who wish to avoid pregnancy and for those who want to become pregnant.

BASAL BODY TEMPERATURE (BBT) METHOD. A woman's temperature tends to be slightly lower during menstruation and for about a week afterward. Just before ovulation it dips; then rises sharply (one-half to one whole degree) following ovulation. It stays high until just before the next menstruation period.

A woman practicing this method must record her temperature every morning upon waking for 6 to 12 months to have an accurate idea of her temperature pattern. When she is quite sure she recognizes the rise in temperature and can predict about when in her cycle it will happen, she can begin using the method. She will abstain from intercourse or use an alternate contraceptive method for three to four days before the expected risk and for four days after it has taken place. If she limits intercourse to only the "safe" time after her temperature has risen, the method is more effective. The method requires high motivation and control. For greater accuracy it may be combined with the mucus method described in the next section.

MUCUS METHOD (BILLINGS OR OVULATION METHOD). In many women, there is a noticeable change in the appearance and character of cervical mucus prior to ovulation. After menstruation, most women experience a moderate discharge of cloudy, yellowish or white mucus. Then, for a day or two, a clear, slippery mucus is secreted. Ovulation occurs immediately after the clear, slippery mucus secretions. The pre-ovulatory mucus is elastic in consistency, rather like raw egg white, and a drop can be stretched between two fingers into a thin strand (at least 6 cm.). This elasticity is called spinnbarkeit. Following ovulation, the amount of discharge decreases markedly. The four days before and the four days after these secretions are considered the unsafe days. An alternate contraceptive method may be used during this time. The method requires training and high motivation to be successful. Clinics are offered in some cities. (For more information, check with your local family planning or women's health clinic.) This method may be combined with the BBT method for greater effectiveness.

SYMPTO-THERMAL METHOD. When the BBT and mucus methods are used together, it is called the sympto-thermal method. Additional signs that may be useful in determining ovulation are mid-cycle pain in the lower abdomen on either side (mittelschmerz) and a very slight discharge of blood from the cervix ("spotting"). Women who wish to rely on fertility awareness methods of contraception should enroll in a class at a clinic. Learning to read one's own unique fertility signs is a complex process requiring one-to-one counseling and close monitoring.

CALENDAR METHOD. This method is based on calculating safe days based on the range of a woman's longest and shortest menstrual cycles. It is not practical or safe for women with irregular cycles. For women with regular cycles, the calendar method is reasonably effective because the period of time when an ovum is receptive to fertilization is only about 24 hours. As sperm generally live two to four days, the maximum period of time in which fertilization could be expected to occur may be calculated with the assistance of a calendar.

Ovulation generally occurs 14 (plus or minus two) days before a woman's menstrual period. Taking this into account, and charting her menstrual cycles for a minimum of eight months to determine the longest and shortest cycles, a woman can determine her expected fertile period.

During the fertile period, a woman must abstain from sexual intercourse or use an alternative method of contraception. A woman using this method must be meticulous in her calculations, keep her calendar up to date, and be able to maintain an awareness of what day it is. Statistically only about one-third of all women have cycles regular enough to satisfactorily employ this method.

EFFECTIVENESS OF FERTILITY AWARENESS METHODS. It is problematic to calculate the effectiveness of fertility awareness methods. With this type of contraception, in a sense, the user *is* the method; the method's success or failure rests largely on the woman's diligence. For those who have used fertility awareness with unfailing dedication, it has been demonstrated to be as much as 99 percent effective. Many studies, however, show fairly high failure rates. Some researchers believe that this is due to risk-taking during the fertile phase.

Additionally, there is always some difficulty in predicting ovulation with pinpoint accuracy; thus, there is a better chance of pregnancy as a result of intercourse prior to ovulation than as a result of intercourse following it. Furthermore, there is evidence that sperm may survive as long as five days. This suggests that unprotected intercourse any time prior to ovulation may be risky. All fertility awareness methods increase in effectiveness if intercourse is unprotected only during the safe period *following* ovulation.

ADVANTAGES. Fertility awareness (or natural family planning) methods are acceptable to most religious groups. They are free and pose no health risks. If a woman wishes to become pregnant, awareness of her own fertility cycles is very useful.

POSSIBLE PROBLEMS. These methods are not suitable for women with irregular menstrual cycles or couples who are not highly motivated to use them. Some couples who practice abstinence during fertile periods may begin to take risks out of frustration. These couples may benefit by exploring other forms of sexual expression; counseling can help.

Sterilization

Among married couples in the United States, sterilization (of one or both partners) is the most popular form of birth control. Approximately 27 percent of couples have chosen to be sterilized.

STERILIZATION FOR WOMEN. In 1984, the most recent year for which figures are available, about 64 percent of sterilizations were done on women. Most female sterilizations are tubal ligations, "tying the tubes." The two most common operations are laparoscopy and minilaparotomy. Less commonly performed types of sterilization for women are culpotomy, culdoscopy, and hysterectomy. Generally, this surgery is not reversible; only women who are completely certain that they want no (or no more) children should choose this method.

Sterilization for women is quite expensive. Surgeon, anesthesiologist, and hospital fees are substantial. The newer procedures in which the woman returns home on the same day have the advantage of being one-half to one-third as expensive as abdominal surgery, but still may cost hundreds or even thousands of dollars. Many health insurance policies will cover all or part of the cost of sterilization for both men and women. In some states, Medicaid pays for certain patients.

LAPAROSCOPY. Sterilization by laparoscopy usually requires a day or less in the hospital or clinic. General anesthesia is usually recommended. The woman's abdomen is inflated with gas to make the organs more visible. The surgeon inserts a rodlike instrument with a viewing lens (the laparoscope) through a small incision at the edge of the navel and locates the fallopian tubes (the ducts between the ovaries and the uterus). Through this incision or a second one, the surgeon inserts another instrument that closes the tubes. The tubes are usually closed by electrocauterization. Special small forceps that carry an electric current clamp the tubes and cauterize (burn) them. The tubes may also be closed off or blocked with tiny rings, clips, or plugs. There is a recovery period of several days to a week. During this time the women will experience some tenderness and some bleeding from the vagina. Rest is important.

MINILAPAROTOMY. Local or general anesthesia is used with minilaparotomy. A small incision is made in the lower abdomen, through which the fallopian tubes are brought into view. They are then tied off or sealed with electric current, clips, or rings. Recovery is the same as with laparoscopy.

CULPOTOMY AND CULDOSCOPY. In these operations, an incision is made at the back of the vagina. In culpotomy, the tubes are viewed through the incision and then tied or otherwise blocked, and cut. Culdoscopy is the same procedure but uses a viewing instrument called a culdoscope. The advantage of these procedures is that they leave no visible scars. They require more expertise on the part of the surgeon, however, and have higher complication rates than laparoscopy and minilaparotomy.

HYSTERECTOMY. Hysterectomy is not performed for sterilization except under special circumstances. Since it involves removal of the entire uterus, it is both riskier and more costly than other methods. It involves greater recovery time and, for some women, is potentially more difficult psychologically. It may be appropriate for women who have a uterine disease or other problem that is likely to require a future hysterectomy anyway.

EFFECTIVENESS OF STERILIZATION FOR WOMEN. Surgical contraception is essentially 100 percent effective. In *extremely* rare instances (less than ¼ of a percent), probably due to improperly done surgery, a tube may reopen or grow back together, allowing an egg to pass through.

Once sterilization is done, no other method of birth control will ever be necessary. (A woman who risks exposure to STDs, however, may wish to protect herself with a spermicide, condom, or women's condom.)

Sterilization does not reduce or change a woman's feminine characteristics. It is not the same as menopause and does not hasten the approach of menopause, as some people believe. A woman still has her menstrual periods until whatever age menopause naturally occurs for her. Her ovaries, uterus (except in the case of hysterectomy), and hormonal system have not been changed. The only difference is that sperm cannot now reach her eggs. (The eggs, which are released every month as before, are reabsorbed by the body.) Sexual enjoyment is not diminished. In fact, a high percentage of women report that they feel more relaxed during intercourse since anxiety about pregnancy has been eliminated. There do not seem to be any harmful side effects associated with female sterilization.

Sterilization should be considered irreversible. The most recently developed methods of ligation using clips, rings, or plugs may be more reversible than those employing electrocauterization, but the overall success rate for reversals is quite low; it is also very costly and not covered by most insurance plans. Only between 15 and 25 percent of women who seek to have their tubal ligations reversed succeed in conceiving.

The tubal ligation itself is a relatively safe procedure. With electrocauterization, there is a chance that other tissues in the abdomen may be damaged, especially if the surgeon is not highly skilled. These "bowel burns" may require further surgery but often heal on their own. Anesthesia complications are the most serious risk. The risk of death is quite low—four deaths per 100,000 operations. Infection is also a possibility; it may be treated with antibiotics.

STERILIZATION FOR MEN. A vasectomy is a minor surgical procedure that can be done in a doctor's office under local anethesia. It takes approximately half an hour. In this procedure, the physician makes a small incision (or two incisions) in the skin of the scrotum. Through the incision, each vas deferens (sperm-carrying tube) is lifted, cut, tied, and often cauterized with electricity. After a brief rest, the man is able to walk out of the office; complete recuperation takes only a few days.

A man may retain some viable sperm in his system for days or weeks following a vasectomy. He should use other birth control until his semen has been checked, about eight weeks following the operation.

EFFECTIVENESS. Vasectomies are 99.85 percent effective. In very rare cases, the ends of a vas deferens may rejoin; this is virtually impossible if the operation is correctly performed.

ADVANTAGES. No birth control method will ever be needed again, unless the man wishes to use a condom to prevent getting or spreading an STD. Sexual enjoyment will not be diminished; he will still have erections and orgasms and ejaculate semen. Vasectomy is relatively inexpensive as surgical procedures go.

POSSIBLE PROBLEMS. Compared to other birth control methods, the complication rates for vasectomy are very low. Most problems occur when proper antiseptic measures are not taken during the operation or when the man exercises too strenuously in the few days after it. Hematomas (bleeding under the skin) and granulomas (clumps of sperm) can be treated with ice packs and rest. Epididymitis (inflammation of the tiny tubes that connect the testicle and vas deferens) can be treated with heat and scrotal support.

One-half to two-thirds of men develop sperm antibodies following vasectomy. The body produces these antibodies in response to the presence of sperm that have been absorbed by body tissues. There is no physiological evidence that this poses any threat to health.

A few men, those who equate fertility with virility and potency, may experience psychological problems following vasectomy. However, according to the authors of *Contraceptive Technology* (Hatcher et al., 1986), "Most well-adjusted males will experience no adverse psychological changes following elective sterilization, if

they understand what to expect . . . and are given an opportunity to express their fears and have their questions answered. . . ."

Among men who seek to have their vasectomies reversed, about 50 percent experience success. The cost is high and not covered by insurance in many cases. Vasectomy should be considered permanent.

Unreliable Methods of Contraception

COITUS INTERRUPTUS (WITHDRAWAL). The oldest form of contraception known is coitus interruptus, which involves the withdrawal of the penis from the vagina prior to ejaculation. This method is widely used throughout the world today and can be considered somewhat successful for *some* people. Success may depend on technique, on combination with rhythm methods, or on physical characteristics of the partners (such as the tendency toward infertility in one or both partners).

A problem with this method is its riskiness. Secretions from the man's Cowper's glands, urethra, or prostate, which sometimes seep into the vagina before ejaculation, can carry thousands of healthy sperm. Also, the first few drops of ejaculate carry most of the sperm. If the man is slow to withdraw or allows any ejaculate to spill into (or near the opening of) the vagina, the woman may get pregnant. The highest observed effective rate using coitus interruptus is 84 percent. The actual user effectiveness rate is 77 percent. Although it is generally considered an unreliable method of birth control, coitus interruptus is certainly better than nothing.

DOUCHING. To douche, a woman flushes the vagina with liquid. As a contraceptive method it is faulty because after the ejaculation, douching is already too late. By the time a woman can douche, the sperm may already be swimming through the cervix into the uterus. The douche liquid may even push the sperm into the cervix. Douching with any liquid, especially if done often, tends to upset the normal chemical balance in the vagina and may cause irritation or infection. There is also evidence that frequent douching can result in ectopic pregnancy.

LACTATION. When a woman, after giving birth, breastfeeds her child, she may not begin to ovulate as long as she continues to nourish her child exclusively by breastfeeding. However, although some women do not ovulate while lactating, others do. Cycles may begin immediately after delivery or in a few months. The woman never knows when she will begin to be fertile. This is considered a method in some other countries, but the success ratings are extremely low.

MYTHICAL METHODS OF CONTRACEPTION. There are many myths among young and old about contraception. The young hear many rumors. Some of the old, who should know better, still believe misconceptions hatched in "the old days" when contraceptive devices were not as easily obtained or as dependable as they are today. (The dependability of condoms, always the most easily purchased device, was greatly improved when the product came under the supervision of the Federal Trade Commission.) Today, when satisfactory methods are so easy to obtain, it is senseless for anyone to use risky ones.

Widely known methods that are *totally* useless include:

1. Standing up during or after intercourse (sperm have no problem swimming "upstream").
2. Taking a friend's pill the day of, or the day after, intercourse (doesn't work—may even be dangerous).
3. Only having intercourse occasionally (it is when, not how often, that makes a difference; once is enough if the woman is fertile at that time).
4. Using plastic wrap or plastic bags for condoms (too loose, undependable, and unsanitary).

❑ ABORTION

Most people, when they hear the word "abortion," think of a medical procedure or operation to end an unwanted pregnancy. But the word carries a wider range of meanings than most people realize. Anytime a growing embryo or fetus is expelled from the uterus, an abortion has taken place. Such expulsion can happen naturally, or it can be made to happen in one of several ways. Many abortions happen spontaneously because the woman wears an IUD, because she suffers physical shock, because the fetus is not properly developed, or, more commonly, because physical conditions within the uterus break down and end the development of the embryo or fetus. Approximately one-third of all abortions reported in a year are spontaneous ("miscarriages"). Of the approximately 6 million pregnancies that occur in this country each year, more than half are unintentional. Of these, almost half are terminated by induced abortions.

Abortions can be induced in several ways. Surgical methods are most common, but the use of medications to induce abortion is also possible. Methods for early abortions (those performed in the first three months) differ from late abortions (those performed after the third month).

To facilitate the dilation of the cervix, many physicians insert a laminaria, a small stick of seaweed, into the cervical opening. The laminaria expands gradually, dilating the cervix gently in the process. It must be placed at least six hours prior to the abortion.

Surgical Methods of Abortion

Surgical methods include vacuum aspiration, dilation and curettage (D & C), dilation and evacuation (D & E), and hysterotomy, as well as several other methods.

VACUUM ASPIRATION (FIRST-TRIMESTER METHOD). This method is performed under local anesthesia. The cervix is dilated with a series of graduated rods (laminaria may have been used to begin dilation). Then a small tube attached to a vacuum is inserted through the cervix. The uterus is gently vacuumed, removing the fetus, placenta, and endometrial tissue. The patient returns home the same day. She will experience cramping, bleeding, and, possibly, emotional reactions over the following days. Serious complications are unusual for a legal, properly performed abortion. Those problems that may arise are discussed in the section entitled "Adjustment Following Abortion."

DILATION AND CURETTAGE (D & C) FIRST-TRIMESTER METHOD). The cervix is dilated and the uterine wall scraped with a small spoon-shaped instrument (curette). Local or general anesthesia is given. It is generally considered less desirable than vacuum aspiration as it causes more bleeding, is more painful, and is sometimes less effective. Possible problems are discussed below.

DILATION AND EVACUATION (D & E) (SECOND-TRIMESTER METHOD). This method is usually performed between the 13th and 20th week of pregnancy. Local or general anesthesia is used. The cervix is slowly dilated and the fetus removed by alternating curettage with the injection of a solution toxic to the fetus. Patients are usually given an intravenous solution of the hormone oxytochin to encourage contractions and limit blood loss. Because it is a second trimester procedure, a D & E is somewhat riskier and often more traumatic than a first trimester abortion.

HYSTEROTOMY (SECOND-TRIMESTER METHOD). The fetus is removed through an incision made in the woman's abdomen. This is essentially a cesarean section—major surgery, requiring several days in the hospital. Its use is limited.

Other Methods of Abortion

Abortion can also be induced medically with injections or suppositories containing certain substances. These abortions are performed during the second trimester and generally require hospitalization. Prostaglandins, saline solutions, and urea are common abortifacients. They are used singly or in varying combinations.

Many cells of the body contain prostaglandins. A prostaglandin is a type of fatty acid that is active in many kinds of body processes, including reproduction. Prostaglandins are injected into the amniotic sac or administered as vaginal suppositories to induce abortion. Some of the side effects associated with their use are gastrointestinal symptoms, cervical lacerations, and temperature elevation.

Saline solutions and solutions of urea are toxic to the fetus and can be injected amniotically. These solutions are relatively inexpensive; they are generally considered more effective when used in combination with prostaglandins.

Mifepristone, known popularly as RU-486, is an antiprogesterone steroid that acts as an abortifacient if taken orally or injected within the first six weeks of pregnancy. It has recently become available for use in the United States.

Adjustment Following Abortion

Following an abortion, most women have some bleeding and cramps for about two weeks. Some women will have light menstrual-type bleeding as long as one to two weeks. The only cause for worry about bleeding is if it is heavier two days in a row than the heaviest day of normal menstrual flow. In order to protect herself against infection, a woman should not have sexual intercourse until she has had her follow-up visit. She should not use tampons for a week (sanitary napkins may be used instead) and should not douche for a week. Her usual period will begin about four to six weeks following the abortion. It is important to use contraception even if her period has not yet begun again since it is still possible to get pregnant. If her period does not begin within eight weeks of her abortion, she should call her clinic or physician.

Although many women feel a great sense of relief once an abortion is completed, many also experience a profound sense of loss. Some women are surprised at the intensity of their feelings. They need to understand that this grieving process is normal. Counseling can help.

Complication rates are low for legal abortions performed by qualified practitioners, especially for first-trimester abortions. About 91 percent of abortions are performed before the 13th week of pregnancy; 99 percent are performed by 20 weeks, before the fetus is viable (able to survive outside the womb).

Properly done, first-trimester abortions are statistically six times safer than childbirth. Later abortions are significantly more dangerous. The possible complications include infection and hemorrhage, often due to retained material in the uterus.

Men are often forgotten people in an abortion; attention is usually focused on the woman who is undergoing the agony of decision. If men are thought of, they are often regarded with hostility and blame. And yet they, like the women, may be undergoing their own private travail, experiencing guilt and anxiety, feeling ambiguous about the possibility of parenthood.

A common feeling men experience is powerlessness. They may try to remain cool and rational, believing that if they reveal their confused feelings they will be unable to give their partners emotional support. Since the drama is within the woman and her body, a man may feel he must not influence her decision.

There is the lure of fatherhood, all the same. A pregnancy forces the man to confront his own feelings about parenting. Parenthood for males, as for females, is a profound passage into adulthood. There is a mixture of pride and fear about being a potential father and a potential adult.

After the abortion, many men feel residual guilt, sadness, and remorse. It is not uncommon for some men to temporarily experience erectile or ejaculatory difficulties following an abortion. It is fairly common for couples to split up after an abortion: the stress, conflict, and guilt can be overwhelming. Many abortion clinics now provide counseling for men, as well as women, involved in abortion.

❑ SEXUALLY TRANSMITTED DISEASES (STDS)

Many people associate sexually transmitted disease (STD), also known as venereal disease (VD), with "loose" or "unclean" sexual behavior that they assume is practiced mostly by people in lower socioeconomic groups. They assume they will not become infected if they stay away from "those types." This view is dangerously wrong. Reports of infection come from all economic and education levels, and the total number rises each year. There are an estimated 13 million cases of STDs yearly (not including AIDS). Some clinics report that the incidence of STDs is highest among gay men, lowest among lesbian women, highest among both sexes between the ages of 20 and 24, and next highest among 15- to 20-year-olds. STDs are increasing dramatically among inner-city black and Latino populations and also, to some degree, among all groups of sexually active men and women.

VD and STD are general terms that refer to several different types of diseases closely associated with sexual contact. The most prevalent in the Untied States today are chlamydia, gonorrhea, genital warts, and genital herpes. Hepatitis B and syphilis are also increasingly widespread. Opportunistic infections associated with AIDS are a threat to everyone who does not practice "safe sex" or who uses intravenous drugs.

Chlamydia

Chlamydia is the most common venereal disease in America, affecting 4 to 5 million persons a year. The symptoms of chlamydia are similar to gonorrhea for both men and women. A man most often has a whitish discharge coming from his urethra; a woman is usually asymptomatic—that is, shows no symptoms. Chlamydia is a parasite, neither a virus nor a bacterium, which causes a variety of infections. Approximately 55 percent of the urinary tract infections seen in STD clinics are from chlamydia.

The risk of getting chlamydia from an infected partner is less than that of getting gonorrhea. The use of IUDs, however, is likely to increase the chance of getting chlamydia, gonorrhea, and/or PID (pelvic inflammatory disease). It is possible for a person to be infected with both gonorrhea and chlamydia; a treatment for gonorrhea will cure the gonorrhea but not the chlamydia.

Since chlamydia does not respond to penicillin, a man with a discharge should insist that a culture be taken to determine whether he is infected with chlamydia or gonorrhea or both. If he has chlamydia, the correct treatment for him and his partner is tetracycline. If the woman is pregnant, however, tetracycline must *not* be used; instead erythromycin should be used. Since there is a high incidence of persons suffering from both gonorrhea and chlamydia at the same time, tetracycline may become the treatment of choice for uncomplicated gonococcal infections.

Chlamydia is a serious disease, although traditionally it has not been treated as an important infection. For men, the serious consequences include sterility; for women, PID may be a consequence, possibly leading to hospitalization, tubal pregnancies, or sterility. Infected women who deliver may pass their infection on to their babies, causing serious eye infections and pneumonia.

Gonorrhea

This is an old disease, second only to the common cold in age and prevalence around the world. In the U.S., 1.8 million new cases are reported annually. In its early stage a man will usually notice a discharge of fluid from his penis two to seven days after sexual contact, a frequent desire to urinate, and a burning sensation when he does so. He will usually go to a doctor at this stage. If untreated, the male commonly suffers various complications, including inflammation of the testes, arthritis, skin infections, urinary disorders, and sterility.

Most women with gonorrhea are asymptomatic—that is, they show no symptoms. For this reason, if a man discovers that he has gonorrhea, it is imperative that he tell his partner so that she may be treated. Many cases in women go undetected until secondary symptoms of pain in the lower abdomen develop. This is the stage of pelvic inflammatory disease (PID). By this time the disease has moved into the fallopian tubes and glands surrounding the female organs. The result may be severe damage to tubes or ovaries, with resulting sterility.

The infection can usually be halted in men and women by penicillin or tetracycline. However, some strains of the gonococcus bacteria are resistant to the usual cures; it is important to have a follow-up exam so that additional treatment can be given if necessary.

Genital Warts

About one million cases of genital warts are reported each year. Genital warts are caused by the human papilloma virus (HPV), a class of virus of which common skin warts are a member. Genital warts are usually small, ranging in size from a pencil point to a quarter inch in diameter; they may even be invisible to the naked eye. They may be white, gray, or pink and brown. They may be flat or round, smooth or bumpy; some look like tiny cauliflowers, others look like small fingers. In men, the warts are most commonly found on the penis; they may also be found in the anus. In women, they are usually found in the cervix, vagina, vulva, and anus.

Some venereal warts appear to be associated with cervical, vaginal, vulval, and penile cancers. It is not clear which strains of HPV are implicated in these cancers; some strains of flat venereal warts are the most likely culprits.

Detection of HPV in males can be done using a vinegar wash at a dermatologist's office. HPV can be detected in women using a Pap test. External warts are easily removed by direct application of podophyllin. Internal warts can be removed through freezing or laser therapy. Once the warts are removed, the chances of developing cervical cancer diminish; it is not known what affect removal has on the incidence of other cancers of the lower genital tract. Even after the warts are removed, HPV remains in the person's system. In 80 percent of cases they eventually reappear.

Genital Herpes

An estimated 30 million Americans carry the herpes virus. A half million new cases of genital herpes are reported each year in the United States. No cure has been found for the disease, so it has spread rapidly and uncontrollably. Genital herpes is caused by a virus, generally herpes simplex type II (although 15 percent of genital herpes is caused by herpes simplex I, the virus responsible for oral and facial cold sores and fever blisters).

About 2 to 20 days after infection, blisters form on the penis or urethra in men and on the cervix, vagina, vulva, or anus in women. The sores are quite painful, and women may report pain during urination. Herpes sores may also appear around the mouth if a person has engaged in oral sex with someone who has an active case of herpes.

Once the disease is contracted, the carrier may experience repeated attacks. Although there is no cure, there are some treatments that reduce the pain and healing time of lesion outbreaks. These also reduce the chance of spreading the disease, which is most contagious during the prodromal (presymptom) stage that precedes blistering by about three days and during the blistering stage. Various ointments also help the lesions to heal quickly. The most effective of these on the market now is acyclovir (this is the generic name; brand names will be different). Acyclovir also minimizes the pain for men but not for women. It is also available as an oral medication. It must be prescribed by a physician. Pregnant women with herpes need to be aware of possible risk to their newborn infants. Informed health practitioners can provide information regarding precautions and alternatives.

Syphilis

The incidence of syphilis is currently at its highest since 1948, with an estimated 130,000 cases per year. It is increasing principally among heterosexuals. It is caused by bacteria that are easy to identify with a blood test and can be treated with penicillin or certain other antibiotics. The disease has four distinct stages that are alike for both women and men. The progression of the disease in its early stage is not painful and is not easily noticed by the person who has it. It is extremely important to arrest the disease in its early stage to avoid irreversible damage to body tissue.

PRIMARY STAGE. A sore called a *chancre* (pronounced *shanker*) appears between ten days and three months after infection at the place of infection. This may be an internal site for a woman. It may look like a pimple, a blister, an ulcer, or a cold sore. It does not hurt. It will heal itself in one to ten weeks.

SECONDARY STAGE. After the chancre heals, the disease spreads to other parts of the body. A rash breaks out (usually on the trunk of the body), but this rash is not painful or itchy. A person may also be bothered with low fever, sore throats, headaches, or other discomforts easily mistaken for ordinary ones. Sometimes lesions form in a mouth during this stage. If so, the mouth will be full of syphilis bacteria and the disease can be passed by kissing.

LATENT STAGE. Beginning six months to two years after infection, the disease becomes latent. During this time the person does not infect others but still tests positive. This stage may continue indefinitely—even until death.

TERTIARY STAGE. The syphilis bacteria sometimes concentrate in certain parts of the body. Then the disease breaks loose. It may be in any part—liver, skin, heart, or central nervous system. Later lesions and ulcers appear. Tissue damage and several disabling diseases can develop. Direct damage, as well as that arising from complications, may prove fatal.

Hepatitis

Hepatitis is a disease of the liver, causing blood pigments that are normally destroyed by the liver to accumulate in the blood. It is one of the most prevalent sexually transmitted diseases among gay men. As a result of hepatitis, jaundice (the yellowing of eyes and skin) develops; other symptoms may include fatigue, nausea, and darkening of the urine. If left unchecked, hepatitis can disable the liver and cause death. Most people with hepatitis, however, recover in a few weeks without permanent damage if they seek treatment promptly.

Infectious hepatitis (Type A hepatitis) may be contracted in a number of ways, through unsanitary conditions, contaminated water or food, transfusion with contaminated blood, or feces. Persons engaging in anal/oral sex may contract infectious hepatitis from licking the anus. Immune serum globulin (ISG) injected before or after exposure may offer some protection against (or lessen the severity of) the infection.

Serum hepatitis (Type B hepatitis) is caused by the virus entering a person through a break in the skin or through mucous membranes and may be spread by infected needles and transfusions. It is also transmitted through saliva, blood, urine, semen, and vaginal secretions. There is some evidence that women may acquire serum hepatitis sexually; there is less evidence that heterosexual men acquire the infection sexually. Hepatitis B may be prevented through a widely available immunization.

Vaginitis

There are a variety of urethral and vaginal infections that are considered venereal because they are aggravated or perpetuated by sexual contacts. Sometimes only one partner suffers from the discomfort, while the other seems to be resistant. Partner 2 acts as a carrier and continually reinfects partner 1. These diseases fall under the general category of vaginitis and include trichomoniasis, candidiasis (yeast infection), and bacterial infections such as Gardnerella.

Here are some hints that may help a woman avoid vaginitis:

❒ Do not use vaginal deodorants, especially deodorant suppositories or tampons, because they upset the natural chemical balance within the vagina. Use douches rarely and then only for good reason, such as a diagnosed yeast infection. Despite what pharmaceutical companies advertise, the healthy vagina does not have an unpleasant odor. If the vagina does have an unpleasant odor, then something is wrong and you should check with a physician or health practitioner.

❒ Regularly wash and rinse the vulva and anus. Be careful about using bubble baths or strongly perfumed soaps, since they may cause irritation.

❒ After a bowel movement, wipe the anus from the front to the back to prevent the spreading of germs from the anus to the vagina.

❒ Wear cotton underpants or underpants that have a cotton crotch, since nylon underpants and pantyhose keep heat and moisture in, encouraging bacterial growth.

❒ When lubricating the vagina, use only water-soluble lubricants. Vaseline is not water-soluble and tends to form a film on the walls of the vagina, which keeps heat and moisture in, encouraging infection.

❒ Have your male partner treated also. Vaginitis is often sexually transmitted. Be on the safe side and have your partner treated to prevent reinfection.

Yeast Infection (Candidiasis)

Symptoms of candidiasis include intense itching of the vagina or vulva and a whitish, lumpy discharge. The fungus *Candida albicans* is normally present in the healthy vaginas of many women. It may also be transmitted sexually. This is not a problem unless a chemical imbalance results in an over abundance of *Candida*. If a woman suspects she has a yeast infection, she may want to try treating it herself:

❒ Plain yogurt applied to the vulva and vagina twice a day may eliminate symptoms. (The yogurt must contain live lactobacillus culture; this means pasteurized supermarket yogurt won't work. A trip to the health food store may be in order. Health stores may also stock homeopathic treatments for yeast.)

❒ Douching with a weak vinegar and water solution (two tablespoons vinegar to one quart of water) once every two or three days may also eliminate the symptoms.

❒ Nutrition can play a part. If you have recurring candidiasis, you might try increasing your intake of plain (health-food type) yogurt; you can also cut down on foods with high sugar or carbohydrate content.

❒ Stress can upset the vagina's chemical state, as can a change in the body's hormone levels. Pregnant women and women who use oral contraception are more susceptible to yeast infections, as are women who are taking antibiotics.

❒ Antifungal medicines such as clotrimazole (Gyne-Lotrimin) and miconazole (Monostat) are now available over the counter in cream or vaginal suppository form. If you have had a yeast infection before and recognize the symptoms, you may want to purchase one of these products. If you are not sure that you have a yeast infection, see your doctor or clinic.

❒ Since women with candidiasis may have trichomonas as well, they should be tested for both.

Symptoms often disappear in two or three days, but curing candidiasis usually requires one to four weeks of treatment.

Cystitis

Cystitis (bladder infection) in women is often related to sexual activity although it is not transmitted from one partner to another. It occurs when friction irritates the urethra, allowing bacteria to easily enter the urinary tract. Frequent painful urination often indicates the presence of cystitis

PREVENTING CYSTITIS. The following measures will lessen the likelihood of a cystitis attack:

❑ Urinate frequently. Holding back urine can weaken the muscles involved in urination; it can allow the buildup of concentrated, highly acidic urine.

❑ Urinate before intercourse and soon afterwards to flush bacteria from the urethra.

❑ Drink plenty of fluids (water is best), especially just prior to and just after intercourse.

❑ Eat a well-balanced diet and get plenty of rest, especially if your resistance is low.

❑ If you use a diaphragm and are troubled by cystitis, consider trying another form of contraception.

TREATING CYSTITIS.

❑ If you feel an attack coming on, drink copious amounts of water (at least sixteen glasses a day). It won't hurt you as long as you urinate frequently! A pinch of baking soda in a glass of water can help neutralize the urine's acidity and ease the burning sensation. Avoid coffee, tea, colas, and alcohol, since they may irritate the urinary tract.

❑ Itchiness may be relieved by spraying or sponging water on the vulva and urethral opening. If urination is especially painful, try urinating while sitting in a few inches of warm water (in the bathtub or a large pan).

❑ If symptoms persist or in case of fever, consult your doctor or clinic. Sulfa drugs or other specific antibiotics will usually clear up the symptoms in several days. (A caution about using sulfa drugs: about 10–14 percent of African Americans have an inherited deficiency of a blood enzyme called glucose-6-phosphate-dehydrogenase (G6PD); sulfa drugs may cause a serious anemic disease in these people.)

❑ HIV AND AIDS

The AIDS virus (HIV—human immunodeficiency virus) affects people in a variety of ways. A few people have lived with an AIDS diagnosis for four or more years and continue to lead energetic and productive lives; others may die within a few days or weeks of their diagnosis. Some are sick throughout the course of disease, while others have periods of health alternating with periods of illness and disability.

AIDS is a very complex disease. Many of its symptoms resemble common signs of cold, the flu, and so on. The symptoms, however, are more severe and last over a significant period of time. But even if the symptoms are severe and long-lasting, they may be the result of illnesses other than AIDS. *AIDS cannot be self-diagnosed.* A person concerned with symptoms he or she thinks might be AIDS should arrange to be tested or consult a physician familiar with AIDS. (See the Self-Help Resource Directory for information about AIDS hotlines and referral services.)

When AIDS begins, a person may have several of the following symptoms. Remember, however, that these are also symptoms of other common and less serious infections.

❑ Persistent and unexplained fatigue

❑ Unexplained fever, shaking chills, or night sweats lasting several weeks or more

❑ Unexplained weight loss, usually more than 10 pounds

❑ Unexplained swollen glands, usually in the neck, armpits, or groin, lasting more than two months

❑ Pinkish or purple blotches on or under the skin, inside the mouth, nose, eyelids, or rectum, which may initially resemble bruises but do not disappear

❑ Persistent diarrhea

❑ Persistent white spots or unusual blemishes about the mouth

❑ Persistent dry cough, especially if accompanied by shortness of breath, not caused by a common respiratory infection

AIDS Antibody Testing

There are no widely available tests for the presence of HIV. The AIDS antibody tests (ELISA and Western Blot), however, are simple and *reasonably* accurate blood tests that show whether the body has developed anitbodies in response to the AIDS virus.

Interpreting the results of the antibody test, however, is not straightforward. If the AIDS antibody is absent, the test will be *negative.* But a negative test can mean one of several things: (1) the person has not been infected with HIV, (2) the person has had contact with HIV but has not become infected (but is in danger of becoming infected with repeated exposure), or (3) the person has become infected within the previous two to eight weeks with HIV, but the body has not yet produced antibodies.

If the antibody is present, the test will be *positive.* If the test is positive, then the person has been infected with HIV and there is an *active* virus present. If the virus is present, the person is capable of transmitting it to others under certain conditions.

A person with a positive HIV diagnosis should consult right away with a physician experienced in treating HIV and AIDS. Early intervention is very important in maximizing the quality of health and life.

Transmission

HIV is not casually transmitted. Casual contact—such as playing, shaking hands, sharing food or glasses, sitting on toilet seats, even biting and spitting—is an unlikely means of passing the virus. Large numbers of people who have had casual contact with people with HIV or AIDS, such as friends, family members, co-workers, or fellow students, have not tested positive for HIV. Antibody tests of family members show no transmission through casual contact; only some husbands, wives, or lovers of those infected with HIV showed AIDS antibodies.

Nonsexually, HIV is transmitted through blood, primarily from the use of unsterilized needles by intravenous (IV) drug users. Previously, it was transmitted through infected donor blood; but since 1983 the nation's donor supply has been tested against AIDS.

Sexually, HIV is transmitted through semen, vaginal secretions and blood. It is transmitted sexually to heterosexuals or homosexuals through various sexual practices—especially anal intercourse. (It is transmitted through anal intercourse because of the ease with which the delicate membranes of the rectum can be ruptured. The virus then enters the blood stream via infected semen.) Although gay men are the largest group that has been struck by the disease, it is not a gay disease but a viral disease. Its association with gay men is a result of their engaging in anal intercourse significantly more frequently than heterosexuals. In recent years, the rate of HIV infection is decreasing among gay men and increasing among heterosexuals, especially women.

❑ SAFE SEX PRACTICES

In the age of AIDS, it is necessary for each of us to practice safe sex to prevent the spread of HIV (as well as other sexually transmitted diseases). Unless you know that both you and your partner are not carrying HIV, do not allow semen, vaginal secretions, or blood to come into contact with the penis, vagina, anus, or mouth. HIV has also been found in saliva, urine, and tears, but there is little or no risk of transmitting HIV through these fluids.

The following sexual practices are safe because there is no exchange of semen, vaginal secretions, or blood:

❑ Kissing
❑ Masturbation alone or with a partner
❑ Touching, hugging, caressing, massaging

The following sexual practices are *generally* safe because there is unlikely to be an exchange of semen, vaginal secretions, or blood:

❑ Vaginal intercourse with a latex condom or women's condom
❑ Oral sex with condom or latex barrier (dental dam)

The following sexual practices are *definitely unsafe* because there is an exchange of semen, vaginal secretions, or blood:

❑ Vaginal intercourse without a condom
❑ Anal intercourse with or without a condom
❑ Oral/anal sex
❑ Oral sex without a barrier
❑ Sharing objects inserted into the anus or vagina

In addition to the previously described sexual behaviors, individuals put themselves at higher risk if they engage in the following:

❑ Sex with gay or bisexual men
❑ Sex with multiple partners
❑ Sex with IV drug users
❑ Sex with prostitutes

The practice of safe sex calls for many of us to reevaluate the place of sexuality in our lives. We may have to change some of our sexual patterns. But whatever changes we must make will ultimately enhance our sexual activities by making them safe for ourselves and others.

❑   Managing Your Money   ❑

The Management Process

A plan for money management is important for everyone. However, no readymade plan fits every family, couple, or individual. Every household is different—not only in the number and characteristics of its members, but also in its values, needs, wants, and resources. Only you can decide how your money should be spent, taking into consideration your income, the number and ages of your household members, where you live and work, your preferences, your responsibilities, and your goals for the future. By following a money management plan, you can be confident that expenses will be met and savings will be available. A plan can let you know where you stand financially and prevent emergencies from causing a financial strain.

Remember three basic concepts when developing a personal money management plan:

❑ *Set realistic objectives.* Objectives set too high may lead to frustrations that could cause you to abandon your plan.
❑ *Be flexible.* Your plan will require adjustments to keep up with your changing life cycle and financial situation. Do not make a plan so tight that each new development requires an entirely new plan.
❑ *Be specific.* State your objectives concisely. If goals are vague, objectives may never be met, and you and other household members may have different ideas of what the end product will be.

Evaluating Your Current Situation with a Net Worth Statement

The first step in developing a money management plan is to evaluate your current situation. An excellent way to do this is to prepare a *net worth statement.* Worksheet 1 can be used to add together your assets (what you own) and subtract from that the sum of your liabilities (what you owe). Space is provided for you to calculate your net worth statement now and again one year from now.

To determine the value of your *assets*, start with cash available. Include your checking and savings accounts, as well as your home bank. Now list all your investments, including bonds, mutual funds, life insurance cash values, and others. List additional assets using the current market value for your house, real estate, automobiles, jewelry, antiques, and other personal items.

To determine your *liabilities*, list the amount that you owe to all your creditors and lenders. Remember to include current bills, charge accounts, mortgage balance, and loans against your life insurance.

By subtracting liabilities from assets, you can determine your *net worth.* Look closely at your final net worth figure. Do you own more than you owe? Consider what you would like this figure to be a year from now. What do you need to do to achieve that goal?

Prepare a new net worth statement at the same time each year to reflect the changes in your finances. The market value of your assets (house, stock, or cars) may have declined or risen. You may have paid off one loan or gained another. A new net worth statement next year will help you decide if the money management plan you are developing now has helped put you ahead.

Planning to Reach Your Goals

An important step in developing a money management plan is to set household and individual goals. Goals are wants, needs, and future objectives for your household and its members. Goals may be long-term, intermediate, or immediate.

Long-term goals are those you hope to reach in 10 to 20 years or perhaps even longer. Long-term goals are often considered first so that they can be incorporated into the plan from the start. They are guided by expected changes in your household's life cycle and must sometimes be adjusted for future expected income and price changes. Long-term goals include such things as paying off a mortgage, putting children through college, or providing for a comfortable retirement.

Intermediate goals are those to be reached within the next five years or so. These goals may reflect the changes that will occur due to your increased income or larger family. Intermediate goals might include such things as a down payment on a house, a new car, or increased life insurance.

Immediate goals are those to be reached within the next five years or so. These are basic needs that must be met even at the expense of some future goals. Immediate goals may include paying current bills, maintaining health insurance, and buying food and clothing.

Addressing goals in this order ensures savings for long-term and intermediate goals and prevents immediate goals from pushing future ones aside. If your income is low, you may be able to meet only immediate goals. But you still should make intermediate and long-term plans that could help you to get ahead in the future.

Decide Which Goals Are Most Important to You

Think carefully about your financial goals. Many of us would like to be financially secure, own a large home, drive a fancy car, educate ourselves or our children, take long vacations, and so on. Realistically, however, most of us cannot have it all. We must select and work toward those goals that are most important to us and the ones we will be able to obtain. The following process may help you work through your goal-selection decisions.

Set goals. Keep a listing of the goals that you and your family hope to achieve. Use Worksheet 2.

Rank goals. List your goals in their order of importance to you and your household.

Assign dollar values to goals. You will not be able to assign a dollar value to all goals now, but to most you will. For example, if you plan to buy a new car next year and you know the amount of the down payment, put this on your worksheet.

Reevaluate your goals. After developing your budget, take another look at Worksheet 2. You may need to drop, postpone, or revise some of your goals. Decide how much change you are willing and

able to make. For example, are you willing to change jobs or give up other goals in order to achieve a goal that is more important to you? Think about the tradeoffs of saving for long-term and intermediate goals versus using income for current expenses. How much choice do you have? Can you, and do you want to, cut down on some immediate goals (current expenses) to improve your chances of meeting your long-term goals? Refer to your goals often as you plan.

Common Goals Throughout the Life Cycle

Some goals are universal to all households, such as providing for sufficient food, comfortable shelter, and financial security. But most goals change as household members progress through the life cycle. When you are young and single, goals generally relate to your own personal development. When you are married and have children, your first priorities may switch from yourself to your children—establishing an education fund, for example. Different types of households use different ways to meet the same goal. For example, a retired couple may provide for their continued financial security during times of high inflation by cutting expenses. A young couple may seek higher paying employment instead.

Look over the following description of household types and determine which group your household resembles. Do you have goals similar to the ones stated for your group? Look at the goals for the other groups. They may help you anticipate future needs. This listing is not meant to be all-inclusive. However, it can be a starting point in determining your current and long-term goals and how those goals may change in years to come.

HOUSEHOLD TYPE 1: SINGLES. This household type consists of adults who have never married, or who are widowed or divorced. It includes persons from age 18 to 54 who are considered to be self-supporting, even though they may be living with relatives or friends and sharing some household expenses. Income for this group may not be high, particularly for the younger members. Important goals involve the individual's personal, educational, and financial development.

HOUSEHOLD TYPE 2: SINGLE PARENTS. Members of this household group may also have never married or are widowed or divorced. Unlike Type I household, they are parents living with dependent children. The critical financial goals for single parents often relate to the care of their children and themselves.

HOUSEHOLD TYPE 3: YOUNG COUPLES. This household type is often called the beginning family or the beginning marriage stage. It is a period of personal and financial adjustment for two persons. Ages of couples in this group typically range from about 18 to 34. There are no children and there are often two incomes. Important goals involve setting up a household and adjusting to each other's needs.

HOUSEHOLD TYPE 4: YOUNG FAMILIES. In this growing-family stage, parents are typically young—age 18 to 34—and have depen-

WORKSHEET 1: NET WORTH STATEMENT

ASSETS (WHAT YOU OWN)	FIRST YEAR	SECOND YEAR	LIABILITIES (WHAT YOU OWE)	FIRST YEAR	SECOND YEAR
Liquid					
Cash			Current bills		
Bank			Charge accounts		
Checking			Credit cards		
Savings			Taxes		
Certificates			Installments		
Other			Mortgages		
Savings bonds			Other		
Other bonds					
Corporate					
Municipal					
Utility					
Life insurance					
Mutual funds					
Other					
Other assets					
Retirement plans					
Private pension plan					
Profit-sharing plan					
Home					
Other real estate					
Car(s)					
Furniture					
Large appliances					
Antiques and art					
Jewelry					
Silverware					
Stamp or coin collection					
Debts others owe you					
Other					
Total Assets			**Total Liabilities**		

Net worth (Total assets minus total liabilities)

First Year: _____ – _____ = _____

Second Year: _____ – _____ = _____

WORKSHEET 2: PROJECTING GOALS

LONG-TERM AND INTERMEDIATE

Goal	Cost of Goal	Number of Years before Needed	Amount Already Saved	Amount to Save Each Year	Amount to Save Each Month
1.					
2.					
3.					
4.					
5.					
6.					
7.					
8.					
9.					
10.					
Total					

IMMEDIATE

Goal	Cost of Goal	Number of Years before Needed	Amount Already Saved	Amount to Save Each Year	Amount to Save Each Month
1.					
2.					
3.					
4.					
5.					
6.					
7.					
8.					
9.					
10.					
Total					

dent children in the household. There may be two incomes. Critical goals include protecting the family income and rearing the children.

HOUSEHOLD TYPE 5: MIDDLE FAMILIES. This household type is sometimes referred to the contracting family. Parents are typically 35 to 54 years old. Children are "leaving the nest" for college, careers, and marriage. Unique goals for this household include providing for children's college or vocational education, weddings, and the parents' eventual retirement.

HOUSEHOLD TYPE 6: MIDDLE COUPLES. This group consists of persons age 35 to 54 without children. This type of household often contains two earners. Income is often quite high, making investment maximization and tax minimization important financial goals.

HOUSEHOLD TYPE 7: OLDER SINGLES. This group contains persons age 55 and older who may be retired. There is no spouse present in the household. The majority of older singles are females. The major financial goal is to provide adequate income and reserves that will last for the balance of the older single's lifetime.

HOUSEHOLD TYPE 8: OLDER COUPLES. This group consists of married couples ages 55 and over who also may be retired. Their major financial goal is maintenance of an adequate level of living for both persons for life.

The Budgeting Process

A budget is a plan for spending and saving. It requires you to estimate your available income for a particular period of time and decide how to allocate this income toward your expenses. A working budget can help you implement your money management plan. A well-planned budget does several things for you and your household. It can help you:

❑ Prevent impulse spending.
❑ Decide what you can or cannot afford.

❑ Know where your money goes.
❑ Increase savings.
❑ Decide how to protect against the financial consequences of unemployment, accidents, sickness, aging, and death.

A working budget need not be complicated or rigid. However, preparing one takes planning, and following one takes determination. You must do several things to budget successfully.

First, communicate with other members of your household, including older children. Consider each person's needs and wants so that all family members feel they are a part of the plan. Everyone may work harder to make the budget a success and be less inclined to overspend if they realize the consequences. When families fail to communicate about money matters, it is unlikely that a budget will reflect a workable plan.

Second, be prepared to compromise. This is often difficult. Newlyweds, especially, may have problems. Each may have been living

WORKSHEET 3: ESTIMATING YOUR INCOME

SOURCE	JANUARY	FEBRUARY	MARCH	APRIL	MAY	JUNE
Net salary:*						
Household member 1						
Household member 2						
Household member 3						
Household member 4						
Social Security payments						
Pension payments						
Annuity payments						
Veterans' benefits						
Assistance payments						
Unemployment compensation						
Allowances						
Alimony						
Child support						
Gifts						
Interest						
Dividends						
Rents from real estate						
Other						
Monthly Totals						

* Net salary is the amount that comes into the household for spending and saving after taxes, Social Security, and other deductions.

on an individual income and not be accustomed to sharing, or may have been in school and dependent on parents. If, for example, one wants to save for things and the other prefers buying on credit, the two will need to discuss the pros and cons of both methods and decide on a middle ground that each can accept. A plan cannot succeed unless there is a financial partnership.

Third, exercise willpower. Try not to indulge in unnecessary spending. Once your budget plan is made, opportunities to overspend will occur daily. Each household member needs to encourage the others to stick to the plan.

Fourth, develop a good recordkeeping system. At first, all members of the household may need to keep records of what they spend. This will show how well they are following the plan and will allow intermediate adjustments in the level of spending. Recordkeeping is especially important during the first year of a spending plan, when you are trying to find a budget that works

best for you. Remember, a good budget is flexible, requires little clerical time, and most importantly, works for you.

Choosing a Budget Period

A budget may cover any convenient period of time—a month, three months, or year, for example. Make sure the period you use is long enough to cover the bulk of household expenses and income. Remember, not all bills come due monthly and every household experiences some seasonal expenses. Most personal budgets are for 12 months. You can begin the 12-month period at any time during the year. If this is your first budget, you may want to set up a trial plan for a shorter time to see how it works.

After setting up your plan, subdivide it into more manageable operating periods. For a yearly budget, divide income and expenses

JULY	AUGUST	SEPTEMBER	OCTOBER	NOVEMBER	DECEMBER	YEARLY TOTALS

by 12, 24, 26, or 52, depending on your pay schedule or when your bills come due. Most paychecks are received weekly or every two weeks. Although most bills come due once a month, not all are due at the same time in the month. Try using each paycheck to pay your daily expenses and expenses that will be due within the next week or two. This way you will be able to pay your bills on time. You may also want to allocate something from each paycheck toward large expenses that will be coming due soon.

Developing a Successful Budget

STEP 1: ESTIMATE YOUR INCOME. Total the money you expect to receive during the budget period. Use Worksheet 3 as a guide in estimating your household income. Begin with regular income that you and your family receive—wages, salaries, income earned from a farm or other business, Social Security benefits, pension payments, alimony, child support, veterans' benefits, public assistance payments, unemployment compensation, allowances, and any other income. Include variable income, such as interest from bank accounts and investments, dividends from stock and insurance, rents from property you own, gifts, and money from any other sources.

If your earnings are irregular, it may be difficult to estimate your income. It is better to underestimate than overestimate income when setting up a budget. Some households have sufficient income, but its receipt does not coincide with the arrival of bills. For these households, planning is very important.

STEP 2: ESTIMATE YOUR EXPENSES. After you have determined how much your income will be for the planning period, estimate your expenses. You may want to group expenses into one of three categories: fixed, flexible, or set-asides. Fixed expenses are payments that are basically the same amounts each month. Fixed regular expenses include such items as rent or mortgage payments, taxes, and credit installment payments. Fixed irregular expenses are large payments due once or twice a year, such as insurance premiums. Flexible expenses vary from one month to the next, such as amounts spent on food, clothing, utilities, and transportation. Set-asides are variable amounts of money accumulated for special purposes, such as for season expenses, savings and emergency funds, and intermediate and long-term goals.

Use old records, receipts, bills, and cancelled checks to estimate future expenses, if you are satisfied with what your dollars have done for you and your family in the past. If you are not satisfied, now is the time for change. Consider which expenses can be cut back and which expenses need to be increased. If you spent a large amount on entertainment, for example, your new budget may reallocate some of this money to a savings account to contribute to some of your future goals.

If you do not have past records of spending, or if this is your first budget, the most accurate way to find out how much you will need to allow for each expense is to keep a record of your household spending. Carry a pocket notebook in which you jot down expenditures during a week or pay period and total the amounts at the end of each week. You may prefer to keep an account book in a convenient place at home and make entries in it. Kept faithfully

for a month or two, the record can help you find out what you spend for categories such as food, housing, utilities, household operation, clothing, transportation, entertainment, and personal items. Use this record to estimate expenses in your plan for future spending. You also need to plan for new situations and changing conditions that increase or decrease expenses. For example, the cost of your utilities may go up.

Total your expenses for a year and divide to determine the amounts that you will have to allocate toward each expense during the budgeting period. Record your estimate for each budgetary expense in the space provided on Worksheet 4. Begin with the regular fixed expenses that you expect to have. Next, enter those fixed expenses that come due once or twice a year. Many households allocate a definite amount each budget period toward these expenses to spread out the cost.

One way to meet major expenses is to set aside money regularly before you start to spend. Keep your set-aside funds separate from other funds so you will not be tempted to spend them impulsively. If possible, put them in an account where they will earn interest. You may also plan at this point to set aside a certain amount toward the long-term and intermediate goals you listed on Worksheet 2. Saving could be almost as enjoyable as spending, once you accept the idea that saving money is not punishment but a systematic way of reaching your goals. You do without some things now in anticipation of buying what will give you greater satisfaction later.

You may want to clear up debts now by doubling up on your installment payments or putting aside an extra amount in your savings fund to be used for this purpose. Also, when you start to budget, consider designating a small amount of money for emergencies. Extras always come up at the most inopportune times. Every household experiences occasional minor crises too small to be covered by insurance but too large to be absorbed into the day-to-day budget. Examples may be a blown-out tire or an appliance that needs replacing. Decide how large a cushion you want for meeting emergencies. As your fund reaches the figure you have allowed for emergencies, you can start saving for something else. Now, record money allocated for occasional major expenses, future goals, savings, emergencies, and any other set-asides in the space provided for them on Worksheet 4.

After you have entered your fixed expenses and your set-asides, you are ready to consider your flexible expenses. Consider including here a personal allowance or "mad money" for each member of the household. A little spending money that does not have to be accounted for gives everyone a sense of freedom and takes some of the tedium out of budgeting.

STEP 3: BALANCE. Now you are ready for the balancing act. Compare your total expected income with the total of your planned expenses for the budget period. If your planned budget equals your estimated future income, are you satisfied with this outcome? Have you left enough leeway for emergencies and errors? If your expenses add up to more than your income, look again at all parts of the plan. Where can you cut down? Where are you overspending? You may have to decide which things are most important to you and which ones can wait. You may be able to do some trimming on your flexible expenses.

WORKSHEET 4: EXPENSE ESTIMATE AND BUDGET BALANCING SHEET, FIXED EXPENSES (PREPARE FOR EACH MONTH)

MONTH _____

	Amount Estimated	Amount Spent	Difference
Rent			
Mortgage			
Installments:			
Credit card 1			
Credit card 2			
Credit card 3			
Automobile loan			
Personal loan			
Student loan			
Insurance:			
Life			
Health			
Property			
Automobile			
Disability			
Set-asides:			
Emergency fund			
Major expenses			
Goals			
Savings and investments			
Allowances			
Education:			
Tuition			
Books			
Transportation:			
Repairs			
Gas and oil			
Parking and tolls			
Bus and taxi			
Recreation			
Gifts			
Other			

TOTAL FIXED EXPENSES FOR MONTH

Once you have cut back your flexible expenses, scan your fixed expenses. Maybe you can make some sizable reductions here, too. Rent is a big item in a budget. Some households may want to consider moving to a lower priced apartment or making different living arrangements. Others turn in a too-expensive car and seek less expensive transportation. Look back at Worksheet 2. You may need to reallocate some of this income to meet current expenses. Perhaps you may have to consider saving for some of your goals at a later date.

If you have cut back as much as you think you can or are willing to do and your plan still calls for more than you make, consider ways to increase your income. You may want to look for a better-paying job, or a part-time second job may be the answer. If only one spouse is employed, consider becoming a dual-earner family. The children may be able to earn their school lunch and extra spending money by doing odd jobs in your neighborhood, such as cutting grass or babysitting. Older children can work part-time on weekends to help out. Another possibility, especially for short-term problems, is to draw on savings. These are decisions each individual household has to make.

If your income exceeds your estimate of expenses—good! You may decide to satisfy more of your immediate wants or to increase the amount your family is setting aside for future goals.

Carrying Out Your Budget

After your plan is completed, put it to work. This is when your determination must really come into play. Can you and your family resist impulse spending?

BECOME A GOOD CONSUMER. A vital part of carrying out the budget is being a good consumer. Learn to get the most for your money, to recognize quality, to avoid waste, and to realize time costs as well as money costs in making consumer decisions.

KEEP ACCURATE RECORDS. Accurate financial records are necessary to keep track of your household's actual money inflow and outgo. A successful system requires cooperation from everyone in the household. Receipts can be kept and entered at the end of each budget period in a "Monthly Expense Record" (Worksheet 5). It is sometimes a good idea to write on the back of each receipt what the purchase was for, who made it, and the date. Decide which family member will be responsible for paying bills or making purchases and decide who will keep the record system up to date.

The household business recordkeeping system does not need to be complex. The simpler it is, the more likely it will be kept current. Store your records in one place—a set of folders in a file drawer or other fire-resistant box is a good place. You can assemble a folder for each of several categories including budget, food, clothing, housing, insurance, investments, taxes, health, transportation, and credit. Use these folders for filing insurance policies, receipts, warranties, cancelled checks, bank statements, purchase contracts, and other important papers. Many households also rent a safe deposit box at the bank for storing deeds, stock certificates, and other valuable items.

WORKSHEET 5: MONTHLY EXPENSE RECORD

MONTH:

YEAR:

DATE	EXPENSE ITEM	MORTGAGE/ RENT	HOUSEHOLD	UTILITIES	FOOD	CLOTHING	TRANSPORTATION	CHILD CARE	MEDICAL
TOTAL									

SAVINGS DEBTS	INSURANCE	EDUCATION	PERSONAL CARE	RECREATION	GIFTS	BUSINESS RELATED	OTHER: TAXES, ALLOWANCES, LEGAL FEES

Evaluating Your Budget

The information on Worksheet 4 can help you determine whether your actual spending follows your plan. If your first plan did not work in all respects, do not be discouraged. A budget is not something you make once and never touch again. Keep revising until results satisfy you.

A

AaBC-X model of family stress See *Double ABC-X model of family stress.*

aberration A departure from what is culturally defined as "normal" behavior.

abortion The termination of a pregnancy either through miscarriage (spontaneous abortion) or through human intervention (induced abortion).

abstinence Refraining from sexual intercourse, often on religious or moral grounds.

abuelo [fem. -a] [Spanish] Grandfather; grandmother.

abuelos [Spanish] Grandparents.

abuse Mistreatment; wrong, bad, injurious, or excessive use.

acculturation The process of adapting to the patterns or customs of a different, usually dominant, culture.

acquaintance rape Rape in which the assailant is personally known to the victim.

adaptability Ability to adjust relationships, roles, and rules to changing circumstances.

adolescence The psychological state occurring during puberty.

adoption The process by which an individual or couple legally become the parents of a child not biologically their own.

adultery Sexual intercourse between a married person and someone other than his or her spouse.

affiliate To take in or adopt as a member.

affiliated family A family in which non-related individuals are treated as family members.

affinity 1. Relationship by marriage. 2. A close relationship.

affirmative action Programs that attempt to place qualified members of minorities in government, corporate, and educational institutions from which they have been historically excluded because of their minority status.

afterbirth The placenta and fetal membranes expelled from the uterus during the third stage of labor.

afterplay Erotic activity, such as kissing, caressing, sex talk, and oral/genital contact, following coitus.

agape According to sociologist John Lee's styles of love, altruistic love.

agglutination test A urine analysis test used to determine the presence of human chorionic gonadotropin (HCG) secreted by the placenta, which is an indication of pregnancy.

AIDS Acquired Immune Deficiency Syndrome. A generally fatal infection caused by the human immunodeficiency virus (HIV), which suppresses the immune system. Transmitted primarily through semen and blood.

alcoholism An illness characterized by preoccupation with alcohol and loss of control over its consumption so as to usually lead to intoxication, repetition, progression, and a tendency for relapse.

alimony Court-ordered monetary support to a spouse or former spouse following separation or divorce.

alpha-feto protein (AFP) screening Test(s) of a pregnant woman's blood that can reveal neural tube defects in the fetus.

amniocentesis A process in which amniotic fluid is removed by syringe to determine possible birth defects.

amniotic fluid The fluid surrounding the developing embryo or fetus within the amniotic sac.

amniotic sac A fluid-filled membrane pouch enclosing the fetus.

ampulla The upper part of the vas deferens, which contracts during emission.

anal intercourse Penetration of the anus by the penis.

androgynous gender role A gender role concept emphasizing flexibility in combining instrumental and expressive traits in accordance with individual differences.

androgyny The state of having flexible gender roles combining instrumental and expressive traits in accordance with unique individual differences.

annulment The legal invalidation of a marriage as if the marriage never occurred.

anus The orifice for the elimination of fecal matter.

artificial insemination Introduction of semen into the vagina by artificial means, usually a syringe.

artificial insemination by donor (AID) Artificial insemination using semen from someone other than the woman's partner, usually because of sterility or high risk of birth defect; also known as *therapeutic donor insemination (TDI)*.

Asian American Collective term relating to those of Asian descent, such as Chinese American, Japanese American, Korean American, or Cambodian American.

assimilation Process by which individuals or groups adopt another group's culture and lose their original identity.

asymptomatic Not showing symptoms.

attachment Close, enduring emotional bonds.

atypical sexual behavior A sexual behavior that departs from the norm; a sexual variation.

authoritarian parenting A parenting style characterized by the demand for absolute obedience.

authoritative parenting A parenting style that recognizes the parent's legitimate power and also stresses the child's feelings, individuality, and need to develop autonomy.

autoeroticism Self stimulation or erotic behavior involving only the self; usually refers to masturbation, but also includes erotic dreams and fantasies.

B

barrier method Any of a number of contraceptive methods that place a physical barrier between sperm and egg, such as the condom, diaphragm, and cervical cap.

Bartholin's glands Two small secretory glands on either side of the vaginal entrance.

basal body temperature (BBT) method   A contraceptive method based on variations of the woman's resting body temperature, which rises 24 to 72 hours before ovulation.

basic conflict   Pronounced disagreement about fundamental marital roles, tasks, and functions. Cf. *nonbasic conflict.*

battered woman   A woman who has been repeatedly and systematically subjected to battering by her spouse or partner.

battering   Violent acts, such as hitting, slapping, beating, stabbing, or shooting.

BBT method   See *basal body temperature.*

bereavement   The response to a loved one's death, including customs, rituals, and the grieving process.

Billings method   See *mucus method.*

binuclear family   A postdivorce family with children, consisting of two nuclear families, one headed by the mother, the other by the father.

bipolar gender roles   The idea that male and female gender roles are polar opposites, with males possessing exclusively instrumental traits and females possessing exclusively expressive traits.

birth canal   The vagina, through which the fetus exits at birth.

birth control   Devices, drugs, techniques or surgical procedures used to prevent conception or implantation or to terminate pregnancy.

birth rate   See *crude birth rate.*

bisexual   Sexual involvement with both sexes, usually sequentially rather than during the same time period.

blastocyst   An early stage of the fertilized egg, containing about 100 cells; the blastocyst implants itself into the uterine lining.

blended family   A family consisting of two adults and one or more children from an earlier marriage or relationship. Also known as a *reconstituted family* or *stepfamily.*

boundary   In systems theory, the emotional or physical separation between subsystems or roles required for adequate functioning.

Braxton Hicks contractions   Uterine contractions that occur periodically throughout pregnancy and also initiate effacement and dilation of the cervix at the beginning of labor.

breakthrough bleeding   Erratic bleeding, also called "spotting," which takes place at times other than the usual menstrual period.

breech presentation   A fetal position in which the baby enters the birth canal buttocks or feet first.

bride price   The goods, services, or money a family receives in exchange for giving their daughter in marriage.

bundling   A colonial Puritan courtship custom in which a couple slept together with a board separating them.

C

calendar method   A fertility awareness method based on calculating "safe" days according to the range of a woman's longest and shortest menstrual cycles; also known as the *rhythm method.*

candidiasis   A yeast infection caused by the *Candida albicans* organism; also called *moniliasis* and *yeast infection.*

case study   The in-depth examination of an individual or small group in clinical treatment in order to gather data and formulate hypotheses. Also known as *clinical study.*

celibacy   Abstinence.

cervical cap   A thimble-shaped cap that fits snugly over the cervix to prevent conception.

cervix   The narrow, lower end of the uterus that opens into the vagina.

cesarean section   Surgical delivery of the child through an incision in the mother's abdominal and uterine walls.

chancre   A painless sore or ulcer that may be the first symptom of syphilis.

chastity   The state of being morally or sexually pure.

Chicano   [fem. **-a**] A Mexican-American.

child-free marriage   A marriage in which the partners have chosen not to have children.

child neglect   Failure to provide adequate or proper physical or emotional care for a child.

child snatching   The kidnapping of one's own children, usually by the non-custodial parent.

child support   Court-ordered financial support by the non-custodial parent to pay or assist in paying expenses incurred by the custodial parent in childrearing.

chlamydia   A common sexually transmitted disease affecting the urinary tract or other organs.

chorionic villus sampling   Surgical removal through the cervix of a tiny piece of embryonic membrane to be analyzed for genetic defects.

chromosomes   The genetic material in the cell nucleus guiding the cell's development and division.

cilia   Hairlike filaments in the fallopian tubes that propel the ovum toward the uterus.

circumcision   The surgical removal of the foreskin.

Circumplex Model   Model of family functioning in which cohesion, adaptability, and communication are the most important dimensions.

clinical study   The in-depth examination of an individual or small group in clinical treatment in order to gather data and formulate hypotheses. Also known as *case study.*

clitoral glans   See *glans clitoridis.*

clitoral hood   A fold of skin from the labia covering the clitoris.

clitoris   An erotically sensitive organ located at the upper end of the vulva above the urethral opening.

cognition   The mental processes, such as thought and reflection, that occur between the moment we receive a stimulus and the moment we respond to it.

cognitive development   A model of child development in which growth is viewed as the mastery of specific ways of perceiving, thinking, and doing that occur at discrete stages.

cognitive social learning   A theory emphasizing the learning of behavior from others through positive and negative reinforcement.

cohabitation   The sharing of living quarters by two heterosexual, gay, or lesbian individuals who are involved in an ongoing emotional and sexual relationship.

cohesion   Binding together.

cohort   A group of persons experiencing a specific event at the same time, such as a birth cohort consisting of persons born in the same year.

coitus   Sexual intercourse.

coitus interruptus   The withdrawal of the penis from the vagina immediately before ejaculation; considered ineffective as a contraceptive measure.

colostrum   A nutritionally rich fluid secreted by the breasts the first few days following childbirth.

comadre   [Spanish] The godmother of one's child (literally, co-mother).

compadrazgo   [Spanish] The Latino institution of godparentage (literally, co-parentage).

compadre   [Spanish] The godfather of one's child (literally, co-father).

compadres   [Spanish] The godparents of one's child.

commuter marriage   A marriage in which couples who prefer living together live apart in pursuit of separate goals.

companionate family   A family characterized by shared decision-making, emotional expressiveness, and democratic child-rearing.

companionate love   A form of love emphasizing intimacy and commitment.

companionate marriage   A marriage characterized by shared decision-making and emotional and sexual expressiveness.

comparable worth   An economic model arguing that occupations traditionally employing women are compensated at a lower rate than those traditonally employing men as a result of sex discriminatiom and that to overcome income differences between men and women, pay should be based on experience, knowledge and skills, mental demands, accountability, and working conditions, not on specific occupations per se.

complementary marriage model   A model in which male employment outside the home and female work within the home are viewed as separate but interdependent.

conception   The union of sperm and ovum; impregnation.

condom   A sheath made from latex rubber or animal intestine that fits over the erect penis to prevent the deposit of sperm in the vagina; used as a contraceptive device and also as prophylaxis against sexually transmitted diseases (latex condoms only).

conflict-habituated marriage   An enduring marriage marked by continuous conflict.

conflict theory   A theory examining how individuals, groups, or organizations with competing interests interact with each other or the social structure and how these interactions lead to change.

congenital   From birth.

conjugal   Of marriage.

conjugal extended family   Extended family formed through marriages.

conjugal family   Family consisting of husband, wife, and children. See also *nuclear family*.

consanguineous   Of the same ancestry.

consanguineous extended family   An extended family formed through blood ties.

contraception   Devices, techniques or drugs used to prevent conception.

contraceptive sponge   A barrier device containing a spermicide that is inserted into the vagina prior to intercourse.

contraction   Tightening of a muscle.

contraindication   A symptom, sign or condition that indicates that a particular drug or device should not be used.

conventionality   In marriage and family research, the tendency of subjects to give conventional or conformist responses.

coping   The process of utilizing resources in response to stress

corona   The rim at the base of the glans penis.

corpora cavernosa   Two cylindrical bodies in the penis which fill with blood to produce an erection.

corpus spongiosum   A spongy cylindrical body in the penis which contains the urethra and fills with blood to produce an erection.

courtship   The process by which a commitment to marriage is developed.

couvade   The psychological or ritualistic assumption of symptoms of pregnancy and childbirth by the male.

Cowper's glands   Two glands in the male which secrete a clear substance during sexual excitement.

crisis   A turning point; a crucial time, stage, or event. See also *predictable crisis* and *unpredictable crisis*.

crisis model   A theoretical construct for studying family strengths, based on the family's ability to function during times of high stress.

crude birth rate (CBR)   The number of births in a single year, divided by the mid-year population, and multiplied by 1000. See also *fertility* and *fertility rate*.

crude death rate (CDR)   The number of deaths in a single year, divided by the mid-year population, and multiplied by 1000. See also *fertility* and *fertility rate*.

culpotomy   A technique of female sterilization in which the fallopian tubes are cut through an incision at the back of the vagina.

culture of poverty   The view that the poor form a qualitatively different culture from the larger society and that their culture accounts for their poverty.

cunnilingus   Oral stimulation of the female genitals.

custodial   Having physical or legal custody of a child. Cf. *non-custodial*.

custody   The care of a child. See also *joint custody*, *sole custody*, and *split custody*.

cycle of violence   The recurring three-phase battering cycle of (1) tension building, (2) explosion, (3) reconciliation.

cystitis   A urinary tract infection usually affecting women.

D

dating   A process in which two individuals meet to engage in activities together; dating may be either exclusive or non-exclusive.

Day of the Dead   See *el Dia de los Muertos*.

D&C   Dilation and curettage.

D&E Dilation and evacuation.

death rate See *crude death rate*.

deferred parenthood The intentional postponement of childbearing until after certain goals have been fulfilled.

demographics The demographic characteristics of a population, such as family size, marriage and divorce rates, and ethnic and racial composition.

demography The study of population and population characteristics, such as family size, marriage and divorce rates, and ethnic and racial composition.

denial The conscious or unconscious refusal to recognize painful acts, situations, or ways of being.

dependent variable A variable that is observed or measured.

DES Diethylstilbestrol.

desire Erotic sensations or feelings which motivate a person to seek out or receive sexual experiences.

developmental interaction A socialization theory stressing the reciprocal nature of parents' and children's growth; development is seen as a lifelong process.

developmental perspective An approach which emphasizes the family's changing roles and relationships over time, beginning with marriage and ending when both spouses have died.

developmental task Appropriate activities and responsibilities individuals learn at different stages in the life cycle.

deviant Departing from social or cultural norms.

devitalized marriage An enduring marriage characterized by a lack of intimacy in contrast to earlier years.

el Dia de los Muertos [Spanish] The Day of the Dead, Latino and Latin American holiday with Indian and Catholic roots honoring the dead, celebrated on November 1.

Diagnostic and Statistic Manual of Mental Disorders (DSM-IV) A manual published by the American Psychiatric Association establishing categories of psychiatric disorders and listing criteria for diagnosing such disorders.

diaphragm A flexible rubber cup placed in the vagina to block the passage of sperm, preventing conception.

diethylstilbestrol (DES) A synthetic estrogen ($C_{18}H_{20}O_2$) designed to prevent miscarriage that is associated with various reproductive abnormalities in the adult children of women who have taken it.

dilation Opening of the cervix.

dilation and curettage (D&C) First trimester abortion technique in which the embryo is removed from the uterus with a sharp instrument (curette).

dilation and evacuation (D&E) Second trimester abortion technique in which suction and forceps are used to remove the fetus.

disability A physical or developmental limitation. Preferred usage over "handicap."

discrimination The process of acting differently toward a person or group because the individual or group belongs to a minority.

displaced homemaker A full-time homemaker who has lost economic support from her husband as a result of divorce or widowhood.

distress Psychological and physical tension, such as intense upset, mood changes, headaches, and muscular tension.

division of labor The interdependence of persons with specialized tasks and abilities. Within the family, labor is traditionally divided along gender lines. Increasing female employment is leading to pressure for a more egalitarian or equitable division of household labor. See also *complementary marriage model*.

divorce The legal dissolution of marriage. Cf. *separation*.

domestic partners act Law granting certain legal rights similar to those of married couples to committed cohabitants, whether heterosexual, gay, or lesbian.

double ABC-X model Model describing stress, in which A*a* represents stressor pile up, B represents family coping resources, C represents perception of stressor pile up, and X represents outcome.

double standard of aging The devaluation of women in contrast to men in terms of attractiveness as they age.

douching Introducing water or liquid into the vagina for medical, or hygienic, or contraceptive reasons.

Down's syndrome A chromosomal error characterized by mental retardation.

dowry The property a woman brings to her husband upon marriage. [Archaic] A man's gift to his bride. Cf. *bride price*.

DSM-IV See *Diagnostic and Statistical Manual of Mental Disorders*.

dual-career family A type of dual-earner family in which both husband and wife are committed to careers.

dual-earner family A family in which both husband and wife are employed. Also known as dual-worker family.

dual-worker family A dual-earner family.

duration of marriage effect Accumulation over time of various factors, such as poor communication, unresolved conflict, and role overload, on marital satisfaction.

dyad A two-member group; a couple.

Dyadic Adjustment Scale A survey instrument developed by Graham Spanier which measures relationship satisfaction.

dysfunction Impaired or inadequate functioning, as in sexual dysfunction.

dyspareunia Painful sexual intercourse.

E

eclampsia Life threatening condition of late pregnancy brought on by untreated high blood pressure.

ecological model of family violence Model that examines the child's development within the family context and the family's development within the community to assess the risk of violence.

economic adequacy The psychological perception that one has sufficient income and economic resources.

ectopic pregnancy A pregnancy in which the fertilized egg implants in a fallopian tube instead of the uterus.

edema Fluid retention and swelling.

effacement Thinning of the cervix during labor.

egalitarian gender roles Gender roles in which men and women are treated equally.

ego dystonic homosexuality A psychiatric disorder in which an individual has a persistent desire to switch from a gay or lesbian to a heterosexual orientation because of the distress his or her homosexuality causes.

ejaculate [noun] Semen.

ejaculation The expulsion of semen during orgasm.

embryo In human beings, the early development of life between about one week and two months after conception.

emission The first stage of male orgasm during which the semen moves into the urethra.

empty nest syndrome A crisis experienced by parents as a result of grown children leaving home.

endogamy Marriage within one's social group. See also *exogamy.*

endometriosis A condition in which endometrial tissue grows outside the uterus.

engagement A pledge to marry.

epididymis Structure within the testis where sperm mature and are stored prior to ejaculation.

episiotomy An incision from the vagina toward the anus made to prevent tearing during childbirth.

equity theory A theory emphasizing that social exchanges must be fair or equally beneficial over the long run.

erectile dysfunction Inability or difficulty in achieving erection.

erection An erect penis.

eros 1. From the Greek eros [love], the fusion of love and sexuality. 2. According to sociologist John Lee's styles of love, the passionate love of beauty.

erotic Pertaining to sexuality, sensuality or sexual sensations.

estrogen Any of a group of hormones produced primarily by the ovaries which are significant in controlling the menstrual cycle, maintaining the vaginal lining, and producing breast growth during puberty. Also present in smaller amounts in the male.

ethnic group A large group of people distinct from others because of cultural characteristics, such as language, religion, and customs, transmitted from one generation to another.

ethnic stratification The hierarchal ranking of groups in superior and inferior positions according to ethnicity.

ethnicity Ethnic affiliation or identity.

ethnocentrism The emotionally-charged belief that one's ethnic group, nation, or culture is superior to all others. See also *racism.*

exchange/social control model of family violence Model that views abuser as weighing costs versus rewards and using violence if social controls (costs) are not strong enough to discourage it.

exchange theory See *social exchange theory.*

excitement phase In the sexual response cycle, the second stage, denoting sexual arousal.

exogamy Marriage outside one's social group. See also *endogamy.*

expressive traits Supportive or emotional traits or characteristics.

extended family The family unit of the parent/child nuclear family and other kin, such as grandparents, uncles, aunts, and cousins. See also **conjugal extended family** and *consanguineous extended family.*

extramarital Outside or in addition to the marital relationship.

F

FAE See *fetal alcohol effect.*

fallopian tubes Two tubes that extend from the ovaries to the uterus. After ovulation, an ovum moves through a fallopian tube, where fertilization may take place.

la familia [Spanish] Family. In Latino culture, a pattern of social organization which emphasizes the family and strong feelings centering on the family. See also *familialism.*

familialism A pattern of social organization in which family and strong feelings for the family are important.

family A unit of two or more persons, of which one or more may be children, who are related by blood, marriage, or affiliation, and who cooperate economically and share a common dwelling place.

family ecosystem Family interactions and adaptations with the larger social environment, such as schools, neighborhoods, or the economy.

family hardship Difficulties specifically associated with a stressor. See *also* **stressor.**

family life cycle A developmental approach which emphasizes the family's changing roles and relationships over time, beginning with marriage and ending when both spouses have died.

family of marriage The family an individual forms by marrying. Also called **family of procreation.** Cf. *family of orientation.*

family migration The geographical movement of a family.

family of orientation The family in which a person is reared as a child. Cf. *family of marriage*

family of origin See *family of orientation.*

family policy A set of objectives concerning family well being and specific measures initiated by government to achieve them.

family power Power exercised by individuals in their family roles as mother, father, child, or sibling.

family of procreation See *family of marriage.*

family role A social role within the family, such as husband or wife, father or mother. See also *kinship role.*

family rule A family's patterned or characteristic response to events, situations, or persons. See also *family systems theory, meta-rule,* and *hierarchy of rules.*

family stress An upset in the steady functioning of the family.

family systems theory A theory holding that family structure is created by the pattern of interactions between its various parts and that individual actions are strongly influenced by the family context.

family tree Diagramatic representation of family and ancestors.

family work The unpaid work that is undertaken by family members to sustain the family, such as housework, laundry, and other chores.

fantasy The realm of imagination.

FAS See *fetal alcohol syndrome.*

fecundity A person's maximum biological capacity to reproduce.

feedback A process in which the factors that produce a result are themselves modified by the result.

fellatio Oral stimulation of the male genitals.

feminism 1. The principle that women should have equal political, social, and economic rights with men. 2. The social movement to obtain for women political, social, and economic equality with men.

feminization of poverty The shift of poverty to females.

fertility The ability to conceive; a person's actual reproductive performance.

fertility awareness methods Contraceptive method based on predicting a woman's fertile period and either avoiding intercourse or using an additional method of contraception during that interval.

fertility rate The number of live births per 1000 women aged 15–44 years. See *birth rate*.

fertilization Union of the egg and sperm. Also known as conception.

fetal alcohol effect (FAE) Growth retardation caused by the mother's chronic ingestion of alcohol during pregnancy.

fetal alcohol syndrome (FAS) A syndrome that may be characterized by unusual facial characteristics, small head and body size, poor mental capacities and abnormal behavior patterns and is caused by the mother's chronic ingestion of alcohol during pregnancy.

fetus The unborn young of a vertebrate; the human embryo becomes a fetus at about the eighth week.

fictive kin Nonrelated individuals who are treated as if they were related; pseudokin.

field of eligibles A group of individuals of the same general background and age who are potential marital partners.

filial crisis Psychological conflict and stress experienced by adult children when aged parents become dependent on them.

fimbriae Delicate, hairlike projections extending from the end of the fallopian tube toward the ovary.

flextime Flexible work schedules determined by employee/employer agreement.

foreplay Erotic activity prior to coitus, such as kissing, carressing, sex talk, and oral/genital contact; petting.

foreskin The sleeve of skin covering the tip of the penis; prepuce.

G

gamete A reproductive cell (sperm or ovum) that can unite with another gamete to form a zygote.

gamete intrafallopian transfer (GIFT) Sperm and eggs collected from parents and deposited in fallopian tube for fertilization.

gay Pertaining to same sex relationships, especially among males. Cf. *lesbian*.

gay male A male sexually oriented toward other males.

gender Biologically, the division into male and female; sex.

gender identity The psychological sense of whether one is male or female.

gender role The traits and behaviors based on biological gender assigned to males and females by a culture.

gender role attitudes The beliefs people have of themselves and others regarding appropriate male and female zpersonality traits and behaviors.

gender role behavior The actual activities or behaviors in which males or females engage according to their gender roles.

gender role stereotype A rigidly held and oversimplified belief that all males and females possess distinctive psychological and behavioral traits as a result of their gender.

gender schema The cognitive organization of individuals, behaviors, traits, objects, and such by gender.

gender theory A theory in which gender is viewed as the basis of hierarchal social relations and justifies greater power to males.

generation 1. The approximately 30-year period between the birth of one generation and the next. 2. A group of people born and living during the same general time period.

genital herpes A sexually transmitted disease caused by the herpes simplex virus type II, similar to cold sores or fever blisters but appearing on the genitals.

genitals The external sex or reproductive organs.

genital warts Warts on the genitals caused by human papilloma virus (HPV), a sexually transmitted virus.

genogram A diagram of the emotional relationships of a family through several generations.

gestational edema-proteinuria-hypertension complex A condition of pregnancy characterized by high blood pressure, toxemia, or pre-eclampsia.

getting together A courtship process in which men and women congregate ("get together") in groups to socialize or engage in common activities or projects. Cf. *dating*.

GIFT See *gamete intrafallopian transfer*.

glans clitoridis The visible, erotically sensitive tip of the clitoris. Also known as *clitoral glans*.

glans penis The erotically sensitive tip of the penis.

gonad An ovary or testis.

gonadotropin A type of hormone secreted by the pituitary gland that affects the gonads.

gonorrhea A sexually transmitted disease caused by the *Neisseria gonorrhoeae* bacterium that initially infects the urethra in males and the cervix in females, or the throat or anus in either sex, depending on the mode of sexual interaction.

Gräfenberg spot An erotically sensitive area on the anterior wall of the vagina midway between the introitus and cervix.

grandparenting Performing the functions of a grandparent.

grieving process Emotional responses and expressions of feeling over the death of a loved one.

guilt The state or feeling that one has done something wrong.

H

halo effect The tendency to infer positive characteristics or traits based on a person's physical attractiveness.

handicap See *disability*.

Hegar's sign A softening of the uterus just above the cervix which may be an early indication of pregnancy.

hierarchy of rules The ranking of rules in order of significance.

health The state of physical and mental well-being.

hepatitis A liver disease causing blood pigments to accumulate. Type B (serum) hepatitis may be sexually transmitted.

herpes simplex type II See *genital herpes*.

heterogamy Marriage between those with different social or personal characteristics. See also *homogamy*.

heterosexuality Sexual orientation toward members of the other sex.

heterosociality Close association with members of the other sex.

Hispanic A person of Spanish or Latin American origin or background; may be of any race. See also *Latino.*

HIV Human immunodeficiency virus.

HIV-positive Infected with HIV.

homemaker 1. A person who manages the home. 2. A housewife.

homeostasis A social group's tendency to maintain internal stability through coordinated responses to compensate for environmental changes.

homogamy Marriage between those with similar social or personal characteristics. See also *heterogamy.*

homophobia Fear or hatred of gay males or lesbians.

homosexuality Sexual orientation toward members of the same sex. See also *gay male* and *lesbian.*

homosociality The tendency to associate mostly with members of the same sex.

hormone A chemical substance, secreted by the endocrine glands into the bloodstream, which organizes and regulates physical development.

hospice A place or program caring for the terminally ill, emphasizing both patient care and family support.

housewife 1. A person who manages the home. 2. A homemaker.

HSD See *hypoactive sexual desire.*

human chorionic gonadotropin (HCG) A hormone secreted by the placenta.

human immunodeficiency virus (HIV) The virus causing AIDS.

human papilloma virus (HPV) The virus causing warts, including genital warts.

hymen Thin membrane that may partially cover the vaginal opening prior to first intercourse.

hypoactive sexual desire (HSD) Inactive or limited sexual desire. Formerly known as *inhibited sexual desire.*

hypothesis An unproven theory or proposition tentatively accepted to explain a collection of facts. See *working hypothesis.*

hysterectomy The surgical removal of the uterus or part of the uterus.

hysterotomy A surgical method of abortion in which the fetus is removed through an abdominal incision.

I

identity An individual's core sense of self.

identity bargaining The process of role adjustment, involving identifying with a role, interacting with others in that role, and negotiating changes in the role.

illegitimate Not based on law, right, or custom. Formerly, born outside of marriage.

incest Sexual intercourse between individuals too closely related to marry, usually interpreted to mean father/daughter, mother/son, or brother/sister.

independent variable A variable that may be changed.

induced abortion The termination of a pregnancy through human intervention.

ie [pronounced *ee-eh*] The basic family unit in traditional Japanese society consisting of past, present, and future members of the extended family and their households.

infertility The inability to conceive after trying for a year or more.

inhibited sexual desire See *hypoactive sexual desire.*

institution An enduring social structure built around a significant and distinct cluster of social values. Institutions include the family, religion, education, and government.

intrafamilial sexual abuse Sexual activities within the family or extended family involving an adult or adolescent and a younger child. See also *incest.*

instrument In social science, a research tool or device, such as a questionnaire, used to gather data about behaviors, attitudes, beliefs, or other such dimensions of an individual, group, or society.

instrumental traits Task-oriented traits or characteristics.

intermarriage Marriage between people of different ethnic or racial groups.

intermittent extended family A family in which adult children (or other relatives) periodically live with their aging parents.

interpersonal competence The ability to develop and share an intimate, growing relationship.

inter-role conflict Conflict experienced when the role expectations of two or more roles are contradictory or incompatible. Also known as role interference and role conflict. See *role strain.*

intrauterine device (IUD) A device inserted into the uterus to prevent conception or implantation of the fertilized egg.

introitus The vaginal opening.

in vitro fertilization The fertilization of an egg outside the body; "test tube" fertilization.

ISD Inhibited sexual desire. See *hypoactive sexual desire.*

I-statement In communication, a statement beginning with "I" that describes the speaker's feelings, such as "I feel upset when I see last week's dishes in the sink."

IUD See *intrauterine device.*

J

joint custody Custody in which both parents are responsible for the care of the child. Joint custody takes two forms: *joint legal custody,* in which the child lives primarily with one parent but both parents jointly share in important decisions regarding the child's education, religious training, and general upbringing, and *joint physical custody* in which the child lives with both parents in separate households and spends more or less equal time with each parent. See *also sole custody* and *split custody.*

joint legal custody See *joint custody.*

K

Kaposi's sarcoma An opportunistic skin cancer associated with AIDS.

kin   Relatives.

kinship   Family relationship.

kinship system   The social organization of related persons conferring rights and obligations based on an individual's status.

kiss   Touching or caressing with the lips.

L

labia majora   Two folds of spongy flesh extending from the mons veneris along the midline between the legs and enclosing the clitoris, labia minora, and urethral and vaginal openings.

labia minora   Two folds of skin within the labia majora; their upper portion forms a single fold over the clitoris known as the clitoral hood.

labor   The physical efforts of childbirth.

lactation   The production of milk.

la familia   See under *familia*.

Lamaze method   A childbirth method in which the mother uses exercises and breathing techniques to assist her labor.

laparoscopy   Tubal ligation technique using a laparoscope (viewing instrument) to locate the fallopian tubes, which are then closed or blocked.

latchkey children   See *self-care*.

Latino [fem. *-a*]   A person of Latin American origin or ancestry; may be of any race. See also *Hispanic*, and *Spanish-speaking*.

legitimacy   The state or quality of being sanctioned by custom, rights, or law.

lesbian   A female sexually oriented toward other females.

life course   A developmental perspective of individual change focusing on (1) *individual time*, an individual's own life span, *(2) social time*, social transition points, such as marriage, and (3) *historical time*, the times in which a person lives.

life cycle   The developmental stages, transitions, and tasks individuals undergo from birth to death.

lochia   A bloody vaginal discharge that appears for several weeks following childbirth.

lone-parent family   [Canadian usage] Single-parent family.

low birth weight (LBW)   Generally, weighing less than 5.5 pounds at birth, often as a result of prematurity.

ludis   According to sociologist John Lee's styles of love, playful love.

M

macho [Spanish]   In traditional Latin American usage, masculine, strong, or daring. In popular U. S. usage, excessively or stereotypically masculine.

madrina [Spanish]   Godmother.

majority group   A social category composed of people holding superordinate status and power and having the ability to impose their will on less powerful minority groups. Cf. *minority group*.

mania   According to sociologist John Lee's styles of love, obsessive love.

marital disruption   Marital instability that includes marital separation as well as divorce.

marital exchange   The process by which individuals trade resources with each other to secure the best marital partner. Traditionally, men exchanged their higher status and greater economic resources for women's physical attractiveness, expressive qualities, and childbearing and houskeeping abilities.

marital power   The power exercised by individuals as husband and wife. Cf. *family power*.

marital rape   Forced sexual contact by a husband with his wife.

marriage   Socially recognized union between a man and woman in which economic cooperation and legitimate sexual interactions and reproduction may take place.

marriage contract   1. The legal and moral rights and responsibilities entailed by marriage. 2. An explicit contract delineating specific terms of marriage which, depending on the terms, may be legally binding. 3. A non-legally binding agreement between partners, covering such areas as conflict resolution, division of household labor, employment, and childrearing responsibilities.

marriage gradient   The tendency for men to marry younger women of lower socioeconomic status and for women to marry older men of higher socioeconomic status.

marriage market   An exchange process in which individuals bargain with each other using their resources in order to find the best available partner for marriage. See *marital exchange*.

marriage squeeze   The phenomenon in which there are greater numbers of marriageable women than marriageable men according to their age and status. See also *marriage gradient*.

masturbation   Manual or mechanical stimulation of the genitals by self or partner; a form of autoeroticism.

matriarchal   Pertaining to the mother as the head and ruler of a family. Cf. *patriarchal*.

matriarchic   Pertaining to female rule. Cf. *patriarchic*.

matriarchy   A form of social organization in which the mother or eldest female is recognized as the head of the family, kinship group, or tribe, and descent is traced through her. Cf. *patriarchy*.

matrilineal   Descent or kinship traced through the mother. Cf. *patrilineal*.

mean world syndrome   The belief, resulting from television viewing, that the world is more dangerous and violent than it is in actuality.

meatus   The urethral opening.

menarche   The first menstrual period, beginning in puberty.

menopause   Cessation of menses for at least one year as a result of aging.

menses   The monthly menstrual flow.

menstrual cycle   The hormonally induced female cycle which begins with the development of an ovum in the ovarian follicle and the menstrual flow and ends with the degeneration of the corpus luteum.

menstruation   The discharge of blood and built-up uterine lining through the vagina that occurs approximately every four weeks among nonpregnant women between puberty and menopause.

meta-analysis   The re-analysis of combined statistical data from previous studies.

meta-rule   An abstract, general, unarticulated rule at the apex of the hierarchy of rules upon which other rules are based.

Mexican American   A U.S. citizen of Mexican ancestry.

midwife   A person who attends and facilitates birth.

mifepristone   See *RU-486*.

minilaparotomy   A method of tubal ligation in which the fallopian tubes are viewed and tied off through a single small incision in the lower abdomen.

minipill   A form of oral contraceptive containing only progesterone.

minority group   A social category composed of people who differ from the majority, who are relatively powerless, and who are subject to unfair and unequal treatment by the majority. Cf. *majority group*.

miscarriage   A spontaneous abortion.

model   A person who demonstrates a behavior observed and imitated by others.

modeling   A process in which learning takes place by imitating others.

monogamy   1. The practice of having only one husband or wife at a time. 2. [colloq.] Sexual exclusiveness.

mons veneris   The mound of fatty tissue over the pubic bone of the female, covered with pubic hair following puberty.

morality   A set of social, cultural, or religious norms defining right and wrong.

morning-after pill   See *postcoital birth control*.

morning sickness   Nausea experienced by many women during the first trimester of pregnancy.

mucus method   A contraceptive method that relies on predicting a woman's fertile period by observing changes in the appearance and character of her cervical mucus; also called Billings or ovulation method.

myotonia   The process of increasing muscular tension.

N

natural childbirth   See *prepared childbirth*.

natural family planning   A fertility awareness method of birth control that relies solely on predicting a woman's fertile period and avoiding intercourse on those days.

negative reinforcement   The process by which an unpleasant stimulus following a response decreases the likelihood that the response will be repeated.

nocturnal orgasm   Nonvoluntary ejaculation or orgasm occurring during sleep; also known as "wet dream."

no-fault divorce   The dissolution of marriage because of irreconcilable differences for which neither party is held responsible.

nonbasic conflict   Pronounced disagreement about non-fundamental or situational issues. Cf. *basic conflict*.

non-custodial   Not having physical or legal custody of a child. Cf. *custodial*.

nonmarital sex   Sexual intercourse outside of marriage by older singles.

nonverbal communication   Communication of emotion by means other than words, such as touch, body movement, and facial expression.

norm   A shared model or expectation of how a group *should* act or behave.

normal   Conforming to group or cultural norms.

normative   Establishing a norm or standard.

nuclear family   The basic family building block, consisting of at least a mother and child. In popular usage, thought of as consisting of a mother, father, and at least one child, all of whom are biologically related to each other; used interchangeably with *traditional family*.

nursing   Breastfeeding.

O

obstetrician   A physician specializing in pregnancy and childbirth.

occupational stratification   The hierarchal ranking in occupations in superior and inferior positions.

opportunistic disease   An infection that is normally resisted by the healthy immune system, such as *Kaposi's sarcoma* and *pneumocystis carinii pneumonia* associated with AIDS.

oral contraception   Contraceptive taken orally; the pill.

oral-genital sex   The erotic stimulation of the genitals by the tongue or mouth; fellatio, cunnilingus, or mutual oral stimulation.

orgasm   The release of physical tensions after the build-up of sexual excitement; usually accompanied by ejaculation in physically mature males.

orgasmic dysfunction   Inability to have orgasm.

orgasmic phase   The phase of the sexual response cycle characterized by orgasm.

orgasmic platform   The swelling of the outermost one-third of the vagina caused by vasocongestion during sexual arousal.

os   The cervical opening.

ovaries   The female gonads which produce estrogen and progesterone and release ova.

ovulation method   See *mucus method*.

ovum   The egg produced by the ovary. [plural] Ova

P

Pacific Islander   Collective term referring to those of native Hawaiian, Filipino, Guamamian, Samoan or other Melanesian, Micronesian, or Polynesian descent.

padrino   [Spanish] Godfather.

Pap smear   Pap test.

Pap test   The sampling of cervical cells to diagnose cancer or a precancerous condition.

parenting   The rearing of children.

passing   [colloquial] Pretending to be heterosexual when actually gay or lesbian.

passionate love   Intense, impassioned love. Cf. *companionate love*.

passive-congenial marriage   An enduring marriage characterized by low expectations and low levels of satisfaction from the beginning.

patriarchal   Pertaining to the father as the head and ruler of a family. Cf. *matriarchal*.

patriarchic   Pertaining to male rule. Cf. *matriarchic*.

patriarchy   A form of social organization in which the father or eldest male is recognized as the head of the family, kinship group, or tribe, and descent is traced through him. Cf. *matriarchy*.

patriarchy model of family violence   Model in which violence is seen as inherent in male-dominated societies.

patrilineal   Descent or kinship traced through the father. Cf. *matrilineal*.

pedophilia   Adult sexual attraction to children; the adult's use of children for sexual purposes.

peer   A person of equal status, as in age, class, position, or rank.

pelvic inflammatory disease (PID)   An infection of the fallopian tubes, often caused by gonorrhea or chlamydia, that may spread to the ovaries and uterus; severe cases may result in sterility. Also known as *salpingitis*.

penis   The male sexual organ through which semen is ejaculated and urine is passed.

perineum   The small band of muscular tissue separating the anus and the genitals.

permissive   A parenting style stressing the child's autonomy and freedom of expression over the needs of the parents.

period   Menses.

permissiveness with affection   Sexual norm permitting nonmarital sexual activity for both men and women in an affectionate relationship.

permissiveness without affection   Sexual standard permitting nonmarital sexual activity without regard as to the nature of the relationship.

personality conflict   Conflict based on personality characteristics; such conflicts are unlikely to be resolved. Cf. *situational conflict*.

petting   Foreplay; sexual contact usually referring to the manual or oral stimulation of the genitals or breasts.

phallus   Penis.

physical abuse   Intentional violent mistreatment. See *violence*.

PID   See *pelvic inflammatory disease*.

placenta   The organ of exchange between the embryo or fetus and the pregnant female through which nutrients and waste pass; the placenta also serves as an endocrine gland producing large amounts of progesterone and estrogen to maintain pregnancy.

pleasuring   The giving and receiving of sensual pleasure through touch.

plural marriage   The practice of having more than one husband or wife at the same time; polygamy.

pneumocystis carinii pneumonia   An opportunistic pneumonia associated with AIDS.

polyandry   The practice of having more than one husband at the same time. See also *polygamy*; cf. *polygyny*.

polygamy   The practice of having more than one husband or wife at the same time; plural marriage. See also *polyandry*, *polygyny*, and *consanguineous extended family*.

polygyny   The practice of having more than one wife at the same time. See also *polygamy*; cf. *polyandry*.

positive reinforcement   The process by which a stimulus following a response has the effect of increasing the likelihood that the response will be repeated.

POSSLQ   Person of opposite sex sharing living quarters; from U. S. Census terminology.

postcoital birth control   Birth control that is administered after intercourse has taken place, but before a diagnosis of pregnancy is possible; usually involves the administering of high-estrogen oral contraceptives. Also called "morning-after birth control."

postmarital sex   Sexual intercourse among previously married individuals.

postpartum period   The period of time following childbirth, around three months.

power   The ability to exert one's will, influence, or control over others.

power conflict   Pronounced disagreements concerning dominance.

powwows   Native American intertribal social gatherings centering around drumming and traditional dances.

pragma   According to sociologist John Lee's styles of love, practical love.

predictable crisis   Within the individual or family life cycle, normal but critical events, such as birth or death. Cf. *unpredictable crisis*.

pre-eclampsia   Increasingly high blood pressure during late pregnancy. See also *gestational edema-proteinuria-hypertension complex*.

premarital sex   Sexual intercourse prior to marriage.

prenatal   Before birth.

prepared childbirth   Birth philosophy stressing education and minimal use of anesthetics or other drugs; natural childbirth.

prepuce   Foreskin.

principle of least interest   A theory of power in which the person less interested in sustaining a relationship has the greater power.

pro-choice movement   Social movement that adovocates women's right to choose abortion.

profamily movement   A social movement emphasizing conservative family values, such as traditional gender roles, authoritarian childrearing, premarital virginity, and opposition to abortion.

progesterone   A hormone produced by the ovaries.

prolactin   A hormone that stimulates the production of milk by the mammary glands.

pro-life movement   Social movement that advocates against abortion.

prophylactic   [adjective] Protecting against disease. [noun] Condom.

propinquity   Spacial nearness.

prostaglandin   A hormone controlling muscle contractions.

prostaglandin injection   Abortion technique in which a prostaglandin solution is injected into the uterus, causing delivery of an unviable fetus.

prostate gland   A gland at the base of a man's bladder which produces most of the seminal fluid in the ejaculate.

prototype   A model.

pseudokin   See *fictive kin*.

pseudomutuality   The maintenance of a relationship with the pretense that it is mutually fulfilling.

psychiatric model of family violence   Model that assumes the source of violence to be in personality of abuser.

psychoanalytic model The Freudian model of child socialization, in which maturity is seen as the ability to gain control over one's unconscious impulses.

psychosexual Pertaining to the psychological aspects of sexuality.

psychosexual development The growth of the psychological aspects (such as attitudes and emotions) of sexuality that accompany physical growth.

puberty The period in which the individual develops secondary sex characteristics and becomes capable of reproducing.

pubococcygeus muscle The muscle that surrounds and supports the vagina.

PWA Person with AIDS.

Q

quickening The time of first movement of the fetus which may be felt by the pregnant woman.

R

race A large group of people defined as distinct because of genetically-transmitted physical characteristics, especially facial structure and skin color.

racism The practice of discrimination and subordination based on the belief that race determines character and abilities. Cf. *sexism.*

rape Sexual act against a person's will or consent as defined by law; may or may not include penile penetration of the vagina. Also known as *sexual assault.* See also *acquaintance rape* and *marital rape.*

rape trauma syndrome A group of symptoms experienced by a rape survivor, including fear, self-blame, anxiety, crying, sleeplessness, anger, or rage.

rating-and-dating The process described by sociologist Willard Waller in which men and women rated potential dates on a scale of one to ten and tried to date the highest rated individuals.

reconstituted family See *blended family* or *stepfamily.*

refractory period Following orgasm, the period during which the penis cannot respond to additional stimulation.

reinforcement A behavior that strengthens the action or response preceding it.

relative love and need theory A theory of power in which the person gaining the most from a relationship is the most dependent.

relocation camps During World War II, camps in which Japanese Americans and Japanese Canadians of all ages were imprisoned without cause by their respective governments.

remarriage A marriage in which at least one partner has been previously married.

reproductive organs External and internal structures involved in reproduction.

resource Anything that can be called into use or used to advantage, such as love, money, or approval, to exert influence or power.

resource model of family violence Model that views force as used to compensate for lack of personal, social, and economic resources.

rhythm method See *calendar method.*

Roe v. Wade U. S. Supreme Court decision (1972) affirming a woman's constitutional right to abortion based on the right to privacy.

role The pattern of behavior expected of a person in a group or culture as a result of his or her social status, such as husband or wife in a family.

role conflict See *inter-role conflict.*

role interference See *inter-role conflict.*

role making The creation or modification of existing roles.

role modeling A significant means by which children are taught attitudes and behavior by learning to imitate adults whom they admire; role models may be "positive" or "negative."

role overload The experience of having more prescribed activities in one or more roles than can be comfortably or adequately performed. See *role strain.*

role playing The changing of one's roles in response to the roles of others.

role strain Difficulties, tensions, or contradictions experienced in performing a role. See also *inter-role conflict* and *role overload.*

role taking The tendency to take on roles in different social situations and to modify behaviors accordingly.

roleless role A role for which there are no clear guidelines for behavior, such as stepparent, widow, and ex-in-law roles.

romantic love Intense, passionate love. Cf. *companionate love.*

RU–486 An antiprogesterone steroid (mifepristone) that acts as an abortifacient if taken within the first six weeks of pregnancy; also used as monthly birth control pill if taken shortly before an expected menstrual period.

rule of thumb Prior to the 19th century, the legally sanctioned practice of disciplining one's wife with a rod, provided it was not wider than the husband's thumb.

S

safe sex Sexual practices, including the use of latex condoms, intended to prevent the transmission of bodily fluids, especially semen, that may contain HIV.

saline injection Abortion technique in which a saline solution is injected into the uterus to induce delivery of an unviable fetus.

salpingitis Infection of the fallopian tube. See *pelvic inflammatory disease.*

sample A group randomly and systematically selected from a larger group.

scapegoating The conscious or unconscious singling out and blaming of an individual or group.

script A mental map, plan, or pattern of behavior. See also *role.*

scrotum The pouch of skin holding the testes.

secondary sex characteristics The physical characteristics other than external genitals that distinguish the sexes from each other, e.g. breasts and body hair.

self-care Children under age fourteen caring for themselves at home without supervision by an adult or older adolescent.

self-disclosure The revelation of intimate feelings to another.

self-esteem Feelings about the value of the self; high self-esteem includes feeling unique, having a sense of power, and feeling connected to others.

semen The fluid containing sperm which is ejaculated, produced mostly by the prostate gland. Also known as *ejaculate*.

seminal fluid The fluid containing sperm; semen.

seminiferous tubules Tiny sperm-producing tubes within the testes.

separation The physical parting of two married persons. Cf. *divorce*.

separation distress A psychological state following separation, characterized by depression, anxiety, intense loneliness, and feelings of loss.

sequential work/family role staging A pattern combining employment and family work in dual-earner families in which women leave employment during pregnancy and while their children are young and return to it at a later time.

sex 1. Biologically, the division into male and female. 2. Sexual activities.

sex hormones Hormones such as testosterone and estrogen which are responsible for the development of secondary sex characteristics and for activating sexual behavior.

sexism 1. The belief that biological differences between males and females provide legitimate bases for female subordination. 2. The economic and social domination of women by men. Cf. *racism*.

sex organs Internal and external reproductive organs; commonly refers only to the penis, vulva, and vagina.

sex ratio The ratio of men to women in a group or society.

sexual assault A legal term referring to rape. See also *acquaintance rape*, *marital rape*, and *rape*.

sexual behavior Behavior that is characterized by conscious psychological/erotic arousal (such as desire) and that may also be accompanied by physiological arousal (such as erection or lubrication) or activity (such as masturbation or coitus).

sexual desire The psychological component that motivates sexual behavior.

sexual disorder Psychological impairment of the capacity for sexual arousal, such as hypoactive sexual desire.

sexual dysfunction Impaired physiological response in excitement or orgasmic phase of the sexual response cycle, such as erectile or orgasmic difficulties.

sexual harassment Deliberate or repeated unsolicited verbal comments, gestures, or physical contact that is sexual in nature and unwelcomed by the recipient.

sexual identity The individual's sense of his or her sexual self.

sexual intercourse Coitus; heterosexual penile/vaginal penetration.

sexuality The state of being sexual, which encompasses the biological, social, and cultural aspects of sex.

sexually transmitted disease (STD) An infection that can be transmitted through sexual activities, such as sexual intercourse, oral/genital sex, or anal sex.

sexual orientation Sexual attraction and interactions directed toward members of the other or same sex. Usually dichotomized as heterosexuality/homosexuality, but may also include bisexuality.

sexual preference See *sexual orientation*.

sexual stratification The hierarchical ranking in superior and inferior positions according to gender.

sexual variation A departure from the sexual norms; atypical sexual behavior.

sibling A brother or sister.

SIDS See *sudden infant death syndrome*.

single-parent family A family with children, created by divorce or unmarried motherhood, in which only one parent is present.

situational conflict Conflict arising as the result of specific acts, events, behaviors, or situations, which are amenable to resolution. Cf. *personality conflict*.

social exchange theory A theory which emphasizes the process of mutual giving and receiving of rewards, such as love or sexual intimacy, in social relationships.

social integration The degree of interaction between individuals and the larger community.

social molding A child socialization theory that views human emotions as formed by the influences of culture, society, and the family.

social-situational model of family violence Model in which violence is seen as arising from a combination of family stress and cultural norms.

social structure A network of interconnected roles and statuses that give structure to interactions.

social support Instrumental and emotional assistance, such as physical care and love.

socialization The shaping of individual behavior to conform to social or cultural norms.

socialization agent Individuals, groups, institutions, or media, such as parents, schools, or television, which socialize the child.

socioeconomic status (SES) Social status ranking determined by a combination of occupational, educational, and income levels.

sole custody Child custody arrangement in which only one parent has both legal and physical custody of the child. See also *joint custody* and *split custody*.

sonogram The picture produced by ultrasonography.

Spanish-speaking Pertaining to Hispanic origin or ancestry.

spells of poverty The periodical movement in and out of poverty.

sperm The male gamete produced by the testis.

spermatogenesis The production of sperm.

spermicide A substance toxic to sperm, used for contraception, usually with a barrier device; available in a variety of forms, such as jelly, cream, aerosol foam, film, and supppository tablets. Spermicide containing nonoxynol-9 provides some protection against certain STDs, including gonorrhea, chlamydia, and HIV.

spinnbarkeit The elastic condition of cervical mucus just prior to ovulation.

split custody Custody of two or more children in which custody is divided between the parents, the mother generally receiving the girls and the father receiving the boys.

spontaneous abortion The natural but fatal explusion of the embryo or fetus; miscarriage.

spotting See *breakthrough bleeding*.

status The position an individual occupies within a group.

STD   Sexually transmitted disease.

stepfamily   A family consisting of two adults and one or more children from an earlier marriage or relationship. Also known as *blended family* or *reconstituted family*.

stereotype   A rigidly held, conventional view of individuals, groups, or ideas, that fails to allow for individual differences or critical judgement.

sterilization   Intervention (usually surgical) making a person incapable of reproducing.

stigmatization   The process of labeling and internalizing perceptions of self, other individuals, groups, behaviors, feelings, or ideas as deviant.

stimulus-value-role   A theory of romantic development: *stimulus* brings people together; *value* is the compatibility of basic values; *role* is role fit.

strain   Tension lingering from previous stressors or tensions inherent in family roles. See also *stressor*.

storge   According to sociologist John Lee's styles of love, companionate love.

stress   Psychological or emotional distress or disruption.

stressor   A stress-causing event.

stressor pileup   The occurrence of a number of stresses within a short period of time which strains family coping abilities.

structural functionalism   A sociological theory that examines how society is organized and maintained by examining the functions performed by its different structures. In marriage and family studies, structural functionalism examines the functions the family performs for society, the functions the individual performs for the family, and the functions the family performs for its members.

subsystem   A system that is part of a larger system, such as the parent/child system being a subsystem of the family system.

sudden infant death syndrome (SIDS)   The death of an apparently healthy infant during its sleep from unknown causes.

surrogate mother   A woman who bears a child for another woman (often for money) and relinquishes custody upon birth; the pregnancy usually results from artificial insemination, in vitro fertilization, or embryo transplant.

sweating   The secretion of a mucuslike liquid from the vaginal walls during the excitement phase of the sexual response cycle.

symbiotic personality   A personality characterized by excessive dependency and need for closeness.

symbolic interactionism   A theory which focuses on the subjective meanings of acts and how these meanings are communicated through interactions and roles to give shared meaning.

symmetrical work/family role allocation   The interface between family and employment in which family work is divided more equitably and females have greater commitment to work roles than in the traditional division of labor. Cf. *sequential work/family role staging* and *traditional-simultaneous/work family life cycle*.

syphilis   A sexually transmitted disease whose first symptom is a painless chancre on the genitals, anus, or mouth; caused by the *Treponema pallidum* bacterium. Life threatening if untreated.

T

TDI   See *therapeutic donor insemination*.

tenting   The expansion and elevation of the innermost two-thirds of the vagina during sexual excitement.

teratogenic   Capable of producing fetal defects.

testes   The two male gonads which produce testosterone and manufacture sperm. [singular] Testis. Also known as testicles.

testicles   See *testes*.

testosterone   A hormone secreted in males by the testes; also secreted in smaller amounts in females by the ovaries. Sometimes referred to as the "male hormone."

thanatology   The study of death and dying.

theoretical effectiveness   The maximum effectiveness of a drug, device or method if used consistently, correctly, and according to instructions.

therapeutic donor insemination (TDI)   Artificial insemination with donated semen, often used if the male is sterile or has a genetically transferable disorder.

tithingman   In colonial New England, a man appointed by the church to supervise his neighbors' morality and behavior.

total marriage   An enduring marriage characterized by a high degree of interdependence in most areas.

toxemia   A condition of pregnancy characterized by high blood pressure and edema. See also *gestational edema-proteinuria-hypertension complex*.

toxic shock syndrome (TSS)   A potentially fatal infection caused by the *Staphylococcus aureus* bacterium and characterized by high fever, vomiting, diarrhea, and rash; TSS has been associated with the use of superabsorbent tampons.

traditional family   In popular usage, an intact, married two-parent family with at least one child, which adheres to conservative family values; an idealized family. Popularly used interchangeably with *nuclear family*.

traditional-simultaneous work/family life cycle   The interface between family and employment in which the husband is regarded as the primary economic provider with little responsibility for family work and the wife, regardless of her employment status, is primarily responsible for family work. Cf. *sequential work/family role staging* and *symmetrical work/family role allocation*.

trait   A distinguishing personality characteristic or quality.

transactional pattern   Habitual patterns of interaction.

transition   1. Passing from one stage or phase to another. 2. The entrance of the fetus' head into the birth canal, marking the end of the first stage of labor.

traumatic sexualization   The process of developing inappropriate or dysfunctional sexual attitudes, behaviors, and feelings by a sexually-abused child.

traveling time   The time immediately following the Civil War when former slaves traveled throughout the South in search of relatives separated by sale.

trial marriage   Cohabitation with the purpose of determining marital compatibility.

tubal ligation   A surgical method of female sterilization in which the fallopian tubes are tied off or closed, usually by laparoscopy.

tubal pregnancy See *ectopic pregnancy*.

two-component theory of emotions The theory, according to Stanley Schacter, that for a person to experience an emotion, both physiological arousal and an appropriate emotional explanation for the arousal must be present.

typology Systematic categorization according to types.

U

ultrasonography Technological method used to view the fetus in utero by reflecting high frequency sound waves off it; ultrasound.

ultrasound See *ultrasonography*.

umbilical cord A hollow cord which connects the circulation system of the embryo or fetus to the placenta.

underclass The socioeconomic class marked by persistent poverty and poor employability.

underemployment Working at a job below one's qualifications, inability to work as many hours as desired, or working for less pay than in previous employment.

unpredictable crisis An unforseen crisis, such as terminal illness in a child. Cf. *predictable crisis*.

unrequited love Love that is not returned.

urethra In the male, the duct inside the penis, through which semen is ejaculated and urine expelled; in the female, the duct through which urine is expelled.

urethritis An infection of the urethra.

user effectiveness The actual effectiveness of a drug, device, or method based on statistical information.

uterus A hollow, muscular organ within the pelvic cavity in which the fertilized egg develops into the fetus; the womb.

V

vacuum aspiration First trimester abortion method in which the contents of the uterus are removed by suction.

vagina The passage leading from the vulva to uterus that expands during intercourse to receive the erect penis or during childbirth to permit passage of the child; the birth canal.

vaginismus The involuntary constriction of the vaginal muscles which prohibits penetration.

vaginitis Vaginal infection, most commonly *Trichomonas vaginalis*, *candidiasis*, or *Gardnerella vaginalis*, which may be sexually transmitted. Men may also acquire these infections but often remain asymptomatic.

variable A situation or behavior that may be changed or varied.

variation Departure from social or cultural norms.

varicocele A varicose vein above the testicle.

vas deferens One of two ducts that carry sperm from the testes to the seminal vesicles. [plural] Vasa deferentia.

vasectomy A surgical form of male sterilization in which the vas deferens is severed.

vasocongestion The increased supply of blood, especially to the genitals during sexual excitation.

VD See *sexually transmitted disease*.

venereal disease See *sexually transmitted disease*.

venereal warts Warts in the genital or anal area which may be sexually transmitted; caused by the human papilloma virus (HPV).

vernix A milky substance often covering infants at birth.

viability Ability to live and continue to grow outside the uterus.

violence The use of physical force to hurt, injure, or kill.

virginity The state of not having engaged in sexual intercourse.

vital marriage An enduring marriage characterized by the partners' lives being closely intertwined in important matters.

vulva The external female genitalia, including the mons veneris, labia majora and labia minora, clitoris, and the vaginal and urethral openings.

W

wedding The act of marrying; a marriage ceremony or celebration.

well-being, emotional The state of feeling happy, hopeful, energetic, and zestful.

well-being, physical The state of feeling fit and able; for the disabled or chronically ill, includes the ability to function within limits.

withdrawal See *coitus interruptus*.

wolf child A child abandoned at an early age who is then reared alone among animals; feral child.

womb Uterus.

work spillover Effect that employment has on time, energy, and psychological functioning of workers and their families.

working hypothesis An unproven theory or proposition used as the basis for further investigation. See *hypothesis*.

workplace/family linkages Ways in which employment affects families.

Z

ZIFT See *zygote intrafallopian transfer*.

zygote The fertilized egg.

zygote intrafallopian transfer (ZIFT) Eggs and sperm united in a petri dish and then transferred to the fallopian tube to begin cell division.

Abbott, Douglas A., Margaret Berry, and William H. Meredith. "Religious Belief and Practice: A Potential Asset in Helping Families." *Family Relations* 39 (October 1990): 443–44.

Abel, Ernest L. "Smoking and Pregnancy." *Journal of Psychoactive Drugs* 16:4 (October–December 1984): 327–338.

Adams, Bert. "The Family: Problems and Solutions." *Journal of Marriage and the Family* 47:3 (August 1985): 525–529.

Adams, David. "Identifying the Assaultive Husband in Court: You Be the Judge. *Response to the Victimization of Women and Children;* 1990; 13(1): 13–16.

Adler, Alfred. "Individual Psychology Therapy." In W. S. Sahakian, ed., *Psychotherapy and Counseling.* Chicago: Rand McNally, 1976.

Adler, Jerry, et al. "The Joy of Gardening." *Newsweek* (July 26, 1982).

Adler, Jerry. "Learning From the Loss." *Newsweek* (March 24, 1986): 66–67.

Adler, Nancy, Susan Hendrick, and Clyde Hendrick. "Male Sexual Preference and Attitudes toward Love and Sexuality." *Journal of Sex Education and Therapy* 12:2 (Fall–Winter 1989): 27–30.

Ahrons, Constance, and Roy Rodgers. *Divorced Families: A Multidisciplinary View.* New York: W. W. Norton, 1987.

Ahrons, Constance, and Lynn Wallisch. "The Relationship Between Former Spouses." In Daniel Perlman and Steve Duck, eds. *Intimate Relationships: Development, Dynamics, and Deterioration.* Newbury Park, Calif.: Sage Publications, 1987.

"AIDS and Children: A Family Disease." *World AIDS Magazine* (November 1989).

Ainsworth, Mary, et al. *Patterns of Attachment: A Psychological Study of the Strange Situation.* Hillsdale, New Jersey: Erlbaum, 1978.

Albert, Alexa, and Kris Bulcroft. "Pets, Families, and the Life Course." *Journal of Marriage and the Family* 50:2 (May 1988): 543–552.

Aldous, Joan. "American Families in the 1980s: Individualism Run Amok?" *Journal of Family Issues* 8:4 (December 1987): 422–425.

_____.*Family Careers: Developmental Change in Families.* New York: Wiley, 1978.

_____. "New Views on the Family Life of the Elderly and Near-Elderly." *Journal of Marriage and the Family* 49 (May 1987): 227–234.

_____. Perspectives on Family Change." *Journal of Marriage and the Family* 52:3 (August 1990): 571–583.

_____, ed. *Two Paychecks.* Beverly Hills, Calif.: Sage Publications, 1982.

Aldous, Joan, and Wilfried Dumon. "Family Policy in the 1980s: Controversy and Consensus." In Alan Booth, ed. *Contemporary Families: Looking Forward, Looking Back.* Minneapolis, Minn.: National Council on Family Relations, 1991.

Aldous, Joan, and David Klein. "Sentiment and Services: Models of Intergenerational Relationships in Midlife." *Journal of Marriage and the Family* 53:3 (August, 1991): 595–608.

Allen, Katherine. *Single Women/Family Ties.* Newbury Park, Calif.: Sage Publications, 1989.

Allen, Katherine, and Robert Pickett. "Forgotten Streams in the Family Life Course." *Journal of Marriage and the Family* 49:3 (August 1987): 517–528.

Allen, W. R. "The Search for Applicable Theories of Black Family Life." *Journal of Marriage and the Family* 40 (February 1978): 117–129.

Allen, W. R., et al. *Black American Families.* Westport, Conn.: Greenwood Press, 1986.

Allgeier, Elizabeth, and Naomi McCormick, eds. *Gender Roles and Sexual Behavior.* Palo Alto, Calif.: Mayfield, 1982.

Altman, Dennis. *AIDS in the Mind of America.* Garden City, N.Y.: Anchor/Doubleday, 1985.

_____. *The Homosexualization of America, The Americanization of the Homosexual.* New York: St. Martin's Press, 1982.

Alvirez, David, and Frank Bean. "The Mexican-American Family." In C. H. Mindel and R. W. Habenstein, eds. *Ethnic Families in America.* New York: Elsevier, 1976.

Alwin, Duane, et al. "Living Arrangements and Social Integration." *Journal of Marriage and the Family* 47:2 (May 1985): 319–334.

Amato, Paul. "Parental Divorce and Attitudes toward Marriage and Family Life." *Journal of Marriage and the Family* 50 (May, 1988): 453–461.

The American Fertility Society. "New Guidelines for the Use of Semen Donor Insemination: 1990." *Fertility and Sterility* 53:3 (suppl. 1) (March 1990): 1S–13S.

American Psychiatric Association on Nomenclature and Statistics. *Diagnostic and Statistical Manual,* 4th ed. Washington, D. C.: American Psychiatric Association, 1991.

Anderson, Carol. "The Community Connection: The Impact of Social Networks on Family and Individual Functioning." In Froma Walsh, ed. *Normal Family Processes.* New York: Guilford Press, 1982.

Anderson, Stephen. "Parental Stress and Coping During the Leaving Home Transition." *Family Relations* 37 (April 1988): 160–165.

Anderson, Stephen, and Paul Nuttall. "Parent Communications Training Across Three Stages of Childrearing." *Family Relations* 36:1 (January 1987): 40–44.

Andre, Rae. *The Homemakers: The Forgotten Workers.* Chicago: University of Chicago Press, 1981.

Andrews, Lori. *New Conceptions: A Consumer's Guide to the Newest Infertility Treatments.* New York: St. Martin's Press, 1984.

Aneshensel, C., and L. I. Pearlin. "Structural Contexts of Sex Differences in Stress." In R. C. Barnett, L. Biener, and G. K. Baruch, eds., *Gender and Stress.* New York: MacMillan, 1987.

Aneshensel, Carol, Eva Fielder, and Rosina Becerra. "Fertility and Fertility-Related Behavior among Mexican-American and Non-Hispanic White Females." *Journal of Health and Social Behavior* 30:1 (March 1989): 56–78.

Anson, Ofra. "Marital Status and Women's Health Revisited: The Importance of a Proximate Adult." *Journal of Marriage and the Family* 51 (February 1989): 185–194.

Antill, J. K. "Sex Role Complementarity versus Similarity in Married Couples." *Journal of Personality and Social Psychology* 45 (1983): 145–155.

Applebome, Peter. "Although Urban Blight Worsens, Most People Don't Feel Its Impact." *The New York Times,* January 26, 1991: 1, 12.

Archer, Sally. "Career and/or Family: The Identity Process for Adolescent Girls." *Youth and Society* 16:3 (1985): 289–314.

Arditti, Joyce. "Noncustodial Fathers: An Overview of Policy and Resources." *Family Relations* 39:4 (October 1990): 460–465.

Arehart-Treichel, Joan. "Pets: The Health Benefits." *Science News* 121 (March 27, 1982): 220–223.

Arendell, Terry. *Mothers and Divorce: Legal, Economic, and Social Dilemmas.* Berkeley, Calif.: University of California Press, 1987.

Aries, Philippe. *Centuries of Childhood.* New York: Vintage Books, 1962.

_____. "The Sentimental Revolution." *Wilson Quarterly* 6:4 (1982): 46–53.

Arms, Suzanne. *Adoption: A Handful of Hope.* Berkeley, Calif.: Celestial Arts, 1990.

Armstrong, George. "Pope Sets Forth Annulment Policy." *San Jose Mercury News.* February 14, 1987: 14D.

Armstrong, Penny and Sheryl Feldman. *A Wise Birth.* New York: William Morrow and Co., 1990.

Aron, Arthur, and Elaine Aron. "Love and Sexuality." In Kathleen McKinney and Susan Sprecher, eds., *Sexuality in Close Relationships.* Hillsdale, N.J.: Erlbaum, 1991.

Aron, Arthur, Elaine Aron, and Joselyn Allen. "Unrequited Love as Self Expansion." Paper presented at Iowa Conference on Personal Relationships, Iowa City, 1989.

Aron, Arthur, Elaine Aron, Meg Paris, Paula Tucker, and Geraldine Rodriguez. "Falling in Love: A Review of the Literature." Second Iowa Conference on Personal Relationships, Iowa City, May 12, 1989.

Aron, Arthur, D. G. Dutton, E. N. Aron, and A. Iverson. "Experiences of Falling in Love." *Journal of Social and Personal Relationships* 6(1989): 243–257.

Askham, J. "Identity and Stability Within the Marriage Relationship." *Journal of Marriage and the Family* 38 (1976): 535–547.

"At a Glance." *OURS: The Magazine of Adoptive Families* 23:6 (Nov.–Dec. 1990): 63.

Atkinson, Alice, and Diedre James. "The Transition between Active and Adult Parenting: An End and a Beginning." *Family Perspective* 25:1 (1991): 57–66.

Atkinson, Jean. "Gender Roles in Marriage and the Family." *Journal of Family Issues* 8:1 (March, 1987): 5–41.

Atkinson, Maxine, and Jacqueline Boles. "WASP (Wives as Senior Partners)." *Journal of Marriage and the Family* 46:3 (November 1984): 861–870.

Atkinson, Maxine, and Becky Glass. "Marital Age Heterogamy and Homogamy, 1900 to 1980." *Journal of Marriage and the Family* 47:3 (August 1985): 685–691.

Atwater, Lynn. "Long-Term Cohabitation Without a Legal Ceremony Is Equally Valid and Desirable." In Harold Feldman and Margaret Feldman, eds., *Current Controversies in Marriage and the Family.* Beverly Hills, Calif.: Sage Publications, 1985.

Auletta, Ken. *The Underclass.* New York: Random House, 1982.

Awad, George, and Ruth Parry. "Access Following Marital Separation." *Canadian Journal of Psychiatry* 25(5) (August 1980): 357–365.

Axelson, Leland, and Paula Dail. "The Changing Character of Homelessness in the United States." *Family Relations* 37:4 (October 1988): 463–469.

Axelson, Marta, and Jennifer Glass. "Household Structure and Labor Force Participation of Black, Hispanic, and White Mothers." *Demography* 22 (1985): 381–394.

Bachrach, Christine. "Contraceptive Practice Among American Women, 1973–1982." *Family Planning Perspectives* 16(6) (November/December, 1984): 253–258.

Bahr, Kathleen. "Student Responses to Genogram and Family Chronology." *Family Relations* 39 (July 1990): 243–249.

Bahr, Stephen. "The Economics of Family Life: An Overview." *Journal of Family Issues* 3:2 (June 1982a): 139–146.

_____. "Effects on Power and Division of Labor in the Family." In Lois Hoffman and Ivan Nye, eds., *Working Mothers.* San Francisco, Calif.: Jossey-Bass, 1974.

_____, ed. *Economics of the Family.* Lexington, Mass.: Lexington Books, 1980.

_____. "The Economics of Family Life." Special issue, *Journal of Family Issues* 3:2 (June 1982b).

Baird, Donna, D. and Allen J. Wilcox. "Cigarette Smoking Associated with Delayed Conception." *Journal of the American Medical Association* 253(20) (1985): 2979–2983.

_____. "Future Fertility after Prenatal Exposure to Cigarette Smoke." *Fertility and Sterility* 46:3 (September 1986): 368–372.

Baker, Sharon, Stanton Thalberg, and Diane Morrison. "Parents' Behavioral Norms as Predictors of Adolescent Sexual Activity and Contraceptive Use." *Adolescence* 23 (Summer 1988): 265–282.

Balswick, Judith. "Explaining Inexpressive Males: A Reply to L'Abate." *Family Relations* 29 (1980): 231–233.

Bane, Mary Jo, and David Ellwood. "Slipping Into and Out of Poverty: The Dynamic of Spells." *Journal of Human Resources* 21 (1986): 1–24.

Bane, Mary Jo, and Paul A. Jargowsky. "The Links Between Public Policy and Family Structure: What Matters and What Doesn't." In Andrew J. Cherlin, ed., *The Changing American Family and Public Policy.* Washington, D.C.: The Urban Institute Press, 1988.

Baptiste, David. "The Image of the Black Family Portrayed by Television." *Marriage and Family Review* 10:1 (April 1983): 41–63.

Barbach, Lonnie. *For Each Other: Sharing Sexual Intimacy.* Garden City, N.Y.: Doubleday, 1982.

Barden, J. C. "Many Parents in Divorces Abduct Their Own Children." *The New York Times,* May 6, 1990: 10.

Barkan, Susan, and Michael Bracken. "Delayed Childbearing: No Evidence for Increased Low Risk of Low Birth Weight and Preterm Delivery." *American Journal of Epidemiology* 125:1 (1987): 101–109.

Barkas, J. L. *Single in America.* New York: Atheneum, 1980.

Baron, Larry. "Sex Differences in Attitudes and Experiences of Romantic Love." *Dissertation Abstracts International* 43 (1983): 3722A.

Barranti, Crystal C. Ramirez. "The Grandparent/Grandchild Relationship: Family Resource in an Era of Voluntary Bonds." *Family Relations* 34:3 (July 1985): 343–352.

Barrow, Georgia. *Aging, Ageism, and Society.* St. Paul, Minn.: West, 1989.

Barth, Robert, and Bill Kinder. "The Mislabeling of Sexual Impulsivity." *Journal of Sex and Marital Therapy* 13:1 (Spring, 1987): 15–23.

Basow, Susan. *Gender Stereotypes: Traditions and Alternatives,* 2d ed. Monterey, Calif.: Brooks/Cole, 1986.

Bass, Ellen, and Louise Thornton, eds. *I Never Told Anyone: Stories and Poems by Survivors of Child Sexual Abuse.* New York: Harper & Row, 1983.

Bassuk, Ellen, et al. "Characteristics of Sheltered Homeless Families." *American Journal of Public Health* 76 (1986): 1097–1101.

Bassuk, Ellen, and Lenore Rubin. "Homeless Children: A Neglected Population." *American Journal of Orthopsychiatry* 57:2 (April 1987): 279–286.

Baumrind, Diana. "Current Patterns of Parental Authority." *Developmental Psychology Monographs* 4:1 (1971): 1–102.

_____. "Parental Disciplinary Patterns and Social Competence in Children." *Youth and Society* 9:3 (March 1978): 239–276.

Bean, Frank, and Marta Tienda. *The Hispanic Population of the United States.* New York: Russell Sage Foundation, 1987.

Beauvoir, Simone de. *The Coming of Age.* New York: Putnam's, 1972.

_____. *The Second Sex.* New York: Knopf, 1948 and 1952.

Beavers, Robert, W. "Healthy, Midrange, and Severely Dysfunctional Families." In Froma Walsh, ed., *Normal Family Processes.* New York: Guilford Press, 1982.

Beavers, Robert W., and Robert Hampson, *Successful Families.* New York: Norton Publishing Co., 1990.

Becerra, Rosina. "The Mexican American Family." In Charles Mindel, Robert Habenstein, and Roosevelt Wright, Jr., eds., *Ethnic Families in America: Patterns and Variations,* 3d ed. New York: Elsevier North Holland, Inc., 1988.

Beck, Melinda. "Miscarriages." *Newsweek* (August 15, 1988): 46–49.

Beck, Rubye, and Scott Beck. "The Incidence of Extended Households among Middle-Aged Black and White Women." *Journal of Family Issues* 10:2 (June 1989): 147–168.

Becker, Howard. *Outsiders*. New York: Free Press, 1963.

Beeghley, Leonard, and Sellers, Christine. "Adolescent and Sex: A Structural Theory of Premarital Sex in the United States." *Deviant Behavior* 7:4 (1986): 313–336.

Begum, Nasa. Disabled Women and the Feminist Agenda. Feminist Review; Spring 1992; (40): 70–85.

Beier, Ernst, and Daniel Stenberg. "Marital Communication." *Journal of Communication* 27:3 (Summer 1977): 92–97.

Belcastro, Philip. "Sexual Behavior Differences between Black and White Students." *Journal of Sex Research* 21:1 (February 1985): 56–67.

Bell, Alan, and Martin Weinberg. *Homosexualities: A Study of Diversities among Men*. New York: Simon & Schuster, 1978.

Bell, Alan, et al. *Sexual Preference: Its Development in Men and Women*. Bloomington: Indiana University Press, 1981.

Bell, Colleen, et al. "Normative Stress and Young Families: Adaptation and Development." *Family Relations* 29:4 (1980): 453–458.

Bell, Robert, John Daly, and Christina Gonzales. "Affinity-Maintenance in Marriage and Marriage Satisfaction." *Journal of Marriage and the Family* 49:2 (May 1987): 445–455.

Bellah, Robert, et al. *Habits of the Heart*. Berkeley, Calif.: University of California Press, 1985.

Beller, Andrea. "Occupational Segregation and the Earnings Gap." In U.S. Commission on Civil Rights, *Comparable Worth: Issue for the 80's*, Vol. 1. Washington, D.C., 1984.

_____. "Occupational Segregation by Sex: Determinants and Changes." *Journal of Human Resources* 17 (Summer 1982): 371–392.

Belsky, Jay. "Patterns of Marital Change and Parent-Child Interaction." *Journal of Marriage and the Family* 53:2 (May 1991): 487–498.

_____. "Transition to Parenthood." *Medical Aspects of Human Sexuality* (20) (Sept. 1986): 56–59.

_____. "Exploring Individual Differences in Marital Change Across the Transition to Parenthood: The Role of Violated Expectations." *Journal of Marriage and the Family* 47:4 (November 1985c): 1037–1044.

_____. "Stability and Change in Marriage Across the Transition to Parenthood: A Second Study." *Journal of Marriage and the Family* 47:4 (November 1985b): 855–865.

_____. "The Work-Family Interface and Marital Change Across the Transition to Parenthood." *Journal of Family Issues* 6 (June 1985a): 205–220.

_____. "Infant Day Care, Child Development, and Family Policy." *Society* 27:5 (July–August 1990): 10–12.

_____, et al. *The Child in the Family*. Reading, Mass.: Addison-Wesley, 1984.

Bem, Sandra. "Androgyny vs. the Tight Little Lives of Fluffy Women and Chesty Men." *Psychology Today* 9:4 (September 1975): 58–59ff.

_____. "Bem Sex-Role Inventory: Professional Manual." Palo Alto, Calif.: Consulting Psychologists Press, 1981.

_____. "Gender Schema Theory: A Cognitive Account of Sex Typing." *Psychological Review* 88 (1981): 354–364.

_____. "Gender Schema Theory and Its Implications for Child Development: Raising Gender-Aschematic Children in a Gender Schematic Society." *Signs* 8:4 (Summer 1983): 598–616.

_____. "The Measurement of Psychological Androgyny." *Journal of Consulting and Clinical Psychology* 42 (1974): 155–162.

_____. "Sex Role Adaptability: One Consequence of Psychological Androgyny." *Journal of Personality and Social Psychology* 31:4 (1975): 634–643.

Bengston, Vern and Joan Roberston, eds. *Grandparenthood*. Beverly Hills, Calif.: Sage Publications, 1985.

Benin, Mary, and Agostinelli, Joan. "Husbands' and Wives' Satisfaction with the Division of Labor." *Journal of Marriage and the Family* 50:2 (May 1988): 349–361.

Benin, Mary, and Barbara Nienstedt. "Happiness, Job Satisfaction, and Life Cycle." *Journal of Marriage and the Family* 47:4 (November 1985): 975–984.

Berardo, Donna, et al. "A Residue of Tradition: Jobs, Careers, and Spouses' Time in Housework." *Journal of Marriage and the Family* 49 (May 1987): 381–390.

Berardo, Felix. "Trends and Directions in Family Research in the 1980s." In Alan Booth, ed., *Contemporary Families: Looking Forward, Looking Back*. Minneapolis: National Council on Family Relations, 1991.

Berardo, Felix, and Constance Sheehan. "Family Scholarship: A Reflection of the Changing Family?" *Journal of Family Issues* 5:4 (December 1984): 577–598.

Berger, Mark J., and Donald P. Goldstein. "Infertility Related to Exposure to DES in Utero: Reproductive Problems in the Female." In Miriam Mazor and Harriet Simons, eds., *Infertility: Medical, Emotional, and Social Considerations*. New York: Human Sciences Press, 1984.

Berk, Richard, P. Newton, and Sarah F. Berk. "What a Difference a Day Makes: An Empirical Study of the Impact of Shelters for Battered Women." *Journal of Marriage and the Family* 48 (August 1986): 481–490.

Berk, Sarah. *The Gender Factory: The Apportionment of Work in American Households*. New York: Plenum Press, 1985.

Berliner, Arthur. "Sex, Sin, and the Church: The Dilemma of Homosexuality." *Journal of Religion and Health* 26:7 (Summer 1987): 137–142.

Berman, William. "Continued Attachment After Legal Divorce." *Journal of Family Issues* 6:3 (September 1985): 375–392.

Bernard, Jessie. *The Future of Marriage*, 2d ed. New York: Columbia University Press, 1982.

Berscheid, Ellen. "Emotion." In H. H. Kelley et al., eds. *Close Relationships*. New York: Freeman, 1983

_____. "Interpersonal Attraction." In G. Lindzey and Elliot Aronson, eds. *Handbook of Social Psychology*. New York: Random House, 1985.

_____ "Some Comments on Love's Anatomy: Or, Whatever Happened to Old-fashioned Lust?" In Robert Sternberg and Michael Barnes, eds., *The Psychology of Love*. New Haven, Conn.: Yale University Press, 1988.

Berscheid, Ellen, and Elaine H. Walster. "A Little Bit About Love." In T. L. Huston, ed., *Foundations of Interpersonal Attraction*. New York: Academic Press, 1974.

_____. *Interpersonal Attraction*. Reading, Mass.: Addison-Wesley, 1978.

Berstein, Barton, and Sheila K. Collins. "Remarriage Counseling: Lawyer and Therapist's Help with the Second Time Around." *Family Relations* 34:3 (July 1985): 387–391.

Best, Joel. *Threatened Children: Rhetoric and Concern About Child-Victims*. Chicago: The University of Chicago Press, 1990.

Bielby, William, and James Baron. "Woman's Place Is With Other Women: Sex Segregation in the Workplace." Unpublished paper, National Research Council, Workshop on Job Segregation by Sex, 1982.

Billingsley, Andrew. *Black Families in White America*. Englewood Cliffs, N.J.: Prentice-Hall, 1968.

_____. "The Impact of Technology on Afro-American Families." *Family Relations* 37 (October 1988): 420–425.

Billy, John, Nancy Landale, William Grady, and Denise Zimmerle. "Effects of Sexual Activity on Adolescent Social and Psychological Development." *Social Psychology Quarterly* 51:3 (September 1988): 190–212.

Binion, Victoria. "Psychological Androgyny: A Black Female Perspective." *Sex Roles* 22: 7–8 (April 1990).

Binsacca, B. D., et al. "Factors Associated with Low Birthweight in an Inner-City Population." *American Journal of Public Health* 77:4 (Apr. 1987): 505–506.

Bird, Gerald, and Gloria Bird. "Determinants of Mobility in Two-Earner Families: Does the Wife's Income Count?" *Journal of Marriage and the Family* 47:3 (August 1985): 753–758.

_____. "Satisfaction in Family, Employment, and Community Roles." *Psychological Reports* 55:2 (October 1984): 675–678.

Blair, Sampson, and Daniel Lichter. "Measuring the Division of Household Labor: Gender Segregation and Housework among American Couples." *Journal of Family Issues* 12:1 (March 1991): 91–113.

Blakely, Mary Kay. "Surrogate Mothers: For Whom Are They Working?" *Ms.* (March 1987): 18, 20.

Blakeslee, Sandra. "Scientists Find Key Biological Causes of Alcoholism." *New York Times*, August 14, 1984:19ff.

Blassingame, John. *The Slave Community*. New York: Oxford Unversity Press, 1972.

Blieszner, Rosemary, and Janet Alley. "Family Caregiving for the Elderly: An Overview of Resources." *Family Relations* 39:1 (January 1990): 97–102.

Block, Jeanne. "Differential Premises Arising from Differential Socialization of the Sexes: Some Conjectures." *Child Development* 54 (1983): 1335–1354.

Bloom, Bernard, et al. "Sources of Marital Dissatisfaction Among Newly Separated Persons." *Journal of Family Issues* 6:3 (September 1985): 359–373.

Blumberg, Rae Lesser, ed. *Gender, Family, and the Economy*. Newbury Park, Calif: Sage Publications, 1990.

Blumenfeld, Warren, and Diane Raymond. *Looking at Gay and Lesbian Life*. Boston: Beacon Press, 1989.

Blumstein, Philip. "Identity Bargaining and Self-Conception." *Social Forces* 53:3 (1975): 476–485.

Blumstein, Philip, and Pepper Schwartz. *American Couples*. New York: McGraw-Hill, 1983.

Bobo, Lawrence. *General Social Survey: 1990*. Chicago: National Opinion Research Center, 1991.

Bodnar, John. *The Transplanted: A History of Immigrants in Urban America*. Bloomington: Indiana University Press, 1985.

Bohannan, Paul. *Divorce and After*. New York: Doubleday, 1971.

Boken, Halcyone. "Gender Equality in Work and Family." *Journal of Family Issues* 5:2 (June 1984): 254–272.

Boken, Halcyone, and Anamarie Viveros-Long. *Balancing Jobs and Family Life: Do Flexible Work Schedules Work?* Philadelphia: Temple University Press, 1981.

Boland, Joseph, and Diane Follingstad. "The Relationship Between Communication and Marital Satisfaction: A Review." *Journal of Sex and Marital Therapy* 13:4 (Winter 1987): 286–313.

Boles, Abner J., and Harriet Curtis-Boles. "Black Couples and the Transition to Parenthood." *The American Journal of Social Psychiatry* 6:1 (Winter 1986): 27–31.

Boone, Margaret S. *Capital Crime: Black Infant Mortality in America*. Newbury Park, Calif.: Sage Publications, 1989.

Booth, Alan. "Who Divorces and Why: A Review." *Journal of Family Issues* 6:3 (September 1985): 255–293.

_____, ed. *Contemporary Families: Looking Forward, Looking Back*. Minneapolis, Minn.: National Council on Family Relations, 1991.

Booth, Alan, and John Edwards. "Age at Marriage and Marital Instability." *Journal of Marriage and the Family* 47:2 (February 1985): 67–74.

Booth, Alan, David Johnson, Lynn White, and John Edwards. "Divorce and Marital Instability over the Life Course." *Journal of Family Issues* 7 (1986): 421–442.

Booth, Alan, et al. "Predicting Divorce and Permanent Separation." *Journal of Family Issues* 6:3 (September 1985): 331–346.

Borhek, Mary. "Helping Gay and Lesbian Adolescents and Their Families: A Mother's Perspective." *Journal of Adolescent Health Care* 9:2 (March 1988):123–128.

Borland, Dolores. "A Cohort Analysis Approach to the Empty-nest Syndrome Among Three Ethnic Groups of Women: A Theoretical Position." *Journal of Marriage and the Family* 44 (February 1982): 117–129.

Boss, Pauline. "Family Stress." In Marvin B. Sussman and Suzanne K. Steinmetz, eds., *Handbook of Marriage and the Family*. New York: Plenum Press, 1987.

Boston Women's Health Book Collective. *The New Our Bodies, Ourselves*. New York: Simon & Schuster, 1984.

_____. *Our Bodies, Ourselves*. Boston: Little, Brown, 1978a.

_____. *Ourselves and Our Children*. New York: Random House, 1978b.

Boswell, John. *Christianity, Social Tolerance, and Homosexuality*. Chicago: University of Chicago Press, 1980.

Botkin, B. A., ed. *Lay My Burden Down: A Folk History of Slavery*. Chicago: University of Chicago Press, 1945.

Bourne, Richard, and Eli Newberger, eds. *Critical Perspectives on Child Abuse*. Lexington, Mass.: Lexington Books, 1979.

Bowen, Gary. "Corporate Supports for the Family Lives of Employees: A Conceptual Model for Program Planning and Evaluation." *Family Relations* 37 (April 1988): 183–188.

Bowker, Lee. *Beating Wife Beating*. Lexington, Mass.: Lexington Books, 1983.

Bowlby, John. *Attachment and Loss*. Three volumes. New York: Basic Books, 1969, 1973, 1980.

Bowman, Madonna, and Constance Ahrons. "Impact of Legal Custody Status on Father's Parenting Post-divorce." *Journal of Marriage and the Family* 47:2 (May 1985) 481–485.

Bozett, Frederick W., ed. *Gay and Lesbian Parents*. New York: Praeger, 1987a.

_____. "Gay Fathers." In Frederick W. Bozett, ed., *Gay and Lesbian Parents*. New York: Praeger, 1987b.

_____. "Children of Gay Fathers." In Frederick W. Bozett, ed., *Gay and Lesbian Parents*. New York: Praeger, 1987c.

Bradford, William. *History of Plymouth Plantation*. Cambridge, Mass.: Harvard University Press, 1945.

Bradley, Buff, et al. *Single Living Your Own Way*. Reading, Mass.: Addison-Wesley, 1977.

Bradley, E. Jane, and R. C. L. Lindsay. "Methodological and Ethical Issues in Child Abuse Research." *Journal of Family Violence* 2:3 (1987): 239–255.

Brand, H. J. "The Influence of Sex Differences on the Acceptance of Infertility." *Journal of Reproductive and Infant Psychology* 7:2 (April–June 1989): 129–131.

Brandenburg, H., et al. "Fetal Loss Rate After Chorionic Villus Sampling and Subsequent Amniocentesis." *American Journal of Medical Genetics* 35:2 (February 1990): 178–180.

Bray, James, and Sandra Berger. "Noncustodial Father and Paternal Grandparent Relationship in Stepfamilies." *Family Relations* 39:4 (October 1990): 414–419.

Breault, K. D., and Augustine Kposowa. "Explaining Divorce in the United States: A Study of 3,111 Counties, 1980." *Journal of Marriage and the Family* 49:3 (August 1987): 549–558.

Brenner, Harvey. "Influence of the Social Environment on Psychopathology: The Historic Perspective." In James Barrett et al., eds. *Stress and Mental Disorder*. New York: Raven, 1979.

_____. *Mental Illness and the Economy*. Cambridge, Mass.: Harvard University Press, 1973.

Bretschneider, Judy, and Norma McCoy. "Sexual Interest and Behavior in Healthy 80- to 102-Year-Olds." *Archives of Sexual Behavior* 17:2 (April 1988): 109–128.

Brigman, K. M. "Churches Helping Families." *Family Perspectives* 18:2 (1984): 77–84.

Bringle, Robert; Buunk, Bram. Extradyadic Relationships and Sexual Jealousy. In: McKinney, Kathleen; Susan Sprecher, eds. *Sexuality in Close Relationships*. Hillsdale, NJ: Lawrence Erlbaum Associates; 1991.

Bristor, Martha Wingerd. "The Birth of a Handicapped Child—A Holistic Model for Grieving." *Family Relations* 33:1 (January 1984): 25–32.

Broderick, Carlfred, and James Smith. "The General Systems Approach to the Family." In Wesley Burr et al., eds., *Contemporary Theories About the Family: General Theories/Theoretical Orientations*. New York: Free Press, 1979.

Brody, Elaine. "Parent Care as a Normative Family Stress." *Gerontologist* 25 (1985): 19–29.

Brody, Jane. "Assessing the Question of Male Circumcision." *The New York Times*, August 14, 1985: 18.

Brodzinsky, David M., and Loreen Huffman. "Transition to Adoptive Parenthood." *Marriage and Family Review* 12:3–4 (1988): 267–286.

Brodzinsky, David M. and Marshall D. Schechter, eds. *The Psychology of Adoption*. New York: Oxford University Press, 1990.

Broman, Clifford. "Gender, Work-Family Roles, and Psychological Well-Being of Blacks." *Journal of Marriage and the Family* 53:2 (May 1991): 509–520.

_____. "Household Work and Family Life Satisfaction among Blacks." *Journal of Marriage and the Family* 50:3 (August, 1988): 743–748.

_____. "Satisfaction among Blacks: The Significance of Marriage and Parenthood." *Journal of Marriage and the Family* 50:1 (February 1988): 45–51.

Bronfenbrenner, Urie. *The Ecology of Human Development*. Cambridge, Mass.: Harvard University Press, 1979.

_____. "The Parent/Child Relationship and Our Changing Society." In L. Eugene Arnold, ed., *Parents, Children and Change*. Lexington, Mass.: Lexington Books, 1985.

Bronfenbrenner, Urie, and Ann Crouter. "Work and Family Through Time and Space." In Sheila Kamerman and C. D. Hayes, eds., *Families That Work: Children in a Changing World*. Washington, D.C.: National Academy Press, 1982.

Brown, Elizabeth, and William R. Hendee. "Adolescents and Their Music." *Journal of the American Medical Association* 262:12 (Sept. 22/29, 1989): 1659–1663.

Brown, Patricia Leigh. "Where to Put the TV Set?" *The New York Times*, October 4, 1990: B4.

Browne, Angela, and David Finkelhor. "Initial and Long-Term Effects: A Review of the Research." In David Finkelhor, ed., *Sourcebook on Child Sexual Abuse*. Beverly Hills, Calif.: Sage Publications, 1986.

Brownmiller, Susan. *Against Our Will: Men, Women, and Rape*. New York: Simon & Schuster, 1975.

_____. *Femininity*. New York: Fawcett Columbine, 1983.

Brubaker, Timothy. "Families in Later Life: A Burgeoning Research Area." In Alan Booth, ed. *Contemporary Families: Looking Forward, Looking Back*. Minneapolis, Minn.: National Council on Family Relations, 1991.

Bruce, Martha, and Philip Leaf. "Psychiatric Disorders and 15-Month Mortality in a Community Sample of Adults." *American Journal of Public Health* 79 (1989): 727–730.

Bryant, Lois, Marilyn Coleman, and Lawrence Ganong. "Race and Family Structure Stereotyping: Perceptions of Black and White Nuclear Families and Stepfamilies." *Journal of Black Psychology* 15 (1988): 1–16.

Bryant, Z. Lois, and Marilyn Coleman. "The Black Family as Portrayed in Introductory Marriage and Family Textbooks." *Family Relations*. 37:3 (July 1988): 255–259.

Buchta, Richard. "Attitudes of Adolescents and Parents of Adolescents Concerning Condom Advertisements on Television." *Journal of Adolescent Health Care* 10:3 (May 1989): 220–223.

Budiansky, Stephen. "The New Rules of Reproduction." *U.S. News and World Report* (April 18, 1988): 66–69.

Buehler, Cheryl. "Initiator Status and the Divorce Transition." *Family Relations* 36 (January 1987): 82–86.

Bullard, David; Knight, Susan, eds. Sexuality and Disability: Personal Perspectives. St. Louis, MO: C. V. Mosby; 1981.

Bullough, Vern. *Sexual Variance in Society and History*. New York: John Wiley & Sons, 1976.

Bumpass, Larry, Teresa Castro Martin, and James Sweet. "The Impact of Family Background and Early Marital Factors on Marital Disruption." *Journal of Family Issues* 12:1 (March 1991): 22–44.

Bumpass, Larry, and James A. Sweet. "Children's Experience in Single Parent Families: Implications of Cohabitation and Marital Transition." *Family Planning Perspectives* 21:6 (November–December 1989): 256–260.

_____. "Differentials in Marital Stability." *Sociological Review* 37 (1972): 754–766.

Bumpass, Larry, James Sweet, and Teresa Castro Martin. "Changing Patterns of Remarriage." *Journal of Marriage and the Family* 52:3 (August 1990): 747–756.

Burgess, Ann W., ed. *Rape and Sexual Assault II*. New York: Garland Press, 1988.

Burgess, Ernest. "The Family as a Unity of Interacting Personalities." *The Family* 7:1 (March 1926): 3–9. Reprinted in Jerold Heiss, ed., *Family Roles and Interaction*. Chicago: Rand McNally, 1968.

Burns, Ailsa. "Perceived Causes of Marriage Breakdown and Conditions of Life." *Journal of Marriage and the Family* 46:3 (August 1984): 551–562.

Burns, Scott. *The Household Economy*. New York: Harper & Row, 1972.

Burr, Wesley. *Theory Construction and the Sociology of the Family*. New York: John Wiley and Sons, 1973.

Burr, Wesley, et al. *Contemporary Theories About the Family*. 2 vols. New York: Free Press, 1979.

Burroughs, Louise, et al. "Careers, Contingencies, and Locus of Control Among White College Women." *Sex Roles* 11(3/4) (1984): 289–302.

Buss, D. M. "Toward a Psychology of Person-Environment (PE) Correlation." *Journal of Personality and Social Psychology* 47 (1984): 361–377.

Butter, I. H., and B. J. Kay. "Self Certification in Law Midwives Organizations—A Vehicle for Professional Autonomy." *Social Science & Medicine* 30:12 (1990): 1329–1339.

Buunk, Bram, and Barry van Driel. *Variant Lifestyles and Relationships*. Newbury Park, Calif.: Sage Publications, 1989.

Byrd, W., et al. "A Prospective Randomized Study of Pregnancy Rates Following Intrauterine and Intracervical Insemination Using Frozen Donor Sperm." *Fertility and Sterility* 53:3 (March 1990): 521–527.

Byrne, Donn and Karen Murnen. *"Maintaining Love Relationships."* In Robert Sternberg and Michael Barnes, eds., *The Psychology of Love*. New Haven, Conn.: Yale University Press, 1988.

Cabai, Robert. "Gay and Lesbian Couples: Lessons on Human Intimacy." *Psychiatric Annals* 18:1 (January 1988):21–25.

Cado, Suzana, and Harold Leitenberg. "Guilt Reactions to Sexual Fantasies during Intercourse." *Archives of Sexual Behavior* 19:1 (1990): 49–63.

Callahan, Sidney, and Daniel Callahan. "Abortion: Understanding the Differences." *Family Planning Perspectives* 16:5 (September/October 1984): 219–221.

Callan, Victor. "The Personal and Marital Adjustment of Mothers and of Voluntarily and Involuntarily Childless Wives." *Journal of Marriage and the Family* 49:4 (November 1987): 847–856.

_____. "Perceptions of Parents, the Voluntarily and Involuntarily Childless: A Multidimensional Scaling Analysis." *Journal of Marriage and the Family* 47:4 (November 1985): 1045–1050.

Camarillo, Albert. *Chicanos in a Changing Society: From Mexican Pueblos to American Barrios in Santa Barbara and Southern California*. Cambridge, Mass.: Harvard University Press, 1979.

_____. *Latinos in the United States*. Santa Barbara, Calif.: ABC-Clio, 1986.

_____. *Mexican-Americans in Urban Society: A Selected Bibliography*. Berkeley, Calif.: Floricanto Press, 1986.

Canter, Lee, and Marlene Canter. *Assertive Discipline for Parents*. Santa Monica, Calif.: Canter and Associates, 1985.

Caplan, Lincoln. *An Open Adoption*. New York: Farrar, Straus & Giroux, 1990.

Cappell, Charles and Robert B. Heiner. "The Intergenerational Transmission of Family Agression." *Journal of Family Violence* 5:2 (June 1990): 121–134.

Carballo-Dieguez, Alex. "Hispanic Culture, Gay Male Culture, and AIDS: Counseling Implications." *Journal of Counseling and Development* 68:1 (September–October 1989): 26–30.

Cargan, Leonard, and Matthew Melko. *Singles: Myths and Realities*. Beverly Hills, Calif.: Sage Publications, 1982.

Carl, Douglas. "Acquired Immune Deficiency Syndrome: A Preliminary Examination of the Effects on Gay Couples and Coupling." *Journal of Marital and Family Therapy* 12:3 (July 1986): 241–247.

Carnes, Patrick. *Out of the Shadows*. Minneapolis, Minn.: CompCare Publications, 1983.

Carroll, Jerry. "Tracing the Causes of Infertility." *San Francisco Chronicle* (March 5, 1990): B3*ff*.

Carroll, Jerry, et al., "Differences in Males and Females in Motives for Engaging in Sexual Intercourse." *Archives of Sexual Behavior* 14 (1985): 131–139.

Carson, David K. et al. "Family of Origin Characteristics and Current Family Relationships of Female Adult Incest Victims." *Journal of Family Violence* 5:2 (June 1990): 153–172.

Carter, D. Bruce, ed. *Current Conceptions of Sex Roles and Sex Typing*. New York: Praeger, 1987b.

_____. "Sex Role Research and the Future: New Directions for Research." In D. Bruce Carter, ed., *Current Conceptions of Sex Roles and Sex Typing*. New York: Praeger, 1987a.

_____. "Societal Implications of AIDS and HIV Infections, HIV Antibody Testing, Health Care, and AIDS Education." *Marriage and Family Review* 13:1–2 (1989): 129–188.

Carter, Betty, and Monica McGoldrick, eds. *The Changing Family Life Cycle*, 2d ed. Boston: Allyn and Bacon: 1989.

Cassell, Carol. *Swept Away*. New York: Simon and Schuster, 1984.

Cate, Jim, Linda Graham, Donna Boeglin, and Steven Tielker. "The Effect of AIDS on the Family System." *Families in Society* 71:4 (April 1990): 195–201.

Cazenave, N. A. "'A Woman's Place': The Attitudes of Middle Class Black Men." *Phylon: The Atlanta University Review of Race and Culture* 44 (1983): 13–32.

Centers for Disease Control. "Statewide Prevalence of Illicit Drug Use by Pregnant Women—Rhode Island." *Morbidity and Mortality Weekly Report* 39:14 (April 3, 1990): 225–227.

Chasnoff, Ira J. "Drug Use in Pregnancy: Parameters of Risk." *Pediatric Clinics of North America* 35:6 (December 1988): 1403–1412.

Chatters, Linda M., Robert Joseph Taylor, and Harold W. Neighbors. "Size of Informal Helper Network Mobilized during a Serious Personal Problem among Black Americans." *Journal of Marriage and the Family* 51 (August 1989): 667–676.

Chaze, William. "New, Nationwide Drive to Curb Child Abuse." *U.S. News and World Report* (October 1, 1984).

Cherlin, Andrew J. "The Changing American Family and Public Policy." In Andrew J. Cherlin, ed., *The Changing American Family and Public Policy*. Washington, D.C.: The Urban Institute Press, 1988.

_____. *Marriage, Divorce, and Remarriage*. Cambridge, Mass.: Harvard University Press, 1981.

_____. "Remarriage as Incomplete Institution." *American Journal of Sociology* 84 (1978): 634–650.

_____. *The Changing American Family and Public Policy*. Washington, D.C.: The Urban Institute Press, 1988.

Cherlin, Andrew, and Frank Furstenberg, Jr. *The New American Grandparent*. New York: Basic Books, 1986.

Chesser, Barbara Jo. "Analysis of Wedding Rituals: An Attempt to Make Weddings More Meaningful." *Family Relations* (April 1980).

Chiasson, M. A., R. L. Stoneburner and S. C. Joseph. "Human Immunodeficiency Virus Transmission Through Artificial Insemination." *Journal of Acquired Immune Deficiency Syndromes* 3:1 (1990): 69–72.

Chilman, Catherine. "Working Poor Families: Trends, Causes, Effects, and Suggested Policies." *Family Relations* 40:2 (April 1991): 191–198.

Chilman, Catherine, et al., eds. *Variant Family Forms*. Beverly Hills, Calif.: Sage Publications, 1988.

Christenen, Andrew. "Dysfunctional Interaction Patterns in Couples." In Patricia Noller and Mary Anne Fitzpatrick, eds., *Perspectives on Marital Interaction*. Philadelphia, Penn.: Multilingual Matters, 1988.

Christensen, Donna, Carla Dahl, and Kathryn Rettig. "Noncustodial Mothers and Child Support: Examining the Larger Context." *Family Relations* 39:4 (October 1990): 388–394.

Christopher, F., and R. Cate. "Factors Involved in Premarital Decisionmaking." *Journal of Sex Research* 20 (1984): 363–376.

Christopher, F. Scott, Richard A. Fabes, and Patricia M. Wilson. "Family Television Viewing: Implications for Family Life Education." *Family Relations* 38:2 (April 1989): 210–214.

Ciancannelli, Penelope, and Bettina Berch. "Gender and the GNP." In Myra Marx Ferree and Beth Hess, eds., *Analyzing Gender*. Newbury Park, Calif.: Sage Publications, 1987.

Cimons, Marlene. "American Infertility Rate Not Growing, Study Finds." *The New York Times*, December 7, 1990: A3.

Claes, Jacalyn A. and David M. Rosenthal. "Men Who Batter Women: A Study in Power." *Journal of Family Violence* 5:3 (September 1990): 215–224.

Clark-Nicolas, Patricia, and Bernadette Gray–Little. "Effect of Economic Resources on Marital Quality in Black Married Couples." *Journal of Marriage and the Family* 53:3 (August 1991): 645–656.

Cleek, Margaret, and T. Allan Pearson. "Perceived Causes of Divorce: An Analysis of Interrelationships." *Journal of Marriage and the Family* 47:2 (February 1985): 179–191.

Clemens, Audra, and Leland Axelson. "The Not-So-Empty-Nest: The Return of the Fledgling Adult." *Family Relations* 34 (April 1985): 259–264.

Clemes, Harris, and Reynold Bean. *How to Raise Children's Self-Esteem*. San Jose, Calif.: Enrich, 1983.

Cleveland, Peggy, et al. "If Your Child Has AIDS...: Responses of Parents with Homosexual Children." *Family Relations* 37:2 (April 1988): 150–153.

Clingempeel, W. Glenn, and Eulalee Brand. "Quasi-kin Relationships, Structural Complexity, and Marital Quality in Stepfamilies: A Replication, Extension, and Clinical Implications." *Family Relations* 34:3 (July 1985): 401–409.

Clingempeel, W. Glenn, et al. "Stepparent-Stepchild Relationships in Stepmother and Stepfather Families: A Multimethod Study." *Family Relations* 33 (1984): 465–473.

Cochran, Susan, Jasen Keidan and Ari Kalechstein. "Sexually Transmitted Diseases and Acquired Immunodeficiency Syndrome (AIDS): Changes in Risk Reduction Behaviors among Young Adults." *Sexually Transmitted Diseases* 16:1 (January–March 1989): 80–86.

Coggle, Frances, and Grace Tasker. "Children and Housework." *Family Relations* 31 (July 1982): 395–399.

Cohen, Nancy Weiner, and Lois J. Estner. "Silent Knife: Cesarean Section in the United States." *Society* 21:1(147) (November–December 1983): 95–111.

Cohen, Theodore. "Remaking Men: Men's Experiences Becoming and Being Husbands and Fathers and Their Implications for Reconceptualizing Men's Lives." *Journal of Family Issues* 8:1 (March, 1987): 57–77.

Cohler, Bertram, and Scott Geyer. "Psychological Autonomy and Interdependence within the Family." In Froma Walsh, ed., *Normal Family Processes*. New York: Guilford Press, 1982.

Cole, Charles, and Anna Cole. "Husbands and Wives Should Have an Equal Share in Making the Marriage Work." In Harold Feldman and Margaret Feldman, eds., *Current Controversies in Marriage and the Family*. Beverly Hills, Calif.: Sage Publications, 1985.

Cole, Cynthia, and Hyman Rodman. "Latchkey Children: A Review of Policy and Resources" *Family Relations*. 36 (January 1987): 101–105.

Coleman, Elizabeth. "Sexual Compulsion vs. Sexual Addiction: The Date Continues." *SIECUS Report* 14 (1986): 7–10.

Coleman, Marilyn, and Lawrence Ganong. "The Cultural Stereotyping of Stepfamilies." In Kay Pasley and Marilyn Ihinger-Tallman, eds. *Remarriage and Stepparenting: Current Research and Theory*. New York: Guilford Press, 1987.

_____. "Remarriage and Stepfamily Research in the 1980s: Increased Interest in an Old Form." In Alan Booth, ed. *Contemporary Families: Looking Forward, Looking Back*. Minneapolis: National Council on Family Relations, 1991.

Coleman, Peter. *Gay Christians: A Moral Dilemma*. Philadelphia: Trinity Press, 1989.

Coles, Robert. *The Spiritual Life of Children*. Boston: Houghton-Mifflin, 1990.

Collier, J., M. Z. Rosaldo, and S. Yanagisako. "Is There a Family? New Anthropological Views." In B. Thorne and M. Yalom, eds., *Rethinking the Family: Some Feminist Questions*. New York: Longman, 1982.

Collins, Glenn. "Insensitivity to the Disabled." *The New York Times*, August 11, 1986: 18.

_____. "U.S. Day-Care Guidelines Rekindle Controversy." *New York Times*, February 4, 1985:20.

Condit, Celeste. *Decoding Abortion Rhetoric*. Urbana, Ill: University of Chicago Press, 1990.

Condrad, Peter, and Joseph Schneider. *Deviance and Medicalization: From Badness to Sickness*. St. Louis, Mo.: C. V. Mosby, 1980.

Condron, John, and Jerry Bode. "Rashomon, Working Wives, and Family Division of Labor: Middletown, 1980." *Journal of Marriage and the Family* 44:2 (May 1982): 421–426.

Condry, J. and S. Condry. "The Development of Sex Differences: A Study of the Eye of the Beholder." *Child Development* 47:4 (1976): 812–819.

Conway, Colleen. "Psychophysical Preparations for Childbirth." In Leota McNall, ed. *Contemporary Obstetric and Gynecological Nursing*. St. Louis, Mo.: C. V. Mosby, 1980.

Cook, Alicia, et al. "Changes in Attitudes Toward Parenting Among College Women: 1972 and 1979 Samples." *Family Relations* 31 (January 1982): 109–113.

Cook, Mark, ed., *The Bases of Human Sexual Attraction*. New York: Academic Press, 1981.

Cooke, Betty D., et al. "Examining the Definition and Assessment of Social Support: A Resource for Individuals and Families." *Family Relations* 37 (April 1988): 211–216.

Cooney, Teresa, and Peter Uhlenberg. "The Role of Divorce in Men's Relation with Their Adult Children after Mid-life." *Journal of Marriage and the Family* 52:3 (August 1990): 677–688.

Corby, Nan, and Judy Zarit. "Old and Alone: The Unmarried in Later Life." In Ruth Weg, ed., *Sexuality in the Later Years: Roles and Behavior*. New York: Academic Press, 1983.

Corea, Gena. *The Mother Machine: Reproductive Technology from Artificial Insemination to Artificial Wombs*. New York: Harper and Row, 1985.

Cortese, Anthony. "Subcultural Differences in Human Sexuality: Race, Ethnicity, and Social Class." In Kathleen McKinney and Susan Sprecher, eds., *Human Sexuality: The Societal and Interpersonal Context*. Norwood, N.J.: Ablex Publishing Corporation, 1989.

Cosby, Bill. "The Regular Way." *Playboy* (December 1968): 288–289.

Coulanges, Fustel de. *The Ancient City*. 1867. Reprint. New York: Anchor Books, 1960.

Cowan, Carolyn P., and Philip A. Cowan. "Who Does What When Partners Become Parents: Implications for Men, Women, and Marriage." *Marriage and Family Review* 12:3–4 (1988): 105–131.

Cowan, Philip, and Carolyn Cowan. "Becoming a Family: Research and Intervention." In Irving Sigel and Gene Brody, eds., *Methods of Family Research: Biographies of Research Projects*. Hillsdale, N.J.: Lawrence Erlbaum Associates, Publishers, 1990.

Cramer, D. "Gay Parents and Their Children: A Review of Research and Practical Implications." *Journal of Counseling and Development* 64 (1986): 504–507.

Cramer, David, and Arthur Roach. "Coming Out to Mom and Dad: A Study of Gay Males and Their Relationships with Their Parents." *Journal of Homosexuality* 14:1–2 (1987): 77–88.

Crandell, Barbara, et al. "Follow-up of 2000 Second-Trimester Amniocenteses." *Obstetrics and Gynecology* 56 (November 1980): 625–628.

Croby, Nan, and Judy Zarit. "Old and Alone: The Unmarried in Later Life." In Ruth Weg, ed., *Sexuality in the Later Years: Roles and Behavior*. New York: Academic Press, 1983.

Cromer, B. A. [and others]. Knowledge, Attitudes, and Behavior Related to Sexuality in Adolescents with Chronic Disability. Developmental Medicine and Child Neurology; July 1990; 32(7): 602–610.

Crosby, John, ed. *Reply to Myth: Perspectives on Intimacy*. New York: John Wiley, 1985.

Cuber, John, and Peggy Haroff. *Sex and the Significant Americans*, rev. ed. Baltimore: Penguin Books, 1965, 1974.

Culp, R. E., et al. "A Comparison of Observed and Reported Adult-Infant Interactions: Effects of Perceived Sex." *Sex Roles* 9 (1983): 475–479.

Cummings, Judith. Disabled Model Defies Sexual Stereotypes. The New York Times. New York; June 8, 1987: 17.

Curie-Cohen, M., et al. "Current Practice of Artificial Insemination by Donor in the United States." *New England Journal of Medicine* 300:11 (March 15, 1979): 585–590.

Curran, Dolores. *Traits of a Healthy Family*. New York: Ballantine Books, 1983.

Daley, Suzanne. "Girls' Self-Esteem Is Lost on Way to Adolescence, New Study Finds." *The New York Times*, January 9, 1991: B1.

Daniluk, Judith, and Al Herman. "Parenthood Decision-Making." *Family Relations* 33 (October 1984): 607–612.

Danzinger, Sheldon, and Robert Plotnick. "Poverty and Policy: Lessons of the Last Two Decades." *Social Services Review* 60 (1986): 34–51.

Darling, Carol, and Kenneth Davidson. "Enhancing Relationships: Understanding the Feminine Mystique of Orgasm." *Journal of Sex & Marital Therapy* 12:3 (Fall 1986): 186–196.

Darling, Rosalyn, and J. Darling. *Children Who Are Different: Meeting the Challenges of Birth Defects in Society*. St. Louis, Mo.: C. V. Mosby, 1982.

Darling, Rosalyn Benjamin. "The Economic and Psychosocial Consequences of Disability: Family-Society Relationships." *Marriage and Family Review* 11:1–2 (Fall–Winter, 1987): 45–61.

Darling-Fisher, Cynthia, and Linda Tiedje. "The Impact of Maternal Employment Characteristics on Fathers' Participation in Child Care." *Family Relations* 39:1 (January 1990): 20–26.

Daro, Deborah, and Anne Cohen. "Child Maltreatment Evaluations Efforts: What Have We Learned?" In Gerald Hotaling, David Finkelhor, John Kirkpatrick, and Murray Straus, eds., *Coping with Family Violence: Research and Perspectives.* Newbury Park, Calif.: Sage Publications, 1988.

Davidson, Kenneth, and Carol Darling. "The Stereotype of Single Women Revisited." *Health Care for Women International* 9:4 (October–December, 1988): 317–336.

——. "Changing Autoerotic Attitudes and Practices among College Females: A Two-Year Follow-up Study." *Adolescence* 23 (Winter, 1988): 773–792.

Davidson, Kenneth, and Linda Hoffman. "Sexual Fantasies and Sexual Satisfaction: An Empirical Investigation of Erotic Thought." *Journal of Sex Research* 22 (May 1986): 184–205.

Davidson, J. Kenneth, Carol Darling, and Colleen Conway-Welch. "The Role of the Gräfenberg Spot and Female Ejaculation in the Female Orgasmic Response: An Empirical Analysis." *Journal of Sex and Marital Therapy* 15 (Summer 1989): 102–120.

Davis, Keith. "Near and Dear: Friendship and Love Compared." *Psychology Today* 19:2 (February 1985): 22–30.

Davis, L. *The Black Family in the United States.* Westport, Conn.: Greenwood Press, 1986.

Davitz, J. R. *The Language of Emotion.* New York: Academic Press, 1969.

Dawson, Deborah. "Family Structure and Children's Health and Well-Being." *Journal of Marriage and the Family* 53:3 (August 1991): 574–584.

Dean, Gillian, and Douglas Gurak. "Marital Homogagy: The Second Time Around." *Journal of Marriage and the Family* 40:3 (August 1978): 559–570.

DeBuono, Barbara, Stephen Zinner, Maxim Daamen, and William McCormack. "Sexual Behavior in College Women in 1975, 1986, and 1989." *New England Journal of Medicine* 322:12 (March 22, 1990): 821–825.

DeCecco, John, ed. *Gay Relationships.* New York: Haworth Press, 1988.

DeCecco, John, and Michael Shively. "From Sexual Identity to Sexual Relationships: A Conceptual Shift." *Journal of Homosexuality* 9(2/3) (Winter 1983/Spring 1984): 1–26.

Degler, Carl. *At Odds.* New York: Oxford University Press, 1980.

Delamater, J. D., and P. MacCorquodale. *Premarital Sexuality: Attitudes, Relationships, Behavior.* Madison: University of Wisconsin Press, 1979.

DeMaris, Alfred. "The Dynamics of Generational Transfer in Courtship Violence: A Biracial Exploration." *Journal of Marriage and the Family* 52 (February 1990): 219–231.

DeMaris, Alfred, and Gerald Leslie. "Cohabitation with the Future Spouse: Its Influence Upon Marital Satisfaction and Communication." *Journal of Marriage and the Family* 46:1 (February 1984): 77–84.

D'Emilio, John, and Estelle Freedman. *Intimate Matters: A History of Sexuality in America.* New York: Harper and Row, 1988.

Demo, David, and Alan Acock. "The Impact of Divorce on Children." In Alan Booth, ed., *Contemporary Families: Looking Forward, Looking Back.* Minneapolis: National Council on Family Relations, 1991.

Demo, David H., et al. "Family Relations and Self-Esteem." *Journal of Marriage and the Family.* 49:4 (November 1987): 705–716.

Demos, Vasilikie. "Black Family Studies in the *Journal of Marriage and the Family* and the Issue of Distortion: A Trend Analysis." *Journal of Marriage and the Family* 52 (August, 1990): 603–612.

Dentzer, Susan. "Do the Elderly Want to Work?" *U.S. News & World Report,* May 14, 1990: 48–50.

Denzin, Norman. "Toward a Phenomenology of Domestic Family Violence." *American Journal of Sociology* 90(30) (1984): 483–513.

DeParle, Jason. "Suffering in the Cities Persists as U.S. Fights Other Battles." *The New York Times,* January 27, 1991: 1, 15.

Depner, Charlene, and James Bray. "Modes of Participation for Noncustodial Parents: The Challenge for Research, Policy, Practice, and Education." *Family Relations* 39:4 (October 1990): 378–381.

Derdeyn, A. and E. Scott. "Joint Custody: A Critical Analysis and Appraisal." *American Journal of Orthopsychiatry* 54 (April 1984): 199–209.

De Simone-Luis, Judith, et al. "Children of Separation and Divorce: Factors Influencing Adjustment." *Journal of Divorce* 3:1 (Fall 1979): 37–42.

Desmond, Edward. "Out in the Open." *Time.* November 30, 1987: 80–90.

DeSpelder, Lynne Ann, and Albert Strickland, 3d ed. *The Last Dance: Encountering Death and Dying.* Palo Alto, Calif.: Mayfield Publishing Co. 1990.

DeVault, Marjorie. "Doing Housework: Feeling and Family Life." In Naomi Gerstel and Harriet Gross, eds., *Families and Work.* Philadelphia: Temple University Press, 1987.

De Witt, Karen. "U.S. Plan on Child Care Is Reported to be Stalled." *The New York Times,* January 17, 1991: A12.

Dick-Read, Grantly. *Childbirth Without Fear.* 4th ed. New York: Harper & Row, 1972.

Dilworth-Anderson, Peggye, and Harriette Pipes McAdoo. "The Study of Ethnic Minority Families: Implications for Practioners and Policymakers." *Family Relations* 37 (July 1988): 265–267.

Dinnerstein, Leonard, and David Reimers. *Ethnic Americans: A History of Immigration.* 3d ed. New York: Harper and Row, 1988.

Dion, Karen. "Physical Attractiveness, Sex Roles, and Heterosexual Attraction." In Mark Cook, ed., *The Bases of Human Sexual Attraction.* New York: Academic Press, 1981.

Dion, Karen, et al. "What Is Beautiful Is Good." *Journal of Personality and Social Psychology* 24 (1972): 285–290.

Dobash, R. Emerson, and Russell Dobash. *Violence Against Wives: A Case Against the Patriarchy.* New York: Free Press, 1979.

Dodson, Fitzhugh. "How to Discipline Effectively." In Eileen Shiff, ed., *Experts Advise Parents.* New York: Dell Publishing Co., 1987.

Dodson, Jualynne. "Conceptualizations of Black Families." In Harriette Pipes McAdoo, ed., *Black Families,* 2d ed. Newbury Park, Calif.: Sage Publications, 1988.

Doherty, William, and Thomas Campbell. *Families and Health.* Newbury Park, Calif.: Sage Publications, 1988.

Donovan, P. "New Reproductive Technologies: Some Legal Dilemmas." *Family Planning Perspectives* 18 (1986): 57ff.

Dooley, Karen, and Ralph Catalano. "Stress Transmission: The Effects of Husbands' Job Stressors on the Emotional Health of Their Wives." *Journal of Marriage and the Family* 53:1 (February 1991): 165–177.

Dorr, Aimee, Peter Kovaric, and Catherine Doubleday. "Parent-Child Coviewing of Television." *Journal of Broadcasting and Electronic Media* 33:1 (Winter 1989): 35–51.

Dorris, Michael. *The Broken Cord.* New York: Harper and Row, 1989.

——. "A Desperate Crack Legacy." *Newsweek* (June 25, 1990): 8.

Dreikurs, Rudolph, and V. Soltz. *Children: The Challenge.* New York: Hawthorne Books, 1964.

Drugger, Karen. "Social Location and Gender-Role Attitudes: A Comparison of Black and White Women." *Gender & Society* 2:4 (December 1988): 425–448.

DSM-IV. See American Psychiatric Association on Nomenclature and Statistics.

Duck, Steve, and Daniel Perlman. *Understanding Personal Relationships: An Interdisciplinary Approach.* Beverly Hills, Calif.: Sage Publications, 1985.

Duncan, Greg, and Saul Hoffman. "A Reconsideration of the Economic Consequences of Divorce." *Demography* 22 (1985): 485–498.

Duncan, Greg, and Willard Rodgers. "Longitudinal Aspects of Childhood Poverty." *Journal of Marriage and the Family* 50:4 (November 1988): 1007–1022.

Duncan, Greg, et al. *Years of Poverty, Years of Plenty.* Ann Arbor: Survey Research Center, Institute for Social Research, University of Michigan, 1984.

Dunford, Franklyn, David Huizinga, and Delbert Elliott. "The Role of Arrest in Domestic Assault: The Omaha Police Experiment." *Criminology* 28:2 (1990): 183–206.

Dutton, Donald, and Arthur Aron. "Some Evidence for Heightened Sexual Attraction under Conditions of High Anxiety." *Journal of Personality and Social Psychology* 30:4 (October 1974): 510–517.

Duvall, Evelyn. "Family Development's First Forty Years." *Family Relations* 37:2 (April 1988): 127–134.

Duvall, Evelyn, and Brent Miller. *Marriage and Family Development,* 6th ed. New York: Harper and Row, 1985.

Dworetsky, John P. *Introduction to Child Development,* 4th ed. St. Paul, Minn.: West Publishing Company, 1990.

Eakins, P. S. "Free-Standing Birth Centers in California." *Journal of Reproductive Medicine* 34:12 (December 1989): 960–970.

Edelman, Marian Wright. "Children at Risk." *Proceedings of the Academy of Political Science* 37:2 (1989): 20–30.

_____. "Children at Risk." In Frank J. Macchiarola and Alan Gartner, eds., *Caring for America's Children.* New York: The Academy of Political Science, 1989.

_____. Forward to Clifford Johnson, Andrew Sum, and James Weill *Vanishing Dreams: The Growing Economic Plight of America's Young Families.* Washington, D.C.: Children's Defense Fund, 1988.

Edelman, Marian, and Lisa Mihaly. "Homeless Families and the Housing Crisis in the United States." *Children and Youth Services Review* 11:1 (1989): 91–108.

Edleson, Jeffrey, et al. "Men `w no Batter Women." *Journal of Family Issues* 6:2 (June 1985): 229–247.

Edwards, G. R. "A Critique of Creationist Homophobia." *Journal of Homosexuality* 18:3–4 (1989): 95–118.

Ehrenkranz, Joel R., and Wylie C. Hembree. "Effects of Marijuana on Male Reproductive Function." *Psychiatric Annals* 16:4 (April 1986): 243–248.

Ehrenreich, Barbara. *The Hearts of Men.* Garden City, New York: Anchor/Doubleday, 1984.

Ehrenreich, Barbara, and Deirdre English. *For Her Own Good: 150 Years of the Experts' Advice to Women.* Garden City, N.Y.: Anchor, 1979.

Eichler, Margrit. *Families in Canada Today.* Toronto: Gage, 1983.

_____. "Reflections on Motherhood, Apple Pie, the New Reproductive Technologies and the Role of Sociologists in Society." *Society-Société* 13:1 (February 1989): 1–5.

Elder, Glen H., Jr. *Children of the Great Depression.* Chicago: University of Chicago Press, 1974.

Elder, Glen, and Jeffrey Liker. "Hard Times in Women's Lives: Historical Influences Across Forty Years." *American Journal of Sociology* 88:2 (September 1982): 241–269.

Ellis, Albert. *Sex without Guilt.* Secaucus, N.J.: Lyle Stuart, 1958.

Ellis, Albert, "The Justification of Sex Without Love." In John Crosby, ed., *Reply to Myth: Perspectives on Intimacy.* New York: John Wiley, 1985.

Ellis, Desmond. "Policing Wife Abuse: The Contribution Made by 'Domestic Disturbance' Deaths and Injuries among Police Officers." *Journal of Family Violence* 4:2 (1987): 319–333.

Ellison, Christopher. "Family Ties, Friendships, and Subjective Well-Being among Black Americans." *Journal of Marriage and the Family* 52 (May 1990): 298–310.

Ellwood, David. *Poor Support: Poverty in the American Family.* New York: Basic Books, 1988.

Emery, Robert, and Melissa Wyer. "Child Custody Mediation and Litigation: An Experimental Evaluation of the Experience of Parents." *Journal of Consulting and Clinical Psychology* 55:2 (1987): 179–186.

Enkin, Murray W. "Smoking and Pregnancy: A New Look." *Birth Issues in Perinatal Care and Education* 11:4 (Winter 1984): 225–229.

Erikson, Erik. *Childhood and Society.* New York: Norton, 1963.

_____. *Identity, Youth and Crisis.* New York: Norton, 1968.

_____. *Vital Involvements in Old Age: The Experience of Old Age in Our Time.* Boston: W. W. Norton, 1986.

Erkut, Sumru. "Exploring Sex-Differences in Expectancy, Attribution, and Academic Achievement." *Sex Roles* 9:2 (1983): 217–231.

Etaugh, Claire, and Barbara Petroski. "Perceptions of Women: Effects of Employment Status and Marital Status." *Sex Roles* 12 (1985): 329–339.

Etaugh, Claire, and J. Malstrom. "The Effect of Marital Status on Person Perception." *Journal of Marriage and the Family* 4 (1981): 801–805.

Evans, H. L., et al. "Sperm Abnormalities and Cigarette Smoking." *Lancet* 1:8221 (March 21, 1981): 627–629.

Fabes, Richard, and Jeremiah Strouse. "Perceptions of Responsible and Irresponsible Models of Sexuality." *Journal of Sex Research* 23:1 (February, 1987): 70–84.

Fabes, Richard, Patricia Wilson, and F. Scott Christopher. "A Time to Reexamine the Role of Television in Family Life." *Family Relations* 38:3 (July 1989): 337–341.

Fagot, Beverly, and Mary Leinbach. "Socialization of Sex Roles within the Family." In D. Bruce Carter, ed. *Current Conceptions of Sex Roles and Sex Typing.* New York: Praeger, 1987.

Faidley, Joyce. "Judge Mirrors Spouse-Abuse Myths." *Los Angeles Times,* July 9, 1989.

Faludi, Susan. "Barren, the Burden." *West* (April 16, 1989): 14–23.

Farber, Bernard, Charles H. Mindel, and Bernard Lazerwitz. "The Jewish American Family." In Charles H. Mindel, Robert W. Habenstein, and Roosevelt Wright, Jr., eds., *Ethnic Families in America: Patterns and Variations,* 3d ed. New York: Elsevier, 1988.

Fay, Robert, Charles Turner, Albert Klassen, and John Gagnon. "Prevalence and Patterns of Same-Gender Sexual Contact among Men." *Science* 243:4889 (January 20, 1989): 338–348.

Featherstone, Helen. *A Difference in the Family.* New York: Basic Books, 1980.

Fehr, Beverly. "Prototype Analysis of the Concepts of Love and Commitment." *Journal of Personality and Social Psychology* 55:4 (1988): 557–579.

Fein, Robert. "Research on Fathering." In Arlene Skolnick and Jerome Skolnick, eds., *The Family in Transition.* Boston: Little, Brown, 1980.

Feirstein, Bruce. "Real Men Don't Eat Quiche." New York: Pocket Books, 1982.

Feldman, Harold, and Margaret Feldman. "The Family Life Cycle: Some Suggestions for Recycling." *Journal of Marriage and the Family* 37 (May 1975): 277–284.

Feldman, Shirley, and Sharon Churnin. "The Transition from Expectancy to Parenthood." *Sex Roles* 11(1/2) (1984): 61–78.

Ferber, Marianne. "Labor Market Participation of Young Married Women: Causes and Effects." *Journal of Marriage and the Family* 44:2 (May 1982): 457–468.

Ferber, Marianne, and Bonnie Birnbaum. "Economics of the Family: Who Maximizes What?" *Family Economics Review* (Summer–Fall, 1980): 13–16.

Ferguson, P. M.; Ferguson, D. L. Sex, Sexuality, and Disability. Journal of the Association for Persons with Severe Handicaps; Spring 1992; 17(1): 27–28.

Ferman, Lawrence. "After the Shutdown: The Social and Psychological Costs of Job Displacement." *Industrial and Labor Relations Report* 18:2 (1981): 22–26.

Ferree, Myra Marx. "Beyond Separate Spheres: Feminism and Family Research." In Alan Booth, ed., *Contemporary Families: Looking Forward, Looking Back*. Minneapolis, Minn.: National Council on Family Relations, 1991.

Figley, Charles, ed. *Treating Families Under Stress*. New York: Brunner/Mazel, 1989.

Figley, Charles, and Hamilton McCubbin, eds. *Stress and the Family*, 2 vols. New York: Brunner/Mazel, 1983.

Fincham, Frank, and Thomas Bradbury. "The Assessment of Marital Quality." *Journal of Marriage and the Family* 49:4 (November 1987): 797–810.

Finkelhor, David. *Child Sexual Abuse: New Theory and Research*. New York: Free Press, 1984.

_____. "Common Features of Family Abuse." In David Finkelhor et al., eds., *The Dark Side of Families*. Beverly Hills, Calif.: Sage Publications, 1983.

_____. "Prevention Approaches to Child Sexual Abuse." In Mary Lystad, ed., *Violence in the Home: Interdisciplinary Perspectives*. New York: Brunner/Mazel, 1986b.

_____. "Prevention: A Review of Programs and Research." In David Finkelhor, ed., *Sourcebook on Child Sexual Abuse*. Beverly Hills, Calif.: Sage Publications, 1986a.

_____. *Sexually Victimized Children*. New York: Free Press, 1979.

Finkelhor, David, and Larry Baron. "High Risk Children." In David Finkelhor ed., *Sourcebook on Child Sexual Abuse*. Beverly Hills, Calif.: Sage Publications, 1986.

Finkelhor, David, and Angela Browne. "Initial and Long-Term Effects: A Conceptual Framework." In David Finkelhor, ed., *Sourcebook on Child Sexual Abuse*. Beverly Hills, Calif.: Sage Publications, 1986.

Finkelhor, David, Gerald Hotaling, and Andrea Sedlak. "Abduction of Children by Family Members." *Journal of Marriage and the Family* 53:3 (August 1991): 805–817.

Finkelhor, David, Gerald Hotaling, and Andrea Sedlak. *Missing, Abducted, Runaway, and Throwaway Children in America*. Washington, D.C.: U.S. Department of Justice, 1990.

Finkelhor, David, and Karl Pillemer. "Elder Abuse: Its Relationship to Other Forms of Domestic Violence." In Gerald T. Hotaling et al., eds., *Family Abuse and Its Consequences*. Newbury Park, Calif.: Sage Publications, 1988.

Finkelhor, David, and Kerst Ÿllo. "Forced Sex in Marriage: A Preliminary Research Report." National Institute of Mental Health, 1980.

_____. *License to Rape: The Sexual Abuse of Wives*. New York: Holt, Rinehardt, 1985.

Finkelhor, David, et al. eds. *The Dark Side of Families*. Beverly Hills, Calif.: Sage Publications, 1983.

Finkelhor, David, et al. "Sexual Abuse in Day Care: A National Study." National Center on Child Abuse and Neglect, University of New Hampshire: Family Research Laboratory, 1988.

Finkelhor, David, et al. "Sexual Abuse in a National Survey of Adult Men and Women." *Child Abuse and Neglect* 14:1 (1990): 19–28.

Firestone, Juanita, and Beth Anne Shelton. "An Estimation of the Effects of Women's Work on Available Leisure Time." *Journal of Family Issues* 9:4 (December 1988): 478–495.

Fischer, David Hackett. *Old Age in America*. Boston: Little, Brown, 1978.

Fischl, Margaret, et al. "Evaluation of Heterosexual Partners, Children, and Household Contacts of Adults with AIDS." *JAMA: Journal of the American Medical Association* 257:5 (February 6, 1987): 640–647.

Fischman, Joshua. "The Children's Hours." *Psychology Today* (October 1986): 16ff.

Fisher, William, and Donn Byrne. "Social Background, Attitudes, and Sexual Attraction." In Mark Cook, ed., *The Bases of Human Sexual Attraction*. New York: Academic Press, 1981.

Fisher, William, et al. "Erotophobia-Erotophilia as a Dimension of Personality." *Journal of Sex Research* 25:1 (February, 1988): 123–151.

Fishman, Barbara. "The Economic Behavior of Stepfamilies." *Family Relations* 32 (1983): 359–365.

Fitting, Melinda, Peter Rabins, M. Jane Lucas, and James Eastham. "Caregivers for Demented Patients: A Comparison of Husbands and Wives." *Gerontologist* 26 (1986): 248–252.

Fitzpatrick, Joseph. "The Puerto Rican Family." In Charles Mindel and Robert Habenstein, eds., *Ethnic Families in America*, 2d ed. New York: Elsevier North Holland, 1981.

Fitzpatrick, Joseph, and Lourdes Parker. "Hispanic-Americans in the Eastern United States." *Annals of the American Academy of Political and Social Science* 454 (March 1981): 98–110.

Flaherty, Mary Jean, Lorna Facteau, and Patricia Garver. "Grandmother Functions in Multigenerational Families." In Robert Staples, ed., *The Black Family: Essays and Studies*, 4th ed. Belmont, Calif.: Wadsworth Publishing Company, 1990.

Floge, Liliane. "The Dynamics of Child-Care Use and Some Implications for Women's Employment." *Journal of Marriage and the Family* 47:1 (February 1985): 143–154.

Flynn, Clifton P. "Sex Roles and Women's Response to Courtship Violence." *Journal of Family Violence* 5:1 (Mar. 1990): 83–94.

Fogel, Daniel. *Junipero Serra, the Vatican, and Enslavement Theology*. San Francisco, Calif.: ISM Press, 1988.

Foote, Nelson, and Leonard Cottrell. *Identity and Interpersonal Competence*. Chicago: University of Chicago Press, 1955.

Forrest, J. D., and S. Singh. "The Sexual and Reproductive Behavior of American Women, 1982–1988." *Family Planning Perspectives* 22:5 (September–October 1990): 206–214.

Ford, Clellan, and Frank Beach. *Patterns of Sexual Behavior*. New York: Harper and Row, 1972.

Forsstrom-Cohen, Barbara, and Alan Rosenbaum. "The Effects of Parental Marital Violence on Young Adults." *Journal of Marriage and the Family* 47:2 (May 1985): 467–472.

Forste, Renata, and Tim Heaton. "Initiation of Sexual Activity among Female Adolescents." *Youth and Society* 19:3 (March 1988): 250–268.

Forstein, Marshall. "Homophobia: An Overview." *Psychiatric Annals* 18:1 (January 1988): 33–36.

Foucault, Michel. *The History of Sexuality*. New York: Pantheon Books, 1979.

Francke, Linda Bird, et al. "Childless By Choice." *Newsweek* (January 14, 1980): 96.

Fraser, Antonia. *The Weaker Vessel*. New York: Alfred Knopf, 1984.

Freed, Doris, and Timothy Walker. "Family Law in the Fifty States." *Family Law Quarterly* 21 (1988): 417–573.

Freedman, Estelle, and Barrie Thorne. "Introduction to 'The Feminist Sexuality Debates.'" *Signs: Journal of Women in Culture and Society* 10:1 (1984): 102–105.

Freeman, Ellen. "Adolescent Contraceptive Use." *American Journal of Public Health* 70 (August 1980): 790–797.

French, J. P., and Bertram Raven. "The Bases of Social Power." In I. Cartwright, ed., *Studies in Social Power*. Ann Arbor: University of Michigan Press, 1959.

Freud, Sigmund. *New Introductory Lectures on Psychoanalysis*. New York: Doubleday, 1933.

Friday, Nancy. *Men in Love*. New York: Delacorte Press, 1980.

Friedan, Betty. *The Feminine Mystique*. New York: Norton, 1963.

_____. *The Second Wave*. New York: Norton, 1980.

Friedman, H., M. Rohrbaugh, and S. Krakauer. *Family Process* 27 (1988): 293–303.

Friedman, Henry. "The Father's Parenting Experience in Divorce." *American Journal of Psychiatry* 137(10) (October 1980): 1177–1182.

Friedman, Rochelle, and Bonnie Gradstein. *Surviving Pregnancy Loss.* Boston: Little, Brown and Company, 1982.

Friend, Richard. "GAYging: Adjustment and the Older Gay Male." *Alternative Lifestyles* 3:2 (May 1980): 231–248.

Frisbie, W. Parker. "Variation in Patterns of Marital Instability among Hispanics." *Journal of Marriage and the Family* 48 (February 1986): 99–106.

Fromm, Erich. *The Art of Loving.* New York: Perennial Library, 1974.

Fuller, Mary Lou. "Help Your Family Understand 'It's a Small, Small World.'" *PTA Today* (December 1989–January 1990): 9–10.

Fulton, Julie. "Parental Reports of Children's Post-Divorce Adjustment." *Journal of Social Issues* 35:4 (1979): 126–139.

Furstenberg, Frank, K., Jr. "The New Extended Family: The Experience of Parents and Children after Remarriage." In Kay Pasley and Marilyn, Ihinger-Tallman, eds., *Remarriage and Stepparenting: Current Research and Theory.* New York: Guilford Press, 1987.

_____. "Recycling the Family: Perspectives for a Neglected Family Form." *Marriage and Family Review* 2:3 (1979): 12–22.

_____. "Reflections on Remarriage." *Journal of Family Issues* 1:4 (1980): 443–453.

Furstenberg, Frank K., Jr. and Andrew Cherlin. *Divided Families.* Cambridge, Mass.: Harvard University Press, 1991.

Furstenberg, Frank K., Jr., Philip Morgan, and Paul Allison. "Paternal Participation and Children's Well-Being after Marital Disruption." *American Sociological Review* 52 (1986): 695–701.

Furstenberg, Frank K., Jr., and Christine Nord. "The Life Course of Children of Divorce: Marital Disruption and Parental Contact." Paper presented at the annual meeting of the Population Association of America, San Diego, April 29–May 1, 1982.

_____. "Parenting Apart: Patterns of Childrearing after Marital Disruption." *Journal of Marriage and the Family* 47:4 (November 1985): 893–904.

Furstenberg, Frank K., Jr., and Graham Spanier. *Recycling the Family: Remarriage after Divorce,* rev. ed. Newbury Park, Calif.: Sage Publications, 1987.

Furstenberg, Frank, Jr., Philip Morgan, Kristin Moore, and James Peterson. "Race Differences in the Timing of Adolescent Intercourse." *American Sociological Review* 52:4 (August 1987): 511–518.

Furstenberg, Frank, K., Jr., et al. "Sex Education and Sexual Experience among Adolescents." *American Journal of Public Health* 75:11 (November 1985): 1331–1332.

Gaesser, David, and Susan Whitbourne. "Work Identity and Marital Adjustment in Blue-Collar Men." *Journal of Marriage and the Family* 47:3 (August 1985): 747–751.

Gagnon, John. "Attitudes and Responses of Parents to Pre-Adolescent Masturbation." *Archives of Sexual Behavior* 14:5 (1985): 451–466.

_____. *Human Sexualities.* New York: Scott, Foresman, 1977.

_____. "Sexual Scripts: Permanence and Change." *Archives of Sexual Behavior* 15:2 (April, 1986): 97–120.

Gagnon, John, and William Simon. "The Sexual Scripting of Oral Genital Contacts." *Archives of Sexual Behavior* 16:1 (February 1987): 1–25.

Gaines, Judith. "A Scandal of Artificial Insemination." *The Good Health Magazine/The New York Times Magazine* (October 7, 1990): 23ff.

Galligan, Richard. "Innovative Techniques (in studying marriage and the family): Siren or Rose?" *Journal of Marriage and the Family* 44:4 (November 1982): 875–888.

Gallup, George H., Jr., "One-fourth Report Family Problems Related to Alcohol." *San Jose Mercury News,* April 26, 1987: 22A.

Gallup, George H., Jr., and Frank Newport. "Parenthood—A Nearly Universal Desire." *San Francisco Chronicle,* June 4, 1990: B3.

Ganong, Lawrence, and Marilyn Coleman. "A Comparison of Clinical and Empirical Literature on Children in Stepfamilies." *Journal of Marriage and the Family* 48 (May 1986): 309–318.

_____. "The Effects of Remarriage on Children: A Review of the Empirical Literature." *Family Relations* 33 (1984): 389–405.

_____. "Sex, Sex Roles, and Family Love." *Journal of Genetic Psychology* 148 (March, 1987): 45–52.

Ganong, Lawrence, Marilyn Coleman, and Dennis Mapes. "A Meta-Analytic Review of Family Structure Stereotypes." *Journal of Marriage and the Family* 52 (May 1990): 287–289.

_____. "Stepparent: A Pejorative Term?" *Psychological Reports* 53:3 (June 1983): 919–922.

Garbarino, James. *Children and Families in the Social Environment.* Hawthorne, N.Y.: Aldine de Gruyter, 1982.

_____. "The Human Ecology of Child Maltreatment." *Journal of Marriage and the Family* 39:4 (Nov. 1977): 721–735.

Garfinkel, Irwin, and Sara McLanahan. *Single Mothers and Their Children: A New American Dilemma.* Washington, D.C.: The Urban Institute Press, 1986.

Garfinkel, Irwin, and Donald Oellerich. "Noncustodial Fathers' Ability to Pay Child Support." *Demography* 26 (1989): 219–233.

Gecas, Viktor, and Monica Seff. "Families and Adolescents." In Alan Booth, ed., *Contemporary Families: Looking Forward, Looking Back.* Minneapolis, Minn.: National Council on Family Relations, 1991.

_____. "Social Class, Occupational Conditions, and Self-Esteem." *Sociological Perspectives* 32 (1989): 353–364.

Gelfand, Donald, and Charles Barresi, eds. *Ethnic Dimensions of Aging.* New York: Springer Publishing, 1987.

Gelles, Richard J. "Applying Research on Family Violence to Clinical Practice." *Journal of Marriage and the Family* 44 (February 1982): 9–20.

_____. "Child Abuse and Violence in Single-Parent Families: Parent Absence and Economic Deprivation." *American Journal of Orthopsychiatry* 59:4 (Oct. 1989): 492–501.

_____. "An Exchange/Social Control Theory." In David Finkelhor et al., eds. *The Dark Side of Families.* Beverly Hills, Calif.: Sage Publications, 1983.

_____. "Parental Child Snatching: A Preliminary Estimate of the National Incidence." *Journal of Marriage and the Family* 46:3 (August 1984): 735–739.

Gelles, Richard J., and Jon R. Conte. "Domestic Violence and Sexual Abuse of Children: A Review of Research in the Eighties." In Alan Booth, ed. *Contemporary Families: Looking Forward, Looking Back.* Minneapolis, MN: National Council on Family Relations, 1991.

Gelles, Richard J., and Claire Pedrick Cornell. *Intimate Violence in Families,* 2nd ed. Newbury Park, Calif.: Sage Publications, 1985, 1990.

Gelles, Richard J., and John W. Harrop. "The Nature and Consequences of the Psychological Abuse of Children: Evidence from the Second National Family Violence Survey." Paper presented at the Eighth National Conference on Child Abuse and Neglect, 1989.

Gelles, Richard J., and Murray A. Straus. *Intimate Violence.* New York: Simon and Schuster, 1988.

Gelman, David. "Who's Taking Care of Our Parents?" *Newsweek* (May 6, 1985): 61–70.

Genevie, Lou, and Eva Margolies. *The Motherhood Report: How Women Feel about Being Mothers.* New York: MacMillan, 1987.

Genovese, Eugene. *Roll, Jordan, Roll.* New York: Harper & Row, 1976.

George, Kenneth, and Andrew Behrendt. "Therapy for Male Couples Experiencing Relationship Problems and Sexual Problems." *Journal of Homosexuality* 14:1–2 (1987): 77–88.

Gerson, Kathleen. *Hard Choices: How Women Decide About Work, Career, and Motherhood.* Berkeley: University of California Press, 1985.

Gerstel, Naomi. "Divorce and Stigma." *Social Forces* 34 (1987): 172–186.

Gerstel, Naomi, and Harriet Gross. *Commuter Marriage: A Study of Work and Family*. New York: The Guilford Press, 1984.

_____. *Families and Work*. Philadelphia: Temple University Press, 1987.

Getlin, Josh. "Legacy of a Mother's Drinking." *Los Angeles Times*, July 24, 1989: V1ff.

Giarretto, Henry. "Humanistic Treatment of Father-Daughter Incest." In Ray Helfer and Henry C. Kempe, eds., *Child Abuse and Neglect: The Family and the Community*. Cambridge, Mass.: Ballinger, 1976.

Gibbs, Nancy. "The Baby Chase." *Time* (October 9, 1989): 86–89.

Gibson, Rose. "Blacks at Middle and Late Life: Resources and Coping." *Annals of the American Academy* 464 (November 1982): 79–90.

Gil, David. "Sociocultural Aspects of Domestic Violence." In Mary Lystad, ed., *Violence in the Home: Interdisciplinary Perspectives*. New York: Brunner/Mazel, 1986.

Gilbert, Lucia, et al. "Perceptions of Parental Role Responsibilities: Differences Between Mothers and Fathers." *Family Relations* 31 (April 1982): 261–269.

Gilligan, Carol. *In a Different Voice: Psychological Theory and Women's Development*. Cambridge, Mass.: Harvard University Press, 1982.

Gilman, Lois. *The Adoption Resource Book*, rev. ed. New York: Harper & Row, 1987.

Givens, Ron. "A New Prohibition." *Newsweek On Campus* (April 1985): 7–13.

Glass, Robert H., and Ronald J. Ericsson. *Getting Pregnant in the 1980s*. Berkeley: University of California Press, 1982.

Glazer-Malbin, Nona, ed. *Old Family/New Family*. New York: Van Nostrand, 1975.

Glenn, Norval. "Duration of Marriage, Family Composition, and Marital Happiness." *National Journal of Sociology* 3 (1989): 3–24.

_____. "Interreligious Marriage in the United States: Patterns and Recent Trends." *Journal of Marriage and the Family* 44:3 (August 1982): 555–566.

_____. "Quantitative Research on Marital Quality in the 1980s: A Critical Review." In Alan Booth, ed., *Contemporary Families: Looking Forward, Looking Back*. Minneapolis: National Council on Family Relations, 1991.

Glenn, Norval, and Kathryn Kramer. "The Marriages and Divorces of the Children of Divorce." *Journal of Marriage and the Family* 49 (November 1987): 811–825.

_____. "The Psychological Well-Being of Adult Children of Divorce." *Journal of Marriage and the Family* 47:4 (November 1985): 905–912.

Glenn, Norval, and Sara McLanahan. "Children and Marital Happiness: A Further Specification of the Relationship." *Journal of Marriage and the Family* 43:1 (February 1982): 63–72.

Glenn, Norval, and Beth Ann Shelton. "Regional Differences in Divorce in the United States." *Journal of Marriage and the Family* 47:3 (August 1985): 641–652.

Glenn, Norval, and Michael Supancic. "The Social and Demographic Correlates of Divorce and Separation in the United States: An Update and Reconsideration." *Journal of Marriage and the Family* 46 (August 1984): 563–575.

Glick, Paul. "American Household Structure in Transition." *Family Planning Perspectives* 16(5) (September/October 1984): 205–211.

_____. "The Family Life Cycle and Social Change." *Family Relations* 38:2 (April 1989): 123–129.

_____. "Fifty Years of Family Demography." *Journal of Marriage and the Family* 50 (November 1988): 861–873.

_____. "Remarried Families, Stepfamilies and Stepchildren: A Brief Demographic Analysis." *Family Relations* 38 (1989): 24–27.

_____. "Updating the Life Cycle of the Family." *Journal of Marriage and the Family* 39:1 (February 1977): 5–14.

Glick, Paul, and Sung Ling Lin. "Recent Changes in Divorce and Remarriage." *Journal of Marriage and the Family* 49:4 (November 1986): 737–747.

Glick, Paul, and Graham Spanier. "Married and Unmarried Cohabitation in the United States." *Journal of Marriage and the Family* 42:1 (February 1980): 19–30.

Gnezda, Therese. "The Effects of Unemployment on Family Functioning." Prepared statement presented to the Select Committee on Children, Youth and Families. House of Representatives, Hearings on the New Unemployed. Detroit, Michigan, March 4, 1984. 35–714O. Washington, D.C.: U.S. Government Printing Office, 1984.

Goelman, Hillel, Ellen Shapiro, and Alan Pence. "Family Environment and Family Day Care." *Family Relations* 39:1 (January 1990): 14–19.

Goetting, Ann. "Divorce Outcome Research." *Journal of Family Issues* 2:3 (September 1981): 20–25.

_____. "The Developmental Tasks of Siblingship over the Life Cycle." *Journal of Marriage and the Family* 48:4 (November 1986): 703–714.

_____. "Parental Satisfaction: A Review." *Journal of Family Issues* 7:1 (March 1986): 83–109.

_____. "Patterns of Support among In-Laws in the United States: A Review of Research." *Journal of Family Issues* 11:1 (March 1990): 67–90.

_____. "The Six Stages of Remarriage: Developmental Tasks of Remarriage After Divorce." *Family Relations* 31 (April 1982): 213–222.

Goldsmith, Jean. "The Postdivorce Family." In Froma Walsh, ed., *Normal Family Processes*. New York: Guilford Press, 1982.

Goldsmith, Marsha. "Possible Herpes Virus Role in Abortion Studied." *Journal of the American Medical Association* 251(23) (1984): 3067–3070.

Goldstein, David, and Alan Rosenbaum. "An Evaluation of the Self-Esteem of Maritally Violent Men." *Family Relations* 34:3 (July 1985): 425–428.

Goldstein, R. "The Gay Family." *Voices* 11:27 (1986): 21–24.

Goleman, Daniel. "How Viewers Grow Addicted to Television." *The New York Times*, October 16, 1990: C1, C8.

_____. "Marriage: Research Reveals Ingredients of Happiness." *New York Times*, April 16, 1985:19–20.

_____. "Spacing of Siblings Strongly Linked to Success in Life." *New York Times*, May 28, 1985:17–18.

Gondolf, Edward W., "The Effect of Batterer Counseling on Shelter Outcome." *Journal of Interpersonal Violence* 3:3 (September 1988): 275–289.

_____. "Evaluating Progress for Men who Batter." *Journal of Family Violence* 2 (1987): 95–108.

_____. "Who Are These Guys? Toward A Behavioral Typology of Batterers." *Violence and Victims* 3:3 (Fall 1989): 187–203.

Gongla, Patricia, and Edward Thompson, Jr. "Single-Parent Families." In Marvin Sussman and Suzanne Steinmetz, eds., *Handbook of Marriage and the Family*. New York: Plenum Press, 1987.

Goode, William. The Family, 2d ed. Englewood Cliffs, N.J.: Prentice-Hall, 1982.

_____. "Force and Violence in the Family." *Journal of Marriage and the Family* 33 (November 1971): 624–636.

_____. "The Theoretical Importance of Love." *American Sociological Review* 24 (February 1959): 38–47.

_____. *World Revolution and Family Patterns*. New York: Free Press, 1963.

Gordon, Michael. *The American Family: Past, Present, and Future*. New York: Random House, 1978.

Gordon, Sol. "What Kids Need to Know." *Psychology Today* (October 1986): 46ff.

Gordon, Thomas. *P.E.T. in Action*. New York: Bantam Books, 1979.

Gottman, J. M. *Marital Interactions: Experimental Investigations*. New York: Academic Press, 1979.

Gough, Kathleen. "Is the Family Universal: The Nayar Case." In Norman Bell and Ezra Vogel, eds., *A Modern Introduction to the Family*. New York: Free Press, 1968.

Gould, Jeffrey B., Becky Davey, and Randall S. Stafford. "Socioeconomic Differences in Rates of Cesarean Section." *New England Journal of Medicine* 321:4 (July 27, 1989): 233–239.

Gove, Walter, Michael Hughes, and Carolyn Style. "Does Marriage Have Positive Effects on the Psychological Well-Being of the Individual?" *Journal of Health and Social Behavior* 24 (1983): 122–131.

Gove, Walter, Carolyn Style, and Michael Hughes. "The Effect of Marriage on the Well-Being of Adults." *Journal of Family Issues* 11:1 (March 1990): 4–35.

Grauerholz, Elizabeth. "Balancing the Power in Dating Relationships." *Sex Roles* 17:9/10 (1987): 563–571.

Green, Richard. "Sexual Identity of 37 Children Raised by Homosexual or Transsexual Parents." *American Journal of Psychiatry* 135:6 (June 1978): 692–697.

_____. The *"Sissy-Boy Syndrome" and the Development of Homosexuality*. New Haven, Conn.: Yale University Press, 1987.

Green, Richard, et al. "Lesbian Mothers and Their Children: A Comparison with Solo Parent Heterosexual Mothers and Their Children." *Archives of Sexual Behavior* 15 (1986): 167–184.

Greenberg, Dan, and Marsha Jacobs, *How to Make Yourself Miserable*. New York: Random House, 1966.

Greenberger, Ellen, and Robin O'Neil. "Parents' Concerns about Their Child's Development: Implications for Father's and Mother's Well-being and Attitudes toward Work." *Journal of Marriage and the Family* 52 (August 1990): 621–635.

Greenstein, Theodore. "Marital Disruption and the Employment of Married Women." *Journal of Marriage and the Family* 52 (1990): 657–676.

_____. "Occupation and Divorce." *Journal of Family Issues* 6:3 (September 1985): 347–357.

Greer, Germaine. *Sex and Destiny*. New York: Harper & Row, 1984.

Greeson, Larry, and Rose Ann Williams. "Social Implications of Music Videos for Youth: An Analysis of the Content and Effects of MTV." *Youth and Society* 18:2 (December 1986):177–189.

Gregor, Thomas. *Anxious Pleasures: The Sexual Lives of an Amazonian People*. Chicago: University of Chicago Press, 1985.

Greif, Geoffrey. "Children and Housework in the Single Father Family." *Family Relations* 34:3 (July 1985): 353–357.

_____. "Single Fathers Rearing Children." *Journal of Marriage and the Family* 47:1 (February 1985): 185–191.

Griego, Diana, and Louis Kilzer. "The Truth About Missing Kids: Exaggerated Statistics Stir National Paranoia." *The Denver Post*, May 12, 1985: 1–A, 14–A.

Griswold Del Castillo, Richard. *La Familia: Chicano Families in the Urban Southwest, 1848 to the Present*. Notre Dame, Ind.: University of Notre Dame, 1984.

Gross, Jane. "ROTC Under Siege for Ousting Homosexuals." *The New York Times*, May 6, 1990: 12.

Grosskopf, D. *Sex and the Married Woman*. New York: Wallaby, 1983.

Grossman, Frances, William Pollack, Ellen Golding, and Nicolina Fedele. "Affiliation and Autonomy in the Transition to Parenthood." *Family Relations* 36:3 (July 1987): 263–269.

Grossman, Frances, et al. *Pregnancy, Birth and Parenthood: Adaptations of Mothers, Fathers, and Infants*. San Francisco: Jossey-Bass, 1980.

Groth, Nicholas. *Men Who Rape: The Psychology of the Offender*. New York: Plenum Press, 1980.

Groth, Nicholas, and H. Jean Birnbaum. "Adult Sexual Orientation and Attraction to Underage Persons." *Archives of Sexual Behavior* 7:3 (May 1978): 175–181.

Groth, Nicholas, and Thomas Gary. "Heterosexuality, Homosexuality, and Pedophilia: Sexual Offenses Against Children." In Anthony Scacco, ed., *Male Rape: A Casebook of Sexual Aggression*." New York: AMS Press, 1982.

Grover, Kelly, et al. "Mate Selection Processes and Marital Satisfaction." *Family Relations* 34:3 (July, 1985): 383–386.

Gruson, Lindsey. "Groups Play Matchmaker to Preserve Judaism." *New York Times*, April 1, 1985.

Gubman, Gayle, and Richard Tessler. "The Impact of Mental Illness on Families." *Journal of Family Issues* 8:2 (June 1987): 226–245.

Guelzow, Maureen, et al. "Analysis of the Stress Process for Dual-Career Men and Women." *Journal of Marriage and the Family* 53:1 (February 1991): 151–164.

Guhl, Beverly. *Purrfect Parenting*. Tucson, Ariz: Fisher Books, 1987.

Guidubaldi, John. "The Status Report Extended: Further Elaborations on the American Family." *School Psychology Review* 9:4 (Fall 1980): 374–379.

Guillemin, Jeanne Harley, and Lynda Lytle Holmstrom. "The Business of Childbirth." *Society* 23:5(183) (July–Aug. 1986).

Gump, J. "Reality and Myth: Employment and Sex Role Ideology in Black Women." In F. Denmark and J. Sherman, eds., *The Psychology of Women*. New York: Psychological Dimensions, 1980.

Gutek, Barbara. *Sex and the Workplace*. San Francisco, Calif.: Jossey-Bass Publishers, 1985.

Gutek, Barbara, et al. "Sexuality and the Workplace." *Basic and Applied Social Psychology* 1:3 (1980): 255–265.

Guttman, Herbert. *The Black Family: From Slavery to Freedom*. New York: Pantheon, 1976.

Gwartney-Gibbs, Patricia. "The Institutionalization of Premarital Cohabitation: Estimates from Marriage License Applications." *Journal of Marriage and the Family* 48 (May 1986): 423–434.

Haferd, Laura. "Paddling Returns to Child Rearing." *San Jose Mercury News*, December 20, 1986: 12D.

Hafstrom, Jeanne, and Vicki Schram. "Chronic Illness in Couples: Selected Characteristics, Including Wife's Satisfaction with and Perception of Marital Relationships." *Family Relations* 33 (1984): 195–203.

Halleck, Seymour. "Sex and Power." *Medical Aspects of Human Sexuality* (October 1969): 8–24.

Hahlweg, Kurt, and Michael Goldstein, eds. *Understanding Major Mental Disorder: The Contribution of Family Interaction Research*. New York: Family Process Press, 1987.

Hällstrom, Tore, and Sverker Samuelsson. "Changes in Women's Sexual Desire in Middle Life: The Longitudinal Study of Women in Gothenburg [Sweden]." *Archives of Sexual Behavior* 19:3 (1990): 259–267.

Hampton, Robert L., Richard J. Gelles and John W. Harrop. "Is Violence in Black Families Increasing? A Comparison of 1975 and 1985 National Survey Rates." *Journal of Marriage and the Family* 51:4 (Nov. 1989): 969–980.

Handlin, Oscar. *Boston's Immigrants*. Revised and enlarged edition. Cambridge, Mass.: Belknap University Press, 1979.

Hanley, Robert. "Surrogate Deals for Mothers Held Illegal in New Jersey." *The New York Times*, February 4, 1988: 1ff.

Hansen, Gary. "Balancing Work and Family: A Literature and Resource Review." *Family Relations* 40:3 (July 1991): 348–353.

_____. "Extradyadic Relations During Courtship." *Journal of Sex Research* 23:3 (August 1987): 383–390.

_____. "Perceived Threats and Marital Jealousy." *Social Psychology Quarterly*; September 1985; 48(3): 262–268.

Hanson, F. W., et al. "Ultrasonagraphy–Guided Early Amniocentesis in Singleton Pregnancies." *American Journal of Obstetrics and Gynecology* 162:6 (June 1990): 1381–1383.

Hanson, Sandra, and Theodora Oooms. "The Economic Costs and Rewards of Two-Earner, Two-Parent Families." *Journal of Marriage and the Family* 53:3 (August 1991): 622–644.

Hansson, Robert, et al. "Adult Children with Frail Elderly Parents: When to Intervene?" *Family Relations* 39:2 (April 1990): 153–158.

Haring-Hidore, Marilyn, et al. "Marital Status and Subjective Well-Being: A Research Synthesis." *Journal of Marriage and the Family* 47:4 (November 1985): 947–953.

Harriman, Lynda. "Marital Adjustment as Related to Personal and Marital Changes Accompanying Parenthood." *Family Relations* 35:2 (April 1986): 233–239.

_____. "Personal and Marital Changes Accompanying Parenthood." *Family Relations* 32 (July 1983): 387–394.

Harris, Kathleen, and S. Philip Morgan. "Fathers, Sons, and Daughters: Differential Paternal Involvement in Parenting." *Journal of Marriage and the Family* 53:3 (August, 1991).

Harris, M. B., and P. H. Turner. "Gay and Lesbian Parents." *Journal of Homosexuality* 12:12 (1985–1986): 101–113.

Harris, Myron. "Children as Hostages." In Stuart Irving, ed., *Children of Separation and Divorce*. New York: Grossman, 1972.

Harris, Sandra. "The Family and the Autistic Child." *Family Relations* 33:1 (January 1984): 67–77.

Harrison, Patricia, Norman Hoffman, and Glenace Edwall. "Differential Drug Use Patterns among Sexually Abused Adolescent Girls in Treatment for Chemical Dependency." *International Journal of the Addictions* 24:6 (June 1989): 499–514.

Harry, Joseph. "Decision Making and Age Differences among Gay Male Couples." In John DeCecco, ed., *Gay Relationships*. New York: Haworth Press, 1988.

_____. "Gay Male and Lesbian Relationships." In Eleanor Macklin and R. Ruben, eds., *Contemporary Families and Alternative Lifestyles: Handbook on Research and Theory*. Beverly Hills, Calif.: Sage Publications, 1983.

Hartup, W. and Z. Rubin, eds. *Relationships and Development*. Hillsdale, N. J.: Erlbaum, 1986.

Harvard Law Review editors. *Sexual Orientation and the Law*. Cambridge, Mass.: Harvard University Press, 1990.

Haskell, Molly. "2000–Year–Old Misunderstanding: Rape Fantasy." *Ms.* 5 (November 1976): 84–86ff.

Hatcher, Robert, et al. *Contraceptive Technology*. New York: Irvington Publishers, 1986.

Hatfield, Elaine. "Passionate and Companionate Love." In Robert Sternberg and Michael Barnes, eds., *The Psychology of Love*. New Haven, Conn.: Yale University Press, 1988.

Hatfield, Elaine, and Richard Hapson. "Passionate Love/Sexual Desire: Can the Same Paradigm Explain Both?" *Archives of Sexual Behavior* 16:3 (June 1987): 259–278.

Hatfield, Elaine, and Susan Sprecher. *Mirror, Mirror: The Importance of Looks in Everyday Life*. New York: State University of New York, 1986.

Hatfield, Elaine, and G. William Walster. *A New Look at Love*. Reading, Mass.: Addison-Wesley, 1981.

_____. *A New Look at Love*. Reading, Mass.: 1978.

Hawkins, Robert O. "The Relationship between Culture, Personality, and Sexual Jealousy in Men in Heterosexual and Homosexual Relationships." *Journal of Homosexuality*; 1990; 19(3): 67–84.

Hayes, Robert M. "Homeless Children." In Frank J. Macchiarola and Alan Gartner, eds., *Caring for America's Children*. New York: The Academy of Political Science, 1989.

Hazan, Cindy, and Philip Shaver. "Romantic Love Conceptualized as an Attachment Process." *Journal of Personality and Social Psychology* 52 (1987)L 511–524.

Hearst, Norman, and Stephen Hulley. "Preventing the Heterosexual Spread of AIDS. Are We Giving Our Patients the Best Advice?" *JAMA* 259:16 (April 22/29 1988): 2428–2432.

Heaton, Tim, and Stan Albrecht. "Stable Unhappy Marriages." *Journal of Marriage and the Family* 53:3 (August 1991): 747–758.

Heaton, Tim B., and E. L. Pratt. "The Effects of Religious Homogamy on Marital Satisfaction and Stability." *Journal of Family Issues* 7:2 (June 1990): 191–207.

Heaton, Tim, et al. "The Timing of Divorce." *Journal of Marriage and the Family* 47:3 (August 1985): 631–639.

Heer, D. M. "The Prevalence of Black-White Marriage in the United States, 1960 and 1970." *Journal of Marriage and the Family* 36 (1974): 246–259.

Hefferan, Colleen. "New Methods for Studying Household Production." *Family Economics Review* 3 (1982a): 16–25.

Hefner, R., M. Rebecca, and B. Oleshansky. "Development of Sex-Role Transcendence." *Human Development* 18 (1975): 143–158.

Heilbrun, Alfred, Dawna Wydra, and Lisa Friedberg. "Parent Identification and Gender Schema Development." *Journal of Genetic Psychology* 150:3 (September 1989): 293–300.

Heilbrun, Carolyn. *Toward a Recognition of Androgyny*. New York: Norton, 1982.

Hemminki, Kari, et al. "Spontaneous Abortion in an Industrialized Community in Finland." *American Journal of Public Health* 73:1 (January 1983): 32–37.

Hendrick, Clyde, and Susan Hendrick. "Research on Love: Does It Measure Up?" *Journal of Personality and Social Psychology* 56:5 (May 1989): 784–794.

_____. "Lovers Wear Rose Colored Glasses." *Journal of Social and Personal Relationships* 5:2 (May 1988a): 161–183.

_____. "A Theory and Method of Love." *Journal of Personality and Social Psychology* 50 (1986): 392–402.

Hendrick, Clyde, et al. "Do Men and Women Love Differently?" *Journal of Personality and Social Psychology* 48 (1984): 177–195.

Hendrick, Susan. "Self-Disclosure and Marital Satisfaction." *Journal of Personality and Social Psychology* 40 (1981): 1150–1159.

Hendrick, Susan, and Clyde Hendrick. "Multidimensionality of Sexual Attitudes." *Journal of Sex Research* 23:4 (November 1987): 502–526.

Hendricks, Glenn, Bruce Downing, and Amos Deinard, eds. *The Hmong in Transition*. Staten Island, New York: Center for Migration Studies of New York, 1986.

Henton, June, et al. "Romance and Violence in Dating Relationships." *Journal of Family Issues* 4 (September, 1983): 467–482.

Herek, Gregory. "Beyond 'Homophobia' A Social Psychological Perspective on Attitudes Toward Lesbians and Gay Men." *Journal of Homosexuality* 10(1/2) (Fall 1984): 1–21.

_____. "On Heterosexual Masculinity: Some Psychical Consequences of the Social Construction of Gender." *American Behavioral Scientist* 29:5 (May–June 1986): 563–567.

_____. "The Social Psychology of Homophobia: Toward a Practical Theory." *Review of Law and Social Change* 14:4 (1986): 923–934.

Herman, Judith. *Father-Daughter Incest*. Cambridge, Mass.: Harvard University Press, 1981.

Herold, Edward, and Leslie Way. "Oral-Genital Sexual Behavior in a Sample of University Females." *Journal of Sex Research* 19:4 (November 1983): 327–338.

Hess, Robert, and Kathleen Camara. "Post-Divorce Relationships as Mediating Factors in the Consequences of Divorce for Children." *Journal of Social Issues* 35:4 (1979): 79–96.

Hetherington, E. Mavis. "Divorce: A Child's Perspective." *American Psychologist* 34(10) (October 1979): 851–858.

Hetherington, E. Mavis, M. Cox, and R. Cox. "Family Interactions and the Social, Emotional, and Cognitive Development of Children Following Divorce." In V. C. Vaugh and T. B. Brazelton, eds., *The Family: Setting Priorities*. New York: Science and Medicine Publishers, 1979.

Hetherington, E. Mavis, et al. "The Aftermath of Divorce." In J. J. Stevens, Jr., and M. Matthews, eds., *Mother-Child, Father-Child Relations*. Washington, D.C.: NAEYC, 1977.

_____. "The Development of Children in Mother-headed Families." In David Reiss and Howard Hoffman, eds., _The American Family: Dying or Developing?_ New York: Plenum Press, 1979.

Hetherington, S. E. "A Controlled Study of the Effect of Prepared Childbirth Classes on Obstetric Outcomes." _Birth_ 17:2 (June 1990): 86–90.

Hevesi, Dennis. "Homeless in New York City: A Day on the Streets." _The New York Times,_ November 17, 1986: 13.

_____. "TV News: Children's Scary Window on New York." _The New York Times,_ September 11, 1990: A21.

Hewitt, J. "Preconceptional Sex Selection." _British Journal of Hospital Medicine_ 37:2 (February 1987): 149ff.

Heyl, Barbara. "Homosexuality: A Social Phenomenon." In Kathleen McKinney and Susan Sprecher, eds., _Human Sexuality: The Societal and Interpersonal Context._ Norwood, N.J.: Ablex Publishing Corporation, 1989.

Hill, Charles, Letitia Peplau, and Zick Rubin. "Breakups Before Marriage: The End of 103 Affairs." _Journal of Social Issues_ 32 (1976): 147–168.

Hill, Martha. "The Changing Nature of Poverty." _Annals of the American Academy of Political Science_ 479 (May 1985): 31–37.

Hill, Reuben. "Generic Features of Families Under Stress." _Social Casework_ 49 (February/March 1958): 139–150.

_____. "Whither Family Research in the 1980's: Continuities, Emergents, Constraints, and New Horizons." _Journal of Marriage and the Family_ 43:2 (May 1981): 255–257.

Hill, Robert B. _The Strengths of Black Families._ New York: Emerson Hall Publishers, 1972.

Hilton, Jeanne, and Virgina Haldeman. "Gender Differences in the Performance of Household Tasks by Adults and Children in Single-Parent and Two-Parent, Two-Earner Families." _Journal of Family Issues_ 12:1 (March 1991): 114–130.

Hilton, N. Zoe. "When Is an Assault Not an Assault? The Canadian Public's Attitudes Toward Wife and Stranger Assault." _Journal of Family Violence_ 4:4 (Dec. 1989): 323–337.

Hilts, Philip. "Growing Concern over Pelvic Infection in Women." _The New York Times,_ October 11, 1990a.

_____. "Life Expectancy for Blacks in U. S. Shows Sharp Drop." _The New York Times,_ November 29, 1990b: A1, B7.

Hiltz, Roxanne. "Widowhood: A Roleless Role." _Marriage and Family Review_ 1(6) (November/December 1978).

Hinds, Michael. "Better Traps Being Built for Delinquent Parents." _The New York Times,_ December 9, 1989:10.

Hite, Shere. _The Hite Report._ New York: Macmillan, 1976.

_____. _The Hite Report on Male Sexuality._ New York: Knopf, 1981.

Hochschild, Arlie, with Anne Machung. _The Second Shift: Working Parents and the Revolution at Home._ New York: Viking Press, 1989.

Hodges, William, et al. "Divorce and the Preschool Child." _Journal of Divorce_ 3:1 (Fall 1979): 55–67.

Hoeffer, B. "Children's Acquisition of Sex-Role Behavior in Lesbian-Mother Families." _American Journal of Orthopsychiatry_ 51 (1981): 536–544.

Hoegerman, G., et al. Drug Exposed Neonates." _Western Journal of Medicine_ 152:1 (May 1990): 559–.

Hoelter, Jon W. "Factoral Invariance and Self-Esteem—Reassessing Race and Sex Differences." _Social Forces_ 61:3 (March 1983): 834–846.

Hoelter, Jon, and Lynn Harper. "Structural and Interpersonal Family Influences on Adolescent Self-Conception." _Journal of Marriage and the Family_ 49 (February 1987): 129–139.

Hofferth, Sandra. "Updating Children's Life Course." _Journal of Marriage and the Family_ 47:1 (9 February 1985): 93–115.

Hofferth, Sandra, and Deborah A. Phillips. "Child Care in the United States, 1970 to 1995." _Journal of Marriage and the Family_ 49:3 (August, 1987): 559–572.

Holmes, Steven. "On the Edge of Despair When Jobless Benefits End." _The New York Times,_ January 28, 1991: A11.

Holmes, T., and R. Rahe. "The Social Readjustment Rating Scale." _Journal of Psychosomatic Medicine_ 11 (1967): 213–218.

Holtzen, D. W., and A. A. Agresti. "Parental Responses to Gay and Lesbian Children." _Journal of Social and Clinical Psychology_ 9:3 (Fall 1990): 390–399.

Hopkins, Ellen. "Childhood's End." _Rolling Stone_ (October 18, 1990): 66–72ff.

Horowitz, A., and L. Shindelman. "Reciprocity and Affection: Past Influences on Present Caregiving." _Journal of Gerontological Social Work_ 5 (1983): 5–20.

Hort, Barbara, Beverly Fagot, and Mary Leinbach. "Are People's Notions of Maleness More Stereotypically Framed than Their Notions of Femaleness?" _Sex Roles_ 23:3–4 (February 1990): 197–212.

Hotaling, Gerald T., and David Finkelhor. "Estimating the Number of Stranger-Abduction Homicides of Children: A Review of Available Evidence." _Journal of Criminal Justice_ 18:5 (1990): 385–399.

Hotaling, Gerald, David Finkelhor, John Kirkpatrick, and Murray Straus, eds. _Coping with Family Violence: Research and Perspectives._ Newbury Park, Calif.: Sage Publications, 1988.

Hotaling, Gerald T., and David B. Sugarman. "A Risk Marker Analysis of Assaulted Wives." _Journal of Family Violence_ 5:1 (March 1990): 1–14.

Hotaling, Gerald T., et al., eds. _Family Abuse and Its Consequences._ Newbury Park, Calif.: Sage Publications, 1988.

Houseknecht, Sharon K., "Childlessness and Marital Adjustment." In Jeffrey Rosenfeld, eds., _Relationships: The Marriage and Family Reader._ Glencoe, Ill.: Scott, Foresman, 1982.

_____. "Voluntary Childlessness." In Marvin B. Sussman and Suzanne K. Steinmetz, eds., _Handbook of Marriage and the Family._ New York: Plenum Press, 1987.

Houseknecht, Sharon K., Suzanne Vaughan, and Ann Statham. "The Impact of Singlehood on the Career Patterns of Professional Women." _Journal of Marriage and the Family_ 49:2 (May, 1987): 353–366.

Howard, Judith. "A Structural Approach to Interracial Patterns in Adolescent Judgments about Sexual Intimacy." _Sociological Perspectives_ 31:1 (January 1988): 88–121.

Huang, Lucy. "The Chinese American Family." In Charles Mindel, Robert Habenstein, and Roosevelt Wright, Jr., eds. _Ethnic Families in America: Patterns and Variations,_ 3d ed. New York: Elsevier North Holland, Inc., 1988.

Huber, Joan, and Glenna Spitze. _Sex Stratification: Children, Housework, and Jobs._ New York: Academic Press, 1983.

Hunt, Morton, and Beatrice Hunt. _The Divorce Experience._ New York: McGraw-Hill, 1977.

Hupka, Ralph B. "Jealousy: Compound Emotion or Label for a Particular Situation." _Motivation and Emotion;_ 1984; 84(23):141–145.

Hurst, Marsha, and Pamela S. Summey. "Childbirth and Social Class: The Case of Cesarean Delivery." _Social Science and Medicine_ 18:8 (1984): 621–631.

Huston, Ted, et al. "From Courtship to Marriage: Mate Selection as an Interpersonal Process." In Steve Duck and Robin Gilmore, eds., _Personal Relationships. 2: Developing Personal Relationships._ London: Academic Press, 1981.

Ihinger–Tallman, Marilyn. "Sibling and Stepsibling Bonding in Stepfamilies." In Kay Pasley and Marilyn Ihinger-Tallman, eds., _Remarriage and Stepparenting: Current Research and Theory._ New York: Guilford Press, 1987.

Ihinger–Tallman, Marilyn, and Kay Pasley. "Divorce and Remarriage in the American Family: A Historical Review." In Kay Pasley and Marilyn Ihinger–Tallman, eds. _Remarriage and Stepparenting: Current Research and Theory._ New York: Guilford Press, 1987.

_____. *Remarriage*. Newbury Park, Calif.: Sage Publications, 1987.

_____, eds. *Remarriage and Stepparenting: Current Research and Theory*: New York, Guilford Press, 1987.

Imber, Johnathan. "The Future of Abortion Politics." *Contemporary Sociology* 19:2 (March 1990): 176–181.

Indivik, Julie, and Mary Fitzpatrick. "'If You Could Read My Mind, Love...,': Understanding and Misunderstanding in the Marital Dyad." *Family Relations* 44:4 (November 1982): 43–51.

Irving, Howard, et al. "Shared Parenting: An Empirical Analysis Utilizing a Large Data Base." *Family Process* 23 (1984): 561–569.

Isensee, Rik. *Love Between Men: Enhancing Intimacy and Keeping Your Relationship Alive*. New York: Prentice-Hall Press; 1990.

Ishwaran, Karigonder. *Marriage and Divorce in Canada*. Toronto: Methuen, 1983.

_____, ed. *Canadian Families: Ethnic Variations*. Toronto: McGraw-Hill Ryerson, 1980.

Itard, Jean. *The Wild Boy of Aveyron*. Reprinted in Lucien Malson, ed., *Wolf Children and the Problem of Human Nature*. New York: Monthly Review Press, 1972.

Jacoby, Arthur, and John Williams. "Effects of Premarital Sexual Standards and Behavior on Dating and Marriage Desirability." *Journal of Marriage and the Family* 47:4 (November 1985): 1059–1065.

Jacques, Jeffrey, and Karen Chason. "Cohabitation: Its Impact on Marital Success." *Family Coordinator* 28:1 (1979): 35–39.

Jaramillo, Patricio, and Jesse Zapata. "Roles and Alliances within Mexican-American Families." *Journal of Marriage and the Family* 49:4 (November 1987): 727–736.

Jenista, Jerri Ann. "Adoption of Foreign-Born Children by U.S. Citizens in 1984 by Country of Origin" (table). *OURS* 20:4 (July/August 1987): 15.

Jenks, Richard. "Swinging: A Replication and Test of a Theory." *Journal of Sex Research* 21:2 (May 1985): 199–210.

Joe, Tom, and Douglas W. Nelson. "New Future for America's Children." In Frank J. Macchiarola and Alan Gartner, eds., *Caring for America's Children*. New York: The Academy of Political Science, 1989.

Joesch, Jutta. "The Effect of the Price of Child Care on AFDC Mothers' Paid Work Behavior." *Family Relations* 40:2 (April 1991): 161–166.

John, Robert. "The Native American Family." In Charles Mindel, Robert Habenstein, and Roosevelt Wright, Jr., eds., *Ethnic Families in America: Patterns and Variations*, 3d ed. New York: Elsevier North Holland, Inc., 1988.

Johnson, Beverly. "Single Parent Families." *Family Economics Review* (Summer–Fall, 1980): 22–27.

Johnson, Carolyn, and Sharon Price-Bonham. "Women and Retirement: A Study and Implications." *Family Relations* (July 1980): 381–385.

Johnson, Clifford, Andrew Sum, and James Weill. *Vanishing Dreams: The Growing Economic Plight of America's Young Families*. Washington, D.C.: Children's Defense Funds, 1988.

Johnson, Coleen. "The Impact of Illness on Later-Life Marriages." *Journal of Marriage and the Family* 47 (1985): 165–172.

_____. "Postdivorce Reorganization of Relationships between Divorcing Children and their Parents." *Journal of Marriage and the Family* 50 (February 1988): 221–23.

Johnson, David, Lynn White, John Edwards, and Alan Booth. "Dimensions of Marital Quality: Toward Methodological and Conceptual Refinement." *Journal of Family Issues* 7 (1986): 31–49.

Johnson, Dirk. "At Colleges, AIDS Alarms Muffle Older Dangers." *The New York Times*, March 8, 1990: B8.

Johnson, G. Timothy, and Stephen Goldfinger, eds. *The Harvard Medical School Health Letter Book*. Cambridge, Mass.: Harvard University Press, 1981.

Johnson, Leanor Boulin. "Perspectives on Black Family Empirical Research: 1965–1978." In Harriette Pipes McAdoo, ed., *Black Families*. Newbury Park, Calif.: Sage Publications, 1988.

Johnston, Thomas F. "Alaskan Native Social Adjustment and the Role of Eskimo and Indian Music." *Journal of Ethnic Studies* 3/4 (Winter 1976): 21–36.

Jones, Carl. "Sharing the Childbirth Miracle." *Nurturing News*. 8:2 (1985): 5, 15ff.

Jones, Jacqueline. *Labor of Love, Labor of Sorrow: Black Women, Work, and the Family from Slave to the Present*. New York: Basic Books, 1985.

Jones, Jennifer, and David Barlow. "Self-Reported Frequencies of Sexual Urges, Fantasies, and Masturbatory Fantasies in Heterosexual Males and Females." *Archives of Sexual Behavior* 19:3 (1990): 269–279.

Jones, Maggie. *A Child by Any Means*. London: Piatkus, 1989.

Jorgensen, Stephen, and Russell Adams. "Predicting Mexican–American Family Planning Intentions: An Application and Test of a Social Psychological Model." *Journal of Marriage and the Family* 50 (February, 1988): 107–119.

Jorgensen, Stephen R., and J. C. Gaudy. "Self-Disclosure and Satisfaction in Marriage: The Relation Examined." *Family Relations* 29:3 (1980): 281–287.

Jorgensen, Stephen R., and A. C. Johnson. "Correlates of Divorce Liberality." *Journal of Marriage and the Family* 42 (1980): 617–622.

Justice, Blair, and Rita Justice. *The Abusing Family*, rev. ed. New York: Insight Books, 1990.

_____. *The Broken Taboo: Incest*. New York: Human Sciences Press, 1979.

Kach, Julie, and Paul McGee. "Adjustment to Early Parenthood." *Journal of Family Issues* 3:3 (September 1982): 375–388.

Kagan, Jerome. *The Nature of the Child*. New York: Basic Books, 1984.

_____. "The Psychological Requirements for Human Development." In Nathan Talbot, ed., *Raising Children in Modern America*. Boston: Little, Brown, 1976.

Kain, Edward. *The Myth of Family Decline: Understanding Families in a World of Rapid Change*. Lexington, Mass.: Lexington Books, 1990.

Kalmuss, Debra. "The Intergenerational Transmission of Marital Aggression." *Journal of Marriage and the Family* 46:1 (February 1984): 11–20.

Kamerman, Sheila, and C. D. Hayes, eds. *Families That Work: Children in a Changing World*. Washington, D.C.: National Academy Press, 1982.

Kanter, Rosabeth. "Why Bosses Turn Bitchy." *Psychology Today* 9(12) (May 1976): 56–59.

Kantor, David, and William Lehr. *Inside Families*. San Francisco, Calif.: Jossey-Bass, 1975.

Kantrowitz, Barbara. "The Crack Children." *Newsweek* (February 12, 1990): 62–63.

_____. "Who Keeps 'Baby M'?" *Newsweek* (January 19, 1987): 44–49.

Kantrowitz, Barbara, and David A. Kaplan. "Not the Right Family." *Newsweek* (March 19, 1990): 50–51.

Kaplan, A. "Clarifying the Concept of Androgyny: Implications for Therapy." *Psychology of Women* 3 (1979): 223–230.

Kaplan, A., and J. P. Bean. "From Sex Stereotypes to Androgyny: Considerations of Societal and Individual Change." In A. Kaplan and J. P. Bean, eds., *Beyond Sex-Role Stereotypes*. Boston: Little, Brown, 1976.

_____, eds. *Beyond Sex-Role Stereotypes*. Boston: Little, Brown, 1979.

Kaplan, Helen Singer. *Disorders of Desire*. New York: Simon & Schuster, 1979.

_____. *Sexual Aversion, Sexual Phobias, and Panic Disorders*. New York: Brunner/Mazel, 1987.

Karan, L. D. "AIDS Prevention and Chemical Dependence Treatment Needs of Women and Their Children." *Journal of Psychoactive Drugs* 21:4 (October–December 1989): 395–399.

Katchadourian, Herant. *Midlife in Perspective*. San Francisco, Calif.: W. H. Freeman, 1987.

Katz, Alvin, and Reuben Hill. "Residential Propinquity and Marital Selection: A Review of Theory, Method and Fact." *Marriage and Family Living* 20 (February 1958): 27–35.

Katz, Michael B. *The Underserving Poor: From War on Poverty to War on Welfare*. New York: Pantheon Books, 1990.

Kavanaugh, Robert. *Facing Death*. Baltimore, Md.: Penguin Books, 1972.

Kaye, K., et al. "Birth Outcomes for Infants of Drug Abusing Mothers." *New York State Journal of Medicine* 144:7 (May 1989): 256–261.

Kearl, Michael C. *Endings: A Sociology of Death and Dying*. New York: Oxford University Press, 1989.

Keith, Pat, et al. "Older Men in Employed and Retired Families." *Alternative Lifestyles* 4:2 (May 1981): 228–241.

Kelley, Harold. "Love and Commitment." In Harold Kelley et al., eds., *Close Relationships*. San Francisco, Calif.: Freeman, 1983.

Kelley, Harold. H., et al., eds. *Close Relationships*. San Francisco, Calif.: Freeman, 1983.

Kelley, Robert, and Patricia Voydanoff. "Work/Family Role Strain Among Employed Parents." *Family Relations* 34:3 (July 1985): 367–374.

Kelly, Susan. "Changing Parent-Child Relationships: An Outcome of Mother Returning to College." *Family Relations* 31 (April 1982): 287–294.

Kempe, C. Henry, and Ray Helfer, eds. *The Battered Child*, rev. ed. Chicago: University of Chicago Press, 1980.

Kennedy, David. *Birth Control in America*. New Haven: Yale University Press, 1970.

Kennedy, Donald. "Why Adoptions Get Harder Every Year." *U.S. News and World Report* (September 20, 1982).

Kennedy, Gregory. "College Students' Expectations of Grandparent and Grandchild Role Behaviors." *Gerontologist* 30:1 (1990): 43–48.

Keshet, Jamie. "From Separation to Stepfamily." *Journal of Family Issues* 1:4 (December 1980): 517–532.

Kessler-Harris, Alice. *A History of Wage-Earning Women in America*. New York: Oxford University Press, 1982.

_____. *Women Have Always Worked: A Historical Overview*. New York: McGraw-Hill, 1981.

Kett, Joseph. *Rites of Passage: Adolescence in America, 1790 to the Present*. New York: Basic Books, 1977.

Kikumura, Akemi, and Harry Kitano. "The Japanese American Family." In Charles Mindel, Robert Habenstein, and Roosevelt Wright, Jr., eds. *Ethnic Families in America: Patterns and Variations*, 3d ed. New York: Elsevier North Holland, Inc., 1988.

Kilborn, Peter. "Big Change Likely as Law Bans Bias Toward Disabled." The New York Times. July 19, 1992: 1, 16.

Kilpatrick, Allie. "Job Change in Dual-Career Families: Danger or Opportunity?" *Family Relations* 31 (July 1982): 363–368.

Kilzer, Louis. "Kid Fingerprinting a Sham, Foes Claim." *The Denver Post*, May 13, 1985a: 1–A, 14–A.

_____. "Public Often Not Told Facts in Missing Children Cases." *The Denver Post*, September 22, 1985b: 1–A, 14–A.

Kilzer, Louis, and Diana Griego. "Missing-Child Reports Bring Out Best, Worst." *The Denver Post*, May 13, 1985: 1–A, 14–A.

Kingston, Paul, and Stephen Nock. "Consequences of the Family Work Day." *Journal of Marriage and the Family* 47:3 (August 1985): 619–629.

Kinsey, Alfred, et al. *Sexual Behavior in the Human Female*. Philadelphia: Saunders, 1953.

_____, et al. *Sexual Behavior in the Human Male*. Philadelphia: Saunders, 1948.

Kirchler, Erich. "Everyday Life Experiences at Home: An Interaction Diary Approach to Assess Marital Relationships." *Journal of Family Psychology* 2 (1989): 311–336.

Kirkpatrick, Martha, et al. "Lesbian Mothers and Their Children: A Comparative Study." *American Journal of Orthopsychiatry* 51:3 (July 1981): 545–551.

Kitson, Gay. "Marital Discord and Marital Separation: A County Survey." *Journal of Marriage and the Family* 47 (1985): 693–700.

Kitson, Gay, and Leslie Morgan. "Consequences of Divorce." In Alan Booth, ed., *Contemporary Families: Looking Forward, Looking Back*. Minneapolis, Minn.: National Council on Family Relations, 1991.

Kitson, Gay, and Marvin Sussman. "Marital Complaints, Demographic Characteristics, and Symptoms of Mental Distress in Divorce." *Journal of Marriage and the Family* 44:1 (1982): 87–101.

Kitzinger, Sheila. *The Complete Book of Pregnancy and Childbirth*. New York: Knopf, 1989.

_____. *Woman's Experience of Sex*. New York: Penguin Books, 1985.

Klatch, Rebecca. "Coalition and Conflict Among Women in the New Right." *Signs* 13:4 (Summer 1988): 671–694.

Klein, Carole. *How It Feels to Be a Child*. New York: Harper Colophon Books, 1977.

Klein, David, and William Smith. "Historical Trends in the Marriage and Family Textbook Literature." *Family Relations* 34 (April 1985): 21–219.

Klinman, Deborah, and Carol Vukelich. "Mothers and Fathers: Expectations for Infants." *Family Relations* 34:3 (July 1985): 305–313.

Klinman, Deborah, et al. *Fatherhood, USA: The First National Guide to Programs, Services and Resources for and about Fathers*. New York: Garland Publishing Co., 1984.

Knapp, Mark, et al. "Compliments: A Descriptive Taxonomy." *Journal of Communication* 34:4 (Autumn 1984): 12–31.

Knaub, P. K., et al. "Strengths of Remarriage." *Journal of Divorce* 7 (1984): 41–55.

Knox, David. *Choices in Relationships*. St. Paul, Minn.: West, 1985.

_____. "Conceptions of Love at Three Developmental Levels." *Family Coordinator* 19 (1970): 151–156.

Knox, David, and K. Wilson. "Dating Behaviors of University Students." *Family Relations* 30 (1981): 83–86.

Koblinsky, Sally, and Christine Todd. "Teaching Self-Care Skills to Latchkey Children: A Review of the Research." *Family Relations* 38:4 (October 1989): 431–435.

Kohen, J. A., et al., "Divorced Mothers: The Costs and Benefits of Female Family Control." In G. Kevinger and O. C. Moles, eds., *Separation and Divorce*. New York: Basic Books, 1979.

Kohlberg, Lawrence. "The Cognitive-Development Approach to Socialization." In A. Goslin, ed., *Handbook of Socialization Theory and Research*. Chicago: Rand McNally, 1969.

Kohn, M. L. "Social Class and Parental Values." *American Journal of Sociology* 64 (1959): 337–351.

Kolata, Gina. "Anti-Acne Drug Faulted in Birth Defects." *The New York Times*, April 22, 1988: 1ff.

_____. *The Baby Doctors*. New York: Delacorte Press, 1989.

_____. "Early Warnings and Latent Cures for Infertility." *Ms*. (May 1979): 86–89.

_____. "Experts Declare Temperance Is Back in Style in America." *The New York Times*, January 1, 1991: B3.

_____. "A Major Operation on a Fetus Works for the First Time." *The New York Times*, May 31, 1990: B1ff.

_____. "Racial Bias Seen in Prosecuting Pregnant Addicts." *The New York Times*, July 20, 1990: A10.

_____. "Tests of Fetuses Rise Sharply Amid Doubts." *The New York Times*, September 22, 1987: 19–20.

Kolker, A. "Advances in Prenatal Diagnosis: Social–Psychological and Policy Issues." *International Journal of Technology Assessment in Health Care* 5:4 (1989): 601–617.

Kolodny, Robert, et al. *Textbook of Sexual Medicine*. Boston: Little, Brown, 1979.

Komarovsky, Mirra. *Blue-Collar Marriage*, 2d ed. New Haven, Conn.: Yale University Press, 1987.

_____. "The New Feminist Scholarship: Some Precursors and Polemics." *Journal of Marriage and the Family*. 50:3 (August, 1988): 585–594.

_____. *Women in College*. New York: Basic Books, 1985.

Koop, Everett. "The U.S. Surgeon General on the Health Effects of Abortion." *Population and Development Review* 15:1 (March 1989): 172–175.

Koss, Mary. "Hidden Rape: Sexual Aggression and Victimization in a National Sample of Students in Higher Education." In A. W. Burgess, ed., *Rape and Sexual Assault II*. New York: Garland Press, 1988.

Koss, Mary, et al. "The Scope of Rape: Incidence and Prevalence of Sexual Aggression and Victimization in a National Sample of Higher Education Students." *Journal of Consulting and Clinical Psychology* 55:2 (April 1987): 162–170.

Koss, Mary, Thomas Dinero, Cynthia Seibel, and Susan Cox. "Stranger and Acquaintance Rape: Are There Differences in the Victim's Experience?" *Psychology of Women Quarterly* 12:1 (March 1988): 1–24.

Kozol, Jonathan. *Rachel and Her Children: Homeless Families in America*. New York: Crown Publishers, 1988.

Krames, Lester, Rebecca England, and Gordon Flett. "The Role of Masculinity and Femininity in Depression and Social Satisfaction in Elderly Years." *Sex Roles* 19:11–12 (December 1988): 713–721.

Kranichfeld, Marion. "Rethinking Family Power." *Journal of Family Issues* 8:1 (March 1987): 42–56.

Kressel, Kenneth. *The Divorce Process: How Professionals and Couples Negotiate Settlement*. New York: Basic Books, 1985.

Krimmel, Herman. "The Alcoholic and His Family." In Peter Bourne and Ruth Fox, eds., *Alcoholism: Progress in Research and Treatment*. New York: Academic Press, 1973.

Kubey, Robert, and Mihaly Csikszentmihalyi. *Television and the Quality of Life: How Viewing Shapes Everyday Experience*. Hillsdale, N.J.: Lawrence Erlbaum Associates, 1990.

Kübler-Ross, Elisabeth. *AIDS: The Ultimate Challenge*. New York: Macmillan, 1987.

_____, *On Death and Dying*. New York: Macmillan, 1969.

_____. *Working it Through*. New York: Macmillan, 1982.

Kupersmid, Joel, and Donald Wonderly. "Moral Maturity and Behavior: Failure to Find a Link." *Journal of Youth and Adolescence* 9 (June 1980): 249–261.

Kurdek, Lawrence. Sexuality in Homosexual and Heterosexual Couples. In: McKinney, Kathleen; Susan Sprecher, eds. Sexuality in Close Relationships. Hillsdale, NJ: Lawrence Erlbaum Associates; 1991.

Kurdek, Lawrence, and Albert Siesky. "Children's Perceptions of Their Parents' Divorce." *Journal of Divorce* 3:4 (Summer 1980): 339–378.

Kurdek, Lawrence and J. Patrick Smith. "Partner Homogamy in Married, Heterosexual, Cohabiting, Gay, and Lesbian Couples." *Journal of Sex Research* 23:2 (May 1987): 212–232.

Kurdek, Lawrence, et al. "Correlates of Children's Long-Term Adjustment to Their Parents' Divorce." *Developmental Psychology* 17(5) (September 1981): 565–579.

Kutner, Lawrence. "Children Need Help Forming Self-Image." *The New York Times*, February 25, 1988: 21ff.

_____. "Parent & Child." *The New York Times*, November 1, 1990: B8.

Kutscher, Austin H., Arthur C. Carr, and Lillian G. Kutscher, eds. *Principles of Thanatology*. New York: Columbia University Press, 1987.

LaBeff, Emily, et al. "Gender Differences in Self Advertisements for Dates." *Free Inquiry in Creative Sociology* 17:1 (May 1989): 45–50.

Ladas, Alice, et al. *The G Spot*. New York: Holt, Rinehart and Winston, 1982.

Laing, R. D. *The Politics of the Family and Other Essays*. New York: Random House, 1972.

Lainson, Suzanne. "Breast-Feeding: The Erotic Factor." *Ms.* 11(8) (February 1983): 66ff.

Lamaze, Fernand. *Painless Childbirth*. Chicago: H. Regnery, 1970; 1st ed., 1956.

Lamb, Michael. *The Father's Role: Cross–Cultural Perspectives*. Hillsdale, N.J.: Lawrence Erlbaum, 1986.

Lane, K. E., and P. A. Gwartney-Gibbs. "Violence in the Context of Dating and Sex." *Journal of Family Issues* 6 (1985): 45–59.

Laner, Mary R. "Violence or its Precipitators: Which is More Likely to Be Identified as a Dating Problem?" *Deviant Behavior*; October 1990; 11(4): 319–329.

Lantz, Herman. "Family and Kin as Revealed in the Narratives of Ex–Slaves." *Social Science Quarterly* 60:4 (March 1980): 667–674.

Larkin, Ralph. *Suburban Youth in Cultural Crisis*. New York: Oxford University Press, 1979.

LaRossa, Ralph, and Maureen LaRossa. *Transition to Parenthood: How Infants Change Families*. Beverly Hills, Calif.: Sage, 1981.

LaRossa, Ralph, and Jane Wolf. "On Qualitative Family Research." *Journal of Marriage and the Family* 47:3 (August 1985): 531–541.

Lasch, Christopher. *Haven in a Heartless World*. New York: Basic Books, 1977.

Lauer, Robert, and Jeanette Lauer. "The Long-Term Relational Consequences of Problematic Family Backgrounds." *Family Relations* 40:3 (July 1991): 286–291.

Lavee, Yoav, and David Olson. "Family Types and Response to Stress." *Journal of Marriage and the Family* 53:3 (August 1991): 786–798.

Laviola, Marisa. "Effects of Older-Brother Younger-Sister Incest: A Review of Four Cases." *Journal of Family Violence* 4:3 (Sept. 1989): 259–274.

Lawson, Carol. "Fathers, Too, Are Seeking a Balance between Their Families and Careers." *The New York Times*, April 12, 1990: B1ff.

Leboyer, Frederic. *Birth Without Violence*. New York: Knopf, 1975.

Lederer, William, and Don Jackson. *Mirages of Marriage*. New York: Norton, 1968.

Lee, John A. "Love-Styles." In Robert Sternberg and Michael Barnes, eds., *The Psychology of Love*. New Haven, Conn.: Yale University Press, 1988.

_____. *The Color of Love*. Toronto, Canada: New Press, 1973.

Lee, Thomas, Jay Mancini, and Joseph Maxwell. "Contact Patterns and Motivations for Sibling Relations in Adulthood." *Journal of Marriage and the Family* 52 (May 1990): 431–440.

Leifer, Myra. *Psychological Effects of Motherhood: A Study of First Pregnancy*. New York: Praeger, 1990.

Leites, Edmund. "The Duty to Desire: Love, Friendship, and Sexuality in Some Puritan Theories of Marriage." *Journal of Social History* 15:3 (Spring 1982): 383–408.

Leming, Michael R., and George E. Dickinson. *Understanding Dying, Death, and Bereavement*. New York: Holt, Rinehart and Winston, 1985.

Leonard, Kenneth E., and Theodore Jacob. "Alcohol, Alcoholism, and Family Violence." In Vincent B. Van Hasselt et al., eds., *Handbook of Family Violence*. New York: Plenum Press, 1988.

Leslie, Leigh, and Katherine Grady. "Changes in Mothers' Social Networks and Social Support Following Divorce." *Journal of Marriage and the Family* 47:3 (August 1985): 663–673.

Lesnick-Oberstein, M., and L. Cohen. "Cognitive Style, Sensation Seeking, and Assortative Mating." *Journal of Personality and Social Psychology* 46 (1984): 112–117.

Lévi-Strauss, Claude. "The Family." In Harry Shapiro, ed., *Man, Culture, and Society*. New York: Oxford University Press, 1956.

Levine, David. "Sociocultural Causes of Family Violence." *Journal of Family Violence* 1:1 (1986): 3–12.

Levine, Linda, and Lonnie Barbach. *The Intimate Male.* New York: Signet Books, 1983.

Levine, Martin. "The Sociology of Male Homosexuality and Lesbianism: An Introductory (Annotated) Bibliography." *Journal of Sexuality* 5:3 (Spring 1990): 249–275.

Levine, Martin, and Richard Troiden. "The Myth of Sexual Compulsivity." *Journal of Sex Research* 25:3 (August 1988): 347–363.

Levinger, George. "Marital Cohesiveness and Dissolution: An Integrative Review." *Journal of Marriage and the Family* 27 (1965): 19–28.

_____. "A Social Psychological Perspective on Marital Dissolution." In George Levinger and O. C. Moles, eds., *Divorce and Separation.* New York: Basic Books, 1979.

Levinger, George, and O. C. Moles, eds. *Divorce and Separation: Context, Causes, and Consequences.* New York: Basic Books, 1979.

Levinson, Daniel J. *The Seasons of a Man's Life.* New York: Ballantine Books, 1977.

Lewin, Bo. "Unmarried Cohabitation: A Marriage Form in a Changing Society." *Journal of Marriage and the Family* 44:3 (August 1982): 763–773.

Lewin, E., and T. A. Lyons. "Everything in Its Place: The Coexistence of Lesbianism and Motherhood." In W. Paul et al., eds., *Homosexuality: Social, Psychological, and Biological Issues.* Newbury Park, Calif.: Sage Publications, 1982.

Lewin, M. "Unwanted Intercourse: The Difficulty of Saying No." *Psychology of Women Quarterly* 9 (1985): 184–192.

Lewin, Tamar. "Drug Use During Pregnancy: New Issue before the Courts." *The New York Times,* February 5, 1990: A1, A12.

_____. "South Korea Slows Export of Babies for Adoption." *The New York Times,* February 12, 1990.

Lewis, Jerry M., ed. *The Birth of the Family: An Empirical Inquiry.* New York: Brunner/Mazel, 1989.

Lewis, Jerry M., Margaret Tresch Owen, and Martha J. Cox. "Family of Origin." In Jerry M. Lewis, ed., *The Birth of the Family: An Empirical Inquiry.* New York: Brunner/Mazel, 1989.

Lewis, Jerry M., et al. *No Single Thread.* New York: Brunner/Mazel, 1976.

Lewis, Karen. "Children of Lesbians: Their Point of View." *Social Work* 25:3 (May 1980): 198–203.

Lewis, Robert. "The Family and Addictions: An Introduction." *Family Relations* 38:3 (July 1989): 254–257.

Libby, Roger. "Social Scripts for Sexual Relationships." In Sol Gordon and Roger Libby, eds. *Sexuality Today and Tomorrow.* North Scituate, Mass.: Duxbury Press, 1976.

Lieberman, B. "Extrapremarital Intercourse: Attitudes toward a Neglected Sexual Behavior." *Journal of Sex Research;* 1988; 24(291–299).

Lieberson, Stanley, and Mary Waters. *From Many Strands: Ethnic and Racial Groups in Contemporary America.* New York: Russell Sage Foundation, 1988.

Lief, Harold, and Helen Singer Kaplan. "Ego-Dystonic Homosexuality." *Journal of Sex and Marital Therapy* 12:4 (Winter 1986): 259–266.

Liem, Ramsay, and J. Liem. "Social Support and Stress: Some General Issues and Their Application to the Problem of Unemployment." In L. Ferman and J. Gordus, eds., *Mental Health and the Economy.* Kalamazoo, Mich.: Upjohn Institute, 1979.

Liem, Ramsay, and Paula Rayman. "Health and Social Costs of Unemployment." *American Psychologist* 37(10) (October 1982): 1116–1123.

Lindsey, Karen. *Friends as Family.* Boston: Beacon Press, 1982.

Lingren, Herbert, et al. "Enhancing Marriage and Family Competencies Through Adult Life Development." In Nick Stinnet et al., eds., *Family Strengths 4: Positive Support Systems.* Lincoln: University of Nebraska Press, 1982.

Lino, Mark. "Expenditures on a Child by Husband-Wife Families." *Family Economics Review* 3:3 (1990): 2–12.

Litwack, Leon. *Been in the Storm So Long.* New York: Alfred A. Knopf, 1979.

Lloyd, Sally A. "Conflict Types and Strategies in Violent Marriages." *Journal of Family Violence* 5:4 (December 1990): 269–284.

_____. "The Darkside of Courtship: Violence and Sexual Exploitation." *Family Relations* 40:1 (January 1991): 14–20.

Lloyd, Sally A., and Beth C. Emery. "The Dynamics of Courtship Violence." Paper presented at the Annual Meeting of The National Council on Family Relations, Seattle, November 1990.

Lockhart, Lettie. "A Reexamination of the Effects of Race and Social Class on the Incidence of Marital Violence: A Search for Reliable Differences." *Journal of Marriage and the Family* 49 (August, 1987): 603–610.

Loiacano, Darryl. "Sex Identity Issues Among Black Americans: Racism, Homophobia, and the Need for Validation." *Journal of Counseling and Development* 68:1 (September–October 1989): 21–25.

Lombardo, W. K. et al. "Fer Cryin' Out Loud—There is a Sex Difference." *Sex Roles* 9 (1983): 987–995.

London, Richard, James Wakefield, and Richard Lewak. "Similarity of Personality Variables as Predictors of Marital Satisfaction." *Personality and Individual Differences* 11:1 (1990): 39–43.

Lopata, Helena. *Occupation: Housewife.* New York: Oxford University Press, 1972.

_____. *Women As Widows: Support Systems.* New York: Elsevier, 1979.

Lord, Lewis. "Desperately Seeking Baby." *U.S. News & World Report* (October 5, 1987):58–65.

Lord, Lewis, et al. "Coming to Grips with Alcoholism." *U.S. News & World Report* (November 30, 1987): 56–62.

Losh-Hesselbart, Susan. "Development of Gender Roles." In Marvin Sussman and Suzanne Steinmetz, eds., *Handbook of Marriage and the Family.* New York: Plenum Press, 1987.

Lowry, Dennis, and David Towles. "Prime Time TV Portrayals of Sex, Contraception, and Venereal Disease." *Journalism Quarterly* 66:2 (Summer 1989): 347–352.

_____. "Soap Opera Portrayals of Sex, Contraception, and Venereal Disease." *Journal of Communication* 39:2 (Spring 1989): 76–83.

Luker, Kristin. *Abortion and the Politics of Motherhood.* Berkeley: University of California Press, 1984.

_____. *Taking Chances.* Berkeley: University of California Press, 1975.

Lurie, Elinore. "Sex and Stage Differences in Perceptions of Marital and Family Relationships." *Journal of Marriage and the Family* 36:2 (May 1974): 260–269.

Lutz, Patricia. "The Stepfamily: An Adolescent Perspective." *Family Relations* 32:3 (July 1983): 367–375.

Lutzer, John, and James Rice. "Using Recidivism Data to Evaluate Project 12-Ways: An Ecobehavioral Approach to the Treatment and Prevention of Child Abuse and Neglect." *Journal of Family Violence* 2:4 (1986): 283–290.

Lutzer, John and James Rice. "Project 12-Ways: Measuring Outcome of a Large-scale In-Home Service for the Treatment and Prevention of Child Abuse and Neglect." *Child Abuse and Neglect International Journal* 8 (1984): 519–524.

Lyon, Jeff. *Playing God in the Nursery.* New York: W. W. Norton, 1985.

McAdoo, Harriette. "Changes in the Formation and Structure of Black Families: The Impact on Black Women." Center for Research on Women, Wellesley College. Working Paper No. 182. Wellesley, Mass.: 1988.

_____, ed. *Black Families,* 2d ed. Beverly Hills, Calif.: Sage Publications, 1988.

McAdoo, Harriette Pipes, and John McAdoo, eds. *Black Children: Social, Educational, and Parental Environments.* Beverly Hills, Calif: Sage, 1985.

McCormack, M. J., et al. "Patient's Attitudes Following Chorionic Villus Sampling." *Prenatal Diagnosis* 10:4 (April 1990): 253–255.

McCubbin, Hamilton I., "Integrating Coping Behavior in Family Stress Theory." *Journal of Marriage and the Family* 41:2 (May 1979): 237–244.

McCubbin, Hamilton I., Constance Joy, and Elizabeth Cauble. "Family Stress and Coping: A Decade Review." *Journal of Marriage and the Family* 42:4 (November 1980): 855–871.

McCubbin, Hamilton I., and Marilyn A. McCubbin. "Typologies of Resilient Families: Emerging Roles of Social Class and Ethnicity." *Family Relations* 37 (July 1988): 247–254.

McCubbin, Hamilton I., and Anne I. Thompson, eds. *Family Assessment Inventories for Research and Practice.* Madison: University of Wisconsin Press, 1987.

McCubbin, Marilyn A. "Family Stress, Resources, and Family Types: Chronic Illness in Children." *Family Relations* 37 (April 1988): 203–210.

McCubbin, Marilyn A., and Hamilton I. McCubbin. "Theoretical Orientations to Family Stress and Coping." In Charles Figley, ed., *Treating Families Under Stress.* New York: Brunner/Mazel, 1989.

_____. "Family Stress Theory and Assessment." In Hamilton I. McCubbin and Anne I. Thompson, eds., *Family Assessment Inventories for Research and Practice.* Madison: University of Wisconsin Press, 1987.

McEwan, K. L., C. G. Costello, and P. J. Taylor. "Adjustment to Infertility." *Journal of Abnormal Psychology* 96:2 (May 1987): 108–116.

McGoldrick, Monica. "Normal Families: An Ethnic Perspective." In Froma Walsh, ed., *Normal Family Processes.* New York: Guilford Press, 1982.

McGoldrick, Monica, and Randy Gerson. *Genograms in Family Assessment.* New York: Norton, 1985.

McGoldrick, Monica, John Pearce, and Joseph Giordano. *Ethnicity and Family Therapy.* New York: Guilford Press, 1988.

McHale, Susan, and Ted Huston. "The Effect of the Transition to Parenthood on the Marriage and Family Relationship: A Longitudinal Study." *Journal of Family Issues* 6:4 (December 1985): 409–433.

McIntosh, Everton; Tate, Douglas T. "Correlates of Jealous Behaviors." Psychological Reports; April 1990; 66(2): 601–602.

McKim, Margaret K. "Transition to What? New Parents' Problems in the First Year." *Family Relations* 36 (January 1987): 22–25.

McKinney, Kathleen. "Perceptions of Courtship Violence: Gender Difference and Involvement." *Free Inquiry in Creative Sociology* 14:1 (May 1986): 61–66.

McKinney, Kathleen, and Susan Sprecher, eds. *Human Sexuality: The Societal and Interpersonal Context.* Norwood, N.J.: Ablex, 1989.

_____. *Sexuality in Close Relationships.* Hillsdale, N.J.: Erlbaum, 1991.

McLanahan, Sara, and Karen Booth. "Mother-Only Families: Problems, Prospects, and Politics." In Alan Booth, ed., *Contemporary Families: Looking Forward, Looking Back.* Minneapolis: National Council on Family Relations, 1991.

McLanahan, Sara, et al. "Network Structure, Social Support, and Psychological Well-Being." *Journal of Marriage and the Family* 43 (August 1981): 601–612.

McLoughlin, David, and Richard Whitfield. "Adolescents and Their Experience of Parental Divorce." *Journal of Adolescence* 7 (1984): 155–170.

McNeely, R. L., and Barbe Fogarty. "Balancing Parenthood and Employment: Factors Affecting Company Receptiveness to Family-Related Innovations in the Workplace." *Family Relations* 37 (April 1988): 189–195.

McNeil, John. *The Church and the Homosexual.* Boston: Beacon Press, 1988.

MacCorquodale, Patricia. "Gender and Sexuality." In Kathleen McKinney, and Susan Sprecher, eds. *Human Sexuality: The Societal and Interpersonal Context.* Norwood, N.J.: Ablex, 1989.

MacCorquodale, Patricia, and John DeLameter. "Self-Image and Premarital Sexuality." *Journal of Marriage and the Family* (May 1979): 327–33.

Macchiarola, Frank J., and Alan Gartner, eds. *Caring for America's Children.* New York: The Academy of Political Science, 1989.

Maccoby, Eleanor, and Carol Jacklin. *The Psychology of Sex Differences.* Stanford, Calif.: Stanford University Press, 1974.

Mace, David, and Vera Mace. "Enriching Marriage." In Nick Stinnet et al., eds., *Family Strengths.* Lincoln: University of Nebraska Press, 1979.

_____. "Enriching Marriages: The Foundation Stone of Family Strength." In Nick Stinnet et al. *Family Strengths: Positive Models for Family Life.* Lincoln: University of Nebraska Press, 1980.

Macklin, Eleanor, ed. *AIDS and Families.* New York: Harrington Park Publishers, 1989.

_____. "AIDS: Implications for Families." *Family Relations* 37:2 (April 1988): 141–149.

_____. "Nonmarital Heterosexual Cohabitation." *Marriage and Family Review* 1 (March/April 1978): 1–12.

_____. "Nontraditional Family Forms." In Marvin Sussman and Suzanne Steinmetz, eds., *Handbook of Marriage and the Family.* New York: Plenum Press, 1987.

Macklin, Eleanor, and Roger Rubin, eds. *Contemporary Families and Alternative Lifestyles: Handbook on Research and Theory.* Beverly Hills, Calif.: Sage Publications, 1983.

Maddox, Brenda. "Homosexual Parents." *Psychology Today.* (February, 1982): 62–69.

Madsen, William. *Mexican-American Youth of South Texas,* 2d ed. New York: Holt, Rinehart, and Winston, 1973.

Magno, Josefina. "The Hospice Concept of Care: Facing the 1990s." *Death Studies* 14:2 (1990): 109–119.

Makepeace, James. "Courtship Violence Among College Students." *Family Relations* 30:1 (January 1981): 97–102.

_____. "Dating, Living Together, and Courtship Violence." In Maureen Pirog-Good, and Jan Stets, eds., *Violence in Dating Relationships: Emerging Social Issues.* New York: Praeger, 1989.

_____. "Gender Differences in Courtship Violence Victimization." *Family Relations* 35:3 (July 1986): 383–388.

_____. "Social Factor and Victim-Offender Differences in Courtship Violence." *Family Relations* 36 (1987): 87–91.

Malatesta, Victor, Dianne Chambless, Martha Pollack, and Alan Cantor. "Widowhood, Sexuality, and Aging: A Life Span Analysis." *Journal of Sex and Marital Therapy* 14:1 (Spring 1989): 49–62.

Maloney, Lawrence. "Behind Rise in Mixed Marriages." *U.S. News & World Report* (February 10, 1986): 68–69.

Malson, Lucien. *Wolf Children and the Problem of Human Nature.* New York: Monthly Review Press, 1972.

Malveaux, Julianne. "The Economic Status of Black Families." In Harriette Pipes McAdoo, ed., *Black Families,* 2d ed. Newbury Park, Calif.: Sage Publications, 1988.

Mancini, Jay, and Rosemary Blieszner. "Aging Parents and Adult Children: Research Themes in Intergenerational Relations." In Alan Booth, ed. *Contemporary Families: Looking Forward, Looking Back.* Minneapolis: National Council on Family Relations, 1991.

_____. "Research on Aging Parents and Adult Children." *Journal of Marriage and the Family* 51 (May 1989): 275–290.

Marecek, Jeanne, Stephen Finn, and Moda Cardell. "Gender Roles in the Relationships of Lesbians and Gay Men." In John DeCecco, ed., *Gay Relationships.* New York: Haworth Press, 1988.

Maret, Elizabeth, and Barbara Finlay. "The Distribution of Household Labor Among Women in Dual–Earner Marriages." *Journal of Marriage and the Family* 46 (1984): 357–364.

Margolin, Gayla, Linda Gorin Sibner, and Lisa Gleberman. "Wife Battering." In Vincent B. Van Hasselt et al., eds., *Handbook of Family Violence.* New York: Plenum Press, 1988.

Margolin, Leslie. "Abuse and Neglect in Nonparental Child Care: A Risk Assessment." *Journal of Marriage and the Family* 53:3 (August 1991): 694–704.

Margolin, Leslie, and Lynn White. "The Continuing Role of Physical Attractiveness in Marriage." *Journal of Marriage and the Family* 49 (February 1987): 21–27.

Margolin, Malcolm. *The Ohlone Way*. Berkeley: Heyday Books, 1978.

Marin, Peter. "Helping and Hating the Homeless." *Harper's*, (January 1987): 39–49.

Markman, Howard. "Prediction of Marital Distress: A Five-Year Follow-up." *Journal of Consulting and Clinical Psychology* 49 (1981): 760–761.

Markman, Howard, S. W. Duncan, R. D. Storaasli, and P. W. Howes. "The Prediction and Prevention of Marital Distress: A Longitudinal Investigation." In Kurt Hahlweg and Michael Goldstein, eds., *Understanding Major Mental Disorders: The Contribution of Family Interaction Research*. New York: Family Process Press, 1987.

Marmor, Judd. "Homosexuality and the Issue of Mental Illness." In Judd Marmor, ed., *Homosexual Behavior*. New York: Basic Books, 1980.

Marmor, Judd, ed. *Homosexual Behavior*. New York: Basic Books, 1980.

Martelli, Leonard, et al. *When Someone You Know Has AIDS: A Book of Hope for Family and Friends*. New York: Crown, 1987.

Martin, Del. *Battered Wives*. San Francisco, Calif.: New Glide, 1981.

Martin, Don, and Maggie Martin. "Selected Attitudes toward Marriage and Family Life among College Students." *Family Relations* 33 (1984): 293–300.

Martin, Elmer P., and Joanne Mitchell Martin. *The Black Extended Family*. Chicago: University of Chicago Press, 1978.

Martin, Grant. "Relationship, Romance, and Sexual Addiction in Extramarital Affairs." *Journal of Psychology and Christianity* 8:4 (Winter 1989): 5–25.

Martin, Peter, Gunhild O. Hagestad, and Patricia Diedrick. "Family Stories: Events (temporarily) Remembered." *Journal of Marriage and the Family* 50 (May 1988): 533–541.

Maruta, Toshihiko, and Mary Jane McHardy. "Sexual Problems in Patients with Chronic Pain." *Medical Aspects of Human Sexuality* 17:2 (February 1983): 68J–68Uff.

Mason, Karen, and Yu-Hsia Lu. "Attitudes toward Women's Familial Roles: Changes in the United States, 1977–1985." *Gender & Society* 2:1 (March 1988): 39–57.

"Massachusetts Midwife Curb Upheld." *The New York Times*, May 25, 1987: 5.

Masters, John, et al. "The Role of the Family in Coping with Childhood Chronic Illness." In Thomas Burish and Laurence Bradley, eds., *Coping with Chronic Disease*. New York: Academic Press, 1983.

Masters, William, et al. *Masters and Johnson on Sex and Human Loving*. Boston: Little, Brown, 1986.

Masters, William, and Virginia Johnson. *Human Sexual Inadequacy*. Boston: Little, Brown, 1970.

Matiella, Ana Consuelo. *Positively Different: Creating a Bias-Free Environment for Children*. Santa Cruz, Calif.: Network Publications, 1991.

Mattessich, Paul, and Reuben Hill. "Life Cycle and Family Development." In Marvin Sussman and Suzanne Steinmetz, eds., *Handbook of Marriage and the Family*. New York: Plenum Press, 1987.

Matthews, Sarah, and Tana Rosner. "Shared Filial Responsibility: The Family as the Primary Caregiver." *Journal of Marriage and the Family* 50:1 (February 1988): 185–195.

Mays, Vickie, and Susan Cochran. "Acquired Immunodeficiency Syndrome and Black Americans: Special Psychosocial Issues." *Public Health Reports* 102:2 (March/April, 1987): 224–232.

Mazor, Miriam. "Barren Couples." *Psychology Today* 12:12 (May 1979): 101–108, 112.

Mazor, Miriam, and Harriet Simons, eds. *Infertility: Medical, Emotional and Social Considerations*. New York: Human Sciences Press, 1984.

Mead, Margaret. *Male and Female*. New York: William Morrow, 1975.

Meckel, Richard. "Childhood and the Historians: A Review Essay." *Journal of Family History* 9:4 (Winter 1984): 415–424.

Mederer, Helen J., and Richard J. Gelles. "Compassion or Control: Intervention in Cases of Wife Abuse." *Journal of Interpersonal Violence* 4:1 (March 1989): 25–43.

Medoff, Marshall. "Constituencies, Ideology, and the Demand for Abortion Legislation." *Public Choice* 60:2 (February 1989): 185–191.

Mehren, Elizabeth. "Suddenly, I Saw God Smiling." *The New York Times*, December 12, 1990: E1, E5.

Meiners, Jane, and Geraldine Olson. "Household, Paid and Unpaid Work Time of Farm Women." *Family Relations* 37:1 (January 1988): 407–411.

Melichor, Joseph, and David Chiriboga. "Significance of Time in Adjustment to Marital Separation." *American Journal of Orthopsychiatry* 58:2 (April 1988): 221–227.

Melito, Richard. "Adaptation in Family Systems: A Developmental Perspective." *Family Processes* 24 (1985): 89–100.

Menaghan, Elizabeth, and Toby Parcel. "Parental Employment and Family Life: Research in the 1980s." In Alan Booth, ed., *Contemporary Families: Looking Forward, Looking Back*. Minneapolis, Minn.: National Council on Family Relations, 1991.

Menning, Barbara Eck. *Infertility: A Guide for Childless Couples*, 2d ed. New York: Prentice Hall, 1988.

Meredith, William, and George Rowe. "Changes in Lao Hmong Marital Attitudes after Immigration to the United States." *Journal of Comparative Family Studies* 17:1 (Spring 1986): 117–126.

Mertensmeyer, Carol, and Marilyn Coleman. "Correlates of Inter-Role Conflict in Young Rurals and Urban Parents." *Family Relations* 36 (October 1987): 425–429.

Messinger, Lillian. "Remarriage between Divorced People with Children from Previous Marriages: A Proposal for Preparation for Remarriage." *Journal of Marriage and Family Counseling* 2 (1976): 193–200.

Miall, Cherlene E. "The Stigma of Adoptive Parent Status: Perceptions of Community Attitudes Toward Adoption and the Experience of Informal Self-Sanctioning." *Family Relations* 36 (January 1987): 34–39.

Milan, Richard, Jr., and Peter Kilmann. "Interpersonal Factors in Premarital Contraception." *Journal of Sex Research* 23:3 (August, 1987): 321–389.

Milardo, Robert. "Changes in Social Networks of Women and Men Following Divorce: A Review." *Journal of Family Issues* 8 (1987) 78–96.

Miller, B. "Gay Fathers and Their Children." *The Family Coordinator* 28 (1979): 544–552.

Miller, Brent. *Family Research Methods*. Beverly Hills, Calif.: Sage Publications, 1986.

Miller, Brent, Kelly McCoy, Terrance Olson, and Christopher Wallace. "Parental Discipline and Control Attempts in Relation to Adolescent Sexual Attitudes and Behavior." *Journal of Marriage and the Family* 48:3 (August 1986): 503–512.

Miller, Jean B. "Psychological Recovery in Low-Income Single Parents." *American Journal of Orthopsychiatry* 52:2 (April 1982): 346–352.

Miller, John. *The First Frontier*, 2d ed. New York: Dell, 1975.

Miller, Randi, and Michael Gordon. "The Decline of Formal Dating: A Study in Six Connecticut High Schools." *Marriage and Family Relationships* 10:1 (April 1986): 139–154.

Mills, David. "A Model for Stepparent Development." *Family Relations* 33 (1984): 365–372.

Min, Pyong Gap. "The Korean American Family." In Charles Mindel, Robert Habenstein, and Roosevelt Wright, eds., *Ethnic Families in America: Patterns and Variations*, 3d ed. New York: Elsevier North Holland, Inc., 1988.

Mindel, Charles H., Robert W. Habenstein, and Roosevelt Wright, Jr., eds. *Ethnic Families in America: Patterns and Variations*, 3d ed. New York: Elsevier North Holland, Inc., 1976, 1981, 1988.

Minuchin, Salvador. *Families and Family Therapy*. Cambridge, Mass.: Harvard University Press, 1974.

_____. *Family Therapy Techniques*. Cambridge, Mass.: Harvard University Press, 1981.

Mintz, Steven, and Susan Kellogg. *Domestic Revolutions: A Social History of American Family Life*. New York: Free Press, 1988.

Mirandé, Alfredo. *The Chicano Experience: An Alternative Perspective*. Notre Dame, Ind.: University of Notre Dame Press, 1985.

Mirowsky, John, and Catherine Ross. "Belief in Innate Sex Roles: Sex Stratification versus Interpersonal Influence in Marriage." *Journal of Marriage and the Family* 49:3 (August, 1987): 527–540.

Mnookin, R. J. "Child-Custody Adjudication: Judicial Functions in the Face of Indeterminacy." *Law and Contemporary Problems* 39 (1975): 226–292.

Moen, Phyllis. "Unemployment, Public Policy, and Families: Forecasts for the 1980s." *Journal of Marriage and the Family* (November 1983): 751–760.

Moen, Phyllis, and Donna Dempster-McClain. "Employed Parents: Role Strain, Work Time, and Preferences for Working Less." *Journal of Marriage and the Family* 49:3 (August 1987): 579–590.

Moffatt, Betty Clare, et al. *AIDS: A Self-Care Manual*. Los Angeles: IBS Press, 1987.

Moffatt, Michael. *Coming of Age in New Jersey: College and American Culture*. New Brunswick, N.J.: Rutgers University Press, 1989.

Mohr, James. *Abortion in America: Origins and Evolution of National Policy, 1800–1900*. New York: Oxford University Press, 1980.

Monahan, Thomas. "Are Interracial Marriages Really Less Stable?" *Social Forces* 48 (1970): 461–473.

Money, John. *Love and Lovesickness*. Baltimore: Johns Hopkins University Press, 1980.

Money, T. O. [and others]. *Sexual Options for Paraplegics and Quadraplegics*. Boston: Little, Brown; 1975.

Monroe, Pamela, and James Garland. "Parental Leave Legislation in the U.S. Senate: Toward a Model Roll-Call Voting." *Family Relations* 40:2 (April 1991): 208–218.

Montagu, Ashley. *Touching*, 3d ed. New York: Columbia University Press, 1986.

Moody, Kate. *Growing Up on Television*. New York: Times Books, 1980.

Moore, Denis. "Ministering to Everyone." *San Jose Mercury News*, July 21, 1990: 10E, 12E.

Moore, Dianne, and Pamela Erickson. "Age, Gender, and Ethnic Differences in Sexual and Contraceptive Knowledge, Attitudes, and Behaviors." *Family and Community Health* 8:3 (November 1985): 38–51.

Moore, Kristin, and Isabel Sawhill. "Implications of Women's Employment for Home and Family Life." In Juanita Kreps, ed., *Women and the American Economy*. Englewood Cliffs, N.J.: Prentice-Hall, 1976.

Moore, Lisa J. "Protecting Babies from Hepatitis-B." *U.S. News & World Report* (May 9, 1988): 85.

Morbidity and Mortality Weekly Reports. "Update: Acquired Immunodeficiency Syndrome—United States." 39:5 (February 9, 1990): 80–82.

Morgan, Carolyn, and Alexis Walker. "Predicting Sex Role Attitudes." *Social Psychology Quarterly* 46 (1983): 148–153.

Morgan, Edmund. *The Puritan Family*. New York: Harper & Row, 1966; 1st ed., 1944.

Morgan, Leslie. "Outcomes of Marital Separation: A Longitudinal Test of Predictors." *Journal of Marriage and the Family* 50 (May 1988): 493–498.

Morgan, S. Philip, Diane Lye, and Gretchen Condran. "Sons, Daughters, and the Risk of Marital Disruption." *American Journal of Sociology* 94 (1988): 110–129.

Morrison, Donna, and Daniel Lichter. "Family Migration and Female Employment: The Problem of Underemployment among Migrant Women." *Journal of Marriage and the Family* 50 (February 1988): 161–172.

Mosher, Donald. "Sex Guilt and Sex Myths in College Men and Women." *Journal of Sex Research* 15:3 (August 1979): 224–234.

Moss, Peter, et al. "Marital Relations During the Transition to Parenthood." *Journal of Reproductive and Infant Psychology* 4:1–2 (September 1986): 57–67.

Muehlenhard, Charlene. "Misinterpreted Dating Behaviors and the Risk of Date Rape." *Journal of Social and Clinical Psychology* 9:1 (1988): 20–37.

Mugford, Stephen, and Jim Lally. "Sex, Reported Happiness, and the Well-Being of Married Individuals." *Journal of Marriage and the Family* 43:4 (November 1981): 969–975.

Mullan, Bob. *The Mating Trade*. Boston: Routledge & Kegan Paul, 1984.

Murdock, George. *Social Structure*. New York: Free Press, 1965; 1st ed., 1949.

_____. "World Ethnographic Sample." *American Anthropologist* 59 (1957): 664–687.

Murray, Charles. *Losing Ground: American Social Policy, 1950–1980*. New York: Basic Books, 1984.

Murstein, Bernard. "A Clarification and Extension of the SVR Theory of Dyadic Pairing." *Journal of Marriage and the Family* 49 (1987): 929–933.

_____. *Who Will Marry Whom: Theories and Research in Marital Choice*. New York: Springer, 1976.

Musetto, Andrew. "Standards for Deciding Contested Child Custody." *Journal of Clinical Child Psychology* 10:1 (Spring 1981): 51–55.

Mydans, Seth. "U.S. Food Program Tightens Its Belt and Millions on Welfare Feel Pinch." *The New York Times*, June 2, 1990: 10.

_____. "Surrogate Loses Custody Bid in Case Defining Motherhood." *The New York Times*, October 23, 1990.

Myers-Walls, Judith, and Fred Piercy. "Mass Media and Prevention: Guidelines for Family Life Professionals." *Journal of Primary Prevention* 5:2 (Winter 1984): 124–136.

Nace, Edgar, et al. "Treatment Priorities in a Family-Oriented Alcoholism Program." *Journal of Marital and Family Therapy* (January 1982): 143–150.

Nadelson, Carol, and Maria Sauzier. "Intervention Programs for Individual Victims and Their Families." In Mary Lystad, ed., *Violence in the Home: Interdisciplinary Perspectives*. New York: Brunner/Mazel, 1986.

Napier, Augustus, and Carl Whitaker. *The Family Crucible*. New York: Harper & Row, 1978.

Nasaw, David. *Children of the City: At Work and Play*. New York: Basic Books, 1985.

National Academy of Sciences. *Homelessness, Health, and Human Needs*. Washington, D.C.: National Academy Press, 1988.

Needle, Richard, et al. "Drug Abuse: Adolescent Addictions and the Family." In Charles R. Figley and Hamilton McCubbin, eds., *Stress and the Family: Coping with Catastrophe*. Vol. 2. New York: Brunner/Mazel, 1983.

Nelsen, Jane. *Positive Discipline*. New York: Ballantine Books, 1987.

Nelson, Margaret, and Gordon Nelson. "Problems of Equity in the Reconstituted Family: a Social Exchange Analysis." *Family Relations* 31 (April 1982): 223–231.

"Neonatal Herpes Is Preventable." *USA Today* 112, February 1984:8–9.

Neuman, Judith. "Divorced Catholics." *San Jose Mercury News*, June 1, 1985: 1C.

Nevid, Jeffrey. "Sex Differences in Factors of Romantic Attraction." *Sex Roles* 11(5/6) (1984): 401–411.

Newcomb, Michael. "Cohabitation in America: An Assessment of Consequences." *Journal of Marriage and the Family* (August 1979): 597–603.

Newcomb, Michael, and Peter Bentler. "Assessment of Personality and Demographic Aspects of Cohabitation and Marital Success." *Journal of Personality Development* 4:1 (1980): 11–24.

Newcomer, Susan, and Richard Udry. "Oral Sex in an Adolescent Population." *Archives of Sexual Behavior* 14:1 (February 1985): 41–46.

Newton, Niles. *Maternal Emotions.* New York: Basic Books, 1955.

NiCarthy, Ginny. *Getting Free: A Handbook for Women in Abusive Relationships.* Seattle, Wash.: Seal Press, 1986.

Nichols, Margaret. "Lesbian Sexuality: Issues and Developing Theory." In: Boston Lesbian Psychologies Collective, ed. Lesbian Psychologies; Explorations and Challenges. Urbana, IL: University of Chicago Press; 1987.

NICHY (National Information Center for Children and Youth with Handicaps). *News Digest* 14 (October 1990): 1–12.

Noble, Elizabeth. *Having Your Baby by Donor Insemination.* Boston: Houghton Mifflin, 1987.

_____. "Prenatal Exercise." In Stanley E. Sagov et al., eds., *Home Birth: A Practitioner's Guide to Birth Outside the Hospital.* Rockville, Md.: Aspen, 1984.

Nobles, Wade W. "African-American Family Life: An Instrument of Culture." In Harriette Pipes McAdoo, ed., *Black Families,* 2d ed. Newbury Park, Calif.: Sage Publications, 1988.

Nock, Steven. "The Symbolic Meaning of Childbearing." *Journal of Family Issues* 8:4 (December, 1987): 373–393.

Noller, Patricia. *Nonverbal Communication and Marital Interaction.* Oxford, England: Pergamon Press, 1984.

Noller, Patricia, and Mary Anne Fitzpatrick. "Marital Communication." In Alan Booth, ed., *Contemporary Families: Looking Forward, Looking Back.* Minneapolis: National Council on Family Relations, 1991.

_____, eds. *Perspectives on Marital Interaction.* Philadelphia: Multilingual Matters, 1988.

Norton, Arthur J. "Family Life Cycle: 1980." *Journal of Marriage and the Family* 45 (1983): 267–275.

Norton, Arthur, and Jeanne Moorman. "Current Trends in American Marriage and Divorce." *Journal of Marriage and the Family* 49 (1987): 3–14.

Notarius, Clifford, and Jennifer Johnson. "Emotional Expression in Husbands and Wives." *Journal of Marriage and the Family* 44:2 (May 1982): 483–489.

Notman, Malkah T., and Eva P. Lester. "Pregnancy: Theoretical Considerations." *Psychoanalytic Inquiry* 8:2 (1988): 139–159.

Notzon, Francis C., Paul J. Placek, and Selma M. Taffel. "Comparisons of National Cesarean-Section Rates." *New England Journal of Medicine* 316:7 (February 12, 1987): 386–389.

Nye, F. Ivan. "Fifty Years of Family Research." *Journal of Marriage and the Family* 50 (May 1988): 305–316.

_____. *Role Structure and Analysis of the Family.* Beverly Hills, Calif.: Sage Publications, 1976.

Nye, F. Ivan, and Felix Berardo, eds. *Emerging Conceptual Frameworks in Family Analysis.* 2 vols. New York: Praeger, 1981.

Nyquist, Linda, et al. "Household Responsibilities in Middle–Class Couples: The Contribution of Demographic and Personality Variables." *Sex Roles* 12(1/2) (1985): 15–34.

Oakley, Ann. *Sex, Gender, and Society,* rev. ed. New York: Harper and Row, 1985.

Odent, Michel. *Birth Reborn.* New York: Pantheon, 1984.

O'Flaherty, Kathleen, and Laura Eells. "Courtship Behavior of the Remarried." *Journal of Marriage and the Family* 50 (May 1988): 499–506.

Olds, David L., Charles Henderson, Jr., Robert Chamberlin, and Robert Tatelbaum. "Preventing Child Abuse and Neglect: A Randomized Trial of Nurse Home Visitation." *Pediatrics* 78 (July 1986): 65–78.

Olson, David. "Insiders' and Outsiders' Views of Relationships: Research Studies." In George Levinger and H. Rausch, eds., *Close Relations.* Amherst, Mass.: University of Massachusetts Press, 1977.

Olson, David H., et al. *Families.* Beverly Hills, Calif.: Sage Publications, 1983.

O'Reilly, Jane. "Wife Beating: The Silent Crime." *Time* (September 5, 1983).

Orlofsky, Jacob, and Connie O'Heron. "Stereotypic and Nonstereotypic Sex Role Trait and Behavior Orientations: Implications for Personal Adjustment." *Journal of Personality and Social Psychology* 52 (May, 1987): 1034–1042.

Orthner, D. K., and J. F. Pittman. "Family Contributions to Work Commitment." *Journal of Marriage and the Family* 48 (1986): 573–581.

Ortiz, Vilma, and Rosemary Santana Cooney. "Sex Role Attitudes and Labor Force Participation among Young Hispanic Females and Non-Hispanic White Females." *Social Science Quarterly* 65:2 (June 1984): 392–400.

Oster, Sharon. "A Note on the Determinants of Alimony." *Journal of Marriage and the Family* 49 (February 1987): 81–86.

Otto, Luther. "America's Youth: A Changing Profile." *Family Relations* 37:4 (October 1988): 385–391.

Pallow-Fleury, Angie. "Your Hospital Birth: Questions to Ask." *Mothering* (Winter 1983): 83–85.

Panuthos, Claudia, and Catherine Romeo. *Ended Beginnings: Healing Childbearing Losses.* New York: Warner Books, 1984.

Papp, Peggy. *The Process of Change.* New York: Guilford Press, 1983.

Parachini, Allen. "Breast-Feeding: Once on the Rise, Is Slowing." *Los Angeles Times,* December 20, 1985.

_____. "Condom Study Finding Wide Differences Among Brands." *Los Angeles Times,* June 29, 1988: V1, 3.

Pareles, Jon. "Indians' Heritage Survives in Songs." *The New York Times,* December 4, 1990: B1ff.

Parker, Hilda, and Seymour Parker. "Cultural Rules, Rituals and Behavior Regulation." *American Anthropologist* 86:3 (1984): 584–600.

_____. "Father–Daughter Sexual Child Abuse: An Emerging Perspective." *American Journal of Orthopsychiatry* 56:4 (October 1986): 531–549.

Parker, Philip. "Motivation of Surrogate Mothers—Initial Findings." *American Journal of Psychiatry* 140:1 (1983): 117–118.

Parr, Jay. *Childhood and Family in Canadian History.* Toronto: McClelland and Steward, 1982.

Parrot, Andrea, and Michael Ellis. "Homosexuals Should Be Allowed to Marry and Adopt or Rear Children." In Harold Feldman and Margaret Feldman, eds., *Current Controversies in Marriage and the Family.* Beverly Hills, Calif.: Sage Publications, 1985.

Parsons, Jacqueline. "Sexual Socialization and Gender Roles in Childhood." In Elizabeth Allgeier and Naomi McCormick, eds. *Gender Roles and Sexual Behavior.* Palo Alto, Calif.: Mayfield, 1982.

_____, ed. *The Psychobiology of Sex Differences and Sex Roles.* Washington, D.C.: Hemisphere, 1980.

Parsons, Talcott. "Family Structure and the Socialization of the Child." In T. Parsons and R. F. Bales, eds., *Family Socialization and Interaction Process.* Glencoe, Ill.: Free Press, 1955.

Parsons, Talcott, and R. F. Bales. *Family Socialization and Interaction Processes.* Glencoe, Ill.: Free Press, 1955.

Pasley, Kay. "Family Boundary Ambiguity: Perceptions of Adult Stepfamily Family Members." In Kay Pasley and Marilyn Ihinger-Tallman, eds., *Remarriage and Stepparenting: Current Research and Theory.* New York: Guilford Press, 1987.

Pasley, Kay, and Marilyn Ihinger-Tallman, eds. *Remarriage and Stepparenting: Current Research and Theory.* New York: Guilford Press, 1987.

Patterson, G. *Families: Applications of Social Learning to Family Life*. Champaign, Ill.: Research Press, 1971.

Patterson, Joan, and Hamilton McCubbin. "Chronic Illness: Family Stress and Coping." In Charles R. Figley and Hamilton McCubbin, eds., *Stress and the Family: Coping with Catastrophe*, Vol. Two. New York: Brunner/Mazel, 1983.

Paul, W., J. Weinrich, J. Gonsiorek, and M. Hotvedt, eds. *Homosexuality: Social, Psychological, and Biological Issues*. Newbury Park, Calif.: Sage Publications, 1982.

Paulson, David. "Hot Tubs and Reduced Sperm Counts." *Medical Aspects of Human Sexuality* 14 (September 1980): 121.

Paulson, Morris J., Robert H. Coombs, and John Landsverk. "Youth Who Physically Assault Their Parents." *Journal of Family Violence* 5:2 (June 1990): 121–134.

Payton, Isabelle. "Single-Parent Households: An Alternative Approach." *Family Economics Review* (Winter 1982): 11–16.

Pear, Robert. "Rich Got Richer in 80's; Others Held Even." *The New York Times*, January 11, 1991: A1, A11.

_____. "U.S. Reports Poverty Is Down but Inequality Is Up." *The New York Times*, September 27, 1990: A12.

_____. "What Causes the High U.S. Rate of Infant Deaths?" *The New York Times*, March 20, 1985: 19.

Pearson, Jessica, et al. "Legal Change and Child Custody Awards." *Journal of Family Issues* 3:3 (March 1982): 5–24.

Pedhazur, E. J., and T. J. Tetenbaum. "Bem's Sex Role Inventory: A Theoretical and Methodological Critique." *Journal of Personality and Social Psychology* 37 (1979): 996–1016.

Peirce, Kate. "Sex Role Stereotyping of Children: A Content Analysis of the Roles and Attributes of Child Characters." *Sociological Spectrum* 9:3 (Fall 1989): 321–328.

Peek, Charles, et al. "Teenage Violence Toward Parents: A Neglected Dimension in Family Violence." *Journal of Marriage and the Family* 47:4 (November 1985): 1051–1058.

Pennington, Saralie Bisnovich. "Children of Lesbian Mothers." In Frederick W. Bozett, ed., *Gay and Lesbian Parents*. New York: Praeger, 1987.

Peplau, Letitia. "Research on Homosexual Couples." In John DeCecco, ed., *Gay Relationships*. New York: Haworth Press, 1988.

_____. "What Homosexuals Want." *Psychology Today* 15:3 (March 1981): 28–38.

Peplau, Letitia, and Steven Gordon. "The Intimate Relationships of Lesbians and Gay Men." In Elizabeth Allgeier and Naomi McCormick, eds., *Gender Roles and Sexual Behavior*. Palo Alto, Calif.: Mayfield, 1982.

Peplau, Letitia, et al. "Sexual Intimacy in Dating Relationships." *Journal of Social Issues* 33:2 (Spring 1977): 86–109.

Perlman, Daniel, and Steve Duck, eds. *Intimate Relationships: Development, Dynamics, and Deterioration*. Beverly Hills, Calif.: Sage Publications, 1987.

Perlman, David. "Brave New Babies." *San Francisco Chronicle*, March 5, 1990: B3ff.

Perry-Jenkins, Maureen. "Future Directions for Research on Dual-Earner Families: A Young Professional's Perspective." *Family Relations* 37:2 (April 1988): 226–228.

Peters, Stefanie, et al. "Prevalence." In David Finkelhor, ed., *Sourcebook on Child Sexual Abuse*. Beverly Hills, Calif.: Sage Publications, 1986.

Petersen, Larry. "Interfaith Marriage and Religious Commitment among Catholics." *Journal of Marriage and the Family* 48 (November 1986): 725–735.

Peterson, Gary W., and Boyd C. Rollins. "Parent-Child Socialization." In Marvin B. Sussman and Suzanne K. Steinmetz, eds., *Handbook of Marriage and the Family*. New York: Plenum Press, 1987.

Peterson, James R., et al. "Playboy's Readers' Sex Survey." *Playboy* (March, 1983).

Peterson, Marie Ferguson. "Racial Socialization of Young Black Children." In Harriette Pipes McAdoo and John McAdoo, eds., *Black Children: Social, Educational, and Parental Environments*. Beverly Hills, Calif.: Sage Publications, 1985.

Peterson, Yen. *Marital Adjustment in Couples of Which One Spouse Is Physically Handicapped*. Palo Alto, CA: R & E Research Associates, 1979.

Petit, Charles. "New Study to Ask Why So Many Infants Die." *San Francisco Chronicle*, May 9, 1990: A3.

Petit, Ellen, and Bernard Bloom. "Whose Decision Was It? The Effect of Initiator Status on Adjustment to Marital Disruption." *Journal of Marriage and the Family* 46:3 (August 1984): 587–595.

Peyrot, Mark, et al. "Marital Adjustment to Adult Diabetes: Interpersonal Congruence and Spouse Satisfaction." *Journal of Marriage and the Family* 50 (May 1988): 363–376.

Pies, Cheri. "Considering Parenthood: Psychological Issues for Gay Men and Lesbians Choosing Alternative Fertilization." In Frederick W. Bozett, ed., *Gay and Lesbian Parents*. New York: Praeger, 1987.

Pilisuk, Marc. "The Delivery of Social Support: The Social Innoculation." *American Journal of Orthopsychiatry* 52:1 (January 1982): 20–31.

Pill, Cynthia. "Stepfamilies: Redefining the Family." *Family Relations* 39:2 (April 1990): 186–193.

Pillemer, Karl. "The Dangers of Dependency: New Findings on Domestic Violence Against the Elderly." *Social Problems* 33 (1985): 146–158.

Pillemer, Karl, and J. Jill Suitor. "Elder Abuse." In Vincent B. Van Hasselt et al., eds., *Handbook of Family Violence*. New York: Plenum Press, 1988.

Pines, Ayala; Aronson, Elliot. "Antecedents, Correlates, and Consequenfces of Sexual jealousy." *Journal of Personality*; March 1983; 51(1): 108–136.

Pink, Jo Ellen, and Karen Smith Wampler. "Problem Areas in Stepfamilies: Cohesion, Adaptability, and the Stepfather-Adolescent Relationship." *Family Relations* 34:3 (July 1985): 327–335.

Piotrkowski, Chaya. *Work and the Family System*. New York: Free Press, 1979.

_____, et al. "Families and Work." In Marvin Sussman and Suzanne Steinmetz, eds., *Handbook of Marriage and the Family*. New York: Plenum Press, 1987.

Pirog-Good, Maureen A., and Jan E. Stets, eds. *Violence in Dating Relationships: Emerging Social Issues*. New York: Praeger, 1989.

Pivan, Frances Fox, and Richard Cloward. *Regulating the Poor*. New York: Vintage Books, 1972.

Pleck, Joseph. *The Myth of Masculinity*. New York: Norton, 1981.

_____. *Working Wives/Working Husbands*. Beverly Hills, Calif.: Sage Publications, 1985.

_____, et al. "Conflicts Between Work and Family Life." *Monthly Labor Review* 103:3 (1980): 29–32. U.S. Department of Labor, Bureau of Labor Statistics.

Plummer, K., ed. *The Making of the Modern Homosexual*. Totowa, N.J.: Barnes and Noble, 1981.

Plummer, William, and Margaret Nelson. "A Mother's Priceless Gift." *People Weekly* (August 26, 1991).

Pogatchnik, Shawn. "Kids' TV Gets More Violent, Study Finds." *Los Angeles Times*, January 26, 1990: F1, F27.

_____. "7000 Hate Crimes on Gays Reported in 1989." *Los Angeles Times*, June 8, 1990: A2.

Pogrebin, Letty Cottin. "Are Men Discovering the Joys of Fatherhood?" *Ms.* (February 1982): 41–46.

_____. *Family Politics*. New York: McGraw-Hill, 1983.

_____. *Growing Up Free: Raising Your Child in the 1980s*. New York: McGraw-Hill, 1980.

Pollis, Carol. "An Assessment of the Impacts of Feminism on Sexual Science." *Journal of Sex Research* 25:1 (February, 1988): 85–105.

_____. "Value Judgments and World Views in Sexuality Education." *Family Relations* 34 (April 1985): 285–290.

Porter, Nancy L., and F. Scott Christopher. "Infertility: Towards An Awareness of a Need Among Family Life Practitioners." *Family Relations* 33 (April 1984): 309–315.

Postman, Neil. *Amusing Ourselves to Death.* New York: Penguin, 1986.

Poussaint, Alvin. "What Every Black Woman Should Know about Black Men." *Ebony* 37 (August, 1982): 36–40.

Pratt, Clara, and Vicki Schmall. "College Students' Attitudes toward Elderly Sexual Behavior: Implications for Family Life Education." *Family Relations* 38 (April 1989): 137–141.

Press, Robert. "Hunger in America." *Christian Science Monitor,* February 15, 1985: 18–19.

Presser, Harriet. "Some Economic Complexities of Child Care Provided by Grandmothers." *Journal of Marriage and the Family* 51:3 (August 1989): 581–591.

_____. "Shift Work Among American Women and Child Care." *Journal of Marriage and the Family* 48 (August 1986): 551–663.

Price, J. H., and P. A. Miller. "Sexual Fantasies of Black and White College Students." *Psychological Reports* 54 (1984): 1007–1014.

Price, Jane. "Who Waits to Have Children? And Why?" In Jeffrey Rosenfeld, ed., *Relationships: The Marriage and Family Reader.* Glenview, Ill.: Scott, Foresman, 1982.

Price, John. "North American Indian Families." In Charles Mindel and Robert Habenstein, eds. *Ethnic Families in America: Patterns and Variations,* 2d ed. New York: Elsevier North Holland, Inc., 1981.

Price-Bonham, S., and J. O. Balswick. "The Noninstitutions: Divorce, Desertion, and Remarriage." *Journal of Marriage and the Family* 42 (1980): 959–972.

Prigatano, G. P. Work, Love, and Play after Brain Injury. Bulletin of the Menninger Clinic; August 1989; 34(8): 791–792.

Prober, Charles, et al. "Low Risk of Herpes Simplex Virus Infections in Neonates Exposed to the Virus at the Time of Vaginal Delivery to Mothers with Recurrent Genital Herpes Simplex Virus Infections." *New England Journal of Medicine* 316 (January 29, 1987): 129–138.

Pruett, Kyle. *The Nurturing Father: Journey Toward the Complete Man.* New York: Warner Books, 1987.

Puglisi, J. T., and D. W. Jackson. "Sex Role Identity and Self-Esteem in Adulthood." *Journal of Aging and Human Development* 12 (1981): 129–138.

Raabe, Phyllis, and John Gessner. "Employer Family-Supportive Policies: Diverse Variations on the Theme." *Family Relations* 37 (April 1988): 196–202.

Ralebipi, Matabole D. Rocky. "Family Resource Database: Single Parents and Child Care [Bibliography]." *Family Relations* 38 (October 1989): 474–475.

_____. "Family Resource Database: Fathers and Child Care [Bibliography]." *Family Relations* 38 (October 1989): 475–476.

Ramsey, Patricia G. *Teaching and Learning in a Diverse World: Multicultural Education for Young Children.* New York: Teachers College Press, 1987.

Rando, Therese A. "Death and Dying Are Not and Should Not Be Taboo Topics." In Austin H. Kutscher et al., eds., *Principles of Thanatology.* New York: Columbia University Press, 1987.

Rapp, Gail, and Sally Lloyd. "The Role of 'Home as Haven' Ideology in Child Care Use." *Family Relations* 38 (October 1989): 427–430.

Raschke, Helen. "Divorce." In Marvin Sussman and Suzanne Steinmetz, eds., *Handbook of Marriage and the Family.* New York: Plenum Press, 1987.

Raval, H., et al. "The Impact of Infertility on Emotions and the Marital and Sexual Relationship." *Journal of Reproductive and Infant Psychology* 5:4 (October–December 1987): 221–234.

Raven, Bertram, et al. "The Bases of Conjugal Power." In Ronald Cromwell and David Olson, eds. *Power in Families.* New York: Halstead Press, 1975.

Ravinder, Shashi. "Androgyny: Is It Really the Product of Educated Middle-Class Western Societies?" *Journal of Cross Cultural Psychology* 18:2 (June 1987): 208–220.

Rawlings, Steve. "Families Maintained by Female Householders, 1970–1979." Bureau of the Census. *Current Population Reports.* Special Studies, Series P23, No. 107. Washington, D.C.: U.S. Government Printing Office, 1980.

_____. "Household and Family Characteristics: March 1983." U.S. Bureau of the Census. *Current Population Reports.* Series P-20, No. 388. Washington, D.C.: U.S. Government Printing Office, 1984.

_____. "Studies in Marriage and the Family: Single Parents and Their Children." Bureau of the Census. *Current Population Reports.* Special Studies, Series P-23, No.162, Washington, D.C.: U.S. Government Printing Office, 1989.

Reamy, Kenneth, and Susan White. "Sexuality in the Puerperium: A Review." *Archives of Sexual Behavior* 16:2 (1987): 165–187.

Rebelsky, F., and C. Hanks. "Fathers' Verbal Interaction with Infants in the First Three Months of Life." *Child Development* 42 (1971): 63–68.

Reed, David, and Martin Weinberg. "Premarital Coitus: Developing and Established Sexual Scripts." *Social Psychology Quarterly* 47:2 (June 1984): 129–138.

Reedy, M., et al. "Age and Sex Differences in Satisfying Love Relationships across the Adult Life Span." *Human Development* 24 (1981): 52–86.

Regan, Mary, and Helen Roland. "Rearranging Family and Career Priorities: Professional Women and Men of the Eighties." *Journal of Marriage and the Family* 47:4 (November 1985): 985–992.

Regan, Riley. "Alcohol Problems and Family Violence." In Jerry Flanzer, ed. *The Many Faces of Family Violence.* Springfield, Ill.: Charles C. Thomas, 1982.

Reid, Pamela, and L. Comas-Diaz. "Gender and Ethnicity: Perspectives on Dual Status." *Sex Roles* 22:7–8 (April 1990): 397–408.

Reinhold, Robert. "State of the States, 1991: Rocky, Almost Everywhere." *The New York Times,* January 14, 1991: A12.

Reiss, David. "Commentary: The Social Construction of Reality—The Passion Within Us All." *Family Process* 24:2 (June 1985): 254–257.

_____. *The Family's Construction of Reality.* Cambridge, Mass.: Harvard Press, 1981.

Reiss, Ira. *Family Systems in America,* 3d ed. New York: Holt, Rinehart, and Winston, 1980.

_____. *Journey Into Sexuality: An Exploratory Voyage:* Englewood Cliffs, NJ: Prentice-Hall, 1986.

_____. *The Social Context of Premarital Sexual Permissiveness.* New York: Irvington, 1967.

_____, et al. *Journey into Sexuality: An Exploratory Voyage.* Inglewood Cliffs, N.J.: Prentice–Hall, 1986.

_____. "A Multivariate Model of the Determinants of Extramarital Sexual Permissiveness." *Journal of Marriage and the Family* 42 (May 1980): 395–411.

Resnick, Sandven. "Informal Adoption among Black Adolescent Mothers." *American Journal of Orthopsychiatry* 60 (April 1990): 210–224.

Retik, Alan B., and Stuart B. Bauer. "Infertility Related to DES Exposure in Utero: Reproductive Problems in the Male." In Miriam Mazor and Harriet Simons, eds., *Infertility: Medical, Emotional, and Social Considerations.* New York: Human Sciences Press, 1984.

Rettig, K. D., and M. M. Bubolz. "Interpersonal Resource Exchanges as Indicators of Quality of Marriage." *Journal of Marriage and the Family* 45 (1983): 497–510.

Rexroat, Cynthia. "Race and Marital Status Differences in the Labor Force Behavior of Female Family Heads: The Effect of Household Structure." *Journal of Marriage and the Family* 52:3 (August 1990): 591–601.

_____. "Women's Work Expectations and Labor-Market Experiences in Early and Middle Life-Cycle Stages. *Journal of Marriage and the Family* 47:1 (February 1985): 131–142.

Rexroat, Cynthia, and Constance Shehan. "The Family Life Cycle and Spouses Time in Housework." *Journal of Marriage and the Family* 49 (November 1987): 737–750.

Rice, Susan. "Sexuality and Intimacy for Aging Women: A Changing Perspective." *Journal of Women and Aging* 1:1–3 (1989): 245–264.

Rich, Adrienne. "Compulsory Heterosexuality and Lesbian Existence." In Ann Snitow et al., eds., *Powers of Desire: The Politics of Sexuality.* New York: Monthly Review Press, 1983.

_____. *Of Woman Born.* New York: Norton, 1976.

Richardson, B. B. "Racism and Child-Rearing: A Study of Black Mothers." *Dissertation Abstracts* 42(1) (1981): 125–A.

Richardson, Diana. "The Dilemma of Essentiality in Homosexual Theory." *Journal of Homosexuality* 9:2–3 (Winter 1983/Spring 1984): 79–90.

Riegle, Donald. "The Psychological and Social Effects of Unemployment." *American Psychologist* 37(10) (October 1982): 1113–1115.

Rieve, J. E. Sexuality and the Adult with Acquired Physical Disability. Nursing Clinics of North America; March 1989; 1(24):265–276.

Riffer, Roger, and Jeffrey Chin. "Dating Satisfaction among College Students." *International Journal of Sociology and Social Policy* 8:5 (1988): 29–36.

Riportella-Muller, Roberta. "Sexuality in the Elderly: A Review." In Kathleen McKinney and Susan Sprecher, eds., *Human Sexuality: The Societal and Interpersonal Context.* Norwood, N.J.: Ablex Publishing Corporation, 1989.

Rist, Marilee C. "Crack Babies in School." *The American School Board Journal* CLVXXVI (January 1990): 19–24.

Rivlin, Leanne. "The Significance of Home and Homelessness." *Marriage and Family Review* 15:1/2 (1990): 39–57.

Robbins, Tom. *Still Life with Woodpecker.* New York: Bantam, 1980.

Roberts, Elizabeth. "Television and Sexual Learning in Childhood." In National Institute of Mental Health, *Television and Behavior.* Washington, D.C.: Government Printing Office, 1982:209–223.

Roberts, Linda, and Lowell Krokoff. "A Time Series Analysis of Withdrawal, Hostility, and Displeasure in Satisfied and Dissatisfied Marriages." *Journal of Marriage and the Family* 52:1 (February 1990): 95–105.

Roberts, Sam. "The Hunger Beneath the Statistics." *The New York Times,* May 23, 1988: A13.

Robertson, Elizabeth, et al. "The Costs and Benefits of Social Support in Families." *Journal of Marriage and the Family* 53:2 (May 1991): 403–416.

Robinson, Paul. *The Modernization of Sex.* New York: Harper & Row, 1976.

Robinson, Pauline. "The Sociological Perspective." In Ruth Weg, ed., *Sexuality in the Later Years: Roles and Behavior.* New York: Academic Press, 1983.

Rodgers, Roy, and L. Conrad. "Courtship for Remarriage: Influences on Family Reorganization after Divorce." *Journal of Marriage and the Family* 48 (1986): 767–775.

Rodman, Hyman, and Cynthia Cole. "When School-Age Children Care for Themselves: Issues for Family Life Educators and Parents." *Family Relations* 36 (January 1987): 92–96.

Roen, Philip. *Male Sexual Health.* New York: William Morrow and Co., 1974.

Rollins, B. C., and K. L. Cannon. "Marital Satisfaction over the Family Life Cycle: A Reevaluation." *Journal of Marriage and the Family* 36 (May 1974): 271–282.

Rollins, B. C., and H. Feldman. "Marital Satisfaction over the Family Life Cycle." *Journal of Marriage and the Marriage and the Family* 32 (February 1970): 20–28.

Romberg, Rosemary. *Circumcision: The Painful Dilemma.* South Hadley, Mass.: Bergin and Garvey, 1985.

Rooks, J., et al. "Outcomes of Care in Birth Centers." *New England Journal of Medicine* 321 (1989): 1804–1811.

Roopnarine, Jaipaul, Nina Mounts, and Glendon Casto. "Mothers' Perceptions of Their Children's Supplemental Care Experience: Correlation with Spousal Relationship." *American Journal of Orthopsychiatry* 56:4 (October 1986): 581–588.

Roos, Patricia, and Lawrence Cohen. "Sex Roles and Social Support as Moderators of Life Stress Adjustment." *Journal of Personality and Social Psychology* 52:3 (March, 1987): 576–585.

Roscoe, Bruce, and Nancy Benaske. "Courtship Violence Experienced by Abused Wives: Similarities in Patterns of Abuse." *Family Relations* 34:3 (July 1985): 419–424.

Rosenbaum, David. "Jobless Aid Dries Up as Recession Looms." *San Francisco Chronicle,* December 3, 1990: 2.

Rosenblatt, Paul, and Roxanne Anderson. "Human Sexuality in Cross-Cultural Perspective." In Mark Cook, ed., *The Bases of Human Sexual Attraction.* New York: Academic Press, 1981.

Rosenfeld, Alvin. "Sexual Misuse and the Family." *Victimology: An International Journal* 2:2 (Summer 1977): 226–235.

Rosenfeld, Alvin, and Eli Newberger. "Compassion vs. Control: Conceptual and Practical Pitfalls in the Broadened Definition of Child Abuse." In Richard Bourne and Eli Newberger, eds., *Critical Perspectives on Child Abuse.* Lexington, Mass.: Lexington Books, 1979.

Rosenkrantz, D., et al. "Sex Role Stereotypes and Self Concepts in College Students." *Journal of Consulting and Clinical Psychology* 32 (1968): 287–295.

Rosenthal, Carolyn. "Kinkeeping in the Familial Division of Labor." *Journal of Marriage and the Family* 47:4 (November 1985): 965–974.

Rosenthal, Elisabeth. "When a Pregnant Woman Drinks." *The New York Times Magazine,* February 4, 1990: 30ff.

Rosenzweig, Julie, and Dennis Daily. "Dyadic Adjustment/Sexual Satisfaction in Women and Men as a Function of Psychological Sex Role Self-Perception." *Journal of Sex and Marital Therapy* 15: (Spring 1989): 42–56.

Ross, Catherine, John Mirowsky, and Karen Goldsteen. "The Impact of the Family on Health." In Alan Booth, ed., *Contemporary Families: Looking Forward, Looking Back.* Minneapolis: National Council on Family Relations, 1991.

Ross, H. L. "Modes of Adjustment of Married Homosexuals." *Social Problems* 18 (1978): 385–393.

_____. "Odd Couples: Homosexuals in Heterosexual Marriage." *Sexual Behavior* 2 (1972): 42–49.

Ross, L., et al. "Television Viewing and Adult Sex-Role Attitudes." *Sex Roles* 8 (1982): 589–592.

Rossi, Alice. "Transition to Parenthood." *Journal of Marriage and the Family* 30 (February 1968): 26–39.

Rowe, William S. Sexuality and the Developmentally Handicapped; A Guidebook for Health Care Professionals. Lewiston, NY: E. Mellen Press; 1987.

Rowland, Robyn. "Technology and Motherhood: Reproductive Choice Reconsidered." *Signs: Journal of Women in Culture and Society* 12:3 (1987): 512–528.

Rubenstein, C. "Wellness Is All." *Psychology Today* (October 1982): 27–37.

Rubenstein, Carin, and Carol Tavris. "Special Survey Results: 26,000 Women Reveal the Secrets of Intimacy." *Redbook* 159 (September 1987): 147–149ff.

Rubin, A. M., and J. R. Adams. "Outcomes of Sexually Open Marriages." *Journal of Sex Research* 22 (1986): 311–319.

Rubin, Lillian. *Erotic Wars*. New York: Farrar, Straus, and Giroux, 1990.

_____. *Intimate Strangers*. New York: Harper & Row, 1983.

_____. *Worlds of Pain*. New York: Basic Books, 1976.

Rubin, Nora Jean. *How to Care for Your Parents: A Handbook for Adult Children*. Washington, D.C.: Storm King Press, 1987.

Rubin, Zick. Introduction to Robert Sternberg and Michael Barnes, eds., *The Psychology of Love*. New Haven, Conn.: Yale University Press, 1988.

_____. *Liking and Loving: An Invitation to Social Psychology*. New York: Holt, Rinehart, and Winston, 1973.

_____. "Loving and Leaving: Sex Differences in Romantic Attachments." *Sex Roles* 7 (1981): 821–835.

_____. "Self Disclosure in Dating Relationships: Sex Roles and the Ethic of Openness." *Journal of Marriage and the Family* 42 (1980): 305–317.

_____, et al. "The Eye of the Beholder: Parents' View of Sex of Newborn." *American Journal of Orthopsychiatry* 44 (Fall 1974): 512–519.

Runyan, William. "In Defense of the Case Study Method." *American Journal of Orthopsychiatry* 52:3 (July 1982): 440–446.

Rush, D., et al. "The National WIC Evaluation." *American Journal of Clinical Nutrition* 48:2 (Suppl.) (August 1988): 439–483.

Russell, C. "Transition to Parenthood." *Journal of Marriage and the Family* 36 (May 1974): 294–302.

Russell, Diana E. H. *Rape in Marriage*, rev. ed. Bloomington, Ind.: Indiana University Press, 1982, 1990.

_____. *Rape in Marriage*. Bloomington, Ind.: Indiana University Press; 1990.

_____. *The Secret Trauma: Incest in the Lives of Girls and Women*. New York: Basic Books, 1986.

_____. *Sexual Exploitation: Rape, Child Sexual Abuse, and Workplace Harassment*. Beverly Hills, Calif.: Sage Publications, 1984.

Sabatelli, Ronald, and Erin Cecil–Pigo. "Relational Interdependence and Commitment in Marriage." *Journal of Marriage and the Family* 47:4 (November 1985): 931–938.

Safilios-Rothschild, Constantina. "Family Sociology or Wives' Sociology? A Cross-Cultural Examination of Decisionmaking." *Journal of Marriage and the Family* 31 (May 1969): 290–301.

_____. *Love, Sex, and Sex Roles*. Englewood Cliffs, N.J.: Prentice-Hall, 1977.

_____. "A Macro- and Micro-Examination of Family Power and Love: An Exchange Model. *Journal of Marriage and the Family* 38 (1976): 355–362.

_____. "The Study of the Family Power Structure." *Journal of Marriage and the Family* 32 (November 1970): 539–543.

_____, ed. *Toward a Sociology of Women*. Lexington, Mass.: Xerox, 1972.

Salgado de Snyder, V. Nelly, Richard Cervantes, and Amado Padilla. "Gender and Ethnic Differences in Psychosocial Stress and Generalized Distress among Hispanics." *Sex Roles* 22:7–8 (April 1990): 441–453.

Salholz, Eloise. "The Future of Gay America." *Newsweek* (March 12, 1990): 20–25.

Salovey, P.; Rodin, J. "Provoking Jealousy and Envy: Domaine Relevance and Self-Esteem Threat." *Journal of Social and Clinical Psychology*; Winter 1991; 10(4): 395–413.

Saluter, Arlene. "Marital Status and Living Arrangements: March 1989." Bureau of the Census. *Current Population Reports*. "Population Characteristics." Series P-20, No. 445. Washington, D.C.: U.S. Government Printing Office, 1991.

_____. "Singleness in America." Bureau of the Census. *Current Population Reports*. "Special Studies." Series P-23, No. 162. Washington, D.C.: U.S. Government Printing Office, 1989.

Sampson, Ronald. *The Problem of Power*. New York: Pantheon Books, 1966.

Samuels, Michael, and Nancy Samuels. *The Well Pregnancy Book*. New York: Summit Books, 1986.

Samuels, Shirley. *Ideal Adoption: A Comprehensive Guide to Forming an Adoptive Family*. New York: Insight Books, 1990.

Samuelson, Robert. "Childcare Revisited." *Newsweek* (August 8, 1988): 53.

Sánchez-Ayéndez, Melba. "The Puerto Rican American Family." In Charles Mindel, Robert Habenstein, and Roosevelt Wright, Jr., eds., *Ethnic Families in America: Patterns and Variations*, 3d ed. New York: Elsevier North Holland, Inc., 1988.

Santrock, John. *Life-Span Development*. Dubuque, Iowa: William C. Brown. 1983.

Santrock, John, and Karen Sitterle. "Parent-Child Relationships in Stepmother Families." In Kay Pasley and Marilyn Ihinger-Tallman, eds., *Remarriage and Stepparenting: Current Research and Theory*. New York: Guilford Press, 1987.

Santrock, John, and Richard Warsack. "Father Custody and Social Development in Boys and Girls." *Journal of Social Issues* 35:4 (1979): 112–125.

Satir, Virginia. *Conjoint Family Therapy*. Palo Alto, Calif.: Science and Behavior Books, 1967.

_____. *The New Peoplemaking*, rev. ed. Mountain View, Calif.: Science and Behavior Books, 1988.

Saunders, Daniel. "When Battered Women Use Violence: Husband-Abuse or Self-Defense." *Victim and Violence* 1:1 (1986): 47–60.

Scales, Peter. "Sex in Politics and Policy." *Marriage and Family Review* 6:3–4 (Fall/Winter 1983): 47–59.

Scanzoni, John. "Reconsidering Family Policy: Status Quo or Force for Change?" *Journal of Family Issues* 3:3 (September 1982): 277–300.

_____. *Sexual Bargaining*. Englewood Cliffs, N.J.: Prentice-Hall, Inc., 1980, 2d ed.

_____. "Social Processes and Power in Families." In W. Burr et al., eds. *Contemporary Theories about the Family*, Vol. 1. New York: Free Press, 1979.

Scanzoni, John, Karen Polonko, Jay Teachman, and Linda Thompson. *The Sexual Bond: Rethinking Families and Close Relationships*. Newbury Park, Calif.: Sage Publications, 1989.

Schaap, Cas, Bram Buunk, and Ada Kerkstra. "Marital Conflict Resolutions." In Patricia Noller and Mary Anne Fitzpatrick, eds., *Perspectives on Marital Interaction*. Philadelphia: Multilingual Matters, 1988.

Schlesinger, Benjamin. *Canadian Family Studies: A Selected, Annotated Bibliography*. Chicago: CPL Bibliographies, 1983.

Schmitt, Bernard, and Robert Millard. "Construct Validity of the Bem Sex Role Inventory: Does the BSRI Distinguish between Gender-Schematic and Gender Aschematic Individuals?" *Sex Roles* 19:9–10 (November 1988): 581–588.

Schneck, M. E., et al. "Low-Income Adolescents and Their Infants: Dietary Findings and Health Outcomes." *Journal of the American Dietetic Association* 90:4 (April 1990): 555–558.

Schneider, David. *American Kinship: A Cultural Account*, 2d ed. Chicago: University of Chicago Press, 1980.

Schneider, Peter. "Lost Innocents: The Myth of Missing Children." *Harper's Magazine* (February, 1987): 47–53.

Schooler, Carmi, et al. "Work for the Household: Its Nature and Consequences for Husbands and Wives." *American Journal of Sociology* 90:1 (July 1984): 97–124.

_____. "Psychological Effects of Complex Environments During the Life Span: A Review and Theory." In Carmi Schooler and K. Warner Schaie, eds., *Cognitive Functioning and Social Structure over the Life Course.* Norwood, N.J.: Ablex, 1987.

Schooler, Carmi, and K. Warner Schaie, eds. *Cognitive Functioning and Social Structure over the Life Course.* Norwood, N.J.: Ablex, 1987.

Schumm, Walter. "Marriage and Parenthood Are Necessary for a Happy Life for Both Men and Women." In H. Feldman and M. Feldman, eds., *Current Controversies in Marriage and the Family.* Beverly Hills, Calif.: Sage, 1985.

_____, et al. "His and Her Marriage Revisited." *Journal of Family Issues* 6 (June 1985): 211–227.

Schvaneveldt, Jay. "The Interactional Framework in the Study of the Family." In F. Ivan Nye and Felix Berardo, eds., *Emerging Conceptual Frameworks in Family Analysis,* 2d ed. New York: Praeger, 1981.

Schvaneveldt, Jay, Shelley Lindauer, and Margaret Young. "Children's Understanding of AIDS: A Developmental Viewpoint." *Family Relations* 39:3 (July 1990): 330–335.

Schwebel, Andrew, Mark Fine, and Maureena Renner. "A Study of Perceptions of the Stepparent Role." *Journal of Family Issues* 23:1 (March 1991): 43–57.

Scott, Clarissa, Lydia Shifman, Lavenda Orr, and Roger Owen. "Hispanic and Black American Adolescents' Beliefs Relating to Sexuality and Contraception." *Adolescence* 23:91 (Fall 1988): 667–688.

Scott, David, and Bernard Wishy, eds. *America's Families: A Documentary History.* New York: Harper & Row, 1982.

Scott, Jacqueline. "Conflicting Beliefs about Abortion: Legal Approval and Moral Doubts." *Social Psychology Quarterly* 52:4 (December 1989): 319–328.

Scott, Jacqueline, and Duane F. Alwin. "Gender Differences in Parental Strain: Parental Role or Gender Role?" *Journal of Family Issues* 10:4 (December 1989): 482–503.

Scott, Jacqueline, and Howard Schuman. "Attitude Strength and Social Action in the Abortion Dispute." *American Sociological Review* 53:5 (October 1989): 785–793.

Scott, Janny. "Low Birth Weight's High Cost." *Los Angeles Times,* December 3, 1990b, A1.

_____. "Trying to Save the Babies." *Los Angeles Times,* December 24, 1990a: A1, 18ff.

Scott, Joan. "Gender: A Useful Category of Historical Analysis." *American Historical Review* 91 (1986): 1053–1075.

Scott, S. G., et al. "Therapeutic Donor Insemination with Frozen Semen." *Canadian Medical Association Journal* 143:4 (August 15, 1990): 273–278.

Scott-Jones, Diane, and Sherry Turner. "Sex Education, Contraceptive and Reproductive Knowledge, and Contraceptive Use among Black Adolescent Females." *Journal of Adolescent Research* 3:2 (Summer 1988): 171–187.

Sears, David. "College Sophomores in the Laboratory: Influences of Narrow Data Base on Social Psychology's View of Human Nature." *Journal of Personality and Social Psychology* 51 (August, 1986): 515–530.

Seidman, Steven. "Constructing Sex as a Domain of Pleasure and Self-Expression: Sexual Ideology in the Sixties." *Theory, Culture, and Society* 6:2 (May 1989): 293–315.

Select Committee on Children, Youth and Families, U.S. House of Representatives. *Families and Child Care: Improving the Options.* Report 98–1180. 98th Congress, 2nd Session. Washington, D.C.: U.S. Government Printing Office, 1985.

Sennett, Richard. *Authority.* New York: Knopf, 1980.

Serdahely, William, and Georgia Ziemba. "Changing Homophobic Attitudes through College Sexuality Education." *Journal of Homosexuality* 10:1–2 (Fall 1984): 148ff.

Settles, Barbara H. "A Perspective on Tomorrow's Families." In Marvin Sussman and Suzanne Steinmetz, eds., *Handbook of Marriage and the Family.* New York: Plenum Press, 1987.

Sexton, Christine, and Daniel Perlman. "Couples' Career Orientation, Gender Role Orientation, and Perceived Equity as Determinants of Marital Power." *Journal of Marriage and the Family* 51:4 (November 1989): 933–941.

Shanis, B. S., J. H. Check, and A. F. Baker. "Transmission of Sexually Transmitted Diseases by Donor Semen." *Archives of Andrology* 23:3 (1989): 249–257.

Shannon, Thomas. *Surrogate Motherhood.* New York: Crossroad Publishing Co., 1988.

Shapiro, David. "No Other Hope for Having a Child." *Newsweek* (January 19, 1987): 50–51.

Shapiro, Joanna. "Family Reactions and Coping Strategies in Response to the Physically Ill or Handicapped Child: A Review." *Social Science and Medicine* 17 (1983): 913–931.

Shapiro, Johanna, and Ken Tittle. "Maternal Adaptation to Child Disability in a Hispanic Population." *Family Relations* 39:2 (April 1990): 179–185.

Shaver, Phillip, et al. "Love as Attachment: The Integration of Three Behavioral Systems." In Robert Sternberg and Michael Barnes, eds. *The Psychology of Love.* New Haven, Conn.: Yale University Press, 1988.

Shaw, David. "Despite Advances, Stereotypes Still Used by Media." *Los Angeles Times,* December 12, 1990: A31.

Sheehan, Nancy, and Paul Nuttall. "Conflict, Emotion, and Personal Strain Among Family Caregivers." *Family Relations* 37:1 (January 1988): 92–98.

Shelp, Earl. *Born to Die?* New York: The Free Press, 1986.

Sherman, Beth. "Spanking: Experts Say No." *San Jose Mercury,* June 24, 1985.

Sherman, Lawrence, and Richard Berk, Jr. "The Special Deterrent Effects of Arrest for Domestic Violence." *American Sociological Review* 49 (1984): 261–272.

"Shifting the Burden." *Los Angeles Times,* April 16, 1990: A5.

Shilts, Randy. *And the Band Played On: Politics, People, and the AIDS Epidemic.* New York: St. Martins Press, 1987.

Shimkin, Demitri, Edith Shimkin, and Dennis Frate. *The Extended Family in Black Societies.* The Hague, Netherlands: Mouton Publishers, 1978.

Shostak, Arthur B. "Singlehood." In Marvin Sussman and Suzanne Steinmetz, eds., *Handbook of Marriage and the Family.* New York: Plenum Press, 1987.

_____. "Tomorrow's Family Reforms: Marriage Course, Marriage Test, Incorporated Families, and Sex Selection Mandate." *Journal of Marital and Family Therapy* 7:4 (October 1981): 521–528.

Sidorowicz, Laura, and G. Sparks Lunney. "Baby X Revisited." *Sex Roles* 6:1 (February 1980): 67–73.

Signorielli, Nancy. "Children, Television, and Gender Roles—Messages and Impact." *Journal of Broadcasting and Electronic Media* 33:3 (Summer 1989): 325–331.

_____. "Television and Conceptions about Sex Roles—Maintaining Conventionality and the Status Quo." *Sex Roles* 21:5–5 (September 1989): 341–350.

Silver, Donald, and B. Kay Campbell. "Failure of Psychological Gestation." *Psychoanalytic Inquiry* 8:2 (1988): 222–233.

Simmel, Georg. *The Sociology of Georg Simmel.* Edited by K. Wolff. New York: Free Press, 1950.

Simon, William, and John Gagnon. "Sexual Scripts." *Society* 221:1 (November–December 1984): 53–60.

Simpson, George Eaton, and J. Milton Yinger. *Racial and Cultural Minorities: An Analysis of Prejudice and Discrimination*. New York: Plenum Press, 1985.

Simpson, Jeffrey. "The Dissolution of Romantic Relationships: Factors Involved in Relationship Stability and Emotional Distress." *Journal of Personality and Social Psychology* 53:4 (1987): 683–694.

Simpson, Jeffrey, et al. "The Association between Romantic Love and Marriage: Kephart (1967) Twice Revisited." *Personality and Social Psychology Bulletin* 12 (1986): 363–372.

Singer, Dorothy, G. "A Time to Reexamine the Role of Television in Our Lives." *American Psychologist* 38 (1983): 815–816.

Singer, Peter, and Deane Wells. *Making Babies: The New Science and Ethics of Conception*. New York: Charles Scribner's Sons, 1985.

Sinnott, Jan. *Sex Roles and Aging: Theory and Research from a Systems Perspective*. New York: Karger, 1986.

Skolnick, Arlene, and Jerome Skolnick, eds. *Family in Transition*. Boston: Little, Brown, 1980.

Slater, Philip. *The Pursuit of Loneliness*. Boston: Beacon Press, 1971.

Sluzki, C. E., and V. Eliseo. "The Double Bind as a Universal Pathogenic Situation." *Family Process* 10 (1971): 397–410.

Small, Stephen, and Dave Riley. "Toward a Multidimensional Assessment of Work Spillover into Family Life." *Journal of Marriage and the Family* 52:1 (February 1990): 51–61.

Smelser, Neil, and Erik Erikson, eds. *Themes of Work and Love in Adulthood*. Cambridge, Mass.: Harvard University Press, 1980.

Smith, Daniel, and Michael Hindus. "Premarital Pregnancy in America: 1640–1971." *Journal of Interdisciplinary History* 4 (Spring 1975): 537–570.

Smith, E. J. "The Black Female Adolescent: A Review of the Educational, Career, and Psychological Literature." *Psychology of Women Quarterly* 6 (1982): 261–288.

Smith, Ken, and Cathleen Zick. "The Incidence of Poverty among the Recently Widowed: Mediating Factors in the Life Course." *Journal of Marriage and the Family* 48 (1986): 619–630.

Snarey, John, et al. "The Role of Parenting in Men's Psychosocial Development." *Developmental Psychology* 23:4 (July 1987): 593–603.

Sobol, Thomas. "Understanding Diversity." *Educational Leadership* 48:3 (November 1990): 27–30.

Sonenstein, F. L., J. H. Pleck, and L. C. Ku. "Sexual Activity, Condom Use, and AIDS Awareness among Adolescent Males." *Family Planning Perspectives* 21:4 (July/August 1989): 152–158.

Sontag, Susan. "The Double Standard of Aging." *Saturday Review* 55 (September 1972): 29–38.

Sophie, Joan. "Internalized Homophobia and Lesbian Identity." *Journal of Homosexuality* 18:3–4 (1989): 95–118.

_____. "Internalized Homophobia and Lesbian Identity." *Journal of Homosexuality* 14:1–2 (Fall/Winter 1987): 53–65.

Sorenson, James, and Guilermo Bernal. *A Family Like Yours: Breaking the Pattern of Drug Abuse*. San Francisco, Calif.: Harper and Row, 1987.

Sorosky, Arthur, Annette Baran, and Ruben Pannor. *The Adoption Triangle: The Effects of the Sealed Record on Adoptees, Birth Parents, and Adoptive Parents*. Garden City, N.Y.: Anchor Press, 1978.

South, Scott, and Glenna Spitze. "Determinants of Divorce over the Marital Life Course." *American Sociological Review* 47 (1986): 583–590.

Spanier, Graham B. "Improve, Refine, Recast, Expand, Clarify—But Don't Abandon." *Journal of Marriage and the Family* 47:4 (November 1985): 1073–1074.

_____. "Measuring Dyadic Adjustment." *Journal of Marriage and the Family* 38 (February 1976): 15–28.

Spanier, Graham B. and Frank Furstenberg, Jr. "Remarriage After Divorce: A Longitudinal Analysis of Well-being." *Journal of Marriage and the Family* 44:3 (August 1982): 709–720.

_____. "Remarriage and Reconstituted Families." In Marvin Sussman and Suzanne Steinmetz, eds. *Handbook of Marriage and the Family*. New York: Plenum Press, 1987.

Spanier, Graham B. and R. L. Margolis. "Marital Separation and Extramarital Sexual Behavior." *Journal of Sex Research* 19 (1983): 23–48.

Spanier, Graham B. and Linda Thompson. "A Confirmatory Analysis of the Dyadic Adjustment Scale." *Journal of Marriage and the Family* 44:3 (August 1982): 731–738.

_____. *Parting: The Aftermath of Separation and Divorce*, rev. ed. Beverly Hills, Calif.: Sage Publications, 1984, 1987.

_____. "Relief and Distress after Marital Separation." *Journal of Divorce* 7 (1983): 31–49.

Spanier, Graham B. et al. "Marital Trajectories of American Women: Variations in the Life Course." *Journal of Marriage and the Family* 47:4 (November 1985): 993–1003.

Spector, I. P., and Carey, M. P. "Incidence and Prevalence of the Sexual Dysfunctions—A Critical Review of the Empirical Literature." *Archives of Sexual Behavior* 19:4 (August 1990): 389–408.

Spence, Janet, and L. L. Sawin. "Images of Masculinity and Feminity." In V. O'Leary, et al., eds., *Sex, Gender, and Social Psychology*. Hillsdale, N.J.: Erlbaum, 1985.

Spence, Janet, et al. "Ratings of Self and Peers on Sex Role Attributes and the Relation to Self-Esteem and Conceptions of Masculinity and Femininity." *Journal of Personality and Social Psychology* 32 (1975): 29–39.

_____. "Sex Roles in Contemporary Society." In G. Lindzey and Elliot Aronson, eds., *Handbook of Social Psychology*. New York: Random House, 1985.

Spencer, Margaret Beale. "Racial Variations in Achievement Prediction." In Harriette Pipes McAdoo and John McAdoo, eds., *Black Children: Social, Educational, and Parental Environments*. Beverly Hills, Calif.: Sage Publications, 1985.

Spiegel, Lynn. *Installing the Television Set: Television and the Family Ideal in Postwar America*. Chicago: University of Chicago Press, 1991.

Spitze, Glenna. "The Division of Task Responsibility in U.S. Households: Longitudinal Adjustments to Change." *Social Forces* 64 (1986): 689–701.

_____. "Women's Employment and Family Relations: A Review." In Alan Booth, ed., *Contemporary Families: Looking Forward, Looking Back*. Minneapolis: National Council on Family Relations, 1991.

Spitze, Glenna, and Scott South. "Women's Employment, Time Expenditure, and Divorce." *Journal of Family Issues* 6:3 (September 1985): 307–329.

Spock, Benjamin. *Baby and Child Care*. New York: Pocket Books, 1945, 1965, and 1976.

Spock, Benjamin, and Michael Rothenberg. *Dr. Spock's Baby and Child Care*. New York: Pocket Books, 1985.

Sponaugle, G. C. "Attitudes Toward Extramarital Relations." In Kathleen McKinney and Susan Sprecher, eds., *Human Sexuality: The Societal and Interpersonal Context*. Norwood, N.J.: Ablex Publishing Corporation, 1989.

Sprecher, Susan. "Sex Differences in Bases of Power in Dating Relationships." *Sex Roles* 12(34) (1985): 449–462.

_____, et al. "Sexual Relationships." In Kathleen McKinney and Susan Sprecher, eds., *Human Sexuality: The Societal and Interpersonal Context*. Norwood, N.J.: Ablex Publishing Corporation, 1989.

_____. "A Revision of the Reiss Premarital Sexual Permissiveness Scale." *Journal of Marriage and the Family* 50:3 (August, 1988): 821–828.

Sprey, Jetse. "Current Theorizing on the Family: An Appraisal." *Journal of Marriage and the Family* 50 (November 1988): 875–890.

Springer, D., and D. Brubaker. *Family Caregivers and Dependent Elderly: Minimizing Stress and Maximizing Independence.* Beverly Hills, Calif.: Sage Publications, 1984.

Stanton, M. Colleen. "The Fetus: A Growing Member of the Family." *Family Relations* 34:3 (July 1985): 321–326.

Stanton, M. D. "Family Treatment Approaches to Drug Abuse Problems: A Review." *Family Processes* 18 (1979): 251–280.

Staples, Robert. "The Black American Family." In Charles Mindel, Robert Habenstein, and Roosevelt Wright, Jr., eds. *Ethnic Families in America: Patterns and Variations,* 3d ed. New York: Elsevier North Holland, Inc., 1988.

_____. "The Black American Family. In Charles Mindel and Robert Habenstein, eds. *Ethnic Families in America.* 1st ed. New York: Elsevier North Holland, 1976.

_____. "The Emerging Majority: Resources for Nonwhite Families in the United States." *Family Relations* 37:3 (July 1988): 348–354.

_____, ed. *The Black Family: Essays and Studies,* 3d ed. Belmont, Calif.: Wadsworth Publishing Co., 1988, 1991.

Staples, Robert, and A. Mirandé. "Racial and Cultural Variations among American Families: A Decennial Review of the Literature." *Journal of Marriage and the Family* 42 (1980): 887–922.

Statistics Canada. *Canada Yearbook.* Ottawa: Supply and Services, 1990.

Steck, L., D. Levitan, D. McLane, and H. H. Kelley. "Care, Need, and Conceptions of Love." *Journal of Personality and Social Psychology* 43 (1982): 481–491.

Steele, Brandt F. "Psychodynamic Factors in Child Abuse." In C. Henry Kempe and Ray Helfer, eds., *The Battered Child.* Chicago: University of Chicago Press, 1980.

Steelman, Lala Carr, and Brian Powell. "The Social and Academic Consequences of Birth Order: Real, Artifactual, or Both?" *Journal of Marriage and the Family* 47 (1985): 117–124.

Stein, Peter, ed. *Single.* Englewood Cliffs, N.J.: Prentice-Hall, 1976.

Stein, Peter, and Meryl Fingrud. "The Single Life Has More Potential for Happiness than Marriage and Parenthood for Both Men and Women." In Harold Feldman and Margaret Feldman, eds., *Current Controversies in Marriage and the Family.* Beverly Hills, Calif.: Sage Publications, 1985.

Steinberg, Laurence, and Susan Silverberg. "Marital Satisfaction in Middle Stages of Family Life Cycle." *Journal of Marriage and the Family* 49:4 (November 1987): 751–760.

Steinglass, Peter. "A Life History Model of the Alcoholic Family." In David Olson and Brent Miller, eds., *Family Studies Review Yearbook,* Vol. 1. Beverly Hills, Calif.: Sage, 1983.

_____, et al. *The Alcoholic Family.* New York: Basic Books, 1987.

Steinman, Susan. "The Experience of Children in a Joint-Custody Arrangement: A Report of a Study." *American Journal of Orthopsychiatry* 51:3 (July 1981): 403–414.

Steinmetz, Suzanne. "Family Violence." In Marvin Sussman and Suzanne Steinmetz, eds., *Handbook of Marriage and the Family.* New York: Plenum Press, 1987.

Stephen, Beverly. "How Today's Woman Plans Her Wedding." *San Francisco Chronicle,* April 19, 1982.

Stephen, Timothy. "Fixed-Sequence and Circular-Causal Models of Relationship Development: Divergent Views on the Role of Communication in Intimacy." *Journal of Marriage and the Family* 47:4 (November 1985): 955–963.

Stephen, Timothy, and Teresa Harrison. "A Longitudinal Comparison of Couples with Sex-Typical and Non-Sex-Typical Orientations to Intimacy." *Sex Roles* 12(1/2) (1985): 195–205.

Sternberg, Robert. "Triangulating Love." In Robert Sternberg and Michael Barnes, eds., *The Psychology of Love.* New Haven, Conn.: Yale University Press, 1988.

_____. *The Psychology of Love.* New Haven, Conn.: Yale University Press, 1988.

Sternberg, Robert, and Michael Barnes. "Real and Ideal Others in Romantic Relationships: Is Four a Crowd?" *Journal of Personality and Social Psychology* 49 (1985): 1589–1596.

Stets, Jan; Pirog-Good, Maureen. "Violence in Dating Relationships." *Social Psychology Quarerly;* September 1987; 50(3): 237–246.

Stets, Jan E., "Verbal and Physical Agression in Marriage." *Journal of Marriage and the Family* 52 (May 1990): 501–514.

Stets, Jan E., and Maureen A. Pirog-Good. "Patterns of Physical and Sexual Abuse for Men and Women in Dating Relationships: A Descriptive Analysis." *Journal of Family Violence* 4:1 (March 1989): 63–76.

Stets, Jan E., and Murray A. Straus. "The Marriage License as a Hitting License: A Comparison of Assaults in Dating, Cohabitating and Married Couples." *Journal of Family Violence* 4:2 (June 1989): 161–180.

Stevens, Gillian, and Robert Schoen. "Linguistic Intermarriage in the United States." *Journal of Marriage and the Family* 50:1 (February 1988): 267–280.

Stinnet, Nick. "In Search of Strong Families." In Nick Stinnet et al., eds., *Building Family Strengths.* Lincoln: University of Nebraska Press, 1979.

_____, et al., eds. *Building Family Strengths.* Lincoln: University of Nebraska Press, 1979.

Stinnett, Nick, and John DeFrain. *Secrets of Strong Families.* Boston: Little, Brown and Company, 1985.

Stockard, Janice. *Daughters of the Canton Delta: Marriage Patterns and Economic Strategies in South China, 1860–1930.* Stanford, Calif.: Stanford University Press, 1989.

Stone, Katherine M., et al. "National Surveillance for Neonatal Herpes Simplex Virus Infections." *Sexually Transmitted Diseases* 16:3 (July–September 1989): 152–160.

Strasser, Susan. *Never Done: A History of American Housework.* New York: Pantheon Books, 1982.

Straus, Murray. "Preventing Violence and Strengthening the Family." In Nick Stinnett, et al., eds. *Family Strengths* 4. Lincoln: University of Nebraska Press, 1980.

Straus, Murray, and Richard Gelles. "Societal Change and Change in Family Violence from 1975 to 1985 as Revealed by Two National Surveys." *Journal of Marriage and the Family* 48 (August 1986): 465–479.

Straus, Murray, Richard Gelles, and Suzanne Steinmetz. *Behind Closed Doors.* Garden City, N.Y.: Anchor Books, 1980.

Strong, Bryan, and Christine DeVault. "Inside America's New Families." *Family Life Educator* 1:3 (Spring 1983): 9–11.

_____. *Understanding Our Sexuality,* 2d ed. St. Paul, Minn.: West Publishing Co., 1988.

Strube, Michael J., and Linda Barbour. "Factors Related to the Decision to Leave an Abusive Relationship." *Journal of Marriage and the Family* 46:4 (November 1984): 837–844.

Sue, D. "Erotic Fantasies of College Students during Coitus." *Journal of Sex Research* 15 (1979): 299–305.

Sugarman, David B., and Gerald T. Hotaling. "Dating Violence: Prevalence, Context, and Risk Markers." In Maureen Pirog-Good and Jan Stets, eds. *Violence in Dating Relationships: Emerging Social Issues.* New York: Praeger, 1989.

Suitor, J. Jill. "Marital Quality and Satisfaction with Division of Household Labor." *Journal of Marriage and the Family* 53:1 (February 1991): 221–230.

Suitor, J. Jill, and Karl Pillemer. "The Presence of Adult Children: A Source of Stress for Elderly Couples' Marriages?" *Journal of Marriage and the Family* 49:4 (November 1987): 717–725.

Sullivan, Harry Stack. *The Collected Works of Harry Stack Sullivan.* New York: Norton, 1952.

Sunoff, Alvin. "A Conversation with Jerome Kagan." *U.S. News and World Report* (March 25, 1985): 63–64.

Surra, Catherine. "Research and Theory on Mate Selection and Premarital Relationship in the 1980s." In Alan Booth, ed., *Contemporary Families: Looking Forward, Looking Back*. Minneapolis: National Council on Family Relations, 1991.

Sussman, Marvin B., and Susan K. Steinmetz, eds. *Handbook of Marriage and the Family*. New York: Plenum Press, 1987.

Swensen, C. H., Jr. "The Behavior of Love." In H. A. Otto, ed., *Love Today: A New Exploration*. New York: Association Press, 1972.

Swenson, Clifford, and Geir Trahaug. "Commitment and the Long-Term Marriage Relationship." *Journal of Marriage and the Family* 47:4 (November 1985): 939–945.

Swift, Carolyn. "Preventing Family Violence: Family-Focused Programs." In Mary Lystad, ed. *Violence in the Home: Interdisciplinary Perspectives*. New York: Brunner/Mazel, 1986.

Sylviachild, Abby Joan. "Infertility and Adoption." In Janet Isaacs Ashford, ed., *Birth Stories*. Freedom, Calif.: Crossing Press, 1984.

Symons, Donald. *The Evolution of Human Sexuality*. New York: Oxford University Press, 1979.

Synder, M., and J. A. Simpson. "Orientation toward Romantic Relationships." In Daniel Perlman and Steve Duck, eds. *Intimate Relationships: Development, Dynamics, and Deterioration*. Beverly Hills, Calif.: Sage Publications, 1987.

Szapocznik, Jose, and Roberto Hernandez. "The Cuban American Family." In Charles Mindel, Robert Habenstein, and Roosevelt Wright, Jr., eds. *Ethnic Families in America: Patterns and Variations*, 3d ed. New York: Elsevier North Holland, Inc., 1988.

Szinovacz, Maximiliane. "Family Power." In Marvin Sussman and Suzanne Steinmetz, eds., *Handbook of Marriage and the Family*. New York: Plenum Press, 1987.

Talbot, Nathan, ed. *Raising Children in Modern America*. Boston: Little, Brown, 1976.

"Talking to Children about Prejudice." *PTA Today* (December 1989–January 1990): 7–8.

Tallmer, Margot. "Grief as a Normal Response to the Death of a Loved One." In Austin H. Kutscher, et al., eds., *Principles of Thanatology*. New York: Columbia University Press, 1987.

Tanfer, Koray. "Patterns of Premarital Cohabitation among Never-Married Women in the United States." *Journal of Marriage and the Family* 49 (August 1987): 683–697.

Tanke, E. D. "Dimensions of the Physical Attractiveness Stereotype: A Factor/Analytic Study." *Journal of Psychology* 110 (1982): 63–74.

Tavris, Carol, and Susan Sadd. *The Redbook Report on Female Sexuality*. New York: Dell, 1977.

Tavris, Carol, and Carole Wade. *The Longest War: Sex Differences in Perspective*, 2d ed. New York: Harcourt Brace Jovanovich, 1984.

Taylor, Ella. "From the Nelsons to the Huxtables: Genre and Family Imagery in American Network Television." *Qualitative Sociology* 12:1 (Spring 1989a); 13–28.

_____. *Prime-Time Families: Television Culture in Postwar America*. Berkeley, Calif.: University of California Press, 1989b.

Taylor, Patricia. "It's Time to Put Warnings on Alcohol." *The New York Times*, March 20, 1988: B2.

Taylor, Robert J. "Need for Support and Family Involvement among Black Americans." *Journal of Marriage and the Family* 52 (August 1990): 584–590.

_____. "Receipt of Support from Family among Black Americans." *Journal of Marriage and the Family* 48 (February 1986): 67.

Taylor, Robert J., Linda M. Chatters, M. Belinda Tucker, and Edith Lewis. "Developments in Research on Black Families." In Alan

Booth, ed., *Contemporary Families: Looking Forward, Looking Back*. Minneapolis: National Council on Family Relations, 1991.

Teachman, Jay. "Receipt of Child Support in the United States." *Journal of Marriage and the Family* 53:3 (August 1991): 759–772.

Teachman, Jay, and Alex Heckert. "The Impact of Age and Children on Remarriage." *Journal of Family Issues* 6 (June 1985): 185–203.

Teachman, Jay D., and Karen A. Polonko. "Cohabitation and Marital Stability in the United States." *Social Forces* 69:1 (September 1990): 207–220.

_____. "Timing of the Transition to Parenthood: A Multidimensional Birth-interval Approach." *Journal of Marriage and the Family* 47:4 (November 1985): 867–879.

Teeser, Abraham, and Richard Reardon. "Perceptual and Cognitive Mechanisms in Human Sexual Attraction." In Mark Cook, ed., *The Bases of Human Sexual Attraction*. New York: Academic Press, 1981.

Tennov, Denise. *Love and Limerence: The Experience of Being in Love*. New York: Stein and Day, 1979.

Testa, Ronald, Bill Kinder, and Gail Ironson. "Heterosexual Bias in the Perception of Loving Relationships of Gay Males and Lesbians." *Journal of Sex Research* 23:2 (May 1987): 163–172.

Textor, Martin. "Family Therapy with Drug Addicts: An Integrated Approach." *American Journal of Orthopsychiatry* 57:4 (October 1987): 495–507.

Thayer, Leo O. *On Communication*. Norwood, N.J.: Ablex Publishing, 1987.

Theroux, Phyllis. "Tell Them I'm Carrying Their Baby." *The New York Times Book Review*, July 8, 1990: 7.

Thompson, Anthony. "Emotional and Sexual Components of Extramarital Relations." *Journal of Marriage and the Family* 46:1 (February 1984): 35–42.

_____. "Extramarital Sex: A Review of the Research Literature." *Journal of Sex Research* 19:1 (February 1983): 1–22.

Thompson, Edward, Christopher Grisanti, and Joseph Pleck. "Attitudes toward the Male Role and Their Correlates." *Sex Roles* 13:7–8 (October 1985): 413–427.

Thompson, Linda and Alexis Walker. "Gender in Families: Women and Men in Marriage, Work, and Parenthood." In Alan Booth, ed., *Contemporary Families: Looking Forward, Looking Back*. Minneapolis: National Council on Family Relations, 1991.

Thompson, Linda, et al. "Developmental Stage and Perceptions of Intergenerational Continuity." *Journal of Marriage and the Family* 47:4 (November 1985): 913–920.

Thomson, Keith. "Research on Human Embryos: Where to Draw the Line." *American Scientist* 73:2 (March–April 1985): 187–189.

Thorne, B., and M. Yalom, eds. *Rethinking the Family: Some Feminist Questions*. New York: Longman, 1982.

Thornton, Arland. "The Courtship Process and Adolescent Sexuality." *Journal of Family Issues* 11:3 (September 1990): 239–273.

_____. "Changing Attitudes toward Family Issues in the United States." *Journal of Marriage and the Family* 51:4 (November 1989): 873–893.

_____, et al. "Causes and Consequences of Sex-Role Attitudes and Attitude Change." *American Sociological Review* 48 (1983): 211–227.

Tienda, Marta, and Ronald Angel. "Headship and Household Composition among Blacks, Hispanics, and Other Whites." *Social Forces* 61 (1982): 508–531.

Tienda, Marta, and Jennifer Glass. "Household Structure and Labor Force Participation of Black, Hispanic, and White Mothers." *Demography* 22 (1985): 381–394.

Tietjen, Anne M., and Christine F. Bradley. "Social Support and Maternal Psychosocial Adjustment during the Transition to Parenthood." *Canadian Journal of Behavioural Science* 17:2 (April 1985): 109–121.

Ting-Toomey, Stella. "An Analysis of Verbal Communication Patterns in High and Low Marital Adjustment Groups." *Human Communications Research* 9:4 (Summer 1983): 306–319.

Tooth, Geoffrey. "Why Children's TV Turns Off So Many Parents." *U.S. News and World Report* (February 18, 1985): 65.

Torres, José. "A Letter to a Child Like Me." *Parade Magazine* (February 26, 1991): 8–9.

Torrey, Barbara. "Aspects of the Aged: Clues and Issues." *Population and Development Review* 14:3 (September 1988): 489–497.

Toufexis, Anastasia. "Older—but Coming on Strong." *Time* (February 22, 1988): 76–79.

Trafford, Abigail. "Medical Science Discovers the Baby." *U.S. News and World Report* (November 10, 1980): 59–62.

Tran, Than Van. "The Vietnamese American Family." In Charles H. Mindel, Robert W. Habenstein, and Roosevelt Wright, Jr., eds., *Ethnic Families in America: Patterns and Variations*, 3d ed. New York: Elsevier, 1988.

Treas, Judith, and Vern L. Bengtson. "The Demography of Mid- and Late-Life Transitions." *Annals of the American Academy* 464 (November 1982): 11–21.

_____. "The Family in Later Years." In Marvin Sussman and Suzanne Steinmetz, eds., *Handbook of Marriage and the Family*. New York: Plenum Press, 1987.

Tribe, Laurence. *Abortion: Clash of Absolutes*. New York: Norton, 1990.

Troiden, Richard. *Gay and Lesbian Identity: A Sociological Analysis*. New York: General Hall, 1988.

Troiden, Richard, and Erich Goode. "Variables Related to the Acquisition of a Gay Identity." *Journal of Homosexuality* 5 (Summer 1980): 383–392.

Troll, Lillian. "The Contingencies of Grandparenting." In Vern Bengston and Joan Roberston, eds., *Grandparenthood*. Beverly Hills, Calif.: Sage Publications, 1985a.

_____. *Early and Middle Adulthood*, 2d ed. Monterey, Calif.: Brooks/Cole Publishing Co., 1985b.

Trost, Jan. "Abandon Adjustment!" *Journal of Marriage and the Family* 47:4 (November 1985): 1072–1073.

True, Reiko Homma. "Psychotherapeutic Issues with Asian American Women." *Sex Roles* 22:7–8 (April 1990): 477–485.

Trzcinski, Eileen, and Matia Finn-Stevenson. "A Response to Arguments against Mandated Parental Leave: Findings from the Connecticut Survey of Parental Leave Policies." *Journal of Marriage and the Family* 53:2 (May 1991): 445–460.

Tucker, Sandra. "Adolescent Patterns of Communication about Sexually Related Topics." *Adolescence* 24:94 (Summer 1989): 269–278.

Turner, P. H., L. Scadden, and M. B. Harris. "Parenting in Gay and Lesbian Families." Paper presented at the first meeting of the Future of Parenting Symposium, Chicago, Ill., March, 1985.

Turner, R. "Rising Prevalence of Cohabitation in the United States May Have Partially Offset Decline in Marriage Rates." *Family Planning Perspectives* 22:2 (March–April 1990): 90–91.

Turner, R. Jay, and William R. Avison. "Assessing Risk Factors for Problem Parenting: The Significance of Social Support." *Journal of Marriage and the Family* 47:4 (November 1985): 881–892.

Turner, R. Jay, and J. W. Gartrell. "Social Factors and Psychiatric Outcome: Toward a Resolution of Interpretive Controversies." *American Sociological Review* 43 (1978): 1–23.

"U.S. Assailed on Infant Mortality." *The New York Times*, February 3, 1987: 18.

Udry, J. Richard. "Marriage Alternatives and Marital Disruption." *Journal of Marriage and the Family* 43 (November 1981): 889–897.

_____. *The Social Context of Marriage*. Philadelphia: Lippincott, 1974.

Ulrich, Patricia. "The Determinants of Depression in Two-Income Marriages." *Journal of Marriage and the Family* 50 (February 1988): 121–131.

Umberson, Debra. "Family Status and Health Behaviors: Social Control as a Dimension of Social Integration." *Journal of Health and Social Behavior* 28 (1987): 306–319.

_____. "Parenting and Well-Being: The Importance of Context." *Journal of Family Issues* 10:4 (December 1989): 427–439.

Umberson, Debra, and Walter R. Gove. "Parenthood and Psychological Well-Being: Theory, Measurement, and Stage in the Family Life Course." *Journal of Family Issues* 10:4 (December 1989): 440–462.

Unger, Donald G., and Marvin B. Sussman. "Introduction: A Community Perspective on Families." *Marriage and Family Review* 15:1/2 (1990).

Urwin, Charlene. "AIDS in Children: A Family Concern." *Family Relations* 37:2 (April 1988): 154–159.

U.S. Bureau of the Census. "Changes in American Family Life." *Special Studies*. Series P-23, No. 163. Washington, D.C.: U.S. Government Printing Office, 1989.

_____. "The Hispanic Population in the United States: March, 1990." *Current Population Reports*. Series P-20, No. 449. Washington, D.C.: U.S. Government Printing Office, 1991.

_____. "Marital Status and Living Arrangements: March, 1987." *Current Population Reports*. Series P-20. Washington, D.C.: U.S. Government Printing Office, 1988.

_____. "Marital and Living Arrangements: March, 1988." *Current Population Reports*. Series P-20. Washington, D.C.: U.S. Government Printing Office, 1989.

_____. "Marital and Living Arrangements: March, 1989." *Current Population Reports*. Series P-20. Washington, D.C.: U.S. Government Printing Office, 1990.

_____. "Marital and Living Arrangements: March, 1990." *Current Population Reports*. Series P-20. Washington, D.C.: U.S. Government Printing Office, 1991.

_____. *Statistical Abstract of the United States*, 109th ed. Washington, D.C., 1989.

_____. *Statistical Abstract of the United States*, 110th ed. Washington, D.C., 1990.

_____. *Statistical Abstract of the United States*, 111th ed. Washington, D.C.: U.S. Government Printing Office, 1991.

_____. "Studies in Marriage and the Family." *Special Studies*. Series P-23, No. 162. Washington, D.C.: U.S. Government Printing Office, 1989.

_____. "Who's Minding the Kids?" Washington, D.C.: U.S. Government Printing Office, 1987.

U.S. Bureau of Labor Statistics. "Employment and Earnings." Washington, D.C.: U.S. Government Printing Office, 1988.

U.S. Commission on Civil Rights. *Child Care and Equal Opportunity for Women*. Clearinghouse Publication No. 67, June 1981.

Urwin, Charlene. "AIDS in Children: A Family Concern." *Family Relations* 37:2 (April 1988): 154–159.

Valentine, Deborah. "The Experience of Pregnancy: A Developmental Process." *Family Relations* 31 (April 1982): 243–248.

Vance, Carole, ed. *Pleasure and Danger: Exploring Female Sexuality*. Boston: Routledge and Kegan Paul, 1984.

Vandell, Deborah, and Mary Anne Corasaniti. "After School Care: Choices and Outcome for Third Graders." Paper presented to Association for the Advancement of Science, May 27, 1985.

Vanderford, Marsha. "Vilification and Social Movements: A Case Study of Pro-Life and Pro-Choice Rhetoric." *Quarterly Journal of Speech* 75:2 (May 1989): 166–182.

Van Hasselt, Vincent B., et al., eds. *Handbook of Family Violence*. New York: Plenum Press, 1988.

Vann, Richard. "The Youth of Centuries of Childhood." *History and Theory* 21:2 (1982): 279–297.

Vasquez-Nuthall, E., I. Romero-Garcia, and B. De Leon. "Sex Roles and Perceptions of Femininity and Masculinity of Hispanic Women: A Review of the Literature." *Psychology of Women Quarterly* 11 (1987): 409–426.

Vaughan, Diane. *Uncoupling: Turning Points in Intimate Relationships*. New York: Oxford University Press, 1986.

Veevers, Jean. *Childless by Choice*. Toronto: Buttersworth, 1980.

_____. "Voluntary Childlessness." *Family Coordinator* 22 (April 1973): 199–206.

Vega, William. "Hispanic Families." In Alan Booth, ed., *Contemporary Families: Looking Forward, Looking Back*. Minneapolis: National Council on Family Relations, 1991.

Velsor, Ellen, and Angela O'Rand. "Family Life Cycle, Work Career Patterns, and Women's Wages at Midlife." *Journal of Marriage and the Family* 46:2 (May 1984): 365–373.

Vemer, Elizabeth, Marilyn Coleman, Lawrence Ganong, and Harris Cooper. "Marital Satisfaction in Remarriage: A Meta-analysis." *Journal of Marriage and the Family* 53:1 (August 1989): 713–726.

Ventura, Jacqueline N. "The Stresses of Parenthood Reexamined." *Family Relations*, 36 (January 1987): 26–29.

Vera, Hernan, et al. "Age Heterogamy in Marriage." *Journal of Marriage and the Family* 47:3 (August 1985): 553–566.

Verbrugge, Lois. "From Sneezes to Adieu: Stages of Health for American Men and Women." *Social Science and Medicine* 22 (1986): 1195–1212.

_____. "Marital Status and Health." *Journal of Marriage and the Family* 41 (May 1979): 267–285.

Verdery, E. Augustus. "Treatment of the Alcoholic by the Nonphysician." In Peter Bourne and Ruth Fox, eds., *Alcoholism: Progress in Research and Treatment*. New York: Academic Press, 1973.

Verwoerdt, A., et al. "Sexual Behavior in Senescence." *Geriatrics* 24 (February 1969): 137–157.

Verzaro-Lawrence, Marce. "Shared Childrearing: A Challenging Alternative Lifestyle." *Alternative Lifestyles* 4:2 (May 1981): 205–217.

Viorst, Judith. *Necessary Losses*. New York: Fawcett Gold Medal, 1987.

Visher, E. B., and J. Visher. *Stepfamilies: A Guide to Working with Stepparents and Stepchildren*. New York: Brunner/Mazel, 1979.

Voeller, Bruce. "Society and the Gay Movement." In Judd Marmor, ed., *Homosexual Behavior*. New York: Basic Books, 1980.

Voydanoff, Patricia. "Economic Distress and Family Relations: A Review of the Eighties." In Alan Booth, ed., *Contemporary Families: Looking Forward, Looking Back*. Minneapolis: National Council on Family Relations, 1991.

_____. *Work and Family Life*. Newbury Park, Calif.: Sage Publications, 1987.

_____. "Work Role Characteristics, Family Structure Demands, and Work/Family Conflict." *Journal of Marriage and the Family* 50:3 (August 1988): 749–761.

Voydanoff, Patricia, and Brenda Donnelly. "Work and Family Roles and Psychological Distress." *Journal of Marriage and the Family* 51:4 (November 1989): 933–941.

Voydanoff, Patricia, and Linda Majka, eds. *Families and Economic Distress: Coping Strategies and Social Policy*. Beverly Hills, Calif.: Sage Publications, 1988.

Wakefield, Jerome. "The Semantics of Success: Do Masturbation Exercises Lead to Partner Orgasm?" *Journal of Sex and Marital Therapy* 13 (Spring 1987): 3–14.

Walker, Alexis J. "Reconceptualizing Family Stress." *Journal of Marriage and the Family* 47:4 (November 1985): 827–837.

_____, et al. "Feminist Programs for Families." *Family Relations* 37:1 (January 1988): 17–22.

Walker, Alexis J., Hwa-Yong Shin, and David Bird. "Perceptions of Relationship Change and Caregiver Satisfaction." *Family Relations* 39:2 (April 1990): 147–152.

Walker, Alexis J., and Linda Thompson. "Feminism and Family Studies." *Journal of Family Issues* 5:4 (December 1984): 545–570.

Walker, Kathryn. "At Home: Organizing Eases the Load." *U.S. News and World Report* (January 25, 1982).

Walker, Lenore. *The Battered Woman Syndrome*. New York: Harper Colophon, 1979.

_____. *The Battered Woman*. New York: Springer Publishing Co., 1984.

_____. "Psychological Causes of Family Violence." In Mary Lystad, ed., *Violence in the Home: Interdisciplinary Perspectives*. New York: Brunner/Mazel, 1986.

Waller, Willard. "The Rating and Dating Complex." *American Sociological Review* 2 (1937): 727–734.

Waller, Willard, and Reuben Hill. *The Family: A Dynamic Interpretation*. New York: Dryden Press, 1951.

Wallerstein, Judith. "Children of Divorce: Report of a Ten-Year Follow-Up of Early Latency-Age Children." *American Journal of Orthopsychiatry* 57:2 (April 1987): 199–211.

Wallerstein, Judith, and Joan Kelly. *Surviving the Breakup: How Children and Parents Cope with Divorce*. New York: Basic Books, 1980b.

_____. "Effects of Divorce on the Visiting Father-Child Relationship." *American Journal of Psychiatry* 137(12) (December 1980a): 1534–1539.

Wallerstein, Judith, and Sandra Blakeslee. *Second Chances: Men, Women, and Children a Decade After Divorce*. New York: Ticknor & Fields, 1989.

Walling, Mary, Barbara Andersen, and Susan Johnson. "Hormonal Replacement Therapy for Postmenopausal Women: A Review of Sexual Outcomes and Related Gynecologic Effects." *Archives of Sexual Behavior* 19:2 (1990): 119–127.

Walsh, A.; Walsh, P. A. Love, Self-Esteem and Multiple Sclerosis. Social Science and Medicine; September 1989; 53(5): 414–431.

Walsh, Froma, ed. *Normal Family Processes*. New York: Guilford Press, 1982.

Walster, Elaine, and G. William Walster. *A New Look at Love*. Reading, Mass.: Addison-Wesley, 1978.

Wardle, Francis. "Helping Children Respect Differences." *PTA Today* (December 1989–January 1990): 5–6.

Warren, Carol. "Homosexuality and Stigma." In Judd Marmor, ed. *Homosexual Behavior*. New York: Basic Books, 1980.

Warren, Mary Anne. "The Abortion Struggle in America." *Bioethics* 3:43 (October 1989): 320–332.

Waterson, E. J., and I. M. Murray-Lyon. "Preventing Alcohol Related Birth Damage: A Review." *Social Science and Medicine* 30:3 (1990): 349–364.

Watkins, Susan Cotts, and Jane Menken. "Demographic Foundations of Family Change." *American Sociological Review* 52 (1987): 346–358.

Watson, Roy. "Premarital Cohabitation vs. Traditional Courtship: Their Effects on Subsequent Marital Adjustment." *Family Relations* 32:1 (January 1983): 139–147.

Watson, Russell. "A Hidden Epidemic." *Newsweek* (May 14, 1984a): 30–36.

_____. "What Price Day Care?" *Newsweek* (September 10, 1984b): 14–21.

Wedemeyer, Nancy, and Harold Grotevant. "Mapping the Family System: A Technique for Teaching Family Systems Theory Concepts." *Family Relations* 31 (April 1982): 185–193.

Weeks, M. O'Neal, and Bruce Gage. "A Comparison of the Marriage-Role Expectations of College Women Enrolled in a Functional Marriage Course in 1961, 1972, and 1978." *Sex Roles* 11(5/6) (1984): 377–388.

Weeks, Jeffrey. *Sexuality and Its Discontents.* London: Routledge & Kegan Paul, 1985.

Weg, Ruth. "Introduction: Beyond Intercourse and Orgasm." *Sexuality in the Later Years: Roles and Behavior.* New York: Academic Press, 1983b.

———. "The Physiological Perspective." In Ruth Weg, ed. *Sexuality in the Later Years: Roles and Behavior.* New York: Academic Press, 1983c.

———, ed. *Sexuality in the Later Years: Roles and Behavior.* New York: Academic Press, 1983a.

Wegscheider, Sharon. *Another Chance: Hope and Health for the Alcoholic Family,* 2d ed. Palo Alto, Calif.: Science and Behavior Books, 1989.

Weinberg, Daniel. "Measuring Poverty." *Family Economic Review* 2 (1985): 9–13.

Weinberg, Martin, and Colin Wilson. "Black Sexuality: A Test of Two Theories." *Journal of Sex Research* 25:2 (May 1988): 197–218.

Weiner, L., B. A. More, and P. Garrido. "FAS/FAE: Focusing Prevention on Women at Risk." *International Journal of the Addictions* 24:5 (May 1989): 385–395.

Weingarten, Helen. "Marital Status and Well-Being: A National Study Comparing First-Married, Currently Divorced and Remarried Adults." *Journal of Marriage and the Family* 47:3 (August 1985): 653–662.

———. "Remarriage and Well-Being." *Journal of Family Issues* 1:4 (December 1980): 533–559.

Weishaus, Sylvia, and Dorothy Field. "A Half Century of Marriage: Continuity or Change?" *Journal of Marriage and the Family* 50:3 (August 1988): 763–774.

Weiss, David, and Joan Jurich. "Size of Community as a Predictor of Attitudes toward Extramarital Sexual Relations." *Journal of Marriage and the Family* 47:1 (February 1985): 173–178.

Weiss, David. "Open Marriage and Multilateral Relationships: The Emergence of Nonexclusive Models of the Marital Relationship." In Eleanor Macklin and Roger Rubin, eds., *Contemporary Families and Alternative Lifestyles.* Beverly Hills, Calif.: Sage Publications, 1983.

Weiss, Robert. "The Fund of Sociolability." *Transactions* (July/August 1969): 36–43.

———. *Going It Alone.* New York: Basic Books, 1979.

———. *Marital Separation.* New York: Basic Books, 1975.

———. "Men and the Family." *Family Processes* 24 (1985): 49–58.

———. "The Study of Loneliness." In Peter Stein, ed. *Single Life.* New York: St. Martin's Press, 1981.

Weitzman, Lenore. *The Divorce Revolution: The Unexpected Social and Economic Consequences for Women and Children in America.* New York: The Free Press, 1985.

———. *The Marriage Contract.* Englewood Cliffs, N.J.: Prentice-Hall, 1978.

———. *The Marriage Contract: Spouses, Lovers, and the Law.* New York: Macmillan, 1981.

Weitzman, Lenore, and Ruth Dixon. "The Transformation of Legal Marriage through No-Fault Divorce." In Arlene Skolnick and Jerome Skolnick, eds., *Family in Transition.* Boston: Little, Brown, 1980.

Weizman, R., and J. Hart. "Sexual Behavior in Healthy Married Elderly Men." *Archives of Sexual Behavior* 16:1 (February 1987): 39–44.

Welch, Mary, and Dorothy Herman. "Why Miscarriage Is So Misunderstood." *Ms.* (February 1980): 14–22.

Wertz, Richard, and Dorothy Wertz. *Lying-In: A History of Childbirth in America.* New York: Harper & Row, 1978.

Whitbourne, Susan, and Joyce Ebmeyer. *Identity and Intimacy in Marriage: A Study of Couples.* New York: Springer-Verlag, 1990.

White, Charles. "Sexual Interest, Attitudes, Knowledge, and Sexual History in Relation to Sexual Behavior of the Institutionalized Aged." *Archives of Sexual Behavior* 11 (February 1982): 11–21.

White, Gregory. "Jealousy and Partner's Perceived Motives for Attraction to a Rival." *Social Psychology Quarterly* 44:1 (March 1981): 24–30.

———. "Inducing Jealousy: A Power Perspective." Personality and Social Psychology Bulletin 6:2 (June 1980a): 222–227.

———. "Physical Attractiveness and Courtship Progress." *Journal of Personality and Social Psychology* 39:4 (October 1980b): 660–668.

White, James. "Premarital Cohabitation and Marital Stability in Canada." *Journal of Marriage and the Family* 49 (August 1987): 641–647.

White, Joseph, and Thomas Parham. *The Psychology of Blacks: An African-American Perspective,* 2d ed. Englewood Cliffs, N.J.: Prentice-Hall, Inc., 1990.

White, Lynn. "Determinants of Divorce." In Alan Booth, ed., *Contemporary Families: Looking Forward, Looking Back.* Minneapolis: National Council on Family Relations, 1991.

White, Lynn, and Alan Booth. "Divorce over the Life Course: The Role of Marital Happiness." *Journal of Family Issues* 12:1 (March 1991): 5–22.

———. "The Transition to Parenthood and Marital Quality." *Journal of Family Issues* 6 (1985): 435–449.

White, Lynn, David Brinkerhoff, and Alan Booth. "The Effect of Marital Disruption on Child's Attachment to Parents." *Journal of Family Issues* 6 (1985): 5–22.

White, Lynn, and Bruce Keith. "The Effect of Shift Work on the Quality and Stability of Marital Relations." *Journal of Marriage and the Family* 52:2 (May 1990): 453–462.

Whitehead, Barbara Dafoe. "How to Rebuild a 'Family-Friendly' Society." *Des Moines Sunday Register,* October 7, 1990: 3C.

Whiteside, Mary F. "Family Rituals as a Key to Kinship Connections in Remarried Families." Family Relations 38 (January 1989): 34–39.

Whitman, David. "The Coming of the 'Couch People.'" *U.S. News & World Report* (August 3, 1987): 19–21.

Wiehe, Vernon. *Sibling Abuse: The Hidden Physical, Emotional, and Sexual Trauma.* Lexington, Mass.: Lexington Books, 1990.

Wiehe, Vernon R. "Religious Influence on Parental Attitudes Toward the Use of Corporal Punishment." *Journal of Family Violence* 5:2 (June 1990): 173ff.

Wilcox, Allen, et al. "Incidents of Early Loss of Pregnancy." *New England Journal of Medicine* 319:4 (July 28, 1988): 189–194.

Wilcox, Clyde. "Political Action Committees and Abortion: A Longitudinal Analysis." *Women and Politics* 9:1 (1989): 1–19.

Wilkerson, Isabel. "Infant Mortality: Frightful Odds in Inner City." *The New York Times,* June 26, 1987: 1ff.

Wilkie, Colleen F., and Elinor W. Ames. "The Relationship of Infant Crying to Parental Stress in the Transition to Parenthood." *Journal of Marriage and the Family* 48:3 (August 1986): 545–550.

Wilkinson, Doris, Esther Ngan-Ling Chow, and Maxine Baca Zinn, eds. Special issue: "Transforming Social Knowledge: The Interlocking of Race, Class, and Gender." *Gender & Society,* September 1992.

Williams, John, and Arthur Jacoby. "The Effects of Premarital Heterosexual and Homosexual Experience on Dating and Marriage Desirability." *Journal of Marriage and the Family* 51 (May 1989): 489–497.

Williams, Juanita. "Middle Age and Aging." In Juanita Williams, ed., *Women: Behavior in a Biosocial Context.* New York: Norton, 1977.

Wilson, Julius W., ed. *The Ghetto Underclass: Social Science Perspectives.* Newbury Park, Calif.: Sage Publications, 1989.

Wilson, Melvin N., Timothy Tolson, Ivora Hinton, and Michael Kiernan. "Flexibility and Sharing of Childcare Duties in Black Families." *Sex Roles* 22:7–8 (April 1990): 409–425.

Wilson, Pamela. "Black Culture and Sexuality." *Journal of Social Work and Human Sexuality* 4:3 (Spring 1986): 29–46.

Wilson, Sarah Jane. *Women, the Family, and the Economy*, 2d ed. Toronto: McGraw-Hill Ryerson, 1986.

Winch, Robert. *Mate Selection: A Study of Complementary Needs*. New York: Harper & Row, 1958.

Winn, Rhoda, and Niles Newton. "Sexuality and Aging: A Study of 106 Cultures." *Archives of Sexual Behavior* 11:4 (August 1982): 283–298.

Wise, P. H., and A. Meyer. "Poverty and Child Health." *Pediatric Clinics of North America* 35:6 (December 1988): 1169–1186.

Wisensale, Steven. "Approaches to Family Policy in State Government: A Report on Five States." *Family Relations* 39:2 (April 1990b): 136–140.

_____. "The Family in the Think Tank." *Family Relations* 40:2 (April 1990a): 199–207.

Wisensale, Steven, and Michael Allison. "Family Leave Legislation: State and Federal Initiatives." *Family Relations* 38:2 (April 1989): 182–189.

Wishy, Bernard. *The Child and the Republic*. Philadelphia: Lippincott, 1968.

Woititz, Janet. *Adult Children of Alcoholics*. Deerfield, Fla: Health Communications, Inc., 1983.

Wolf, Rosalie S., and Karl A. Pillemer. "Intervention, Outcome, and Elder Abuse." In Gerald T. Hotaling et al., eds. *Coping with Family Violence*. Newbury Park, Calif.: Sage Publications, 1988.

Wolkind, Stephen, and Eva Zajicek, eds. *Pregnancy: A Psychological and Social Study*. New York: Grune and Stratton, 1981.

Wong, Morrison G. "The Chinese American Family." In Charles H. Mindel, Robert W. Habenstein, and Roosevelt Wright, Jr., eds., *Ethnic Families in America: Patterns and Variations*, 3d ed. New York: Elsevier, 1988.

Woodward, Kenneth. "New Rules for Making Love and Babies." *Newsweek* (March 23, 1987): 42–43.

"Work Interruptions and Earnings." *Family Economics Review* 2 (1985): 30–31.

Wyatt, Gail Elizabeth. "The Aftermath of Child Sexual Abuse of African American and White Women: The Victim's Experience." *Journal of Family Violence* 5:1 (March 1990): 61–81.

Wyatt, Gail, Stefanie Peters, and Donald Guthrie. "Kinsey Revisited II: Comparisons of the Sexual Socialization and Sexual Behavior of Black Women over 33 Years." *Archives of Sexual Behavior* 17:4 (August 1988): 289–332.

Wynn, Ruth, and Christine Fletcher. "Sex Role Development and Early Educational Experiences." In D. Bruce Carter, ed., *Current Conceptions of Sex Roles and Sex Typing*. New York: Praeger, 1987.

Ybarra, Lea. "When Wives Work: The Impact on the Chicano Family." *Journal of Marriage and the Family* (February 1982): 169–178.

Yogev, Sara, and Jane Brett. "Perceptions of the Division of Housework and Child Care and Marital Satisfaction." *Journal of Marriage and the Family* 47:3 (August 1985): 609–618.

Yulsman, Tom. "A Little Help for Creation." *The Good Health Magazine, The New York Times*, October 7, 1990: 22ff.

Yura, Michael. "Family Subsystem Functions and Disabled Children: Some Conceptual Issues." *Marriage and Family Review* 11:1–2 (1987): 135–151.

Zarit, Stephen, P. Todd, and J. Zarit. "Subjective Burden of Husbands and Wives as Caregivers: A Longitudinal Study." *Gerontologist* 26 (1986): 260–266.

Zaslow, Martha, et al. "Depressed Mood in New Fathers." Unpublished paper presented to the Society for Research in Child Development. Boston, April 1981.

Zavella, Patricia. *Women's Work and Chicano Families*. Ithaca, N.Y.: Cornell University Press, 1987.

Zilbergeld, Bernie. *Male Sexuality*. New York: Bantam Books, 1979.

Zimmerman, Shirley L. "State Level Public Policy Choices as Predictors of State Teen Birth Rates." *Family Relations* 37 (July 1988): 315–321.

_____. "The Welfare State and Family Breakup: The Mythical Connection." *Family Relations* 40:2 (April 1991): 139–147.

_____. *Understanding Family Policy: Theoretical Approaches*. Beverly Hills, Calif.: Sage, 1988.

Zimmerman, Shirley L., and Phyllis Owens. "Comparing the Family Policies of Three States: A Content Analysis." *Family Relations* 38:2 (April 1989): 190–195.

Zinn, Maxine Baca. "Family, Feminism, and Race." *Gender & Society* 4 (1990): 68–82.

Zvonkovic, Anisa, et al. "Making the Most of Job Loss: Individual and Marital Features of Job Loss." *Family Relations* 37:1 (January 1988): 56–61.

PHOTO CREDITS

3. © Arthur Glauberman, Photo Researchers; 6. © Michael Hayman, Photo Researchers; 7. Courtesy Christine DeVault; 11. © Julie Bidwell, Stock Boston; 19. © Carmen Lomas Garza, photo by Wolfgang Dietze; 23. © Michael Tweed, NYT Pictures; 26. © Sue Bennett, Photographer; 33. © Robert A. Isaacs, Photo Researchers; 41. © Elizabeth Crews, Stock Boston; 45. Max Seabaugh; 57. © Jean-Claude Lejeune, Stock Boston; 60. © Laurie DeVault; 64. © Rosemary Kaul, *Los Angeles Times*; 79. Photo by Richard Berquist; 83. Olive Pierce Photography, Stock Boston; 86. © Spencer Grant, Stock Boston; 94. © Laurie DeVault; 104. Carol Guzy, © *Miami Herald*; 113. © Spencer Grant, Stock Boston; 114. AP Wide World Photos; 120. © Spencer Grant, Photo Researchers; 125. © Jim Whitmer, Stock Boston; 130. © Richard Frieman, Photo Researchers; 137. Courtesy Miriam Grosman; 143. © Nancy Durrell McKenna, Photo Re-

searchers; 149. © Laurie DeVault; 152. © Laurie DeVault; 154. © Eugene Richards, Magnum Photos, Inc.; 158a. Profs. P. M. Motta & J. van Blerkom/Science Photo Library; 158b. © Omikron, Photo Researchers; 158c. Omikron, Photo Researchers; 158d. Dr. M. A. Ansary/Science Photo Library; 159e. Stock Boston; 159f. © Petit Format/Science Source; 168. © Laurie DeVault; 171. © Jill Fineberg, Photo Researchers; 177. *The New York Times*/Duane Hall; 183. © Wendy Surr; 188. © Michael Wiesbrot, Stock Boston; 201. © Judy Gelles, Stock Boston; 208. © Laurie DeVault; 209. Judy Griesedieck, *San Jose Mercury News*; 213. © Eddie Adams/*Time Magazine*; 215. © Jeffry W. Myers, Stock Boston; 219. Photo by Karen T. Borchers, reprinted from *Matrix Newsmagazine*, June, 1988; 229. © Rhoda Sidney, Stock Boston; 231. © *Miami Herald*; 232. © 1991, Marty Katz; 250. © Dan Ford Connolly, Picture Group; 263. © Michael Weis-

brot, Stock Boston; 265. © John Coletti, Stock Boston; 274. © James McGoon; 275. © Jim Whitmer, Stock Boston; 282. Rick McCawley, *Miami Herald*; 289. AP/Wide World Photos; 293. © Bob Daemmrich, Stock Boston; 297. © Laurie DeVault; 317. © Frank Siteman, Stock Boston; 327. © Donna Feratto, Black Star; 330. © Gilles Peress, Magnum Photos, Inc.; 342. © Laurie DeVault; 349. Paul Fortin, Stock Boston; 352. Courtesy of the Library of Congress; 365. © Laurie DeVault; 369. © Spencer Grant, Stock Boston; 370. Courtesy Christine DeVault; 379. © Laurie DeVault; 395. © Bob Daemmrich, Stock Boston; 399. © Bob Daemmrich, Stock Boston; 402. © Peter Southwick, Stock Boston; 406. Carol Guzy Grossman, © *Miami Herald*; 408. © Charles Kennard, Stock Boston; 410. Nancy Durrell McKenna from *Woman's Experience of Sex* by Sheila Kitzinger.

Acknowledgments: Jealousy section of Chapter 3, *Love, Commitment, and Intimacy,* adapted from Bryan Srong and Christine DeVault, *Human Sexuality: The Intimate Environment.* Mountain View, CA: Mayfield Publishing Company, 1994 [in press].